MASTER THE CATHOLIC HIGH SCHOOL ENTRANCE EXAMS 2018

About Peterson's®

Peterson's®, a Nelnet company, has been your trusted educational publisher for over 50 years. It's a milestone we're quite proud of, as we continue to offer the most accurate, dependable, high-quality educational content in the field, providing you with everything you need to succeed. No matter where you are on your academic or professional path, you can rely on Peterson's for its books, online information, expert test-prep tools, the most up-to-date education exploration data, and the highest quality career success resources—everything you need to achieve your education goals. For our complete line of products, visit www.petersons.com.

For more information, contact Peterson's, 3 Columbia Circle, Suite 205, Albany, New York 12203-5158; 800-338-3282 Ext. 54229; or find us online at www.petersons.com.

Peterson's makes every reasonable effort to obtain from reliable sources accurate, complete, and timely information about the tests covered in this book. Nevertheless, changes can be made in the tests or the administration of the tests at any time and Peterson's makes no representation or warranty, either expressed or implied as to the accuracy, timeliness, or completeness of the information contained in this book.

ISBN: 978-0-7689-4145-6

Printed in the United States of America

10 9 8 7 6 5 4 3 2 1   19 18 17

Twenty-second Edition

Petersonspublishing.com/publishingupdates

Check out our website at www.petersonspublishing.com/publishingupdates to see if there is any new information regarding the tests and any revisions or corrections to the content of this book. You should also carefully read the material you receive from the Archdiocese when you register for the test. We've made sure the information in this book is accurate and up-to-date; however, the test format or content may have changed since the time of publication.

Contents

Credits

Excerpt from *A Christmas Carol,* by Charles Dickens

Excerpt from *Rip Van Winkle,* by Washington Irving

Excerpt from *The Nightingale,* by Hans Christian Andersen

The Rhodora, by Ralph Waldo Emerson

Before You Begin

WHY YOU SHOULD USE THIS BOOK

If you're in the eighth grade and are preparing to continue your education at a Catholic high school, then this book is just what you need. An essential part of getting into the school of your choice is taking and passing an entrance exam. This book has been specially designed to assist you with preparing for and taking the two most commonly used Catholic high school entrance exams, the COOP and the HSPT®. If you live within the Archdiocese of New York, or the Diocese of Brooklyn and Rockland Counties, you probably will have to take the Test for Admissions into Catholic High Schools, commonly known as the TACHS. Exercises are included here to prepare you for that test also. You'll find help with answering questions in every test subject and plenty of practice to get you ready for your exam.

Master the Catholic High School Entrance Exams will help you develop and sharpen your test-taking skills. This book includes descriptions and examples of each type of entrance exam and six full-length practice exams—two TACHS, two COOPs, and two HSPT® exams. The TACHS, COOP, and HSPT® practice exams simulate the type of questions you can expect to find on the actual exams. However, the test-makers may have instituted changes after this book was published. To see if new information regarding the tests is available, check www.petersonspublishing.com/publishingupdates. In addition, this book provides skills review and practice questions in each of the subject areas covered by typical entrance exams. Use these sections to help you strengthen your weak areas.

HOW THIS BOOK IS ORGANIZED

Divided into sections, this book provides five main parts that can help you with your preparation. Use Part I to learn more about each exam type and how it's scored. You'll find examples of typical questions from each exam. Take our Diagnostic Test in Part II to determine your strengths and weaknesses so you can best plan your test preparation. Use Part III to review the verbal skill sections of the TACHS, COOP, and HSPT® exams, such as analogies, verbal logic, reading, and composition. Use Part IV to review quantitative and nonverbal skills, such as mathematics. Part V includes practice exams for the TACHS, the COOP, and the HSPT®. The Appendix includes a Word list and a useful Synonyms/Antonyms list to help boost your test-prep confidence on the Language Arts sections of the admissions tests.

HOW TO USE THIS BOOK

Diagnostic Test Method

One way to use this book is to start with a diagnostic test. A diagnostic test is a test that helps you understand your strengths and weaknesses on the exam. It "diagnoses" the skills that need the most improvement.

In this method, you take a diagnostic test first, and then you use the results of your diagnostic to develop a study plan. Use the Diagnostic Test in Part II, Chapter 5. This test will give you a sampling of the kinds of questions you are likely to see on your test, and it will show you where you might need to focus your test-prep efforts.

Once you've taken your diagnostic test, score yourself to see your strengths and weaknesses. How did you do? Make a list of your strong and weak areas. If you scored well on Math but poorly on Verbal Skills, then you can count Math as a strength. Your Verbal Skills, on the other hand, will need some work. Rank the different sections in terms of your strongest and weakest skills.

Use your ranking list to develop your study plan. Your plan should prioritize boosting your weaker skills. You don't need to spend as much time brushing up on your strengths. However, you should plan to spend *some* time on "strong skills" exercises—just to stay in shape!

Once you've got a study plan, put it to work. Read the introduction to your test in Part I. Then, focus on improving your weak skills by studying the sections in Parts III and IV. After you've reviewed the content sections, take a practice test in Part V. This test should show an improvement in your score!

Front-to-Back Method

Another way to use this book is the front-to-back method. In this method, you work through the book the way it is organized.

Start at Part I of the book and carefully read through the introductory section on your exam. This will help you understand the exam and how it's scored. Next, study the content sections in Parts III and IV. Focus on the sections that relate to your exam. If you know your strong and weak skills, you might devote extra time to sections where you need the most improvement.

After you've reviewed the content, take a practice test or two in Part V. Even taking one test will help you be more prepared for exam day. Sometimes, the process of taking the test itself can actually help increase your score. This is because you become more familiar with the test, which increases your confidence.

After you complete each test, review your answers with the explanations provided. If you still don't understand how to answer a certain question, you might ask a teacher for help. A review session with a friend might prove helpful, too.

WHAT TO STUDY: TACHS, COOP, AND HSPT®

Parts III and IV of this book provide TACHS, COOP, and HSPT® content for you to review. Use the table below to determine which chapters to study for your test.

No.	Chapter	TACHS	COOP	HSPT®
	Part III: Verbal Skills			
6	Synonyms	X		X
7	Antonyms			X
8	Analogies		X	X
9	Verbal Logic		X	X
10	Reading	X	X	X
11	Spelling	X	X	X
12	Punctuation and Capitalization	X	X	X
13	English Usage	X	X	X
14	Language Composition and Expression	X	X	X
	Part IV: Quantitative and Nonverbal Skills			
15	Quantitative Reasoning		X	
16	Mathematics	X	X	X
17	Series Reasoning	X	X	X
18	Comparisons			X

SPECIAL STUDY FEATURES

Master the Catholic High School Entrance Exams is designed to be as user-friendly as it is complete. To this end, it includes several features to make your preparation much more efficient.

Overview

Each chapter begins with a bulleted overview listing the topics to be covered in the chapter. This will allow you to quickly target the areas in which you are most interested.

Summing It Up

Each chapter ends with a point-by-point summary that captures the most important points contained in the chapter. They are a convenient way to review key points.

Bonus Information

As you work your way through the book, keep your eye on the margins to find bonus information and advice. Information can be found in the following forms:

Note

Notes highlight critical information about each test's format.

Tip

Tips draw your attention to valuable concepts, advice, and shortcuts. By reading the tips, you will learn how to approach different question types, pace yourself, and use process-of-elimination techniques.

Alert!

Wherever you need to be careful of a common pitfall or test-taker trap, you'll find an *Alert!* This information reveals and eliminates the misperceptions and wrong turns so many students take on the exam.

By taking full advantage of all the features presented in *Master the Catholic High School Entrance Exams*, you will become much more comfortable with the test that you need to take and will be more confident about getting a good score.

Word List and List of Synonyms and Antonyms

Questions that require a good knowledge of vocabulary appear throughout all of these exams. The broader, more varied, and more accurate your vocabulary knowledge, the better your chances of answering questions quickly and correctly. To help you with this task, we've put together a list of about 500 commonly used words that may appear on your exam, including hundreds of related words—words that are variants of the primary words or words that share a common word root. We've also included a list of synonyms and antonyms for many of the terms on the word list as well as additional terms. You'll find the Word List and the List of Synonyms and Antonyms at the back of the book. We hope they will enhance your vocabulary study for any of the Catholic High School entrance exams.

YOU'RE WELL ON YOUR WAY TO SUCCESS

Remember that knowledge is power. By using this book you will be studying the most comprehensive guide available.

GIVE US YOUR FEEDBACK

Peterson's publishes a full line of books—test prep, education exploration, financial aid, and career preparation. Peterson's publications can be found at high school guidance offices, college libraries and career centers, and your local bookstore and library. In addition, you can find Peterson's products online at www.petersons.com.

We welcome any comments or suggestions you may have about this publication. Please call our customer service department at 800-338-3282 Ext. 54229 or send an e-mail message to custsvc@ petersons.com. Your feedback will help us make educational dreams possible for you—and others like you.

LOOKING FOR SOME FUN, "ON-THE-GO" TEST PREP?

Prepping for your Catholic High School entrance exam doesn't need to stop when you're away from your desk and aren't able to use this book. Peterson's has joined forces with NerdCoach, creators of mobile, video-game inspired study tools to make test prep fun and portable. The new, fun NerdCoach app (for the iPhone or iPad) drills students in the cognitive skills that are essential for mastering any of the Catholic high school exams featured in this guide.

The NerdCoach games are potent 1-minute study sessions. The games are designed like video games and are so much fun you might not realize that you're actually learning!

So, whether you have 5 minutes before the school bus arrives or 15 minutes until dinner is ready, the NerdCoach app games enable you to sharpen your test skills anywhere, anytime. And, they're the perfect companion to this guide!

For more information, visit www.nerdcoach.com/mtc.

TOP 10 WAYS TO RAISE YOUR SCORE

When it comes to taking your entrance exam, some test-taking skills will do you more good than others. There are concepts you can learn, techniques you can follow, and tricks you can use that will help you to do your very best. Here are our picks for the top 10 ways to raise your score:

1. **Regardless of which plan you will follow, get started by reading Part I to familiarize yourself with the test formats.**

2. **Make sure to complete the exercises in each chapter you read.**

3. **When you are one third of the way through your preparation, take a practice test.** Make sure you are applying new test-taking strategies.

4. **It's a good idea to have a dictionary nearby while taking the practice test or studying the review sections of this book.** If you come across a word you don't know, circle it and look it up later.

5. **Revisit problematic chapters and chapter summaries.**

6. **After you have completed all of the study sections, take your second practice test.** You should find the second practice test much easier now, and, after your study and practice, you should be able to answer more questions than you could on the first practice test.

7. **If you have the time, you might find it instructive to take the practice tests for the other exams.** For example, if you're required to take the COOP exam, you might also test yourself with the HSPT® exam.

8. **During the last phase of your study, review the practice tests.**

9. **Be sure to read the test-taking techniques in Chapter 4 for additional tips to help you on the day of the exam.**

10. **The night before your exam, RELAX.** You'll be prepared.

PART I
TACKLING THE EXAMS

All About the New York City Test for Admission into Catholic High Schools (TACHS)

chapter 1

OVERVIEW

- **The TACHS exam format**
- **About the TACHS questions**
- **Summing it up**

The Test for Admission into Catholic High Schools (TACHS) is the entrance examination for eighth-grade students wishing to attend a Catholic high school in New York City beginning in the ninth grade.

If you are currently in the eighth grade or will be in the eighth grade and are planning to attend a Catholic high school in the ninth grade, this is the exam you will take as part of your admissions process. You may take the exam only once. If you are planning to attend a New York City Catholic high school as a tenth-, eleventh- or twelfth-grader, you will not need to take the TACHS. Instead, you will need to apply directly to the high school you wish to attend.

The TACHS tests basic knowledge in the areas of reading, language arts, math, and general reasoning ability. The specific details of each of these sections will be discussed later. The TACHS is an instrument used to help high schools make decisions about admissions and placement of eighth-graders into the high school setting as ninth-graders. Therefore, the exam is not designed to trick applicants or present any extremely difficult challenges for applicants. Rather, the TACHS tests knowledge and skills that have been determined to be standard for eighth-grade students. Knowing this ahead of time should help you relax and do your best on the exam.

Results from the exam will be sent to up to three Catholic high schools of your choice. If you are currently enrolled in a Catholic elementary school, your school will also receive the results of your exam. If you are not currently enrolled in a Catholic school, results of the exam will be sent to your home.

You can register for the exam online or by phone or paper registration. Be sure to complete and submit the Eligibility Form for Students Needing Extended Testing Time, if applicable. Upon registration, you will receive an Admit Card that will confirm your test site. You must bring this Admit Card with you on the day of the test. Complete registration information, including important dates, registration procedures, registration fees, and testing locations can be found online at www.tachsinfo.com.

THE TACHS EXAM FORMAT

The multiple-choice answer format is used throughout the TACHS exam. Most answer choices are given in sets of four, and the sets are grouped as (A), (B), (C), (D) or as (J), (K), (L), (M). For example, the first question might use (A), (B), (C), (D) as the answer choices, and the next question might use (J), (K), (L), (M). Answer choices in the Spelling section are given in groups of five, and the sets are grouped as (A), (B), (C), (D), (E) or as (J), (K), (L), (M), (N). This design should help you keep your place as you flip back and forth between the test booklet and the answer sheet.

ABOUT THE TACHS QUESTIONS

Let's take a look at each one of the sections of the exam, so you have a good idea about what to expect when you take the exam.

Reading

The Reading section of the TACHS contains two parts. Part 1 of the Reading section deals with vocabulary. Here you will be presented with vocabulary words within the context of short phrases. You will be asked to select from a group of possible answers the word that means the same or nearly the same as the underlined vocabulary word in the short phrase. Vocabulary words that appear on the exam may be nouns, verbs, and modifiers. Approximately the same number of each will appear on the exam.

To <u>roam</u> the plains

(A) follow

(B) wander

(C) disguise

(D) destroy

The correct answer is (B), *wander.* Other synonyms include "stray," "ramble," and "rove."

Part 2 of the Reading section measures ability in reading comprehension, or how well you understand what you read. In Part 2, you will be presented with a number of reading passages of varying length. Some passages may be only a few lines while others may be up to a page in length. Reading passages will vary in content. Some passages may be fiction and may include fables, stories, and excerpts from previously published works. Other passages will be nonfiction and may include such topics as social studies and science. The exam will test your ability to comprehend what you read and will not test your understanding of science and social studies, for example. For the most part, you will be asked to make inferences or generalizations about what you read. You may be asked to identify the meaning of a word or phrase in context, to identify the main idea of the passage, and to determine what might come next in the story or to "read between the lines."

Paul Grisham, as a young boy, sold newspapers on the street corner to help his family. He went to work before sunrise, worked until it was time for school, and then returned home after school. Paul walked everywhere he went, regardless of the weather. The work ethic he developed as a youngster contributed to his eventual financial success as an adult.

Based on the information in the passage above, which of the following can be inferred about Paul's family when he was a child?

(A) Paul's family had very little money.

(B) Paul's family was very wealthy.

(C) Paul's family lived in the country.

(D) Paul's family was very large.

The correct answer is (A). Paul worked before school and "walked everywhere he went." It can be inferred from the passage that he worked, because he needed the money, and walked, because the family had no other means of transportation.

Written Expression

The Written Expression section of the TACHS tests different skills and abilities in the language arts. This section covers spelling, capitalization, punctuation, usage, and expression.

The first portion of the TACHS Written Expression section tests your knowledge of **spelling.** You will be presented with four words, one of which may be spelled incorrectly. You will also be presented with a fifth choice, *(No mistakes)*, in case all four words are correct. This actually tests your knowledge of four words at a time. Spelling errors you may see on the test include common mistakes in adding unnecessary letters, omitting letters, or reversing letters.

(A) demolition

(B) cordial

(C) ocasional

(D) pleasant

(E) *(No mistakes)*

The correct answer is (C). The correct spelling is *occasional*.

The second portion of the Written Expression section tests your skill and ability in **capitalization.** You will be given three choices that include words that are capitalized and words that are not. You will be asked to find mistakes in capitalization. You will also be presented with a fourth choice, *(No mistakes)*, in the event that there are no capitalization errors. Capitalization errors include capitalizing when unnecessary and not capitalizing when necessary for such things as names, holidays, organizations, and titles.

(A) The services for easter

(B) will be held at St. John's

(C) located at 123 Main Street.

(D) *(No mistakes)*

The correct answer is (A). *Easter* should be capitalized.

The third portion of the Written Expression section tests your skill and ability in **punctuation.** You will be given several lines of writing in which you are to identify punctuation errors. You will be given a fourth choice, *(No mistakes)*, in the event that there are no punctuation errors. You may find errors in punctuation dealing with commas, semicolons, periods, and apostrophes.

(A) The city council met last night

(B) and decided to lower taxes.

(C) in the Brooksmith neighborhood.

(D) *(No mistakes)*

The correct answer is (B). There should be no period at the end of choice (B).

The fourth portion of the Written Expression section measures your ability in **usage.** You will be presented with several lines of text. You will need to select the line containing a usage error—misuse of verbs, pronouns, modifiers, or word choice—or you can select "(No mistakes)" if you believe there is no error. Here is an example:

(J) The sky became darker as the storm rolled in.

(K) I thought I heard thunder in the distance.

(L) Me and Brooke ran as fast as we could.

(M) *(No mistakes)*

The correct answer is (L). The sentence should read: Brooke and I ran as fast as we could.

The fifth portion of the Written Expression section tests your ability in **expression.** For these questions, you will choose the best or most fitting way of stating an idea in a sentence or paragraph. Errors include the organization of sentence and paragraph elements, conciseness, clarity, and appropriateness of expression. Following are two examples.

(A) Clarisse, though a fast runner, a match for her cousin Arnold she was not.

(B) Though she was fast; Clarisse was a runner but was no match for her cousin Arnold.

(C) Though Clarisse was a fast runner, she was no match for her cousin Arnold.

(D) As a runner, though fast, a match for her cousin Arnold Clarisse was not.

The correct answer is (C). In this sentence, the clause "though Clarisse was a fast runner" is followed by a comma, which is the correct punctuation. Choice (B) is incorrect, because it contains a semicolon instead of a comma after the introductory phrase "though she was fast."

(1) Jacob is highly allergic to peanuts and must avoid eating this food. (2) <u>Additionally</u>, he must be careful not to consume any products made with peanuts or peanut oil.

What is the best way to write the underlined part of sentence 2?

(A) Furthermore

(B) Because

(C) However

(D) *(No change)*

The correct answer is (A). "Furthermore" is the closest in meaning to "Additionally."

Math

The Math section of TACHS measures your ability to solve math problems in a variety of ways. For each math question, you will be given answer choices from which to choose. The first portion tests your knowledge of math concepts such as fractions, factors, multiples, multiplication, division, and decimals.

The fraction $\frac{9}{10}$ can also be expressed as which of the following decimals?

(A) 0.9

(B) 0.09

(C) 0.009

(D) 9.0

The correct answer is (A). 9 divided by 10 is 0.9.

The second portion of this section tests your ability to solve word problems using the basic math concepts mentioned above.

Gail has $\frac{2}{3}$ as many French fries as Mindy. Mindy has 12 French fries. How many French fries does Gail have?

(A) 8

(B) 9

(C) 10

(D) Not given

The correct answer is (A). $\frac{2}{3} \times 12 = 8$

The third portion of this section measures your ability to estimate, or do the math in your head, without using a pencil and paper.

The closest estimate of 3.9 × 4.1 is _____.

(A) 9

(B) 12

(C) 16

(D) 20

The correct answer is (C). $3.9 \times 4.1 \approx 4 \times 4 \approx 16$

The fourth portion of this section measures your ability to interpret data, or to work with charts and graphs.

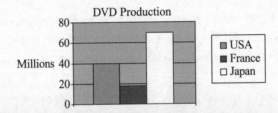

The chart above shows the annual production of DVDs in various countries as measured in millions. Based on the information in the chart, about how many DVDs does Japan produce each year?

(A) 70

(B) 70,000,000

(C) 60

(D) 60,000,000

The correct answer is (B). Japan is represented by the white bar that places yearly DVD production at 70 million, or 70,000,000.

Ability

The Ability section of the exam tests your abstract reasoning ability. You will be presented with visual tasks that require you to generalize from one item or series of items to another. These are reasoning skills that are going to be tested, not academic abilities, so don't worry if this sounds unlike anything you've been taught in school. Identifying patterns and looking ahead for the logical outcome of series of changes to shapes is all that will be required of you in this section.

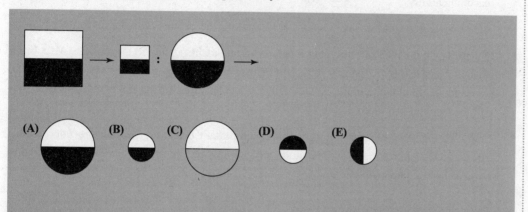

The correct answer is (B). The first pair share a similar item but with the second rectangle being smaller than the first. The same logic must hold true for the second pair. Choice (B) is a smaller version of the black and white circle in the series above.

SUMMING IT UP

- The Test for Admission into Catholic High Schools (TACHS) is for eighth-grade students wishing to attend a Catholic high school in New York City beginning in the ninth grade.

- The TACHS tests basic knowledge in the areas of reading, language arts, math, and general reasoning ability.

- The TACHS uses a multiple-choice answer format, and the testing time is approximately 2 hours.

- On test day, remember to bring your Admit Card and identification to the test site. Also, bring several sharpened No. 2 pencils with good erasers. Don't bring any notes, books, or scratch paper. In addition, you will not be able to bring a calculator, watch, or any electronic devices into the examination room.

- Complete registration information, including important dates, registration procedures, registration fees, and testing locations, along with sample test questions, can be found online at www.tachsinfo.com.

All About the Cooperative Admissions Examination Program (COOP)

OVERVIEW

- **The COOP exam format**
- **How the COOP is scored**
- **About the COOP questions**
- **Summing it up**

The two most widely used entrance exams for Catholic high schools are the COOP and the HSPT®.

What exactly is the COOP exam? The Cooperative Admissions Examination Program (called COOP, for short) is a multiple-choice-style exam designed to determine the academic aptitude and skills achievement of eighth-graders seeking admission to selective high schools. The COOP tests a student's understanding of language, reading, and mathematics, among other things.

The COOP is administered only to students planning to enter ninth grade. It is given once each year, during either October or November. If you plan on taking the COOP, you must first pre-register for this exam, either through your parochial elementary school, or, if currently enrolled in public school, as directed on the application form obtained from a parochial school. The Cooperative Admissions Office now offers the option of applying online for the COOP Examination, including paying the nonrefundable $60 examination fee by credit card when applying online; the examination fee includes reporting scores to three high schools. To access the COOP online application registration form, go to www.coopexam.org, select "Online Application Registration," and follow the instructions. Please note that there are different deadline dates for the online and mail-in applications.

Once registered, you'll receive a handbook of instructions that includes some sample questions to familiarize you with the exam. Upon registration you will also receive an admission ticket that you must bring with you to the assigned testing location on the assigned testing date.

THE COOP EXAM FORMAT

The multiple-choice answer format is used throughout the COOP exam. Most answer choices are given in sets of four, and the sets are grouped either as (A), (B), (C), (D) or as (F), (G), (H), (J). For example, the first question might use (A), (B), (C), (D) as the answer choices, and the next question might use (F), (G), (H), (J). The test is designed this way to make it easy for you to keep your place as you flip back and forth between the test booklet and the answer sheet.

In the past, various sections of the test have offered five answer choices, so (E) and (K) are added to the answer group range. Note that there is no choice (I). (I) has been omitted to avoid any possible confusion with the number "1." Each year, the publisher of the COOP (CTB/McGraw-Hill) changes 30 percent of the content of the exam. Most of the changes consist of substituting new questions for old ones. Changes also include new question styles, changing numbers of questions or time limits of test sections, or eliminating or combining test sections. The following chart was accurate at the time this book was written. Your own exam might not adhere precisely to these section titles, the number of questions, or the exact timing, but this chart is similar enough for you to use as your guide.

TIMETABLE AND ANALYSIS OF THE COOP

Test Number and Topic	Number of Questions	Time Allotted
1 Sequences	20	15 minutes
2 Analogies	20	7 minutes
3 Quantitative Reasoning	20	15 minutes
4 Verbal Reasoning—Words	20	15 minutes
15-minute break		
5 Verbal Reasoning—Context	20	15 minutes
6 Mathematics	40	35 minutes
7 Reading and Language Arts	40	40 minutes

TIP

On the COOP exam, all questions count the same. You won't get more points for answering a really difficult math question than you get for answering a very simple analogy. Remember that the more time you spend wrestling with the answer to one "stumper," the less time you have to whip through several easier questions.

HOW THE COOP IS SCORED

Raw scores for each test section of the COOP are determined by crediting one point for each question answered correctly. There is no deduction or penalty for any question answered incorrectly. Because each part of the exam contains a different number of questions, your raw score is converted to a scaled score according to a formula devised by the test administrators. The use of scaled scores enables schools to compare your performance on one part of the exam with your performance on other parts of the exam. Your scores are compared to the scores of other students taking the exam and are reported as percentiles. Your percentile rank shows where you stand compared to others who took the test. A percentile rank is reported for each part of the test.

There is no passing grade on the COOP, nor is there a failing grade. All of the high schools to which you have applied receive your scaled scores and your percentile rankings. Each has its own standards, and each makes its own admissions decisions based on test scores, school grades, recommendations, and other factors.

ABOUT THE COOP QUESTIONS

The following questions are examples of what you can expect on the COOP. Each question is preceded by directions like those on the actual exam and is followed by an explanatory answer. Later in this book, you will find two COOP Practice Tests you can take to prepare for the actual exam.

Test 1. Sequences

Directions: There are three forms of questions designed to measure sequential reasoning ability. In each case, you must choose the answer that would best continue the pattern or sequence.

1.
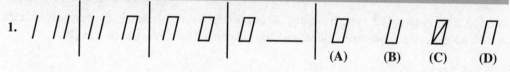
   (A)   (B)   (C)   (D)

Each frame contains two figures. The second figure within each frame has one more line than the first figure. In the final frame, the first figure has four lines; the second must have five, as in choice (C). **The correct answer is (C).**

2. 2 4 6 | 3 5 7 | 15 17 _____
   (F) 18
   (G) 16
   (H) 19
   (I) 15

Within each frame, the pattern is simply the number plus 2, plus 2. 17 plus 2 equals 19. **The correct answer is (H).**

3. Abcde   aBcde   abCde   _____   abcdE
   (A) AbcdE
   (B) abCDe
   (C) aBcDe
   (D) abcDe

In each group of letters, the single capitalized letter moves progressively one space to the right. **The correct answer is (D).**

Test 2. Analogies

Directions: Analogy questions test your ability to recognize and understand relationships. In these questions, you must choose the picture that would go in the empty box so that the bottom two pictures are related in the same way that the top two are related.

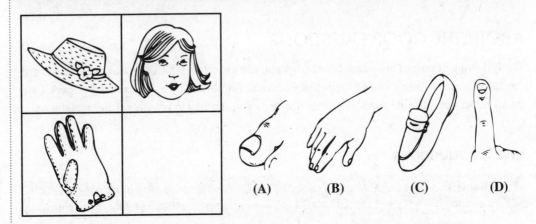

The relationship of hat to head is that a hat is a head covering; therefore, the best answer is the drawing of a hand, because a glove is a hand covering. **The correct answer is (B).**

Test 3. Quantitative Reasoning

Three different question styles are used to measure your aptitude for thinking with numbers. The following questions are typical of what you can expect on this test.

Directions: Find the relationship of the numbers in one column to the numbers in the other column. Then find the missing number.

1. $2 \rightarrow \blacksquare \rightarrow 4$

   $3 \rightarrow \blacksquare \rightarrow 9$

   $4 \rightarrow \blacksquare \rightarrow ?$

   (A) 8

   (B) 12

   (C) 13

   (D) 16

If you think of the first pattern as 2 times itself (2) = 4, the second as 3 times itself (3) = 9, then the third would be 4 times itself (4) = 16. **The correct answer is (D).**

Directions: Find the fraction of the grid that is shaded.

2.

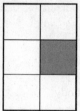

(F) $\frac{1}{2}$

(G) $\frac{1}{4}$

(H) $\frac{1}{6}$

(J) $\frac{1}{8}$

There are six squares. One of them is shaded. We know that 1 over 6 is $\frac{1}{6}$. **The correct answer is (H).**

Directions: Look at the scale that shows sets of shapes of equal weight. Find an equivalent pair of sets that would also balance the scale.

3.

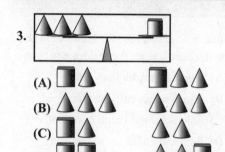

The scale indicates that 1 cube = 3 cones. The only answer that maintains this relationship is choice (B), since it shows that 3 cones = 3 cones. **The correct answer is (B).**

Test 4. Verbal Reasoning—Words

Two different question styles are used to measure how well you reason with words. Each question style has its own directions.

Directions: Find the word that names a necessary part of the underlined word.

1. claustrophobia

   (A) closet

   (B) fear

   (C) door

   (D) space

Claustrophobia is the fear of being in small, enclosed places. While the person who suffers from claustrophobia would surely be uncomfortable in a closet or behind a closed door, the *necessary* ingredient of claustrophobia is *fear*. **The correct answer is (B).**

Directions: The words in the top row are related in some way. The words in the bottom row are related in the same way. Find the word that completes the bottom row of words.

2. best better good
   worst worse _____

   (F) bad

   (G) worser

   (H) okay

   (J) good

The words in the top row are in a comparative series, with the superlative on the left. Likewise, the words in the bottom row must be a similar comparative series. The comparison descends from *worst* to *worse* to *bad*. **The correct answer is (F).**

Test 5. Verbal Reasoning—Context

Directions: Find the statement that must be true according to the given information.

1. Julie is in second grade. Laura is in third grade. Julie's sister Anne rides a tricycle.

   (A) Laura is smarter than Julie.

   (B) Anne is physically handicapped.

   (C) Julie is behind Laura in school.

   (D) Julie and Laura are sisters.

The only certainty is that Julie is behind Laura in school, choice (C). The fact that Laura is ahead in school does not necessarily mean that she is smarter, choice (A), possibly only older. Anne might be a normal, healthy 2-year-old, so choice (B) is incorrect. Julie and Anne are sisters, but Laura's relationship to them is not given, so choice (D) is wrong. **The correct answer is (C).**

Directions: Here are some words translated from an artificial, imaginary language. Read the words and answer the question.

2. *ababawayla* means somewhere
   parimoodu means nobody
   pariwayla means somebody
   Which word means *nowhere*?

   (F) waylapari

   (G) pariababa

   (H) mooduababa

   (J) ababamoodu

You will notice that elements of words are repeated among the English words as well as among the artificial words. By noticing the pattern of repetition, you can define and isolate word elements. In this sample, *wayla* means some, *pari* means body, *ababa* means where, and *moodu* means no. The order of the elements of words in this artificial language is the reverse of the order in English but is consistent within the language. Your answer choice must reflect that order, which is the reason that choice (H) is not correct. **The correct answer is (J).**

Test 6. Mathematics

The computations in this test are not complicated, but you must have a firm grasp of the meaning of mathematics and a little bit of common sense in order to answer the questions.

1. 350 students are taking this examination in this school today; $\frac{4}{7}$ of these students are girls. How many boys are taking the exam in this school?

    (A) 150

    (B) 200

    (C) 500

    (D) 550

    The correct answer is (A). If $\frac{4}{7}$ are girls, $\frac{3}{7}$ are boys. $\frac{3}{7}$ of $350 = \frac{3}{7} \times \frac{350}{1} = 150$.

2. Which number sentence is true?

    (F) $-12 > 9$

    (G) $-5 > -8$

    (H) $-3 = 3$

    (J) $2 < -6$

    The correct answer is (G). Draw a number line to prove this to yourself, if necessary.

3. Mrs. Breen came home from the store and put two half-gallon containers of milk into the refrigerator. Jim came home from school with a few friends, and they all had milk and cookies.

    When they had finished, only $\frac{1}{2}$ of one container of milk remained. How much milk did the boys drink?

    (A) $1\frac{1}{2}$ pints

    (B) $1\frac{1}{2}$ quarts

    (C) 3 quarts

    (D) $1\frac{1}{2}$ gallons

The correct answer is (C). There are 4 quarts in a gallon; so there are 2 quarts in each half-gallon container. If only $\frac{1}{2}$ of one of the containers remained, then the boys drank 3 quarts.

4. Look at the figure below. Then choose the statement that is true.

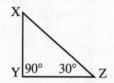

    (F) $m \angle X < m \angle Y < m \angle Z$

    (G) $m \angle X > m \angle Y > m \angle Z$

    (H) $m \angle X = m \angle Z + m \angle Y$

    (J) $m \angle Z < m \angle X < m \angle Y$

The correct answer is (J). Because the sum of the angles of a triangle is 180°, angle X must be 60°. 60 is greater than 30 (angle Z), and it is smaller than 90 (angle Y).

5. Look at the graph below. Then read the question and choose the correct answer.

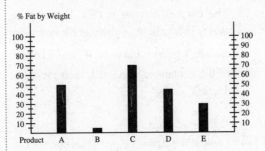

% Fat by Weight

According to FDA regulations, in order to print the designation "light" on its labels, a product must contain no more than 45% fat by weight. Which of these products may be labeled "light"?

(A) D only

(B) B and E only

(C) B, D, and E only

(D) A and C only

The correct answer is (C). The regulations state that a "light" product contains *no more than 45% fat*. Product D, which contains exactly 45% fat, may be labeled "light" along with B and E.

6. The piece of property shown below is to be divided into uniform building lots of 100 × 100 sq. ft. Twenty percent of the property must be left undeveloped. How many houses may be built on this property?

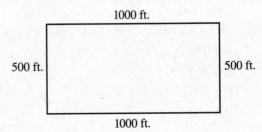

(F) 20

(G) 40

(H) 50

(J) 100

The correct answer is (G). The entire property is 1000 ft. × 500 ft., which equals 500,000 sq. ft. Twenty percent must be left undeveloped. 500,000 × 20% = 100,000. 500,000 − 100,000 = 400,000 sq. ft. to be developed. Each building lot is 100 × 100 = 10,000 sq. ft. 400,000 divided by 10,000 = 40 houses.

Test 7. Reading and Language Arts

Directions: Read the passage and the questions following it. Answer each question based upon what you have read.

As he threw his head back in the chair, his glance happened to rest upon a bell, a disused bell, that hung in the room and communicated, for some purpose now forgotten, with a chamber in the highest story of the building. It was with great astonishment, and with a strange inexplicable dread, that, as he looked, he saw this bell begin to swing. Soon it rang out loudly, and so did every bell in the house.

This was succeeded by a clanking noise, deep down below as if some person were dragging a heavy chain over the casks in the wine merchant's cellar. Then he heard the noise much louder on the floors below; then coming up the stairs; then coming straight toward his door.

It came in through the heavy door, and a specter passed into the room before his eyes. And upon its coming in, the dying flame leaped up, as though it cried, "I know him! Marley's ghost!"

—from *A Christmas Carol*
by Charles Dickens

> **NOTE**
> It's an "open-book" test. In COOP reading comprehension questions, the answers will be directly stated or implied in the passage.

1. The bell that began ringing

   (A) was large and heavy.

   (B) did so by itself.

   (C) was attached to every bell in the house.

   (D) rested first on his glance.

   The correct answer is (B). The bell began to ring by itself. The bell might have been large and heavy, but we have no way of knowing this from the passage. The ringing of every bell in the house would likely be due to the same supernatural factors that caused the first bell to ring.

2. The man who was listening to the bell

   (F) dragged a chain across the wine casks.

   (G) sat perfectly still.

   (H) was apparently very frightened.

   (J) is Marley's ghost.

   The correct answer is (H). Obviously, this was a frightening experience. Also, *inexplicable dread* indicates fear.

3. The man in the story

   (A) first heard noises in his room.

   (B) is probably a wine merchant.

   (C) recognized Marley's ghost.

   (D) set the room on fire.

   The correct answer is (C). If the man imagined the flame crying out the identity of the specter, he must have recognized it himself.

4. How would you describe the mood being created by the author?

   (F) Festive

   (G) Depressing

   (H) Exciting

   (J) Spooky

   The correct answer is (J). Unexplained bells, creaking, clanking, and ghosts all create a spooky mood. The man in the story might have found the scene depressing, and you, the reader, might find the story exciting, but the overall mood is best described as *spooky*.

Directions: Choose the word that best completes the sentence.

5. I would bring grandma to visit you,

   _____ I have no car.

   (A) while

   (B) because

   (C) but

   (D) moreover

   (E) therefore

   The correct answer is (C). The conjunction *but* is the only choice that makes any sense in the context of the sentence.

Directions: Choose the sentence that is complete and correctly written.

6. **(F)** Cold-blooded reptiles with no mechanism for controlling body temperature.

   (G) Reptiles, which have no mechanism for controlling body temperature, are described as cold-blooded animals.

   (H) Reptiles are described as cold-blooded animals, this means that they have no mechanism for controlling body temperature.

   (J) Reptiles are described as cold-blooded animals and they have no mechanism for controlling body temperature.

   (K) Cold-blooded animals with no mechanism for controlling temperature, a description of reptiles.

   The correct answer is (G). Choice (F) is a sentence fragment. Choice (H) is a comma splice of two independent clauses. Choice (J) is a run-on sentence. Choice (K) has no verb, so it is nothing more than a sentence fragment.

Directions: Choose the sentence that uses verbs correctly.

7. **(A)** While we were waiting for the local train, the express roared past.

   (B) The sky darkens ominously and rain began to fall.

   (C) The woman will apply for a new job because she wanted to earn more money.

   (D) I wish I knew who will be backing into my car.

   (E) The wind blows, the thunder clapped, lightning will fill the sky, and it rains.

   The correct answer is (A). All other choices mix tenses in illogical order.

Directions: Choose the underlined word that is the simple subject of the sentence.

8. The first step in improving your writing
            (F)   (G)   (H)
   is to know what makes a good sentence.
               (J)   (K)

   The correct answer is (F). In this sentence, *step* is the simple subject.

Directions: Choose the underlined word or group of words that is the simple predicate (verb) of the sentence.

9. A decrease in the incidence of
      (A)   (B)
   contagious diseases proves that
                      (C)
   sanitation is worthwhile.
            (D)   (E)

   The correct answer is (C). The subject of the sentence is *decrease*, and the decrease *proves* the value of sanitation.

Directions: Choose the sentence that best combines the two underlined sentences into one.

10. Fish in tropical waters are colorful. They swim among coral reefs.

    (F) In tropical waters there are coral reefs swimming with colorful fish.

    (G) Fish swim among coral reefs in tropical waters, and they are colorful.

    (H) When fish swim among coral reefs, they are colorful in tropical waters.

    (J) Colorful fish swim among coral reefs in tropical waters.

    (K) Colorful tropical waters are home to swimming fish and coral reefs.

    The correct answer is (J). That sentence is the simplest and most straightforward one.

Directions: Choose the topic sentence that best fits the paragraph.

11. _____ However, in reality, they are adaptable, intelligent, and often beautiful. A squid's body appears to be all head and feet. These feet, commonly referred to as arms, have little suction cups on them.

    (A) Because the squid is shy, it is often misunderstood.

    (B) Scientists consider squid the most intelligent mollusks.

    (C) Squid are considered a tasty treat by the other inhabitants of the sea.

    (D) The body of the squid is uniquely adapted for locomotion and for grabbing in its liquid environment.

    (E) Squid are considered by many to be ugly, unpleasant creatures.

    The correct answer is (E). The second sentence contradicts the topic statement about the squid's appearance.

Directions: Choose the sentence that does *not* belong in the paragraph.

12. (1) Computers have definitely changed the way that we view time and space. (2) Author Dragana Kovacic discusses this notion in her article "Digital Technology and the Information Revolution." (3) According to Kovacic, computers have expanded our image of space by making it possible to reach any point on the planet through the Internet. (4) Despite our increasing reliance on the Internet for communication, information, and entertainment, nearly 25 percent of Americans do not have Internet access in their homes. (5) They have also compressed our view of time by allowing us to access information immediately.

    (A) Sentence 2

    (B) Sentence 3

    (C) Sentence 4

    (D) Sentence 5

    The correct answer is (C). The paragraph is about the ways that computers have changed our perceptions of time and space, not about the digital divide or lack of Internet access, so Sentence 4, choice (C), does not belong in the paragraph.

SUMMING IT UP

- The Cooperative Admissions Examination Program (COOP) tests eighth-graders' understanding of language, reading, and mathematics.

- When you register, you will receive an admission ticket. Be sure to bring it with you to the exam.

- The COOP uses a multiple-choice answer format.

- There is no deduction or penalty for wrong answers on the COOP. Therefore, if you don't know the answer, guess.

All About the High School Placement Test (HSPT®)

OVERVIEW

- **The HSPT® exam format**
- **How to prepare for the HSPT®**
- **How the HSPT® is scored**
- **About the HSPT® questions**
- **The HSPT® optional tests**
- **Summing it up**

The Scholastic Testing Service High School Placement Test, called HSPT® for short, is a five-part, multiple-choice test of verbal, quantitative, reading, mathematics, and language skills. The exam takes approximately 2 hours and 30 minutes. It contains 298 questions that are designed to indicate how well a student performs tasks that can be expected of an eighth-grader.

There are two different kinds of HSPT® exams: the Closed HSPT® and the Open HSPT®. The Closed HSPT® is administered by the school, but it is scored by the Scholastic Testing Service (STS). Closed HSPT® scores are compared to national standard distribution norms, so nationwide percentiles can be computed. The Open HSPT® is administered and scored by the school, so STS does not deal directly with student results. The Open HSPT® uses old versions of the Closed HSPT®.

Scholastic Testing Service provides, along with the High School Placement Test, a choice of one optional test in Mechanical Aptitude, Science, or Catholic Religion. Because many schools do not choose any of these tests, and because the results on the optional test are not included as part of the HSPT® composite score, this book doesn't cover the optional tests. However, to give you some idea of what you can expect on an optional test, an outline of the Science test is provided at the end of this section. This outline shows you the typical structure and scope of the optional tests. If you are required to take one of the optional tests, be sure to seek study advice from the school to which you are applying.

THE HSPT® EXAM FORMAT

Like the COOP exam, the HSPT® exam uses a multiple-choice format. Each question offers three or four answer choices, lettered (A), (B), (C), and (D). Take a look at the following Timetable and Analysis of the HSPT® chart to see the timing, number of questions, and question types of the basic HSPT® exam. Questions on the HSPT® exam are numbered consecutively from 1 to 298. This numbering system helps you avoid the pitfall of answering questions in the wrong section of the answer sheet. For example, because there is only one question 25, you aren't able to mark your answer to question 25 in the wrong part of the sheet.

TIMETABLE AND ANALYSIS OF THE HSPT®

Test Section	Number of Questions	Time Allotted
Verbal Skills	60	16 minutes
Verbal Analogies	10	
Synonyms	15	
Logic	10	
Verbal Classifications	16	
Antonyms	9	
Quantitative Skills	52	30 minutes
Number Series	18	
Geometric Comparison	9	
Nongeometric Comparison	8	
Number Manipulation	17	
Reading	62	25 minutes
Comprehension	40	
Vocabulary	22	
Mathematics	64	45 minutes
Concepts	24	
Problem-Solving	40	
Language Skills	60	25 minutes
Punctuation and Capitalization	12	
Usage	28	
Spelling	10	
Composition	10	

HOW TO PREPARE FOR THE HSPT®

As noted on the website www.ststesting.com/hspt/, STS offers the following tips to help students best prepare for the HSPT®:

- Carefully listen to and read the directions for each subtest.

- Pace yourself—there are time limits for each subtest. Test administrators should state when time is halfway through so you can determine if you'll be able to finish at your current pace. Avoid spending too much time on one question.

- Read each question carefully.

- For the Mathematics subtest, you will need to work out the problem; you won't be able to use a calculator. You may use scratch paper or your test booklet to do any calculations.

- Answer every question. If you're not sure, just take your best guess. you won't be penalized for answering incorrectly.

Check your work. If you still have time, go back and review your answers. Make sure each item has only one response. Of course, while taking the test, check that the answer you are marking on your answer sheet matches the item number in the test booklet.

HOW THE HSPT® IS SCORED

As was just noted, your score on the HSPT® is based on the number of questions you answer correctly. No points are subtracted for incorrect answers, so it pays to answer as many questions as possible—even if you have to guess.

Scholastic Testing Service converts your raw scores to standard scores that are reported on a scale of 200 to 800. Your HSPT® score report includes your standard scores, your national and local percentile rank, your grade equivalent, and your Cognitive Skills Quotient.

Scholastic Testing Service will compare your performance with that of the other 120,000 students taking the exam in some 1,000 schools throughout the United States, many of these among the 1,570 Catholic secondary schools in the country. Scholastic Testing Service will also compare your performance with that of other students in your own area. All of this information is sent to the high schools you have indicated on your answer sheet. It is up to each school to decide what is an acceptable score for admission to the freshman class.

ABOUT THE HSPT® QUESTIONS

The following questions are typical of what you can expect on the HSPT® exam. Each question is followed by an explanatory answer. In Part V, you will find two full-length HSPT® Practice Tests you can take to prepare for the actual exam.

Part 1. Verbal Skills

Verbal Analogies

Throw is to ball as shoot is to
(A) policeman.
(B) kill.
(C) arrow.
(D) hunting.

The correct answer is (C). This is an action-to-object relationship. You *throw* a ball, and you *shoot* an arrow.

Synonyms

Meager most nearly means
(A) well received.
(B) long overdue.
(C) valuable.
(D) scanty.

The correct answer is (D). *Meager* means lacking in quality or quantity. *Sparse* or *scanty* are synonyms for *meager*.

NOTE

Don't worry that you don't see directions or instructions about how to answer these question types. In Part III of this book, you'll find in-depth reviews of each question type contained in the entrance exams discussed here.

Logic

Bill runs faster than Mike. Jeff runs faster than Bill. Jeff is not as fast as Mike. If the first two statements are true, the third statement is

(A) true.

(B) false.

(C) uncertain.

The correct answer is (B). If the first two statements are true, Jeff runs faster than both Bill and Mike.

Verbal Classification

Which word does *not* belong with the others?

(A) Car

(B) Plane

(C) Van

(D) Truck

The correct answer is (B). A plane is the only vehicle that flies; all others are modes of ground transportation.

Antonyms

Loyal means the *opposite* of

(A) lovely.

(B) unfaithful.

(C) unlucky.

(D) usual.

The correct answer is (B). *Loyal* means faithful. The best antonym is *unfaithful*.

Part 2. Quantitative Skills

Number Series

Look at this series: 10, 14, 18, 22, 26, ... What number should come next?

(A) 28

(B) 29

(C) 30

(D) 32

The correct answer is (C). The pattern in this series is to add 4 to each number. $26 + 4 = 30$.

Geometric Comparisons

Examine hourglasses (A), (B), and (C) and find the best answer.

(A)   (B)   (C)

(A) (B) shows the most time passed.

(B) (A) shows the most time passed.

(C) (C) shows the most time passed.

(D) (A), (B), and (C) show the same time passed.

The correct answer is (B). Be especially careful to avoid response errors when answering these questions. The correct answer is hourglass (A), but you must mark the letter of the correct statement, which, of course, is choice (B).

Nongeometric Comparisons

Examine (I), (II), and (III) and find the best answer.

  (I) $(4 \times 2) - 3$

 (II) $(4 \times 3) - 2$

(III) $(4 + 3) - 2$

(A) (I) is greater than (III).

(B) (I), (II), and (III) are equal.

(C) (III) is greater than (II).

(D) (I) and (III) are equal.

The correct answer is (D). Determine the numerical value of (I), (II), and (III). Then test each answer choice to see which one is true.

  (I) $(4 \times 2) - 3 = 8 - 3 = 5$

 (II) $(4 \times 3) - 2 = 12 - 2 = 10$

(III) $(4 \times 3) - 2 = 7 - 2 = 5$

Number Manipulation

What number is 5 more than $\frac{2}{3}$ of 27?

(A) 14

(B) 32

(C) 9

(D) 23

The correct answer is (D).

First find $\frac{2}{3}$ of 27: $\frac{2}{3} \times 27 = 18$.

Then add: $18 + 5 = 23$.

Part 3. Reading

Comprehension

Most of us know that physical exercise is important for a healthy lifestyle. We know that people who exercise live longer lives and resist many fatal diseases. We know, in short, that exercise is a good thing. What we might not realize, however, is exactly how *many* benefits physical activity provides. Research conducted by the Harvard University School of Public Health has shed light on this issue by describing the effects of exercise in detail.

The Harvard studies show that physical exercise helps prevent many diseases, including obesity, stroke, heart disease, and many types of cancers. Exercise increases our balance as well as the strength of our muscles and bones. Exercise helps us concentrate, enables us to burn more fat, keeps our joints healthy, and fortifies our immune systems. If all that weren't enough, exercise also has an important psychological benefit: it causes us to feel more positive and to maintain better moods.

Which of the following is true regarding the Harvard University School of Public Health?

(A) It conducted research studies showing that physical activity prevents many diseases.

(B) It ran many tests on exercise and published a book on the benefits of exercise.

(C) It developed technology to measure what happens to the joints of people who exercise.

(D) It ran scientific studies to examine how athletes can be harmed by too much exercise.

The correct answer is (A). To answer a question like this one, it is helpful to re-read the part of the passage that contains the reference to the Harvard School of Public Health. This reference occurs at the end of the first paragraph and the beginning of the second one. We learn that the Harvard School of Public Health has conducted research about the benefits of exercise. According to paragraph two, the school's studies have shown that "physical exercise helps prevent many diseases," so choice (A) is correct. Choice (B) is incorrect because we're never told that the Harvard School of Public Health published a book on the benefits of exercise, just simply that it conducted research studies.

Vocabulary

As used in the previous passage, the word *fortifies* probably means

(A) slows.

(B) releases.

(C) analyzes.

(D) strengthens.

The correct answer is (D). The passage discusses the benefits of exercise, emphasizing its positive effects on our health. This particular sentence describes health improvements brought about by exercise, so we can conclude that exercise improves the immune system in some way. We are looking for a word that is close in meaning to "improves." Choice (D), *strengthens*, is correct.

Part 4. Mathematics

Concepts

To the nearest tenth, 52.693 is written

(A) 52.7

(B) 53

(C) 52.69

(D) 52.6

The correct answer is (A). To "round off" to the nearest tenth means to "round off" to one digit to the right of the decimal point. The digit to the right of the decimal point is 6. However, the next digit is 9, which means you must round up to 52.7.

Problem-Solving

On a map, 1 inch represents 500 miles. How many miles apart are two cities that are $1\frac{1}{2}$ inches apart on the map?

(A) 750

(B) 1000

(C) 1250

(D) 1500

The correct answer is (A). If 1 inch = 500 miles, then $\frac{1}{2}$ inch = 250 miles. Therefore, $1\frac{1}{2}$ inches = 500 + 250 = 750 miles.

Part 5. Language Skills

Punctuation and Capitalization

Find the sentence that has an error in capitalization or punctuation. If you find no mistake, mark choice (D) as your answer.

(A) Sally asked, "What time will you be home?"

(B) Doug hopes to enter John F. Kennedy High School next Fall.

(C) The letter arrived on Saturday, January 15.

(D) No mistakes

The correct answer is (B). This sentence has an error in capitalization. The word *fall* should not be capitalized.

Usage

Find the sentence that has an error in usage. If you find no mistake, mark (D) as your answer.

(A) Many children adopt the beliefs of their parents.

(B) "Is he always so amusing?" she asked.

(C) All the officers declined except she.

(D) No mistakes

The correct answer is (C). This sentence has an error in usage. The word *she* should be *her* since it acts as the object of the preposition *except*.

Spelling

Find the sentence that has an error in spelling. If you find no mistake, mark choice (D) as your answer.

(A) We recieved a letter from the principal.

(B) The library closes at 5 o'clock tomorrow.

(C) I have an appointment with the doctor on Wednesday.

(D) No mistakes

The correct answer is (A). The word *recieved* is spelled incorrectly; the correct spelling is *received*.

Composition

Choose the best word or words to join the thoughts together.

I left my key at school; _____ I had to ring the bell to get in the house.

(A) however

(B) nevertheless

(C) therefore

(D) None of these

The correct answer is (C). *Nevertheless* and *however* are used to express a contrast. *Therefore* is used to express a result. The second half of this sentence is clearly a result of the first half.

THE HSPT® OPTIONAL TESTS

Some schools might require that you take one of the three optional tests described at the beginning of this section: Mechanical Aptitude, Science, or Catholic Religion. Not every school you apply to will require this extra test. However, if you do have to take an optional test, the test is chosen by the school, and, like the basic HSPT® exam, the test will involve multiple-choice questions and answers.

Your score on the optional test will not be included with your score on the basic HSPT® exam. Rather, the school will receive a report on your overall performance on the optional exam and a topic-by-topic evaluation of your performance. The school will use this information to place you in appropriate classes. It might also use the information to determine the background of the student body as a whole in preparing the curriculum for the following year.

The optional science test consists of 40 questions covering a wide variety of topics. The questions are not neatly categorized. For example, a biology question might be followed by a physics question, and then a laboratory methods question might be followed by a chemistry question. The outline below gives you an idea of how many topics are covered and approximately how many questions there are on each topic.

DISTRIBUTION OF TOPICS ON HSPT® OPTIONAL SCIENCE TEST

Topic/Content	Number of Items
Biological Sciences:	
Plants	2
Animals	2
Life Processes	2
Health and Safety	1
Ecology	2
Earth Sciences:	
Astronomy	2
Geology	2
Weather	1
Air	2
Water	2
Physical Sciences:	
Matter and Energy	2
Machines and Work	2
Magnetism and Electricity	2
Sound	1
Heat and Light	1
Chemistry	2
Implications of Scientific Technology:	
Societal Benefits	3
Technical Applications	3
Principles of Scientific Research and Experimentation:	
Laboratory Methods	3
Research Practices	3

SUMMING IT UP

- The HSPT® is a five-part multiple-choice test of verbal, quantitative, reading, mathematics, and language skills.

- The test takes approximately 2 hours and 30 minutes and contains 298 questions.

- No points are subtracted for incorrect answers, so it pays to answer as many questions as possible, even if you have to guess.

- Some schools might require that you take one of the three optional tests: Mechanical Aptitude, Science, or Catholic Religion. Your score on the optional test will not be included with your score on the basic HSPT® exam. Rather, the school will receive a report on your overall performance on the optional exam and a topic-by-topic evaluation of your performance.

- The optional science test consists of 40 questions covering a wide variety of topics, including biological, earth, and physical sciences.

Test-Taking Techniques

OVERVIEW

- **What to expect when you take the exam**
- **Tips for answering questions**
- **Summing it up**

No test preparation book would be complete without a rundown of surefire test-taking techniques. Some of the techniques and tips listed here are common sense, but it never hurts to be reminded. For example, you should always assemble your materials the night before the exam, get a good night's sleep, get up early enough so that you don't need to rush, and eat breakfast. Here are some more tips:

- The only materials you need to bring to your exam are a few sharpened #2 pencils with clean erasers, positive identification, and your admission ticket (if you were issued one).

- Unless you were expressly instructed to bring a calculator, do not bring one to your exam. Calculators are not permitted on most high school entrance exams.

- It is important to wear a watch even though the room will most likely have a clock. The clock might not be conveniently located to keep track of time. If calculators are not allowed, be sure that your watch is not a calculator watch, because all calculator watches will be confiscated for the duration of the exam. If your watch has an alarm, be sure to turn it off.

- Enter the room early enough to choose a comfortable seat. After you're settled, relax. You'll concentrate more and perform better on the test if you're relaxed and comfortable. Besides, you studied hard for the exam, so what do you have to worry about, right?

WHAT TO EXPECT WHEN YOU TAKE THE EXAM

The first thing you will do in the exam room is fill out forms. You will be given detailed instructions for this procedure. Listen, read, and follow the directions; filling out forms is not timed, so don't rush. The exam will not begin until everyone has finished.

Next, the administrator will give you general instructions for taking the exam. You will be told how to recognize the stop and start signals. You will also find out what to do if you have a problem, such as all your pencils breaking or you find a page missing from your test booklet. Pay attention to the instructions. If you have any questions, ask them before the test begins.

When the signal is given, open your test booklet and read:

- **Read** all directions carefully. The directions will probably be very similar to those in this book, but don't take anything for granted. Test-makers do periodically change the exams.

- **Read** every word of every question. Be alert for little words that might have a big effect on your answer—words such as *not, most, all, every,* and *except.*

- **Read** all of the choices before you select an answer. It is statistically true that the most errors are made when the correct answer is the last choice given. Too many people mark the first answer that seems correct without reading through all of the choices to find out which answer is best.

TIPS FOR ANSWERING QUESTIONS

One of the best test tips we can offer is this: Try to answer every question on the exam, especially if you're running out of time. If you answer every question—even if you guess wildly—you are more likely to earn a high score. (The TACHS is an exception to this rule. Remember that there is a penalty for wrong answers on these tests, so an educated guess can help, while a wild guess might not.) There is no penalty for wrong answers on the COOP or HSPT®, so even a wild guess gives you a 20 or 25 percent chance for credit! Here are some basic tips for making an educated guess.

- If you're uncertain as to the answer to a question, guess—you can always mark the question and return to it for another try later if you have the time.

- An educated guess is worth more than a random guess. To make an educated guess, look carefully at the question and eliminate any answers that you are sure are wrong. Chances are that you can spot some obviously wrong answers among the choices to vocabulary, reading, and language questions. You will probably find some of the choices to math questions to be so far off as to make you chuckle. When it boils right down to it, you have a better chance of guessing correctly when you have three options instead of four or five. Your odds improve even more if you can guess between two choices.

- Keep alert for the moment during the exam when time is about to run out. In those last few seconds, pick one response—preferably not the first, because the first answer tends to be the correct one less often than the others—and mark all remaining blanks on your answer sheet with that same answer. By the law of averages, you should pick up a free point or two.

Another way to make sure you do as well as you can on the exam is to make sure that you don't lose any points through carelessness. Here's a list of eleven suggestions that apply to any paper-and-pencil entrance exam, including the practice exams you'll take later in Part V.

1 Mark your answers by completely blackening the answer space of your choice. Be sure not to make any marks outside the lines.

2 Mark only **one** answer for each question, even if you think that more than one answer is correct. If you mark more than one answer, you lose all credit for that question.

3 If you change your mind, erase the answer completely. Leave no doubt as to which answer you mean.

4 Answer every question in the right place on the answer sheet. Make sure that the number of the answer blank matches the number of the question you are answering. You could lose a lot of time if you have to go back and change a lot of answers.

5 Don't spend too much time on any question, even if it poses an interesting challenge. Pick an answer and move on. You can always mark the question in your test booklet and go back to it later if time permits.

6 You are not required to answer every question; however, if you do skip one, **be sure to skip its answer space.** Otherwise, you might throw off your entire answer sheet. For that reason, it's safer to guess than to skip. Just mark the guesses in your test booklet so that you can go back and deliberate some more if you have time.

7 If you use scratch paper (you may on the HSPT but not on the COOP), be sure to mark the answer on the answer sheet. Only the answer sheet is scored; the test booklet and the scratch paper are not.

8 Stay alert. Getting a good night's sleep the night before and eating breakfast on the morning of the test will help you to be alert.

9 If you don't finish a section before the time is up, don't worry. Few people can actually answer every question. If you are accurate, you might earn a high score even without finishing every test section.

10 Don't let your performance on a section affect your performance on any other part of the exam. For example, if you don't think you did very well on mathematics, forget about that section after you are finished and start on the next section. Worrying about a previous section will cause you a lot of stress.

11 Check and recheck. If you finish any part before the time is up, go back and check to be sure that each question is answered in the right space and that there is only one answer for each question. Return to the difficult questions and rethink them.

SUMMING IT UP

- Always assemble everything you will need the night before the exam. You will need a few #2 pencils and a watch (calculator watches are not permitted). Don't bring a calculator unless you have been instructed to do so.

- Get a good night's sleep and get up early enough so you can eat breakfast, so you don't have to rush, and so you can arrive at the testing center with plenty of time to spare. Enter the room early enough to find a comfortable seat and relax.

- **READ.** Read all of the directions carefully, read every word of every question, and read all of the choices before selecting an answer.

- **PRACTICE.** Practice all of the question-answering tips in this chapter when you study and when you take the practice exams. This way, they will come as second nature when you take the exam.

PART II

DIAGNOSTIC TEST

Diagnostic Test

VERBAL SKILLS

Synonyms

Directions: In the following questions, choose the word that means the same as or about the same as the underlined word.

1. an articulate speaker
   - (A) expressive
   - (B) boastful
   - (C) daring
   - (D) unusual

2. curtail the program
   - (A) begin
   - (B) appreciate
   - (C) enrich
   - (D) shorten

3. lucrative profession
   - (A) demanding
   - (B) profitable
   - (C) common
   - (D) exciting

4. great elation
   - (A) achievement
   - (B) joy
   - (C) interest
   - (D) appeal

5. strong adversary
   - (A) effort
   - (B) support
   - (C) opponent
   - (D) attraction

6. adjourn the meeting
   - (A) discontinue
   - (B) organize
   - (C) direct
   - (D) schedule

7. effective technique
   - (A) discipline
   - (B) equipment
   - (C) instructor
   - (D) method

Antonyms

Directions: Choose the best answer.

1. Lavish means the *opposite* of
   - (A) plain.
   - (B) elegant.
   - (C) profitable.
   - (D) attractive.

2. Partial means the *opposite* of
   - (A) open.
   - (B) orderly.
   - (C) whole.
   - (D) normal.

3. Deteriorate means the *opposite* of
   - (A) liken.
   - (B) expect.
   - (C) improve.
   - (D) oppose.

4. Flair means the *opposite* of
   - (A) secret.
   - (B) unjust.
   - (C) darkness.
   - (D) inability.

5. Squander means the *opposite* of
   - (A) undo.
   - (B) save.
   - (C) approve.
   - (D) proceed.

6. Accurate means the *opposite* of
   - (A) mistaken.
   - (B) expected.
   - (C) useful.
   - (D) absent.

7. Escalate means the *opposite* of
   - (A) punctual.
   - (B) arise.
   - (C) obey.
   - (D) decrease.

Analogies

Directions: Mark one answer—the answer you think is best—for each problem.

1. Brown is to dirt as blue is to
   - (A) tree.
   - (B) sky.
   - (C) cloud.
   - (D) black.

2. Stove is to cook as bed is to
   - (A) run.
   - (B) sheet.
   - (C) sleep.
   - (D) laugh.

3. Glass is to window as wall is to
   - (A) house.
   - (B) beach.
   - (C) winter.
   - (D) car.

4. First is to last as beginning is to
   (A) entrance.
   (B) question.
   (C) cup.
   (D) end.

5. Dirty is to clean as interested is to
   (A) bored.
   (B) certain.
   (C) silly.
   (D) funny.

Verbal Logic

Directions: For questions 1 and 2, find the statement that is true according to the given information.

1. Katie and Laurel play on the softball team together. Saturday afternoon, they had a softball game. Their team won the game 10 – 7.
   (A) Katie and Laurel's team has never lost a game.
   (B) Katie and Laurel play softball every Saturday.
   (C) Katie is a better softball player than Laurel.
   (D) Katie's and Laurel's team wins some of its games.

2. Arthur rode his bike to school on Thursday. On the way, he stopped at the store. The store owner, Mr. Clemson, asked Arthur how he was doing, and Arthur said that he was afraid he was going to be late to school.
   (A) Arthur rides his bike to school every day.
   (B) Arthur got in trouble for being late to school.
   (C) Arthur spoke with Mr. Clemson on Thursday.
   (D) Arthur was late to school on Thursday.

Directions: For questions 3–5, mark one answer—the answer you think is best—for each problem.

3. Which word does *not* belong with the others?
   (A) hammer
   (B) screwdriver
   (C) basket
   (D) wrench

5. Which word does *not* belong with the others?
   (A) hopeful
   (B) perspective
   (C) positive
   (D) optimistic

4. Which word does *not* belong with the others?
   (A) watch
   (B) sing
   (C) talk
   (D) whisper

Reading

QUESTIONS 1–5 REFER TO THE FOLLOWING PASSAGE.

In order to better understand what it is that makes people purchase particular items, or be drawn to certain products, the business world conducts psychological research about buyer behavior. Researchers want to learn as much as they can about the actions that people take when they are in the purchasing process. Much of market research revolves around uncovering the factors that influence how and why people make purchasing decisions.

One of the ways in which companies conduct market research is through the use of surveys. A survey is a questionnaire that asks respondents for information, including their demographic characteristics. A survey might ask if a person is male or female, for instance. It might also ask for the individual's approximate age, income level, marital information, the number of persons living in the household, and the number of children living at home. All of this information gives the company administering the survey a general profile or picture of the background of the person responding.

Then, depending on the type of products or services that the company specializes in, a survey will typically ask respondents about their behavioral patterns in a certain area. For example, a company that produces fabric softener might ask survey respondents if they own a washing machine or not, how often they do the laundry, how many loads per week they do, or perhaps whether or not they use fabric softener.

As another example, a fast-food company might be interested in the types of food that people most frequently buy when they go through a drive-through. Or, they might ask if respondents prefer sandwiches with chicken or beef. They might inquire about what kinds of salad dressing a person eats most frequently.

All of this information is collected so that companies can track the behavior of buyers. Businesses want to know about respondents' demographic characteristics so they can build a profile of the kind of person who most frequently buys their products or shops at their stores. If companies can track how their buyers make decisions, they can gain a much stronger understanding of the psychological motivations that drive people's purchases. They can also tailor their advertisements in order to attract the attention of their target customers, designing their ads so that they will have the greatest appeal for potential buyers.

Market research involves more than administering questionnaires and surveys, however. Companies and corporate researchers can also investigate what colors and designs people find most appealing in product packaging. They can further inquire about the types of advertising and marketing messages that buyers are most likely to remember, and to respond to, as they make their purchasing decisions.

Companies can also hold focus groups, where they ask groups of people about their preferences, opinions, or responses concerning different types of products—from food to cleaning supplies to electronics. Businesses collect the responses of these focus groups and use the data to construct advertisements and marketing campaigns in ways that are designed to be appealing, based on the focus groups' results.

Sometimes market researchers even ask buyers to test new products. They might ask a subject to use a certain new shampoo, for instance, and then report back about their reactions to the product. The results of consumer tests such as these can influence whether a new product ever actually makes it onto the shelves for people to buy or not.

1. What is the passage mainly about?
   (A) It focuses on how people make decisions concerning a company's products.
   (B) It mainly discusses how advertisers test new products.
   (C) It explains the various ways that companies conduct market research.
   (D) It discusses people's preferences concerning their shopping decisions.

2. According to the passage, what is one of the main ways that companies collect market research information?
   (A) Through the use of surveys
   (B) Through the use of secret shoppers
   (C) Through the use of role playing
   (D) Through the use of psychological evaluations

3. The word demographic, as underlined and used in paragraph 2, most nearly means
   (A) superior.
   (B) problematic.
   (C) likeable.
   (D) group.

4. Why does the author mention fabric softener in paragraph 3?
   (A) To describe how many consumers make decisions concerning purchases
   (B) To give an example of a product that might be the subject of market research
   (C) To discuss the product that is the most common subject of market research
   (D) To explain why buyers like the product, based on historical market research

5. According to the passage, why do market research surveys collect demographic information?
   (A) To be able to track customers' purchases with the company over time
   (B) To keep careful records in a database so that the company can sell this information
   (C) To compile information about people most likely to purchase the company's products
   (D) To be able to tell why purchasers like certain colors better than other colors

QUESTIONS 6-10 REFER TO THE FOLLOWING PASSAGE.

Sound consists of three significant dimensions: speed, loudness, and frequency. Sound can travel through different media, such as air, for example. But it can also travel through water and even solids. After all, can you remember being inside a building but hearing a fire truck's siren outside? That is an example of how sound can travel through a solid. The sound travels through the solid matter of the building—its bricks or limestone, for instance.

It can take sound longer to travel through liquids, and especially through solids, than it might take the same sound to travel through gases or the air. This explains why it sometimes seems as if you can hear a siren sooner when you are standing outside than you can when you are inside a building. This can also be what causes sounds to seem odd or modified when heard underwater.

Sound is made up of waves. This wave structure explains why the loudness of a sound can change as a person moves in relation to the sound. To go back to the siren example, as a fire truck drives closer to a building, the sound of its siren becomes louder. This increase in intensity has to do with the amplitude, or size, of the sound wave. As the fire truck moves away from the building, the sound of the siren becomes softer, since the listener is now farther away from the sound source.

Finally, the frequency of a sound makes the sound seem higher or lower in pitch. Only sounds that fall into a certain range are discernible by human hearing. That range is 20 to 20,000 hertz (Hz). Instrumental orchestras must tune before performing to make sure that their instruments are pitched at a specific frequency, so that the notes all match when the instruments play together. The tuning note that often sounds prior to an orchestra performance is an A. Usually, the frequency of this note is pitched right around 440 Hz. That is at the lower end of the frequency range that many human beings can hear.

6. What is the passage mainly about?
   (A) It focuses on how sound properties change because of position.
   (B) It mainly discusses the properties associated with sound.
   (C) It explains ideas about why sounds become louder.
   (D) It talks generally about why pitches are used in certain ways for music.

7. The word media, as underlined and used in paragraph 1, most nearly means
   (A) substances.
   (B) artistic materials.
   (C) newspapers.
   (D) communication devices.

8. According to the passage, sound waves can take longer to travel through which of the following?
   (A) Air and gases
   (B) Liquids and solids
   (C) Air and liquids
   (D) Gases and solids

9. According to the passage, what causes an approaching fire truck's siren to first sound louder and then to become softer again?
   (A) The pitch of the siren as the truck moves past
   (B) The listener's location inside or outside a building
   (C) The frequency of the siren as the truck moves past
   (D) The proximity of the listener to the siren

10. Why does a siren seem to be heard sooner when a person is standing outside a building, according to the passage?
    - **(A)** The sound waves do not have to travel through the solid medium of a building.
    - **(B)** The sound waves do not have to travel through the liquid medium of a river.
    - **(C)** The person is physically more distant from the siren, so the siren is louder.
    - **(D)** The pitch of the siren sounds different to a listener outside the building.

Spelling

Directions: For each of the following questions, decide which one of the answer choices contains a spelling mistake. If you find no error, choose (E) as your answer.

1. **(A)** cantaloupe
   (B) porcupine
   (C) acquire
   (D) explaination
   (E) *No mistakes*

2. **(A)** definitly
   (B) license
   (C) noticeable
   (D) publicly
   (E) *No mistakes*

3. **(A)** seperate
   (B) until
   (C) calendar
   (D) leisure
   (E) *No mistakes*

4. **(A)** jewelry
   (B) accommodate
   (C) priviledge
   (D) restaurant
   (E) *No mistakes*

5. **(A)** camouflage
   (B) foreign
   (C) defendant
   (D) grammar
   (E) *No mistakes*

6. **(A)** apology
   (B) precede
   (C) disappoint
   (D) existance
   (E) *No mistakes*

7. **(A)** development
   (B) pronounciation
   (C) recommend
   (D) knowledge
   (E) *No mistakes*

8. **(A)** occasion
   (B) pleasant
   (C) necessery
   (D) labeled
   (E) *No mistakes*

Punctuation and Capitalization

Directions: In the following questions, look for errors in punctuation. Mark the answer choice that contains the error. If you find no mistakes, mark (D) as your answer.

1. **(A)** "I'm not sure who lives there," she said.
   (B) Zach is a student here, isn't he?
   (C) You cannot drive on this street. It is for pedestrian's only.
   (D) *No mistakes*

2. **(A)** He finished his homework on Friday so that he could relax all weekend.
   (B) Who's in charge of the graduation committee this year?
   (C) Amy missed the bus she was late for school.
   (D) *No mistakes*

3. **(A)** Mr. Wolfe, who was my French teacher last year, is leading the trip to Paris.
   (B) I don't like living in a small town. I prefer the city life.
   (C) How many students in this class ride the bus to school?
   (D) *No mistakes*

4. **(A)** When we finished the hike, we were all very tired?
   (B) "We parked the car behind the building," she said.
   (C) If the weather is bad, we'll have to change our plans.
   (D) *No mistakes*

Directions: For each of the following question, decide which one of the first three answer choices contains a capitalization mistake. If none of the answer choices contains a mistake, choose (D) as your answer.

5. **(A)** During our next summer vacation,
   (B) we plan to go to New York
   (C) and visit the Empire State building.
   (D) *No mistakes*

6. **(A)** Last Saturday night,
   (B) we went to a restaurant
   (C) and enjoyed a meal of Mexican food.
   (D) *No mistakes*

7. **(A)** On a clear evening, you can see Venus.
   (B) I hope to visit Italy one day soon.
   (C) This Store has the best prices in town.
   (D) *No mistakes*

8. **(A)** I enjoyed a cup of starbucks coffee with my breakfast.
   (B) Their house is just half a mile north of the park.
   (C) *The Grapes of Wrath* is one of my favorite novels.
   (D) *No mistakes*

English Usage

Directions: For questions 1–4, what is the best way to rewrite the underlined part of sentence 2?

1. (1) The Apollo 11 mission was affected by many technical difficulties before the lunar module finally landed on the moon. (2) <u>Also,</u> the moonwalk proceeded effortlessly.
   - (A) Consequently,
   - (B) Nevertheless,
   - (C) As a matter of fact,
   - (D) *No change is needed.*

2. (1) I purchased the bicycle last week and the skateboard less than a month ago. (2) Unfortunately, <u>neither one of them are</u> functioning properly.
   - (A) neither one of them is
   - (B) both of them isn't
   - (C) neither the bicycle nor the skateboard are
   - (D) *No change is needed.*

3. (1) Abraham Lincoln delivered his Second Inaugural Address only days before the Union won the Civil War. (2) <u>Furthermore,</u> he never gloated about his imminent victory anywhere in the speech.
   - (A) Indeed,
   - (B) Even so,
   - (C) In addition,
   - (D) *No change is needed.*

4. (1) Athletes who hope to compete in the Olympics undergo grueling training, give up all their hobbies, and forego most social activities. (2) Nevertheless, so few of them <u>won medals or even made the team.</u>
   - (A) had won medals or had even made the team
   - (B) win medals or even made the team
   - (C) win medals or even make the team
   - (D) *No change is needed.*

5. Choose the word to join the thoughts together.

   Alan and his family always visit the Statue of Liberty _____ they are in New York.
   - (A) unless
   - (B) until
   - (C) whenever
   - (D) None of these

6. Choose the word or words to join the thoughts together.

   Marla has a photographic memory; _____, she usually forgets my birthday.
   - (A) nevertheless
   - (B) unless
   - (C) even though
   - (D) None of these

7. Choose the word to join the thoughts together.

   We decided not to go skating on Tuesday; _____, we went to the movies.
   - (A) also
   - (B) however
   - (C) instead
   - (D) None of these

8. Choose the word or words to join the thoughts together.

   The pilot navigated the storm with ease _____ he landed the jet haphazardly.
   - (A) unless
   - (B) although
   - (C) because
   - (D) None of these

Language Composition and Expression

Directions: In the following questions, choose which of the four sentences is constructed best and expresses the idea most clearly.

1. **(A)** They were anxious, the explorers were, because dangerous terrain they knew they were entering.

   (B) The explorers, because they knew that they were entering dangerous terrain, were anxious.

   (C) The explorers were anxious because they knew that they were entering dangerous terrain.

   (D) The explorers, knowing that they were entering dangerous terrain, were anxious.

2. **(A)** At the tournament, John, because he lost his confidence, fared poorly despite months of practice.

   (B) Despite months of practice, John lost his confidence and fared poorly at the tournament.

   (C) John, at the tournament, despite months of practice, lost his confidence and fared poorly.

   (D) Losing his confidence, at the tournament despite months of practice, John fared poorly.

3. **(A)** Putting aside their differences on the project allowed Marc and Jason to collaborate on it.

   (B) Marc and Jason, once they put aside their differences on the project, collaborated.

   (C) Collaborating on the project, Marc and Jason were able to once they put aside their differences.

   (D) Marc and Jason were able to collaborate on the project once they put aside their differences.

4. **(A)** The Louisiana Purchase and the Gold Rush sparked westward expansion in the nineteenth century.

   (B) Sparking westward expansion were the Louisiana Purchase and the Gold Rush in the nineteenth century.

   (C) The Louisiana Purchase in the nineteenth century and the Gold Rush sparked westward expansion.

   (D) In the nineteenth century, westward expansion of the Louisiana Purchase and the Gold Rush sparked.

5. All high school students should perform mandatory community service.

   (A) High school students are generally irresponsible because they have too much free time on their hands. They are in dire need of things to keep them busy.

   (B) More and more people are living to advanced ages. High school students would perform an invaluable service by volunteering in senior citizen centers.

   (C) High school curricula should develop civic responsibility as well as academic proficiency. Mandatory community service would help achieve these noble aims.

   (D) Studies indicate that teenagers who participate in a diverse range of activities do well in college. High school curricula should therefore include more varied activities.

6. Students should be allowed to grade teachers just as teachers grade students.

   (A) Grades are subjective, often arbitrary estimations of ability. People who grade others frequently base their grades on irrelevant factors.

   (B) Some students work harder when they receive less-than-satisfactory grades; some do not. Teachers might work harder if they were graded on their teaching.

   (C) Many corporations allow workers to rate the performance of their managers. This form of two-way communication benefits everyone.

   (D) Grades help people recognize their areas of strength and weakness. Teachers would only benefit from honest evaluations by their students.

7. The voting age should be lowered to sixteen.

   (A) By age sixteen, most people have a keen understanding of the electoral process. Research indicates that more and more teenagers follow political issues because of social media.

   (B) Governmental legislation often affects the lives of people who are minors. Sixteen-year-olds are mature enough to vote to select those candidates who best represent their interests.

   (C) Many scientists believe that people experience significant brain development at age sixteen. As a result, 16-year-olds have better decision-making skills than they did a year earlier.

   (D) In a democracy, voting isn't a privilege, it's a fundamental right. Teenagers are denied too many rights that others take for granted.

QUANTITATIVE AND NONVERBAL SKILLS

Quantitative Reasoning

Directions: For questions 1–5, find the relationship of the numbers in one column to the numbers in the other column. Then find the missing number.

1. $3 \rightarrow \square \rightarrow 6$
    $4 \rightarrow \square \rightarrow 8$
    $1 \rightarrow \square \rightarrow ?$

0	2	3	9
(A)	(B)	(C)	(D)

2. $5 \rightarrow \square \rightarrow 8$
    $1 \rightarrow \square \rightarrow 4$
    $7 \rightarrow \square \rightarrow ?$

6	7	10	12
(A)	(B)	(C)	(D)

3. $10 \rightarrow \square \rightarrow 6$
    $12 \rightarrow \square \rightarrow 8$
    $15 \rightarrow \square \rightarrow ?$

–1	3	7	11
(A)	(B)	(C)	(D)

4. $25 \rightarrow \square \rightarrow 5$
    $10 \rightarrow \square \rightarrow 2$
    $15 \rightarrow \square \rightarrow ?$

3	4	5	10
(A)	(B)	(C)	(D)

5. $11 \rightarrow \square \rightarrow 4$
    $14 \rightarrow \square \rightarrow 7$
    $13 \rightarrow \square \rightarrow ?$

3	6	7	9
(A)	(B)	(C)	(D)

Directions: For questions 6–10, find the fraction of the grid that is shaded.

6.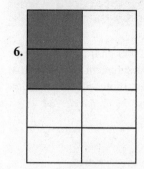
$\frac{1}{4}$ $\frac{1}{3}$ $\frac{3}{8}$ $\frac{1}{2}$
(A)   (B)   (C)   (D)

7.
$\frac{1}{2}$ $\frac{2}{3}$ $\frac{4}{5}$ $\frac{5}{6}$
(A)   (B)   (C)   (D)

8.
$\frac{1}{6}$ $\frac{1}{4}$ $\frac{2}{3}$ $\frac{3}{4}$
(A)   (B)   (C)   (D)

9.
$\frac{3}{4}$ $\frac{2}{3}$ $\frac{1}{2}$ $\frac{1}{6}$
(A)   (B)   (C)   (D)

10.
$\frac{2}{3}$ $\frac{1}{2}$ $\frac{2}{5}$ $\frac{1}{3}$
(A)   (B)   (C)   (D)

diagnostic test

Mathematics

Directions: For questions 1–15, four answers are given for each problem. Choose the best answer.

1. Which of the following is *not* a factor of 36?
   - (A) 4
   - (B) 9
   - (C) 6
   - (D) 10

2. The closest estimate of $56{,}012 \div 7019$ is
   - (A) 8
   - (B) 80
   - (C) 800
   - (D) 8000

3. 0.12% is equal to
   - (A) 1.2
   - (B) 0.12
   - (C) 0.012
   - (D) 0.0012

4. Which of the following is a pair of reciprocals?
   - (A) $(12, -12)$
   - (B) $(0, 0)$
   - (C) $\left(3\frac{3}{4}, \frac{4}{15}\right)$
   - (D) $(5^2, 2^5)$

5. The ratio of 1 hour to 120 seconds is
   - (A) 120 to 1
   - (B) 30 to 1
   - (C) 18 to 1
   - (D) 6 to 24

6. Find the area of a triangle whose dimensions are $b = 16$ centimeters, $h = 13$ centimeters.
   - (A) 104 sq. centimeters
   - (B) 140 sq. centimeters
   - (C) 144 sq. centimeters
   - (D) 208 sq. centimeters

7. Alicia invests \$2000 and earns 8 percent interest on her investment in one year. What is the total amount of her investment after one year?
   - (A) \$2008
   - (B) \$2080
   - (C) \$2160
   - (D) \$2225

8. If Andrea spends $1\frac{3}{4}$ hours per day training for a marathon and she trains 5 days per week, how many hours does Andrea train for the marathon each week?
   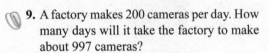
   - (A) $5\frac{1}{4}$
   - (B) $6\frac{1}{2}$
   - (C) $8\frac{3}{4}$
   - (D) 9

9. A factory makes 200 cameras per day. How many days will it take the factory to make about 997 cameras?
   - (A) 5
   - (B) 11
   - (C) 53
   - (D) Not given

10.

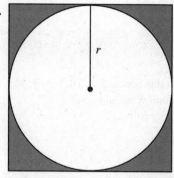

In the figure shown, the length of *r* is 3 centimeters. The area of the shaded portion of the square is approximately

(A) $5\frac{1}{4}$ sq. centimeters

(B) $7\frac{3}{4}$ sq. centimeters

(C) 10 sq. centimeters

(D) $17\frac{1}{6}$ sq. centimeters

11. For five weeks over the summer, Neera earned weekly paychecks at her part-time job. The amount of each paycheck was $101.65, $79.23, $84.67, $121.33, and $77.62. What was her average paycheck for those five checks?

(A) $101.3

(B) $99.47

(C) $94.16

(D) $92.90

12. Solve for *x*: $3.7x - 1.2 = 58$

(A) 12

(B) 15.35

(C) 16

(D) 18.70

13. Write 784 in expanded form, using exponents.

(A) $(7 \times 10^2) + (8 \times 10) + 4$

(B) $(7 \times 10^3) + (8 \times 10^2) + (4 \times 10)$

(C) $(7 \times 10^0) + (8 \times 10) + (4 \times 10)$

(D) None of the above

14. Increased by 175%, the number 24 becomes

(A) 38

(B) 42

(C) 48

(D) 66

15. If $xy - 7 = 56$, and $x = 7$, $y =$

(A) 3

(B) 7

(C) 9

(D) 12

Series Reasoning

Directions: For questions 1–5, choose the answer that would continue the pattern or series.

1. QXR SXT UXV _____ YXZ
   - (A) WXV
   - (B) WXZ
   - (C) WXX
   - (D) WXY

2. ARD DAR RDA ARD _____
   - (A) RDA
   - (B) DAR
   - (C) ARD
   - (D) RAD

3. Look at this series: 28, 23, 18, 13, ... What number should come next?
   - (A) 8
   - (B) 6
   - (C) 3
   - (D) 1

4. Look at this series: 7, 8, 10, 11, 13, 14, ... What number should come next?
   - (A) 14
   - (B) 16
   - (C) 17
   - (D) 19

5. Look at this series: 2, 4, 7, 14, 17, 34, ... What number should come next?
   - (A) 35
   - (B) 36
   - (C) 37
   - (D) 39

Comparisons

Directions: Mark one answer—the answer you think is best—for each problem.

1. Examine (A), (B), and (C) and find the best answer.

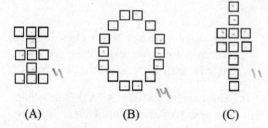

(A)   (B)   (C)

   (A) (A) and (B) each have more squares than (C).

   (B) (A) and (C) have the same number of squares.

   (C) (C) has more squares than (B).

   (D) (B) and (C) each have fewer squares than (A).

2. Examine the square and find the best answer.

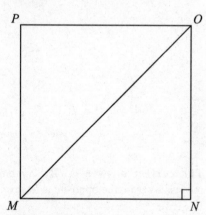

   (A) *MN* is equal to *MO*.

   (B) *MO* minus *MN* is equal to *ON*.

   (C) m∠*OMP* is greater than m∠*ONM*.

   (D) *MO* is greater than *MP*.

3. Examine (A), (B), and (C) and find the best answer.

   (A) 8^2 64

   (B) 9×7 63

   (C) 67

   (A) (C) is less than (A).

   (B) (A), (B), and (C) are all equal.

   (C) (A) is greater than (B).

   (D) (B) is greater than (A) and (C).

4. Examine (A), (B), and (C) and find the best answer.

   (A) 6×10^2 600

   (B) $\dfrac{6}{10}$ 0.6

   (C) 0.60 0.6

   (A) (B) is equal to (C).

   (B) (A) is less than (B).

   (C) (C) is greater than (A) and (B).

   (D) (B) is greater than (A).

5. Examine (A), (B), and (C) and find the best answer.

   (A) $6(4 + 2)$ 36

   (B) $(4 + 2)^2$ 36

   (C) $(6 \times 4) + 2$ 26

   (A) (C) is greater than (B).

   (B) (C) is less than (A) and (B).

   (C) (A) is less than (B).

   (D) (A), (B), and (C) are all equal.

ANSWER KEY AND EXPLANATIONS

Synonyms

1. A	3. B	5. C	7. D
2. D	4. B	6. A	

1. **The correct answer is (A).** *Expressive* is a synonym for *articulate*. Other synonyms include "eloquent," "fluent," and "well-spoken."

2. **The correct answer is (D).** *Shorten* is a synonym for *curtail*. Other synonyms include "limit," "reduce," and "curb."

3. **The correct answer is (B).** *Profitable* is the closest in meaning to the word *lucrative* among the four choices. Other synonyms include "productive," "high-paying," and "money-making."

4. **The correct answer is (B).** *Joy* is a synonym for the word *elation*. Other synonyms include "happiness," "delight," and "ecstasy."

5. **The correct answer is (C).** *Opponent* is a synonym for *adversary*. Other synonyms include "enemy," "competitor," and "rival."

6. **The correct answer is (A).** *Discontinue* is a synonym of *adjourn*. Other synonyms include "stop," "finish," and "suspend."

7. **The correct answer is (D).** *Method* is a synonym for the word *technique*. Other synonyms include "procedure" and "system."

Antonyms

1. A	3. C	5. B	7. D
2. C	4. D	6. A	

1. **The correct answer is (A).** *Lavish* means extravagant; the opposite is *plain*.

2. **The correct answer is (C).** *Partial* means incomplete; the opposite is *whole*.

3. **The correct answer is (C).** *Deteriorate* means to worsen; the opposite is *to improve*.

4. **The correct answer is (D).** *Flair* means skill; the opposite is *inability*.

5. **The correct answer is (B).** *Squander* means to waste; the opposite is *to save*.

6. **The correct answer is (A).** *Accurate* means correct; the opposite is *mistaken*.

7. **The correct answer is (D).** *Escalate* means to increase; the opposite is *to decrease*.

Analogies

1. B	3. A	5. A
2. C	4. D	

1. **The correct answer is (B).** Characteristic relationship. Brown is the color of dirt; blue is the color of the sky.

2. **The correct answer is (C).** Object-purpose relationship. The purpose of a stove is to use it to cook; the purpose of a bed is to use it to sleep.

3. **The correct answer is (A).** Part-whole relationship. Glass is part of a window; a wall is part of a house.

4. **The correct answer is (D).** Sequence relationship. The first item in a series comes before the last item; the beginning of an event comes before the end.

5. **The correct answer is (A).** Antonym relationship. Dirty is the opposite of clean; interested is the opposite of bored.

Verbal Logic

1. D	3. C	5. B
2. C	4. A	

1. **The correct answer is (D).** Katie's and Laurel's team won the game on Saturday, so it must be true that their team wins some of its games. We can't know for sure that their team has never lost a game, just that it has won at least once.

2. **The correct answer is (C).** The only statement that must be true is that Arthur spoke with Mr. Clemson on Thursday. We know this because they had a conversation at the store. Arthur might ride his bike to school daily, and he might have been late to school on Thursday, but these are only possibilities, not certainties, based on the information given.

3. **The correct answer is (C).** A *hammer*, a *screwdriver*, and a *wrench* are all tools. A *basket* is not a tool, so it does not belong with the other three words.

4. **The correct answer is (A).** To *sing*, to *talk*, and to *whisper* all involve using your voice. To *watch* requires using your eyesight, not your voice, so *watch* does not belong with the other three words.

5. **The correct answer is (B).** The word *perspective* refers to a particular viewpoint. The other three words all reflect positive attitudes or qualities.

Reading

1. C	3. D	5. C	7. A	9. D
2. A	4. B	6. B	8. B	10. A

1. **The correct answer is (C).** The passage is mainly about the various ways that companies conduct market research. Choice (A) is incorrect because the passage explains how companies find out this information, instead of how people make their decisions. The passage mainly describes various ways to conduct market research, so choices (B) and (D) can be eliminated.

2. **The correct answer is (A).** In the beginning of the passage, the author explains that one of the main ways that companies conduct market research is through the distribution of surveys. The passage focuses on how market research is conducted, so choices (C) and (D) can be eliminated.

3. **The correct answer is (D).** The second sentence in paragraph 2 uses *demographic* to refer to characteristics of a group. Gender and marital status are group characteristics mentioned in the sentence that follows, giving a clue as to the context. This eliminates choice (B), *problematic*. Choices (A) and (C) also do not fit the context and can be eliminated.

4. **The correct answer is (B).** The author mentions fabric softener in paragraph 3 to give an example of a product that might be the subject of market research. This example helps explain why a survey might contain certain types of questions.

5. **The correct answer is (C).** The author states in paragraph 5 that companies ask for demographic information from survey respondents so they can understand what type of person is most likely to purchase their products. With this information, companies can build consumer profiles of potential customers.

6. **The correct answer is (B).** The passage is mainly about the various properties of sound. Choice (A) is incorrect because this represents just one component of the passage. The author discusses the speed, loudness, and frequency of sound, so choice (C) can be eliminated.

7. **The correct answer is (A).** Air is a medium, or intervening substance, through which sound is transmitted; therefore, choice (A) is the correct answer. Choices (B), (C), and (D) do not fit the context of the passage.

8. **The correct answer is (B).** The passage explains in paragraph 2 that sound waves can take longer to move through liquids and solids than through gases or air. Choices (A), (C), and (D) can be eliminated.

9. **The correct answer is (D).** The author describes how a siren gradually gets louder as it moves toward a building and then becomes softer again as it passes the building. This is because of the listener's proximity in relation to the siren's distance on a moving fire truck.

10. **The correct answer is (A).** The passage mentions in paragraph 2 that a siren sometimes seems to be heard sooner when the listener is outside because the sound does not have to travel through the solid medium of a building. It takes longer for sound waves to travel through solids than through the air.

Spelling

1. D	3. A	5. E	7. B
2. A	4. C	6. D	8. C

1. **The correct answer is (D).** The correct spelling is *explanation*.

2. **The correct answer is (A).** The correct spelling is *definitely*.

3. **The correct answer is (A).** The correct spelling is *separate*.

4. **The correct answer is (C).** The correct spelling is *privilege*.

5. **The correct answer is (E).** *No mistakes*

6. **The correct answer is (D).** The correct spelling is *existence*.

7. **The correct answer is (B).** The correct spelling is *pronunciation*.

8. **The correct answer is (C).** The correct spelling is *necessary*.

Punctuation and Capitalization

1. C	3. D	5. C	7. C
2. C	4. A	6. D	8. A

1. **The correct answer is (C).** There should not be an apostrophe before the *s* in *pedestrians* because it is a plural noun.

2. **The correct answer is (C).** Choice (C) is a run-on sentence. It contains two independent clauses joined with no punctuation. One way to correct this sentence would be to add a comma followed by a coordinating conjunction: *Amy missed the bus, and she was late for school.*

3. **The correct answer is (D).** *No mistakes*

4. **The correct answer is (A).** The sentence should end with a period because it is a statement, not a question.

5. **The correct answer is (C).** The word *building* is included in the proper noun *Empire State Building*.

6. **The correct answer is (D).** *No mistakes*

7. **The correct answer is (C).** The word store should not be capitalized because it is not part of a proper noun.

8. **The correct answer is (A).** *Starbucks* is the name of a company. Therefore, it is a proper noun and should be capitalized.

English Usage

1. B	3. B	5. C	7. C
2. A	4. C	6. A	8. B

1. **The correct answer is (B).** The word "nevertheless" generally means "in spite of the fact that was just stated." It is correct in this instance because it indicates that the moonwalk proceeded effortlessly in spite of the fact that the mission was affected by many technical difficulties.

2. **The correct answer is (A).** The words "neither one" indicate that the subject is singular. "Is" agrees with a singular subject. Choices (B) and (C) have faulty subject-verb agreement.

3. **The correct answer is (B).** The words "even so" generally mean "in spite of the fact that was just stated." It is correct in this instance because it indicates that Lincoln didn't gloat about his victory in spite of the fact that the Union was about to win the war.

4. **The correct answer is (C).** Sentence 2 incorrectly shifts to the past tense, so both verbs should be switched from past to present tense. It is important to read all of the answer choices before selecting one. On a quick glance, you might have picked choice (B), which would have been incorrect because only the first verb was changed to the present tense.

5. **The correct answer is (C).** The word "whenever" joins the thoughts together in a timeframe that is logical. Choices (A) and (B) represent impossibilities.

6. **The correct answer is (A).** The word "nevertheless" generally means "in spite of the fact that was just stated." It is correct in this instance because it indicates that Marla forgets the author's birthday in spite of the fact that she has a photographic memory. "Nevertheless" is also the only choice that requires a semicolon before it and a comma after it.

7. **The correct answer is (C).** The word "instead" generally means "as an alternative." It is correct in this instance because it indicates that the authors decided to go to the movies as an alternative to skating.

8. **The correct answer is (B).** The word "although" indicates a contrast between the first thought and the second thought, as it does in this instance. Choice (A) makes no sense, and choice (C) indicates an illogical cause and effect.

Language Composition and Expression

1. C	3. D	5. C	7. B
2. B	4. A	6. D	

1. **The correct answer is (C).** This sentence expresses the ideas clearly: *The explorers were anxious because they knew that they were entering dangerous terrain.* Its independent and dependent clauses are separate, distinct, and straightforwardly written.

2. **The correct answer is (B).** This sentence expresses the ideas clearly: *Despite months of practice, John lost his confidence and fared poorly at the tournament.* The subject immediately follows a brief introductory phrase, and it is not separated from the predicate by any clauses or phrases.

3. **The correct answer is (D).** This sentence expresses the ideas directly and concisely: *Marc and Jason were able to collaborate on the project once they put aside their differences.* The plural subject begins the sentence and is immediately followed by the verb, which helps to clearly convey the action taking place.

4. **The correct answer is (A).** This sentence expresses the ideas directly and concisely: *The Louisiana Purchase and the Gold Rush sparked westward expansion in the nineteenth century.* The plural subject begins the sentence and is immediately followed by the verb, which helps to clearly convey the action taking place.

5. **The correct answer is (C).** Both sentences tell us why community service is beneficial to high school students and support the argument that it should be mandatory. Choice (A) is a statement of opinion and a biased generalization. Choice (B) digresses into a narrow aspect of community service—the elderly—and fails to express why community service should be mandatory. Choice (D) does not specifically address or develop the statement introduced in the topic sentence.

6. **The correct answer is (D).** Both sentences in choice (D) support the idea that it would be beneficial to teachers if students in particular graded them. Choice (A) offers generalizations about grading but does not support the topic sentence. Choice (B) never mentions that students in particular should do the grading. Choice (C) completely digresses from students, teachers, and schools. It would better serve as a secondary argument.

7. **The correct answer is (B).** The first sentence tells us why people who are minors have reason to vote. The second sentence explains why 16-year-olds ought to be able to vote. Choice (A) never addresses voting. Choice (C) offers scientific information that would better serve as a secondary argument. Choice (D) does not develop the statement introduced in the topic sentence.

answers diagnostic test

Quantitative Reasoning

1. B	3. D	5. B	7. B	9. C
2. C	4. A	6. A	8. D	10. D

1. **The correct answer is (B).**
   $3 \times 2 = 6$
   $4 \times 2 = 8$
   $1 \times 2 = \mathbf{2}$

2. **The correct answer is (C).**
   $5 + 3 = 8$
   $1 + 3 = 4$
   $7 + 3 = \mathbf{10}$

3. **The correct answer is (D).**
   $10 - 4 = 6$
   $12 - 4 = 8$
   $15 - 4 = \mathbf{11}$

4. **The correct answer is (A).**
   $25 \div 5 = 5$
   $10 \div 5 = 2$
   $15 \div 5 = \mathbf{3}$

5. **The correct answer is (B).**
   $11 - 7 = 4$
   $14 - 7 = 7$
   $13 - 7 = \mathbf{6}$

6. **The correct answer is (A).** There are eight squares. Two of them are shaded. We know that 2 over 8 is $\frac{2}{8}$, or $\frac{1}{4}$.

7. **The correct answer is (B).** There are six squares. Four of them are shaded. We know that 4 over 6 is $\frac{4}{6}$, or $\frac{2}{3}$.

8. **The correct answer is (D).** There are eight squares. Six of them are shaded. We know that 6 over 8 is $\frac{6}{8}$, or $\frac{3}{4}$.

9. **The correct answer is (C).** There are four squares. One complete square and two half-squares are shaded. If we add $1 + \frac{1}{2} + \frac{1}{2}$, the answer is 2. We know that 2 over 4 is $\frac{2}{4}$, or $\frac{1}{2}$.

10. **The correct answer is (D).** There are six squares. Two of them are shaded. We know that 2 over 6 is $\frac{2}{6}$, or $\frac{1}{3}$.

Mathematics

1. D	4. C	7. C	10. B	13. A
2. A	5. B	8. C	11. D	14. D
3. D	6. A	9. A	12. C	15. C

1. **The correct answer is (D).** 36 cannot be divided evenly by 10.

2. **The correct answer is (A).** 56,012 ÷ 7019 is approximately 56,000 ÷ 7000, or 8.

3. **The correct answer is (D).** To convert a percentage to a decimal number, move the decimal to the left two places. The percentage 0.12% can be written in decimal form as 0.0012.

4. **The correct answer is (C).** The reciprocal of a fraction is the fraction "inverted." To find the answer, you would have to rewrite $3\frac{3}{4}$ as an improper fraction, $\frac{15}{4}$. The fraction $\frac{15}{4}$ is the reciprocal of $\frac{4}{15}$.

5. **The correct answer is (B).** The components of this problem must be stated in the same units. There are 60 minutes in an hour and 60 seconds in a minute. Therefore, 1 hour equals 60 × 60, or 3600 seconds. The ratio of 3600 to 120 is simplified to 30 to 1.

6. **The correct answer is (A).** The area of a triangle is found using the formula $A = \frac{1}{2}bh$. Since the base measures 16 centimeters and the height measures 13 centimeters, the area equals $\frac{1}{2} \times (16) \times (13)$, or 104 square centimeters.

7. **The correct answer is (C).** The amount of interest earned in one year is $2000 × 0.08, or $160. The total value of Alicia's investment after one year is $2000 + $160, or $2160.

8. **The correct answer is (C).** $1\frac{3}{4} \times 5 = 8\frac{3}{4}$ hours each week.

9. **The correct answer is (A).** The factory makes 200 cameras per day, so it would make 1000 cameras in 5 days. It would take 5 days for the factory to make about 997 cameras.

10. **The correct answer is (B).** To find the area of the shaded portion, subtract the area of the circle from the area of the square. The area of the circle can be found using the formula $A = \pi r^2$. The area of the circle is therefore $\pi \times (3)^2$, or 3.14 × 9, which equals approximately 28.26 square centimeters.

    The diameter of the circle is equal to the length of the side of the square. The radius of the circle measures 3 centimeters, so the diameter of the circle is twice that, or 6 centimeters. The area of the square can be found using the formula $A = s^2$. The area of the square is 6 × 6, or 36 square centimeters.

    The area of the shaded portion equals 36 − 28.26, or 7.74 square centimeters, which is closest to $7\frac{3}{4}$ square centimeters.

11. **The correct answer is (D).** To find the average, add the sum of the paychecks and divide by 5. The sum of the paychecks is $101.65 + $79.23 + $84.67 + $121.33 + $77.62, which equals $464.50. The average paycheck equals $464.50 ÷ 5, or $92.90.

12. **The correct answer is (C).** Solve the equation by isolating the variable x on one side:

$$3.7x - 1.2 = 58$$
$$3.7x = 58 + 1.2$$
$$3.7x = 59.2$$
$$x = \frac{59.2}{3.7}$$
$$x = 16$$

13. **The correct answer is (A).** The number 784 can be written as $(7 \times 10^2) + (8 \times 10) + 4$. The number 10^2 equals 100, so $7 \times 10^2 = 700$. The value of 8×10 is 80. Add the three numbers together to double check the result: $700 + 80 + 4 = 784$.

14. **The correct answer is (D).** This question doesn't ask you to determine 175% of 24; instead, it asks you to *increase* 24 by 175%. First, calculate 175% of 24 using multiplication: $24 \times 1.75 = 42$. Next, add 42 to 24. The correct answer is 66.

15. **The correct answer is (C).** Substitute 7 into the equation for x. Then solve for y:

$$xy - 7 = 56$$
$$7y - 7 = 56$$
$$7y = 56 + 7$$
$$7y = 63$$
$$y = \frac{63}{7}$$
$$y = 9$$

Series Reasoning

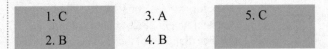

1. C	3. A	5. C
2. B	4. B	

1. **The correct answer is (C).** This series consists of the letters of the alphabet in alphabetical order, beginning with the letter Q. The letter X appears in the middle of each set of three letters.

2. **The correct answer is (B).** This series consists of the three letters *A-R-D* in constant rotation. In each succeeding group of letters, the last letter of the previous group moves to the beginning of the group, and the other two letters move to the right, so the letter that was last in the previous group becomes the first letter of the next. After *ARD*, the *D* must move to the beginning, and the next group must begin with *D* followed by *AR*.

3. **The correct answer is (A).** The pattern in this series is made by subtracting 5 from each number.

4. **The correct answer is (B).** The pattern in this series is +1, +2, +1, +2, and so on.

5. **The correct answer is (C).** The pattern in this series is ×2, +3, ×2, +3, and so on.

Comparisons

1. B	3. C	5. B
2. D	4. A	

1. **The correct answer is (B).** Count the number of squares in (A), (B), and (C). The figures in (A) and (C) each have 11 squares, and the figure in (B) has 14 squares.

2. **The correct answer is (D).** The diagonal *MO* forms two right triangles. The hypotenuse of a right triangle is always its longest side, so *MO* must be greater than *MP*.

3. **The correct answer is (C).** Calculate the value of (A) and (B). The value of (A) is 8 × 8, or 64. The value of (B) is 9 × 7, or 63. The only true statement is that (A) is greater than (B).

4. **The correct answer is (A).** Calculate the value of (A) and (B). The value of (A) is 6×10^2, or 6 × 100, which equals 600. The value of (B) is 6 ÷ 10, or 0.60. Therefore, (B) is equal to (C).

5. **The correct answer is (B).** Calculate the value of (A), (B), and (C). The value of (A) is 6 × (4 + 2), or 6 × 6, which equals 36. The value of (B) is (4 + 2) × (4 + 2), or 6 × 6, which also equals 36. The value of (C) is (6 × 4) + 2, or 24 + 2, which equals 26. Therefore, (C) is less than (A) and (B).

answers diagnostic test

DIAGNOSTIC SCORE SHEET

Directions: Use the score sheet below to convert your test scores to percentages. This will allow you to determine your strong and weak areas of performance. Use the study reference guide below to find which chapters of the book to review to improve your skills.

Subject	No. Incorrect	No. Correct ÷ No. Questions	× 100 = _____ %
Synonyms	_____	_____ ÷ 7 = _____	_____ × 100 = _____ %
Antonyms	_____	_____ ÷ 7 = _____	_____ × 100 = _____ %
Analogies	_____	_____ ÷ 5 = _____	_____ × 100 = _____ %
Verbal Logic	_____	_____ ÷ 5 = _____	_____ × 100 = _____ %
Reading	_____	_____ ÷ 10 = _____	_____ × 100 = _____ %
Spelling	_____	_____ ÷ 8 = _____	_____ × 100 = _____ %
Punctuation and Capitalization	_____	_____ ÷ 8 = _____	_____ × 100 = _____ %
English Usage	_____	_____ ÷ 8 = _____	_____ × 100 = _____ %
Language Composition and Expression	_____	_____ ÷ 7 = _____	_____ × 100 = _____ %
Quantitative Reasoning	_____	_____ ÷ 10 = _____	_____ × 100 = _____ %
Mathematics	_____	_____ ÷ 15 = _____	_____ × 100 = _____ %
Series Reasoning	_____	_____ ÷ 5 = _____	_____ × 100 = _____ %
Comparisons	_____	_____ ÷ 5 = _____	_____ × 100 = _____ %
TOTAL EXAM	_____	_____ ÷ 100 = _____	_____ × 100 = _____ %

Study Reference Guide

Subject	Chapter	Page
Synonyms	Chapter 6: Synonyms	p. 73
Antonyms	Chapter 7: Antonyms	p. 87
Analogies	Chapter 8: Analogies	p. 95
Verbal Logic	Chapter 9: Verbal Logic	p. 107
Reading	Chapter 10: Reading	p. 121
Spelling	Chapter 11: Spelling	p. 159
Punctuation and Capitalization	Chapter 12: Punctuation and Capitalization	p. 167
English Usage	Chapter 13: English Usage	p. 181
Language Composition and Expression	Chapter 14: Language Composition and Expression	p. 199
Quantitative Reasoning	Chapter 15: Quantitative Reasoning	p. 209
Mathematics	Chapter 16: Mathematics	p. 221
Series Reasoning	Chapter 17: Series Reasoning	p. 297
Comparisons	Chapter 18: Comparisons	p. 315

PART III

VERBAL SKILLS

Synonyms

OVERVIEW

- Tips for answering synonym questions
- Exercises: Synonyms
- Answer keys and explanations
- Summing it up

Synonym questions test your understanding of words. You are asked to choose another word that has the same, or nearly the same, meaning as the given word. On the HSPT®, synonyms are tested in the Verbal Skills section and the Reading section under Vocabulary. On the TACHS, synonyms are tested in the Reading section under Vocabulary. Each exam may indicate the synonym in a different fashion. For example, some exams will identify the word they want you to match by italicizing or capitalizing the word, then ask you to choose a synonym from the answer choices. Other exams will use the word in a sentence, usually identifying the synonym in question by italicizing, underlining, or capitalizing the word, and then you must select a matching synonym from the answer choices. For example:

The surface of the *placid* lake was smooth as glass.

(A) cold

(B) muddy

(C) deep

(D) calm

In this example, the word *calm* is the correct choice. As you can see, the nice thing about a sentence example is that it might give you contextual clues that make it easier to figure out the synonym's meaning. In the example, when you read that the lake was "smooth as glass," you could infer that, although the lake might have been muddy, deep, or cold, it definitely must have been calm. That made choice (D) the best choice for this question. **The correct answer is (D).**

chapter 6

TIPS FOR ANSWERING SYNONYM QUESTIONS

Here's a tip to use when choosing the answer for a synonym question: If the given word is in sentence, you should always try substituting the choices in the place of the indicated word. This process can help you find and check your answer.

Sometimes the italicized or underlined word has multiple meanings, which can make the contextual clues of the sentence even more important. Consider the following question:

The camel is sometimes called the ship of the *desert*.

(A) abandon

(B) ice cream

(C) sandy wasteland

(D) leave

Here, the sentence is absolutely necessary to the definition of the word. Without the sentence, you would not know whether the word *desert* is to be pronounced *de-sert'*, which means to leave or to abandon, or *des'-ert*, which means a sandy wasteland. If you are not sure of your spelling, the sentence can also spare you the confusion of *desert* with *dessert*, which is the last course of a meal. **The correct answer is (C).**

On the other hand, the phrase or sentence might be of little or no use at all in helping you to choose the synonym. The sentence might help you to determine the part of speech of the indicated word, but not its meaning, as in:

The robbery suspect had a *sallow* complexion.

(A) ruddy

(B) pale

(C) pock-marked

(D) freckled

The sentence shows you the proper use of the word *sallow*. It is an adjective used to describe a complexion, but the sentence gives no clue that *sallow* means *pale*. You either know the meaning of the word or you must guess. When the given word isn't part of a sentence, or if the sentence doesn't help define the word, you might have to guess. But before you guess blindly, you need to make sure there are no other clues that could lead you to the correct answer. **The correct answer is (B).**

Perhaps you have seen the word used but were never sure what it meant. Look carefully. Do you know the meaning of any part of the word? If you can associate the word with something else you've read or you know, you might be able to find the answer. An example:

Remedial most nearly means

(A) reading.

(B) slow.

(C) corrective.

(D) special.

Your association is probably "remedial reading." That association can help you, but be careful! *Remedial* does not mean *reading*. *Remedial* is an adjective, and *reading* is the noun it modifies. Slow readers might receive remedial reading instruction in special classes that are intended to correct bad reading skills. Do you see the word *remedy* in *remedial*? You know that a *remedy* is a *cure* or a *correction* for an ailment. If you combine all the information you now have, you can choose *corrective* as the word that most nearly means *remedial*. **The correct answer is (C).**

Sometimes you can find the correct answer to a synonym question by eliminating the answers that you know are wrong. If you can eliminate even one of the answers, you have a 33 percent chance of choosing the correct answer. Eliminate two incorrect answers, and you have a 50/50 chance of choosing the right answer from the two remaining choices. For example:

Infamous most nearly means

(A) well known.

(B) poor.

(C) disgraceful.

(D) young.

The first word you see when you look at *infamous* is *famous*. *Famous*, of course, means well known. Because *in*, meaning *not*, is a negative prefix, you should be looking for a negative word as the meaning of *infamous*. With that in mind, you can eliminate choice (A). There is no choice meaning *not famous*, so you must look for negative fame. A person who is not well known might or might not be poor. You should carefully consider the other choices before choosing *poor*, choice (B). Choice (D), *young*, probably can be eliminated for the same reasons. Though many young people are not famous, the terms aren't necessarily synonymous. *Disgrace* is a negative kind of *fame*. A person who behaves *disgracefully* is well known for his bad behavior; he is *infamous*. Therefore, choice (C) becomes the best answer for this question. **The correct answer is (C).**

All of the previous suggestions can help you use clues to determine the meaning of words and find their synonyms. But many synonym questions might give you no clues at all. The best way to minimize the number of synonym questions that you simply cannot answer is to learn as many vocabulary words as you can. One way to increase your vocabulary is to work with a dictionary when preparing for your exam. Try to read as much as you can during the time before your exam. When you run into a word that's totally unfamiliar to you, look it up. If you run across a word you don't know while doing the practice exams, circle the word and look it up later. Look up words you find in the reading passages, new words from among answer choices, words you find in the explanations, and words you meet in the study chapters. Looking up words for yourself is the best way to learn them.

If you understand every word in this book, you are well on your way toward a broad-based vocabulary and should be able to handle not only the synonym questions, but the other verbal questions as well.

Now try the following exercises. Answer keys and explanations follow Exercise 2.

EXERCISES: SYNONYMS

Exercise 1

Directions: In the following questions, choose the word that means the same as or about the same as the underlined word.

1. a display of affluence
   - (A) power
   - (B) wealth
   - (C) glibness
   - (D) junction

2. the gloss of her lips
   - (A) goblet
   - (B) shadow
   - (C) brightness
   - (D) blush

3. a wary neighbor
   - (A) boastful
   - (B) cautious
   - (C) weak
   - (D) flexible

4. a thrilling encounter
   - (A) meeting
   - (B) bar
   - (C) ledge
   - (D) spaceship

5. to concede one's guilt
   - (A) hide
   - (B) invent
   - (C) admit
   - (D) contradict

6. to emerge from hiding
   - (A) bury
   - (B) come out
   - (C) join
   - (D) show anger

7. to teem with humanity
   - (A) abound
   - (B) play
   - (C) group
   - (D) adolescent

8. to permit to attend
   - (A) discourage
   - (B) allow
   - (C) drive
   - (D) card

9. an indifferent politician
   - (A) confused
   - (B) involved
   - (C) charismatic
   - (D) neutral

10. a recurrent theme
    - (A) refined
    - (B) resultant
    - (C) electrifying
    - (D) returning

11. on the verge of disaster
    (A) boat
    (B) force
    (C) brink
    (D) violence

12. to ponder deeply
    (A) peruse
    (B) think
    (C) delay
    (D) reveal

13. to aspire for success
    (A) hope
    (B) breathe
    (C) exhaust
    (D) plot

14. an era of apathy
    (A) mistake
    (B) war
    (C) place
    (D) age

15. temerity to speak out
    (A) fear
    (B) nerve
    (C) flutter
    (D) cowardice

16. a feat of skill
    (A) body part
    (B) celebration
    (C) big meal
    (D) achievement

17. zest for adventure
    (A) relish
    (B) fluency
    (C) garment
    (D) haste

18. a plaintive sound
    (A) musical
    (B) famous
    (C) mournful
    (D) patient

19. to view with consternation
    (A) dismay
    (B) telescope
    (C) relief
    (D) pretense

20. flagrant disobedience
    (A) disguised
    (B) glaring
    (C) repeated
    (D) perfumed

Exercise 2

Directions: Choose the word or phrase that has the same or nearly the same meaning as the underlined word or group of words.

1. The veracity of her story is without doubt.
   - (A) persistence
   - (B) truthfulness
   - (C) poetry
   - (D) horror

2. The drawings were completely identical.
   - (A) twin
   - (B) unclear
   - (C) breathtaking
   - (D) same

3. In our cellar, we accumulate old clothes.
   - (A) affirm
   - (B) donate
   - (C) refurbish
   - (D) collect

4. This legislation will transform the railroad system.
   - (A) improve
   - (B) electrify
   - (C) change
   - (D) sell

5. Candy will gratify the baby.
   - (A) satisfy
   - (B) fatten
   - (C) excite
   - (D) teach

6. The arena was girded with ribbons.
   - (A) protected
   - (B) established
   - (C) decorated
   - (D) encircled

7. How shall we quell the rebellion?
   - (A) begin
   - (B) cushion
   - (C) crush
   - (D) fire

8. His face looked pale and sickly.
   - (A) wan
   - (B) gabled
   - (C) paltry
   - (D) ponderous

9. The father was stern and impersonal with his children.
   - (A) morose
   - (B) gruff
   - (C) opinionated
   - (D) endeared

10. The meaning of the text was inscrutable to laymen.
    - (A) comprehensible
    - (B) loud
    - (C) mysterious
    - (D) enjoyable

11. Let us hoist the banner now.
    - (A) raise
    - (B) lower
    - (C) wave
    - (D) fold

12. The town took drastic measures to ensure its security.
    - (A) well-informed
    - (B) ill-advised
    - (C) haphazard
    - (D) extreme

13. The newscaster <u>alluded to</u> the weather fore-cast.

    (A) changed

    (B) complained about

    (C) praised

    (D) referred to

14. The strength of the cord <u>exceeds</u> government standards.

    (A) surpasses

    (B) equals

    (C) challenges

    (D) falls short of

15. The <u>austere</u> forest cabin appealed to the pioneers.

    (A) simple

    (B) sturdy

    (C) extravagant

    (D) hidden

16. I wish that you would stop <u>beating around the bush.</u>

    (A) running in circles

    (B) avoiding the subject

    (C) sweeping the driveway

    (D) repeating the same thing over and over

17. I generally accept Jim's pronouncements with <u>a grain of salt.</u>

    (A) some question

    (B) criticism

    (C) pleasure

    (D) relief

18. That explanation is little more than <u>an old wives' tale.</u>

    (A) a deliberate falsehood

    (B) a half-truth

    (C) feminist propaganda

    (D) folklore

19. The medicine man shared his <u>tried and true</u> remedy with me.

    (A) new and unusual

    (B) tested and proven

    (C) experimental

    (D) unorthodox but effective

20. You should not <u>look a gift horse in the mouth.</u>

    (A) question authority

    (B) quibble over details

    (C) expose yourself to danger

    (D) be suspicious of good fortune

exercises

ANSWER KEYS AND EXPLANATIONS

Exercise 1

1. B	5. C	9. D	13. A	17. A
2. C	6. B	10. D	14. D	18. C
3. B	7. A	11. C	15. B	19. A
4. A	8. B	12. B	16. D	20. B

1. **The correct answer is (B).** *Affluence* is a synonym for wealth. *Influence* is a synonym for power, choice (A); *glibness*, choice (C), means being talkative in a smooth, somewhat insincere way; and *confluence* is a synonym for junction, choice (D).

2. **The correct answer is (C).** *Gloss* is brightness, polish, or shine.

3. **The correct answer is (B).** To be *wary* means to be cautious or careful, particularly in dangerous situations.

4. **The correct answer is (A).** An *encounter* is a face-to-face meeting.

5. **The correct answer is (C).** To *concede* is to admit or to acknowledge.

6. **The correct answer is (B).** To *emerge* is to come out. The word *emerge* is almost opposite to the word *merge*, which means join.

7. **The correct answer is (A).** To *teem* is to abound or to overflow. If you selected choice (C), group, you might have been thinking about the homonym team. Choice (D), adolescent, is incorrect because the word is *teem* not *teen*.

8. **The correct answer is (B).** The word *permit*, pronounced *per-mit'*, means allow. If the word were pronounced *per'-mit*, it would mean license (which is not offered as a choice), but in no event would it mean discourage, drive, or card.

9. **The correct answer is (D).** To be *indifferent* is to be neutral or disinterested in something.

10. **The correct answer is (D).** That which is *recurrent* returns from time to time.

11. **The correct answer is (C).** *Verge* means brink or threshold.

12. **The correct answer is (B).** To *ponder* is to think or to consider. *Peruse*, choice (A), means to read.

13. **The correct answer is (A).** To *aspire* is to hope or to desire. To *breathe* is to respire.

14. **The correct answer is (D).** An *era* is an age or period. Read carefully to avoid careless mistakes such as reading *err* or *area* and incorrectly selecting choice (A), mistake, or choice (C), place.

15. **The correct answer is (B).** *Temerity* is audacity or nerve. *Timorousness* is timidity, fear, or cowardice.

16. **The correct answer is (D).** A *feat* is an achievement. Beware of homonyms when choosing synonyms.

17. **The correct answer is (A).** *Zest* means relish or gusto.

18. **The correct answer is (C).** *Plaintive* means mournful or melancholy.

19. **The correct answer is (A).** *Consternation* is amazement or dismay that throws one into confusion.

20. **The correct answer is (B).** *Flagrant* means glaring or conspicuously objectionable. The word meaning *perfumed,* choice (D), is *fragrant*.

Exercise 2

1. B	5. A		9. B	13. D		17. A
2. D	6. D		10. C	14. A		18. D
3. D	7. C		11. A	15. A		19. B
4. C	8. A		12. D	16. B		20. D

1. **The correct answer is (B).** *Veracity* is truthfulness or accuracy. Persistence, choice (A), would be a synonym for *tenacity*.

2. **The correct answer is (D).** *Identical* means same. Identical twins are genetically the same, but choice (A), twin, is not a synonym for *identical*.

3. **The correct answer is (D).** To *accumulate* is to collect or to amass.

4. **The correct answer is (C).** To *transform* means to change. A *transformer* converts electrical currents, but the word transform has nothing to do with electricity, choice (B). If the railroad system is *transformed*, it may be improved (choice (A)), but the change in itself is no guarantee.

5. **The correct answer is (A).** To *gratify* is to indulge, to please, or to satisfy.

6. **The correct answer is (D).** *Girded* means encircled.

7. **The correct answer is (C).** To *quell* is to put down, to suppress, or to crush.

8. **The correct answer is (A).** *Wan* means pale, sickly, or feeble.

9. **The correct answer is (B).** *Gruff* means rough or stern.

10. **The correct answer is (C).** Something that is *inscrutable* is mysterious or not easy to interpret.

11. **The correct answer is (A).** To *hoist* is to raise or to lift.

12. **The correct answer is (D).** *Drastic* means extreme or severe.

13. **The correct answer is (D).** To *allude* is to make indirect reference or to refer.

14. **The correct answer is (A).** To *exceed* is to surpass.

15. **The correct answer is (A).** Something that is a*ustere* is simple and not fancy in appearance and character.

16. **The correct answer is (B).** *Beating around the bush* is talking about irrelevant topics and raising side issues to avoid talking about or committing oneself on a particular subject.

17. **The correct answer is (A).** When one takes something with *a grain of salt,* one does not accept it at face value but questions details, motives, or conclusions.

18. **The correct answer is (D).** *An old wives' tale* is a story or explanation that has been handed "from woman to woman" as an oral tradition until it becomes folklore.

19. **The correct answer is (B).** *Tried and true* means tested and proven.

20. **The correct answer is (D).** Quite literally, the expression means that because one does not know the disposition of a gift horse, one should not risk sticking one's head in its mouth; furthermore, accept a gift as a gift without questioning its value (checking the quality of its teeth). In other words, be happy with what you get and don't be suspicious of good fortune.

MORE SYNONYM PRACTICE
Courtesy of *Peterson's egghead's Guide to Vocabulary*

Elaborate: very involved or complex; to explain something in detail

Example
An *elaborate* wedding is one that has lots of expensive decorations.

Tara's lists
Tara kept *elaborate* lists of statistics about her favorite sports teams. The lists were detailed and complex. She liked to keep track of how the teams were performing.

Elated: very happy

Example
A student might be *elated* when she graduates from high school.

Her parents might be more **elated!**

A happy day
One day Janet came home from school and burst in the door with great news. One of her best friends was moving to her neighborhood. Janet was *elated*! She walked through the house with a huge smile on her face.

Practice 3 – Synonyms

Directions

Match the words to their synonyms below.

Synonyms

___ **A.** thrilled
___ **B.** sadness
___ **C.** untruthful
___ **D.** improve
___ **E.** unique
___ **F.** control
___ **G.** remove
___ **H.** fancy

Words

1. deceptive
2. dismay
3. dominate
4. detach
5. elaborate
6. elated
7. distinct
8. enhance

You'll find the answers on the next page.

Practice 3 – Synonyms
Check your answers against the solutions below.

Answer Key

1. C
2. B
3. F
4. G
5. H
6. A
7. E
8. D

Explanations

1. **The correct answer is C.** *Deceptive* means lying. Untruthful is a synonym of *deceptive*.

Someone who is **deceptive** is being dishonest.

2. **The correct answer is B.** *Dismay* means sadness. Sadness is a synonym of *dismay*.

3. **The correct answer is F.** *Dominate* means to rule or control. Control is a synonym of *dominate*.

4. **The correct answer is G.** *Detach* means to separate or pull apart. Remove is a synonym of *detach*. You can *detach* a post-it note from a mirror.

5. **The correct answer is H.** *Elaborate* means involved or complex. Fancy is a synonym of *elaborate*.

6. **The correct answer is A.** *Elated* means very happy. Thrilled is a synonym of *elated*.

7. **The correct answer is E.** *Distinct* means separate or unique. Unique is a synonym of *distinct*.

8. **The correct answer is D.** *Enhance* means to increase or improve. Improve is a synonym of *enhance*.

Congrats! You've **enhanced** your vocabulary!

Did you find this helpful—and a fun way to boost your vocabulary? Check out *egghead's Guide to Vocabulary* at **www.petersons.com**.

SUMMING IT UP

- When choosing the answer for a synonym question, if the given word is in a sentence, you should try substituting the answer choices in the place of the indicated word.

- When the given word is in a sentence, there are several ways to select the best answer. Look for contextual clues to determine which meaning of the word is being used. Determine which part of speech the word is, and look for an answer choice of the same part of speech.

- When you don't know the meaning, try to take apart the word. Look for prefixes, suffixes, and the root word.

- Eliminate answers that you know are wrong and concentrate on the others.

Antonyms

chapter 7

OVERVIEW

- **Tips for answering antonym questions**
- **Exercises: Antonyms**
- **Answer keys and explanations**
- **Summing it up**

Antonym questions are similar to synonym questions in that they test your understanding of words. However, antonym questions are a bit trickier because they challenge you to demonstrate your mental flexibility as well as your verbal skills. On the HSPT®, antonym questions appear on the Verbal Skills portion of the exam.

The task in an antonym question is to define the indicated word and pick its opposite. That sounds simple enough, right? Here's why it gets tricky. Where there is no true opposite, you must choose the word or phrase that is most nearly opposite. Where there appears to be two or more opposites, you must choose the best opposite. You must guard against choosing an associated word or phrase that is different in meaning but is not a true opposite. After struggling to define a word, you must then take care to choose its *antonym,* not its *synonym* (the word or phrase that is most similar in meaning).

Let's try an example. Suppose the test question looks like this:

Inaudible means the *opposite* of
(A) invisible.
(B) bright.
(C) loud.
(D) clear.

You do not know the meaning of the word *inaudible*, but you might recognize some of the word's parts. You might know that the prefix *in-* typically means *not*. You also might recognize a part of audio in the word, and you know that the *audio* of your TV is the sound. You might also see *-able* in *-ible* and thereby reconstruct not soundable or not heard.

BEWARE! This is the point at which your reasoning can easily lead you astray. If you associate the word with your TV, you might think, "The opposite of not heard is not seen or invisible, choice (A)." Wrong. These are not true opposites. Or you might associate *not heard* with *not seen* and choose choice (B), *bright,* as the opposite of *not seen.* Wrong again. Or you might think of *inaudible* as hard to hear and choose choice (D), *clear*. Clear would not be a bad answer, but choice (C), *loud,* is better and is indeed the best answer. The best opposite of *inaudible* is *loud.* You can now see how tricky finding the answer can be! To find the right answer to an antonym question, you need to be certain that you remember exactly what you're looking for as you reject or choose an answer choice.

TIPS FOR ANSWERING ANTONYM QUESTIONS

Thankfully, there is a sound approach to handling antonym questions if you're not sure of the correct answer. After reading the word and its four answer choices very carefully, run through the following four possibilities.

Possibility #1

You know the meaning of the word, but no answer choice seems correct.

- Perhaps you misread the word. Are there other words that look similar to the word in the question? For example, did you read *revelation* for *revaluation* or *compliment* for *complement?*

- Perhaps you read the word correctly but accented the wrong syllable. Some words have alternative pronunciations with vastly different meanings. Remember *de-sert'* and *des'-ert?*

- Perhaps you are dealing with a single word that can be used as two different parts of speech and therefore has two entirely unrelated meanings. A *moor* (noun) is a boggy wasteland. To *moor* (verb) is to secure a ship or a boat in place. The proper noun *Moor* refers to the Moslem conquerors of Spain.

- Perhaps the word can appear as a number of parts of speech with numerous meanings and shades of meaning within each of these. *Fancy* (noun) can mean inclination, love, notion, whim, taste, judgment, or imagination. *Fancy* (verb) can mean to like, to imagine, and to think. *Fancy* (adjective) can mean whimsical, ornamental, and extravagant. Your task is to choose from among the four choices one word or phrase that is opposite to *one* of these meanings of the word *fancy*.

Possibility #2

You do not know the meaning of the word, but it appears to contain prefix, suffix, or root clues. Examine those clues. For example, the word *inaudible* uses the prefix *in-*, which means *not*, so look for the best opposite of "not audible."

Possibility #3

You do not know the meaning of the word and can see no clues, but you have a feeling that the word has some specific connotation, be it sinister, gloomy, or positive. Play your hunch. Choose a word with the opposite connotation.

Possibility #4

You are stumped. There is no penalty for guessing on the HSPT® exam, so when all else fails, guess. If you can eliminate one or more of the choices, you improve the odds of guessing correctly. Eliminate choices as you can, choose from the remaining options, and move on. There's no need to waste time on a question for which you cannot figure out the answer.

Now try the following exercises using the tactics outlined. Answer keys and explanations follow Exercise 2.

EXERCISES: ANTONYMS

Exercise 1

Directions: Choose the best answer.

1. Accelerate means the *opposite* of
   (A) stop.
   (B) slow.
   (C) quicken.
   (D) hasten.

2. Docile means the *opposite* of
   (A) active.
   (B) health.
   (C) probable.
   (D) teachable.

3. Candor means the *opposite* of
   (A) frankness.
   (B) doubt.
   (C) deception.
   (D) enthusiasm.

4. Nomadic means the *opposite* of
   (A) secret.
   (B) anonymous.
   (C) stationary.
   (D) famous.

5. Heed means the *opposite* of
   (A) agree.
   (B) ignore.
   (C) listen.
   (D) analyze.

6. Defy means the *opposite* of
   (A) desire.
   (B) embrace.
   (C) fight.
   (D) abscond.

7. Gorge means the *opposite* of
   (A) duck.
   (B) diet.
   (C) stuff.
   (D) valley.

8. Curtail means the *opposite* of
   (A) curry.
   (B) open.
   (C) shorten.
   (D) extend.

9. Initiate means the *opposite* of
    (A) instruct.
    (B) begin.
    (C) terminate.
    (D) invade.

10. Craven means the *opposite* of
    A) brave.
    (B) greedy.
    (C) hungry.
    (D) nervous.

11. Clamor means the *opposite* of
    (A) ugliness.
    (B) beauty.
    (C) silence.
    (D) dishonor.

12. Rouse means the *opposite* of
    (A) lull.
    (B) alarm.
    (C) complain.
    (D) weep.

13. Credible means the *opposite* of
    (A) believable.
    (B) unbelievable.
    (C) honorable.
    (D) dishonorable.

14. Thorough means the *opposite* of
    (A) around.
    (B) circumvented.
    (C) incomplete.
    (D) inside.

15. Wooden means the *opposite* of
    (A) iron.
    (B) slippery.
    (C) rubbery.
    (D) green.

Exercise 2

Directions: Choose the best answer.

1. Succumb means the *opposite* of
    (A) arrive.
    (B) yield.
    (C) eat.
    (D) conquer.

2. Divert means the *opposite* of
    (A) instruct.
    (B) include.
    (C) bore.
    (D) amuse.

3. Admonish means the *opposite* of
    (A) review.
    (B) scare.
    (C) praise.
    (D) tease.

4. Diminish means the *opposite* of
    (A) lessen.
    (B) begin.
    (C) complete.
    (D) expand.

5. Brazen means the *opposite* of
   (A) frozen.
   (B) meek.
   (C) rustproof.
   (D) leaky.

6. Intent means the *opposite* of
   (A) alfresco.
   (B) busy.
   (C) uninterested.
   (D) shy.

7. Erode means the *opposite* of
   (A) weaken.
   (B) restore.
   (C) combat.
   (D) color.

8. Lavish means the *opposite* of
   (A) filthy.
   (B) elegant.
   (C) squander.
   (D) conserve.

9. Aloof means the *opposite* of
   (A) sociable.
   (B) humble.
   (C) public.
   (D) ignorant.

10. Elated means the *opposite* of
   (A) on time.
   (B) tardy.
   (C) ideal.
   (D) depressed.

11. Furnish means the *opposite* of
   (A) dress.
   (B) decorate.
   (C) remove.
   (D) polish.

12. Ostracize means the *opposite* of
   (A) include.
   (B) shun.
   (C) hide.
   (D) delight.

13. Exorbitant means the *opposite* of
   (A) priceless.
   (B) worthless.
   (C) reasonable.
   (D) straight.

14. Chastise means the *opposite* of
   (A) dirty.
   (B) cleanse.
   (C) praise.
   (D) straighten.

15. Profit means the *opposite* of
   (A) gain.
   (B) money.
   (C) suffer.
   (D) disgust.

exercises

ANSWER KEYS AND EXPLANATIONS

Exercise 1

1. B	4. C	7. B	10. A	13. B
2. A	5. B	8. D	11. C	14. C
3. C	6. B	9. C	12. A	15. C

1. **The correct answer is (B).** To *accelerate* is to quicken or to hasten. Its best opposite is to *slow*. *Accelerate* implies that the object was already in motion. *Stop* would be the opposite if the original word had meant *to put into motion*.

2. **The correct answer is (A).** *Docile* means calm and easily led. Of the choices offered, its best opposite is *active*.

3. **The correct answer is (C).** *Candor* is frankness; its opposite is *deception*.

4. **The correct answer is (C).** *Nomadic* means wandering; its opposite is *stationary*, staying in one place. The word *nomadic* has nothing to do with names.

5. **The correct answer is (B).** To *heed* means to pay close attention to something. To *ignore* something is the opposite of this.

6. **The correct answer is (B).** To *defy* is to challenge; its opposite is *embrace*.

7. **The correct answer is (B).** To *gorge* oneself is to overeat; the opposite is to *diet*.

8. **The correct answer is (D).** To *curtail* is to shorten; the opposite is to *extend*.

9. **The correct answer is (C).** To *initiate* is to begin; its opposite is to end or to *terminate*.

10. **The correct answer is (A).** *Craven* means fearful or having a lack of courage. Being *brave* is the direct opposite of this.

11. **The correct answer is (C).** *Clamor* is noise; its opposite is *silence*. You must read carefully. *Clamor* is not *glamour*.

12. **The correct answer is (A).** To *rouse* is to awaken; to *lull* is to soothe and to cause to sleep.

13. **The correct answer is (B).** *Credible* means believable; its opposite is *unbelievable*.

14. **The correct answer is (C).** One meaning of *thorough* is covering everything or all important points; its opposite would be *incomplete*.

15. **The correct answer is (C).** *Wooden* means stiff and unbending; its opposite, *rubbery*, means flexible.

Exercise 2

1. D	4. D	7. B	10. D	13. C
2. C	5. B	8. D	11. C	14. C
3. C	6. C	9. A	12. A	15. C

1. **The correct answer is (D).** To *succumb* is to yield or to give in; its opposite is to *conquer.*

2. **The correct answer is (C).** To *divert* is to amuse (think of *diversion*); its opposite is to *bore.* To divert also means *to change the direction of,* but no opposite to this meaning is offered.

3. **The correct answer is (C).** To *admonish* means to criticize or reprimand; its opposite is to *praise.*

4. **The correct answer is (D).** To *diminish* is to lessen. Therefore, its opposite is *expand.*

5. **The correct answer is (B).** *Brazen* means bold or impudent; its opposite is *meek.*

6. **The correct answer is (C).** To be *intent* is to be engrossed or determined; the opposite is to be *uninterested.*

7. **The correct answer is (B).** To *erode* means to whither or wear away, often gradually and over a period of time. The opposite of this is to *restore* or bring back to a pristine condition.

8. **The correct answer is (D).** To *lavish* is to spend profusely or to squander; its opposite is to *conserve.*

9. **The correct answer is (A).** One who is *aloof* is distant or reserved; an opposite type of person is *sociable.*

10. **The correct answer is (D).** One who is *elated* is joyful and jubilant; its opposite is one who is *depressed.*

11. **The correct answer is (C).** To *furnish* is to provide; its opposite is to *remove.*

12. **The correct answer is (A).** To *ostracize* is to shut out or to exclude; its opposite is to *include.*

13. **The correct answer is (C).** *Exorbitant* means excessive; its opposite is *reasonable.*

14. **The correct answer is (C).** To *chastise* is to scold; its opposite is to *praise.*

15. **The correct answer is (C).** To *profit* is to benefit; its opposite is to *suffer.*

SUMMING IT UP

- Antonym questions are trickier than synonym questions because they ask you to define the indicated word and choose its opposite—or the word or phrase that is most nearly opposite.

- When you think you know the meaning of the given word but can't find the answer, go back and check the following: Did you misread the word? Did you accent the wrong syllable? Can the word be used as two different parts of speech? Does the word have multiple meanings?

- If you don't know the meaning of the word, look for prefixes, suffixes, and root words. Be sure you are clear on the context and look for the opposite meaning.

- When you have to guess, try to eliminate some answer choices. Consider connotation and the part of speech.

Analogies

OVERVIEW

- Tips for answering analogy questions
- Exercises: Analogies
- Answer keys and explanations
- Summing it up

Verbal analogy questions test your ability to see a relationship between words and to apply that relationship to other words. It is a test of your ability to think things out clearly and logically. Analogies are tested on the COOP and on the HSPT®.

Depending on the exam, verbal analogy questions might be presented in a number of different forms. In the HSPT® exam, you are given two example words that are related to each other in a certain way. Then you are given a third word and four answer choices. The correct answer choice will have the same relationship to the third word as that shared by the example words. For example:

Man is to boy as woman is to

(A) child.

(B) sister.

(C) girl.

(D) offspring.

The completed analogy reads "man is to boy as woman is to girl." A woman is an adult girl, just as a man is an adult boy. **The correct answer is (C).**

The Analogies section on the COOP exam takes a different form, using pictures instead of words. After you have named the object in each picture, you must proceed as with a verbal analogy question, defining and completing the relationships. The Verbal Reasoning—Words section of the COOP exam uses yet another form for analogy questions. Here, you must define the relationship among three words and then complete a second group of three words, this time choosing the third word for the second group. Regardless of which form an analogy question might take, the task is always the same: Define relationships and then apply the relationships to different words.

TIPS FOR ANSWERING ANALOGY QUESTIONS

The first step in tackling an analogy question is to define the first set of words and determine their relationship. Most often you will know the meanings of both words (if you're not sure, make a guess and move on to the next step). Your next step will be to determine how those words are related. Define a specific relationship between the words. Here's an example: Suppose you are confronted with an analogy question that begins *brim* is to *hat*. *Brim* and *hat* are immediately associated in your mind; a *brim* is a part of a *hat,* so the relationship between the two is that of a part to the whole.

Now take a look at the third word in the analogy question and the four choices available. By process of elimination, you must find among the choices a word that bears the same relationship to the third word that the second word bears to the first. The analogy question would look like this:

Brim is to hat as hand is to

(A) glove.

(B) finger.

(C) foot.

(D) arm.

To figure out the answer, consider each answer choice in turn. *Hand* is certainly associated with choice (A), *glove,* but in no way is a hand part of a glove. *Hand* and choice (B), *finger,* are certainly associated and, indeed, a *finger* is part of a *hand.* But BEWARE! Reexamine the relationship of the first two words: *Brim* is a part of *hat,* or in other words, *hat* is the whole of which *brim* is a part. The relationship in choice (B) is the reverse of the relationship of the first two words. *Hand* is the whole and *finger* is the part. Your answer must maintain the same relationship in the same sequence as the original pair.

The relationship of *hand* and choice (C), *foot,* is only one of association, not of part to whole. This answer is no more likely to be correct than choice (A). In fact, because you have found two answers that have equal chances of being incorrect, you now know that neither of them is the answer you are looking for. There must be a best answer.

A *hand* is part of an *arm* in the same way that a *brim* is part of a *hat*, or the *arm* is the whole of which a *hand* is a part in the same way that *hat* is the whole of which a *brim* is the part. When you've determined this, you know that choice (D) is the *best* answer. **The correct answer is (D).**

So the process is the following five steps:

1 Define the initial terms.

2 Describe the initial relationship.

3 Eliminate incorrect answers.

4 Refine the initial relationship, if necessary.

5 Choose the best of the remaining answer choices.

Usually your biggest problem in solving an analogy question will be that of narrowing your choices down to the *best* answer. Sometimes, however, your difficulty will be in finding even one correct answer. If this happens, you might have to shift gears and completely redefine your initial relationship. Let's look at another analogy example.

Consider an analogy that begins *letter* is to *word*. Initially, you will probably think, "A letter is part of a word; therefore, the relationship is that of part to whole." If the relationship of the third word to any of the choices is also part to whole, then all is well. However, suppose the question looks like this:

Letter is to word as song is to

(A) story.

(B) music.

(C) note.

(D) orchestra.

Three of the choices offer an association relationship, so, clearly, you must go along with a more refined definition of the relationship. None of the choices offers a whole of which a song might be a part (such as an opera). Therefore, you must return to the original pair of words and consider other relationships between letter and word. If letter is not "letter of the alphabet," but rather "written communication," then a word is part of a letter and the relationship of the first to the second is whole to part. Then the answer becomes clear: A song is the whole of which *note*, choice (C), is the part. The relationship of *song* and *note* is the same as that of *letter* and *word*. **The correct answer is (C).**

Analogy questions are a real challenge and can even be fun. Following is a list of a few of the most common, very general relationships.

- Part to whole, e.g., *branch* to *tree*

- whole to part, e.g., *ocean* to *water*

- cause and effect, e.g., *germ* to *disease*

- effect and cause, e.g., *honors* to *study*

- association, e.g., *bat* to *ball*

- degree, e.g., *hut* to *mansion*

- sequence, e.g., *elementary* to *secondary*

- function, e.g., *teacher* to *student*

- characteristic, e.g., *wise* to *owl*

- antonym, e.g., *bad* to *good*

- synonym, e.g., *spring* to *jump*

- purpose, e.g., *mask* to *protection*

TIP

Know the six most common analogy connections:

1. Characteristic
2. Purpose
3. Antonym
4. Part to whole
5. Whole to part
6. Degree

Analogy questions also offer many opportunities for errors if every answer is not given careful consideration. The following are some of the most common pitfalls to avoid:

- Reversal of sequence of the relationship:

  o Part to whole is *not* the same as whole to part.

  o Cause to effect is *not* the same as effect to its cause.

TIP

Turn the analogy pairs into sentences to help you see the connection. Then fit the answer pairs into the same sentence until you find the one that works best.

- o   Smaller to larger is *not* the same as larger to smaller.

- o   Action to object is *not* the same as object to action.

- Confusion of relationship:

   - o   Part to part (*geometry* to *calculus*) with part to whole (*algebra* to *mathematics*)

   - o   Cause and effect (*fire* to *smoke*) with association (*man* to *woman*)

   - o   Degree (*drizzle* to *downpour*) with antonyms (*dry* to *wet*)

   - o   Association (*walk* to *limp*) with synonyms (*eat* to *consume*)

- Grammatical inconsistency: The grammatical relationship of the first two words must be retained throughout the analogy. A wrong analogy would be *imprisoned* is to *convict* as *cage* is to *parrot*. While the meaningful relationship exists, the analogy is not parallel in construction. A correct analogy of this sort would have to read *prison* is to *convict* as *cage* is to *parrot,* or *imprisoned* is to *convict* as *caged* is to *parrot*. In analogy questions, you have to create a pair that is grammatically consistent with the first pair, as well as meaningfully correct.

- Concentration on the meanings of words instead of on their relationships: In this type of error, you see *feathers* to *beak,* and you think *bird* instead of part-to-part relationship. Then, you choose as your answer *wing* to *bird* instead of *wing* to *foot.*

Remember: The key to answering verbal analogy questions lies in the relationship between the first two words!

If you are having trouble determining the relationship between the words of the initial pair, you might find it useful to mentally reverse their order. If this works, just remember to mentally reverse the order of the third and fourth terms as well, to maintain parallelism in your answer.

Now try the following verbal analogies exercises and study the answer key and explanations that follow the exercises.

EXERCISES: ANALOGIES

Exercise 1

Directions: In the following questions, the first two words are related to each other in a certain way. The third and fourth words must be related to each other in the same way. Choose from among the four choices the word that is related to the third word in the same way that the second word is related to the first.

1. Gasoline is to petroleum as sugar is to
   (A) sweet.
   (B) oil.
   (C) plant.
   (D) cane.

2. Fly is to spider as mouse is to
   (A) cat.
   (B) rat.
   (C) rodent.
   (D) trap.

3. Volcano is to crater as chimney is to
   (A) smoke.
   (B) fire.
   (C) flue.
   (D) stack.

4. Petal is to flower as fur is to
   (A) coat.
   (B) rabbit.
   (C) warm.
   (D) woman.

5. Retreat is to advance as timid is to
   (A) bold.
   (B) cowardly.
   (C) fearful.
   (D) shy.

6. Ledger is to accounts as journal is to
   (A) pen.
   (B) territory.
   (C) book.
   (D) observations.

7. Picture is to see as speech is to
   (A) view.
   (B) enunciate.
   (C) hear.
   (D) soliloquize.

8. Soprano is to high as bass is to
   (A) guitar.
   (B) bad.
   (C) low.
   (D) fish.

9. Addition is to addend as subtraction is to
   (A) difference.
   (B) sum.
   (C) subtrahend.
   (D) minus.

10. Obese is to eat as elected is to
    (A) advertise.
    (B) run.
    (C) count.
    (D) fraud.

11. Acute is to chronic as temporary is to
    (A) persistent.
    (B) sick.
    (C) pretty.
    (D) narrow.

12. Sleeves are to shirt as legs are to
    (A) shoes.
    (B) slacks.
    (C) hats.
    (D) closets.

13. Chariot is to charioteer as automobile is to
    (A) passenger.
    (B) engine.
    (C) motor.
    (D) driver.

14. Team is to league as player is to
    (A) piano.
    (B) team.
    (C) tournament.
    (D) football.

15. Honor is to citation as speeding is to
    (A) citation.
    (B) hurry.
    (C) race.
    (D) stop.

Exercise 2

Directions: In the following questions, the first two words are related to each other in a certain way. The third and fourth words must be related to each other in the same way. Choose from among the four choices the word that is related to the third word in the same way that the second word is related to the first.

1. Net is to fisherman as gun is to
   (A) bullet.
   (B) policeman.
   (C) deer.
   (D) hunter.

2. *Hamlet* is to Shakespeare as telephone is to
   (A) Bell.
   (B) telegraph.
   (C) iPhone.
   (D) Verizon.

3. Distracting is to noise as soothing is to
   (A) medicine.
   (B) music.
   (C) volume.
   (D) bleeding.

4. Year is to calendar as hour is to
   (A) decade.
   (B) minute.
   (C) clock.
   (D) month.

5. Father is to brother as mother is to
   (A) daughter.
   (B) sister.
   (C) aunt.
   (D) niece.

6. Words are to books as notes are to
   (A) songs.
   (B) letters.
   (C) pianos.
   (D) fragrances.

7. Pungent is to odor as shrill is to
   (A) whisper.
   (B) sound.
   (C) piercing.
   (D) shriek.

8. Present is to birthday as reward is to
   (A) accomplishment.
   (B) medal.
   (C) punishment.
   (D) money.

9. Mouse is to mammal as lizard is to
   (A) fish.
   (B) scale.
   (C) camouflage.
   (D) reptile.

10. Sky is to ground as ceiling is to
    (A) floor.
    (B) roof.
    (C) top.
    (D) plaster.

11. Food is to nutrition as light is to
    (A) watt.
    (B) bulb.
    (C) electricity.
    (D) vision.

12. Actor is to play as musician is to
    (A) guitarist.
    (B) performer.
    (C) instrument.
    (D) concert.

13. Square is to triangle as cube is to
    (A) circle.
    (B) line.
    (C) ball.
    (D) pyramid.

14. Abacus is to calculator as propeller is to
    (A) jet.
    (B) airplane.
    (C) mathematics.
    (D) flight.

15. Dizziness is to vertigo as fate is to
    (A) adversity.
    (B) order.
    (C) destiny.
    (D) pride.

exercises

ANSWER KEYS AND EXPLANATIONS

Exercise 1

1. D	4. B	7. C	10. B	13. D
2. A	5. A	8. C	11. A	14. B
3. C	6. D	9. C	12. B	15. A

1. **The correct answer is (D).** The relationship is that of the product to its source. *Gasoline* comes from *petroleum*; *sugar* comes from *cane*.

2. **The correct answer is (A).** The relationship is that of the eaten to the eater. The fly is eaten by the *spider;* the *mouse* is eaten by the *cat.* You have to refine this analogy to eating in order to solve it. If you were to consider only catching, then you would not be able to distinguish between the *cat* and the *trap.*

3. **The correct answer is (C).** The relationship is functional. The *crater* is the vent for a *volcano*; the *flue* is the vent for a *chimney.*

4. **The correct answer is (B).** The relationship is that of part to whole. A *petal* is part of a *flower; fur* is part of a *rabbit.* Fur might be part of a coat, but it is not a necessary part, so *rabbit* makes a better analogy.

5. **The correct answer is (A).** The relationship is that of antonyms. *Retreat* is the opposite of *advance; timid* is the opposite of *bold.*

6. **The correct answer is (D).** This analogy involves a functional relationship. A *ledger* is used to store and maintain *accounts* for businesses. A *journal* is used to store and maintain *observations* for individuals.

7. **The correct answer is (C).** This is another variety of object-to-action relationship. You *see* a *picture;* you *hear* a *speech.*

8. **The correct answer is (C).** The relationship is that of synonyms or definition. A *soprano* voice is *high;* a *bass* voice is *low.* Bass has a number of possible meanings. You must define the word in light of the relationship of the first two words.

9. **The correct answer is (C).** The relationship is that of the whole to a part. The *addend* is one term of an *addition* problem; the *subtrahend* is one term of a *subtraction* problem.

10. **The correct answer is (B).** This is an essential cause-and-effect relationship. You cannot become *obese* if you do not *eat;* you cannot be *elected* if you do not run.

11. **The correct answer is (A).** The relationship is that of antonyms. *Acute* means sudden and short; *chronic* means always present. *Temporary* is the opposite of *persistent.*

12. **The correct answer is (B).** This is a part to whole relationship—*sleeves* are a part of a *shirt. Legs,* therefore, must be a part of the correct answer. Review the answer choices: legs are a part of *slacks,* which completes the analogy.

13. **The correct answer is (D).** The relationship is that of object and actor. The *charioteer* drives the *chariot;* the *driver* drives the *automobile.* You must consider the action in this analogy in order to differentiate between *driver* and *passenger.*

14. **The correct answer is (B).** The relationship is that of the part to the whole. The *team* is part of the *league;* the *player* is part of the *team.*

15. **The correct answer is (A).** This analogy is probably more difficult than any you will get. The trick lies in the fact that citation has two distinct meanings. The relationship is that of cause to effect. When you are to be

honored, you receive a *citation*, which is a formal document describing your achievements. When you are stopped for *speeding*, you receive a *citation*, which is an official summons to appear in court.

Exercise 2

1. D	4. C		7. B	10. A		13. D
2. A	5. B		8. A	11. D		14. A
3. B	6. A		9. D	12. D		15. C

1. **The correct answer is (D).** The relationship does not fall into a category with a precise name. The *fisherman* uses a *net* for his sport; the *hunter* uses a *gun* for his sport. The policeman also uses a gun but not for sport. You must refine your relationship so as to eliminate all but one choice.

2. **The correct answer is (A).** This is a creation-creator relationship. *Shakespeare* is the creator (author) of *Hamlet*; the *telephone* is an invention of *Alexander Graham Bell*.

3. **The correct answer is (B).** The relationship is that of effect to its cause. *Noise* is *distracting*; *music* is *soothing*.

4. **The correct answer is (C).** This is a functional relationship. *Years* are measured on a *calendar*; *hours* are measured on a *clock*.

5. **The correct answer is (B).** The relationship of *father* to his same-sex sibling, *brother*, is analogous to the relationship of *mother* to her same-sex sibling, *sister*.

6. **The correct answer is (A).** The relationship is of parts to wholes. *Words* are parts of *books*; *notes* are parts of *songs*.

7. **The correct answer is (B).** The relationship is that of adjective to the noun it modifies. An odor may be described as *pungent*, though there are many other adjectives that may also be used. A *sound* may be described

as *shrill*, though certainly not all sounds are shrill. *Shriek* is not the best answer because a shriek is always shrill.

8. **The correct answer is (A).** This is a purpose relationship. The purpose of a *present* is to celebrate a *birthday*; the purpose of a *reward* is to celebrate an *accomplishment*.

9. **The correct answer is (D).** The relationship is one of classification. A *mouse* is a *mammal*; a *lizard* is a *reptile*.

10. **The correct answer is (A).** The relationship is one of antonyms. *Sky* is the opposite of *ground*; *ceiling* is the opposite of *floor*.

11. **The correct answer is (D).** The relationship is that of cause and effect. *Food* promotes *nutrition*; *light* promotes *vision*.

12. **The correct answer is (D).** This analogy highlights a part to whole relationship. An *actor* is a part of a *play* performance, and a *musician* is a part of a *concert* performance.

13. **The correct answer is (D).** You might loosely state the relationship as *four* is to *three*. A *square* is a four-sided plane figure in relation to a *triangle*, which is a three-sided plane figure. A *cube* is a solid figure based on a square; a *pyramid* is a solid figure based on a triangle.

14. **The correct answer is (A).** The relationship is sequential. An *abacus* is an earlier, more primitive *calculator*; a *propeller* is an earlier, less sophisticated means of propulsion than a *jet*.

15. **The correct answer is (C).** The relationship is that of synonyms. *Vertigo* is *dizziness*; *destiny* is *fate*. One's fate may well be to suffer adversity, but fate is not necessarily negative.

SUMMING IT UP

- Analogies are tested on the COOP and on the HSPT®.

- Questions in the Analogy section of the COOP use pictures instead of words. Once you have named the object in each picture, proceed the same way you would with a verbal analogy.

- Follow the steps: define the initial terms, describe the initial relationship, eliminate incorrect answers, refine the initial relationship, and choose the best answer.

- Study and learn the twelve types of analogy questions: part to whole, whole to part, cause and effect, effect and cause, association, degree, sequence, function, characteristic, antonym, synonym, and purpose.

Verbal Logic

OVERVIEW

- HSPT® Logic
- HSPT® Verbal Classification
- COOP Extraction of Information
- COOP Logic
- COOP Artificial Language
- Exercises: Verbal Logic
- Answer keys and explanations
- Summing it up

You'll definitely be tested on your logical thinking on both the COOP and HSPT® exams. A test of your reasoning skills will show how you think through a problem or scenario. The HSPT® exam tests several types of verbal logic, one under the Logic test section and the other under the Verbal Classifications section, both of which appear under Verbal Skills. In the COOP exam, verbal logic questions are found in the Verbal Reasoning sections.

One measure of verbal logic requires you to extract indisputable information from a series of short sentences. Another asks you to consider a single word and to decide which of four choices is an absolutely necessary component of that word. The third measure of logical thinking is an exercise in translating an artificial language. Let's look at how each exam handles a typical test question for each of these areas of measurement.

HSPT® LOGIC

HSPT® Logic questions take a slightly different form than other questions on the exam. In these questions, you're given a series of sentences. You are asked to determine if, based on the truth of the other sentences, the final sentence is (A) true, (B) false, or (C) uncertain. If it is not possible to determine if the final sentence is true or false, then the correct answer is choice (C).

chapter 9

Let's look at an example of an HSPT® Logic question:

> The black horse jumped over more hurdles than the spotted horse. The white horse jumped over more hurdles than the spotted horse. The white horse jumped over more hurdles than the black horse. If the first two statements are true, the third statement is
>
> **(A)** true.
>
> **(B)** false.
>
> **(C)** uncertain.
>
> From the first two statements, we know that both the black horse and the white horse jumped over more hurdles than the spotted horse. This is all that we know. The first two statements do not give us any information about the comparative achievements of the black horse and the white horse. The answer, therefore, is choice (C). The third statement can be neither affirmed nor denied on the basis of the first two statements. **The correct answer is (C).**

HSPT® VERBAL CLASSIFICATION

Here's another type of Verbal Logic question you'll find on the HSPT®. In Verbal Classification questions, you are presented with four words and asked to determine which of the words doesn't fit with the other three. Here's an example:

> Which word does *not* belong with the others?
>
> **(A)** crack
>
> **(B)** cleave
>
> **(C)** split
>
> **(D)** pare
>
> The first three words are synonyms. All refer to dividing something by opening it into two or more pieces. Choice (D), on the other hand, refers to opening by peeling off the outer layer (to pare is to peel). The key to answering this kind of question lies in figuring the relationship among three of the words. The relationships might be of synonyms, degrees, parts of speech, functions, or along any of a myriad of dimensions. **The correct answer is (D).**

COOP EXTRACTION OF INFORMATION

The COOP Extraction of Information questions present you with a series of related statements and four answer choices. You must choose the answer statement that is supported by the series of statements that precede the choices. That process probably sounds a lot more complicated than it really is, so let's look at an example:

Directions: Find the statement that is true according to the given information.

The little red house on our block is very old. It was once used as a church, and Abraham Lincoln might have worshipped there. It also served as a schoolhouse.

(A) At one time, schools were used for worship.

(B) Abraham Lincoln prayed in school.

(C) The house has an interesting history.

(D) Red is a popular color for schools.

Take one statement at a time. Choice (A) cannot be supported by the paragraph. The paragraph states that the house was once used as a church, not that it was used as a church and a school at the same time. Choice (B) also cannot be supported by the paragraph. If Abraham Lincoln worshipped in the house, he did so when it was a church. Although Abraham Lincoln might have prayed in school as a child, such information is extraneous to the paragraph. Choice (C) is clearly correct. The house does have a long and interesting history dating back to or before the Civil War and having been at various times a church, a school, and a house. Chances are that choice (C) is the correct answer, but check out choice (D) before choosing your answer. Choice (D) makes a statement of fact that is true in its own right, but it is not supported by the information in the passage. You must therefore select choice (C). **The correct answer is (C).**

COOP LOGIC

The COOP Logic questions ask that you choose a word that names a necessary part or component of an italicized or underlined word. Here's an example:

Which word names a *necessary* part of the underlined word?

    colander

(A) water

(B) holes

(C) food

(D) dirt

A *colander* is a perforated dish or bowl for draining off liquids, as in rinsing pasta, fruit, or vegetables. The *holes,* choice (B), are absolutely necessary; all other choices are related, but none is necessary to the existence of the colander. **The correct answer is (B).**

COOP ARTIFICIAL LANGUAGE

The COOP Artificial Language questions test your ability to transfer information that you have about one word to help define another, related word. The trick here is that all the words you deal with in these questions are nonsense-words, so you have to carefully read the definitions you're given and use those clues to help find the right answer choice. Here's an example:

Here are some words translated from an artificial language.

> *lobobatoba* means insult
> *lomonatoba* means inspect
> *lobobatabo* means result

Which word means *respect?*

(A) tabolomona

(B) tobatabo

(C) lomonatabo

(D) lobobalomona

Look first at the English words. Notice that each word consists of a prefix and a stem and that among the four words there are only two prefixes and two stems. Now look at the three artificial-language words. Notice that each appears to have two parts, one beginning with *l* and ending with *a* and the other beginning with *t*.

Now return to the first pair of words and separate each into its two halves.

> loboba toba = in sult
> lomona toba = in spect

You now have gathered useful information. In the artificial language, the stem comes first and is followed by the prefix. Furthermore, you now know that

> *toba* means *in*
> *loboba* means *sult*
> *lomona* means *spect*

Confirm this information by looking at the third pair of words:

> loboba tabo = re sult

You already knew that *loboba* means *sult*; now you also know that *tabo* means *re*. At this point, you can figure the answer. Look at the four choices. Immediately eliminate choices (A) and (B) because you know that the stem must be followed by the prefix, and in these two choices the order of the parts of the words is reversed. If you look quickly ahead, you will see that in choice (D) you are offered joined stems with no prefix. You can confidently pick choice (C) as the answer to this question. Confirm: *tabo* means *re*; *lomona* means *spect*. **The correct answer is (C).**

At first glance, the artificial-language type of a Verbal Logic question seems rather weird, even intimidating. Actually, with concentration and practice, the procedure can become mechanical and not at all difficult.

Try your hand at using the reasoning processes we have just taught you as you tackle the following exercises. Answer keys and explanations follow Exercise 3.

EXERCISES: VERBAL LOGIC

Exercise 1

Directions: Choose the best answer.

1. George is older than Bob. Fred is younger than George. Bob is older than Fred. If the first two statements are true, the third statement is
   (A) true.
   (B) false.
   (C) uncertain.

2. Group A sings higher than Group C. Group B sings lower than Group C. Group A sings higher than Group B. If the first two statements are true, the third statement is
   (A) true.
   (B) false.
   (C) uncertain.

3. Percolator coffee is weaker than electric-drip coffee. Extractor coffee is stronger than electric-drip coffee. Electric-drip coffee is stronger than extractor coffee. If the first two statements are true, the third statement is
   (A) true.
   (B) false.
   (C) uncertain.

4. Red kites fly higher than yellow kites. Yellow balloons fly higher than red kites. Yellow kites fly higher than yellow balloons. If the first two statements are true, the third statement is
   (A) true.
   (B) false.
   (C) uncertain.

5. The New York team lost fewer games than the Boston team. The Boston team won more games than the Baltimore team, but not as many games as the New York team. The Baltimore team lost the fewest games. If the first two statements are true, the third statement is
   (A) true.
   (B) false.
   (C) uncertain.

6. The history book has more pages than the poetry book, but fewer pages than the math book. The math book has more pages than the science book but fewer pages than the English book. The poetry book has the fewest pages. If the first two statements are true, the third statement is
   (A) true.
   (B) false.
   (C) uncertain.

7. Which word does *not* belong with the others?
   (A) ceiling
   (B) window
   (C) floor
   (D) wall

8. Which word does *not* belong with the others?
   (A) orange
   (B) apple
   (C) tomato
   (D) carrot

9. Which word does *not* belong with the others?

(A) emotion

(B) love

(C) anger

(D) disappointment

10. Which word does *not* belong with the others?

(A) destroy

(B) brick

(C) construct

(D) connect

11. Which word does *not* belong with the others?

(A) medicine

(B) healing

(C) therapy

(D) surgery

12. Which word does *not* belong with the others?

(A) orange

(B) brown

(C) red

(D) purple

Exercise 2

Directions: Choose the statement that is true according to the given information.

1. Mr. Stonehill worked in the corporate headquarters of a large corporation. Another company acquired Mr. Stonehill's company and sold off the operating divisions one by one. There can be no corporate headquarters without any operating divisions. Mr. Stonehill is

(A) unemployed.

(B) working for one of the operating divisions.

(C) no longer working in corporate headquarters.

(D) working for the new company.

2. Mr. Moffitt is a high school chemistry teacher. As a young man, Mr. Moffitt worked in the textile dyes division of a chemical company. Besides teaching chemistry, Mr. Moffitt operates a business cleaning Oriental carpets.

(A) Mr. Moffitt changes jobs often.

(B) Mr. Moffitt teaches students how to clean carpets.

(C) Mr. Moffitt is a wealthy man.

(D) Mr. Moffitt is well-qualified for the work he does.

3. Sally and Susie are twins. Sally lives near her parents in a Chicago suburb with her husband and children. Susie lives in a remote area of Alaska and raises dogs.

(A) Susie does not get along with her parents.

(B) Twins may have different interests and tastes.

(C) Sally does not like dogs.

(D) There are special bonds between twins.

4. Wilbur Greenville is employed at the Happy Meat bologna factory in his hometown of Willowridge. He has been working at the factory longer than anyone else. Wilbur Greenville is retiring from the factory today, after 38 years of dedicated employment.

(A) Wilbur Greenville is the oldest employee at the Happy Meat bologna factory.

(B) Wilbur Greenville enjoys eating bologna sandwiches for lunch.

(C) Wilbur Greenville won't be working at the factory next month.

(D) Wilbur Greenville was born in the town of Willowridge.

5. Eight children went trick-or-treating together on Halloween. Each child carried a lighted flashlight and a big bag. Jill and Mary did not wear masks.

   (A) The children went trick-or-treating at night.

   (B) Six children wore masks.

   (C) The bags were heavy.

   (D) The youngest children were Jill and Mary.

Directions: For questions 6–10, find the correct answer.

6. Here are some words translated from an artificial language.

   pritibondo means construct
   kwalaropipiwi means diverge
   kwalarobondo means converge

   Which word means *destruct*?

   (A) pritipepewe

   (B) kwalaropepewe

   (C) bondopriti

   (D) pipiwipriti

7. Here are some words translated from an artificial language.

   hohoysiri means larger
   hohosiriyi means smaller
   hohohoysiri means largest

   Which word means *smallest*?

   (A) ysirisiriyi

   (B) siriyihoho

   (C) ysirihoho

   (D) hohohosiriyi

8. Here are some words translated from an artificial language.

   skesshituhrabi means fast
   jhunbundhistli means slow
   hnuskesshituhrabi means fastest

   Which word means *slowest*?

   (A) jhunbundhistlihnu

   (B) skessbundhistli

   (C) hnujhunbundhistli

   (D) skesshitudhistli

9. Here are some words translated from an artificial language.

   eselklup means black dog
   eselrifoulof means white puppy
   finiklupulof means gray cat

   Which word means *gray kitten*?

   (A) finikluprifo

   (B) finirifoklupulof

   (C) finiulofklup

   (D) klupulofrifofini

10. Here are some words translated from an artificial language.

    nipilazokople means base hit
    frixzokople means home run
    nipilazokoptaha means first down

    Which word means *touchdown*?

    (A) nipilazokoptaha

    (B) zokopfrixtaha

    (C) frixlezokop

    (D) frixzokoptaha

Exercise 3

Directions: Choose the word that names a necessary part of the underlined word.

1. mother
   - (A) nurturing
   - (B) home
   - (C) responsibility
   - (D) child

2. essay
   - (A) words
   - (B) organization
   - (C) paper
   - (D) outline

3. fantasy
   - (A) entertainment
   - (B) dream
   - (C) imagination
   - (D) music

4. carpenter
   - (A) house
   - (B) wood
   - (C) saw
   - (D) repair

5. history
   - (A) past
   - (B) social studies
   - (C) documents
   - (D) culture

6. editorial
   - (A) newspaper
   - (B) rebuttal
   - (C) publisher
   - (D) opinion

7. skeleton
   - (A) anatomy
   - (B) death
   - (C) bones
   - (D) skull

8. tree
   - (A) water
   - (B) forest
   - (C) sap
   - (D) green

9. disappointment
   - (A) loss
   - (B) discouragement
   - (C) failure
   - (D) expectation

10. heirloom
   - (A) antique
   - (B) nostalgia
   - (C) ancestor
   - (D) jewelry

ANSWER KEYS AND EXPLANATIONS

Exercise 1

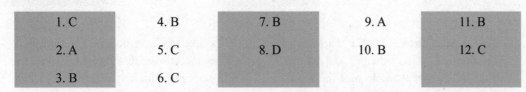

1. C	4. B	7. B	9. A	11. B
2. A	5. C	8. D	10. B	12. C
3. B	6. C			

1. **The correct answer is (C).** We know only that George is the oldest. There is no way to tell whether Bob is older than Fred, or Fred is older than Bob.

2. **The correct answer is (A).** Group A sings the highest of the three.

3. **The correct answer is (B).** Extractor coffee is the strongest, electric-drip comes next, and percolator coffee is the weakest.

4. **The correct answer is (B).** Balloons appear to fly higher than kites.

5. **The correct answer is (C).** We know for certain that the Baltimore team *won* the fewest games, but without information about how many games were played, we have no knowledge of how many games the Baltimore team *lost*.

6. **The correct answer is (C).** The English book has the most pages, followed by the math book. The history book has more pages than the poetry book. However, we do not have enough information to rank the science book; it might have more or fewer pages than the poetry book.

7. **The correct answer is (B).** The window is transparent or, at the very least, translucent and probably is movable as well. All of the other choices are solid, opaque, and fixed.

8. **The correct answer is (D).** The carrot is a root vegetable. All of the other choices are seed-bearing fruits.

9. **The correct answer is (A).** The other three choices (love, anger, and disappointment) are all actual emotions.

10. **The correct answer is (B).** This is a verbal classification question, so you must determine which of the words doesn't fit with the other three. *Brick* is a noun; the other three choices are verbs.

11. **The correct answer is (B).** Medicine, therapy, and surgery are all procedures leading to healing.

12. **The correct answer is (C).** Red is a primary color; all of the others (orange, brown, and purple) are red-based mixtures.

Exercise 2

1. C	3. B	5. A	7. D	9. B
2. D	4. C	6. A	8. C	10. D

1. **The correct answer is (C).** There is no information as to whether or not Mr. Stonehill is now working, nor for whom. However, if the operating divisions have been sold, there is no corporate headquarters. If there is no corporate headquarters, most certainly Mr. Stonehill does not work there.

2. **The correct answer is (D).** With the credentials required of all schoolteachers and with his specialized experience in a chemical company, Mr. Moffitt is clearly qualified to teach high school chemistry. The training that Mr. Moffitt received working in the textile dyes division applies beautifully to his sideline occupation, cleaning Oriental carpets. The other choices, while all possible, are in no way supported by the paragraph.

3. **The correct answer is (B).** The only statement definitely supported by the paragraph is that twins may have different interests and tastes.

4. **The correct answer is (C).** The only statement that's irrefutably true is that Wilbur Greenville won't be working at the factory next month, as we're told "Wilbur Greenville is retiring from the factory today." There is no evidence that definitively suggests that Wilbur Greenville is the oldest employee (just the longest serving), or that he likes eating bologna sandwiches, or that he was born in Willowridge, even though he lives there now.

5. **The correct answer is (A).** If all eight children carried *lighted* flashlights, we might be pretty sure that it was dark. The information that Jill and Mary did not wear masks implies that the other children did but does not prove it. Some of the others might

also have not worn masks or might have worn sheets over their heads. Sometimes the youngest children wear masks while older youngsters apply complicated makeup. Jill and Mary were not necessarily the youngest. The children carried big bags, but there is no information about the weight of each bag, so we don't know if they were heavy, choice (C).

6. **The correct answer is (A).** In this language, prefix and stem appear in reverse order. Among these words, the stems are *priti* meaning *struct* and *kwalaro* meaning *verge*. Within the three given words, *bondo* means *con*, and *pipiwi* means *di*. Because the word you must translate includes the stem *struct*, it must begin with *priti*. Only choice (A) begins with *priti*, so you need look no further. With no further information, you might conclude that because *pipiwi* means *di*, *pepewe* could reasonably stand for *de*.

7. **The correct answer is (D).** In this language, stem and suffix appear in reverse order. *Hoho* is the comparative suffix (*er*) and hohoho the superlative suffix (*est*). *Ysiri* means *large* and *siriyi* means *small*. The choice of answer is easy because only choice (D) begins with *hohoho*.

8. **The correct answer is (C).** In this language, the prefix *hnu-* indicates an extreme comparative degree; adding *hnu-* to *skesshituhrabi*, the word for fast, creates *hnuskesshituhrabi*, the word for fastest. If we want to create the word for slowest, we need to add the prefix *hnu-* to the word for slow, *jhunbundhistli*.

9. **The correct answer is (B).** Because *esel* is the only word segment appearing in both the first and second words, *esel* must mean

dog. The noun appears before its modifier. *Klup* means *black*. For the moment, we cannot tell within the second word which segment means *white* and which signifies that the dog is young. Moving on to the third word, we find *klup* in the middle. Because the noun comes first, we know that *fini* means *cat*. Black cat *ulof*? But we want gray cat. *Ulof* also appears in the second word that defines a white puppy. *Ulof* must mean *white*, and the juxtaposition of *blackwhite* (*klupulof*) means gray. The remaining segment of the second word, *rifo*, must indicate that the dog is young. Now put together the answer. It must begin with *cat*, *fini*. The second segment, *rifo*, makes it young, hence a kitten. Finally, *klupulof* (blackwhite) makes it *gray*.

10. **The correct answer is (D).** This question takes even more logical thinking than most others. Because the English words do not have common elements, you must first figure out the basis on which the artificial-language words are formed. The first two words are both related to baseball and both end in *le*, which does not appear in the word related to football. The first and third words begin with *nipila*, and both refer to an initial advance toward scoring in a sport, though not the same sport. Appearing in all three words is *zokop*. Evidently, *zokop* has something to do with either sports or balls. The meaning of *zokop* is unimportant, but because the word you must translate relates to football, *zokop* must appear in the word. If *nipila* refers to the initial advance toward a score and *frix* appears only in the word meaning home run, chances are that *frix* is a scoring word portion. Now, remembering that *taha* appeared only in the word relating to football and was not otherwise accounted for, you can construct the word for *touchdown*. The degree of scoring comes first. A touchdown is a scoring play, so our word must begin with *frix*. *Zokop* must come into the middle of all words having to do with scoring activities in football or baseball. A touchdown is a scoring play in football, so our word ends in *taha*.

Exercise 3

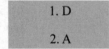 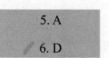

1. D	3. C	5. A	7. C	9. D
2. A	4. B	6. D	8. A	10. C

1. **The correct answer is (D).** One cannot be a mother without having or having had a child. All the other choices are usual and desirable adjuncts of motherhood, but they are not necessary to its existence.

2. **The correct answer is (A).** An essay is created of words. The most commonly seen essays are well organized and appear on paper, but a poor essay might be disorganized, and an essay might appear on electronic media rather than paper.

3. **The correct answer is (C).** Fantasy is based on imagination. Fantasy might be dreamlike, might entertain, and might be musical or embellished by music, but imagination is what is crucial to fantasy.

4. **The correct answer is (B).** A carpenter works with wood. What the carpenter does with wood or how the carpenter accomplishes a goal is immaterial to the existence of the carpenter.

5. **The correct answer is (A).** History is that which is past. You might study culture, choice (D), and read through documents, choice (C), as part of the history curriculum in your social studies, choice (B), class; however, the past is the essential part of history.

6. **The correct answer is (D).** An editorial is an expression of opinion. We tend to first think of editorials as being essays that are published in newspapers, but editorials—that is, statements of opinion—may also be broadcast on radio or television. Although an editorial might lead to a rebuttal, choice (B), or might be a rebuttal of a previously expressed opinion, choice (D), the rebuttal is not necessary to the editorial.

7. **The correct answer is (C).** The skeleton is the bony structure of the body. After death and decomposition, the skeleton might become visible, but death, choice (B), is not necessary to the existence of the skeleton. The skull, choice (D), is a part of the skeleton, necessary in a living person, but not necessary to the existence of any skeleton. The bones, choice (C), themselves, however, are the necessary component.

8. **The correct answer is (A).** Although the amount needed varies by type, all trees require some water to grow from seeds into trees. However, a tree can grow outside of the forest, choice (B); some trees don't produce sap, choice (C); and not all trees are green, choice (D).

9. **The correct answer is (D).** Disappointment is what occurs when expectations are not fulfilled. This is the necessary connection.

10. **The correct answer is (C).** An heirloom is an object handed down from an ancestor. Without an ancestor to hand down the object, the object might be an antique, but it is not an heirloom.

SUMMING IT UP

- The HSPT® exam tests several measures of verbal logic in its Verbal Skills section, one under the Logic test section and the other under the Verbal Classifications section.

- In the COOP, the verbal logic test is found in the Verbal Reasoning sections.

- On the HSPT® Logic questions, you only have three answer choices. NEVER mistakenly choose (D).

25 min for 62 ?s

1. Read questions first!
2. Skim B Scan
3. Read Newspaper!

Reading

OVERVIEW

- How to improve your reading skills
- Tips for answering reading comprehension questions
- Exercises: Reading
- Answer keys and explanations
- Summing it up

Both the COOP and the HSPT® include sections on reading comprehension. They are called Reading and Language Arts on the COOP and Reading on the HSPT® (under the Comprehension section). The TACHS tests reading comprehension in the Reading section. The format for reading questions on all three exams differs from the other question types you've learned about so far. The exams present reading passages followed by a series of questions based on the passages. The questions test not only how well you understand what you read but also how well you can interpret the meaning of the passage and the author's intent. These questions also test how well you draw conclusions based on what you have read.

To do well on the reading comprehension sections of an exam, reading quickly is crucial. You won't be able to answer questions based on a passage if you have not had time to read it. Even if you are able to read the passage through once, you must have enough time left over to reread the selection for detail questions.

HOW TO IMPROVE YOUR READING SKILLS

One of the best techniques for increasing your reading speed and comprehension is also one of the techniques that will help you improve your vocabulary—**reading.** The best way to increase your reading speed between now and the actual exam is to read as much as possible. Read everything in sight—newspapers, magazines, novels, billboards, and so on. Newspaper reading is an especially good way to improve your reading skills. Don't stop with just the opening paragraph of each article. Push yourself to read the whole story and give it your full attention as you read. If your mind wanders, you will not comprehend what you read.

chapter 10

To read with understanding, your eyes must occasionally stop on the page. Most people stop on each word because that is the way reading is taught in the early grades. But once you know how to read well, this method wastes a great deal of time. The key to increasing your reading speed is to take in more words each time your eyes stop. If a line had ten words in it and you were able to read the line by stopping only twice instead of ten times, you would be reading five times as fast as you do now. Try to train yourself.

If you have a habit of softly speaking words as you read, *break that habit now*! This habit is called *subvocalizing*, and no matter how fast you can talk, you can read faster if you stop subvocalizing. Some people chew gum to stop subvocalizing. For others, just being aware of the habit is enough to help them correct it. Not only will it slow you down, but if you're reading aloud during your exam, the administrator will ask you to stop, so you don't disturb other test-takers.

In building your reading speed, try moving your index finger or pencil underneath the line you are reading. Because your eyes tend to move as quickly as your pencil, you will not stop on every word. You will not regress (look back), and you probably will not subvocalize. However, what you might do is concentrate on your pencil and not on the reading passage. This is why you must practice this technique before using it on your test. Start your finger or your pencil at the second or third word in the line and stop it before the last word in the line. Your peripheral vision (what you see at the edges) will pick up the first and last words in the lines, and you will save time by not having to focus on them.

Become more aware of words. Earlier in this part, you were advised to use a dictionary while you read to help increase your vocabulary. That exercise can help you with reading comprehension questions as well. Vocabulary and reading comprehension are very closely interrelated. You cannot have a large vocabulary without reading. You cannot understand what you read without an understanding of the words. When you look up words, study the roots, prefixes, and suffixes so that you can apply all that you know whenever you meet unfamiliar words. In addition, don't forget to check out the Word List at the back of this book.

TIPS FOR ANSWERING READING COMPREHENSION QUESTIONS

- Begin by reading over the questions—not the answer choices, just the questions themselves. With an idea of what the questions will be asking, you will be able to focus your reading.

- Skim the passage to get a general idea of the subject matter and of the point that is being made. Pay special attention to the first and last sentences in each paragraph. Those sentences often state the main idea of the passage.

- Reread the passage, giving attention to details and the point of view. Be alert for the author's hints as to what he or she thinks is important. Phrases such as *Note that . . .*, *Of importance is . . .*, and *Do not overlook . . .* give clues to what the writer is stressing.

- If the author has quoted material from another source, be sure that you understand the purpose of the quote. Does the author agree or disagree?

- Carefully read each question or incomplete statement. Determine exactly what is being asked. Watch for negatives or all-inclusive words such as *always*, *never*, *all*, *only*, *every*, *absolutely*, *completely*, *none*, *entirely*, and *no*. These words can affect your choice of answer.

- Read all four answer choices. Do not rush to choose the first answer that might be correct. Eliminate those choices that are obviously incorrect. Reread the remaining choices and refer to the passage, if necessary, to determine the *best* answer.

- Don't confuse a *true* answer with the *correct* answer. You can do this best if you avoid inserting your own judgments into your answers. Even if you disagree with the author, or spot a factual error in the passage, you must answer on the basis of what is stated or implied in the passage.

- Don't spend too much time on any one question. If looking back at the passage does not help you to find or figure out the answer, choose from among the answers remaining after you eliminate the obviously wrong ones, and go on to the next question or passage.

Now try these exercises. Correct answer keys and explanations follow Exercise 2.

NOTE

Many people find it helps them to focus their reading if they read the questions before reading the passage.

EXERCISES: READING

Exercise 1

Directions: The following questions are based on a number of reading passages. Each passage is followed by a series of questions. Read each passage carefully, then answer the questions based on it. You may reread the passage as often as you wish. When you have finished answering the questions based on one passage, go right on to the next passage.

QUESTIONS 1–4 REFER TO THE FOLLOWING PASSAGE.

Henry Ford was a natural businessman, even as a youngster. Ford grew up in Michigan in the 1860s. When he was 11 years old, he was given a watch for his birthday. Young Ford was so enthralled by the watch that he managed to develop his own timepiece a year later. He set about attempting to sell the homemade watches at every opportunity for $1 each. That might not seem like much to us now, but remember that Ford only made about $1.10 per day when he took his first job at age 17.

According to the biography produced by the Edison and Ford Winter Estates, the most notable event that inspired the invention of the automobile happened when Ford was 13. Ford and his father were riding together in a wagon when they saw a steam engine moving down the road. The engine had been attached to wheels to propel itself. When Ford saw the engine, he became very excited and asked the engine's driver all about the machine. From this the idea of a self-propelled vehicle took root in Ford's mind.

Ford gained his first experience in the auto industry when he was 17, when he moved to Detroit and took his first job. Ford was fired after only a short time at that job. He angered the senior employees in the company because he was able to make repairs in about 30 minutes that took the other employees five hours!

1. Which of the following best describes Henry Ford?

   (A) Even as a youngster, Ford was better at mechanics than at business.

   (B) From the time of his first job, Ford was an efficient worker.

   (C) Ford was fired from his first job for not working very hard.

   (D) As a business owner, Ford had a way of making his workers dissatisfied.

2. Which of the following describes Ford's first experience as a business owner?

   (A) He gained his first experience working in the auto industry when he was 17.

   (B) As early as age 13, he was very interested in how steam engines operated.

   (C) He started his first business selling watches when he was just 11 years old.

   (D) He started an auto business that earned more than $1 million within four years.

3. Which statement best expresses the main idea of this selection?

   (A) Henry Ford's innovation helped develop the American auto industry.

   (B) Henry Ford started his career as a watchmaker.

   (C) Henry Ford had a strong aptitude for business and industry from childhood.

   (D) Ford started life as a low-wage laborer in an auto factory.

4. Which of the following best describes Ford's watch-making business?

   (A) Ford sold his watches very cheaply.

   (B) Ford was able to make several watches a day.

   (C) Ford was able to earn enough money from his watches to leave home.

   (D) Ford sold his watches for a relatively high price.

exercises

QUESTIONS 5–13 REFER TO THE FOLLOWING PASSAGE.

The music of Mozart has had a significant impact on the world, and it still does to this day. Although Mozart died very young, at the age of 35, he wrote more compositions during his short lifetime than any other composer in history. He was so skilled as a musician that we find it difficult to comprehend the stories we hear of his talents today. His skill allowed him to leave a musical legacy that not only delighted audiences but had a great impact on the future of music as well.

Perhaps the most notable aspect of Mozart's career is how young he was when he started. From the time that Mozart was three years old, it was clear that he was extraordinarily gifted. He was considered to be a child prodigy because of his stunning musical talents. He began to play the piano at age three, and he composed his first music at the age of four. Mozart had an excellent ear for music, even at this very young age.

Mozart's efforts changed music in many ways. One of the most important changes that Mozart helped to contribute was expanding the different types of music that existed during his time. Before Mozart began composing, there was only one major form of music, known as the *sonata*. A sonata is a musical piece written for one or two solo instruments, consisting of three or four separate parts, called movements. At that time, composers wrote sonatas either for the violin or for the keyboard. The movements within these sonatas were also small, without much development.

Through his writing, Mozart greatly increased the types of music that were written and performed. He helped add forms such as symphonies, concertos, quartets, and trios. Mozart also wrote sonatas, but he added depth to the sonatas and gave them more structure. In part, he was able to do this because he had been exposed to many different types of music during his travels as a young boy. He combined the musical styles that he learned during his stays in Germany, France, Italy, and other regions in Austria.

5. Which statement best reflects the main idea of the passage?

   (A) Mozart started his musical career when he was extremely young: he learned to play the piano when he was only three years old.

   (B) Mozart was an extremely talented musician and composer whose contributions have had a significant impact on music.

   (C) Mozart greatly increased the types of music that were written and performed, adding symphonies, concertos, quartets, and trios to the sonata form that already existed.

   (D) Mozart wrote a great number of musical works during his lifetime, but his music was not appreciated until after his death.

6. The word *prodigy* in this context means a

   (A) person with exceptional skills.

   (B) person who is slower than most.

   (C) person with a scientific mind.

   (D) person who shows great kindness.

7. How did Mozart's sonatas differ from previous sonatas written before Mozart's time?

   (A) Mozart's sonatas were more entertaining than the previous sonatas.

   (B) Mozart's sonatas had more depth and more structure than the previous sonatas.

   (C) Mozart's sonatas were composed more quickly than the previous sonatas.

   (D) Mozart's sonatas were more difficult to play than the previous sonatas.

8. According to the passage, which statement is true of Mozart's compositions?

   (A) No other composer in history has equaled his output.

   (B) He wrote more symphonies than any other composer in history.

   (C) His compositions all had at least three parts.

   (D) All of his compositions were sonatas.

9. According to the passage, what did Mozart accomplish before the age of five?

   (A) He learned to play the trumpet and piano.

   (B) He composed a sonata for the violin and piano.

   (C) He was introduced to the royal court in Vienna.

   (D) He learned to play the piano and wrote his first composition.

10. According to the passage, many of Mozart's musical compositions had three or four separate parts, known as

    (A) elements.

    (B) solos.

    (C) movements.

    (D) aspects.

11. According to the passage, a sonata is a musical composition for

    (A) an orchestra with a piano solo.

    (B) a stringed instrument and a woodwind.

    (C) trios and quartets.

    (D) one or two instruments.

12. According to the passage, as a boy, Mozart traveled through which countries outside of his homeland?

    (A) England, France, and Italy

    (B) France, Italy, and Germany

    (C) Germany, Austria, and Italy

    (D) Austria, France, and Italy

13. According to the passage, Mozart's travels as a young boy

    (A) brought him fame and wealthy patrons.

    (B) exposed him to disease, causing his death at the age of 35.

    (C) exposed him to many different types of music.

    (D) helped him learn several languages.

QUESTIONS 14-20 REFER TO THE FOLLOWING PASSAGE.

When I was growing up during the Depression, I lived on a farm in New Jersey with my grandmother and grandfather. Aunt Frieda was my youngest aunt; she lived in New York City with her husband, my Uncle Stuart, and she frequently wrote letters to my grandmother and grandfather. My grandparents didn't speak any English, so I always translated the correspondence for them from English into Italian.

One day, when I was about fifteen, I saw that the letters from my Aunt Frieda were coming written in Uncle Stuart's handwriting. I realized that Aunt Frieda wasn't really writing them, but I didn't say anything to my grandmother or grandfather because I didn't want to worry them. My grandmother was a real worrier, and I didn't want her to get upset, so I continued to read the letters to her as if they were coming from Aunt Frieda.

That went on for several weeks, until we had a visit from my Aunt Grace, who was Aunt Frieda's older sister. Aunt Grace told me that she had just visited Aunt Frieda. I asked my Aunt Grace what was wrong with Aunt Frieda, and Aunt Grace replied, "Your Aunt Frieda has had an eye operation. She's recuperating just fine, and she's planning a visit to see *Nana* very soon."

Shortly after that, I received a letter from Uncle Stuart informing me that he and Aunt Frieda were coming to visit. On the day they arrived, the moment I saw their car, I said to my grandmother, "*Nana*, I have something to tell you about Aunt Frieda. Now I don't want to worry you—Aunt Frieda is fine, but she's had an operation on her eye. She went to the hospital in Philadelphia to have the surgery done."

My grandmother was beginning to get visibly upset, and I did my best to calm her down. We were all standing on the front porch when Aunt Frieda and Uncle Stuart drove up. When Aunt Frieda exited the car, she was walking <u>gingerly</u>, like someone who couldn't see very well. I kept trying to keep my grandmother calm.

Nana behaved outwardly, but she cried silently to herself. When my Aunt Frieda got out of the car, all that my *Nana* said was, "Your own mother—you keep a secret from your own mother—your mother was supposed to be there by your side!" She kept repeating it over and over, but that was all she said.

I imagine that part of the reason why *Nana* would become so upset when she felt powerless was because she was accustomed to having everything go her way. Unlike my grandmother, my grandfather was a very quiet man who lived a routine, predictable life: he did his work, ate dinner, and went to bed. My grandmother, on the other hand, was absolutely in charge, and it was clear that she controlled the money, the decisions—she controlled everything. She was smart as a whip, too.

14. The word *gingerly* in this context means

(A) confidently.

(B) cautiously.

(C) recklessly.

(D) naturally.

15. How is the author's grandfather different from his grandmother?

(A) His grandfather doesn't have many dreams, while his grandmother dreams often.

(B) His grandfather becomes sick easily, while his grandmother is very healthy.

(C) His grandfather tends to be controlling, while his grandmother is usually relaxed.

(D) His grandfather tends to be very quiet, while his grandmother gets easily agitated.

16. How did the author know that Aunt Frieda had stopped writing letters to his grandmother?

(A) His Aunt Grace told him that Aunt Frieda had stopped writing.

(B) Aunt Frieda's letters were written in Italian and not in English.

(C) His grandmother stopped receiving any letters from Aunt Frieda.

(D) The letters began coming in Uncle Stuart's handwriting.

17. From the passage, we can infer that the author considered *Nana* to be

(A) cut off from her children because she couldn't speak English.

(B) withdrawn and fearful of the outside world.

(C) the authority figure in the household.

(D) submissive to her husband's decisions.

18. When *Nana* sees Aunt Frieda, her main feeling is

(A) confusion, because she did not know about the eye operation.

(B) relief, because the operation was a success.

(C) anger, because she had been tricked into thinking Frieda wrote the letters.

(D) powerlessness, because Frieda did not tell her about the operation.

19. In the passage, the author regards *Nana* as someone who is

(A) fragile but easily soothed.

(B) intelligent but easily worried.

(C) intelligent but lacking in formal education.

(D) educated but easily deceived.

20. When the author asks Aunt Grace why Aunt Frieda is not writing the letters, the tone of Aunt Grace's answer is intended to be

(A) reassuring.

(B) consoling.

(C) alarming.

(D) distressing.

QUESTIONS 21–25 REFER TO THE FOLLOWING PASSAGE.

On entering the amphitheater, new objects of wonder presented themselves. On a level spot in the center was a company of odd-looking personages playing at nine-pins. They were dressed in a quaint, outlandish fashion, some wore short doublets, others jerkins, with long knives in their belts, and most of them had enormous breeches, of a type similar to that of the guide's. Their visages, too, were peculiar, one had a large beard, broad face, and small piggish eyes. The face of another seemed to consist entirely of nose and was surmounted by a white sugar-loaf hat set off with a little red cock's tail. They all had beards of various shapes and colors. There was one who seemed to be the commander. He was a stout old gentleman, with a weather-beaten countenance; he wore a lace doublet, broad belt and hangar, high crowned hat and feather, red stockings, and high-heeled shoes with roses in them. The whole group reminded Rip of the figures in an old <u>Flemish</u> painting, in the parlor of the village parson, which had been brought over from Holland at the time of the settlement.

What seemed particularly odd to Rip was that though these folks were evidently amusing themselves, yet they maintained the gravest faces, the most mysterious silence, and were the most melancholy party of pleasure he had ever witnessed. Nothing interrupted the stillness of the scene but the noise of the balls, which, whenever they were rolled, echoed along the mountains like rumbling peals of thunder.

—from *Rip Van Winkle*
by Washington Irving

21. Looking at this scene, the observer is apparently
    (A) fascinated.
    (B) frightened.
    (C) repulsed.
    (D) bored.

22. The word *Flemish* possibly refers to
    (A) something from the area near Holland.
    (B) the village parson.
    (C) a certain painter.
    (D) an old-fashioned parlor.

23. The characters were probably playing
    (A) a game like bowling.
    (B) soccer.
    (C) a type of baseball.
    (D) golf.

24. The person observing all of this is
    (A) Flemish.
    (B) a parson.
    (C) melancholic.
    (D) Rip.

25. The observer was surprised that the
    (A) men's beards were of so many shapes and colors.
    (B) men appeared to be so serious while they were playing a game.
    (C) leader was so stout.
    (D) rolling balls sounded like thunder.

QUESTIONS 26–31 REFER TO THE FOLLOWING PASSAGE.

Author Ben Wiens defines energy simply as "the ability to create a force over a distance some time in the future." The term energy, Wiens notes, was developed only about 200 years ago, by a scientist named Thomas Young. In Young's time, energy was thought to be the ability to do physical work, like the work that an axe can do when it comes down on a log with force and severs the log in two. In Young's time, according to Wiens, work was defined as "a force acting over a distance." When a person uses his energy to run, for instance, he is showing an example of a force acting over a distance.

As scientists began to research energy more carefully, they realized that energy was more than just the ability to do physical work. They started to see energy as the *potential* to do work as well. One scientist named James Prescott Joule believed that the ability to do work was stored within the molecules of matter. Joule stated in 1830 that molecules contained very small forms of energy. These forms of energy could not be seen by the naked eye, according to Joule, but they did exist.

In 1905, Albert Einstein made an important contribution to our study of energy. During Einstein's time, scientists knew that matter was made up of smaller parts, such as molecules and atoms. Einstein believed, however, that molecules and atoms were not the smallest parts of matter. He stated that molecules and atoms were made up of energy. He saw them as large groups of energy particles. Some of these energy particles were even able to transfer energy between different types of matter.

Thanks to Einstein's work, energy became much better understood by modern scientists. Since the time of Thomas Young, work had been recognized as force acting over a distance. Einstein showed that energy is the *ability to create* force over any distance. In other words, according to Wiens, energy is "the ability to do work some time in the future." It is the stored potential to be able to complete work.

26. Which statement best reflects the main idea of the passage?

(A) Scientists once believed that molecules and energy were the smallest parts of matter, but now they believe that molecules and atoms themselves are made up of even smaller energy particles.

(B) Scientists once defined energy as the ability to do physical work, but they now define it as the stored potential to complete work at some time in the future.

(C) Because of the work of Albert Einstein, modern scientists now have a better understanding of energy than did earlier scientists.

(D) Our understanding of energy developed from the work of three scientists: Thomas Young, James Prescott Joule, and Albert Einstein.

27. The word *severs* in the first paragraph means
    (A) prepares.
    (B) unites.
    (C) splits.
    (D) covers.

28. Which statement reflects the view of both James Prescott Joule and Albert Einstein?
    (A) Molecules are the smallest parts of matter.
    (B) Energy cannot be seen with the naked eye, so it does not exist.
    (C) Energy is the ability to do physical work in the present moment.
    (D) Molecules of matter are made up of energy.

29. According to the passage, Albert Einstein
    (A) showed that energy is the ability to create force over any distance.
    (B) showed that energy was made up of small particles called atoms.
    (C) developed a way to view energy with the naked eye.
    (D) developed the term "energy" about 200 years ago.

30. How did Albert Einstein's view of energy differ from that of Thomas Young?
    (A) Einstein's view was more comprehensive than Young's, because Einstein saw energy as the potential to be able to do work.
    (B) Einstein's view was more concrete than Young's, because Einstein saw energy as the ability to do physical work.
    (C) Einstein's view was the opposite of Young's, because Einstein saw energy as the ability to do physical work.
    (D) Einstein's view was more developed than Young's, because Einstein believed that molecules and atoms were the smallest parts of matter.

31. According to the passage, James Prescott Joule believed that the ability to do work
    (A) could transfer between molecules.
    (B) was constantly changing.
    (C) was unable to be stored.
    (D) was stored within matter.

QUESTIONS 32–36 REFER TO THE FOLLOWING PASSAGE.

In 1911, an American named Hiram Bingham made a magnificent discovery in the Andes Mountains of Peru. Hidden deep in the Andean jungle and surrounded by mountain peaks lay the lost city of Machu Picchu, a sacred religious site built by the Inca Indians. Machu Picchu is located 43 miles northwest of a Peruvian city called Cusco. Cusco was conquered by the Spanish in 1532, but no mention was made of the remarkable city. Until Bingham's discovery in 1911, no one in the West knew that Machu Picchu even existed. Now, almost a century later, Machu Picchu is the best-known archeological site in all of South America.

Archeologists believe that when Machu Picchu was built around 1460, it was not built as a city. Instead, they believe, it was built as the royal estate of an Incan ruler named Pachacuti Inca Yupanqui. Machu Picchu served as this ruler's home and also as a religious retreat. It is located so high in the mountains, at an altitude of 8,000 feet, that it probably did not have any military or business uses.

Judging from the massive size of the "city," it must have housed many people during its day. Machu Picchu is made up of about 200 buildings. Most of these buildings were used as homes, but some were used as temples or for storage. Today, archeologists believe that about 1,200 people lived in the area of Machu Picchu and that most of these people were women, children, and priests.

32. How did Westerners learn of the existence of Machu Picchu?

   (A) The site was discovered in 1911 by an American named Hiram Bingham.

   (B) The site was discovered in 1420 by an Inca ruler named Pachacuti Inca Yupanqui.

   (C) The site was discovered in 1532 by the Spanish, who conquered the Incas.

   (D) The site was discovered in 1532 by an explorer named Cusco.

33. In this passage, Machu Picchu can best be described as

   (A) a mythical city.

   (B) the center of the Aztec Empire.

   (C) the lost city of the Incan Empire.

   (D) an example of Spanish colonization.

34. According to the passage, Machu Picchu is the

   (A) largest archaeological site in South America.

   (B) oldest archaeological site in South America.

   (C) highest archaeological site in South America.

   (D) most famous archaeological site in South America.

35. Archaeologists believe that the purpose of Machu Picchu was to serve as a

 (A) home and religious retreat for the Incan ruler and his court.

 (B) monastery exclusively for the use of Incan priests.

 (C) fortress for Incan warriors.

 (D) marketplace for traders from other parts of the Incan Empire.

36. Located near Machu Picchu, the city of Cusco was

 (A) also lost, abandoned, and rediscovered like Machu Picchu.

 (B) conquered by the Spanish.

 (C) built around 1460.

 (D) the burial site of Pachacuti Inca Yupanqui.

QUESTIONS 37–41 REFER TO THE FOLLOWING PASSAGE.

Glutamate, or glutamic acid, is one of the amino acids present in our bodies. It serves as a neurotransmitter within the human body. As a neurotransmitter, glutamate works by sending signals to certain neurons, or nerve cells, located in the brain, spinal cord, and nervous system. Some researchers, such as Russell Blaylock and James South, have argued that glutamate is not safe to eat when added to food. When present in the blood in high levels, these researchers believe glutamate can destroy some types of brain cells.

How does this process of cell destruction occur? Neurotransmitters as a group fall into two types: those that *cause* nerve cells to act, and those that *stop* nerve cells from acting. Glutamate is one of the neurotransmitters that cause nerve cells to act. Although glutamate is commonly used, it is normally present in the brain in very small amounts. When levels of glutamate become high, this prompts nerve cells in the brain to become too active, which leads to destruction of the cells.

Since glutamate is found naturally in the body, the brain has ways of keeping glutamate levels in the brain from rising too high. One of these ways is a system called the *blood-brain barrier*. The blood-brain barrier was designed, writes Blaylock, to protect the brain against moderate increases of glutamate. It stops working as well when faced with large amounts of glutamate, such as those that enter the bloodstream when a person eats foods containing flavor enhancers.

Glutamate that is found naturally in foods does not pose as much of a risk of creating high levels of glutamate in the brain. This is because glutamate found naturally in foods occurs in its "bound" form, which means that it is bonded with other amino acids.

37. The title that best expresses the main idea of this selection is
    (A) "The Effect of Glutamate on the Brain."
    (B) "Glutamate as a Building Block of Cells."
    (C) "Glutamate: The Most Common Neurotransmitter."
    (D) "FDA Research on Glutamate."

38. How does excess glutamate in the brain destroy brain cells?
    (A) It slows down the activity of nerve cells in the brain.
    (B) It causes deterioration in the blood-brain barrier that protects the brain.
    (C) It causes nerve cells in the brain to become over-active.
    (D) It stops the hypothalamus from functioning.

39. Which type of glutamate does not pose much of a risk of creating high levels of glutamate in the brain?
    (A) Glutamate in its free form
    (B) Monosodium glutamate
    (C) Hydrolyzed vegetable protein
    (D) Glutamate that is bonded with other amino acids

40. As a neurotransmitter, glutamate
    (A) stops nerve cells from acting.
    (B) causes nerve cells to act.
    (C) creates a barrier protecting the brain.
    (D) slows down the brain's processing.

41. Glutamate in the brain
    (A) helps strengthen the blood-brain barrier.
    (B) blocks signals to nerve cells.
    (C) is more potent in its bound form.
    (D) is normally found in very small amounts.

exercises

QUESTIONS 42–45 REFER TO THE FOLLOWING PASSAGE.

Janessa could not have had a tougher time falling asleep last night, and woke up feeling exhausted. She has never been able to control the excitement she felt for an upcoming event, and she tossed and turned in bed until the sun rose that morning. Today was the day of her class trip to the Hopkins Planetarium. She did her best to shake off her tiredness and get ready for what she hoped would be a fun-filled day with her friends.

After getting dressed, Janessa raced down the stairs and nearly tripped over Marmalade, the families' orange tabby cat, which could almost always be found sleeping at the foot of the staircase.

"Slow down Janessa, or you might trip and fall!" Janessa's mom said. "Sit down, catch your breath, and have some breakfast."

"Sorry mom, I'm just excited." Janessa replied. "I've been looking forward to our trip to the planetarium for weeks!" Janessa took her usual seat at the kitchen table and rocked back and forth with excitement as her mom prepared a plate with scrambled eggs, toast, and bacon, which she placed in front of Janessa.

"I know you're excited," said Janessa's mom. "What part are you looking forward to the most?"

"I'm SO glad you asked me that!" Janessa beamed. "I hear they have the best presentation on black hole's anywhere, and when they zoom in on the Milky Way solar system you can see HUNDREDS of stars and…" Janessa swung her hand wildly and knocked her plate onto the ground. It crashed, sending the uneaten food all over the floor.

Janessa's father came racing into the room. "What happened?" he asked.

"I think I got too excited…" Janessa replied. With that, her parents looked at each other and laughed.

"I tried to tell you, when people get too excited, they sometimes get careless" Janessa's mom said. Janessa's parents started cleaning up the mess.

"I know, I know… I just can't help it!" replied Janessa. "Dad, can you drive me to school? I can't wait to get there!"

Janessa's dad laughed and shook his head. "Some lessons are harder to learn than others," he said. "Ok, lets get in the car."

Janessa and her father got in the car and headed toward the school. The whole ride over, Janessa talked about the things she's been learning about in science class: the layers of the Earth, the planets, and photosynthesis. While her father paid careful attention to the road, Janessa spoke enthusiastically about her plans for her science project this year—a real working volcano—and got so excited that she gave herself the hiccups.

"Janessa, your mother and I tried to tell you—you have to try not to get too excited!"

"I know, I know…" Janessa said.

When Janessa arrived at school, she joined her classmates in the auditorium. Her teacher, Mrs. Ashton, had the students line up for the bus, but Janessa could hardly stand still. There was just one last thing before everyone could get on the bus and go to the planetarium. The teacher needed to collect the parent permission slips. Janessa fished around in her pockets, and came up empty. At that moment, she learned the lesson that her parents were trying to teach her that morning.

42. According to the story, why was Janessa so tired that morning?
   (A) She had a big test she was nervous about.
   (B) She felt sick and couldn't fall asleep.
   (C) She was too excited to go to bed.
   (D) Her cat kept waking her up during the night.

43. When Janessa's father says "Some lessons are harder to learn than others," he means
   (A) science is one of the most difficult subjects in school.
   (B) you must study hard to do well on class exams.
   (C) some students are smarter than others.
   (D) sometimes it takes a person a long while to learn something.

44. Janessa was learning all of the following things in science class EXCEPT
   (A) photosynthesis.
   (B) magnetism.
   (C) the layers of the Earth.
   (D) the planets.

45. What lesson did Janessa finally learn at the end of the story?
   (A) When someone gets too excited, they sometimes get careless and make mistakes.
   (B) When someone stays up too late and wakes up tired, they are always more forgetful.
   (C) When you don't eat a good breakfast in the morning, you're more likely to have accidents.
   (D) It's difficult to forgive someone when they make mistakes, so try not to make mistakes very often.

QUESTIONS 46–50 REFER TO THE FOLLOWING PASSAGE.

There used to be a saying in business that "if you make a better mousetrap, the world will beat a path to your door." This advice suggested to manufacturers that they simply had to make a better quality product, and the product would definitely sell. Unfortunately, this piece of advice erroneously ignored the role that prices play in affecting what consumers buy. It turns out that that role is very important.

In 1956, a better mousetrap *was* built by a company called the Pioneer Tool and Die Company. The mousetrap did not require the use of any bait (such as cheese), and it did not have any odor. It was a much higher quality product than the wooden mousetraps that households had been using. However, this mousetrap did not sell very well, and the company eventually stopped producing it. The key reason why consumers failed to buy the mousetrap was its price. The product sold for $29.95, compared to $0.07 for a plain wooden mousetrap.

The Pioneer Tool and Die Company set a high price for their better mousetraps because the mousetraps had more advanced features than regular mousetraps. The company learned from this experience, however, that people really did not care about the "better" qualities that were built into Pioneer mousetraps. At least, consumers did not value these qualities enough to pay a higher price for them. It turns out that consumers were really only willing to pay about 7 cents for an ordinary wooden mousetrap. These ordinary mousetraps sold the best.

When consumers refused to buy Pioneer mousetraps, Pioneer took their mousetraps off the market. It received a strong message from consumers that consumers did not want expensive mousetraps with lots of bells and whistles. Instead, consumers preferred a simple mousetrap at a very inexpensive cost.

46. The word *erroneously* in this context means
(A) bizarrely.
(B) mistakenly.
(C) wisely.
(D) quickly.

47. What happened to the expensive mousetraps produced by Pioneer Tool and Die Company?
(A) They were taken off the market.
(B) The company continues to produce them today.
(C) The company made them less expensive.
(D) The company made them easier to use.

48. Which is the most appropriate title for this passage?
(A) "A Cheaper Mousetrap"
(B) "A Successful Mousetrap"
(C) "An Electric Mousetrap"
(D) "A Better Mousetrap"

49. According to this passage, mousetraps preferred by consumers cost
(A) about $30.00.
(B) less than 10 cents each.
(C) 70 cents each.
(D) nothing, because they could be made at home.

50. The phrase "bells and whistles" in the last paragraph refers to the
(A) sound the Pioneer Tool and Die mousetrap made when it snapped shut.
(B) sleek and modern appearance of the Pioneer Tool and Die mousetrap.
(C) fancy features on the Pioneer Tool and Die mousetrap.
(D) fact that the Pioneer Tool and Die mousetrap did not use cheese for bait.

Exercise 2

Directions: Read each selection, then answer the questions that follow it. Indicate your answer by circling its letter.

QUESTIONS 1–5 REFER TO THE FOLLOWING PASSAGE.

Nowadays, the compound fluoride is found in almost all American homes. It is the main ingredient in most toothpastes and has been used by dentists to help prevent tooth decay. The fluoride that is now used in dental care was developed as a result of the discovery of an element known as fluorine.

The discovery of fluorine began with the early work of Georg Bauer. Bauer was a German physician who studied the diseases of mine workers in the 1500s. In his work, Bauer described how a mineral known as "fluorspar" was used by miners in creating metal from ore. Fluorspar is a mineral found in nature in several different varieties. The purple version of fluorspar looks like amethyst, and the green version looks like emeralds.

In the 1600s and 1700s, scientists working with fluorspar saw that when the mineral was heated, it gave off a gas, which could create etchings in glass. However, it was not until 1771 that fluoric acid was discovered by a Swedish chemist named Carl Wilhelm Scheele. Once fluoric acid was discovered, the next step was to isolate the element fluorine. Many scientists unsuccessfully tried to isolate fluorine in dangerous experiments that cost some researchers their lives. The scientist who gets credit for isolating fluorine was a French chemist named Henri Moissan, who produced the element in 1886. Moisson's work was so significant that he won the Nobel Prize in chemistry in 1906.

Fluorine is a highly destructive, pale yellow gas. It participates in reactions with almost all substances, including gold and platinum. It explodes when it is mixed with hydrogen, and it causes glass, metals, ceramics, carbon, and water to burn with a bright flame. Even the salts of fluorine, known as fluorides, are very dangerous and should never be touched, inhaled, or swallowed.

exercises

1. What does the author mean when he states in paragraph three that certain experiments designed to isolate fluorine "cost some researchers their lives?"

   (A) Some researchers spent their entire lives trying to isolate fluorine.

   (B) Some researchers spent a great deal of money trying to isolate fluorine.

   (C) Some researchers were killed in these experiments for isolating fluorine.

   (D) Some researchers took on large amounts of debt to fund the experiments.

2. Which mineral was most important to the discovery of fluorine?

   (A) Diamond

   (B) Floures

   (C) Emerald

   (D) Fluorspar

3. Which of the following conclusions can be drawn about flourides?

   (A) It is safer for researchers to touch flourides than to breathe in their fumes.

   (B) Researchers should remember that flourides are more harmful than fluorine gas.

   (C) Researchers should ensure that flouride fumes are released into the laboratory.

   (D) Researchers should never come into contact with fluoride compounds.

4. The title that best expresses the main idea of this passage is

   (A) "The Development of Toothpaste."

   (B) "The Discovery of Fluorine."

   (C) "The Dangers of Scientific Experiments."

   (D) "The Isolation of Chemical Elements."

5. In the passage, fluorine is described as an element

   (A) that is dangerous and should be banned before it takes more lives.

   (B) for which no practical use has ever been discovered.

   (C) that is dangerous but also has practical uses.

   (D) that is extremely rare and valuable to most nations.

QUESTIONS 6–11 REFER TO THE FOLLOWING PASSAGE.

The Berlin Wall was built in Berlin, Germany in 1961. It was built during the height of the Cold War, which was a period of tension between communist and democratic countries. At that time, the city of Berlin was divided into two parts. One part, the eastern part, had a communist government, and the other part (the western part) had a democratic government. Between 1949 and 1961, over 2 million people escaped from East Berlin to the western parts of Germany to be free from communism. The Berlin Wall was built to prevent East Germans from escaping.

The wall was an imposing landmark. It was built of concrete right in the middle of the city and topped with barbed wire. It was guarded by police with guns, and it separated East Berlin from West Berlin for twenty-eight years. During this time, it symbolized the strong division between communism and democracy.

Then, in 1989, all that changed. The wall was torn down due to riots by the people of East Berlin. The breach in the wall started during a visit by Mikhail Gorbachev, who was then head of the Soviet Union. Gorbachev was visiting East Germany to celebrate the country's 40th anniversary of communist government. When Gorbachev arrived, he was met with protesters. The East German people were unhappy with communism, and they chose this event to protest. On November 9, 1989, the protesters broke through the Berlin Wall. They demanded to be let into West Germany. The East German government crashed. The wall was quickly torn down, and millions of East Germans poured into West Germany.

For many years, the Berlin Wall had served not just as a symbol of the division between communism and democracy but also as a symbol of the Soviet Union's power. The Soviet Union had been the leader of the communist countries in Eastern Europe. When the Berlin Wall was destroyed, Soviet power soon declined also.

6. According to the author, what caused the fall of the Berlin Wall?

- **(A)** Riots by the people of East Berlin
- **(B)** Protests by the Soviet people
- **(C)** The Cold War between the Soviet Union and the United States
- **(D)** Striking workers in Poland

7. Which statement is true, according to the passage?

- **(A)** The building of the Berlin Wall led to the Cold War.
- **(B)** The Berlin Wall was necessary to protect West Germany from communism.
- **(C)** The destruction of the Berlin Wall led to the decline of the Soviet Union.
- **(D)** Soviet leader Mikhail Gorbachev caused the destruction of the Berlin Wall.

8. The Berlin Wall was built to
   (A) prevent West Germans from entering East Germany.
   (B) control trade between East and West Germany.
   (C) prevent East Germans from escaping to West Germany.
   (D) divide the city into four sections.

9. Soviet leader Mikhail Gorbachev visited East Berlin in November 1989 to
   (A) put down the protests against communism.
   (B) celebrate the 40th anniversary of the Russian Revolution.
   (C) conduct negotiations with West Germany.
   (D) celebrate 40 years of communist rule in East Germany.

10. The wall was built of
    (A) stone topped with steel spikes.
    (B) concrete topped by barbed wire.
    (C) brick topped with iron spikes.
    (D) steel topped by barbed wire.

11. The wall was built in 1961 during a period of tension between democratic and communist nations commonly known as
    (A) the nuclear arms race.
    (B) détente.
    (C) the Red Scare.
    (D) the Cold War.

QUESTIONS 12–18 REFER TO THE FOLLOWING PASSAGE.

Science is so much a part of our world today that we take it for granted as having always existed. As hard as it may be for us to believe, science in fact did not always exist. It was "invented" in the 1600s, and it went through many different developments before becoming the process that we utilize today.

The birth of modern science is usually traced back to the work of an English philosopher named Sir Francis Bacon. Before Bacon's time, scientific theories as we know them did not exist. Instead, the ideas that were considered to be knowledge were based upon faith, and most came from the philosophies of the church. Bacon was very opposed to this approach to knowledge. He disliked the notion that knowledge could be based simply on beliefs or on the ideas of the church. He searched for a way of developing knowledge that he felt was more reliable.

Bacon was very interested in the facts that could be gained from simply observing what goes on around us in the physical world. He believed that observing the physical world would produce much more reliable knowledge than simply making up knowledge based on beliefs. In 1620, Bacon published a book containing his ideas on the importance of developing knowledge through observation of nature. This book, called *The New Organon*, created a foundation for what is now known as "empirical" science, or science that comes from observing that which can be perceived through our senses.

Bacon's approach came to be known by the name *inductivism*. Inductivism is the idea that theories about science can be developed from observing events. In the inductivist approach, the scientist views a series of repeating events and draws a general conclusion from these events. The scientist takes this conclusion to be true *because* it is based on experience. A scientist using the inductivist approach might conclude, for instance, that "all swans are white," based solely on the fact that all swans that he has previously observed are white.

12. The best title for this selection would be
    (A) "Understanding the Scientific Method."
    (B) "Bacon and the Development of Science."
    (C) "Testing Hypotheses and Theories."
    (D) "The History of Sir Francis Bacon."

13. Why did Sir Francis Bacon search for a way to develop knowledge based on observing the physical world?
    (A) He believed that knowledge based on observing similar, repeated events was unreliable.
    (B) He believed that knowledge based on the principle of inductivism was unreliable.
    (C) He believed that knowledge based on faith, or the ideas of the church, was unreliable.
    (D) He believed that knowledge based on the principle of falsification was unreliable.

14. Bacon's approach to science was known as
    (A) inductivism.
    (B) positivism.
    (C) radicalism.
    (D) relativism.

15. Before Bacon, scientific knowledge was based on
    (A) concepts from astronomy.
    (B) rigorous testing.
    (C) legal precepts.
    (D) the ideas of the church.

16. Bacon's book, *The New Organon*, focused on
    (A) refining knowledge that is based on personal beliefs.
    (B) developing knowledge that can be perceived through the senses.
    (C) revising the ideas of political leaders of Bacon's time.
    (D) practicing strict scientific discipline in all research.

17. Which of the following would Bacon be most likely to accept as scientific knowledge?
    (A) Ideas based on church doctrine
    (B) Untested philosophical concepts
    (C) Theories based on empirical facts
    (D) A hypothesis based on opinion

18. Inductivist theories are developed from
    (A) observing events.
    (B) scientific mistakes.
    (C) ongoing debates.
    (D) experimental competitions.

exercises

QUESTIONS 19–23 REFER TO THE FOLLOWING PASSAGE.

The animal kingdom is filled with interesting and wondrous creatures—both big and small—and among them is the awe-inspiring hippopotamus. The hippo, or *Hippopotamus amphibious*, is an herbivorous mammal that typically resides in sub-Saharan regions of Africa. The name "hippopotamus" has ancient Greek origins, meaning "river horse," despite bearing little resemblance to the other animals of the same name. Hippos have existed on Earth for several million years, with the earliest known fossilized examples dating back approximately 16 million years.

If you've ever seen a hippo, there's little chance that you'd forget it. They are among the largest and heaviest land mammals that currently exist on Earth, behind only elephants and rhinoceroses. The average weight of this undeniably prodigious animal, which stands at approximately 5 feet tall, is approximately 3,500 lbs. What do these large animals eat? Surprisingly, their diet largely consists of creeping grass, reeds, green shoots, and other vegetation.

Hippos have a smooth, cylindrical shape that's nearly hairless; high-set eyes, ears, and nostrils; large tusk-filled jaws; and distinctively squat, dainty legs (with webbed feet) for such a rotund animal. Their unique physical characteristics suit their semiaquatic lifestyle quite well—hippos spend a great deal of time staying cool in nearby rivers and lakes.

Some individuals mistakenly assume that these jolly-looking animals come with a sweet, harmless personality. They couldn't be more wrong! Despite appearances, hippos have garnered quite a reputation for unpredictable displays of vicious, aggressive behavior. They are capable of surprising bursts of speed (up to 19 mph), and are more than willing to use the immense power of their huge jaws to crush any foe who threatens their territory or safety. Few animals—living or extinct—can match the sheer bite force of the hippopotamus.

The relationship between humans and hippos could best be characterized as tenuous at best. Despite their penchant for fierceness, hippos are still threatened by poachers who are on the hunt for ivory. And humans aren't free from hippo harm; hippos have been known to randomly attack boats and hurt their unlucky passengers. It's safe to say that hippos and humans are best served when they maintain a safe and respectful distance from each other.

19. What title best expresses the main idea of the passage?
- **(A)** The Wide World of Large Animals
- **(B)** A Closer Look at Sub-Saharan Africa
- **(C)** Getting to Know the Hippopotamus
- **(D)** The Strange Relationship between Humans and Hippos

20. All of the following characteristics of the hippopotamus are mentioned in the passage *except*
- **(A)** a keen intelligence.
- **(B)** aggressive behavior.
- **(C)** surprising speed.
- **(D)** strong jaws.

21. Based on the passage (paragraph 2), what does *prodigious* most likely mean?

    (A) Quite angry

    (B) Very big

    (C) Short tempered

    (D) Fiercely loyal

22. What does the author mean when he states in paragraph 5 that the "relationship between humans and hippos could best be characterized as tenuous at best"?

    (A) There is a history of mutual aggression between humans and hippos.

    (B) Humans have long enjoyed learning more about how hippos live.

    (C) Both humans and hippos enjoy staying cool while swimming in lakes.

    (D) Humans rarely have opportunities to see hippos in their native habitat.

23. According to the information provided in the passage, which of the following meals would most likely appeal to a hippopotamus?

    (A) Meat from a gazelle

    (B) River trout

    (C) A ripe pineapple

    (D) Grazeable grass

exercises

QUESTIONS 24–28 REFER TO THE FOLLOWING PASSAGE.

The Rhodora

In May, when sea-winds pierced our solitudes,

I found the fresh Rhodora in the woods,

Spreading its leafless blooms in a damp nook,

To please the desert and the sluggish brook.

The purple petals, fallen in the pool,

Made the black water with their beauty gay;

Here might the red-bird come his plumes to cool,

And court the flower that cheapens his array.

Rhodora! if the sages ask thee why

This charm is wasted on the earth and sky,

Tell them, dear, that if eyes were made for seeing,

Then Beauty is its own excuse for being:

Why thou wert there, O rival of the rose!

I never thought to ask, I never knew:

But, in my simple ignorance suppose

The self-same Power that brought me there brought you.

—*Ralph Waldo Emerson*

24. The poet is impressed with the beauty of
    (A) the sea.
    (B) the woods.
    (C) a bird.
    (D) a flower.

25. When the poet says that the flower cheapens the array of the red-bird, he means that the
    (A) bird gets nothing from the flower.
    (B) flower gets nothing from the bird.
    (C) color of the flower is brighter than that of the bird.
    (D) bird ruins the flower.

26. In saying "This charm is wasted on the earth and sky," the poet means that
    (A) the earth and sky do not appreciate beauty.
    (B) no one sees a flower that blooms deep in the woods.
    (C) wise men sometimes ask foolish questions.
    (D) the bird does not even notice the beauty of the flower.

27. The poet believes that
    (A) flower petals pollute the water.
    (B) red birds are garish.
    (C) beauty exists for its own sake.
    (D) sea-wind is refreshing.

28. The poet probably
    (A) is an insensitive person.
    (B) dislikes solitude.
    (C) is a religious person.
    (D) is ignorant.

ANSWER KEYS AND EXPLANATIONS

Exercise 1

1. B	11. D	21. A	31. D	41. D
2. C	12. B	22. A	32. A	42. C
3. C	13. C	23. A	33. C	43. D
4. D	14. B	24. D	34. D	44. B
5. B	15. D	25. B	35. A	45. A
6. A	16. D	26. B	36. B	46. B
7. B	17. C	27. C	37. A	47. A
8. A	18. D	28. D	38. C	48. D
9. D	19. B	29. A	39. D	49. B
10. C	20. A	30. A	40. B	50. C

1. **The correct answer is (B).** The passage tells us that Henry Ford was fired from his first job because he worked so quickly. This shows that Ford was a very efficient worker, as choice (B) states. Choice (B) is therefore correct. The passage shows that Ford was very interested in mechanics as a youngster, but it never states that Ford was better at mechanics than at business, so Choice (A) is incorrect.

2. **The correct answer is (C).** The passage tells us in paragraph one that Ford started his first business selling watches when he was only 11 years old. Choice (C) is therefore correct. Choice (A) shows that Ford started working in the auto industry when he was 17, but this company wasn't a business that Ford owned.

3. **The correct answer is (C).** The passage tells us that Henry Ford was a "natural businessman," meaning that an aptitude for and interest in business were part of his life from his earliest years. This idea is developed through various examples of Ford's ambitions and talents throughout his youth. Choice (B) is incorrect because although the passage describes the watch-making business Ford

engaged in as a boy, it also covers his entry into the auto industry in his late teens.

4. **The correct answer is (D).** The passage tells us that Ford sold each watch for $1.00 and points out that Ford only earned $1.10 a day at his first job in the auto industry. Therefore, he sold his watches for almost a full day's wage for a factory worker, making $1.00 a relatively high price for that time. Though the passage later tells us that Ford was an efficient worker, it does not state how long it took him to make a watch, so choice (B) is not the correct answer.

5. **The correct answer is (B).** This main idea question requires you to locate the sentence that best describes the main point of the *entire* passage. This particular passage starts out by describing Mozart's gifts as a musician and a composer, and then it explains his contribution to music. Choice (B) summarizes the main point clearly as it states: "Mozart was an extremely talented musician and composer whose contributions had a significant impact on music."

6. **The correct answer is (A).** This question asks you to define the meaning of *prodigy*,

a word that you may not be familiar with. When you are faced with unfamiliar words, you can use clues from the sentence to help you define them. If necessary, you can re-read the part of the passage that the sentence was taken from to gain more clues about the meaning of the vocabulary word.

The sentence that contains the word *prodigy* tells us that Mozart was highly musically talented. It is in paragraph two, which describes how gifted he was as a child. The word *prodigy* must therefore mean "a child who is talented or gifted." Choice (A) comes closest to this meaning, so it is correct.

7. **The correct answer is (B).** This is a "compare and contrast" question. It asks you to identify the difference between Mozart's sonatas and the sonatas that were written before his time.

Often, you can find the answers to a compare and contrast question written directly in the text. If you look back to the part of the passage that describes sonatas (paragraphs three and four), you will find a sentence that explains how Mozart wrote sonatas: "Mozart also wrote sonatas, but he added depth to the sonatas and gave them more structure." This sentence describes the main difference between Mozart's sonatas and the sonatas that existed previously. It is reflected in answer choice (B), so choice (B) is correct.

8. **The correct answer is (A).** The passage states in the first paragraph that Mozart wrote more compositions than any other composer in history, so choice (A) is the correct answer. The passage does not state how many symphonies he wrote compared to other composers, nor does it state the number of movements he included in his compositions, so choices (B) and (C) are incorrect. The passage does make it clear that Mozart wrote a variety of compositions, so choice (D) is incorrect.

9. **The correct answer is (D).** The passage states that Mozart learned to play the piano at the age of three and composed his first work at the age of four, so the correct answer is choice (D). The passage does not state the nature of the composition, so choice (B) is incorrect. Nor does the passage indicate the he learned to play the trumpet, making choice (A) incorrect also.

10. **The correct answer is (C).** The passage states that the separate parts of a musical composition are called movements, making choice (C) the correct answer. The words *elements* and *aspects* can be synonyms for parts, but the passage does not mention these words when describing musical compositions, so choices (A) and (D) are incorrect.

11. **The correct answer is (D).** The passage states in paragraph three that a sonata is a composition for one or two solo instruments. It does not state that the instruments must be a stringed instrument and a woodwind, so choice (B) is incorrect.

12. **The correct answer is (B).** Although the passage does not specifically state that Mozart was born in Austria, the phrase "other regions in Austria," indicates that Mozart resided in a part of Austria, making choices (C) and (D) incorrect. The other countries mentioned in the passage are Germany, France, and Italy, making choice (B) the correct answer. England is not mentioned, so choice (A) is also incorrect.

13. **The correct answer is (C).** The passage states that Mozart's travels exposed him to many types of music, which helped him compose sonatas with more depth and structure, making choice (C) the correct answer. The passage does not mention that he learned any foreign languages during those travels, so choice (D) is incorrect.

14. **The correct answer is (B).** This "vocabulary" question asks you to identify the meaning of a word that you may not be familiar with. The best way to define such a word is by using the context of the sentence to help you. Sometimes it can also

be helpful to re-read the paragraph that the sentence came from, to get more clues about the meaning of the vocabulary word.

In this case, we're told that Aunt Frieda has recently had surgery on her eye. She is coming to visit her mother after the surgery. When she exits the car, she walks like someone who can't see very well. Someone who can't see very well would probably walk in a *careful* way, so we're looking for an answer choice that has a meaning similar to *careful*. Answer choice (B), *cautiously*, is close in meaning to *careful*, and it makes sense in the context of this sentence, so choice (B) is correct.

15. **The correct answer is (D).** This "compare and contrast" question asks you to identify the difference between two of the characters in the story. In this case, the character of the grandfather is described in the last paragraph of the passage. The author states that his grandfather was "a very quiet man who lived a routine, predictable life." We know that his grandmother, on the other hand, became upset very easily whenever things didn't go her way. Choice (D) summarizes this difference between the characters nicely, so choice (D) is correct.

16. **The correct answer is (D).** This question concerns one specific detail from the passage. The correct answers to detail questions are given directly within the passage. If you can't remember the answer, you can find it by re-reading the necessary part of the passage. At the beginning of paragraph two, the author tells us that "One day, when I was about fifteen, I saw that the letters from my Aunt Frieda were coming written in Uncle Stuart's handwriting. I realized that Aunt Frieda wasn't really writing them . . . ." The author knew that Aunt Frieda wasn't writing the letters because he could tell that the handwriting belonged to his Uncle Stuart. Choice (D) is correct.

17. **The correct answer is (C).** The passage states that *Nana* controlled the family finances and made most of the decisions, so choice (C) is the correct answer. Choice (A) is incorrect because, although she did not speak English, the author translated the letters from her children, so she was not cut off from them.

18. **The correct answer is (D).** The author describes *Nana* as "crying inside" and feeling "powerless" when she sees Aunt Frieda and repeatedly saying that as a mother she should have been with her child at the hospital, making choice (D) the correct answer. Although it might make sense to suspect that she was also a little angry, she does not seem angry at the author about the deception regarding the letters, so choice (C) is incorrect.

19. **The correct answer is (B).** When the letters started coming in Uncle Stuart's handwriting, the author did not inform Nana because she was easily worried, as is noted in paragraph two: "My grandmother was a real worrier, and I didn't want her to get upset…" At the end of the passage, the author remarks that she was also "smart as a whip," making choice (B) the correct answer. The author does not reveal how much formal education she had, so choices (C) and (D) are incorrect.

20. **The correct answer is (A).** Aunt Grace tells the author that Aunt Frieda is "recovering just fine," a reassuring statement that makes choice (A) the correct answer. Choice (B) is incorrect because "console" means to comfort another person at a time of grief, sorrow, or disappointment. Choice (D) is also incorrect because Aunt Grace's response is intended to be reassuring to the author, even though *Nana* later finds the news distressing.

21. **The correct answer is (A).** If necessary, reread the selection. Clearly, the observer is fascinated by the scene before him. He gives no indication of being frightened or repulsed and is far too interested to be bored.

22. **The correct answer is (A).** The Flemish painting was brought over from Holland.

23. **The correct answer is (A).** At the beginning of the selection, the game is being played on a level spot with nine pins. At the end of the passage, balls are rolled, presumably at the pins. This is a variety of bowling.

24. **The correct answer is (D).** The second paragraph begins "What seemed particularly odd to Rip . . . ." Rip must be the observer. All of the other choices *could* be true, but we have no confirming evidence in the selection, whereas the selection does tell us that the man's name is Rip.

25. **The correct answer is (B).** In the first sentence of the last paragraph, Rip found it "particularly odd" that the men maintained such grave faces while evidently amusing themselves.

26. **The correct answer is (B).** This question asks you to identify the main idea, or main point, of the entire passage. The correct answer will be a statement that is broad enough to cover the entire passage, but narrow enough to describe the specific message of the passage. It must also describe this specific message accurately.

    This passage basically provides us with a comparison of two views of energy: the original view, developed 200 years ago, and the current view now held by scientists. Paragraph one tells us that the original view, developed by Thomas Young, held that energy was "the ability to do physical work." The last paragraph tells us that the current view, developed by Albert Einstein, is that energy is "the stored potential to be able to complete work." This point is best summarized in choice (B), so choice (B) is the correct answer.

27. **The correct answer is (C).** The word *severs* is found in the first paragraph of the passage. Here, we are presented with a definition of the term "energy." We are told that the term "energy" was developed by a scientist named Thomas Young, who originally believed that energy was the ability to do physical work. Energy, Young thought, was like the work that an axe does when it comes down on a log and cuts the log into two pieces. The force of the axe acts on the log to break it in two.

    You are looking for an answer choice that reflects a meaning similar to "cuts" or "breaks." The word *splits* is the best choice here. It reflects the action that an axe takes when it separates a log into two pieces. Choice (C) is correct.

28. **The correct answer is (D).** To answer this question, you must identify a statement that reflects the views of *both* Joule and Einstein. The correct answer must express a belief shared by each scientist. If an answer choice contains the view of only one of the scientists, or neither of them, that choice will be incorrect.

    Choice (D) reflects a belief that was held by both Joule and Einstein. Both scientists believed that molecules and atoms were made up of energy. Paragraph two tells us that Joule thought that "molecules contained very small forms of energy." Paragraph three tells us that Einstein thought that "molecules and atoms were made up of energy." Since choice (D) describes both scientists' beliefs, it is the correct answer.

29. **The correct answer is (A).** The last half of the passage is the place to look for the answer to this question. If we go back and re-read paragraphs three and four, we see that Einstein made two important discoveries that helped change our view of energy. First, as paragraph three tells us, he helped us understand that molecules and atoms were made up of large groups of energy particles. Second, as paragraph four states, Einstein broadened our definition of energy to "the ability to create force over any distance." This second discovery is mentioned in choice (A), so choice (A) is correct.

Choice (B) is incorrect because it reflects the opposite of Einstein's view. Einstein did not show that energy was made up of atoms; on the contrary, he showed that molecules and atoms were made up of energy. Choice (B) can be eliminated. Choice (C) is also incorrect, because the passage never states that Einstein invented a way to view energy with the naked eye. Finally, choice (D) is incorrect, because it is false, based on the passage. Einstein did not develop the term "energy." It is true that this term was developed about 200 years ago, as the passage tells us in paragraph one, but it was developed by Thomas Young, not Einstein.

30. **The correct answer is (A).** This question asks you to compare two views about energy that are given in the passage. The first view is that of Einstein, given towards the end of the passage. The second view is that of Thomas Young, given at the beginning of the passage. To answer the question, then, you must understand the difference between the two views.

   The passage tells us in paragraph one that Young saw energy as the ability to do physical work. It then tells us in the last paragraph that Einstein saw energy as the stored potential to complete physical work. In other words, Young believed that energy was the ability to do work now, whereas Einstein saw it as the ability to do work at some time in the future. Einstein's view is stated accurately only in choice (A), so choice (A) is the correct answer.

31. **The correct answer is (D).** Paragraph two describes Joule's beliefs about the ability to do work. It states that Joule believed "the ability to do work was stored within the molecules of matter," so choice (D) is the correct answer.

32. **The correct answer is (A).** To answer this question, you must identify the factor that enabled Western people to learn that Machu Picchu existed. Paragraph one tells

us that Machu Picchu was discovered by an American named Hiram Bingham in 1911, and that "until Bingham's discovery in 1911, no one in the West knew that Machu Picchu even existed." Westerners learned about the site because of Bingham's discovery, so answer choice (A) is correct.

33. **The correct answer is (C).** The passage focuses on the rediscovery of Machu Picchu, after it was lost to history for many centuries, making choice (C) the correct answer. It was not mentioned in Spanish accounts of the Inca, so choice (D) is incorrect. The term *mythical* refers to something that does not exist, making choice (A) incorrect. The Aztecs are not mentioned in the passage, so choice (B) is incorrect.

34. **The correct answer is (D).** The passage states that Machu Picchu is the most well-known archaeological site in South America. The passage does not compare or contrast it with other archaeological sites, so we are not given enough information to determine if it is the largest, oldest, or highest in altitude.

35. **The correct answer is (A).** The passage states that archaeologists believe the site was used as both a home and religious retreat, making choice (A) the correct answer. The high altitude made it unlikely that it could have any military or business value, so choices (C) and (D) are incorrect. The passage makes it clear that women and children also occupied Machu Picchu, so choice (B) is also incorrect.

36. **The correct answer is (B).** The passage states that Cusco was conquered by the Spanish in 1532, though the Spanish apparently made no mention of Machu Picchu in their records. The passage does not state when Cusco was built or where Pachacuti Inca Yupanqui is buried, so choices (C) and (D) are incorrect.

37. **The correct answer is (A).** The passage describes how glutamate works and how

it can destroy certain types of brain cells. It addresses the impact of glutamate on the brain, so answer choice (A) is correct. Choices (B), (C), and (D) are not mentioned in the passage.

38. The correct answer is (C). The correct answer can be found in the last sentence of paragraph two ("When levels of glutamate become high, this prompts nerve cells in the brain to become too active, which leads to destruction of the cells."). Excess glutamate destroys brain cells by causing nerve cells in the brain to become too active, so choice (C) is the correct answer.

39. The correct answer is (D). Paragraph four tells us that glutamate found naturally in foods poses a low risk of causing high levels of glutamate in the brain. It goes on to explain that natural glutamate is bonded with other amino acids, so choice (D) is correct.

40. The correct answer is (B). Paragraph two states that there are two types of neurotransmitters: those that *cause* nerve cells to act and those neurotransmitters that *stop* nerve cells from acting. Glutamate is one of the neurotransmitters that cause nerve cells to act, so answer choice (B) is correct.

41. The correct answer is (D). Paragraph two states that glutamate is normally present in the brain in very small amounts. Choice (B) is incorrect, because the first paragraph states that glutamate *sends* signals to nerve cells rather than blocking them.

42. The correct answer is (C). The passage states that Janessa had a tough time falling asleep last night and woke up tired because she has never been able to control the excitement she feels for an upcoming event, and this was the morning of her class trip, which she was very excited about. There is no mention of an upcoming test, so choice (A) is incorrect. The story did not mention that Janessa was sick or that her cat kept her up that night, so choices (B) and (D) are also incorrect.

43. The correct answer is (D). When Janessa's father said, "Some lessons are harder to learn than others," he was talking about what Janessa's mother had said—that when people get too excited, they sometimes get careless. He meant that sometimes people have to make a mistake multiple times before they learn their lesson, so choice (D) is the correct answer. There is no mention that he thinks science is the toughest subject in school, so choice (A) is incorrect. He also doesn't talk about studying hard to do well on exams, even if he thinks that's true, so choice (B) is incorrect. He also says nothing about some students being smarter than others, so choice (C) is also incorrect.

44. The correct answer is (B). Use the information provided in the passage to answer this question. While riding in the car to school, Janessa talks to her father about the things she's learning in science class. The only topic she doesn't mention among the answer choices is choice (B), magnetism.

45. The correct answer is (A). At the end of the story, after checking her pockets for the trip permission slip and realizing she forgot it at home, Janessa finally realized the truth of what her parents were telling her that morning: if you get too excited, you may get careless and make mistakes, such as forgetting something. Therefore, choice (A) is correct. The lessons in the other answer choices may be important and worth learning, but they are not what Janessa finally realized when she discovered that she didn't have the trip permission slip.

46. The correct answer is (B). To answer this question, it is helpful to first re-read the paragraph that contains the sentence with the word *erroneously*. The sentence comes near the end of the first paragraph. Paragraph one tells us that some people used to believe that "if you build a better product, that product will definitely sell." It was discovered, however, that this idea was false.

Sentence three of the paragraph tells us that the piece of advice was wrong because it "ignored the role that prices play in affecting what consumers buy." We are therefore looking for a definition of *erroneously* that means something like "incorrectly." Choice (B), *mistakenly*, best fits the definition that we're looking for.

47. **The correct answer is (A).** Companies used to believe that people would always buy better products if those products were available on the market. This belief, however, turned out not to be true, as the Pioneer company learned. The Pioneer Tool and Die Company built a very high-quality mousetrap, but people wouldn't buy it because it was too expensive. The company therefore stopped producing or selling it. Choice (A) is correct.

48. **The correct answer is (D).** The passage focuses on the fact that the Pioneer Tool and Die Company built a mousetrap that was better than others on the market, making choice (D) the correct answer. The mousetrap was not inexpensive, nor was it a successful product, so choices (A) and (B) are incorrect. The passage does not indicate if any of the features of the new mousetrap

were powered by electricity, so choice (C) is also incorrect.

49. **The correct answer is (B).** The passage states that the mousetraps most consumers preferred cost about 7 cents each, making choice (B) the correct answer. Although it is possible that mousetraps could be made at home, the passage does not address that issue, so choice (D) is incorrect.

50. **The correct answer is (C).** The passage uses the phrase "bells and whistles" as a metaphor for the fancy features of the Pioneer Tool and Die mousetrap in contrast to the plain and simple one preferred by consumers, making choice (C) the correct answer. The passage does not state anything about the sounds the mousetrap made or its appearance, so choices (A) and (B) are incorrect. Choice (D) is also incorrect, because although this is one feature of the Pioneer mousetrap, the phrase "lots of bells and whistles" refers to multiple features of the device.

Exercise 2

1. C	7. C	13. C	19. C	24. D
2. D	8. C	14. A	20. A	25. C
3. D	9. D	15. D	21. B	26. B
4. B	10. B	16. B	22. A	27. C
5. C	11. D	17. C	23. D	28. C
6. A	12. B	18. A		

1. **The correct answer is (C).** Paragraph three tells us that it was difficult to isolate fluorine because fluorine was very dangerous and destructive. The statement that it "cost some researchers their lives" tells us that certain researchers died during these destructive experiments. Choice (C) is correct.

2. **The correct answer is (D).** This question is what is known as a "detail" question. It asks about a detail from the passage. The correct answer to detail questions will always be contained in the passage. In this case, paragraph two tells us that the discovery of fluorine began with a scientist named Georg Bauer, who first described a mineral known as "fluorspar." The third paragraph then tells us that scientists working with fluorspar saw that when the mineral was heated, it gave off a gas. It took years to isolate the element fluorine, but the process started with the research on fluorspar by Bauer. So, choice (D) is the correct answer.

3. **The correct answer is (D).** This last paragraph of the passage lets us know that fluorides are extremely dangerous and that they should never be touched, inhaled, or swallowed. The last paragraph is warning us that fluorides should not come in contact with the human body. Choice (D) reflects this conclusion, so it is correct.

4. **The correct answer is (B).** The passage deals primarily with the discovery and isolation of fluorine, making choice (B) the correct answer. Choice (D), which refers to chemical elements in general, is incorrect because fluorine is the only element that the passage discusses in detail. Toothpaste and the dangers encountered by those experimenting with fluorine are details in the passage that contribute to the main idea, but choices (A) and (C) do not reflect the emphasis of the passage.

5. **The correct answer is (C).** The passage describes a practical use for fluorine as fluoride in toothpaste in the first paragraph and warns of its dangers in pure form in the last paragraph, making choice (C) the correct answer. The passage does not discuss the rarity or monetary value of fluorine, so choice (D) is incorrect.

6. **The correct answer is (A).** This "cause and effect" question asks you to identify the factor that *caused* the Berlin Wall to fall. To answer it, you should first re-read the paragraph that describes the destruction of the wall. Paragraph three tells us (in the second sentence) that the wall was torn down due to riots by the people of East Berlin, so choice (A) is the correct answer.

7. **The correct answer is (C).** The last paragraph states that the Berlin Wall was a symbol of the Soviet Union, and that the destruction of the wall soon led to a decline of Soviet power. Although Gorbachev was present when protestors first broke though the wall, the passage does not state that he was the cause of that protest, making choice (D) incorrect.

8. **The correct answer is (C).** The first paragraph states that the wall was built to prevent East Germans from escaping to West Germany. The passage states that the city had already been divided before the wall was built, and it was divided into two parts, so choice (D) is incorrect.

9. **The correct answer is (D).** The second paragraph states that Gorbachev's visit was prompted by the 40th anniversary of communist rule in East Germany, so he was there to celebrate 40 years of communist rule, choice (D). The Russian Revolution occurred much earlier in 1917 and is not mentioned in the passage, making choice (B) incorrect.

10. **The correct answer is (B).** The second paragraph of the passage states that the wall was an "imposing landmark" built of concrete topped with barbed wire, so choice (B) is the correct answer.

11. **The correct answer is (D).** The term Cold War is mentioned in the passage in paragraph one. This term refers to the period between roughly the end of World War II in 1945 and the fall of the Soviet Union in 1989, when the democratic countries led by the United States and the communist countries led by the Soviet Union engaged in a conflict without direct military confrontation.

12. **The correct answer is (B).** The passage discusses the development of science and Sir Francis Bacon's contributions to it. Choice (B) best reflects this content. Choice (D) is incorrect, because it is too narrow. Choice (C) is outside the scope of the passage.

13. **The correct answer is (C).** To answer this "cause and effect" question, you must identify the *reason* why Francis Bacon chose to look for a new approach to knowledge. Why did he wish to develop an approach based on the observation of physical events? The answer to this question is revealed for us in paragraphs two and three of the passage. These paragraphs tell us that before Bacon's time, knowledge was based on the beliefs of the church. Bacon did not like the idea of basing knowledge only on faith or belief. The last sentence of paragraph two tells us that Bacon "searched for a way of developing knowledge that he felt was more reliable." This sentence suggests that Bacon felt that knowledge based on the beliefs of the church was *not* very reliable, so choice (C) is correct.

14. **The correct answer is (A).** Paragraph four of the passage tells us that Bacon's approach came to be known by the name *inductivism*, so choice (A) is correct.

15. **The correct answer is (D).** According to paragraph two, scientific knowledge before Bacon's time was based on religious ideas and the doctrine of the church. The ideas that were considered to be knowledge were based upon faith, so (D) is correct.

16. **The correct answer is (B).** The answer to this question is found in paragraph three. *The New Organon*, published in 1620, became the foundation for what we know today as the "empirical" sciences. It addressed how to develop knowledge gained from observing that which can be perceived through the senses, making (B) the correct answer. Choice (D) is incorrect, because the passage does not mention that the book emphasized practicing strict scientific discipline in all research.

17. **The correct answer is (C).** To answer this inference question, you must draw on information given in the passage to make a logical deduction. Bacon did not support scientific ideas based on church doctrine, so choice (A) is incorrect. He advocated that science should be based on empirical research, or what could be observed through the senses, so choice (C) is the correct answer.

18. **The correct answer is (A).** The second sentence of paragraph four tells us that inductivism is the idea that theories about science can be developed from observing events, so choice (A) is correct. Choices (B), (C), and (D) are incorrect, because these factors are not mentioned as important for inductivism.

19. **The correct answer is (C).** The clear focus of the passage is the hippopotamus, including its behavioral and physical characteristics. Therefore, the best choice for a title would be choice (C), "Getting to Know the Hippopotamus." Although Sub-Saharan Africa, choice (B), and a few large animals, choice (A), are mentioned in the passage, they are small supporting details. There is no mention of the relationship between humans and hippos as being strange, so choice D is incorrect.

20. **The correct answer is (A).** The passage discusses a variety of the hippo's common characteristics, including its aggressive behavior, surprising speed, and strong jaws. The only characteristic among the answer choices that isn't mentioned in the passage is a keen intelligence. Therefore, choice (A) is the correct answer.

21. **The correct answer is (B).** The sentence in which the word *prodigious* appears discusses the immense size and weight of the hippopotamus. Based on the context, it can

be determined that *prodigious* means very large. Therefore, choice (B) is the correct answer.

22. **The correct answer is (A).** The tenuous, or uncertain, relationship between humans and hippos, as described by the author, refers to the acts of aggression that have come from both sides. According to the passage, human poachers have hunted hippos for their ivory, and hippos have been known to attack sailing vessels filled with people. Therefore, choice (A) is the correct answer.

23. **The correct answer is (D).** Information on the dietary habits of the hippopotamus is provided in paragraph 2. There we are told that the herbivorous mammal's diet "largely consists of creeping grass," which makes choice (D), grazeable grass, the correct answer. Hippos do not eat meat or fish, and there's no mention of pineapple or other fruits in the passage, so choices (A), (B), and (C) are incorrect.

24. **The correct answer is (D).** The poem really is an ode to the flower.

25. **The correct answer is (C).** The poet is saying that while the bird is splendid, the flower is even more beautiful.

26. **The correct answer is (B).** The flower blooms deep in the woods where, except for the occasional wanderer like himself, no one sees it.

27. **The correct answer is (C).** "Then beauty is its own excuse for being."

28. **The correct answer is (C).** In saying "The self-same Power that brought me there brought you," the poet is expressing his faith in a Supreme Being that created man and nature.

SUMMING IT UP

- This section is called Reading and Language Arts on the COOP and Reading on the HSPT® (under the Comprehension section). It's called "Reading" on the TACHS. Each test presents reading passages followed by a series of questions.

- To do well on this section, you will need to be able to read quickly. If you do not read quickly, study the section "How to Improve Your Reading Skills" in this chapter.

- Study and remember all of the steps for answering reading comprehension questions: read over the question, skim the passage for the main idea, reread the passage with attention to details and point of view, carefully read each question or incomplete statement, read all four answer choices, and don't spend too much time on any one question.

Spelling

OVERVIEW

- **Tips for improving your spelling skills**
- **Twenty-four spelling rules**
- **Exercises: Spelling**
- **Answer keys and explanations**
- **Summing it up**

The COOP, HSPT®, and TACHS exams all include several test questions that check spelling skills. In these questions, you are presented with a series of answer choices. Some of the choices contain sentences; the last choice is "No Mistakes." You are asked to read the sentences and check for errors in capitalization, punctuation, usage, or spelling. If you believe that none of the sentences contains an error, you choose "No Mistakes."

Spelling is a weakness for many students. The ability to spell well does not seem to be directly related to any measurable factor. A few fortunate individuals are just natural spellers—they can hear a word and instinctively spell it correctly. Most people, however, must memorize rules, memorize spellings, and rely on a dictionary.

To help you excel on the spelling questions found on the COOP, the HSPT®, and the TACHS exams, this section includes tips for improving your spelling and a list of spelling rules.

TIPS FOR IMPROVING YOUR SPELLING SKILLS

You can improve your spelling by keeping a list of words that you spell incorrectly or that you must often look up. Add to your list whenever you find a word you cannot spell. When you have a few minutes to study spelling, write each word correctly ten times. If you know how to type, type each word ten times, too. Let your hand get used to the feel of the correct spelling, and let your eye become accustomed to seeing the word spelled correctly. Periodically, ask someone to read your list aloud to you, and try writing them correctly. Frequent self-testing of problem spelling words should help you learn the correct spellings. On the day before the test, read over your list carefully.

Another way to improve your spelling is by developing mnemonic devices. A mnemonic device is a private clue that you develop to help you remember something. For example, if you have trouble spelling the word *friend*, you might find it helpful to remember the sentence, "A friend is true to the *end*." This little sentence will help you remember to place the "i" before the "e." If you have trouble distinguishing between *here* and *hear* try a sentence like "To listen is to hear with an ear." If you confuse the spellings *principle* and *principal*, remember (whether you believe it or not) "The princiPAL is your PAL." And finally, this cute mnemonic device might help you spell "misspells" correctly: " *Miss Pell* never *misspells*. "

When you have trouble spelling a word, try to invent your own mnemonic device, and you will have a built-in "prompter" when you encounter spelling questions on the exam. Much of spelling must simply be learned. However, there are some rules that apply to the spelling of root words and more rules that apply to the adding of suffixes. The following list presents some of the most useful spelling rules and some of the most common exceptions to those rules. Try to learn them all! The explanations that accompany the spelling exercises, as well as the exam questions that test spelling, refer to these rules by number when they apply.

TWENTY-FOUR SPELLING RULES

1 *i* before *e*
Except after *c*
Or when sounded like *ay*
As in *neighbor* or *weigh*.
Exceptions: Neither, leisure, foreigner, seized, weird, heights.

2 If a word ends in *y* preceded by a vowel, keep the *y* when adding a suffix.
Examples: day, days; attorney, attorneys

3 If a word ends in *y* preceded by a consonant, change the *y* to *i* before adding a suffix.
Examples: try, tries, tried; lady, ladies
Exceptions: To avoid double *i*, retain the *y* before *-ing* and *-ish*.
Examples: fly, flying; baby, babyish

4 Silent *e* at the end of a word is usually dropped before a suffix beginning with a vowel.
Examples: dine + ing = dining
　　　　　　locate + ion = location
　　　　　　use + able = usable
　　　　　　offense + ive = offensive
Exceptions: Words ending in *ce* and *ge* retain *e* before *-able* and *-ous* in order to retain the soft sounds of *c* and *g*.
Examples: peace + able = peaceable
　　　　　　courage + ous = courageous

5 Silent *e* is usually kept before a suffix beginning with a consonant.
Examples: care + less = careless
　　　　　　late + ly = lately
　　　　　　one + ness = oneness
　　　　　　game + ster = gamester

6 Some exceptions must simply be memorized. Some exceptions to the last two rules are *truly, duly, awful, argument, wholly, ninth, mileage, dyeing, acreage, canoeing*.

7 A word of one syllable that ends in a single consonant preceded by a single vowel doubles the final consonant before a suffix beginning with a vowel or before the suffix *-y*.

Examples: hit, hitting; drop, dropped; big, biggest; mud, muddy; **but:** *help*, *helping* because *help* ends in two consonants; *need*, *needing*, *needy* because the final consonant is preceded by two vowels.

8 A word of more than one syllable that accents the last syllable and that ends in a single consonant preceded by a single vowel doubles the final consonant when adding a suffix beginning with a vowel.

Examples: begin, beginner; admit, admitted; **but:** *enter*, *entered* because the accent is not on the last syllable.

9 A word ending in *er* or *ur* doubles the *r* in the past tense if the word is accented on the last syllable.

Examples: occur, occurred; prefer, preferred; transfer, transferred

10 A word ending in *er* does not double the *r* in the past tense if the accent falls before the last syllable.

Examples: answer, answered; offer, offered; differ, differed

11 When *-full* is added to the end of a noun, the final *l* is dropped.

Examples: cheerful, cupful, hopeful

12 All words beginning with *over* are one word.

Examples: overcast, overcharge, overhear

13 All words with the prefix *self* are hyphenated.

Examples: self-control, self-defense, self-evident

14 The letter *q* is always followed by *u*.

Examples: quiz, bouquet, acquire

15 Numbers from twenty-one to ninety-nine are hyphenated.

16 *Per cent* is *never* hyphenated. It may be written as one word (*percent*) or as two words (*per cent*).

17 *Welcome* is one word with one *l*.

18 *All right* is always two words. *Alright* is a nonstandard form of English and should not be used.

19 *Already* means *prior to some specified time*. *All ready* means *completely ready*.

Example: By the time I was *all ready* to go to the play, the tickets were *already* sold out.

20 *Altogether* means *entirely*. *All together* means *in sum* or *collectively*.

Example: There are *altogether* too many people to seat in this room when we are *all together*.

21 *Their* is the possessive of *they*.

They're is the contraction for *they are*.

There means *at that place*.

Example: *They're* going to put *their* books over *there*.

22 *Your* is the possessive of *you*.

You're is the contraction for *you are*.

Example: *You're* certainly planning to leave *your* muddy boots outside.

23 *Whose* is the possessive of *who*.

Who's is the contraction for *who is*.

Example: Do you know *who's* ringing the doorbell or *whose* car is in the street?

24 *Its* is the possessive of *it*. *It's* is the contraction for it is.

Example: *It's* I who lost the letter and *its* envelope.

Now try the following exercises. Answer keys and explanations follow Exercise 2.

EXERCISES: SPELLING

Exercise 1

Directions: Look for errors in spelling. Choose the letter of the sentence that contains the error. No question contains more than one sentence with a spelling error. If you find no error, choose (D) as your answer.

1. (A) In the teacher's absence, the pupils had an eraser fight.
   (B) The laws of apartheid prohibited marriage between people of different races.
   (C) We may be haveing a fire drill this afternoon.
   (D) *No mistakes*

2. (A) The Indian squaw carried her papoose strapped to a board on her back.
   (B) Christopher Columbus is credited with the discovary of America.
   (C) Innocent victims should not have to stand trial.
   (D) *No mistakes*

3. (A) Mel's position in the chess match was not advantagious, and he was nervous.
   (B) The welcome committee set up the registration booth by the entrance to the banquet hall.
   (C) The manager was eager to review her subordinate's recommendation for increasing company revenue.
   (D) *No mistakes*

4. (A) Meet me at the bus depot promptly at four.
   (B) On Saturday, we will have dinner at a restaurant.
   (C) The whipping post was in use as punishment in Delaware until recent times.
   (D) *No mistakes*

5. (A) The shepherd would be lonely without his dog.
   (B) The experiment served to confirm the hypothesis.
   (C) The divinity fudge was truly deliscious.
   (D) *No mistakes*

6. (A) The golfer took a break after the nineth hole.
   (B) Let me acquaint you with the new rules.
   (C) The slugger wields a heavy bat.
   (D) *No mistakes*

7. (A) Biology is always a laboratory science.
   (B) The short story is really a memoir.
   (C) My neice will enter college in the fall.
   (D) *No mistakes*

8. (A) The currency of Mexico is the peso.
   (B) The detective had the perfect disguise.
   (C) Is there anything one can buy for a nickel?
   (D) *No mistakes*

9. (A) Our senator is a staunch supporter of the president.
   (B) I heard a rumer that our principal is about to retire.
   (C) A surgeon must have steady hands.
   (D) *No mistakes*

10. **(A)** To grow crops in the desert, we must irrigate daily.

(B) Most convenience stores have very long hours.

(C) There was a lovly centerpiece on the table.

(D) *No mistakes*

Exercise 2

Directions: Look for errors in spelling. Choose the letter of the sentence that contains the error. No question contains more than one sentence with a spelling error. If you find no error, choose (D) as your answer.

1. **(A)** Your not going to believe what happened in class today.

(B) The new mother worried incessantly about her baby.

(C) The new computer programming will take place tonight.

(D) *No mistakes*

2. **(A)** Carter was always running around the house.

(B) Rachel preferred to ride her bike to school.

(C) The cashier wieghed the fruit on the scale.

(D) *No mistakes*

3. **(A)** Mel's position in the chess match was not advantagious, and he was nervous.

(B) The welcome committee set up the registration booth by the entrance to the banquet hall.

(C) The manager was eager to review her subordinate's recommendation for increasing company revenue.

(D) *No mistakes*

4. **(A)** I can never remember how to spell your name.

(B) Next Sunday, we'll be traveling to my grandmother's home in Arizona.

(C) The family was so thrilled that you found they're missing dog.

(D) *No mistakes*

5. **(A)** We carefully stuffed the letters in the envelopes.

(B) Abby was very hopefull that she passed the exam.

(C) The fog made it impossible to see where we were going.

(D) *No mistakes*

6. **(A)** The robbery occured when the Mitchell family was out of town.

(B) I need to explain this to you from the beginning.

(C) The kidnapping suspect was brought to the police station for questioning.

(D) *No mistakes*

7. **(A)** We're honoring the veterans in our community today.

(B) I couldn't tell who's writing was on the board.

(C) When we are all together, there won't be an empty chair.

(D) *No mistakes*

8. **(A)** It's a mystery how some ancient and forgotten civilizations vanished.

(B) Shana was eager to recieve her final exam grade in geometry class.

(C) Milo's loud breathing in the library made it difficult for everyone to concentrate.

(D) *No mistakes*

9. (A) Jason answered every question correctly.

   (B) My teacher is always so cheerful, even on gloomy days.

   (C) Paula's mother is taking a self-defense class.

   (D) *No mistakes*

10. (A) I keep forgetting to tell you the story.

   (B) The attorneys agreed to settle the case before going to trial.

   (C) We all enjoyed the delicious ~~desert~~ Melissa baked for us.

   (D) *No mistakes*

ANSWER KEYS AND EXPLANATIONS

Exercise 1

1. C	3. A	5. C	7. C	9. B
2. B	4. D	6. A	8. D	10. C

1. **The correct answer is (C).** The correct spelling is *having*. Rule 4 states: Silent *e* at the end of a word is usually dropped before a suffix beginning with a vowel.

2. **The correct answer is (B).** The correct spelling is *discovery* (The base word is *discover*. There is no reason to change the *e* to *a*.).

3. **The correct answer is (A).** The correct spelling is *advantageous*. Remember that words ending in *ce* and *ge* retain *e* before *-able* and *-ous* in order to retain the soft sounds of *c* and *g*.

4. **The correct answer is (D).** *(No mistakes)*

5. **The correct answer is (C).** The correct spelling is *delicious* (There is no *s* in the middle of this word.).

6. **The correct answer is (A).** The correct spelling is *ninth*. Rule 6 states that some exceptions to the rules must simply be memorized, and "ninth" is an exception to the rule that a silent *e* is usually kept before a suffix beginning with a consonant.

7. **The correct answer is (C).** The correct spelling is *niece*. Remember Rule 1: "*i* before *e* Except after *c*."

8. **The correct answer is (D).** *(No mistakes)*

9. **The correct answer is (B).** The correct spelling is *rumor* (No rule; just learn the spelling.).

10. **The correct answer is (C).** The correct spelling is *lovely*. Rule 5 states that a silent *e* is usually kept before a suffix beginning with a consonant: love + ly = lovely.

Exercise 2

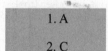 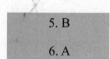

1. A	3. D	5. B	7. B	9. D
2. C	4. C	6. A	8. B	10. C

1. **The correct answer is (A).** The correct spelling is *You're*. Rule 22 states: *Your* is the possessive of *you*. *You're* is the contraction for *you are*.

2. **The correct answer is (C).** The correct spelling is *weighed*. See Rule 1: "*i* before *e* Except after *c* Or when sounded like *ay* as in *neighbor* or *weigh*."

3. **The correct answer is (D).** (*No mistakes*)

4. **The correct answer is (C).** The word they're should be *their*, the possessive of *they*. Rule 21 states: *Their* is the possessive of *they*. *They're* is the contraction for *they are*.

5. **The correct answer is (B).** The correct spelling is *hopeful*. See Rule 11: When -*full* is added to the end of a noun, the final *l* is dropped.

6. **The correct answer is (A).** The correct spelling is *occurred*. Rule 9 states: A word ending in *er* or *ur* doubles the *r* in the past tense if the word is accented on the last syllable.

7. **The correct answer is (B).** The correct spelling is *whose*. Rule 23 states: *Whose* is the possessive of *who*. *Who's* is the contraction for *who is*.

8. **The correct answer is (B).** The correct spelling is *receive*. Remember Rule 1: "*i* before *e* except after *c*."

9. **The correct answer is (D).** (*No mistakes*)

10. **The correct answer is (C).** The correct spelling is *dessert*. A good way to remember this is this mnemonic device: "Dessert is double delicious."

answers exercises

SUMMING IT UP

- The HSPT®, the COOP, and the TACHS exams have several questions specifically testing spelling.

- You are given some choices containing sentences; the last choice says "No mistakes." You must find the spelling error and choose that sentence, or choose "No mistakes" if all sentences are correct.

- Keep a list of words that you spell incorrectly or that you have to look up. Periodically write the words, and have someone test you on them.

- Read the "Twenty-Four Spelling Rules" section, and write some examples for yourself.

Punctuation and Capitalization

chapter 12

OVERVIEW

- **Punctuation rules**
- **Capitalization rules**
- **Exercises: Punctuation and Capitalization**
- **Answer keys and explanations**
- **Summing it up**

Along with spelling, the HSPT®, the TACHS, and the COOP exams also test your knowledge of punctuation and capitalization. To help you review, check out the following list of punctuation and capitalization rules. Because rules can be boring and very difficult to study, we've broken the rules into categories to help you study them in "chunks." Most will be familiar to you, but if you find anything surprising, or if you have trouble understanding any of the rules, be sure to talk to your teacher.

PUNCTUATION RULES

The Period

- Use a period at the end of a sentence that makes a statement, gives a command, or makes a "polite request" in the form of a question that does not require an answer.

  Examples: I am brushing up on my verbal skills.

  Study the chapter on verbs for a quiz tomorrow.

  Would you please read this list of words so that I may practice my spelling lesson.

- Use a period after an abbreviation and after an initial in a person's name.

  Examples: Gen. Robert E. Lee led the Confederate forces.

  Minneapolis and St. Paul are known as the "twin cities."

  Exception: Do not use a period after postal service state name abbreviations.

  Example: St. Louis, MO

- Use a period as a decimal point in numbers.

  Example: A sales tax of 5.5% amounts to $7.47 on a $135.80 purchase.

The Question Mark

- Use a question mark at the end of a direct and genuine question.
  Example: Why do you want to borrow that book?

- Do not use a question mark after an indirect question; use a period.
  Example: He asked if they wanted to accompany him.

- A direct and genuine question must end with a question mark even if the question is only part of the sentence.
  Example: "Daddy, are we there yet?" the child asked.

- Use a question mark (within parentheses) to indicate uncertainty as to the correctness of a piece of information.
  Example: John Carver, (first governor of Plymouth colony?) was born in 1575 and died in 1621.

The Exclamation Mark

- The only reason to use an exclamation mark is to express strong feeling, emotion, or extreme importance.
  Examples: Congratulations! You broke the record.
  Rush! Perishable contents.

The Comma

TIP

Commas are often used to separate introductory phrases, clauses, names, or appositives from the rest of the sentence.

- The salutation of a personal letter is followed by a comma.
  Example: Dear Mary,

- The complimentary close of a letter is ordinarily followed by a comma, though this use is optional.
  Example: Cordially yours,

- An appositive must be set off by commas.   *restrictive/non?*
  Example: Jim Rodgers, my next-door neighbor, is an excellent baby-sitter.

- A noun of address is set apart by commas.
  Example: When you finish your homework, Jeff, please take out the garbage.

- Use commas to set off parenthetical words.
  Example: I think, however, that a move might not be wise at this time.

- When two or more adjectives all modify a noun equally, all but the last must be followed by commas. If you can add the word *and* between the adjectives without changing the sense of the sentence, then use commas.
  Example: The refined, tall, stern-looking man stood at the top of the stairs.

- An introductory phrase of five or more words must be separated by a comma.
  Example: Because the prisoner had a history of attempted jailbreaks, he was put under heavy guard.

- After a short introductory phrase, the comma is optional. The comma should be used where needed for clarity.

  Examples: As a child she was a tomboy. (comma unnecessary)

  To Dan, Phil was friend as well as brother. (comma clarifies)

  In 1978, 300 people lost their lives in one air disaster. (comma clarifies)

- A comma is not generally used before a subordinate clause that ends a sentence, though in long, unwieldy sentences like this one, use of such a comma is optional.

- A comma precedes the coordinating conjunction unless the two clauses are very short.

  Examples: Kevin wanted to borrow a book from the library, but the librarian would not allow him to take it until he had paid his fines.

  Roy washed the dishes and Helen dried.

- Words, phrases, or clauses in a series are separated by commas. The use of a comma before *and* is optional. If the series ends in *etc.*, use a comma before *etc.* Do not use a comma after *etc.* in a series, even if the sentence continues.

  Examples: Coats, umbrellas, and boots should be placed in the closet at the end of the hall.

  Pencils, scissors, paper clips, etc. belong in your top desk drawer.

- A comma separates a short direct quotation from the speaker.

  Examples: She said, "I must be home by six."

  "Tomorrow I begin my new job," he told us.

- Use a comma to indicate that you have omitted a word or words, such as *of* or *of the.*

  Example: President, XYZ Corporation

- Use a comma to separate a name from a title or personal-name suffix.

  Examples: Paul Feiner, Chairman

  Carl Andrew Pforzheimer, Jr.

- Use a comma when first and last names are reversed.

  Example: Bernbach, Linda

- Use a comma to separate parts of dates or addresses.

  Example: Please come to a party on Sunday, May 9, at the Pine Tavern on Drake Road, Cheswold, Delaware.

  Exception: Do not use a comma between the postal service state abbreviation and the zip code.

  Example: Scarsdale, NY 10583

- A comma ordinarily separates thousands, millions, and trillions.

  Example: 75,281,646

- A nonrestrictive adjective phrase or clause must be set off by commas. A nonrestrictive phrase or clause is one that can be omitted without essentially changing the meaning of the sentence.

  Example: Our new sailboat, which has bright orange sails, is very seaworthy.

- A restrictive phrase or clause is vital to the meaning of a sentence and cannot be omitted. Do not set it off with commas.
  Example: A sailboat without sails is useless.

- A comma must be used if the sentence might be subject to different interpretation without it.
  Example: He saw the woman who had rejected him, and blushed.

- If a pause would make the sentence clearer and easier to read, insert a comma.
  Examples: Inside the people were dancing. (confusing)
  Inside, the people were dancing. (clearer)
  After all crime must be punished. (confusing)
  After all, crime must be punished. (clearer)

  The pause rule is not infallible, but it is your best resort when all other rules governing use of the comma fail you.

The Hyphen

- Use a hyphen to divide a word at the end of a line.

- Hyphenate numbers from twenty-one through ninety-nine, except for multiples of ten: twenty, thirty, forty, etc.

- Use a hyphen to join two words serving together as a single adjective before a noun.
  Examples: We left the highway and proceeded on a well-paved road.
  That baby-faced man is considerably older than he appears to be.

- Use a hyphen with the prefixes *ex-*, *self-*, *all-*, and the suffix *-elect*.
  Examples: ex-Senator, self-appointed, all-State, Governor-elect

- Use a hyphen to avoid ambiguity.
  Example: After the custodian recovered the use of his right arm, he re-covered the office chairs.

- Use a hyphen to avoid an awkward union of letters.
  Examples: semi-independent; shell-like

- Refer to a dictionary whenever you are uncertain as to whether you should write two words, a hyphenated word, or one word.

The Dash

- You may use a dash (—) or parentheses () for emphasis or to set off an explanatory group of words.
  Example: The tools of his trade—probe, mirror, cotton swabs—were neatly arranged on the dentist's tray.

  Unless the set-off expression ends a sentence, dashes must be used in pairs.

- Use a dash to mark a sudden break in thought that leaves a sentence unfinished.
  Example: He opened the door a crack and saw—

The Colon

- Use a colon after the salutation in a business letter.
  Example: Dear Board Member:

- Use a colon to separate hours from minutes.
  Example: The eclipse occurred at 10:36 a.m.

- A colon may, but need not always, be used to introduce a list, introduce a long quotation, or introduce a question.
  Example: My question is this: Are you willing to punch a time clock?

The Semicolon

- A semicolon may be used to join two short, related independent clauses.
  Example: Anne is working at the front desk on Monday; Ernie will take over on Tuesday.
  Two main clauses must be separated by a conjunction or by a semicolon or must be written as two sentences. A semicolon never precedes a coordinating conjunction. The same two clauses may be written as follows:
  > Autumn had come and the trees were almost bare.
  > Autumn had come; the trees were almost bare.
  > Autumn had come. The trees were almost bare.

- A semicolon may be used to separate two independent clauses that are joined by an adverb such as *however*, *therefore*, *otherwise*, or *nevertheless*. The adverb must be followed by a comma.
  Example: You may use a semicolon to separate this clause from the next; however, you will not be incorrect if you choose to write two separate sentences.
  If you are uncertain about how to use the semicolon to connect independent clauses, write two sentences instead.

- A semicolon should be used to separate a series of phrases or clauses when each of them contains commas.
  Example: The old gentleman's heirs were Margaret Whitlock, his half-sister; James Bagley, the butler; William Frame, his late cousin; Robert Bone; and his favorite charity, the Salvation Army.

The Apostrophe

- In a contraction, insert an apostrophe in place of the omitted letter or letters.
  Examples: have + not = haven't
  we + are = we're
  let + us = let's
  of the clock = o'clock
  class of 1985 = class of '85

- The apostrophe, when used to indicate possession, means *belonging to everything to the left of the apostrophe.*
  Examples: lady's = belonging to the lady
  ladies' = belonging to the ladies
  children's = belonging to the children

NOTE

Never begin a paragraph with a contraction.

To test for correct placement of the apostrophe, read *of the*.

Examples: childrens' = of the childrens (therefore incorrect)

girls' = of the girls (correct if it is the meaning intended)

Quotation Marks

- All directly quoted material must be enclosed by quotation marks. Words not quoted must remain outside the quotation marks.
  Example: "If it is hot on Sunday," she said, "we will go to the beach."

- An indirect quote must not be enclosed by quotation marks.
  Example: She said that we might go to the beach on Sunday.

- When a multiple-paragraph passage is quoted, each paragraph of the quotation must begin with quotation marks, but ending quotation marks are used only at the end of the last quoted paragraph.

- A period always goes inside the quotation marks, whether the quotation marks are used to denote quoted material, to set off titles—such as chapters in a book or titles of short stories—or to isolate words used in a special sense.
  Examples: Jane explained: "The house is just around the corner."

  The first chapter of *The Andromeda Strain* is entitled "The Country of Lost Borders."

- A comma always goes inside the quotation marks.
  Examples: "We really must go home," said the dinner guests.

  If your skills have become "rusty," you must study before you take the test.

  Three stories in Kurt Vonnegut's *Welcome to the Monkey House* are "Harrison Bergeron," "Next Door," and "EPICAC."

- A question mark goes inside the quotation marks if it is part of the quotation. If the whole sentence containing the quotation is a question, the question mark goes outside the quotation marks.
  Examples: He asked, "Was the airplane on time?"

  What did you really mean when you said "I do"?

- An exclamation mark goes inside the quotation marks if the quoted words are an exclamation, outside if the entire sentence including the quotation is an exclamation.
  Examples: The sentry shouted, "Drop your gun!"

  Save us from our "friends"!

- A colon and a semicolon always go *outside* the quotation marks.
  Example: He said, "War is destructive"; she added, "Peace is constructive."

- Words used in an unusual way may be placed inside quotation marks.
  Example: A surfer who "hangs ten" is performing a tricky maneuver on a surfboard, not staging a mass execution.

- A quotation within a quotation may be set apart by single quotes.
  Example: George said, "The philosophy 'I think, therefore I am' may be attributed to Descartes."

CAPITALIZATION RULES

- Capitalize the first word of a complete sentence.
  Example: Your desk top should appear neat and orderly.

- Capitalize the first word of a quoted sentence.
  Example: The teacher said, "Please write your name at the top of the paper."
  Do *not* capitalize the first word within quotation marks if it does not begin a complete sentence.
  Examples: "I was late," she explained, "because of the snow."
  Some groups would like to restrict certain liberties in the interest of "patriotism."

- Capitalize the letter *I* when it stands alone.

- Capitalize the first letter of the first, last, and each important word in the title of a book, play, article, etc.
  Examples: "The Mystery of the Green Ghost"
  A Night at the Opera

- Capitalize a title when it applies to a specific person, group, or document.
  Examples: The President will give a press conference this afternoon.
  Senators Goldwater and Tower were leading figures in the Conservative Party.
  Our Constitution should be strictly interpreted.
  Do *not* capitalize the same type of title when it does not make a specific reference.
  Examples: Some congressmen are liberal; others are more conservative.
  It would be useful for our club to write a constitution.

- Capitalize days of the week, months of the year, and holidays, but do *not* capitalize the seasons.
  Example: Labor Day, the last holiday of the summer, falls on the first Monday in September.

- Capitalize all proper names, including but not limited to: names of people, buildings, events, places and words formed using those places, organizations, and words referring to a sole God.
  Examples: John F. Smith
  Empire State Building
  Memorial Day
  Panama and Panamanian
  The United Fund
  Allah

- Capitalize the points of the compass only when referring to a specific place or area.
  Example: Many retired persons spend the winter in the South.

- Do *not* capitalize the points of the compass when they refer to a direction.
  Example: Many birds fly south in the winter.

- The only school subjects that are regularly capitalized are languages and specific place names used as modifiers.
  Example: Next year I will study French, biology, English literature, mathematics, European history, and ancient philosophy.

- A noun not regularly capitalized should be capitalized when it is used as part of a proper name.
  Example: Yesterday I visited Uncle Charles, my favorite uncle.

- In a letter:
    a. Capitalize all titles in the address and closing.
    Examples: Mr. John Jones, President Mary Smith, Chairman of the Board
    b. Capitalize the first and last words, titles, and proper names in the salutation.
    Examples: Dear Dr. Williams, My dear Sir:
    c. Capitalize only the first word in a complimentary closing.
    Example: Very truly yours,

EXERCISES: PUNCTUATION AND CAPITALIZATION

Exercise 1

Directions: Among the following sentences, look for errors in capitalization or punctuation. If you find no mistake, mark (D).

1. **(A)** He was not informed, that he would have to work overtime.
   (B) The wind blew several papers off his desk.
   (C) I believe this is the man whom you interviewed last week.
   (D) *No mistakes*

2. **(A)** If an employee wishes to attend the conference, she should fill out the necessary forms.
   (B) Mr. Wright's request cannot be granted under any conditions.
   (C) Charles Dole, who is a member of the committee, was asked to confer with commissioner Wilson.
   (D) *No mistakes*

3. **(A)** He is the kind of person who is always willing to undertake difficult assignments.
   (B) The teacher entered the room and said, "the work must be completed today."
   (C) The special project was assigned to Mary Green and me.
   (D) *No mistakes*

4. **(A)** Mr. Barnes, the bus dispatcher, has many important duties.
   (B) We checked the addresses once more and sent the letters to the mailroom.
   (C) Do you agree that this year's class is the best yet?
   (D) *No mistakes*

5. **(A)** Gerry had never been the type to run away from a challenge however his sister was the exact opposite and did not have a taste for adventure.
   (B) Rhett, an excellent fisherman, brought his new pole, a tackle box full of lures, and a cooler full of cold sodas on his trip to the ocean.
   (C) Mrs. Cromwell asked the waitress for the following items: a sharp steak knife, a glass of cold waiter, and a bottle of ketchup.
   (D) *No mistakes*

6. **(A)** Although I am willing to work on most holidays, I refuse to work on Labor Day.
   (B) Every Tuesday afternoon, Joan volunteers at Children's Hospital.
   (C) If you wish to be considered for the scholarship, you must file your application promptly.
   (D) *No mistakes*

7. **(A)** The new student asked the gym teacher if he could join the baseball team?

   (B) Girl Scout Troop 71 will march in the parade.

   (C) Mrs. Garcia asked Louisa and Henry to help bake cookies for the party.

   (D) *No mistakes*

8. **(A)** I find his study of the birds of North America to be fascinating.

   (B) The doctor suggested that my grandfather go South for the winter to avoid frequent colds.

   (C) Under the new rules, when do we revert to Eastern Standard Time?

   (D) *No mistakes*

9. **(A)** If you would like to spend the night, you may sleep in Tom's room.

   (B) The attack on Pearl Harbor, on December 7, 1941, came as a complete surprise.

   (C) "May I use the computer this afternoon," the boy asked?

   (D) *No mistakes*

10. **(A)** "If it rains on Friday," the boy mused, "the game may be played on Saturday instead."

    (B) The child's new bicycle lay on its side near the curb.

    (C) Whenever I drive on a New York street, I watch for potholes.

    (D) *No mistakes*

Exercise 2

Directions: Among the following sentences, look for errors in capitalization or punctuation. If you find no mistake, mark (D).

1. **(A)** I used to live in St. Paul, Minnesota, but I now reside in St. Augustine, Florida.

   (B) "I love to play the piano from morning till night," said the musician.

   (C) Lily answered the teacher's question correctly she was so proud.

   (D) *No mistakes*

2. **(A)** Every memorial day, my mother takes my picture next to the flag in front of our home.

   (B) Please submit an essay, two letters of recommendation, and the completed application form.

   (C) The reporter asked the senator about the election results.

   (D) *No mistakes*

3. **(A)** "I forgot my running shoes and can't go to the gym today," she explained.

   (B) The conference will be held in November in Asheville, North Carolina.

   (C) Marie shared her extra candy with Sofia, Eddie, and me.

   (D) *No mistakes*

4. **(A)** Saul and his best friend Madison went to see *The Guiding Hand*, the newest movie at the Pekoe County Theater.

   (B) After Nomi's physical examination, Dr. Pembroke said to her, "You are in excellent health."

   (C) Aleck read the first seven chapters of the horror novel he purchased, *no turning back*, and couldn't sleep all night.

   (D) *No mistakes*

5. (A) Some students requested extra test-prep help before the important exam.

   (B) The art teacher asked, "has anyone seen the new exhibit at the museum?"

   (C) Heather recommended that the organization draft a new constitution.

   (D) *No mistakes*

6. (A) On their class trip to independence hall in Philadelphia, the students interviewed the actor who portrayed John Adams.

   (B) Our tour guide said that the school is accredited by the Southern Association of Colleges and Schools.

   (C) Please read the directions carefully, and hand in your test before the bell rings at 3:05.

   (D) *No mistakes*

7. (A) Students may study Chinese, French, German, or Spanish in their first year at our school.

   (B) Mrs. Young frowned as she asked, "Why are you late today?"

   (C) The childrens' shoes were under the leaves in the backyard.

   (D) *No mistakes*

8. (A) Julia handed out the twenty two new books to the students in her class.

   (B) Annual events include Parents' Weekend in the fall and Alumni Weekend in the spring.

   (C) Their dog, Quincy, always barked whenever anyone rang the doorbell.

   (D) *No mistakes*

9. (A) Because Ben lives so far from school, he needs to set his alarm to ring at 5 a.m. each day.

   (B) The event for new students will be held on Monday August 28 in the new gymnasium.

   (C) "Do you think we'll get to the party on time?" she asked me for the third time.

   (D) *No mistakes*

10. (A) "When you finish your homework," my mom said, "please set the table for dinner."

    (B) I was surprised to learn that Adam and Andrew are twins; they certainly don't look alike at all.

    (C) I am always sad when the hummingbirds fly south for the winter.

    (D) *No mistakes*

ANSWER KEYS AND EXPLANATIONS

Exercise 1

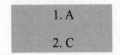
1. A	3. B
2. C	4. D

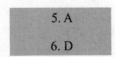
5. A	7. A
6. D	8. B

9. C	
10. D	

1. **The correct answer is (A).** There is no reason for a comma between the verb and its object. The sentence should read: He was not informed that he would have to work overtime.

2. **The correct answer is (C).** Commissioner Wilson is a specific commissioner, and so the *C* must be capitalized.

3. **The correct answer is (B).** The direct quote must begin with a capital *T*.

4. **The correct answer is (D).** *No mistakes.*

5. **The correct answer is (A).** As written, this is a run-on sentence. Remember the following rule: A semicolon may be used to separate two independent clauses that are joined by an adverb such as *however, therefore, otherwise,* or *nevertheless.*

6. **The correct answer is (D).** *No mistakes.*

7. **The correct answer is (A).** This is a declaratory statement, not a direct question; it must end with a period.

8. **The correct answer is (B).** Do not capitalize directions, only place names.

9. **The correct answer is (C).** The boy's question needs to end with a question mark: "May I use the computer this afternoon?" The entire sentence is a simple statement that should end with a period.

10. **The correct answer is (D).** *No mistakes.*

Exercise 2

1. C	3. D
2. A	4. C

5. B	7. C
6. A	8. A

9. B	
10. D	

1. **The correct answer is (C).** This is a run-on sentence. It contains two independent clauses joined with no punctuation. One way to correct this is to add a comma followed by a coordinating conjunction: Lily answered the teacher's question correctly, and she was so proud. Another option would be to use a semicolon: Lily answered the teacher's question correctly; she was so proud.

2. **The correct answer is (A).** Holidays, along with days of the week and months of the year should be capitalized, so the M and D in Memorial Day should be capitalized.

3. **The correct answer is (D).** *No mistakes.*

4. **The correct answer is (C).** Book titles, such as *No Turning Back,* should be capitalized.

answers exercises

5. **The correct answer is (B).** The first word in a quoted sentence should be capitalized. The sentence should read: The art teacher asked, "Has anyone seen the new exhibit at the museum?"

6. **The correct answer is (A).** Independence Hall should be capitalized since it is the name of a building.

7. **The correct answer is (C).** The apostrophe belongs before the s here. As noted earlier, when used to indicate possession, an apostrophe means belonging to everything to the left of the apostrophe. In this case, the children's shoes means the shoes belonging to the children.

8. **The correct answer is (A).** Hyphenate numbers from twenty-one to ninety-nine. The number should appear as twenty-two.

9. **The correct answer is (B).** Commas are needed to separate parts of dates, so the sentence in choice (B) should read: The event for new students will be held on Monday, August 28, in the new gymnasium.

10. **The correct answer is (D).** *No mistakes.*

SUMMING IT UP

- The HSPT®, the COOP, and the TACHS exams test your writing skills regarding punctuation and capitalization.

- To prepare for this section, you must PRACTICE. Read the rules listed in this chapter and practice them.

English Usage

chapter 13

OVERVIEW

- **Principles of grammar**
- **Troublesome words**
- **Exercises: English Usage**
- **Answer keys and explanations**
- **Summing it up**

The HSPT®, the TACHS, and the COOP exams will quiz you on your expertise in language usage. The COOP exam does this in the Reading and Language Arts section. The HSPT® lumps this subject with spelling, punctuation and capitalization, and composition in the Language Skills section. The TACHS tests this subject in the Language section.

Language usage includes a student's grasp of correct English and how it's used. Your expertise in this area is based on years of reading and hundreds of hours of classroom instruction on grammar. In answering language usage questions, you may have to consider problems of agreement, double negatives, and dangling modifiers. Word choice, punctuation, tense, and case may also enter into your decision on which answer is best.

The "Principles of Grammar" that follow may prove useful to you as you prepare for English usage questions. Just remember, a simple, direct statement is more effective than a wordy one.

PRINCIPLES OF GRAMMAR

Subject-Verb Agreement

- A verb must agree with its subject in number.
  Single subjects require singular verbs.
  Example: *She walks* to school every day.
  Plural subjects need plural verbs.
  Example: *They walk* home together.

- The number of the subject is not affected by a prepositional phrase that follows it.
  Examples: The *girl together with* her friends *walks* to school every day.
            One of the apples *is* rotten.

- In sentences beginning with *there* or *here*, the verb must agree with the noun that follows it.
  Examples: There *are* six *boys* in the class.
            Here *is* the *book* you wanted.

- *Each, every, everyone, everybody, someone, somebody, anyone, anybody, no one, nobody, either* and *neither* are singular and require singular verbs and pronouns.
  Example: *Everyone* on the team *thinks he can* win the prize.

- Singular subjects joined by *and* take a plural verb:
  Example: *John and Ted are* good friends.

- Two singular subjects joined by *or* or *nor* take a singular verb.
  Example: Meg or Mary is always first to answer.

- A singular and a plural subject joined by *or* or *nor* take a singular or plural verb, depending on which subject is nearer the verb.
  Examples: Neither Kim nor her *sisters are* ready yet.
            Neither her sisters nor *Kim is* ready yet.

- *Don't* is a contraction for *do not*. It is correct for first- and second-person singular and plural (*I don't, you don't, we don't*) and for third-person plural (*they don't*). Use *doesn't* with third-person singular pronouns or nouns.
  Examples: *It doesn't* matter to me.
            Bill doesn't know that song.

Pronoun Agreement

- A pronoun agrees with the words to which it refers in person (first, second, or third), number (singular or plural), and gender (masculine, feminine, or neuter).
  Examples: When the *boys* left, *they* took *their* books with *them*.
            Each *girl* must have *her* ticket.

- A pronoun following a linking verb must be in the subject form (*I, you, he, she, it, we, they*).
  Example: The woman in the photo *was she*.

- If a pronoun is the object of a preposition or an action verb, the pronoun must be in the object form (*me, you, him, her, it, us, them*).
  Examples: Would you like to go to the movies *with* John and *me*?
            The teacher *selected* Joan and *me* to lead the class.

- When a pronoun is used as an appositive, it must be in the same form as the word to which it refers. An appositive is a noun or pronoun that follows another noun or pronoun to identify or explain it.

Example: Ms. Ross, *my adviser*, suggested that I apply to this school.

If the appositive refers to a subject, use the subject form.

Example: The two pilots, *Captain Miller* and *he*, sat in the cockpit.

(*Captain Miller* and *he* are appositives referring to the subject. Therefore, the subject form, *he*, is required.)

If the appositive refers to an object, use the object form.

Example: The class chose two representatives—*Jeff* and *him*—to attend the meeting. (*Jeff* and *him* are appositives referring to *representatives*, the object of the verb *chose*. Therefore, the object form, *him*, is required.)

- A noun ending in *-ing* (a gerund) takes a possessive pronoun.
  Example: My mother objected to *my getting* home so late.

- Use the pronouns *who* and *whom* the same way you would use *he/she* and *him/her*. Use *who* wherever you could substitute *he* or *she*, and *whom* where you could substitute *him* or *her*.
  Examples: The prize was won by a man *who* everyone agreed was deserving of it.
  (Think: Everyone agreed *he* was deserving of it.)
  The woman *whom* they elected to be chairperson accepted with pleasure.
  (Think: They elected *her* to be chairperson.)

- *This* and *that* are singular and refer to singular words: *this kind* of book, *that sort* of book. *These* and *those* are plural and refer to plural words: *these kinds* of books, *those sorts of books*.

Adjective and Adverb Usage

- Use adverbs to modify action verbs.
  Example: The car drove *slowly* and *carefully* (not *slow* and *careful*) on the icy road.

- Use an adjective after a linking verb.
  Example: The flower smelled *sweet* (not *sweetly*).

- Use the comparative form of an adjective or adverb (the form that ends in *-er* or uses the word *more*) when comparing two things.
  Examples: Jim runs *faster* than Joe.
  Beth is *taller* than Amy.

- Use the superlative form of an adjective or adverb (the form that ends in *-est* or uses the word *most*) when comparing more than two things.
  Examples: Of all the boys on the team, Jim runs *fastest*.
  Beth is the *tallest* girl in the class.

- Avoid double negatives.
  Examples: The rain was so heavy we *could hardly* see.
  (*not*: The rain was so heavy we couldn't hardly see.)
  They *don't have any* homework tonight.
  (*not*: They don't have no homework tonight.)

TIP

One way to decide between *who* and *whom* in a sentence is to remember two things:
1. *Who* is followed by a verb
2. *Whom* is followed by a noun (which can also be a subject or a pronoun).

TROUBLESOME WORDS

There are a few groups of words that span the realms of spelling, punctuation, and usage. You probably have many of these under control. Others might consistently give you trouble. Your choice of the best version of a sentence might hinge upon your understanding the correct uses of the words in these troublesome groups.

- **their, they're, there**
  Their is the possessive of *they*.
  Example: The Martins claimed *their* dog from the pound because it belonged to them.
  They're is the contraction for *they are*.
  Example: Tom and Marie said that *they're* going skiing in February.
  There means at that place.
  Example: You may park your car over *there*.
  This last form is also used in sentences or clauses where the subject comes after the verb.
  Example: *There* is no one here by that name.

- **your, you're**
  Your is the possessive of *you*.
  Example: Didn't we just drive past *your* house?
  You're is the contraction for *you are*.
  Example: When we finish caroling, *you're* all invited inside for hot chocolate.

- **whose, who's**
  Whose is the possessive of *who*.
  Example: The handwriting is very distinctive, but I cannot remember *whose* it is.
  Who's is the contraction for *who is*.
  Example: *Who's* calling at this hour of night?

- **its, it's**
  Its is the possessive of *it*.
  Example: The injured cat is licking *its* wounds.
  It's is the contraction for *it is*.
  Example: *It's* much too early to leave for the airport.

- **which, who, that**
  Which as a relative pronoun refers only to objects.
  Example: This is the vase *which* the cat knocked over.
  Who and *whom* refer only to people.
  Example: The boy *who* won the prize is over there.
  That may refer to either objects or people. *That* is used only in restrictive clauses.
  Example: This is the vase *that* the cat knocked over. The boy *that* won the prize is over there.

- **learn, teach**
  To *learn* is to *acquire* knowledge. To *teach* is to *impart* knowledge.
  Example: My mother *taught* me all that I have *learned*.

- **between, among**

  Between commonly applies to only two people or things.

  Example: Let us keep this secret *between you and me*.

  Among always implies that there are more than two.

  Example: The knowledge is secure *among the members* of our club.

  Exception: Between may be used with more than two objects to show the relationship of each object to each of the others, as in "The teacher explained the difference *between* adjective, adverb, and noun clauses."

- **beside, besides**

  Beside is a preposition meaning *by the side of*.

  Example: He sat *beside* his sick father.

  Besides, an adverb, means *in addition to*.

  Example: *Besides* his father, his mother also was ill.

- **lay, lie**

  The verb to *lay*, except when referring to hens, may be used only if you could replace it with the verb to *put*. At all other times, use a form of the verb to *lie*.

  Examples: You may *lay* the books upon the table.

  Let sleeping dogs *lie*.

- **many/much, fewer/less, number/amount**

  The use of *many/much, fewer/less, number/amount* is governed by a simple rule of thumb. If the object can be counted, use *many, fewer, number*. If the object is thought of as a single mass or unit, use *much, less, amount*.

  Examples: *Many* raindrops make *much* water.

  If you have *fewer* dollars, you have *less* money.

  The *amount* of property you own depends upon the *number* of acres in your lot.

- **I, me**

  The choice of *I* or *me* when the first-person pronoun is used with one or more proper names may be tested by eliminating the proper names and reading the sentence with the pronoun alone.

  Examples: John, George, Marylou, and (me *or* I) went to the movies last night. (By eliminating the names, you can readily choose *I went to the movies*.)

  It would be very difficult for Mae and (I *or* me) to attend the wedding. (Without *Mae*, it is clear that *difficult for me* is correct.)

- **as, like**

  As is a conjunction introducing a subordinate clause, while *like*, in cases where the two words are confused, is a preposition. The object of a preposition is a noun or phrase.

  Examples: Speeding is a traffic violation, *as* you should know. (*You* is the subject of the clause; *should* is its verb.)

  He behaves *like* a fool.

  She prefers green vegetables *like* spinach.

NOTE

The English language has many irregularities; therefore, items like the troublesome words must be memorized in order to use them correctly in a sentence.

- **already, all ready**

  Already means *prior to some specified time.*

  Example: It is *already* too late to submit your application.

  All ready means *completely ready.*

  Example: The cornfield is *all ready* for the seed to be sown.

- **altogether, all together**

  Altogether means *entirely.*

  Example: It is *altogether* too foggy to drive safely.

  All together means *in sum* or *collectively.*

  Example: The family will be *all together* at the Thanksgiving dinner table.

- **two, to, too**

  Two is the numeral 2.

  Example: There are *two* sides to every story.

  To means *in the direction of.*

  Example: We shall go *to* school.

  Too means *more than* or *also.*

  Examples: It's *too* cold to go swimming today.

     We shall go, *too.*

EXERCISES: ENGLISH USAGE

Exercise 1

Directions: In the following questions, choose which of the four sentences is constructed best. The answer keys and explanations follow Exercise 3.

1. **(A)** It is the opinion of the commissioners that programs that include the construction of cut-rate municipal garages in the central business district is inadvisable.

   (B) Having reviewed the material submitted, the program for putting up cut-rate garages in the central business district seemed likely to cause traffic congestion.

   (C) The commissioners believe that putting up cut-rate municipal garages in the central business district is inadvisable.

   (D) Making an effort to facilitate the cleaning of streets in the central business district, the building of cut-rate municipal garages presents the problem that it would encourage more motorists to come into the central city.

2. **(A)** Since the report lacked the needed information, it was of no use to him.

   (B) This report was useless to him because there were no needed information in it.

   (C) Since the report did not contain the needed information, it was not real useful to him.

   (D) Being that the report lacked the needed information, he could not use it.

3. **(A)** In reviewing the typists' work reports, the job analyst found records of unusual typing speeds.

   (B) It says in the job analyst's report that some employees type with great speed.

   (C) The job analyst found that, in reviewing the typists' work reports, that some unusual typing speeds had been made.

   (D) In the reports of typists' speeds, the job analyst found some records that are kind of unusual.

4. **(A)** They do not ordinarily present these kind of reports in detail like this.

   (B) A report of this kind is not hardly ever given in such detail as this one.

   (C) This report is more detailed than what such reports ordinarily are.

   (D) A report of this kind is not ordinarily presented in as much detail as this one is.

5. **(A)** Elephants sucks water through their long, flexible trunks and squirts it into their mouths.

   (B) Every morning, Angel talks to his parrot Rudy while getting dressed for school.

   (C) The high school football team practices diligently every morning during the playing season.

   (D) Each year, the Brookville Public Library hosts an event that celebrates local writers and artists.

6. (A) If properly addressed, the letter will reach my mother and I.

(B) The letter had been addressed to myself and my mother.

(C) I believe the letter was addressed to either my mother or I.

(D) My mother's name, as well as mine, was on the letter.

7. (A) The paper we use for this purpose must be light, glossy, and stand hard usage as well.

(B) Only a light and a glossy, but durable, paper must be used for this purpose.

(C) For this purpose, we want a paper that is light, glossy, but that will stand hard wear.

(D) For this purpose, paper that is light, glossy, and durable is essential.

8. (A) This kind of worker achieves success through patience.

(B) Success does not often come to men of this type except they who are patient.

(C) Because they are patient, these sort of workers usually achieve success.

(D) This worker has more patience than any man in his office.

9. (A) You have got to get rid of some of these people if you expect to have the quality of the work improve.

(B) The quality of the work would improve if they would leave fewer people do it.

(C) I believe it would be desirable to have fewer persons doing this work.

(D) If you had planned on employing fewer people than this to do the work, this situation would not have arose.

10. (A) It is quite possible that we shall reemploy anyone whose training fits them to do the work.

(B) It is probable that we shall reemploy those who have been trained to do the work.

(C) Such of our personnel that have been trained to do the work will be again employed.

(D) We expect to reemploy the ones who have had training enough that they can do the work.

Exercise 2

Directions: Choose the word or group of words that should go into the blank to make a correct sentence.

1. All of the boys and Joyce took _____ baseball gloves to the ball game.

   (A) her

   (B) their

   (C) his

   (D) our

2. Dana was the _____ person who dared go into the haunted house.

   (A) most only

   (B) onliest

   (C) sole only

   (D) only

3. Molly and Brandon always knew that _____ wanted to add a swimming pool to their family home.

   (A) she

   (B) he

   (C) them

   (D) they

4. If Duncan had joined the soccer team, he _____ been the star.

   (A) should have

   (B) could of

   (C) would of

   (D) might have

5. Even before the wind had stopped, the rain _____ down.

   (A) was slowed

   (B) has been slowing

   (C) had been slowing

   (D) had been slowed

6. Last week, I had lunch with the girl _____ won the English prize.

   (A) who

   (B) whom

   (C) which

   (D) what

7. In choosing between chocolate and vanilla ice cream, I like chocolate ice cream _____.

   (A) most

   (B) best

   (C) better

   (D) more better

8. The jury is depending _____ the witness' statements.

   (A) about

   (B) of

   (C) upon

   (D) from

9. I would bring Grandma to visit you, _____ I have no car.

   (A) except

   (B) while

   (C) because

   (D) moreover

10. The little girl next door _____ on her swings all day.

    (A) swinged

    (B) swang

    (C) swung

    (D) has swinged

exercises

11. Neither Kenneth nor Larry _____ book report.

    (A) has completed their
    (B) have completed their
    (C) have completed his
    (D) has completed his

12. We had just finished shoveling the driveway _____ the plow came through again.

    (A) if
    (B) until
    (C) when
    (D) than

13. You must wait for the election results until we _____ the ballots.

    (A) had counted
    (B) have counted
    (C) are counting
    (D) have had counted

Directions: Make a complete sentence by choosing the words that should go into the blank.

14. After completing the lifesaving course _____.

    (A) and taking both the written and practical exams
    (B) gaining months of practical experience as an apprentice
    (C) you will be eligible to take the examination
    (D) at the YMCA under the auspices of the Red Cross

15. Ella, a professional carpenter, _____.

    (A) building is something that Ella really enjoys doing
    (B) built her first bookcase when she was 20 years old
    (C) her first serious building project will be a maple table and chair set
    (D) at work Ella is learning how to build a residential cabin

Directions: Select the sentence that means the same or most nearly the same as the underlined sentences.

16. The hiker was lost. A St. Bernard rescued him. It happened in the Alps.

    (A) The hiker was rescued by a St. Bernard lost in the Alps.
    (B) The lost Alpine hiker was rescued by a St. Bernard.
    (C) The hiker in the lost Alps was rescued by a St. Bernard.
    (D) In the Alps, the hiker was rescued by a lost St. Bernard.

17. Taxes are deducted from all wages. Workers who must work at night are paid overtime. The rate of tax to be withheld is fixed by law.

    (A) The law requires that people who are paid overtime must pay taxes.
    (B) According to the law, people who work at night must be paid overtime and deduct taxes.
    (C) The tax rate on overtime pay is deducted from wages by law and is paid at night.
    (D) By law, a fixed rate of taxes is deducted from all wages, including those paid overtime for night work.

Directions: Choose the word or group of words that makes the second sentence have the same meaning as the underlined sentence.

18. The accident victim was not only frightened but also in pain.

    The accident victim was _____.
    (A) neither frightened nor in pain
    (B) both frightened and in pain
    (C) either frightened or in pain
    (D) only frightened, not in pain

19. I may go to the movies tomorrow if I baby-sit today.

    _____ baby-sitting today, I may go to the movies tomorrow.
    (A) By
    (B) While
    (C) Until
    (D) Once

20. The criminal received consecutive sentences for his three crimes.

    The criminal has to serve his sentences _____.
    (A) all at once
    (B) after a period of delay
    (C) one at a time
    (D) with no opportunity for parole

21. We bought the house; moreover, we bought the adjacent lot.

    We bought _____.
    (A) the house because we bought the lot next door
    (B) the lot because we bought the house next door
    (C) the house but not the lot next door
    (D) the house and the lot next door

Exercise 3

Directions: For questions 1–8, look for errors in grammar, usage, or composition. If you find no mistakes, mark (D).

1. (A) He got off of the horse.
   (B) Your umbrella is better than mine.
   (C) How could I be other than glad?
   (D) *No mistakes*

2. (A) No one was there except Charles.
   (B) Your sample is the most satisfactory of all that I have seen.
   (C) I couldn't hardly do it.
   (D) *No mistakes*

3. (A) There should be no secrets between you and me.
   (B) I knew him to be the ringleader.
   (C) Everyone has studied his lesson.
   (D) *No mistakes*

4. (A) There are a piano and a phonograph in the room.
   (B) This is the man whom you interviewed last week.
   (C) He is reported to be killed.
   (D) *No mistakes*

5. (A) I have met but one person.
   (B) She is the tallest of the two girls.
   (C) The child is able to shape the clay easily.
   (D) *No mistakes*

6. (A) I wish I were going to Mexico with you.
   (B) Please loan me five dollars until payday.
   (C) The audience was enthusiastic.
   (D) *No mistakes*

7. (A) Because of the downpour, the carnival was postponed.
   (B) He walks up and said "Hello."
   (C) I already anticipate the good time I shall have at camp.
   (D) *No mistakes*

8. (A) The couple promised to renew they're wedding vows in Las Vegas every year.
   (B) It's important to place all of your garbage in the proper recycling bins, in order to be environmentally responsible.
   (C) Without a proper identification tag, it's difficult to determine whose piece of luggage this is.
   (D) *No mistakes*

Directions: For questions 9–14, choose the answer that best describes the group of words.

9. The worst feature of my summer camp was the food next was the latrine.
   (A) Run-on sentence
   (B) Complete sentence
   (C) *Not* a complete sentence

10. The man with the wart on the end of his nose gave his seat to the old woman.
    (A) Run-on sentence
    (B) Complete sentence
    (C) *Not* a complete sentence

11. Driving across the country in order to meet a deadline.
    (A) Run-on sentence
    (B) Complete sentence
    (C) *Not* a complete sentence

12. Once upon a time in a corner of the kitchen lived a small black cricket and the cricket made a lot of noise which annoyed the woman who lived in the house and so the woman swept the cricket out the door.
    (A) Run-on sentence
    (B) Complete sentence
    (C) *Not* a complete sentence

13. Bob and his brother Ted, who is a Civil War buff, went to Gettysburg during summer vacation and studied the battlefield together.
    (A) Run-on sentence
    (B) Complete sentence
    (C) *Not* a complete sentence

14. The strong wind suddenly increased to gale force and the sailboat to capsize.
    (A) Run-on sentence
    (B) Complete sentence
    (C) *Not* a complete sentence

Directions: For questions 15–20, choose the sentence that is correctly written.

15. (A) She had done much the people began to realize.
    (B) When the people began to realize how much she had done.
    (C) Soon the people began to realize how much she had done.
    (D) The people began to realize and how much she had done.

16. (A) Mounting the curb, the empty car crossed the sidewalk and came to rest against a building.
    (B) The empty car mounts the curb, crossed the sidewalk, and will come to rest against a building.
    (C) Mounting the curb when the empty car crosses the sidewalk and comes to rest against a building.
    (D) The curb was mounted by the empty car and crossed the sidewalk and came to rest against a building.

17. **(A)** I had forgotten my gloves realizing and returning to the theater.

    (B) Because I will realize that I forgot my gloves, I returned to the theater.

    (C) My gloves forgotten, realized, and returned to the theater.

    (D) Realizing I had forgotten my gloves, I returned to the theater.

18. **(A)** She learned that further practice will have had a good effect on her swimming ability.

    (B) She learned that further practice would have a good effect on her swimming ability.

    (C) Having learned and practiced had a good effect on her swimming ability.

    (D) Learning and practicing to have a good effect on her swimming ability.

19. **(A)** Assisting him his friend who lives in the next house.

    (B) Assisting him and living in the next house his friend.

    (C) His friend who lives in the next house assisting.

    (D) He was assisted by his friend who lives in the next house.

20. **(A)** The driver does all that it will be possible to do.

    (B) The driver, having done all that was possible.

    (C) The driver did all that was possible to do.

    (D) Doing all that is possible to do and driving.

ANSWER KEYS AND EXPLANATIONS

Exercise 1

1. C	3. A	5. A	7. D	9. C
2. A	4. D	6. D	8. A	10. B

1. **The correct answer is (C).** Choice (A) has an agreement error (*programs . . . are*). Choice (B) is incorrect because the program did not review the material. Choice (D) is totally garbled.

2. **The correct answer is (A).** In choice (B), the subject of the second clause is *information*, which is singular. In choice (C), the adverb should be *really*. *Being that*, in choice (D), is not an acceptable form.

3. **The correct answer is (A).** The indefinite pronoun *it* in choice (B) refers to nothing at all, so it means nothing. In choice (C), the *that* after *found* should be omitted. Choice (D) uses colloquial language, which is unacceptable in Standard Written English.

4. **The correct answer is (D).** Choice (A) contains an error of agreement (*these kind*). Choice (B) contains a double negative, *not hardly*. *What* is an extra word in choice (C).

5. **The correct answer is (A).** Remember, plural subjects require plural verb forms to be in proper agreement. The plural subject elephants require the use of plural verbs: *suck* and *squirt*.

6. **The correct answer is (D).** Choices (A) and (C) use the subject-form pronoun, *I*, where the object-form, *me*, is required. In choice (B), the object of the preposition *to* should be *me*, not *myself*.

7. **The correct answer is (D).** The sentences in choices (A), (B), and (C) are not parallel in construction. All the words that modify *paper* should be in the same form.

8. **The correct answer is (A).** In choice (B), *men* is the implied subject of the verb *are*. Inserting the subject into the phrase, you can see that it must read . . . *except to those (men) who are patient*. Choice (C) contains an error of number; to be correct, the phrase must read either *this sort of worker* or *these sorts of workers*. In choice (D), the comparison is incomplete. It must read *than any other man*.

9. **The correct answer is (C).** Choice (A) is wordy. In choice (B), the correct verb should be *have* in place of *leave*. In choice (D), *arose* is incorrect; the correct form is *arisen*.

10. **The correct answer is (B).** In choice (A), *them* should be *him* because it refers to *anyone*, which is singular. Choices (C) and (D) are wordy and awkward.

Exercise 2

1. B	6. A	10. C	14. C	18. B
2. D	7. C	11. D	15. B	19. A
3. D	8. C	12. C	16. B	20. C
4. D	9. A	13. B	17. D	21. D
5. C				

1. **The correct answer is (B).** The subject is plural and the object is plural; therefore, the possessive pronoun must be plural. The subject is in the third person, not the first, so *their*, not *our*, is the correct word.

2. **The correct answer is (D).** *Only* is an exclusive term. It cannot be modified in any way.

3. **The correct answer is (D).** This sentence requires a plural pronoun to replace the plural subject in this sentence, *Molly and Brandon*. The pronoun *they* is the correct choice.

4. **The correct answer is (D).** *Of* is not an auxiliary verb, so choices (B) and (C) are automatically incorrect. Choice (D) is more in tune with the nature of the sentence than is choice (A).

5. **The correct answer is (C).** To show that one past activity (the *slowing*) occurred before another past activity (the *stopping*) requires the *had been* construction (past perfect). *Had been slowed*, choice (D), implies that an external force was working on the rain. *Had been slowing* more accurately describes the end of a storm.

6. **The correct answer is (A).** *Who* is the subject of the verb *won*. (Think: *She* won the prize.) *Which* may only be used to apply to things. *What* is not a pronoun.

7. **The correct answer is (C).** The comparison between two objects requires *more* or *better*. *More better*, choice (D), is redundant and incorrect. *Most* and *best,* choices (A) and (B), refer to comparison among three or more objects.

8. **The correct answer is (C).** The proper idiomatic use is *depend on* or *depend upon*.

9. **The correct answer is (A).** In this sentence, *except* serves as a conjunction. *But* would fit into the blank in the same way. All of the other choices make no sense in the context of the sentence.

10. **The correct answer is (C).** The past tense of *swing* is *swung*.

11. **The correct answer is (D).** The construction *neither/nor* creates a singular subject (or object). Because the subject is singular, both the verb and the possessive pronoun must be singular as well.

12. **The correct answer is (C).** The sentence describes two activities in terms of their relationship in time. Only choice (C) makes sense.

13. **The correct answer is (B).** A present activity that is dependent on a future activity requires that the future activity be stated in the present perfect, *have counted*.

14. **The correct answer is (C).** The sentence fragment is nothing more than an introductory prepositional phrase. The completion must supply both subject and verb.

15. **The correct answer is (B).** The correct answer must be in the proper tense. Since Ella is a professional carpenter, her first building project must have already occurred. *Built* is the correct past tense for this verb, which is appropriate for this sentence.

16. **The correct answer is (B).** The correct answer must give correct information as to who was lost, where he was lost, and how he was rescued.

17. **The correct answer is (D).** The tax rate and the fact of withholding are established by law. Overtime pay is not established by law, but it does constitute wages subject to withholding.

18. **The correct answer is (B).** The term *not only . . . but also* is inclusive.

19. **The correct answer is (A).** The sentence is conditional and in reverse sequence: "I may do something tomorrow *if* I do something today." Reverse the sentence: "By doing something today, I may do something else tomorrow."

20. **The correct answer is (C).** *Consecutive* means *one after the other*. The word that means *all at the same time* is concurrent.

21. **The correct answer is (D).** The word *moreover* simply means *in addition to* or *also*. It does not imply any causality.

Exercise 3

1. A	5. B	9. A	13. B	17. D
2. C	6. B	10. B	14. C	18. B
3. D	7. B	11. C	15. C	19. D
4. C	8. A	12. A	16. A	20. C

1. **The correct answer is (A).** *Off of* is an unacceptable construction: He got off the horse.

2. **The correct answer is (C).** *Hardly* is a negative word, and so *couldn't hardly* is an unacceptable double negative: I could hardly do it.

3. **The correct answer is (D).** *No mistakes.*

4. **The correct answer is (C).** The activity began in the past (he *was* killed) and is completed in the present (is reported *now*). Therefore, the present perfect tense should be used. The sentence should read: "He is reported to *have been killed.*"

5. **The correct answer is (B).** The comparison is between two girls; therefore, *taller* is correct.

6. **The correct answer is (B).** *Loan* is a noun. The sentence requires the verb *lend.*

7. **The correct answer is (B).** The two verbs should be in the same tense. He *walked* up and *said* "Hello."

8. **The correct answer is (A).** *There, their,* and *there* are typically confused words. In this sentence, the possessive *their* is required.

9. **The correct answer is (A).** The two complete, independent clauses must either be separated into two sentences or be joined by a semicolon.

10. **The correct answer is (B).** This sentence is complete.

11. **The correct answer is (C).** This is not a complete sentence. It is a sentence fragment that either needs a subject (*Juan was driving across the country in order to meet a deadline.*) or needs to be joined with an independent clause (*Driving across the country in order to meet a deadline, Juan raced along in his red convertible.*).

12. **The correct answer is (A).** There are actually three independent clauses here. The best correction would be to eliminate the first *and* and to begin a second sentence with "The cricket." The second *and* should be eliminated and be replaced by a comma.

13. **The correct answer is (B).** This sentence is complete.

14. **The correct answer is (C).** The sentence fragment, as organized, calls for a compound verb: *increased* to gale force and (try inserting) *caused the sailboat to capsize.*

15. **The correct answer is (C).** Choice (A) is a run-on sentence. Choice (B) is a sentence fragment. In choice (D), the *and* is superfluous.

16. **The correct answer is (A).** Choice (B) mixes tenses illogically. Choice (C) is a sentence fragment. In choice (D), the curb crosses the street and comes to rest against the building.

17. **The correct answer is (D).** No other choice makes sense.

18. **The correct answer is (B).** Choice (A) confuses tenses; choices (C) and (D) are sentence fragments.

19. **The correct answer is (D).** No other choice is a complete sentence.

20. **The correct answer is (C).** Choice (A) confuses tenses; choices (B) and (D) are sentence fragments.

answers exercises

SUMMING IT UP

- The COOP exam tests English usage in the Reading and Language Arts section. The HSPT® includes it in the Language Skills section with spelling, punctuation, and capitalization. The TACHS includes it in the Language section.

- Study, learn, and practice the "Principles of Grammar" given in this chapter. They will help you not only on the test but also throughout school and life.

Language Composition and Expression

chapter 14

OVERVIEW

- Tips for answering language composition and expression questions
- Exercises: Language Composition and Expression
- Answer keys and explanations
- Summing it up

Your studies of spelling, punctuation, capitalization, and grammar all contribute to your skills in language expression, another crucial part of any entrance exam. Language expression, also called language composition, is a skill that you'll use in all kinds of high school course work and exams and in your college applications, as well.

Although the exams covered in this book do not include essay questions, COOP, TACHS, and HSPT® exams have found a few ways to test your language expression skills. These exams have tucked questions into test sections of English usage and language expression that are designed to tap your potential for composition. Among these are questions that ask you to move a sentence to another location in the paragraph or to remove a sentence that does not belong. Other composition questions require you to identify topic sentences or choose the best development of topic sentences that are given.

The area of language expression is one in which all test-makers are experimenting at this time. New measures might crop up on the next edition of many of the high school exams administered over the next few years.

TIPS FOR ANSWERING LANGUAGE COMPOSITION AND EXPRESSION QUESTIONS

Composition questions make up only a small portion of the exam, but those few questions might be among the most difficult and time-consuming on the test. Though you can't become an expert essayist in just a few weeks, you can familiarize yourself with some of the basic guidelines of composition, and you can learn how to focus your concentration to address these questions on your exam. Language expression questions typically test topic development and appropriateness. The following sections give you some common-sense tips and guidelines to use when you encounter questions dealing with these areas of language expression.

Tackling Topic Development Questions

What do we mean by "development"? The concept is relatively simple, though the task can be a bit more difficult. Topic development requires that you be able to clearly understand the main point or idea of information, and then recognize additional information that logically expands upon or further clarifies that main point or idea. Topic development is much like finishing a story that someone else has started.

Topic development questions come in a number of forms. Here are four tips that will help you tackle these questions on the exams:

1. If the question gives you a topic sentence and asks you to develop that sentence, your task is to choose a second and third sentence that best develop the idea presented in the first sentence. You aren't just choosing some sentences that refer to the same subject presented in the topic sentence. You have to choose the sentences that best expand upon or clarify the topic.

2. The question might give you an essay title and then ask that you choose a topic sentence that would best express the idea of that essay. You have to choose a sentence that relates well to the subject presented by the title and that is broad enough to allow for further development of a paragraph.

3. If the question gives you a title and asks you simply to choose a sentence that belongs under that title, you must weed out the sentences that are related to but not entirely relevant to the topic.

4. The occasional answer choice "None of these" complicates your task and makes the question much more difficult. On the other questions, you know that one of the answers is the best solution to topic development, and you can use the process of elimination to improve your odds of landing on the correct response. When you're faced with a "None of these" response, you might not be able to use your guessing skills to find the right answer. If you can't find the answer to one of these questions, just move on. Don't let it hold you up too long.

Tackling Appropriateness Questions

Questions that ask whether a particular sentence is appropriate to a specific paragraph are, in a way, asking you to perform the same skills you use in topic development, but in reverse! With these questions, rather than choosing the best way to add to the information about a topic, you're asked to choose which information definitely does or does not belong, or to determine where the best placement of that information might be.

If you can write a well-organized composition, you'll know how to allocate ideas into paragraphs. Unfortunately, these are not skills that you can develop right this minute. Take time to go over your returned written class work and learn from your teachers' comments. If you do not understand some comments or the reasons for some low grades, ask your teachers for explanations and help.

EXERCISE: LANGUAGE COMPOSITION AND EXPRESSION

1. Salting highways in winter is undoubtedly helpful to the motorist, yet this practice may actually cause a great deal of harm.

   (A) Salt works more quickly than chemical ice melters because it does not require heat to go into action. Salt mixed with sand offers especially good traction.

   (B) While melting the ice and eliminating slippery conditions, the same salt eats into the road surface itself, creating dangerous potholes. Further, the salty runoff leaches into the soil and kills surrounding vegetation.

   (C) A small amount of salt is a dietary necessity, especially in hot, dry climates. Large amounts of dietary salt, however, lead to water retention and high blood pressure.

   (D) Salt is inexpensive because it occurs abundantly in nature. Highways in the Rocky Mountains should have good safety records because they are so close to Utah, a great source of salt.

2. Mesa Verde is a great flat-topped mountain that rises dramatically above the surrounding Colorado desert.

   (A) In contrast to this desert, Mesa Verde is fertile and well-watered, a green oasis to which men have been drawn since ancient times. Within the sheer cliff walls of these canyons, nature has carved out vast caverns in soft sandstone rock.

   (B) In 1275, a severe 24-year drought hit the Mesa Verde area. The Cliff Dwellers, hounded by their relentless enemies and forces they could not comprehend, abandoned their cities and fields and fled from Mesa Verde.

   (C) At Mesa Verde, the *Anasazi* found favorable growing conditions. The legends call them the *Anasazi*, the Ancient Ones.

   (D) Villages, towns, and ultimately great cities appeared on the mesa tops. Tools and implements became more diverse and elaborate.

Directions: Choose the topic sentence that best fits the paragraph.

3. They set fires for many different reasons. Sometimes a shopkeeper sees no way out of losing his business and sets fire to it to collect the insurance. Another type of arsonist wants revenge and sets fire to the home or shop of someone he feels has treated him unfairly.

   (A) They don't look like criminals, but they cost the nation millions of dollars in property loss and sometimes loss of life.

   (B) Arsonists of this type have even been known to help fight the fire.

   (C) Arsonists are persons who set fires deliberately.

   (D) Some arsonists just like the excitement of seeing the fire burn and watching the firefighters at work.

4. But you ought not to despise it, for it can help you and your family obtain many of the good things of life. It can buy an adequate diet, one of the basics of good health. It can make it easier for your children to secure an education. When necessary, it can provide medicine and medical care.

   (A) Money can offer a great opportunity for you to help others.

   (B) Money can be the means for a comfortable house, for travel, for good books, and for hobbies and recreation.

   (C) Mainly people consider that amassing great wealth is a goal in itself.

   (D) Certainly money should not be your chief aim in life.

Directions: Choose the sentence that does not belong in the paragraph.

5. (1) In a democratic state, people are allowed to have certain freedoms. (2) They can speak their views freely, even if these views are against the government. (3) Andrew Jackson, who served from 1829–1837, was the first president elected by the Democratic Party. (4) They can express their views freely in the media, such as newspapers. (5) Citizens are free to gather together in groups to discuss political or religious issues. (6) They can form political parties, and they can elect the people they choose to govern them. (7) In a democratic state, no one can be arrested for expressing their views about politics. (8) The role of the government is to keep its citizens secure and to protect their freedoms.

   (A) Sentence 2

   (B) Sentence 3

   (C) Sentence 4

   (D) Sentence 5

6. (1) Hermit crabs are aquatic crustaceans that often dwell in saltwater reefs and near shorelines. (2) Hermit crabs typically protect their soft, curved abdomens from potential predators by wearing a shell, which is typically salvaged from sea snails or bivalves. (3) Other creatures that have shells include turtles and armadillos. (4) Did you know that hermit crabs have gills, which need to stay wet so they can breathe?

   (A) Sentence 1

   (B) Sentence 2

   (C) Sentence 3

   (D) Sentence 4

Directions: Choose the best answer.

7. Where should the sentence, "Prior to the Civil War, the steamboat was the center of life in the thriving Mississippi towns," be placed in the paragraph below?

   (1) With the war came the railroads. (2) River traffic dwindled, and the white-painted vessels rotted at the wharves. (3) During World War I, the government decided to relieve rail congestion by reviving the long-forgotten waterways. (4) Today, steamers, diesels, and barges ply the Mississippi.

   (A) Before sentence 1
   (B) Between sentences 2 and 3
   (C) Between sentences 3 and 4
   (D) The sentence does not fit in this paragraph.

8. Where should the sentence, "It can damage the heart and also the blood vessels," be placed in the paragraph below?

   (1) Patients with the condition known as "Type 2" diabetes suffer from the same basic problem as patients with "Type 1" diabetes. (2) In short, their bodies are not able to use the sugar in their blood very effectively. (3) This blood sugar, known as glucose, becomes very high in patients with diabetes, and it can cause many problems. (4) People with Type 2 diabetes usually have high blood pressure as well, which puts even more of a strain on the heart and circulatory system.

   (A) Between sentences 1 and 2
   (B) Between sentences 2 and 3
   (C) Between sentences 3 and 4
   (D) Between sentences 4 and 5

9. Which of the following sentences best fits under the topic, "The Symbolic Use of Bears"?

   (A) Dancing bears provide a comical form of entertainment at street fairs.
   (B) Small children love to hug teddy bears because they are soft and warm.
   (C) The bear has long been the symbol of Russia.
   (D) None of these

10. Which topic is best for a one-paragraph theme?

   (A) Development and Decline of the Whaling Industry
   (B) The Effects of Automation upon the Farming Industry
   (C) The Advantage of Using a Heavier Baseball Bat
   (D) None of these

ANSWER KEY AND EXPLANATIONS

1. B	3. C	5. B	7. A	9. C
2. A	4. D	6. C	8. C	10. C

1. **The correct answer is (B).** Choice (B) picks up where the topic sentence leaves off. It explains how the salt is helpful and then gives examples of the harm caused by salt. Choice (A) is also not a bad one. This choice amplifies the action of salt on ice and tells of its beneficial effects. Choices (C) and (D) do not develop the topic sentence at all. If you were not offered choice (B), you could choose choice (A) over choices (C) and (D) and have an acceptable answer. However, because you must choose the *best* from among all of the choices, choice (B) is the answer.

2. **The correct answer is (A).** The topic sentence introduces both Mesa Verde and the Colorado desert, and choice (A) flows naturally by contrasting Mesa Verde to the desert and then further describing Mesa Verde. A clear second-best choice is (C). However, a transitional sentence would be desirable to introduce the *Anasazi*. Choices (B) and (D) do nothing to develop the topic sentence.

3. **The correct answer is (C).** Most often, a definition makes a good topic sentence. This definition sets a good reference point for the pronoun, "they," which begins the next sentence. Choices (A) and (B) cannot be first sentences since they refer to antecedents that aren't there. Choice (D) might serve as a topic sentence but not as the topic sentence for this particular paragraph. Choice (D) would lead to a very different paragraph development.

4. **The correct answer is (D).** Choice (D) as topic sentence sets up a nice contrast with the "but" that follows it. Choices (A) and (B) set up meaningless contrasts. Choice (C) makes a weak topic sentence, creating confusion of person (people . . . you) and leaving an unclear reference for the "it" that is not to be despised.

5. **The correct answer is (B).** Although this paragraph discusses the types of freedoms associated with democracies, it does not address political parties. Sentence 3 provides information about a prominent member of the Democratic Party, which is not the focus of this paragraph.

6. **The correct answer is (C).** This is an informative passage about the hermit crab; sentence 3 provides only tangential information about other animals that have shells and does not belong in the paragraph.

7. **The correct answer is (A).** The organization of this paragraph is chronological. Because the third sentence discusses relief of rail congestion during World War I, it is clear that the war of the first sentence is the Civil War. Events prior to the Civil War should be mentioned before events that happened during the Civil War.

8. **The correct answer is (C).** The topic sentence introduces the subject of the Type 2 diabetes and indicates that more information about this condition will follow. Elevated blood sugar levels and the resulting problems are mentioned in the second and third sentences, so a description of these problems would logically follow. Therefore the sentence should be placed between sentences (3) and (4).

9. **The correct answer is (C).** Choices (A) and (B) tell of actual uses of bears.

10. **The correct answer is (C).** This is a limited topic that could be dealt with in one paragraph. The topic also lends itself to being one paragraph in a longer, more comprehensive essay.

SUMMING IT UP

- The COOP, the HSPT®, and the TACHS use multiple-choice questions that ask you to move a sentence to another location in the paragraph, remove a sentence that does not belong, identify topic sentences, or choose the best development of topic sentences.

- Topic development requires that you be able to clearly understand the main point or idea of information, and then recognize additional information that logically expands upon or further clarifies that main point or idea.

- Appropriateness questions ask you to choose which information definitely does or does not belong, or to determine where the best placement of that information might be.

PART IV
QUANTITATIVE AND NONVERBAL SKILLS

Quantitative Reasoning

OVERVIEW

- **The best approach**
- **Exercises: Quantitative Reasoning**
- **Answer keys and explanations**
- **Summing it up**

The COOP includes a Quantitative Reasoning section. Unlike the other test components, the Quantitative Reasoning section does not test your knowledge of formulas or facts. Instead, it tests your ability to determine the relationship between elements and the process of deducing these relationships.

This chapter gives you some in-depth instruction for working with reasoning questions by focusing on number relationships, visual problems, and symbol relationships. These are the most common types of quantitative reasoning questions you'll see on the COOP. The information and practice you'll get in this chapter will give you all the help you need to solve any quantitative reasoning questions you may encounter on other standardized tests.

The Quantitative Reasoning section is similar to the Series Reasoning section of the test because you need to use the same skills to work through the questions—concentration, logical thinking, and the ability to be flexible in how you approach the questions. When you begin to work through the quantitative reasoning questions to try to figure out the relationship between the elements, you may find that the answer you come up with is not one of the answer choices! Don't be discouraged. All you need to do is to try another approach to find out what other relationship is reasonable. We're going to show you how.

THE BEST APPROACH

On the COOP, the quantitative reasoning questions will appear as groups of similar questions. In other words, each type of question will be presented in a group. Before each group of questions, there will be instructions telling you how to answer the questions. While it is important that you read the instructions and make sure that you understand them, it is equally important to know that all the questions are really asking you the same thing: "What is the relationship between the elements in each expression?"

chapter 15

Number Relationships

Before each group of number relationship questions, the instructions will say that you must find the relationship between the two numbers in an expression. Each question will consist of three expressions, one on each line. Each of the first two will have a number with an arrow pointing to an empty box, then an arrow pointing to another number. The last line, the "question expression," will have the number on the left with an arrow pointing to an empty box, then an arrow pointing to a question mark. The entire question looks like the following:

$2 \rightarrow \boxed{} \rightarrow 4$ 6   8   10   12
$6 \rightarrow \boxed{} \rightarrow 8$ (A)   (B)   (C)   (D)
$8 \rightarrow \boxed{} \rightarrow ?$

To solve this question, approach each expression separately and calculate which operation and number should go into the box.

For instance, to get from 2 to 4, you could stick in the relationship

+2 (or plus 2)

so that

$2 + 2 = 4$.

Now look at the next expression. To get from 6 to 8, you would also put in the relationship

+2

so that

$6 + 2 = 8$.

This means that the relationship between the numbers in each expression is + 2. So just stick that same relationship into the question expression.

$8 + 2 = 10$.

So, choice (C) is correct.

Now remember that it is sometimes possible for more than one relationship to fit into the box. You'll know if you've chosen the wrong relationship because you won't get the same relationship for the first two expressions.

Let's look at our sample question again:

$2 \rightarrow \boxed{} \rightarrow 4$ 6   8   10   12
$6 \rightarrow \boxed{} \rightarrow 8$ (A)   (B)   (C)   (D)
$8 \rightarrow \boxed{} \rightarrow ?$

Let's say that for the first expression you thought the relationship was

×2 (or times 2)

so that

$2 \times 2 = 4$.

This doesn't work for the second expression.

$6 \times 2 = 12$, not 8.

So you know that $\times 2$ (or times 2) is not the correct relationship, and you should go back to the first expression and look for another relationship that fits.

If you use this method of finding the relationship that applies to each expression, you will be able to work through any number question in the Quantitative Reasoning section.

Visual Problems

Visual problems ask you to assess a drawing visually. Essentially, these questions are asking you to express the relationship of the parts of the drawing in the same terms in which the answer choices are written. Let's take a look at a question:

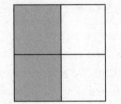

$$\begin{array}{cccc} \dfrac{1}{8} & \dfrac{1}{4} & \dfrac{1}{3} & \dfrac{1}{2} \\ \textbf{(A)} & \textbf{(B)} & \textbf{(C)} & \textbf{(D)} \end{array}$$

In this drawing, the square is separated into four smaller squares. Two of them are shaded and two are white.

The directions for this question type say, "Find the fraction of the grid that is shaded." There are four squares total. Two of the four squares are shaded. You know that $\frac{2}{4}$ is equal to $\frac{1}{2}$. Therefore, the correct answer is (D).

Symbol Relationships

Symbol relationship questions are questions that use symbols or drawings of objects to represent numbers. There are two steps to answering a symbol question. The first is to figure out how the symbols relate to each other. The second is to answer the question in the instructions.

Each question will consist of a drawing with two symbols. Then there will be four answer choices, also containing drawings of the symbols. Look at the symbols and anything else in the drawing to figure out the relationship between the symbols. Take a look at this question:

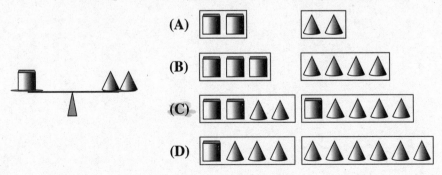

In this question, the symbols are cube and cone shapes.

The instructions say, "Look at the scale that shows sets of shapes of equal weight. Find an equivalent pair of sets that could also balance the scale." In other words, figure out what the relationships are between the answer choice expressions, and choose the one that equals the relationship on the scale.

Choice (A) shows that two cube shapes equal two cone shapes, or 2 cubes = 2 cones. We know that one cube shape equals two cone shapes, or 1 cube = 2 cones.

Choice (B) shows that three cube shapes equal four cone shapes, or 3 cubes = 4 cones. We already know that two cube shapes equal four cone shapes, so this can't be correct.

Choice (C) shows that two cube shapes and two cone shapes equal one cube shape and four cone shapes, or (2 cubes + 2 cones) = (1 cube + 4 cones). This one's a little tricky. There's a cube shape on each side of the equal sign, so let's remove it. We're left with one cube shape and two cone shapes equal four cones, or (1 cube + 2 cones) = 4 cones. Now we've got two cone shapes on each side of the equal sign, so let's remove those. We're left with one cube shape equals two cone shapes. Since one cube equals two cones on our scale, this answer choice is correct. But let's check the last one, choice (D), just to be sure.

Choice (D) shows that one cube shape plus three cone shapes equal six cone shapes. There are three cone-shaped weights on each side of the equal sign, so let's remove them. We're left with one cube-shaped weight equals three cone-shaped weights. Since one cube-shaped weight equals two cone-shaped weights, this can't be correct.

If you use this same method of finding the relationship that applies to each set of symbols, you will be able to work through any symbol question in the Quantitative Reasoning section.

EXERCISES: QUANTITATIVE REASONING

Directions: For numbers 1–7, find the relationship of the numbers in one column to the numbers in the other column. Then find the missing number.

1. $1 \rightarrow \boxed{} \rightarrow 5$
   $5 \rightarrow \boxed{} \rightarrow 9$
   $9 \rightarrow \boxed{} \rightarrow ?$

1	5	13	19
(A)	(B)	(C)	(D)

2. $8 \rightarrow \boxed{} \rightarrow 10$
   $16 \rightarrow \boxed{} \rightarrow 18$
   $12 \rightarrow \boxed{} \rightarrow ?$

12	14	16	18
(A)	(B)	(C)	(D)

3. $12 \rightarrow \boxed{} \rightarrow 8$
   $8 \rightarrow \boxed{} \rightarrow 4$
   $4 \rightarrow \boxed{} \rightarrow ?$

0	1	2	4
(A)	(B)	(C)	(D)

4. $\frac{1}{4} \rightarrow \boxed{} \rightarrow \frac{1}{2}$
   $\frac{1}{2} \rightarrow \boxed{} \rightarrow 1$
   $3 \rightarrow \boxed{} \rightarrow ?$

2	3	5	6
(A)	(B)	(C)	(D)

5. $2 \rightarrow \boxed{} \rightarrow 4$
   $3 \rightarrow \boxed{} \rightarrow 9$
   $4 \rightarrow \boxed{} \rightarrow ?$

8	12	13	16
(A)	(B)	(C)	(D)

6. $21 \rightarrow \boxed{} \rightarrow 7$
   $7 \rightarrow \boxed{} \rightarrow \frac{7}{3}$
   $\frac{7}{3} \rightarrow \boxed{} \rightarrow ?$

14	7	$\frac{7}{9}$	$\frac{1}{3}$
(A)	(B)	(C)	(D)

7. $5 \rightarrow \boxed{} \rightarrow 1$
   $4 \rightarrow \boxed{} \rightarrow 1$
   $3 \rightarrow \boxed{} \rightarrow ?$

1	2	3	4
(A)	(B)	(C)	(D)

Directions: For numbers 8–13, find the fraction of the grid that is shaded.

8.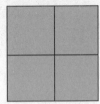

$\frac{1}{4}$ $\frac{1}{3}$ $\frac{1}{2}$ 1

(A)   (B)   (C)   (D)

9.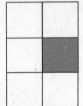

$\frac{1}{3}$ $\frac{1}{4}$ $\frac{1}{5}$ $\frac{1}{6}$

(A)   (B)   (C)   (D)

10.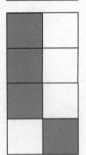

$\frac{1}{2}$ $\frac{1}{3}$ $\frac{1}{5}$ $\frac{1}{8}$

(A)   (B)   (C)   (D)

11.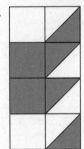

$\frac{1}{2}$ $\frac{1}{4}$ $\frac{1}{8}$ $\frac{1}{16}$

(A)   (B)   (C)   (D)

12.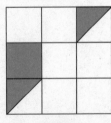

$\frac{1}{2}$ $\frac{1}{3}$ $\frac{2}{7}$ $\frac{2}{9}$

(A)   (B)   (C)   (D)

13.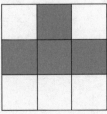

$\frac{1}{2}$ $\frac{4}{9}$ $\frac{5}{9}$ $\frac{8}{9}$

(A)   (B)   (C)   (D)

Directions: For questions 14–20, look at the scale that shows sets of shapes of equal weight. Find an equivalent pair of sets that would also balance the scale.

14.

(A)

(B)

(C)

(D)

15.

(A)

(B)

(C)

(D)

16.

(A)

(B)

(C)

(D)

17.

(A)

(B)

(C)

(D)

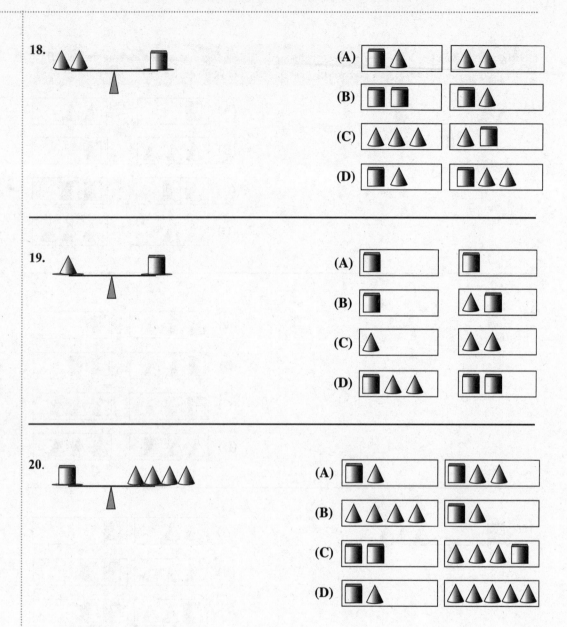

ANSWER KEY AND EXPLANATIONS

1. C	5. D	9. D	13. B	17. B
2. B	6. C	10. A	14. A	18. C
3. A	7. A	11. A	15. B	19. A
4. D	8. D	12. D	16. D	20. D

1. **The correct answer is (C).**

   $1 + 4 = 5$

   $5 + 4 = 9$

   $9 + 4 = 13$

2. **The correct answer is (B).**

   $8 + 2 = 10$

   $16 + 2 = 18$

   $12 + 2 = 14$

3. **The correct answer is (A).**

   $12 - 4 = 8$

   $8 - 4 = 4$

   $4 - 4 = 0$

4. **The correct answer is (D).**

   $\frac{1}{4}$ plus itself $\left(\frac{1}{4}\right) = \frac{1}{2}$

   $\frac{1}{2}$ plus itself $\left(\frac{1}{2}\right) = 1$

   3 plus itself $(3) = 6$

5. **The correct answer is (D).**

   2 times itself $(2) = 4$

   3 times itself $(3) = 9$

   4 times itself $(4) = 16$

6. **The correct answer is (C).**

   10 divided by $5 = 2$

   2 divided by $5 = \frac{2}{5}$

   15 divided by $5 = 3$

7. **The correct answer is (A).**

   5 divided by itself $(5) = 1$

   4 divided by itself $(4) = 1$

   3 divided by itself $(3) = 1$

8. **The correct answer is (D).**

   There are four squares, all of which are shaded. 4 over 4 is $\frac{4}{4}$, or 1.

9. **The correct answer is (D).**

   There are six squares. One of them is shaded. 1 over 6 is $\frac{1}{6}$.

10. **The correct answer is (A).**

    There are eight squares. Four of them are shaded. 4 over 8 is $\frac{4}{8}$, or $\frac{1}{2}$.

11. **The correct answer is (A).**

    There are eight squares. Two complete squares and four half-squares are shaded. $2 + \frac{1}{2} + \frac{1}{2} + \frac{1}{2} + \frac{1}{2}$ equals 4. Four squares are shaded. 4 over 8 is $\frac{4}{8}$, or $\frac{1}{2}$.

12. **The correct answer is (D).** There are nine squares. One complete square and two half-squares are shaded. $1 + \frac{1}{2} + \frac{1}{2}$ is 2. So, 2 over 9 is $\frac{2}{9}$.

13. **The correct answer is (B).** There are nine squares. Four of them are shaded. So, 4 over 9 is $\frac{4}{9}$.

14. **The correct answer is (A).** The scale indicates that 2 cones = 1 cube. The only answer that maintains this relationship is choice (A), since it has 1 cube = 2 cones.

15. **The correct answer is (B).** The scale indicates that 1 cube = 2 cones. The only answer that maintains this relationship is choice (B), since it has 1 cube + 2 cones = 2 cubes.

16. **The correct answer is (D).** The scale indicates that 1 cube = 3 cones. The only answer that maintains this relationship is choice (D), since it has 2 cubes = 1 cube + 3 cones.

17. **The correct answer is (B).** The scale indicates that 1 cube = 3 cones. The only answer that maintains this relationship is choice (B), since it has 1 cube + 1 cone = 4 cones.

18. **The correct answer is (C).** The scale indicates that 1 cube = 2 cones. The only answer that maintains this relationship is choice (C), since it has 3 cones = 1 cone + 1 cube.

19. **The correct answer is (A).** The scale indicates that 1 cube = 1 cone. The only answer that maintains this relationship is choice (A), since it has 1 cube = 1 cube.

20. **The correct answer is (D).** The scale indicates that 1 cube = 4 cones. The only answer that maintains this relationship is choice (D), since it has 1 cube + 1 cone = 5 cones.

SUMMING IT UP

- The Quantitative Reasoning section of the COOP contains approximately 20 questions.

- It does not test your knowledge of formulas or specific facts.

- To answer a quantitative reasoning question, find the relationship between the elements, and then use that relationship to find the answer to the question.

Mathematics

OVERVIEW

- **The number line**
- **Decimals**
- **Fractions**
- **Percentages**
- **Algebra**
- **Equations**
- **Geometry**
- **Coordinate geometry**
- **Word problems**
- **Exercises: Mathematics**
- **Answer keys and explanations**
- **Summing it up**

Whether you love math or hate it, it's always a part of your life. Mathematics questions are found on all scholastic aptitude and achievement tests, including Catholic high school entrance exams. On the COOP exam, these questions are called Mathematics. On the HSPT®, math questions include the categories of Mathematics and Quantitative Skills. On the TACHS, the questions are called Math.

In the pages that follow, we have tried to condense eight years of mathematics instruction into a comprehensive review that touches on most of the topics covered on the exams. This is only a review, not a course. If you find that you're having difficulties with any mathematics topic, talk with a teacher or refer to any of your mathematics textbooks. This chapter really helps you most by letting you know what you *don't* know, so you can focus some of your test-prep time on brushing up your skills in problem areas. The explanations that accompany the mathematics exercises are very complete. These explanations will be a big help to you, because they help you understand the processes involved in finding the right answers to mathematics questions. For extra practice with math questions, do the math sections of all the practice exams that follow.

The following sections in this part outline some of the basic mathematics rules, procedures, and formulas that you've learned over the past eight years in school. You also have an opportunity to practice your skills with some exercises, and you can judge your progress by checking your work against the answer explanations that follow the exercises. Work through these sections and the exercises carefully, and be honest with yourself about the accuracy and speed with which you solve these problems. Note which problems are difficult for you as well as those that are easy. After you've completed this section, you'll know exactly which areas you need to strengthen.

chapter 16

THE NUMBER LINE

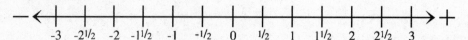

A *number line* is a convenient concept to keep as a mental picture. The number line above shows whole numbers and fractions greater than zero and less than zero. Numbers increase in size as you move to the right and decrease in size as you move to the left. The number line above has an arrow at each end, meaning that the number line goes on infinitely in both positive and negative directions.

Number lines can be drawn up to aid in basic mathematical calculations. Either fractions, whole numbers, or decimals can be used to name the intervals on the line. We suggest that you use number lines when dealing with signed (+, −) numbers and inequalities.

Here is a list of a few basic rules that must be mastered for speed and accuracy in mathematical computation. You should memorize these rules:

Any number multiplied by 0 = 0.

$5 \times 0 = 0$

If 0 is divided by any number, the answer is 0.

$0 \div 2 = 0$

If 0 is added to any number, that number does not change.

$7 + 0 = 7$

If 0 is subtracted from any number, that number does not change.

$4 - 0 = 4$

If a number is multiplied by 1, that number does not change.

$3 \times 1 = 3$

If a number is divided by 1, that number does not change.

$6 \div 1 = 6$

A number added to itself is doubled.

$4 + 4 = 8$

If a number is subtracted from itself, the answer is 0.

$9 - 9 = 0$

If a number is divided by itself, the answer is 1.

$8 \div 8 = 1$

If you have memorized these rules, you should be able to write the answers to the questions in the following exercise as fast as you can read the questions.

Test Yourself 1

Answers follow Test Yourself 19.

1. $1 - 1 =$ **11.** $8 \times 0 =$

2. $3 \div 1 =$ **12.** $0 \div 4 =$

3. $6 \times 0 =$ **13.** $1 + 0 =$

4. $6 - 0 =$ **14.** $3 - 0 =$

5. $0 \div 8 =$ **15.** $5 \times 1 =$

6. $9 \times 1 =$ **16.** $9 \div 1 =$

7. $5 + 0 =$ **17.** $6 + 6 =$

8. $4 - 0 =$ **18.** $4 - 4 =$

9. $2 \div 1 =$ **19.** $5 \div 5 =$

10. $7 - 7 =$ **20.** $6 \times 1 =$

The more rules, procedures, and formulas you are able to memorize, the easier it will be to solve mathematical problems on your exam and throughout life. Become thoroughly familiar with the rules in this section, and try to commit to memory as many as possible.

When multiplying a number by 10, 100, 1000, etc., move the decimal point to the right a number of spaces equal to the number of zeros in the multiplier. If the number being multiplied is a whole number, push the decimal point to the right by inserting the appropriate number of zeros.

$$0.36 \times 100 = 36$$
$$1.2 \times 10 = 12$$
$$5.0 \times 10 = 50$$
$$60.423 \times 100 = 6042.3$$

When dividing a number by 10, 100, 1000, etc., again count the zeros, but this time move the decimal point to the left.

$$123. \div 100 = 1.23$$
$$352.8 \div 10 = 35.28$$
$$16.0 \div 100 = 0.16$$
$$7.0 \div 1000 = 0.007$$

Test Yourself 2

1. $18 \times 10 =$ **6.** $0.12 \div 100 =$

2. $5 \div 100 =$ **7.** $4.5 \times 10 =$

3. $1.3 \times 1000 =$ **8.** $83.28 \div 1000 =$

4. $3.62 \times 10 =$ **9.** $761 \times 100 =$

5. $9.86 \div 10 =$ **10.** $68.86 \div 10 =$

DECIMALS

Decimals are a way of writing fractions using tenths, hundredths, thousandths, and so forth. If you can count money, make change, or understand a batting average, decimals should present no problem.

When writing decimals, the most important step is placing the decimal point. The whole system is based on its location. Remember the decimal places?

1,	2	3	6,	5	4	0	.	1	3	2	4	5	6
MILLIONS	HUNDRED THOUSANDS	TEN THOUSANDS	THOUSANDS	HUNDREDS	TENS	ONES	DECIMAL POINT	TENTHS	HUNDREDTHS	THOUSANDTHS	TEN THOUSANDTHS	HUNDRED THOUSANDTHS	MILLIONTHS

When adding or subtracting decimals, it is most important to keep the decimal points in line. After the decimal points are aligned, proceed with the problem in exactly the same way as with whole numbers, simply maintaining the location of the decimal point.

Example: Add 36.08 + 745 + 4.362 + 58.6 + 0.0061.

Solution:

```
      36.08
     745.
       4.362
      58.6
+      0.0061
    844.0481
```

If you find it easier, you may fill in the spaces with zeroes. The answer will be unchanged.

```
    036.0800
    745.0000
    004.3620
    058.6000
+   000.0061
    844.0481
```

Example: Subtract 7.928 from 82.1.

Solution:

```
    82.1              82.100
-    7.928          -    7.928
   74.172              74.172
```

Test Yourself 3

1. $1.52 + 0.389 + 42.9 =$

2. $0.6831 + 0.01 + 4.26 + 98 =$

3. $84 - 1.9 =$

4. $3.25 + 5.66 + 9.1 =$

5. $17 - 12.81 =$

6. $46.33 - 12.1 =$

7. $51 + 7.86 + 42.003 =$

8. $35.4 - 18.21 =$

9. $0.85 - 0.16 =$

10. $7.6 + 0.32 + 830 =$

When multiplying decimals, you can ignore the decimal points until you reach the product. Then the placement of the decimal point is dependent on the sum of the places to the right of the decimal point in both the multiplier and number being multiplied.

$$
\begin{array}{r}
1.482 \quad \text{(3 places to the right of decimal point)} \\
\times\ 0.16 \quad \text{(2 places to the right of decimal point)} \\
\hline
8892 \\
14820 \\
\hline
0.23712 \quad \text{(5 places to the right of decimal point)}
\end{array}
$$

You cannot divide by a decimal. If the divisor is a decimal, you must move the decimal point to the right until the divisor becomes a whole number, an integer. Count the number of spaces by which you moved the decimal point to the right and move the decimal point in the dividend (the number being divided) the same number of spaces to the right. The decimal point in the answer should be directly above the decimal point in the dividend.

$$
0.06\overline{)4.212} \quad 70.2
$$

Decimal point moves two spaces to the right.

Test Yourself 4

Solve the following problems.

1. $3.62 \times 5.6 =$

2. $92 \times 0.11 =$

3. $18 \div 0.3 =$

4. $1.5 \times 0.9 =$

5. $7.55 \div 5 =$

6. $6.42 \div 2.14 =$

7. $12.01 \times 3 =$

8. $24.82 \div 7.3 =$

9. $0.486 \div 0.2 =$

10. $0.21 \times 12 =$

FRACTIONS

Fractions are used when we wish to indicate parts of things. A fraction consists of a numerator and a denominator.

$$\frac{3}{4} \overset{\leftarrow \ \text{numerator} \ \rightarrow}{\leftarrow \text{denominator} \rightarrow} \frac{7}{8}$$

The denominator tells you how many equal parts the object or number has been divided into, and the numerator tells how many of those parts we are concerned with.

Example: Divide a baseball game, a football game, and a hockey game into convenient numbers of parts. Write a fraction to answer each equation.

   1. If a pitcher played two innings, how much of the whole baseball game did he play?

   2. If a quarterback played three quarters of a football game, how much of the whole game did he play?

   3. If a goalie played two periods of a hockey game, how much of the whole game did he play?

Solution 1: A baseball game is conveniently divided into nine parts (each an inning). The pitcher pitched two innings. Therefore, he played $\frac{2}{9}$ of the game. The denominator represents the nine parts the game is divided into; the numerator, the two parts we are concerned with.

Solution 2: Similarly, there are four quarters in a football game, and a quarterback playing three of those quarters plays in $\frac{3}{4}$ of the game.

Solution 3: There are three periods in hockey, and the goalie played in two of them. Therefore, he played in $\frac{2}{3}$ of the game.

Equivalent Fractions

Fractions having different denominators and numerators might actually represent the same amount. Such fractions are equivalent fractions.

For example, the following circle is divided into two equal parts. Write a fraction to indicate how much of the circle is shaded.

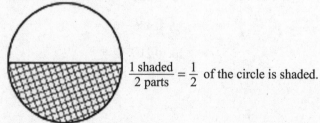

$$\frac{1 \ \text{shaded}}{2 \ \text{parts}} = \frac{1}{2} \ \text{of the circle is shaded.}$$

The circle below is divided into four equal parts. Write a fraction to indicate how much of the circle is shaded.

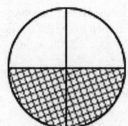

$\dfrac{2 \text{ shaded}}{4 \text{ parts}} = \dfrac{2}{4}$ of the circle are shaded.

This circle is divided into eight equal parts. Write a fraction to indicate how much of the circle is shaded.

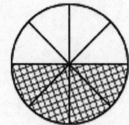

$\dfrac{4 \text{ shaded}}{8 \text{ parts}} = \dfrac{4}{8}$ of the circle are shaded.

In each circle, the same amount was shaded. This should show you that there is more than one way to indicate one half of something.

The fractions $\dfrac{1}{2}$, $\dfrac{2}{4}$, and $\dfrac{4}{8}$ that you wrote are *equivalent fractions* because they all represent the same amount. Notice that the denominator is twice as large as the numerator in every case. Any fraction you write that has a denominator that is exactly twice as large as the numerator will be equivalent to $\dfrac{1}{2}$.

Example: Write other fractions equivalent to $\dfrac{1}{2}$.

Solution: Any fraction that has a denominator that is twice as large as the numerator: $\dfrac{3}{6}$, $\dfrac{5}{10}$, $\dfrac{6}{12}$, $\dfrac{32}{64}$, etc.

Example: Write other fractions equivalent to $\dfrac{1}{4}$.

Solution: Any fraction that has a denominator that is four times as large as the numerator: $\dfrac{2}{8}$, $\dfrac{4}{16}$, $\dfrac{5}{20}$, $\dfrac{15}{60}$, etc.

Example: Write other fractions equivalent to $\dfrac{2}{3}$.

Solution: Any fraction that has a denominator that is one and one-half times as large as the numerator: $\dfrac{4}{6}$, $\dfrac{10}{15}$, $\dfrac{14}{21}$, $\dfrac{16}{24}$, etc.

When the numerator and denominator of a fraction cannot be divided evenly by the same whole number (other than 1), the fraction is said to be in simplest forms. In the examples above, $\dfrac{1}{2}$, $\dfrac{1}{4}$, and $\dfrac{2}{3}$ are in simplest form.

To write equivalent fractions where the numerator is not 1 requires one more step.

Example: What is the equivalent fraction for $\dfrac{4}{5}$ using 10 as a denominator?

Solution: Each $\dfrac{1}{5}$ is equivalent to $\dfrac{2}{10}$; therefore, $\dfrac{4}{5}$ is equivalent to $\dfrac{8}{10}$.

The quickest way to find an equivalent fraction is to divide the denominator of the fraction you want by the denominator you know. Take the result and multiply it by the numerator of the fraction you know. This becomes the numerator of the equivalent fraction.

Example: Rename $\frac{3}{8}$ as an equivalent fraction having 16 as a denominator.

Solution: $16 \div 8 = 2; 2 \times 3 = 6$

Answer: $\frac{6}{16}$

Example: Rename $\frac{3}{4}$ as equivalent fractions having 8, 12, 24, and 32 as denominators.

Solution: $\frac{3}{4} = \frac{6}{8}$ $(8 \div 4 = 2; 2 \times 3 = 6)$

$\frac{3}{4} = \frac{9}{12}$ $(12 \div 4 = 3; 3 \times 3 = 9)$

$\frac{3}{4} = \frac{18}{24}$ $(24 \div 4 = 6; 6 \times 3 = 18)$

$\frac{3}{4} = \frac{24}{32}$ $(32 \div 4 = 8; 8 \times 3 = 24)$

A fraction that has a numerator greater than the denominator is called an *improper fraction*. A number expressed as an integer together with a proper fraction is called a *mixed number*.

Examples of improper fractions include $\frac{3}{2}, \frac{12}{7}$, and $\frac{9}{5}$. Note that each is in simplest form because the numerator and denominator cannot be divided evenly by a number other than 1.

Examples of mixed numbers include $1\frac{1}{2}, 1\frac{5}{7}$, and $1\frac{4}{5}$. These are called mixed numbers because they have a whole number part and a fractional part. These mixed numbers are equivalent to the improper fractions given previously. To rename a mixed number as an improper fraction is easy.

Example: Rename $2\frac{1}{4}$ as an improper fraction.

Solution: The whole number 2 contains 8 fourths. Add to it the $\frac{1}{4}$ to write the equivalent

fraction $\frac{9}{4}$.

An alternative way of figuring this is to multiply the denominator of the fraction by the whole number and add the numerator.

Example: Rename $2\frac{1}{4}$ as an improper fraction.

Solution: $4 \times 2 = 8 + 1 = 9; \frac{9}{4}$

To rename an improper fraction as a mixed number, just proceed backward.

Example: Rename $\frac{9}{4}$ as a mixed number.

Solution: Divide the numerator by the denominator and use the remainder (R) as the fraction numerator:

$9 \div 4 = 2\,R1$ or $9 \div 4 = 2\frac{1}{4}$

Adding and Subtracting Fractions

To add fractions having the same denominators, simply add the numerators and keep the common denominator.

Example: Add $\frac{1}{4} + \frac{3}{4} + \frac{3}{4}$.

Solution: The denominators are the same, so just add the numerators to arrive at the answer, $\frac{7}{4}$ or $1\frac{3}{4}$.

To find the difference between two fractions having the same denominators, simply subtract the numerators, leaving the denominators alone.

Example: Find the difference between $\frac{7}{8}$ and $\frac{3}{8}$.

Solution: $\frac{7}{8} - \frac{3}{8} = \frac{4}{8}$. Simplified to simplest form $\frac{4}{8} = \frac{1}{2}$.

To add or subtract fractions having different denominators, you will have to find a *common denominator*. A common denominator is a number that can be divided by the denominators of all the fractions in the problem without a remainder.

Example: Find a common denominator for $\frac{1}{4}$ and $\frac{1}{3}$.

Solution: 12 can be divided by both 4 and 3:

$\frac{1}{4}$ is equivalent to $\frac{3}{12}$

$\frac{1}{3}$ is equivalent to $\frac{4}{12}$

We can now add the fractions because we have written equivalent fractions with a common denominator.

$$\frac{3}{12} + \frac{4}{12} = \frac{7}{12}$$

Therefore:

$$\frac{1}{4} + \frac{1}{3} = \frac{7}{12}$$

Seven twelfths is in simplest form because 7 and 12 do not have a whole number (other than 1) by which they are both divisible.

Example: Add $\frac{3}{8}$, $\frac{5}{6}$, $\frac{1}{4}$, and $\frac{2}{3}$.

Solution: Find a number into which all denominators will divide evenly. For 8, 6, 4, and 3, the best choice is 24. Now convert each fraction to an equivalent fraction having a denominator of 24:

$$\frac{3}{8} = \frac{9}{24} \ (24 \div 8 = 3; \ 3 \times 3 = 9)$$

$$\frac{5}{6} = \frac{20}{24} \ (24 \div 6 = 4; \ 4 \times 5 = 20)$$

$$\frac{1}{4} = \frac{6}{24} \ (24 \div 4 = 6; \ 6 \times 1 = 6)$$

$$\frac{2}{3} = \frac{16}{24} \ (24 \div 3 = 8; \ 8 \times 2 = 16)$$

Now add the fractions:

$$\frac{9}{24} + \frac{20}{24} + \frac{6}{24} + \frac{16}{24} = \frac{51}{24}$$

The answer, $\frac{51}{24}$, is an improper fraction; that is, the numerator is greater than the denominator. To rename the answer to a mixed number, divide the numerator by the denominator and express the remainder as a fraction.

$$\frac{51}{24} = 51 \div 24 = 2\frac{3}{24} = 2\frac{1}{8}$$

Test Yourself 5

Express your answers as simple mixed numbers.

1. $\frac{2}{4} + \frac{3}{5} + \frac{1}{2} =$

2. $\frac{6}{8} - \frac{2}{4} =$

3. $\frac{1}{3} + \frac{1}{2} =$

4. $\frac{4}{5} - \frac{3}{5} =$

5. $\frac{7}{8} + \frac{3}{4} + \frac{1}{3} =$

6. $\frac{1}{2} + \frac{1}{4} + \frac{2}{3} =$

7. $\frac{5}{6} - \frac{1}{2} =$

8. $\frac{5}{8} - \frac{1}{3} =$

9. $\frac{5}{12} + \frac{3}{4} =$

10. $\frac{8}{9} - \frac{2}{3} =$

Multiplying and Dividing Fractions

When multiplying fractions, multiply numerators by numerators and denominators by denominators.

$$\frac{3}{5} \times \frac{4}{7} \times \frac{1}{5} = \frac{3 \times 4 \times 1}{5 \times 7 \times 5} = \frac{12}{175}$$

When multiplying fractions, try to work with numbers that are as small as possible. You can make numbers smaller by dividing out common factors. Do this by dividing the numerator of any one fraction and the denominator of any one fraction by the same number.

$$\frac{{}^{1}3}{4_{2}} \times \frac{{}^{1}2}{9_{3}} = \frac{1 \times 1}{2 \times 3} = \frac{1}{6}$$

In this case, the numerator of the first fraction and the denominator of the other fraction were divided by 3, while the denominator of the first fraction and the numerator of the other fraction were divided by 2.

To divide by a fraction, multiply by the reciprocal of the divisor.

$$\frac{3}{16} \div \frac{1}{8} = \frac{3}{16_{2}} \times \frac{8^{1}}{1} = \frac{3}{2} = 1\frac{1}{2}$$

Test Yourself 6

Divide out common factor wherever possible and express your answers in simplest form.

1. $\dfrac{4}{5} \times \dfrac{3}{6} =$

2. $\dfrac{2}{4} \times \dfrac{8}{12} \times \dfrac{7}{1} =$

3. $\dfrac{3}{4} \div \dfrac{3}{8} =$

4. $\dfrac{5}{2} \div \dfrac{3}{6} =$

5. $\dfrac{8}{9} \times \dfrac{3}{4} \times \dfrac{1}{2} =$

6. $\dfrac{7}{8} \div \dfrac{2}{3} =$

7. $\dfrac{4}{16} \times \dfrac{8}{12} \times \dfrac{10}{13} =$

8. $\dfrac{1}{6} \times \dfrac{7}{6} \times \dfrac{12}{3} =$

9. $\dfrac{3}{7} \div \dfrac{9}{4} =$

10. $\dfrac{2}{3} \div \dfrac{2}{3} =$

The fraction bar in a fraction means "divided by." To rename a fraction as a decimal, follow through on the division.

$$\frac{4}{5} = 4 \div 5 = 0.8$$

To rename a decimal as a percent, multiply by 100, move the decimal point two places to the right, and attach a percent sign.

$$0.8 = 80\%$$

Test Yourself 7

Rename each fraction, first as a decimal to three places, and then as a percent.

1. $\dfrac{2}{4}$

2. $\dfrac{7}{8}$

3. $\dfrac{5}{6}$

4. $\dfrac{6}{8}$

5. $\dfrac{3}{4}$

6. $\dfrac{2}{3}$

7. $\dfrac{3}{5}$

8. $\dfrac{4}{10}$

9. $\dfrac{1}{4}$

10. $\dfrac{2}{5}$

NOTE

There is a relationship between decimals, fractions, and percents. The following notes will help you to convert numbers from one of these forms to another:

1. To change a % to a decimal, remove the % sign and divide by 100.
2. To change a decimal to a %, add the % sign and multiply by 100.
3. To change a % to a fraction, remove the % sign and divide by 100.
4. To change a fraction to %, multiply by 100 and add the % sign.

PERCENTAGES

One percent is one hundredth of something. The last syllable of the word *percent*, *-cent*, is the name we give to one hundredth of a dollar.

One percent of $1.00, then, is one cent. Using decimal notation, we can write one cent as $0.01, five cents as $0.05, twenty-five cents as $0.25, and so forth.

Twenty-five cents represents twenty-five hundredths of a dollar. Rather than say that something is so many hundredths of something else, we use the word percent. Twenty-five cents, then, is twenty-five percent of a dollar. We use the symbol % to stand for percent.

Percentage ("hundredths of") is a convenient and widely used way of measuring all sorts of things. By measuring in hundredths, we can be very precise and notice very small changes.

Percentage is not limited to comparing other numbers to 100. You can divide any number into hundredths and talk about percentage.

Example: Find 1% of 200.

Solution: 1% of 200 is one hundredth of 200.

$$200 \div 100 = 2$$

Using decimal notation, we can calculate one percent of 200 by:

$$200 \times 0.01 = 2$$

Similarly, we can find a percentage of any number we choose by multiplying it by the correct decimal notation. For example:

Five percent of 50: $0.05 \times 50 = 2.5$
Three percent of 150: $0.03 \times 150 = 4.5$
Ten percent of 60: $0.10 \times 60 = 6.0$

All percentage measurements are not between one percent and 100 percent. We may wish to consider less than one percent of something, especially if it is very large.

For example, if you were handed a book 1,000 pages long and were told to read one percent of it in 5 minutes, how much would you have to read?

$$1000 \times 0.01 = 10 \text{ pages}$$

Quite an assignment! You might bargain to read one half of one percent, or one-tenth of one percent in the 5 minutes allotted to you.

Using decimal notation, we write one-tenth of one percent as 0.001, the decimal number for one thousandth. If you remember that a percent is one hundredth of something, you can see that one tenth of that percent is equivalent to one thousandth of the whole.

In percent notation, one tenth of one percent is written as 0.1%. On high school entrance exams, students often mistakenly think that 0.1% is equal to 0.1. As you know, 0.1% is really equal to 0.001.

Sometimes we are concerned with more than 100% of something. But, you may ask, since 100% constitutes all of something, how can we speak of *more* than all of it?

Where things are growing, or increasing in size or amount, we may want to compare their new size to the size they once were. For example, suppose we measured the heights of three plants to be 6 inches, 9 inches, and 12 inches one week and discover a week later that the first plant is still 6 inches tall, but the second and third ones are now 18 inches tall.

The 6-inch plant grew *zero percent* because it didn't grow at all.
The second plant *added 100%* to its size. It doubled in height.
The third plant *added 50%* to its height.

We can also say:

The first plant is 100% of its original height.
The second plant grew to 200% of its original height.
The third plant grew to 150% of its original height.

Here are some common percentage and fractional equivalents you should remember:

- Ten percent (10%) is one tenth $\left(\frac{1}{10}\right)$, or 0.10.

- Twelve and one-half percent (12.5%) is one eighth $\left(\frac{1}{8}\right)$, or 0.125.

- Twenty percent (20%) is one fifth $\left(\frac{1}{5}\right)$, or 0.20.

- Twenty-five percent (25%) is one quarter $\left(\frac{1}{4}\right)$, or 0.25.

- Thirty-three and one-third percent $\left(33\frac{1}{3}\%\right)$ is one third $\left(\frac{1}{3}\right)$, or $0.33\overline{3}$.

- Fifty percent (50%) is one half $\left(\frac{1}{2}\right)$, or 0.50.

- Sixty-six and two-thirds percent $\left(66\frac{2}{3}\%\right)$ is two thirds $\frac{2}{3}$, or $0.66\overline{6}$.

- Seventy-five percent (75%) is three quarters $\left(\frac{3}{4}\right)$, or 0.75.

Caution: When solving problems involving percentages, be careful of common errors:

- **Read the notation carefully.** 0.50% is *not* fifty percent, but one half of one percent.

- When solving problems for percentage increases or decreases in size, **read the problems carefully.**

- **Use common sense.** If you wish to find less than 100% of a number, your result will be smaller than the number you started with. For example, 43% of 50 is less than 50. Using common sense works in the other direction as well. For example, 70 is 40% of what number? The number you are looking for must be larger than 70, since 70 is only $\frac{40}{100}$ of it. Moreover, you can estimate that the number you are looking for will be a little more than twice as large as 70, since 70 is almost half (50%) of that number.

To find a percent of a number, rename the percent as a decimal and multiply the number by it.

Example: What is 5% of 80?

Solution: 5% of 80 = 80 × 0.05 = 4

To find out what a number is when a percent of it is given, rename the percent as a decimal and divide the given number by it.

Example: 5 is 10% of what number?

Solution: 5 ÷ 0.10 = 50

To find what percent one number is of another number, create a fraction by placing the part over the whole. Simplify the fraction if possible, then rename it as a decimal (remember the fraction bar means *divided by,* so divide the numerator by the denominator) and rename the answer as a percent by multiplying by 100, moving the decimal point two places to the right.

Example: 4 is what percent of 80?

Solution: $\frac{4}{80} = \frac{1}{20} = 0.05 = 5\%$

Test Yourself 8

1. 10% of 32 =

2. 8 is 25% of what number?

3. 12 is what percent of 24?

4. 20% of 360 =

5. 5 is what percent of 60?

6. 12 is 8% of what number?

7. 6% of 36 =

8. 25 is 5% of what number?

9. 70 is what percent of 140?

10. What percent of 100 is 19?

ALGEBRA

If you are finishing the eighth grade this year, you might not yet have had a formal algebra class. Nevertheless, you have probably used algebraic terms and expressions, and you have probably solved simple equations. This section will review the skills you have acquired so far and will show you the kinds of questions you can expect to find on a high school entrance examination.

Signed Numbers

The number line exists to both sides of zero. Each positive number on the right of zero has a negative counterpart to the left of zero. The number line below shows the location of some pairs of numbers (+4, –4; +2, –2; +1, –1).

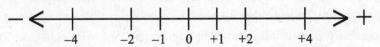

Because each number of a pair is located the same distance from zero (though in different directions), each has the same absolute value. Two vertical bars symbolize absolute value:

$$|+4| = |-4| = 4$$

The absolute value of +4 equals the absolute value of –4. Both are equivalent to 4. If you think of absolute value as the distance from zero, regardless of direction, you will understand it easily. The absolute value of any number, positive or negative, is always expressed as a positive number.

Addition of Signed Numbers

When two oppositely signed numbers having the same absolute value are added, the sum is zero.

$$(+10) + (-10) = 0$$

$$(-1.5) + (+1.5) = 0$$

$$(-0.010) + (+0.010) = 0$$

$$\left(+\frac{3}{4}\right) + \left(-\frac{3}{4}\right) = 0$$

If one of the two oppositely signed numbers is greater in absolute value, the sum is equal to the amount of that excess and carries the same sign as the number having the greater absolute value.

$$(+2) + (-1) = +1$$

$$(+8) + (-9) = -1$$

$$(-2.5) + (+2.0) = -0.5$$

$$\left(-\frac{3}{4}\right) + \left(+\frac{1}{2}\right) = -\frac{1}{4}$$

Test Yourself 9

1. $(+5) + (+8) =$

2. $(+6) + (-3) =$

3. $(+4) + (-12) =$

4. $(-7) + (+2) =$

5. $(-21) + (-17) =$

6. $(-9) + (-36) =$

7. $(+31) + (-14) =$

8. $(-16.3) + (-12.5) =$

9. $\left(-8\frac{1}{2}\right) + \left(+4\frac{1}{4}\right) =$

10. $(+66) + (-66) =$

NOTE

Change the sign of the number being subtracted and follow the rules for addition.

Subtraction of Signed Numbers

Subtraction is the operation that finds the difference between two numbers, including the difference between signed numbers.

When subtracting signed numbers, it is helpful to refer to the number line.

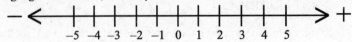

For example, if we wish to subtract +2 from +5, we can use the number line to see that the difference is +3. We give the sign to the difference that represents the direction we are moving along the number line from the number being subtracted to the number from which you are subtracting. In this case, because we are subtracting +2 from +5, we count three units in a positive direction from +2 to +5 on the number line.

When subtracting signed numbers:

- The distance between the two numbers gives you the absolute value of the difference.
- The direction you have to move from the number being subtracted to get to the number from which you are subtracting gives you the sign of the difference.

Example: Subtract –3 from +5.

Solution: Distance on the number line between –3 and +5 is 8 units.
Direction is from negative to positive—a positive direction.
Answer is +8.

Example: Subtract –6 from –8.

Solution: Distance on number line between 6 and 8 is 2 units. Direction is from –6 to –8—a negative direction. Answer is –2.

Example: Subtract +1.30 from –2.70.

Solution: Distance between them on the number line is 4.0. Direction is from +1.30 to –2.70 —a negative direction. Answer is –4.0.

A quick way to subtract signed numbers accurately involves placing the numbers in columns, reversing the sign of the number being subtracted and then adding the two.

Example: Subtract +26 from +15.

Solution:

$$
\begin{aligned}
+15 &= +15 \\
\underline{-+26} &= \underline{-26} \\
&= -11
\end{aligned}
$$

Example: Subtract –35 from +10.

Solution:

$$
\begin{aligned}
+10 &= +10 \\
\underline{--35} &= \underline{+35} \\
&= +45
\end{aligned}
$$

Notice that in each of the examples, the correct answer was found by reversing the sign of the number being subtracted and then adding.

Test Yourself 10

1. $(-6) - (-12) =$

2. $(+17) - (-8) =$

3. $(+45) - (+62) =$

4. $(-34) - (+21) =$

5. $(+4) - (-58) =$

6. $(+75) - (+27) =$

7. $(-12.6) - (-5.3) =$

8. $\left(-15\frac{1}{4}\right) - \left(+26\frac{1}{2}\right) =$

9. $(-35) - (+35) =$

10. $(+56.1) - (+56.7) =$

Multiplication of Signed Numbers

Signed numbers are multiplied as any other numbers would be, with the following exceptions:

The product of two negative numbers is positive.

$$(-3) \times (-6) = +18$$

The product of two positive numbers is positive.

$$(+3.05) \times (+6) = +18.30$$

The product of a negative and positive number is negative.

$$\left(+4\frac{1}{2}\right) \times (-3) = -13\frac{1}{2}$$

$$(+1) \times (-1) \times (+1) = -1$$

Test Yourself 11

1. $(+5) \times (+8) =$

2. $(+12) \times (-3) =$

3. $(-6) \times (-21) =$

4. $(-4) \times (-10) =$

5. $(+3.3) \times (-5.8) =$

6. $(-7.5) \times (+4.2) =$

7. $\left(-6\frac{1}{2}\right) \times \left(-7\frac{1}{4}\right) =$

8. $(+9) \times (-1) =$

9. $(0) \times (-5.7) =$

10. $(-12) \times (-12) =$

NOTE

If the signs are the same, the product is positive. If the signs are different, the product is negative.

Division of Signed Numbers

As with multiplication, the division of signed numbers requires you to observe three simple rules:

1 When dividing a positive number by a negative number, the result is negative.

$$(+6) \div (-3) = -2$$

2 When dividing a negative number by a positive number, the result is negative.

$$(-6) \div (+3) = -2$$

3 When dividing a negative number by a negative number or a positive number by a positive number, the result is positive.

$$(-6) \div (-3) = +2$$

$$(+6) \div (+3) = +2$$

Test Yourself 12

1. $(+3) \div (-1) =$

2. $(+36) \div (+12) =$

3. $(-45) \div (-9) =$

4. $(-75) \div (+3) =$

5. $(+5.6) \div (-0.7) =$

6. $(-3.5) \div (-5) =$

7. $\left(+6\frac{1}{2}\right) \div \left(+3\frac{1}{4}\right) =$

8. $(-8.2) \div (-1) =$

9. $\left(+12\frac{1}{2}\right) \div \left(-12\frac{1}{2}\right) =$

10. $(0) \div (-19.6) =$

EQUATIONS

An equation is an equality. The values on either side of the equal sign in an equation must be equal. In order to learn the value of an unknown in an equation, do the same thing to both sides of the equation so as to leave the unknown on one side of the equal sign and its value on the other side.

Example: $x - 2 = 8$

Solution: Add 2 to both sides of the equation:

$$x - 2 + 2 = 8 + 2$$
$$x = 10$$

Example: $5x = 25$

Solution: Divide both sides of the equation by 5:

$$\frac{{}^1\cancel{5}x}{\cancel{5}_1} = \frac{25}{5}$$
$$x = 5$$

Example: $y + 9 = 15$

Solution: Subtract 9 from both sides of the equation:

$$y + 9 - 9 = 15 - 9$$
$$y = 6$$

Example: $a \div 4 = 48$

Solution: Multiply both sides of the equation by 4:

$${}^1\cancel{4}\left(\frac{a}{\cancel{4}_1}\right) = 48 \times 4$$
$$a = 192$$

Sometimes more than one step is required to solve an equation.

Example: $6a \div 4 = 48$

Solution: First, multiply both sides of the equation by 4:

$$\frac{6a}{4} \times \frac{4}{1} = 48 \times 4$$
$$6a = 192$$

Then divide both sides of the equation by 6:

$$\frac{{}^1\cancel{6}a}{\cancel{6}_1} = \frac{192}{6}$$
$$a = 32$$

Test Yourself 13

Solve for x.

1. $x + 13 = 25$

2. $4x = 84$

3. $x - 5 = 28$

4. $x \div 9 = 4$

5. $3x + 2 = 14$

6. $\frac{x}{4} - 2 = 4$

7. $10x - 27 = 73$

8. $2x \div 4 = 13$

9. $8x + 9 = 81$

10. $2x \div 11 = 6$

GEOMETRY

Area of Plane Figures

Area is the space enclosed by a plane (flat) figure. A rectangle is a plane figure with four right angles. Opposite sides of a rectangle are of equal length and are parallel to each other. To find the area of a rectangle, multiply the length of the base of the rectangle by the length of its height. Area is always expressed in square units.

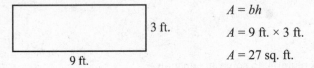

$A = bh$

$A = 9 \text{ ft.} \times 3 \text{ ft.}$

$A = 27 \text{ sq. ft.}$

A square is a rectangle in which all four sides are the same length. The area of a square is found by squaring the length of one side, which is exactly the same as multiplying the square's length by its width.

$A = s^2$

$A = 4 \text{ in.} \times 4 \text{ in.}$

$A = 16 \text{ sq. in.}$

A triangle is a three-sided plane figure. The area of a triangle is found by multiplying the base by the altitude (height) and dividing by two.

$A = \frac{1}{2}bh$

$A = \frac{1}{2}(9 \text{ in.})(5 \text{ in.}) = \frac{45}{2}$

$A = 22\frac{1}{2} \text{ sq. in.}$

A circle is a perfectly round plane figure. The distance from the center of a circle to its rim is its radius. The distance from one edge to the other through the center is its diameter. The diameter is twice the length of the radius.

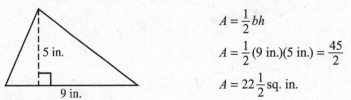

Pi (π) is a mathematical value equal to approximately 3.14, or $\frac{22}{7}$. Pi(π) is frequently used in calculations involving circles. The area of a circle is found by squaring the radius and multiplying it by π. You may leave the area in terms of pi unless you are told what value to assign π.

$A = \pi r^2$

$A = \pi(4 \text{ cm.})^2$

$A = 16\pi$ sq. cm.

Test Yourself 14

Find the area of each figure. Assume that any angle which appears to be a right angle is a right angle.

1.

4 ft.

8 ft.

2.

8 in.

7 in.

3.

1 mile

4.

3 yd.

5 yd.

5.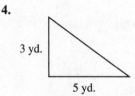

2 cm.

6.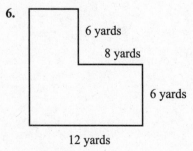

6 yards

8 yards

6 yards

12 yards

7. 3 yd.

8 yd.

10 yd.

8.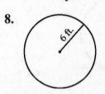

6 ft.

9.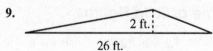

2 ft.

26 ft.

10.

6 meters

5 meters

17 meters

20 meters

ALERT!

Don't confuse the two formulas for calculating the circumference and the area of circles. A good way to keep them straight is to remember the square in πr^2. It should remind you that area must be in square units.

Perimeter of Plane Figures

The *perimeter* of a plane figure is the distance around the outside. To find the perimeter of a polygon (a plane figure bounded by line segments), just add the lengths of the sides.

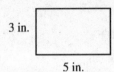

$$P = 3 \text{ in.} + 5 \text{ in.} + 3 \text{ in.} + 5 \text{ in.}$$
$$= 16 \text{ in.}$$

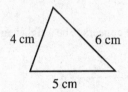

$$P = 4 \text{ cm} + 6 \text{ cm} + 5 \text{ cm}$$
$$= 15 \text{ cm}$$

The perimeter of a circle is called the circumference. The formula for the circumference of a circle is πd or $2\pi r$, which are both, of course, the same thing.

$$C = 2 \times 3 \times \pi = 6\pi$$

Volume of Solid Figures

The volume of a solid figure is the measure of the space within. To find the volume of a solid figure, multiply the area of the base by the height or depth.

The volume of a rectangular solid is length × width × height. Volume is always expressed in cubic units.

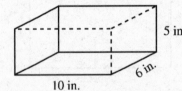

$$V = lwh$$
$$V = (10 \text{ in.}) (6 \text{ in.}) (5 \text{ in.})$$
$$V = 300 \text{ cu. in.}$$

The volume of a cube is the cube of one side.

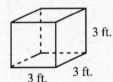

$$V = s^3$$
$$V = (3 \text{ ft.})^3$$
$$V = 27 \text{ cu. ft.}$$

The volume of a cylinder is the area of the circular base (πr^2) times the height.

$V = \pi r^2 h$

$V = \pi(4 \text{ in.})^2 (5 \text{ in.})$

$V = \pi(16)(5) = 80\pi$ cu. in.

Test Yourself 15

1. Find the perimeter.

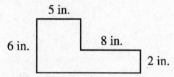

2. Find the volume.

3. Find the circumference.

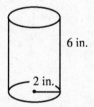

4. Find the volume.

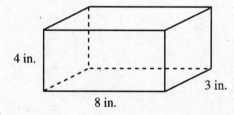

5. Find the volume.

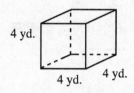

6. Find the perimeter.

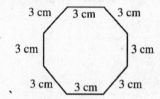

7. Find the perimeter.

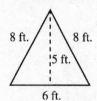

8. Find the perimeter.

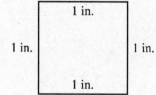

Angles

The sum of the angles of a straight line is 180°.

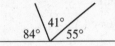

The sum of the angles of a triangle is 180°.

The sum of the angles of a rectangle is 360°.

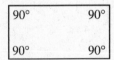

The sum of the angles of a circle is 360°.

The sum of the angles of a polygon of n sides is $(n-2)180°$.

$$(8-2)(180°) = 6 \times 180° = 1080°$$

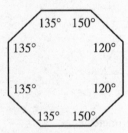

MORE ABOUT ANGLES
Courtesy of *Peterson's egghead's Guide to Geometry*

Adding angle measures

You can add up the degree measures of angles just like you would normal numbers.

Examples

The measure of ∠x is 60°. The measure of ∠y is 12°. The measure of ∠x plus the measure of ∠y is 72°.

$$m\angle x + m\angle y = 72$$

In the figure shown, m∠R = 45 and m∠S = 60.

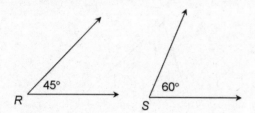

The measure of ∠R plus the measure of ∠S = 45 + 60, or 105.

Bisecting rays

In the last chapter, we learned about bisecting lines, or bisectors, which cross line segments at their midpoint. Angles can also have bisectors. A **bisecting ray** is a ray that divides one larger angle into two equal, smaller angles.

Examples

In the figure shown, ray *BJ* is a bisector. It divides ∠ABC into two equal angles.

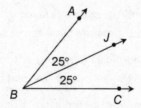

In this figure, ray *YO* bisects ∠XYZ. As the figure shows, m∠XYO = m∠OYZ.

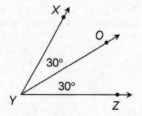

Did you find this helpful? For additional expert geometry explanations and fun exercises, check out *egghead's Guide to Geometry* at **www.petersons.com**.

Test Yourself 16

What is the size of the unlabeled angle?

1.
   50°   50°

2.
   100°
   20°

3. 90°   90°

   90°

4.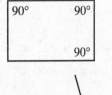
   30°
   95°

5.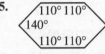
   110° 110°
   140°
   110° 110°

6.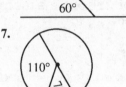
   60°

7.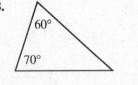
   110°
   70°

8.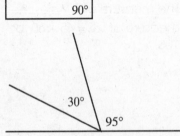
   60°
   70°

COORDINATE GEOMETRY

Coordinate geometry is used to locate and graph points and lines on a plane.

The coordinate system is made up of two perpendicular number lines that intersect at 0. Any point on the plane has two numbers, or coordinates, that indicate its location relative to the number lines.

The *x*-coordinate (abscissa) is found by drawing a vertical line from the point to the horizontal number line (the *x*-axis). The number found on the *x*-axis is the abscissa.

The *y*-coordinate (ordinate) is found by drawing a horizontal line from the point to the vertical number line (the *y*-axis). The number found on the *y*-axis is the ordinate.

The two coordinates are always written in the order (*x,y*).

On the following graph, the *x*-coordinate of point A is 3. The *y*-coordinate of point A is 2. The coordinates of point A are given by the ordered pair (3,2). Point B has coordinates (−1,4). Point C has coordinates (−4,−3). Point D has coordinates (2,−3).

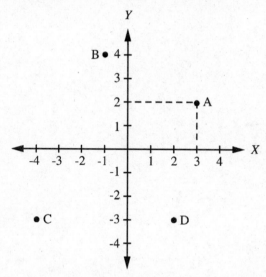

To graph a point whose coordinates are given, first locate the *x*-coordinate on the *x*-axis, then from that position move vertically the number of spaces indicated by the *y*-coordinate.

To graph (4,−2), locate 4 on the *x*-axis, then move −2 spaces vertically (2 spaces down) to find the given point.

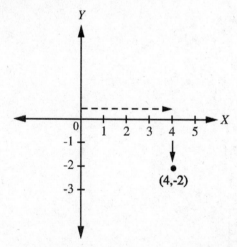

The point at which the *x*-axis and the *y*-axis meet has coordinates (0,0) and is called the origin. Any point on the *y*-axis has 0 as its *x*-coordinate. Any point on the *x*-axis has 0 as its *y*-coordinate.

Test Yourself 17

1. In the graph below, the coordinates of point A are

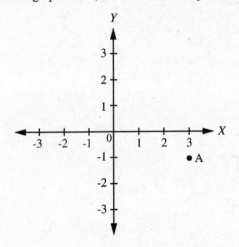

2. The coordinates of point P on the graph are

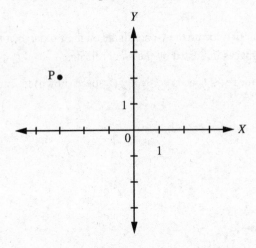

3. Which point is named by the ordered pair (5,1)?

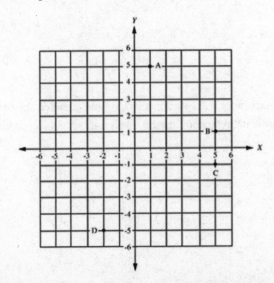

4. Which point might possibly have the coordinates (2,–3)?

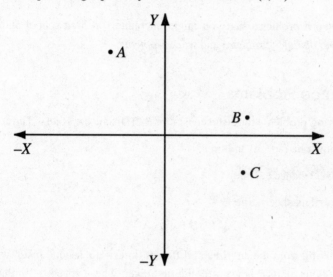

5. The point with the coordinate (3,0) is

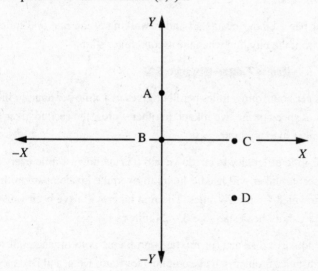

WORD PROBLEMS

Two very common kinds of word problems that you might encounter on high school entrance examinations are *rate, time, and distance problems* and *work problems*.

Rate, Time, and Distance Problems

The basic formula used in solving problems for distance is: $D = RT$ (Distance = Rate × Time)

Use this formula when you know rate (speed) and time.

To find rate, use: $R = \dfrac{D}{T}$ (Rate = Distance ÷ Time)

To find time, use: $T = \dfrac{D}{R}$ (Time = Distance ÷ Rate)

Study the following problems:

Example: Two hikers start walking from the city line at different times. The second hiker, whose speed is 4 miles per hour, starts 2 hours after the first hiker, whose speed is 3 miles per hour. Determine the amount of time and distance that will be consumed before the second hiker catches up with the first.

Solution 1: Since the first hiker has a 2-hour head start and is walking at the rate of 3 miles per hour, he is 6 miles from the city line when the second hiker starts.

Rate × Time = Distance

Subtracting 3 miles per hour from 4 miles per hour gives us 1 mile per hour, or the difference in the rates of speed of the two hikers. In other words, the second hiker gains 1 mile on the first hiker in every hour.

Because there is a 6-mile difference to cut down and it is cut down 1 mile every hour, it is clear that the second hiker will need 6 hours to overtake his companion. In this time, he will have traveled 4 × 6 = 24 miles. The first hiker will have been walking 8 hours, since he had a 2-hour head start, 8 × 3 = 24 miles.

Solution 2: One excellent way to solve distance (or mixture) problems is to organize all of the data in a chart. For distance problems, make columns for Rate, Time, and Distance and separate lines for each moving object. In the problem about the two hikers, the chart technique works like this:

STEP 1: Draw the chart.

	Rate	×	Time	=	Distance
Hiker 1	3		$x + 2$		$3x + 6$
Hiker 2	4		x		$4x$

$3(8) = 4(6)$

$24 = 24$

$3(x + 2) = 4x$

$3x + 6 = 4x$

$6 = x$

$D_1 = D_2$

STEP 2: Since the problem states that Hiker 1 is traveling at 3 miles per hour and Hiker 2 is traveling at 4 miles per hour, enter these two figures in the Rate column.

	Rate	× Time	= Distance
Hiker 1	3 mph		
Hiker 2	4 mph		

STEP 3: The problem does not tell us how long each hiker traveled, but it does say that Hiker 1 started 2 hours before Hiker 2. Therefore, if we use the unknown x to represent the number of hours Hiker 2 traveled, we can set Hiker 1's time as $x + 2$. Enter these two figures in the Time column.

	Rate	× Time	= Distance
Hiker 1	3 mph	$x + 2$	
Hiker 2	4 mph	x	

STEP 4: Using the formula $D = R \times T$, we can easily find each hiker's distance by multiplying the figures for rate and time already in the chart.

For Hiker 1: $3(x + 2) = 3x + 6$

For Hiker 2: $4(x) = 4x$

	Rate	× Time	= Distance
Hiker 1	3 mph	$x + 2$	$3x + 6$
Hiker 2	4 mph	x	$4x$

STEP 5: When the two hikers meet, each will have covered the same distance. Using this information, we can set up an equation:

Distance covered by Hiker 1		Distance covered by Hiker 2
$3x + 6$	$=$	$4x$

Solving this equation for x, we find that $x = 6$. This means that Hiker 1 has walked for $6 + 2 = 8$ hours when Hiker 2 catches up to him.

STEP 6: Because Hiker 1 started 2 hours earlier than Hiker 2, Hiker 2 will have walked for 6 hours to catch up to Hiker 1.

STEP 7: Using this information, we can determine that Hiker 1 walked 8 hours at 3 miles per hour to cover 24 miles. Hiker 2 walked for 6 hours at 4 miles per hour to cover the same 24 miles.

Let's try another example:

Example: The same two hikers start walking toward each other along a road connecting two cities that are 60 miles apart. Their speeds are the same as in the preceding example, 3 and 4 miles per hour, respectively. How much time will elapse before they meet?

Solution 1:   In each hour of travel toward each other, the hikers will cut down a distance equal to the sum of their speeds, $3 + 4 = 7$ miles per hour. To meet, they must cut down 60 miles, and at 7 miles per hour this would be:

$$\frac{D}{R} = T \text{ OR } \frac{60}{7} = 8\frac{4}{7} \text{ hours}$$

Solution 2:   In this problem, we know that the distance traveled by Hiker 1 plus the distance traveled by Hiker 2 equals 60 miles and that the two hikers will have been traveling for the same length of time when they meet. Therefore, we set up an equation to represent this information and solve for x to find the time that will have elapsed before the two hikers meet:

$$3x + 4x = 60$$
$$7x = 60$$
$$x = 8\frac{4}{7}$$

The problem might also have asked: ''How much distance must the slower hiker cover before the two hikers meet?'' In such a case, we should have gone through the same steps plus one additional step: The time consumed before meeting was $8\frac{4}{7}$ hours. To find the distance covered by the slower hiker, we merely multiply his rate by the time elapsed:

$$R \times T = D \qquad 3 \times 8\frac{4}{7} = 25\frac{5}{7}$$

Test Yourself 18

1. A sailor on leave drove to Yosemite Park from his home at 60 miles per hour. On his trip home, his rate was 10 miles per hour less, and the trip took 1 hour longer. How far is his home from the park?

2. Two cars leave a restaurant at the same time and travel along a straight highway in opposite directions. At the end of 3 hours, they are 300 miles apart. Find the rate of the slower car if one car travels at a rate 20 miles per hour faster than the other.

3. At 10:30 a.m., a passenger train and a freight train left from stations that were 405 miles apart and traveled toward each other. The rate of the passenger train was 45 miles per hour faster than that of the freight train. If they passed each other at 1:30 p.m., how fast was the passenger train traveling?

4. Susie left her home at 11 a.m. traveling along Route 1 at 30 miles per hour. At 1 p.m., her brother Richard left home and started after her on the same road at 45 miles per hour. At what time did Richard catch up to Susie?

5. How far can a man drive into the country if he drives out at 40 miles per hour, returns over the same road at 30 miles per hour, and spends 8 hours away from home, including a 1-hour stop for lunch?

6. At 10 a.m., two cars started traveling toward each other from towns 287 miles apart. They passed each other at 1:30 p.m. If the rate of the faster car exceeded the rate of the slower car by 6 miles per hour, find the rate in miles per hour of the faster car.

7. A driver covered 350 miles in 8 hours. Before noon he averaged 50 miles per hour, but after noon he averaged only 40 miles per hour. At what time did he leave?

8. At 3 p.m., a plane left New York City for Los Angeles traveling at 600 mph. At 3:30 p.m., another plane left the same airport on the same route traveling at 650 mph. At what time did the second plane overtake the first?

9. A scout troop left their campsite at 10 a.m. and walked on the park trail at 4 miles per hour. They returned on the same path at 2 miles per hour. If the troop arrived back at their campsite at 4 p.m., how many miles on the path did they walk?

10. Two cars leave the gas station at the same time and proceed in the same direction along the same route. One car averages 36 miles per hour and the other 31 miles per hour. In how many hours will the faster car be 30 miles ahead of the slower car?

Work Problems

Work problems generally involve two or more workers doing a job at different rates. The aim of work problems is to predict how long it will take to complete a job if the number of workers is increased or decreased. Work problems may also involve determining how fast pipes can fill or empty tanks. In solving pipe and tank problems, you must think of the pipes as workers.

In most work problems, a job is broken up into several parts, each representing a fractional portion of the entire job. For each part represented, the numerator should represent the time actually spent working, while the denominator should represent the total time needed for the worker to do the job alone. The sum of all the individual fractions must be 1 if the job is completed. The easiest way to understand this procedure is to carefully study the examples that follow. By following the step-by-step solutions, you will learn how to make your own fractions to solve the practice problems that follow and the problems you may find on your exam.

Example: If A does a job in 6 days, and B does the same job in 3 days, how long will it take the two of them, working together, to do the job?

Solution:

STEP 1: Write the fractions as follows.

$$\frac{\text{Time actually spent}}{\text{Time needed to do entire job alone}} \quad \overset{A}{\frac{x}{6 \text{ days}}} + \overset{B}{\frac{x}{3 \text{ days}}} = 1$$

The variable x represents the amount of time each worker will work when both work together. 1 represents the completed job.

STEP 2: Multiply all the terms by the same number (in this case, 6) in order to clear the fractions so as to work with whole numbers.

$$x + 2x = 6$$

STEP 3: Solve for x.

$$3x = 6$$
$$x = 2 \text{ days}$$

Working together, A and B will get the job done in 2 days.

Example: A and B, working together, do a job in $4\frac{1}{2}$ days. B, working alone, is able to do the job in 10 days. How long would it take A to do the job working alone?

Solution:

STEP 1: Write the fractions as follows.

$$\frac{\text{Time actually spent}}{\text{Time needed to do entire job alone}} \qquad \overset{A}{\frac{4.5 \text{ days}}{x \text{ days}}} + \overset{B}{\frac{4.5 \text{ days}}{10 \text{ days}}} = 1$$

STEP 2: Multiply all the terms by $10x$ to clear the fractions.

$$45 + 4.5x = 10x$$

STEP 3: Solve for x.

$$45 = 5.5x$$
$$x = 8\frac{2}{11} \text{ or } 8.18 \text{ days}$$

It would take A nearly $8\frac{2}{11}$ days to do the job alone.

Example: If A can do a job in 6 days that B can do in $5\frac{1}{2}$ days, and C can do in $2\frac{1}{5}$ days, how long would the job take if A, B, and C were working together?

Solution:

STEP 1: This example is very similar to the first one. The number of workers is greater, but the procedure is the same. First write the fractions as follows.

$$\frac{\text{Time actually spent}}{\text{Time needed to do entire job alone}} \qquad \overset{A}{\frac{x}{6 \text{ days}}} + \overset{B}{\frac{x}{5.5 \text{ days}}} + \overset{C}{\frac{x}{2.2 \text{ days}}} = 1$$

Convert all the decimals to fractions:

$$\frac{x}{6} + \frac{2x}{11} + \frac{5x}{11} = 1$$

Remember that 1 represents the completed job regardless of the number of days involved.

STEP 2: Multiply all terms by 66 to clear the fractions.

$$11x + 12x + 30x = 66$$

STEP 3: Solve for x.

$$53x = 66$$
$$x = 1.245 \text{ days}$$

A, B, and C all working together at their usual rates would get the job done in about $1\frac{1}{4}$ days.

Example: One pipe can fill a pool in 20 minutes, a second pipe can fill the pool in 30 minutes, and a third pipe can fill it in 10 minutes. How long would it take the three pipes together to fill the pool?

Solution:

STEP 1: Treat the pipes as workers and write the fractions as follows.

$$\frac{\text{Time actually spent}}{\text{Time needed to do entire job alone}} \qquad \overset{A}{\frac{x}{20 \text{ mins.}}} + \overset{B}{\frac{x}{30 \text{ mins.}}} + \overset{C}{\frac{x}{10 \text{ mins.}}} = 1$$

STEP 2: Multiply all terms by 60 to clear the fractions.
$$3x + 2x + 6x = 60$$

STEP 3: Solve for x.
$$11x = 60$$
$$x = 5\frac{5}{11} \text{ minutes}$$

If the water flows from all three pipes at once, the pool will be filled in $5\frac{5}{11}$ minutes.

MORE ABOUT WORD PROBLEMS
Courtesy of *Peterson's egghead's Guide to Algebra*

Ratios and proportions

Word problems may present information in terms of a ratio. You must then set up a proportion to find a missing value.

Eric writes thank-you notes for the gifts he received at graduation. He has 30 thank-you notes to write. He writes 10 thank-you notes in the first 2 hours. At that rate, how long will it take Eric to write all 30 notes?

This problem starts with the rate at which Eric writes thank-you notes. This rate can be expressed as a **ratio**: 10 notes for every 2 hours, or 10:2. The ratio can also be written as a fraction: $\frac{10}{2}$.

To solve this problem, you would need to set up a proportion. A **proportion** is an equation containing two ratios.

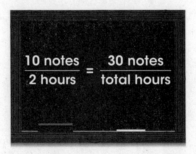

You are looking for the total number of hours it takes Eric to write all 30 notes.

To solve the problem, we now would cross multiply. Let *t* represent the total hours it would take Eric to write 30 notes:

$$\frac{10 \text{ notes}}{2 \text{ hours}} = \frac{30 \text{ notes}}{\text{total hours}}$$

$$\frac{10}{2} = \frac{30}{t}$$

$$10 \times t = 2 \times 30$$

$$10t = 2 \times 30$$

$$10t = 60$$

Divide both sides by 10 to solve for t:

$$10t = 60$$

$$\frac{10t}{10} = \frac{60}{10}$$

$$t = \frac{60}{10}$$

$$t = 6$$

It would take Eric 6 hours to write 30 thank-you notes.

Did you find this helpful? Check out *egghead's Guide to Algebra* at **www.petersons.com** for additional easy-to-follow explanations to help you boost your algebra scores.

Test Yourself 19

1. John can complete a paper route in 20 minutes. Steve can complete the same route in 30 minutes. How long will it take them to complete the route if they work together?

2. Mr. Powell can mow his lawn twice as fast as his son Rick can. Together they do the job in 20 minutes. How many minutes would it take Mr. Powell to do the job alone?

3. Mr. White can paint his barn in 5 days. What part of the barn is still unpainted after he has worked for x days?

4. Mary can clean the house in 6 hours. Her younger sister Ruth can do the same job in 9 hours. In how many hours can they do the job if they work together?

5. A swimming pool can be filled by an inlet pipe in 3 hours. It can be drained by a drainpipe in 6 hours. By mistake, both pipes are opened at the same time. If the pool is empty, in how many hours will it be filled?

6. Mr. Jones can plow his field with his tractor in 4 hours. If he uses his manual plow, it takes three times as long to plow the same field. One day, after working with the tractor for 2 hours, he ran out of gas and had to finish with the manual plow. How long did it take to complete this job after the tractor ran out of gas?

7. Michael and Barry can complete a job in 2 hours when working together. If Michael requires 6 hours to do the job alone, how many hours does Barry need to do the job alone?

8. A girl can sweep the garage in 20 minutes, while her brother needs 30 minutes to do the same job. How many minutes will it take them to sweep the garage if they work together?

9. One printing press can print the school newspaper in 12 hours, while another press can print it in 18 hours. How long will the job take if both presses work simultaneously?

10. If John can do $\frac{1}{4}$ of a job in $\frac{3}{4}$ of a day, how many days will it take him to do the entire job?

TEST YOURSELF ANSWERS AND EXPLANATIONS

Test Yourself 1

1. 0	5. 0	9. 2	13. 1	17. 12
2. 3	6. 9	10. 0	14. 3	18. 0
3. 0	7. 5	11. 0	15. 5	19. 1
4. 6	8. 4	12. 0	16. 9	20. 6

Test Yourself 2

1. 180	3. 1300	5. 0.986	7. 45	9. 76,100
2. 0.05	4. 36.2	6. 0.0012	8. 0.08328	10. 6.886

Test Yourself 3

1. 44.809	3. 82.1	5. 4.19	7. 100.863	9. 0.69
2. 102.9531	4. 18.01	6. 34.23	8. 17.19	10. 837.92

Test Yourself 4

1. 20.272	3. 60	5. 1.51	7. 36.03	9. 2.43
2. 10.12	4. 1.35	6. 3	8. 3.4	10. 2.52

Test Yourself 5

1. $\frac{32}{20} = 1\frac{12}{20} = 1\frac{3}{5}$

2. $\frac{2}{8} = \frac{1}{4}$

3. $\frac{5}{6}$

4. $\frac{1}{5}$

5. $\frac{47}{24} = 1\frac{23}{24}$

6. $\frac{17}{12} = 1\frac{5}{12}$

7. $\frac{2}{6} = \frac{1}{3}$

8. $\frac{7}{24}$

9. $\frac{14}{12} = 1\frac{2}{12} = 1\frac{1}{6}$

10. $\frac{2}{9}$

Test Yourself 6

1. $\frac{2}{5}$

2. $2\frac{1}{3}$

3. 2

4. $\frac{15}{3} = 5$

5. $\frac{1}{3}$

6. $\frac{21}{16} = 1\frac{5}{16}$

7. $\frac{5}{39}$

8. $\frac{7}{9}$

9. $\frac{4}{21}$

10. 1

Test Yourself 7

1. $0.5 = 50\%$
2. $0.875 = 87\frac{1}{2}\%$
3. $0.833 = 83\frac{1}{3}\%$
4. $0.75 = 75\%$
5. $0.75 = 75\%$
6. $0.666 = 66\frac{2}{3}\%$
7. $0.60 = 60\%$
8. $0.40 = 40\%$
9. $0.25 = 25\%$
10. $0.40 = 40\%$

Test Yourself 8

1. $32 \times 0.10 = 3.2$
2. $8 \div 0.25 = 32$
3. $\frac{12}{24} = \frac{1}{2} = 0.5 = 50\%$
4. $360 \times 0.20 = 72$
5. $\frac{5}{60} = \frac{1}{12} = 0.08\overline{33} = 8\frac{1}{3}\%$
6. $12 \div 0.08 = 150$
7. $36 \times 0.06 = 2.16$
8. $25 \div 0.05 = 500$
9. $\frac{70}{140} = \frac{1}{2} = 0.5 = 50\%$
10. $\frac{19}{100} = 0.19 = 19\%$

Test Yourself 9

1. $+13$
2. $+3$
3. -8
4. -5
5. -38
6. -45
7. $+17$
8. -28.8
9. $-4\frac{1}{4}$
10. 0

Test Yourself 10

1. $+6$
2. $+25$
3. -17
4. -55
5. $+62$
6. $+48$
7. -7.3
8. $-41\frac{3}{4}$
9. -70
10. -0.6

Test Yourself 11

1. $+40$
2. -36
3. $+126$
4. $+40$
5. -19.14
6. -31.5
7. $+47\frac{1}{8}$
8. -9
9. 0
10. $+144$

Test Yourself 12

1. -3
2. $+3$
3. $+5$
4. -25
5. -8
6. $+0.7$
7. $+2$
8. $+8.2$
9. -1
10. 0

Test Yourself 13

1. $x = 12$	**3.** $x = 33$	**5.** $x = 4$	**7.** $x = 10$	**9.** $x = 9$
2. $x = 21$	**4.** $x = 36$	**6.** $x = 24$	**8.** $x = 26$	**10.** $x = 33$

Test Yourself 14

1. $A = bh$
$A = 8 \times 4 = 32$ sq. ft.

2. $A = \frac{1}{2}bh$

$A = \frac{1}{2}(7 \times 8)$

$A = \frac{1}{2}(56) = 28$ sq. in.

3. $A = s^2$
$A = 1^2 = 1$ sq. mile

4. $A = \frac{1}{2}bh$

$A = \frac{1}{2}(5 \times 3)$

$A = \frac{1}{2}(15) = 7\frac{1}{2}$ sq. yds.

5. $A = \pi r^2$
$A = \pi 2^2$
$A = 4\pi$ sq. cm

6. $A = bh$
$A = 12 \times 6 + (12 - 8) \times 6$
$A = 12 \times 6 + 4 \times 6$
$A = 72 \times 24 = 96$ sq. yds.

7. $A = bh$
$A = 10 \times 8 = 80$ sq. yds.

$A = \frac{1}{2}bh$

$A = \frac{1}{2}(10 \times 3) = \frac{1}{2}(30)$

$A = 15$ sq. yds.
$80 + 15 = 95$ sq. yds.

8. $A = \pi r^2$
$A = \pi 6^2$
$A = 36\pi$ sq. ft.

9. $A = \frac{1}{2}bh$

$A = \frac{1}{2}(26 \times 2) = \frac{1}{2}(52)$

$A = 26$ sq. ft.

10. $A = bh$
$A = 6 \times 5 + 20 \times (17 - 5)$
$A = 6 \times 5 + 20 \times 12$
$A = 30 + 240 = 270$ sq. meters

Test Yourself 15

1. $P = 6 + 5 + (6 - 2) + 8 + 2 + (8 + 5)$
$P = 38$ in.

2. $V = \pi r^2 h$
$V = \pi \times 2^2 \times 6$
$V = \pi \times 4 \times 6$
$V = 24\pi$ cu. in.

3. $C = 2\pi r$
$C = 2 \times \pi \times 7$
$C = 14\pi$ cm

4. $V = lwh$
$V = 8 \times 3 \times 4$
$V = 96$ cu. in.

5. $V = s^3$
$V = 4^3 = 4 \times 4 \times 4$
$V = 64$ cu.yd.

6. $P = 3 + 3 + 3 + 3 + 3 + 3 + 3 + 3$
$P = 24$ cm

7. $P = 8 + 8 + 6 = 22$ ft.

8. $P = 1 + 1 + 1 + 1 = 4$ in.

Test Yourself 16

1. 80°	**3.** 90°	**5.** 140°	**7.** 180°
2. 240°	**4.** 55°	**6.** 120°	**8.** 50°

Test Yourself 17

1. (3,–1) A vertical line through A meets the x-axis at 3; therefore, the x-coordinate is 3. A horizontal line through A meets the y-axis at –1; therefore, the y-coordinate is –1. The coordinates of point A are (3,–1).

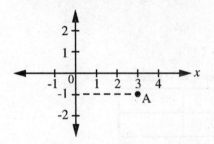

2. Point P has coordinates $x = -3$ and $y = 2$.

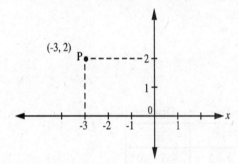

3. Because both coordinates are positive numbers, the point must be located in the upper-right quadrant of the graph. Location along the x-axis is always stated first, so the correct answer is point B.

4. **The correct answer is point C.** Start by moving in a positive direction along the x-axis. Then you must move along the y-axis in a negative direction. The actual number of spaces you move is irrelevant, since point C is the only possible answer.

5. Again, make your moves in order. First move in the positive direction along the x-axis. Because the second coordinate is 0, make no move on the y-axis. Point C is your answer.

Test Yourself 18

To solve any type of motion problem, it is helpful to organize the information in a chart with columns for Rate, Time, and Distance. A separate line should be used for each moving object. Be very careful of units used. If the rate is given in *miles per hour*, the time must be in hours and the distance will be in *miles*.

1. 300 miles

	Rate ×	Time =	Distance
Going	60 mph	x	$60x$
Return	50 mph	$x + 1$	$50x + 50$

Let x = time of trip at 60 mph
The distances are, of course, equal.

$$60x = 50x + 50$$
$$10x = 50$$
$$x = 5$$

$R \times T = D$; 60 mph × 5 hours = 300 miles

2. 40 mph

	Rate	×	Time	=	Distance
Slow Car	x		3		$3x$
Fast Car	$x + 20$		3		$3x + 60$

Let x = rate of slower car

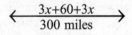
$$\frac{3x+60+3x}{300 \text{ miles}}$$

$$3x + 3x + 60 = 300$$
$$6x = 240 \text{ mph}$$
$$x = 40 \text{ mph}$$

3. 90 mph

	Rate	×	Time	=	Distance
Passenger	$x + 45$		3		$3x + 135$
Freight	x		3		$3x$

Let x = rate of freight train
$$3x + 135 + 3x = 405$$
$$6x = 270$$
$$x = 45$$
$$x + 45 = 45 + 45 = 90 \text{ mph}$$

4. 5 p.m.

	Rate	×	Time	=	Distance
Susie	30		x		$30x$
Richard	45		$x - 2$		$45x - 90$

Let x = time Susie traveled

Richard left 2 hours later than Susie, so he traveled for $x - 2$ hours. Since Richard caught up to Susie, the distances are equal.

$$30x = 45x - 90$$
$$90 = 15x$$
$$x = 6 \text{ hours}$$

Susie traveled for 6 hours. 11 a.m. + 6 hours = 5 p.m. when Richard caught up to her.

5. 120 miles

	Rate ×	Time =	Distance
Going	40	x	$40x$
Return	30	$7 - x$	$210 - 30x$

Let x = time for trip out

Total driving time = $8 - 1 = 7$ hours

Therefore, time for return trip = $7 - x$ hours

$$40x = 210 - 30x$$
$$70x = 210$$
$$x = 3 \text{ hours}$$

$R \times T = D$; 40 mph × 3 hours = 120 miles

6. 44 mph

	Rate ×	Time =	Distance
Slow Car	x	3.5	$3.5x$
Fast Car	$x + 6$	3.5	$3.5(x + 6)$

Let x = rate of slow car

The cars traveled from 10 a.m. to 1:30 p.m., which is 3.5 hours.

$$3.5x + 3.5(x + 6) = 287$$
$$3.5x + 3.5x + 21 = 287$$
$$7x + 21 = 287$$
$$7x = 266$$
$$x = 38 \text{ mph}$$
$$x + 6 = 44 \text{ mph}$$

7. 9 a.m.

	Rate ×	Time =	Distance
Before Noon	50	x	$50x$
After Noon	40	$8 - x$	$40(8 - x)$

Let x = hours traveled before noon

Note that the 8 hours must be divided into two parts.

$$50x + 40(8 - x) = 350$$
$$50x + 320 - 40x = 350$$
$$10x = 30$$
$$x = 3 \text{ hours}$$

If he traveled 3 hours before noon, he left at 9 a.m.

8. 9:30 p.m.

	Rate ×	Time =	Distance
3 p.m. Plane	600	x	$600x$
3:30 p.m. Plane	650	$x - \frac{1}{2}$	$650\left(x - \frac{1}{2}\right)$

Let x = travel time of the 3 p.m. plane.

The later plane traveled $\frac{1}{2}$ hour less.

$$600x = 650\left(x - \frac{1}{2}\right)$$
$$600x = 650x - 325$$
$$325 = 50x$$
$$x = 6\frac{1}{2} \text{ hours}$$

The plane that left at 3 p.m. traveled for $6\frac{1}{2}$ hours. The time then was 9:30 p.m.

9. 8 miles

	Rate ×	Time =	Distance
Going	4	x	$4x$
Return	2	$6 - x$	$2(6 - x)$

Let x = time for a walk on the path

The scout troop was gone for 6 hours. Therefore, time of trip back = $6 - x$.

$$4x = 2(6 - x)$$
$$4x = 12 - 2x$$
$$6x = 12$$
$$x = 2 \text{ hours}$$
$R \times T = D$; 2 hours at 4 mph = 8 miles

10. 6 hours

	Rate ×	Time =	Distance
Faster Car	36	x	$36x$
Slower Car	31	x	$31x$

Let x = travel time

$$36x - 31x = 30$$
$$5x = 30$$
$$x = 6 \text{ hours}$$

Test Yourself 19

1. 12 minutes

	John	Steve
$\dfrac{\text{Time actually spent}}{\text{Time needed to do entire job alone}}$	$\dfrac{x}{20}$ +	$\dfrac{x}{30} = 1$

Multiply all terms by 60 to clear the fractions.

$$3x + 2x = 60$$
$$5x = 60$$
$$x = 12$$

2. 30 minutes

It takes Mr. Powell x minutes to mow the lawn. Rick alone will take twice as long, or $2x$ minutes.

	Mr. Powell	Rick
$\dfrac{\text{Time actually spent}}{\text{Time needed to do entire job alone}}$	$\dfrac{20}{x}$ +	$\dfrac{20}{2x} = 1$

Multiply all terms by $2x$ to clear the fractions.

$$40 + 20 = 2x$$
$$60 = 2x$$
$$x = 30 \text{ minutes}$$

3. $\dfrac{5-x}{5}$

In x days, he has painted $\dfrac{x}{5}$ of the barn. To find what part is still unpainted, subtract the part completed from $1\left(\dfrac{5}{5}\right)$.

$$\frac{5}{5} - \frac{x}{5} = \frac{5-x}{5}$$

4. $3\dfrac{3}{5}$ hours

	Mary	Ruth
$\dfrac{\text{Time actually spent}}{\text{Time needed to do entire job alone}}$	$\dfrac{x}{6}$ +	$\dfrac{x}{9} = 1$

Multiply all terms by 18 to clear the fractions.

$$3x + 2x = 18$$
$$5x = 18$$
$$x = 3\frac{3}{5}$$

5. 6 hours

$$\frac{\text{Time actually spent}}{\text{Time needed to do entire job alone}} \quad \overset{\text{Inlet}}{\frac{x}{3}} - \overset{\text{Drain}}{\frac{x}{6}} = 1$$

Multiply all terms by 6 to clear the fractions.

$$2x - x = 6$$
$$x = 6$$

Note that the two fractions are subtracted because the drainpipe does not help the inlet pipe but rather works against it.

6. 6 hours

$$\frac{\text{Time actually spent}}{\text{Time needed to do entire job alone}} \quad \overset{\text{Tractor}}{\frac{2}{4}} + \overset{\text{Plow}}{\frac{x}{12}} = 1$$

You do not need to calculate the answer. Because half the job $\left(\frac{2}{4}\right)$ was completed by the tractor, the other half $\left(\frac{6}{12}\right)$ was done by the plow, and x, therefore, must equal 6.

7. 3 hours

$$\frac{\text{Time actually spent}}{\text{Time needed to do entire job alone}} \quad \overset{\text{Michael}}{\frac{2}{6}} + \overset{\text{Barry}}{\frac{2}{x}} = 1$$

Multiple all the terms by $6x$ to clear the fractions.

$$2x + 12 = 6x$$
$$12 = 4x$$
$$3 = x$$

8. 12 minutes

$$\frac{\text{Time actually spent}}{\text{Time needed to do entire job alone}} \quad \overset{\text{Girl}}{\frac{x}{20}} + \overset{\text{Brother}}{\frac{x}{30}} = 1$$

Multiply all the terms by 60 to clear the fractions.

$$3x + 2x = 60$$
$$5x = 60$$
$$x = 12$$

9. 7 hours 12 minutes

	Fast Press	Slower Press
$\dfrac{\text{Time actually spent}}{\text{Time needed to do entire job alone}}$	$\dfrac{x}{12}$ +	$\dfrac{x}{18}$ = 1

Multiply all the terms by 36 to clear the fractions.

$3x + 2x = 36$

$5x = 36$

$x = 7.2 \text{ hours} = 7 \text{ hours } 12 \text{ minutes}$ (To restate 7.2 hours as hours and minutes: 0.2 hours $= \dfrac{2}{10}$ or $\dfrac{1}{5} \times 60$ minutes $= 12$ minutes)

10. 3 days

If John completes $\dfrac{1}{4}$ of the job in $\dfrac{3}{4}$ day, it will take him 4 times as long to do the entire job.

$$\dfrac{4}{1} \times \dfrac{3}{4} = 3$$

EXERCISES: MATHEMATICS

Exercise 1

Directions: In the following questions, work out each problem and mark the letter that corresponds to the correct answer. If the correct answer does not appear among the choices, mark (E) for ''Not given.'' Answers are found following Exercise 4.

1.   896
   × 708

   (A) 643,386
   (B) 634,386
   (C) 634,368
   (D) 643,368
   (E) Not given

2.   9)4266

   (A) 447
   (B) 477
   (C) 474
   (D) 475
   (E) Not given

3. $125.25
       0.50
     70.86
  +   6.07

   (A) $201.68
   (B) $202.69
   (C) $200.68
   (D) $202.68
   (E) Not given

4. $1250.37
   −   48.98

   (A) $1201.39
   (B) $1201.49
   (C) $1200.39
   (D) $1201.38
   (E) Not given

5.   29)476.92

   (A) 16.4445
   (B) 17.4445
   (C) 16.4555
   (D) 17.4455
   (E) Not given

6.   28
     19
     17
  +   24

   (A) 87
   (B) 88
   (C) 90
   (D) 89
   (E) Not given

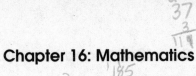

7. $3.7)\overline{2339.86}$

(A) 632.4

(B) 62.34

(C) 642.3

(D) 63.24

(E) Not given

8. $\begin{array}{r} 45286 \\ \times\ \ 4\frac{1}{5} \end{array}$

(A) $190,021\frac{1}{5}$

(B) 190,234

(C) $190,201\frac{1}{5}$

(D) $190,202\frac{2}{5}$

(E) Not given

9. $\begin{array}{r} 8\frac{1}{6} \\ -\ 5\frac{2}{3} \end{array}$

(A) $3\frac{2}{3}$

(B) $2\frac{1}{3}$

(C) $3\frac{1}{6}$

(D) $2\frac{1}{2}$

(E) Not given

10. $\frac{1}{9} \times \frac{2}{3} \times \frac{7}{8} =$

(A) $\frac{6}{108}$

(B) $\frac{7}{108}$

(C) $\frac{14}{27}$

(D) $\frac{12}{52}$

(E) Not given

11. $4\frac{1}{3})\overline{\frac{1}{4}}$

(A) $\frac{3}{52}$

(B) $\frac{5}{52}$

(C) $17\frac{1}{3}$

(D) $\frac{12}{52}$

(E) Not given

12. $\begin{array}{r} 78523 \\ 21457 \\ 3256 \\ +\ \ \ 1478 \end{array}$

(A) 104,715

(B) 105,714

(C) 104,814

(D) 105,814

(E) Not given

13. $\begin{array}{r} 12689 \\ \times\ \ \ \ 37 \end{array}$

(A) 569,493

(B) 468,493

(C) 469,493

(D) 568,493

(E) Not given

14. Find $6\frac{2}{3}\%$ of $13.50

(A) $0.89

(B) $0.91

(C) $0.88

(D) $0.95

(E) Not given

15. Rename $\frac{11}{16}$ as a decimal.

(A) 0.8675

(B) 0.6875

(C) 0.6785

(D) 0.6578

(E) Not given

Exercise 2

Directions: Work each problem on scratch paper or in the margins, then look at the answer choices. If your answer is among those choices, circle the letter before your answer. If your answer is not among the choices, mark (E) for "None of these." Answers are found following Exercise 4.

1.   5239
     $\times$ 706

   (A) 3,698,734
   (B) 3,708,734
   (C) 398,164
   (D) 68,107
   (E) None of these

2.   48207
     $\times$ 926

   (A) 44,639,682
   (B) 45,739,682
   (C) 45,638,682
   (D) 46,739,682
   (E) None of these

3. $4628 \div 7 =$
   (A) 662 R1
   (B) 661
   (C) 661 R1
   (D) 660 R6
   (E) None of these

4. $419\overline{)5063}$
   (A) 11 R408
   (B) 12 R9
   (C) 12 R37
   (D) 14 R81
   (E) None of these

5. $\$59.60 \div \$0.40 =$
   (A) 0.149
   (B) 1.49
   (C) 14.9
   (D) 149
   (E) None of these

6. $3.41 + 5.6 + 0.873 =$
   (A) 4.843
   (B) 9.883
   (C) 15.264
   (D) 17.743
   (E) None of these

7.   58769
     $-$ 4028

   (A) 54,641
   (B) 44,741
   (C) 54,741
   (D) 53,741
   (E) None of these

8. $0.3 \times 0.08 =$
   (A) 0.0024
   (B) 0.024
   (C) 0.240
   (D) 2.40
   (E) None of these

9. $0.33\overline{)9.9}$
   (A) 0.3
   (B) 3
   (C) 30
   (D) 33
   (E) None of these

10. 16% of 570 =
   (A) 85.3
   (B) 89.41
   (C) 90.68
   (D) 92
   (E) None of these

11. 135 is what percent of 900?

   (A) 12%

   (B) 15%

   (C) 17.5%

   (D) 19%

   (E) None of these

Directions: Express all fractions in lowest terms.

12. $\frac{3}{4} + \frac{3}{8} =$

   (A) $\frac{7}{8}$

   (B) $\frac{8}{9}$

   (C) $1\frac{1}{8}$

   (D) $1\frac{3}{8}$

   (E) None of these

13.
$$3\frac{1}{4}$$
$$4\frac{1}{8}$$
$$+ \quad 4\frac{1}{2}$$

   (A) $11\frac{5}{8}$

   (B) $11\frac{3}{4}$

   (C) $11\frac{7}{8}$

   (D) 12

   (E) None of these

14.
$$10\frac{2}{3}$$
$$- \quad 9\frac{1}{2}$$

   (A) $1\frac{1}{3}$

   (B) $1\frac{1}{2}$

   (C) $1\frac{1}{6}$

   (D) $\frac{13}{32}$

   (E) None of these

15.
$$14\frac{7}{24}$$
$$- \quad 5\frac{2}{3}$$

   (A) $8\frac{11}{12}$

   (B) $8\frac{5}{6}$

   (C) $9\frac{1}{3}$

   (D) $9\frac{15}{24}$

   (E) None of these

16. $\frac{8}{15} \times \frac{3}{4} =$

   (A) $\frac{1}{5}$

   (B) $\frac{2}{5}$

   (C) $\frac{3}{5}$

   (D) $\frac{3}{10}$

   (E) None of these

exercises

17. $5\frac{1}{4} \times 2\frac{2}{7} =$

    (A) 12

    (B) $11\frac{3}{28}$

    (C) $11\frac{4}{7}$

    (D) $10\frac{3}{28}$

    (E) None of these

18. $\frac{3}{4}\overline{)\frac{9}{16}}$

    (A) $\frac{27}{64}$

    (B) $\frac{3}{4}$

    (C) $\frac{5}{8}$

    (D) $\frac{7}{16}$

    (E) None of these

19. $(-12) + (+4) =$

    (A) +16

    (B) −8

    (C) +8

    (D) −16

    (E) None of these

20. $(-22) - (-18) =$

    (A) +13

    (B) +6

    (C) −6

    (D) −30

    (E) None of these

21. $(+7) \times (-7) =$

    (A) +49

    (B) 0

    (C) +1

    (D) −14

    (E) None of these

22. $(+56) \div (-7) =$

    (A) −6

    (B) −8

    (C) +8

    (D) +6

    (E) None of these

Exercise 3

Directions: Choose the correct answer to each problem and circle its letter. Answers are found following Exercise 4.

1. Six girls sold the following numbers of boxes of cookies: 42, 35, 28, 30, 24, 27. What was the average number of boxes sold?

   (A) 26

   (B) 29

   (C) 30

   (D) 31

2. The cost of sending a telegram is 52 cents for the first ten words and $2\frac{1}{2}$ cents for each additional word. The cost of sending a 14-word telegram is

   (A) 62 cents.

   (B) 63 cents.

   (C) 69 cents.

   (D) 87 cents.

3. A stock clerk has on hand the following items:

   > 500 pads worth 4 cents each
   > 130 pencils worth 3 cents each
   > 50 dozen rubber bands worth 2 cents per dozen

   If, from this stock, he issues 125 pads, 45 pencils, and 48 rubber bands, what would be the value of the remaining stock?

   (A) $6.43

   (B) $8.95

   (C) $17.63

   (D) $18.47

4. As an employee at a clothing store, you are entitled to a 10% discount on all purchases. When the store has a sale, employees are also entitled to the 20% discount offered to all customers. What would you have to pay for a $60 jacket bought on a sale day?

   (A) $6.00

   (B) $10.80

   (C) $36.00

   (D) $43.20

5. How many square yards of linoleum are needed to cover a floor having an area of 270 square feet?

   (A) 24

   (B) 28

   (C) 30

   (D) 33

6. If a pie is divided into 40 parts, what percent is one part of the whole pie?

   (A) 0.4

   (B) 2.5

   (C) 4.0

   (D) 25

7. A recipe for 6 quarts of punch calls for $\frac{3}{4}$ cups of sugar. How much sugar is needed for 9 quarts of punch?

   (A) $\frac{5}{8}$ of a cup

   (B) $\frac{7}{8}$ of a cup

   (C) $1\frac{1}{8}$ cups

   (D) $2\frac{1}{4}$ cups

8. How many yards of ribbon will it take to make 45 badges if each badge uses 4 inches of ribbon?

   (A) 5

   (B) 9

   (C) 11

   (D) 15

9. Oil once sold at $42\frac{1}{2}$ cents a quart. What was the cost of 4 gallons of oil?

   (A) $6.50

   (B) $6.60

   (C) $6.70

   (D) $6.80

10. A clerk can add 40 columns of figures an hour by using an adding machine. He can add 20 columns of figures an hour without using an adding machine. What is the total number of hours it will take the clerk to add 200 columns of figures if $\frac{3}{5}$ of the work is done by machine and the rest without the machine?

    (A) 6 hours

    (B) 7 hours

    (C) 8 hours

    (D) 9 hours

11. Two rectangular boards, each measuring 5 feet by 3 feet, are placed together to make one large board. How much shorter will the perimeter be if the two long sides are placed together than if the two short sides are placed together?

    (A) 2 feet

    (B) 4 feet

    (C) 6 feet

    (D) 8 feet

12. 1% of 8 =

    (A) 8

    (B) 0.8

    (C) 0.08

    (D) 0.008

13. When 81.3 is divided by 10, the quotient is

    (A) 0.0813

    (B) 0.813

    (C) 8.13

    (D) 813

14. +1 −1 +1 −1 +1 . . . and so on, where the last number is +1 has a sum of

    (A) 0

    (B) −1

    (C) +1

    (D) 2

15. If a plane travels 1000 miles in 5 hours 30 minutes, what is its average speed in miles per hour?

    (A) $181\frac{9}{11}$

    (B) 200

    (C) 215

    (D) $191\frac{1}{5}$

16. A jacket that normally sells for $35 can be purchased on sale for 2,975 pennies. What is the rate of discount represented by the sale price?

    (A) 5%

    (B) 10%

    (C) 15%

    (D) 20%

17. Perform the indicated operations and express your answer in inches: 12 feet minus 7 inches, plus 2 feet 1 inch, minus 7 feet, minus 1 yard, plus 2 yards 1 foot 3 inches.

    (A) 130 inches

    (B) 128 inches

    (C) 129 inches

    (D) 131 inches

18. What is the value of x when $5x = 5 \times 4 \times 2 \times 0$?

    (A) 6

    (B) 8

    (C) 0

    (D) 1

19. A square has an area of 49 sq. in. The number of inches in its perimeter is

    (A) 7

    (B) 28

    (C) 14

    (D) 98

20. $(3 + 4)^3 =$

(A) 21

(B) 91

(C) 343

(D) 490

21. A roll of carpeting will cover 224 square feet of floor space. How many rolls will be needed to carpet a room 36' × 8' and another 24' × 9'?

(A) 2.25

(B) 4.50

(C) 2.50

(D) 4.25

22. A library contains 60 books on arts and crafts. If this is 0.05% of the total number of books on the shelves, how many books does the library own?

(A) 120,000

(B) 12,000

(C) 1,200,000

(D) 1,200

23. A court clerk estimates that the untried cases on the docket will occupy the court for 150 trial days. If new cases are accumulating at the rate of 1.6 trial days per day (Saturday and Sunday excluded) and the court sits 5 days a week, how many days' business will remain to be heard at the end of 60 trial days?

(A) 168 trial days

(B) 188 trial days

(C) 185 trial days

(D) 186 trial days

24. A house plan uses the scale $\frac{1}{4}$ inch = 1 foot, and in the drawing the living room is 7 inches long. If the scale is changed to 1 inch = 1 foot, what will the length of the living room be in the new drawing?

(A) 18 in.

(B) 28 in.

(C) 30 in.

(D) 36 in.

25. A store sold suits for $65 each. The suits cost the store $50 each. The percentage of increase of selling price over cost is

(A) 40%

(B) $33\frac{1}{2}$%

(C) $33\frac{1}{3}$%

(D) 30%

26. A man borrowed $5000 and agreed to pay $11\frac{1}{2}$% annual interest. If he repaid the loan in 6 months, how much interest would he pay?

(A) $2875.00

(B) $5750.00

(C) $287.50

(D) $575.00

27. After deducting a discount of 30%, the price of a coat was $35.00. What was the regular price of the coat?

(A) $116.67

(B) $24.50

(C) $50.00

(D) $42.00

28. Two cars start from the same point at the same time. One drives north at 20 miles an hour, and the other drives south on the same straight road at 36 miles an hour. How many miles apart are they after 30 minutes?

(A) Fewer than 10

(B) Between 10 and 20

(C) Between 20 and 30

(D) Between 30 and 40

29. During his summer vacation, a boy earned $14.50 per day and saved 60% of his earnings. If he worked 45 days, how much did he save?

(A) $391.50

(B) $287.93

(C) $402.75

(D) $543.50

30. The number of cubic feet of soil needed for a flower box 3 feet long, 8 inches wide, and 1 foot deep is

    (A) 24

    (B) 12

    (C) $4\frac{2}{3}$

    (D) 2

31. The scale of a certain map is 4 inches = 32 miles. The number of inches that would represent 80 miles is

    (A) 8

    (B) 12

    (C) 10

    (D) 16

32. The daily almanac report for one day during the summer stated that the sun rose at 6:14 a.m. and set at 6:06 p.m. Find the number of hours and minutes in the time between the rising and setting of the sun on that day.

    (A) 11 hr. 52 min

    (B) 12 hr. 8 min.

    (C) 11 hr. 2 min.

    (D) 12 hr. 48 min.

33. One piece of wire is 25 feet 8 inches long and another is 18 feet 10 inches long. What is the difference in length?

    (A) 6 ft. 10 in.

    (B) 6 ft. 11 in.

    (C) 7 ft. 2 in.

    (D) 7 ft. 4 in.

34. If a vehicle is to complete a 20-mile trip at an average rate of 30 miles per hour, it must complete the trip in

    (A) 20 min.

    (B) 30 min.

    (C) 40 min.

    (D) 50 min.

35. A snapshot measures $2\frac{1}{2}$ inches by $1\frac{7}{8}$ inches. It is to be enlarged so that the longer dimension will be 4 inches. The length of the enlarged shorter dimension will be

    (A) $2\frac{1}{2}$ inches.

    (B) 3 inches.

    (C) $3\frac{3}{8}$ inches.

    (D) $2\frac{5}{8}$ inches.

36. An adult's ski lift ticket costs twice as much as a child's. If a family of three children and two adults can ski for $49, what is the cost of an adult ticket?

    (A) $7

    (B) $10

    (C) $12

    (D) $14

37. A recipe calls for $1\frac{1}{2}$ cups of sugar. It is necessary to make eight times the recipe for a church supper. If 2 cups of sugar equal 1 pound, how many pounds of sugar will be needed to make the recipe for the supper?

    (A) 4

    (B) 6

    (C) 8

    (D) 10

38. In the fraction $\frac{1}{\Delta - 2}$, Δ can be replaced by all of the following except

    (A) 0

    (B) +3

    (C) +2

    (D) −2

39. If one pipe can fill a tank in $1\frac{1}{2}$ hours and another can fill the same tank in 45 minutes, how long will it take for the two pipes to fill the tank together?

(A) 1 hour

(B) $\frac{1}{2}$ hour

(C) $1\frac{1}{2}$ hours

(D) $\frac{1}{3}$ hour

40. Two cars are 550 miles apart and traveling toward each other on the same road. If one travels at 50 miles per hour, the other at 60 miles per hour, and they both leave at 1:00 p.m., what time will they meet?

(A) 4:00 p.m.

(B) 4:30 p.m.

(C) 5:45 p.m.

(D) 6:00 p.m.

Exercise 4

Directions: Choose the correct answer to each problem and circle its letter. Answers are found at the end of this chapter.

1. Any number that is divisible by both 5 and 6 is also divisible by

(A) 11

(B) 9

(C) 7

(D) 3

2. 3,482,613 rounded to the nearest million is

(A) 2,000,000

(B) 3,500,000

(C) 3,000,000

(D) 4,000,000

3. The number that is *not* a factor of 120 is

(A) 5

(B) 6

(C) 7

(D) 8

4. What is the place value of 3 in 4.9236?

(A) Hundredths

(B) Thousandths

(C) Ten thousandths

(D) Hundred thousandths

5. Which symbol belongs in the circle?

0.0983 ○ 0.124

(A) <

(B) >

(C) =

(D) ≅

6. The greatest common factor of 24 and 12 is

(A) 2

(B) 4

(C) 6

(D) 12

7. 1000% is equal to

(A) 0.0001

(B) 0.1

(C) 10

(D) 100

8. In the simplest form, $\frac{12}{16}$ is

   (A) $\frac{3}{4}$

   (B) $\frac{2}{3}$

   (C) $\frac{2}{6}$

   (D) $\frac{4}{8}$

9. $\frac{9}{25}$ is equal to

   (A) 0.036

   (B) 0.04

   (C) 0.36

   (D) 0.45

10. What number belongs in the box?

   $-5 + \Box = 0$

   (A) -5

   (B) 0

   (C) -1

   (D) +5

11. $\sqrt{81}$ is equal to

   (A) 8

   (B) 9

   (C) 18

   (D) 40.5

12. Solve for x: $\frac{x}{2} + 3 = 15$

   (A) 18

   (B) 20

   (C) 22

   (D) 24

13. If $y + 2 > 10$, then y must be

   (A) smaller than 10.

   (B) smaller than 8.

   (C) greater than 8.

   (D) equal to 0.

14. If $a + b = 200°$, and $c + d + e + f = 140°$, what is the number of degrees in angle g?

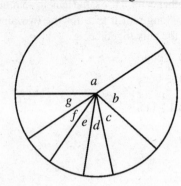

   (A) 10°

   (B) 20°

   (C) 30°

   (D) 45°

15. The area of the shaded portion of the rectangle below is

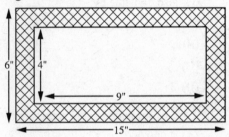

   (A) 54 sq. in.

   (B) 90 sq. in.

   (C) 45 sq. in.

   (D) 36 sq. in.

16. Which point shown below corresponds to (8,3)?

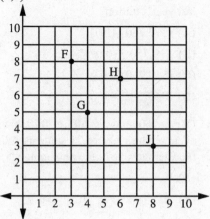

(A) Point F

(B) Point G

(C) Point H

(D) Point J

QUESTIONS 17–23 ARE BASED ON THE FOLLOWING PASSAGE.

Mr. Shea, a shop teacher at the junior high school, owns a ski lodge in Vermont. The lodge is open to guests on weekends and during school vacations. Mr. Shea's regular rates, which include breakfast and dinner, are $25 per night for dormitory-style accommodations. He gives a 30 percent discount to all members of organized student groups from his community.

17. Sixteen members of Boy Scout Troop 60 and two of their leaders went on a ski weekend and stayed at Mr. Shea's lodge. The two-night cost of room and board for each boy was

(A) $25

(B) $35

(C) $50

(D) $60

18. The leaders shared a room instead of sleeping in the dormitory. The total bill for the two of them was $84 for the two nights. The surcharge per person for the semi-private room was

(A) 7%

(B) 20%

(C) 32%

(D) 42%

19. Lift tickets cost $20 per day for adults and $14 per day for juniors (persons under 13 years of age). Five of the boys were 12 years old, while the others were older. What was the total cost of lift tickets for a day of skiing?

(A) $220

(B) $290

(C) $330

(D) $390

20. Among the boys, $\frac{1}{4}$ considered themselves to be expert skiers. Of those who were less experienced, $\frac{3}{4}$ took ski lessons. Of those who took ski lessons, $\frac{1}{3}$ rented ski equipment. How many boys rented ski equipment?

(A) 9

(B) 6

(C) 4

(D) 3

21. The mountain on which the troop skied had 27 trails served by a T-bar lift, two J-bars lifts, and three chair lifts. The proportion of trails to lifts was

(A) 5:1

(B) 7:2

(C) 9:3

(D) 9:2

22. One boy skied the length of a 4.6-mile trail in just under 14 minutes. His average speed was approximately

    (A) 15 mph.

    (B) 20 mph.

    (C) 25 mph.

    (D) 30 mph.

23. The bus chartered for the trip cost $250. The rooms and lift tickets totaled $1,304. The troop contributed $400 from its treasury to help defray expenses of the trip. If the rest was divided equally among the 16 boys and 2 leaders, how much did each individual pay?

    (A) $64.11

    (B) $71.13

    (C) $75.28

    (D) $83.07

QUESTIONS 24–28 REFER TO THE FOLLOWING PASSAGE.

Applesville High School, an accredited 4-year institution (grades 9 to 12), is located on a picturesque 128-acre campus. At Applesville, the student-teacher ratio is 7:1, average class size is 15, and current annual tuition is $19,750. The historic library is located at the center of campus and has a collection of 30,000 volumes.

24. If $\frac{7}{8}$ of the campus is devoted to woods and gardens and the rest is developed for academic use, how many acres are used for academics?

    (A) 16

    (B) 32

    (C) 48

    (D) 96

25. This year, annual tuition is 7% higher than it was last year. Which expression represents last year's tuition?

    (A) ($19,750)(1.07)

    (B) $19,750 – (0.07)($19,750)

    (C) ($19,750)(0.93)

    (D) $19,750/1.07

26. Of the 60 classes offered, 20 have an average class size of 21 students. What is the average size of the remaining classes?

    (A) 9

    (B) 12

    (C) 15

    (D) 21

27. Next year, Applesville will loan its rare book collection (2% of its volumes) to the local university. How many volumes will Applesville's library have on campus next year?

    (A) 29,000

    (B) 29,400

    (C) 29,600

    (D) 29,800

28. Excluding maintenance and administrative personnel, if there are 304 persons (teachers and students) at school, how many teachers work at Applesville High School?

    (A) 7

    (B) 14

    (C) 38

    (D) 152

QUESTIONS 29–32 REFER TO THE FOLLOWING PASSAGE.

On an icy day, the Bergs' car skidded into a telephone pole and suffered two smashed doors and a broken drive shaft. After four weeks in a body shop, the car was fully repaired. The Bergs' insurance company paid the body shop's bill, less the $200 deductible, which the Bergs paid.

29. For what portion of the year were the Bergs unable to use their car?

(A) $\frac{1}{4}$

(B) $\frac{1}{10}$

(C) $\frac{1}{12}$

(D) $\frac{1}{13}$

30. In the year before the accident, the Bergs' insurance premium was $1100. The year following the accident, their premium rose to $1500. The new premium was about what percent of the old premium?

(A) $26\frac{2}{3}\%$

(B) $36\frac{1}{3}\%$

(C) $136\frac{1}{3}\%$

(D) 140%

31. To match the blue paint of the car, the man in the body shop had to add $1\frac{1}{2}$ ounces of black paint for each pint of blue paint. He used three gallons of blue paint on the car. What was the total amount of paint he used?

(A) $2\frac{1}{4}$ pints

(B) $21\frac{3}{4}$ pints

(C) 24 pints

(D) $26\frac{1}{4}$ pints

32. Three men of about equal efficiency were assigned to work on the Bergs' car. One man worked on the car full-time. He was always assisted by one of the other men. If the full-time man needed to complete the job alone, how many weeks would the car have been in the shop?

(A) 2 weeks

(B) 4 weeks

(C) 6 weeks

(D) 8 weeks

ANSWER KEYS AND EXPLANATIONS

Exercise 1

1. C	4. A	7. A	10. B	13. C
2. C	5. E	8. C	11. A	14. E
3. D	6. B	9. D	12. E	15. B

1. The correct answer is (C).

$$\begin{array}{r} 896 \\ \times \quad 708 \\ \hline 7168 \\ 62720 \\ \hline 634368 \end{array}$$

2. The correct answer is (C).

$$\begin{array}{r} 474 \\ 9\overline{)4266} \\ \underline{36} \\ 66 \\ \underline{63} \\ 36 \\ 36 \end{array}$$

3. The correct answer is (D). $202.68

4. The correct answer is (A). $1201.39

5. The correct answer is (E).

$$16.44551 \approx 16.4455$$

$$\begin{array}{r} 29\overline{)476.9200} \\ \underline{29} \\ 186 \\ \underline{174} \\ 129 \\ \underline{116} \\ 132 \\ \underline{116} \\ 160 \\ \underline{145} \\ 150 \\ \underline{145} \\ 50 \end{array}$$

6. The correct answer is (B). 88

7. The correct answer is (A).

$$63\,2.39 \approx 632.4$$

$$\begin{array}{r} 3.7\overline{)2339.8\,60} \\ \underline{222} \\ 119 \\ \underline{111} \\ 88 \\ \underline{74} \\ 146 \\ \underline{111} \\ 350 \\ \underline{333} \\ 17 \end{array}$$

8. **The correct answer is (C).**

$$\frac{1}{5} = 0.20$$

$$
\begin{array}{r}
45286 \\
\times \quad 4.20 \\
\hline
905720 \\
181144 \quad \\
\hline
190201.20 = 190,201\frac{1}{5}
\end{array}
$$

9. **The correct answer is (D).**

$$
\begin{array}{r}
8\frac{1}{6} = 7\frac{7}{6} \\
-5\frac{2}{3} = 5\frac{4}{6} \\
\hline
2\frac{3}{6} = 2\frac{1}{2}
\end{array}
$$

10. **The correct answer is (B).**

$$\frac{1}{9} \times \frac{\cancel{2}^1}{3} \times \frac{7}{\cancel{8}_4} = \frac{7}{108}$$

11. **The correct answer is (A).**

$$\frac{1}{4} \div 4\frac{1}{3} = \frac{1}{4} \div \frac{13}{3} = \frac{1}{4} \times \frac{3}{13} = \frac{3}{52}$$

12. **The correct answer is (E).** 104,714. If you got this wrong, check how you added up each column again.

13. **The correct answer is (C).**

$$
\begin{array}{r}
12689 \\
\times \quad 37 \\
\hline
88823 \\
38067 \quad \\
\hline
469493
\end{array}
$$

14. **The correct answer is (E).**

$$\$13.50 \times 6\frac{2}{3}\% = \$13.50 \times 0.06\frac{2}{3}$$

$$= \frac{\$13.50}{1} \times \frac{0.20}{3}$$

$$= \frac{\$2.70}{3} = \$0.90$$

15. **The correct answer is (B).**

$$
\frac{11}{16} = 16\overline{)\begin{array}{l} 0.6875 \\ 11.0000 \end{array}}
$$

$$
\begin{array}{r}
9\ 6 \\
\hline
1\ 40 \\
1\ 28 \\
\hline
120 \\
112 \\
\hline
80 \\
80
\end{array}
$$

Exercise 2

1. A	6. B	11. B	15. E	19. B
2. A	7. C	12. C	16. B	20. E
3. C	8. B	13. C	17. A	21. E
4. E	9. C	14. C	18. B	22. B
5. D	10. E			

1. The correct answer is (A).

```
      5239
   ×  706
   ‾‾‾‾‾‾
     31434
   366730
   ‾‾‾‾‾‾‾
   3698734
```

2. The correct answer is (A).

```
     48207
   ×   926
   ‾‾‾‾‾‾‾
    289242
     96414
   433863
   ‾‾‾‾‾‾‾‾
   44639682
```

3. The correct answer is (C).

```
      661 R 1
   7)4628
     42
     ‾‾
      42
      42
      ‾‾
       08
        7
       ‾‾
        1
```

4. The correct answer is (E).

```
        12 R 35
   419)5063
       419
       ‾‾‾
       873
       838
       ‾‾‾
        35
```

5. The correct answer is (D).

```
              1 49
   $0.40)$59.60
           40
           ‾‾‾
           19 6
           16 0
           ‾‾‾‾
            3 60
            3 60
```

6. The correct answer is (B).

```
     3.410
     5.600
   +0.873
   ‾‾‾‾‾‾
     9.883
```

7. The correct answer is (C). 54,741

8. The correct answer is (B). 0.024

Add up the places to the right of the decimal point.

9. The correct answer is (C).

```
         30.
   .33)9.90
```

10. The correct answer is (E).

```
      570
   × 0.16
   ‾‾‾‾‾‾
    34 20
    570
   ‾‾‾‾‾‾
    91.20
```

11. **The correct answer is (B).**

    $135 \div 900 = 0.15 = 15\%$

12. **The correct answer is (C).**

    $$\frac{3}{4} = \frac{6}{8}$$
    $$+ \frac{3}{8} = \frac{3}{8}$$
    $$\frac{9}{8} = 1\frac{1}{8}$$

13. **The correct answer is (C).**

    $$3\frac{1}{4} = 3\frac{2}{8}$$
    $$4\frac{1}{8} = 4\frac{1}{8}$$
    $$+ 4\frac{1}{2} = 4\frac{4}{8}$$
    $$11\frac{7}{8}$$

14. **The correct answer is (C).**

    $$10\frac{2}{3} = 10\frac{4}{6}$$
    $$- 9\frac{1}{2} = 9\frac{3}{6}$$
    $$1\frac{1}{6}$$

15. **The correct answer is (E).**

    $$14\frac{7}{24} = 14\frac{7}{24} = 13\frac{31}{24}$$
    $$- 5\frac{2}{3} = 5\frac{16}{24} = 5\frac{16}{24}$$
    $$8\frac{15}{24} = 8\frac{5}{8}$$

16. **The correct answer is (B).**

    $$\frac{{}^{2}\cancel{8}}{\cancel{15}_{5}} \times \frac{{}^{1}\cancel{3}}{\cancel{4}_{1}} = \frac{2}{5}$$

17. **The correct answer is (A).**

    $$5\frac{1}{4} \times 2\frac{2}{7} = \frac{{}^{3}\cancel{21}}{\cancel{4}_{1}} \times \frac{{}^{4}\cancel{16}}{\cancel{7}_{1}} = \frac{12}{1} = 12$$

18. **The correct answer is (B).**

    $$\frac{9}{16} \div \frac{3}{4} = \frac{{}^{3}\cancel{9}}{\cancel{16}_{4}} \times \frac{{}^{1}\cancel{4}}{\cancel{3}_{1}} = \frac{3}{4}$$

19. **The correct answer is (B).** When adding two numbers of unlike sign, subtract and assign the sign of the larger number.

20. **The correct answer is (E).** Minus negative becomes plus positive. The problem then reads: $(-22) + (+18) = -4$

21. **The correct answer is (E).** When multiplying two numbers of unlike signs, the product is always negative. $(7) \times (-7) = -49$

22. **The correct answer is (B).** When you divide two numbers of unlike sign, the quotient is always negative.

    $(+56) \div (-7) = -8$

Exercise 3

1. D	9. D	17. C	25. D	33. A
2. A	10. B	18. C	26. C	34. C
3. D	11. B	19. B	27. C	35. B
4. D	12. C	20. C	28. C	36. D
5. C	13. C	21. A	29. A	37. B
6. B	14. C	22. A	30. D	38. C
7. C	15. A	23. D	31. C	39. B
8. A	16. C	24. B	32. A	40. D

1. **The correct answer is (D).** To find the average, add all the numbers and divide the sum by the number of terms.

   $42 + 35 + 28 + 30 + 24 + 27 = 186$

   $186 \div 6 = 31$

2. **The correct answer is (A).**

   14 words = 10 words + 4 words

   10 words cost 52 cents

   4 words @ 2.5 cents = $4 \times 2.5 = 10$ cents

   52 cents + 10 cents = 62 cents

3. **The correct answer is (D).**

   $500 - 125 = 375$ pads @ $0.04 = $15.00

   $130 - 45 = 85$ pencils @ $0.03 = $2.55

   50 dozen − 4 dozen = 46 dozen rubber bands @ $0.02 = $0.92

   $15 + $2.55 1 $0.92 = $18.47

4. **The correct answer is (D).**

   $60 \times 0.10 = $6 (employee discount)

   $60 − $6 = $54

   $54 \times 0.20 = $10.80 (sale discount)

   $54 − $10.80 = $43.20

5. **The correct answer is (C).**

   9 square feet = 1 square yard

   270 sq. ft. ÷ 9 = 30 sq. yds.

6. **The correct answer is (B).**

   The whole pie is 100%.

   Each part is $\frac{1}{40}$.

   $100 \div 40 = 2.5\%$

7. **The correct answer is (C).** First find out how much sugar is needed for one quart of punch.

   $$\frac{3}{4} \text{ cups} \div 6 = \frac{3}{4} \div \frac{6}{1} = \frac{\cancel{3}^{1}}{4} \times \frac{1}{\cancel{6}_{2}} = \frac{1}{8}$$

   For 9 quarts of punch:

   $$9 \times \frac{1}{8} = \frac{9}{8} = 1\frac{1}{8}$$

8. **The correct answer is (A).** 45 badges × 4 inches each = 180 inches needed. There are 36 inches in one yard. 180 inches ÷ 36 = 5 yards of ribbon needed.

9. **The correct answer is (D).**

   1 gallon = 4 quarts

   4 gals. = 16 qts.

   16 qts. $\times 42\frac{1}{2}$ cents $= 16 \times \$0.425 = \$6.80$

10. **The correct answer is (B).**

$\frac{3}{5}$ of 200 = 120 columns by machine @ 40 columns per hour = 3 hours

200 − 120 = 80 columns without machine @ 20 columns per hour = 4 hours

3 hours + 4 hours = 7 hours to complete the job

11. **The correct answer is (B).** Perimeter = $2l$ + $2w$. If the two long sides are together, the perimeter will be 5 + 3 + 3 + 5 + 3 + 3 = 22.

If the two short sides are together, the perimeter will be 3 + 5 + 5 + 3 + 5 + 5 = 26.

```
       5     5
   3  ┌─────┬─────┐  3
      └─────┴─────┘
```

26 − 22 = 4 feet shorter

12. **The correct answer is (C).** To remove a % sign, divide the number by 100.

Thus, 1% = $\frac{1}{100}$ = 0.01. 1% of 8 is the same as 1% times 8 = 0.01 × 8 = 0.08.

13. **The correct answer is (C).**

```
         8.13
   10)81.30
      80
       1 3
       1 0
         30
         30
          0
```

14. **The correct answer is (C).**

Each −1 cancels out the +1 before it.

Because the final term is +1, which is not canceled out by a −1, the sum is + 1.

15. **The correct answer is (A).**

5 hours 30 minutes = $5\frac{1}{2}$ hours

1000 miles ÷ $5\frac{1}{2}$ hours = $1000 ÷ \frac{11}{2}$ =

$1000 × \frac{2}{11} = 181\frac{9}{11}$ mph

16. **The correct answer is (C).**

2975 pennies = \$29.75

\$35.00 − \$29.75 = \$5.25 amount of discount

Rate of discount = $\frac{5.25}{35} × 100$

$= 0.15 × 100$

$= 15\%$

17. **The correct answer is (C).** First convert all the yards and feet into inches so that all addition and subtraction can be done using the same units.

$$
\begin{array}{rl}
12 \text{ feet} = & 144 \text{ inches} \\
-7 \text{ inches} = & -7 \text{ inches} \\
+2 \text{ feet, 1 inch} = & +25 \text{ inches} \\
-7 \text{ feet} = & -84 \text{ inches} \\
-1 \text{ yard} = & -36 \text{ inches} \\
+2 \text{ yards, 1 foot,} & \\
3 \text{ inches} = & \underline{+87 \text{ inches}} \\
= & 129 \text{ inches}
\end{array}
$$

18. **The correct answer is (C).** Any number multiplied by 0 equals 0. Since one multiplier on one side of the equals sign is 0, the product on that side of the sign must be 0.

$5x = 5 × 4 × 2 × 0$

$5x = 40 × 0$

$5x = 0$

$x = 0$

19. **The correct answer is (B).**

Area of a square $= s^2$

$49 = 7^2$

One side $= 7$ inches

$P = 4s$

$P = 4 \times 7'' = 28$ inches

20. **The correct answer is (C).** First perform the operation within the parentheses. To cube a number, multiply it by itself, two times.

$(3 + 4)^3 = (7)^3 = 7 \times 7 \times 7 = 343$

21. **The correct answer is (A).**

First room:

36 ft. $\times$ 8 ft. = 288 sq. ft.

Second room:

24 ft $\times$ 9 ft. $= \dfrac{216 \text{ sq. ft.}}{504 \text{ sq. ft.}}$

504 $\div$ 224 = 2.25 rolls needed

22. **The correct answer is (A).**

0.05% of the total $(x) = 60$

$0.0005x = 60$

$x = 60 \div 0.0005 = 120{,}000$

23. **The correct answer is (D).** If the court does a day's work every day, it will dispense with 60 days' worth of new cases. The excess work is $0.6 \times 60 = 36$ days of work. Add the 36 newly accumulated hours of excess work to the backlog of 150 days of work to learn that the court will be 186 trial days behind.

24. **The correct answer is (B).** $\dfrac{1}{4}$ in. = 1 ft., so 1 in. = 4 ft. and the living room is $7 \times 4 = 28$ ft. long. When the scale is changed to 1 in. = 1 ft., the 28-ft. living room will be 28 in. on the new drawing.

25. **The correct answer is (D).** To find percent of change, subtract the original figure from the new figure to determine amount of change; then divide the amount of change by the original figure to determine percent of change.

$\$65 - \$50 = \$15 \div 50 = 0.3 = 30\%$

26. **The correct answer is (C).** $11\dfrac{1}{2}\%$ of $5000 is $575. Because he repaid the loan in one-half of a year, his interest payment is $575 $\div$ 2 = $287.50.

27. **The correct answer is (C).** If 30% has been deducted, $35 is 70% of the original price. To find out what a number is when a percent of it is given, rename the percent as a decimal and divide the given number by it.

$\$35 \div 0.70 = \$50$

28. **The correct answer is (C).** One car went 20 mph for $\dfrac{1}{2}$ hour = 10 miles. The other went 36 mph for $\dfrac{1}{2}$ hour = 18 miles. Because they went in opposite directions, add the two distances to find the total number of miles apart: $10 + 18 = 28$.

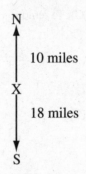

29. **The correct answer is (A).** The boy worked 45 days $\times$ $14.50 per day, so he earned $652.50. He saved 60% of $652.50 = $391.50.

30. **The correct answer is (D).** Rename 8 in. as $\dfrac{2}{3}$ ft. so that all measurements are in the same unit. Then multiply $l \times w \times h$.

3 ft. $\times \dfrac{2}{3}$ ft. $\times$ 1 ft. = 2 cu. ft.

31. **The correct answer is (C).** 4 in. = 32 miles; therefore, 1 in. = 32 ÷ 4 = 8 miles. 80 miles would be represented by 10 in.

32. **The correct answer is (A).** You do not need to do complicated calculations to answer this question: $14 - 6 = 8$. The sun was above the horizon for 8 minutes less than 12 hours, which is 11 hours 52 minutes ($60 - 8 = 52$).

33. **The correct answer is (A).**

    $$\begin{array}{r} 25 \text{ ft. } \quad 8 \text{ in.} = 24 \text{ ft. } 20 \text{ in.} \\ 18 \text{ ft. } 10 \text{ in.} = \underline{18 \text{ ft. } 10 \text{ in.}} \\ 6 \text{ ft. } 10 \text{ in.} \end{array}$$

34. **The correct answer is (C).** No calculations are needed here. Note that a 20-mile trip at 60 mph (which is 1 mile per minute) would take 20 minutes. Because the vehicle is traveling half as fast (30 mph), the 20-mile trip should take twice as long, or 40 minutes.

35. **The correct answer is (B).** This is a proportion problem. Set up the proportion as follows:

    $$\frac{2\frac{1}{2}}{4} = \frac{1\frac{7}{8}}{?}$$

    Substitute x for ?:

    $$\frac{2\frac{1}{2}}{4} = \frac{1\frac{7}{8}}{x}$$

    Cross-multiply:

    $$2\frac{1}{2}x = 4 \times 1\frac{7}{8}$$

    $$\frac{5}{2}x = \frac{60}{8}$$

    Divide both sides by the coefficient of x and calculate:

    $$x = \frac{60}{8} \div \frac{5}{2}$$

    $$x = \frac{60}{8} \times \frac{2}{5}$$

    $$x = 3$$

36. **The correct answer is (D).** A child's ticket costs x dollars. Each adult ticket costs twice as much, or $2x$ dollars. $2(2x) = 2$ adult tickets; $3x = 3$ children tickets. Write a simple equation and solve for x.

    $$2(2x) + 3x = \$49$$

    $$4x + 3x = \$49$$

    $$7x = \$49$$

    $$x = \$7$$

    $7 is the cost of a child's ticket; $14 is the cost of an adult's ticket.

37. **The correct answer is (B).**

    $1\frac{1}{2}$ c. sugar $\times$ 8 = 12 c. sugar

    12 c. ÷ 2 c. per lb. = 6 lb. of sugar

38. **The correct answer is (C).** By substituting +2 for the triangle, the denominator of the fraction becomes zero. A denominator of zero is undefined in mathematics.

39. **The correct answer is (B).** The first pipe can fill the tank in $1\frac{1}{2}$ hours, or $\frac{3}{2}$ hours; that is, it can do $\frac{2}{3}$ of the job in 1 hour. The second pipe can fill the tank in 45 minutes, or $\frac{3}{4}$ of an hour, or it can do $\frac{4}{3}$ of the job in 1 hour. Together the pipes can complete $\frac{4}{3} + \frac{2}{3} = \frac{6}{3}$ of the job in 1 hour. $\frac{6}{3} = 2$, or twice the job in 1 hour. Therefore, together the two pipes could fill the tank in $\frac{1}{2}$ hour.

40. **The correct answer is (D).** The cars are traveling toward each other, so the distance between them is being reduced at $60 + 50$ or 110 miles per hour. At a rate of 110 mph, 550 miles will be covered in 5 hours. If both cars left at 1:00 p.m., they should meet at 6:00 p.m.

Exercise 4

1. D	8. A	15. A	21. D	27. B
2. C	9. C	16. D	22. B	28. C
3. C	10. D	17. B	23. A	29. D
4. B	11. B	18. B	24. A	30. C
5. A	12. D	19. C	25. D	31. D
6. D	13. C	20. D	26. B	32. D
7. C	14. B			

1. **The correct answer is (D).** Not many numbers are divisible by both 5 and 6. Only multiples of 5 × 6 are divisible by both. Multiples of 5 × 6 are multiples of 30, which are all divisible by 3.

2. **The correct answer is (C).** The seventh digit to the left of the decimal point is in the millions place. Because 482 is less than 500, round down.

3. **The correct answer is (C).** 120 is not divisible by 7.

4. **The correct answer is (B).** The place values are: four ones, nine tenths, two hundredths, three thousandths, six ten thousandths.

5. **The correct answer is (A).** Look immediately to the right of the decimal point. 0 is less than 1.

6. **The correct answer is (D).** The greatest number by which both 12 and 24 can be divided is 12.

7. **The correct answer is (C).** To rename a percent as a decimal, move the decimal point two places to the left.

   $1000\% = 10.00$

8. **The correct answer is (A).** To simplify $\frac{12}{16}$ to simplest form, divide both numerator and denominator by 4.

9. **The correct answer is (C).** The fraction bar in a fraction means "divided by."
   $9 \div 25 = 0.36$

10. **The correct answer is (D).** The positive and negative cancel each other out. Addition may be done in any order. To check this problem, reverse the order of the addends.

    $5 - 5 = 0$

11. **The correct answer is (B).** The square root of 81 is 9.

12. **The correct answer is (D).**

    $\frac{x}{2} + 3 = 15$

    $\frac{x}{2} = 15 - 3$

    $\frac{x}{2} = 12$

    $x = 12 \times 2$

    $x = 24$

13. **The correct answer is (C).**

    $y + 2 > 10$

    $y > 10 - 2$

    $y > 8$

14. **The correct answer is (B).** The sum of the angles of a circle = 360°. Angles *a* through *f* total 340°. Angle *g* must be 20°.

15. **The correct answer is (A).** The area of the entire rectangle is 6 in. × 15 in. = 90 sq. in.

The area of the unshaded portion is 4 in. × 9 in. = 36 sq. in.

90 sq. in. – 36 sq. in.= 54 sq. in. in the shaded portion.

16. **The correct answer is (D).** In reading a graph, always read along the horizontal axis first.

17. **The correct answer is (B).** The charge for one night is $25; for two nights, $50. The Boy Scouts receive a 30% discount, so they pay 70%. 70% of $50 = $35.

18. **The correct answer is (B).** As part of the group, the leaders received the same 30% discount as the boys. If they had slept in the dormitory, they would have paid $35 each for the two nights. Their total bill (2 men, 2 nights) would have been $70. However, they paid extra for a semi-private room. To find the percent of increase, subtract the original number from the new number and divide the difference by the original number.

$84 – $70 = $14 ÷ $70 = 20%

19. **The correct answer is (C).** Of the 18 people, there are 13 adults and 5 juniors. The adult tickets cost $20 × 13 = $260. The junior tickets cost $14 × 5 = $70. The total cost of lift tickets for one day is $260 + $70 = $330.

20. **The correct answer is (D).** $\frac{1}{4}$ of 16 = 4 expert skiers. That leaves 16 – 4 = 12 less experienced skiers. $\frac{3}{4}$ of 12 = 9 who took ski lessons. $\frac{1}{3}$ of 9 = 3 who rented equipment.

21. **The correct answer is (D).** There were 27 trails and 6 lifts, which simplifies to 9:2.

22. **The correct answer is (B).** The formula for determining rate is $\frac{D}{T}$. The distance skied is 4.6 miles. The time, just under 14 minutes, is approximately 0.25 hour.

4.6 ÷ 0.25 = 18.4 mph

Because he skied the distance in slightly less than 0.25 hour, his average speed was very close to 20 mph.

23. **The correct answer is (A).** First add up the expenses:

Rooms and lift tickets =	$1304
Bus =	$250
	$1554

Subtract the troop contribution	– 400
	$1154

Now divide by the 18 people:

$2254 ÷ 18 = $64.11 each

24. **The correct answer is (A).** If $\frac{7}{8}$ of the campus is devoted to woods and gardens, then $\frac{1}{8}$ is used for academics.

$\frac{1}{8}$ of 128 acres = $\frac{1}{8} \times 128 = 16$

25. **The correct answer is (D).** Let x = tuition last year. This year's tuition is 7% greater:

$1.07x = \$19,750$

$x = \$19,750/1.07$

26. **The correct answer is (B).** Average class size = (sum of the class sizes) ÷ (total number of classes). If 20 classes have an average size of 21 students, that's 20 × 21 students. Let x = average class size of the other 40 classes. Then:

$$\frac{(20)(21)+40x}{60}=15$$

Multiplying both sides by 60:

$$420+40x=900$$
$$40x=480$$
$$x=12$$

Or, since we know that $\frac{1}{3}$ of the classes have an average size of 21, which is 6 above the given average size of 15, then the remaining $\frac{2}{3}$ of the classes (twice as many as $\frac{1}{3}$) must have an average size of 3 below 15.

$15 – 3 = 12$

27. **The correct answer is (B).** The library has 30,000 volumes. Ten percent of 30,000 = 3000. So, 2% = 3000/5 = 600. The number of volumes left on campus next year will be:

$$30,000 - 600 = 29,400$$

28. **The correct answer is (C).** Based on the information given, the student-teacher ratio is 7:1. This means that for every 7 students, there is 1 teacher. So, we can let $7x$ = number of students and $1x$ = number of teachers. Then:

$$7x + 1x = 304$$
$$8x = 304$$
$$x = 38$$

29. **The correct answer is (D).** 4 weeks is $\frac{4}{52} = \frac{1}{13}$.

30. **The correct answer is (C).** Again find what percent one number is of another by creating a fraction. This time, the part that you want to know about happens to be larger than the whole.

$$\$1500 \div 1100 = 1.3636 \approx 136\frac{1}{3}\%$$

31. **The correct answer is (D).** 3 gallon = 24 pints. $1\frac{1}{2}$ ounces of black paint × 24 = 36 ounces of black paint. 36 ounces $= 2\frac{1}{4}$ pints. 24 pints of blue $+ 2\frac{1}{4}$ pints of black $= 26\frac{1}{4}$ pints of paint.

32. **The correct answer is (D).** You do not have to calculate this problem. If you read carefully, you will see that 2 men worked full-time and the work took 4 weeks. If only one man (half the number) had worked, the job would have taken twice the time, or 8 weeks.

SUMMING IT UP

- If you are having special difficulties with any mathematics topic, talk with a teacher or refer to any of your math textbooks.

- Use the exercises in this chapter to determine what you DON'T know well, and concentrate your study on those areas.

- When adding or subtracting decimals, it is important to keep the decimal points in line.

- The fastest way to find an equivalent fraction is to divide the denominator of the fraction you know by the denominator you want. Take the result and multiply it by the numerator.

- To change a % to a decimal, remove the % sign and divide by 100. To change a decimal to a %, add the % sign and multiply by 100. To change a % to a fraction, remove the % sign and divide by 100. To change a fraction to %, multiply by 100 and add the % sign.

- When solving a percentage problem, be sure to read the notation carefully, read the problem carefully, and use common sense.

- Remember the number line when subtracting signed numbers.

- Memorizing some simple rules will help you to move through the test more quickly and with less anxiety. An example of some of those rules is the following: The product of two negative numbers is positive; the product of two positive numbers is positive; and the product of a negative number and a positive number is negative.

- Memorize the basic equations of geometry. These may not be given to you on the test. For example, to find the area of a rectangle, you must multiply the length times the width, $A = lw$.

Series Reasoning

OVERVIEW

- **Number series**
- **Letter series**
- **Mixed series**
- **Symbol series**
- **Tips for answering series questions**
- **Exercises: Series Reasoning**
- **Answer keys and explanations**
- **Summing it up**

Series reasoning questions crop up on the TACHS, COOP, and HSPT® exams. On the COOP, these questions are called Sequences. On the TACHS, these questions are dealt with in the Ability section. On the HSPT®, you find these questions in the Number Series section under Quantitative Skills. Series reasoning questions—symbol series, number series, letter series, or mixed—are designed to test your ability to reason without words. These questions can be challenging, fun, and sometimes very frustrating.

In some ways, series questions are a lot like analogy questions—you remember, the questions that ask you to find the relationships between words. In series questions, you have to determine the relationship between a series of symbols, numbers, or letters, then choose the next item for the series.

This chapter gives you some in-depth instruction in working with series, by showing you how to complete number and letter series. These are the most common kinds of series questions that you'll encounter on the TACHS, COOP, and the HSPT® exams. The information and practice you get in this chapter will help you develop your own methods and strategies for solving these series questions. And you can use those same strategies to solve mixed series and even symbol series.

All series reasoning questions require the same concentration, the same logical thinking, and the same flexibility of approach. With all series reasoning questions, you run the risk of working out a sequence and then finding that the answer you would choose to complete the sequence is not among the choices. Don't be discouraged! Just start over and try to determine what other relationship is reasonable.

chapter 17

NUMBER SERIES

Number series questions measure your ability to think with numbers and to see the relationship between elements of a series. Even though this type of task might be new and unfamiliar to you, the actual mathematics of number series questions is not complicated. The problems involve nothing more than simple arithmetic and a few other mathematical concepts. What the questions do require of you is concentration; you must be able to see how the numbers in a series are related so that you can supply the next number in that series. You must be flexible enough in your thinking so that if the first pattern you consider for a series turns out to be invalid, you can try a different pattern.

There is a system with which to approach number series questions. Look hard at the series. The pattern might be obvious to you on inspection. A series such as 1, 2, 3, 1, 2, 3, 1 . . . should not require any deep thought. Clearly, the sequence 1, 2, 3 is repeating itself over and over. The next number in the series must be 2. You might also instantly recognize the pattern of a simple series into which one number periodically intrudes. An example of such a series is 1, 2, 15, 3, 4, 15, 5 . . . . The number 15 appears after each set of two numbers in a simple +1 series. The next number in this series is 6, which is followed by 15. Can you see why?

Test Yourself 1

Here are five series questions, which you should be able to answer by inspection. Choose the number that should come next in the series.

The answer keys and explanations appear after Test Yourself 8.

1. 12, 10, 13, 10, 14 . . .
   (A) 15
   (B) 14
   (C) 10
   (D) 9

2. 6, 21, 36, 6, 21 . . .
   (A) 36
   (B) 6
   (C) 51
   (D) 21

3. 9, 1, 9, 3, 9 . . .
   (A) 5
   (B) 6
   (C) 8
   (D) 4

4. 5, 8, 5, 8, 5 . . .
   (A) 5
   (B) 8
   (C) 6
   (D) 9

5. 10, 9, 8, 7, 6 . . .
   (A) 7
   (B) 4
   (C) 5
   (D) 6

Sometimes you might find that your ear is more adept than your eye. You might be able to "hear" a pattern or "feel" a rhythm more easily than you can "see" it. If you cannot immediately spot a pattern, try saying the series softly to yourself. First read the series through. If that does not help, try accenting the printed numbers and speaking the missing intervening numbers even more softly. Try grouping the numbers within the series into twos or threes. After grouping, try accenting the last number, or the first. If you read aloud 2, 4, 6, 8, 10, you will hear that the next number is 12. Likewise, if you see the series 31, 32, 33, 32, 33, 34, 33, and you group that series this way: 31, 32, 33/ 32, 33, 34/ 33 . . ., you will feel the rhythm. The series consists of three-number mini-series. Each mini-series begins with a number one higher than the first number of the previous mini-series. The next number of the above series is 34, then 35, and then the next step will be 34, 35, 36.

Test Yourself 2

You might be able to answer the next five series questions by inspection. If you cannot, try sounding them out.

1. 1, 2, 5, 6, 9, 10, 13 . . .
   (A) 14
   (B) 15
   (C) 16
   (D) 17

2. 2, 3, 4, 3, 4, 5, 4 . . .
   (A) 3
   (B) 4
   (C) 5
   (D) 6

3. 10, 10, 12, 14, 14, 16 . . .
   (A) 16
   (B) 18
   (C) 20
   (D) 22

4. 1, 2, 3, 2, 2, 3, 3, 2, 3 . . .
   (A) 1
   (B) 2
   (C) 3
   (D) 4

5. 22, 20, 18, 20, 18, 16, 18 . . .
   (A) 20
   (B) 16
   (C) 14
   (D) 18

If you cannot hear the pattern of a series, the next step is to mark the degree and direction of change between the numbers. Most series progress by either + (plus) or – (minus) or a combination of both directions, so first try marking your changes in terms of + and –. If you cannot make sense of a series in terms of + and –, try x (times) and ÷ (divided by). You may mark the changes between numbers right on your exam paper, but be sure to mark the letter of the answer on your answer sheet when you figure it out. Only your answer sheet will be scored. The exam booklet will be collected, but it will not be scored.

Test Yourself 3

Try this next set of practice questions. If you cannot "see" or "hear" the pattern, mark the differences between the numbers to establish the pattern. Then continue the pattern to determine the next number of the series.

1. 9, 10, 12, 15, 19, 24 . . .
   (A) 25
   (B) 29
   (C) 30
   (D) 31

2. 35, 34, 31, 30, 27, 26 . . .
   (A) 22
   (B) 23
   (C) 24
   (D) 25

3. 38, 38, 45, 45, 52, 52 . . .
   (A) 20
   (B) 25
   (C) 29
   (D) 32

4. 48, 44, 40, 36, 32, 28 . . .
   (A) 27
   (B) 26
   (C) 25
   (D) 24

5. 20, 30, 39, 47, 54, 60 . . .
   (A) 65
   (B) 66
   (C) 68
   (D) 70

Arithmetical series such as those above might be interrupted by a particular number that appears periodically or by repetition of numbers according to a pattern. For example: 3, 6, 25, 9, 12, 25, 15, 18, 25 . . . and 50, 50, 35, 40, 40, 35, 30, 30, 35 . . . . In these cases, you must search a bit harder to spot both the arithmetic pattern and the pattern of repetition. When choosing your answer, you must be alert to the point at which the pattern was interrupted.

Test Yourself 4

Choose the number that should come next in the series. Do not repeat a number that has already been repeated, but do not forget to repeat before continuing the arithmetical pattern if repetition is called for at this point in the series.

1. 10, 13, 13, 16, 16, 19 . . .
   (A) 16
   (B) 19
   (C) 21
   (D) 22

2. 2, 4, 25, 8, 16, 25, 32 . . .
   (A) 25
   (B) 32
   (C) 48
   (D) 64

3. 38, 38, 45, 45, 52, 52 . . .
   (A) 52
   (B) 59
   (C) 45
   (D) 66

4. 35, 35, 32, 30, 30, 27 . . .
   (A) 25
   (B) 26
   (C) 27
   (D) 28

5. 76, 70, 12, 65, 61, 12 . . .
   (A) 12
   (B) 54
   (C) 55
   (D) 58

LETTER SERIES

In letter series, each question consists of letters that are arranged according to a definite pattern. You must discover what that pattern is and then use that knowledge to determine which of the four alternatives offered is the missing letter or group of letters in the series. Series might be simple alphabetical progressions or intricate combinations that alternate between forward and backward steps.

Because each question is based on the twenty-six letters of the alphabet, it is a good idea to keep a copy of the alphabet in front of you as you work. In addition, it is well worth your time to assign a number to each letter, jotting down the numbers from one to twenty-six directly under the letters to which they correspond. The seconds spent doing this might save you precious minutes as you work through the letter series.

There is more than one method of attack for letter series questions. You may solve these problems by inspection whenever possible. If that fails, try numerical analysis.

Inspection

The first line of attack should always be inspection, for this is the quickest and easiest approach. Look at the letters. Are they progressing in normal or reverse alphabetical order? Are the letters consecutive, or do they skip one or more letters between terms? Are certain letters repeated?

Test Yourself 5

Here are some simple series that you should be able to solve by inspection only.

1. d b f b h b j b l b
   - (A) b
   - (B) m
   - (C) n
   - (D) o

2. a b c c d e f f g h i
   - (A) f
   - (B) j
   - (C) k
   - (D) i

3. gij jlm mop
   - (A) prq
   - (B) prs
   - (C) rst
   - (D) qur

Numerical Analysis

If inspection does not make the answer apparent, switch to a numerical analysis of the series. Assign each letter in the series a numerical value according to its position in the alphabet. Write the direction and degree of difference between letters. Once you have done this, you will find yourself with a pattern of pluses and minuses similar to those you utilized in number series.

Test Yourself 6

Choose the letter or group of letters that will continue the pattern or sequence.

1. c d b e f d g h f i j
   - (A) h
   - (B) k
   - (C) f
   - (D) l

2. a b d g k p
   - (A) q
   - (B) u
   - (C) w
   - (D) v

3. mpt jmq gjn dgk
   - (A) cfj
   - (B) bei
   - (C) kos
   - (D) adh

MIXED SERIES

With mixed series, you must once again ask yourself, "What's happening?" In what direction and in what manner are the numbers progressing? What about the letters? Are changes occurring in the relationships of numbers to letters? According to what pattern?

Test Yourself 7

Choose the answer that will continue the pattern or sequence or that should fill in the blank in the series.

1. $RA_1T_2 \ RA_3T_4 \ RA_1T_2 \ RA_4T_5$ _____
    - **(A)** RA_5T_6
    - **(B)** RA_5T_4
    - **(C)** RA_1T_2
    - **(D)** R_1AT_2

2. $L^2M_2N^2 \ O_3P^3Q_3 \ R^2S_2T^2$ _____ $X^2Y_2Z^2$
    - **(A)** $U_4V^4W_4$
    - **(B)** $T_3U^3V_3$
    - **(C)** $U^3V_3W^3$
    - **(D)** $V^4W_3X^4$

SYMBOL SERIES

In symbol series, the figures might be unfamiliar and thus intimidating, but the task is the same. You must study the relationships of the individual members within a group and then determine what changes occur in that relationship as you move from one group to the next. While this activity is classified as nonverbal reasoning, you must verbalize to yourself exactly what is happening in the creation of the series.

Test Yourself 8

Choose the answer that will continue the pattern or sequence or that should fill in the blank in the series.

1.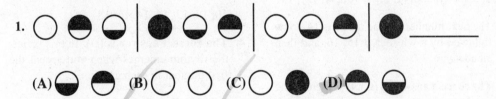

2.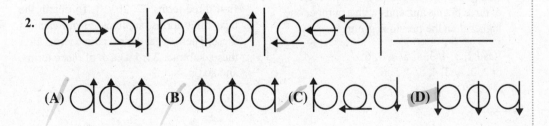

TEST YOURSELF ANSWER KEYS AND EXPLANATIONS

Test Yourself 1

1. C	2. A	3. A	4. B	5. C

1. **The correct answer is (C).** The series is a simple +1 series with the number 10 inserted after each step of the series.

2. **The correct answer is (A).** The sequence 6, 21, 36 repeats itself over and over again.

3. **The correct answer is (A).** This is a simple +2 series with the number 9 appearing before each member of the series.

4. **The correct answer is (B).** In this series, the sequence 5, 8 repeats.

5. **The correct answer is (C).** You should be able to see that this is a descending series; each number is one less than the one before it. You can call this a –1 series.

Test Yourself 2

1. A	2. C	3. B	4. D	5. B

1. **The correct answer is (A).** If you group the numbers in pairs, you can whisper the bracketed "missing numbers" to determine the pattern:

   1, 2, [3, 4,] 5, 6, [7, 8,] 9, 10, [11, 12,] 13

   The next number to read aloud is 14, to be followed by a whispered 15, 16, and then aloud again, 17.

2. **The correct answer is (C).** If you group the numbers into threes and read them aloud, accenting either the first or last number of each group, you should feel that each group of three begins and ends with a number one higher than the previous group.

   Read 2, 3, 4/ 3, 4, 5/ 4, 5, 6;
   or 2, 3, 4/ 3, 4, 5/ 4, 5, 6.

3. **The correct answer is (B).** Once more, group the numbers into threes. This time, be certain to accent the third number in each group in order to sense the rhythm, and thereby the pattern, of the series:

   10, 10, 12/ 14, 14, 16/ 18 . . .

4. **The correct answer is (D).** In this series, the rhythm emerges when you accent the first number in each group:

   1, 2, 3/ 2, 2, 3/ 3, 2, 3/ 4, 2, 3.

5. **The correct answer is (B).** Consider the first three terms 22, 20, 18. To obtain the next three terms, subtract 2 from each of these. Then, to get the next three terms after these, subtract 2 from each of *those* terms, and so on.

Test Yourself 3

1. **The correct answer is (C).** 9^{+1} 10^{+2} 12^{+3} 15^{+4} 19^{+5} 24^{+6} 30

2. **The correct answer is (B).** 35^{-1} 34^{-3} 31^{-1} 30^{-3} 27^{-1} 26^{-3} 23

3. **The correct answer is (B).** 38 38^{+7} 45 45^{+7} 52 52^{+7} 59

4. **The correct answer is (D).** 48^{-4} 44^{-4} 40^{-4} 36^{-4} 32^{-4} 28^{-4} 24

5. **The correct answer is (A).** 20^{+10} 30^{+9} 39^{+8} 47^{+7} 54^{+6} 60^{+5} 65

Test Yourself 4

(r = repeat; ○ = extraneous number repeated periodically)

1. **The correct answer is (B).** 10^{+3} 13^{r} 13^{+3} 16^{r} 16^{+3} 19^{r} 19

2. **The correct answer is (D).** $2^{\times 2}$ $4^{\times 2}$ ㉕ $8^{\times 2}$ $16^{\times 2}$ ㉕ $32^{\times 2}$ 64

3. **The correct answer is (B).** 80^{r} 80^{-5} 75^{r} 75^{-5} 70^{r} 70^{-5} 65

4. **The correct answer is (A).** 35^{r} 35^{-3} 32^{-2} 30^{r} 30^{-3} 27^{-2} 25

5. **The correct answer is (D).** 76^{-6} 70^{-5} ⑫ 65^{-4} 61^{-3} ⑫ 58

Test Yourself 5

1. **The correct answer is (C).** The even terms of the sequence are always "b." The other terms start with "d" and skip a letter each time. So, the odd terms are d, f, h, j, l, n, p, r, . . .

2. **The correct answer is (D).** This is also a consecutive alphabetical progression, but here the third letter of each set is repeated. Thus, we have abcc deff ghii. Because only one *i* is given in the original series, the next letter must be the second *i* needed to complete the third set.

3. **The correct answer is (B).** This is a bit more difficult, but with the grouping already done for you, you should be able to solve it by inspection. The pattern is as follows: From the first letter, skip one, then let the next letter in sequence follow immediately. Start each new three-letter sequence with the last letter of the previous sequence. The missing sequence begins with the *p* of the previous sequence, skips one letter to *r*, then continues immediately with *s*.

Test Yourself 6

| 1. A | 2. D | 3. D |

A	B	C	D	E	F	G	H	I	J	K	L	M	N	O	P	Q	R	S	T	U	V	W	X	Y	Z
1	2	3	4	5	6	7	8	9	10	11	12	13	14	15	16	17	18	19	20	21	22	23	24	25	26

1. The correct answer is (A).

c		d		b		e		f		d		g		h		f		i		j		h
3		4		2		5		6		4		7		8		6		9		10		8
	+1		−2		+3		+1		−2		+3		+1		−2		+3		+1		−2	

Now it is obvious that the series progresses by the formula +1 −2 +3. According to this pattern, the next letter must be 10 −2, or 8, which corresponds to the letter *h*.

2. The correct answer is (D).

a		b		d		g		k		p		v
1		2		4		7		11		16		22
	+1		+2		+3		+4		+5		+6	

The progression is obvious.

3. The correct answer is (D).

m		p		t		j		m		q		g		j		n		d		g		k		a		d		h
13		16		20		10		13		17		7		10		14		4		7		11		1		4		8
	+3		+4		−10		+3		+4		−10		+3		+4		−10		+3		+4		−10		+3		+4	

Within each group of three, the pattern is +3, +4. Between groups of three, subtract 10.

Test Yourself 7

| 1. C | 2. A |

1. The correct answer is (C). A good solid look at the groupings within the series shows that the unit RA_1T_2 intervenes between the other units of the series. With no further information on which to base any other features of the series, you must select choice (C).

2. The correct answer is (A). The first thing that becomes clear in this mixed series is that the letters form a simple alphabetical progression. You can immediately narrow your choices to (A) and (C). On the basis of the information given, there is no way to know whether the numbers in the missing unit should be 3s or 4s, but we do have information about their position with relation to the letters. The pattern of the groups in which the numbers are 2s is superscript, subscript, superscript. In the only given group in which the numbers are not 2s, the pattern is subscript, superscript, subscript. Because, in addition, there is evidence of possible alternation of patterns, the proper choice is (A), in which the pattern of the numbers is subscript, superscript, subscript.

Test Yourself 8

1. D   2. D

1. **The correct answer is (D).** If you look from the first group to the second, you will see that the second group is precisely the reverse of the first. Where the first is empty, upper half full, lower half full, the second is full, lower half full, upper half full. In the third group, the empty first circle of the first group is repeated, but the other two circles are reversed. Because the final group begins with a full circle (in both instances, the group with its first circle full follows a group with its first circle empty), the missing two circles should be the reverse of the second and third circles in the preceding group.

2. **The correct answer is (D).** In each group, all of the arrows go in the same direction, and in each group, the arrows go in a direction different from those in any other group. The arrows in the last group should point down. In all three groups, the middle arrow goes through the middle circle and the outer arrows go along the outer edges of the circles. This is clearest in the second group. Choice (D) fulfills all requirements best.

TIPS FOR ANSWERING SERIES QUESTIONS

- Tackle first the questions that seem easiest for you. Questions generally tend to be arranged in order of difficulty, with the easiest questions first, but problems that might seem easy to some people might be more difficult to others, and vice versa. Answer quickly the questions that require little of your time, and leave yourself extra time for the more difficult questions.

- When you skip a question, put a mark before the question number in the test booklet and leave its answer space blank. When you return to a question that you have skipped, be sure to mark its answer in the correct space. The time you spend checking to make sure that question and answer number are alike is time well spent.

- Follow the procedures outlined in this chapter. First, look for an obvious pattern. Second, sound out the series; if necessary, group the numbers or letters and sound out again. Third, write the direction and amount of change between the numbers or letters.

- If you do any figuring in the test booklet, be sure to mark the letter of the correct answer on your answer sheet. All answers must be marked on the answer sheet.

- If none of the answers given fits the rule you have figured out, try again. Try to figure out a rule that makes one of the four answers a correct one.

- Do not spend too much time on any one question. If a question seems impossible, skip it and come back to it later. A fresh look will sometimes help you find the answer. If you still cannot figure out the answer, guess. Remember that there is no penalty for a wrong answer.

- Keep track of time. Because there is no penalty for a wrong answer, you will want to answer every question. Leave yourself time to go back to the questions you skipped to give them a second look. If you are not finished as the time limit approaches, mark random answers for the remaining questions.

EXERCISES: SERIES REASONING

Exercise 1

Directions: Choose the number that should come next or that should fill the blank in the series. The answer keys and explanations appear after Exercise 3.

1. 75, 75, 72, 72, 69, 69,
   - (A) 63
   - (B) 66
   - (C) 68
   - (D) 69

2. 12, 16, 21, 27, 31,
   - (A) 33
   - (B) 35
   - (C) 36
   - (D) 37

3. 22, 24, 12, 26, 28, 12,
   - (A) 12
   - (B) 30
   - (C) 34
   - (D) 36

4. 13, 22, 32, 43, _____, 68
   - (A) 53
   - (B) 54
   - (C) 55
   - (D) 56

5. $4, 2, 1, \frac{1}{2}, \frac{1}{4},$
   - (A) 0
   - (B) $\frac{1}{8}$
   - (C) $\frac{3}{8}$
   - (D) $\frac{1}{16}$

6. 100, 81, _____, 49, 36
   - (A) 60
   - (B) 64
   - (C) 65
   - (D) 75

7. 32, 25, 86, 32, 25,
   - (A) 5
   - (B) 32
   - (C) 68
   - (D) 86

8. 51, 51, 30, 47, 47, 30, 43,
   - (A) 30
   - (B) 41
   - (C) 43
   - (D) 45

9. 3 3 9 | 15 15 21 | 27 27 _____
   - (A) 1
   - (B) 27
   - (C) 30
   - (D) 33

10. 95 90 86 | 83 78 74 | 51 _____ 42
    - (A) 45
    - (B) 46
    - (C) 47
    - (D) 50

11. 1 5 1 | 2 6 2 | 3 _____ 3
    - (A) 0
    - (B) 3
    - (C) 4
    - (D) 7

12. 50 52 48 | 35 37 33 | _____ 14 10
- **(A)** 9
- **(B)** 11
- **(C)** 12
- **(D)** 15

13. 39 40 80 | 10 11 22 | 17 18 _____
- **(A)** 9
- **(B)** 33
- **(C)** 36
- **(D)** 38

14. 36 12 4 | 63 21 7 | _____ 36 12
- **(A)** 72
- **(B)** 85
- **(C)** 97
- **(D)** 108

Exercise 2

Directions: Choose the letter or group of letters that should come next or that should fill the blank in the series.

1. n n o p p q r r s t
- **(A)** t
- **(B)** u
- **(C)** v
- **(D)** r

2. a j e b u q i y e p a
- **(A)** k
- **(B)** d
- **(C)** f
- **(D)** w

3. d e f d g h i g j k l j m n o
- **(A)** j
- **(B)** m
- **(C)** n
- **(D)** o

4. a c d a a c d b a c d c a c
- **(A)** a
- **(B)** b
- **(C)** c
- **(D)** d

5. a d h l b e i m c f j
- **(A)** l
- **(B)** m
- **(C)** n
- **(D)** o

6. z a z c z f z j z
- **(A)** g
- **(B)** o
- **(C)** z
- **(D)** s

7. hat | mat | rat | bat | _____
- **(A)** jat
- **(B)** qat
- **(C)** pat
- **(D)** uat

8. mnp | hik | bce | _____ | kln
- **(A)** uvx
- **(B)** gij
- **(C)** rqp
- **(D)** xyz

9. ZWT WTQ TQN _____ NKH
- **(A)** PNL
- **(B)** NLJ
- **(C)** MJG
- **(D)** QNK

10. ABC IRS GNO DHI
- **(A)** BDG
- **(B)** FKL
- **(C)** EJK
- **(D)** NYZ

Exercise 3

Directions: Choose the answer that will continue the pattern or sequence or that should fill the blank in the series.

1. $STPR_1$ STP_1R_2 $STPR_3$ _____ $STPR_5$
   - (A) $STPR_4$
   - (B) STP_4R_5
   - (C) $ST_1P_2R_3$
   - (D) STP_2R_3

2. $F^1G_2H^3I_4G_6H^7I_8J^9H_4I^5J_6K^7I^3J_4K^5L_6$_____
   - (A) $J^7K_8L^9M_{10}$
   - (B) $M^5N_6O^7P_8$
   - (C) $J^8K_9L^{10}M_{11}$
   - (D) $K^1L_3M^5N_9$

3. $D_4F_6H_8E_5G_7I_9$ _____ $K_{11}M_{13}O_{15}P_{16}R_{18}T_{20}$
   - (A) $J_{10}K_{11}L_{12}$
   - (B) $J_{10}L_{12}N_{14}$
   - (C) $J_{10}L_{11}N_{12}$
   - (D) $J_{10}K_{12}L_{14}$

4. $R^2D^2R^2D_2R_2D_2R_2D^2D^2R^2$ _____
   - (A) D_2R_2
   - (B) R^2D_2
   - (C) D^2R_2
   - (D) D_2R^2

5.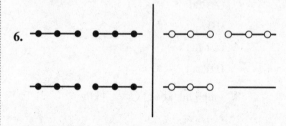

6.

7.

8.

ANSWER KEYS AND EXPLANATIONS

Exercise 1

1. B	4. C	7. D	10. B	13. C
2. C	5. B	8. C	11. D	14. D
3. B	6. B	9. D	12. C	

1. **The correct answer is (B).** The pattern is: repeat the number, –3; repeat the number, –3; repeat the number, –3. The next number must be 69 – 3 = 66.

2. **The correct answer is (C).** The pattern is +4, +5, +6; +4, +5, +6. The next number must be 31 + 5, which is 36.

3. **The correct answer is (B).** The basic pattern is a simple +2. The number 12 is inserted after each two terms of the series.

4. **The correct answer is (C).** The numbers are large, but the progression is simple. If you mark the differences between numbers, you will recognize: +9, +10, +11, supply the +12 term, then continue with +13.

5. **The correct answer is (B).** This is a simple ÷2 series.

6. **The correct answer is (B).** This series consists of the squares of the whole numbers in descending order.

7. **The correct answer is (D).** This series follows no mathematical rule. You must solve it by inspection. The sequence 32, 25, 86 simply repeats.

8. **The correct answer is (C).** The basic pattern is: repeat the number, –4; repeat the number, –4. The number 30 appears each time after the repeat and before the –4.

9. **The correct answer is (D).** The entire series pattern is repeat, +6, +6; repeat, +6, +6. To answer the question, it is enough to recognize that the pattern within each segment of the series is: repeat, +6.

10. **The correct answer is (B).** Within each segment of the series, the pattern is –5, –4. In the final segment, 51 – 5 = 46 – 4 = 42.

11. **The correct answer is (D).** You might see the pattern within each segment as +4, –4, or you might recognize by inspection or vocalization that each segment is simply a step up from the previous one.

12. **The correct answer is (C).** Within each segment, the pattern is +2, –4. Because there is no overall pattern for the series, you must establish the pattern in the first two segments, then apply it in reverse to determine the first term in the last segment. If the second term is two higher than the first, you can subtract 2 from the second term to determine the first.

13. **The correct answer is (C).** The pattern is +1, ×2.

14. **The correct answer is (D).** In the first two segments, you can establish that the pattern is ÷3. When you reach the third segment, multiply the second term by 3 to achieve the number that when divided by 3 equals 36.

Exercise 2

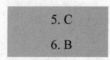

| 1. A | 3. B | 5. C | 7. C | 9. D |
| 2. A | 4. D | 6. B | 8. A | 10. C |

1. **The correct answer is (A).** This pattern alternates double and single letters in alphabetical order: nn o pp q rr s t. The next letter must be the second *t* needed to maintain the pattern.

2. **The correct answer is (A).** In this series, each set of two letters is a vowel followed by a consonant that contains the sound of the vowel with which it is paired: aj eb uq iy ep a. The only consonant offered that contains the sound of *a* is *k*.

3. **The correct answer is (B).** This series is an alphabetical progression of four-letter sequences where each fourth letter repeats the first letter of each sequence: defd ghig jklj mno. The missing letter is therefore the *m* needed to complete the fourth set.

4. **The correct answer is (D).** This pattern consists of the letters *acd* followed by consecutive letters of the alphabet. Thus: acda acdb acdc acd. The next letter must be *d*.

5. **The correct answer is (C).** The best way to visualize this pattern is to assign the letters of the alphabet numbers from 1 to 26. This series then becomes:

a	d	h	l	b	e	i	m	c	f	j	n
1	4	8	12	2	5	9	13	3	6	10	14

$$+3 \quad +4 \quad +4 \quad -10 \quad +3 \quad +4 \quad +4 \quad -10 \quad +3 \quad +4 \quad +4$$

The last number must be $10 + 4$, which is 14, corresponding to the letter *n*.

6. **The correct answer is (B).** Starting at the beginning of the alphabet, the space between letters increases by one with each new letter:

a		c		f		j		o
	+2		+3		+4		+5	

The letter *z* is a constant between each term. The next step in this series must be five letters after *j*, which is *o*.

7. **The correct answer is (C).** In this series, each set of three letters makes a word composed of a consonant plus *at*: hat, mat, rat, bat. The next segment, therefore, must consist of a consonant plus *at* that may be combined to form an English word.

8. **The correct answer is (A).** The easiest way to solve this series is to verify the numerical relationship within segments. In each instance, the sequence is +1, +2. The only option that satisfies this sequence is u + 1 = v + 2 = x.

9. **The correct answer is (D).** Look at the alphabet written out before you. From *Z*, skip over two letters back to *W*, and from *W* skip two more to *T*. In the next group, the procedure is exactly the same, and in each of the following groups as well. In addition, note that each succeeding group begins with the middle letter of the group before it. Thus, the missing group begins with the *Q* in the middle of the preceding group, continues with the skip of two back to *N*, and concludes with the further skip back to *K*.

10. **The correct answer is (C).** It is very important to have written the entire alphabet and to have assigned each letter its numerical equivalent in order to choose the answer to this question.

ABC	IRS	GNO	DHI	EJK
1 2 3	9 18 19	7 14 15	4 8 9	5 10 11
×2 +1	×2 +1	×2 +1	×2 +1	×2 +1

Obviously, you must figure out the relationship on groups other than the first one, then confirm that the relationship of the first three letters is not simple alphabetical succession. It is also clear that no group of three bears any external relationship to any other group of three letters. Only the relationship within a group of three will determine the correct answer. Only choice (C) satisfies the ×2, +1 formula.

Exercise 3

1. D	3. B	5. B	7. C	8. B
2. A	4. C	6. D		

1. **The correct answer is (D).** In all groupings, the letters are the same. You might assume that the answer choice will contain those same letters. When there is only one subscript number, it is at the end. When there are two, they follow the last and the next-to-last letter. Your best guess, if you can find reasonable choices to fit, is that the number pattern appears to alternate: one number, two numbers, one number, two numbers. Choices (B) and (D) might fit into this pattern. Then look for the rationale for the numbers themselves. The numbers of the second group add to make the number of the third. Because the numbers of choice (D) add to make the number in the final group, this is the most logical choice.

2. **The correct answer is (A).** By inspection, you can find the pattern of the letters. Each succeeding group picks up with the second letter of the preceding group and proceeds in alphabetical order. This narrows your answer choices to (A) or (C). Now look at the numbers. Within each set of four, the numbers go in order, but there seems to be no rule by which numbers are assigned to succeeding groups. So you must look for a pattern of some sort. Note that even numbers always appear as subscripts and odd numbers are always superscripts. Now you know why choice (A) is the correct answer.

3. **The correct answer is (B).** Some series questions are easier than others. The numbers that follow the letters are the numbers assigned to the letters according to their position in the alphabet. Immediately, you may narrow the correct answer possibility to choices (A) and (B). Now look at the pattern of the letters. In each group, there is a skip-one pattern. Because choice (A) gives letters in sequence, the correct answer must be (B).

4. **The correct answer is (C).** In the first four groupings, the 2s position themselves in all possible combinations around the R and the

D. The fifth group reverses the positions of R and D and appears to begin anew the circuit of 2s around the letters. The final group, then, should continue the rotation of the 2s, following in the same manner as when the letters were in their original position. Thus, the second $D\ R$ should have the 2s placed in the same manner as the second $R\ D$.

5. **The correct answer is (B).** As the pattern progresses, in each succeeding frame an additional circle is darkened. Thus, in the first, none; in the second, one; in the third, two; and in the fourth, three. Because three circles have already been darkened in the fourth frame, the frame must be completed with undarkened circles, horizontal as in all frames.

6. **The correct answer is (D).** Because frames one and three are identical, you must assume that the pattern is of alternating identities and that frames two and four must also be identical.

7. **The correct answer is (C).** In the first three frames, the farthest-right figure is always a U shape. In the first frame, the next-to-last figure is upended; in the second frame, an additional figure is upended, reading from right to left; in the third frame, three figures are upended. Logically, as the series progresses, the fourth frame should include the four left-hand figures upended, with only the farthest right maintaining its position as a U.

8. **The correct answer is (B).** The darkened figures seem to be following no particular pattern within themselves, but they do seem to be alternating frames with the undarkened figures. The positions of the undarkened arrows in the first and third frames are identical. There is no reason to expect their positions to change the next time they appear in the series. With the alternating dark, light pattern, the undarkened arrows are due to appear in the next frame, and choice (B) maintains their same position as in the two previous appearances.

answers exercises

SUMMING IT UP

- On the COOP, these questions are called Sequences.

- On the TACHS, these questions are in the Ability section.

- On the HSPT®, these questions are in the Number Series section under Quantitative Skills.

- In series questions, you have to determine the relationship between a series of symbols, numbers, or letters, and then choose the next item for the series.

- First read the series through. If that does not help, try accenting the printed numbers and speaking the missing intervening numbers even more softly. Try grouping the numbers within the series into twos or threes. After grouping, try accenting the last number, or the first.

- It is a good idea to keep a copy of the alphabet in front of you as you work. In addition, it is well worth your time to assign a number to each letter, jotting down the numbers from 1 to 26 directly under the letters to which they correspond.

- Study and practice the series reasoning question tactics in this chapter. Remember: Answer the easy ones first; if you skip a question, make a mark on your answer sheet so you don't mark your answer sheet incorrectly; follow the system—look, sound, and group; don't spend too much time on any one question; and keep track of time.

Comparisons

chapter 18

OVERVIEW

- Geometric comparisons
- Nongeometric comparisons
- Exercises: Comparisons
- Answer keys and explanations
- Summing it up

The comparison questions in the Quantitative Skills section of the HSPT® require a little bit of mathematical skill and a lot of patience and logical thinking. You can't rush through any of these questions! To get the maximum number of right answers, you have to study and count when you're answering geometric comparison questions. You begin by performing all of the operations of nongeometric comparison questions. Then you work through the answer choices one by one, eliminating each statement that proves to be false, based on the facts of the problem. When you find what you think is the correct choice, you still need to continue trying all of the other answers, as a check on your own reasoning. To give you a feel for these questions, let's work through a few together.

GEOMETRIC COMPARISONS

1. Examine (A), (B), and (C) and find the best answer.

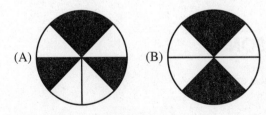

(A) (A) is more shaded than (B).

(B) (B) is more shaded than (A) and less shaded than (C).

(C) (A) and (B) are equally shaded and less shaded than (C).

(D) (A), (B), and (C) are equally shaded.

Begin by studying the three circles. Note that each circle is divided into eight segments. Now count the number of shaded segments in each circle, and write that number next to the letter of the circle. If you have counted accurately, you have written: (A) 4, (B) 4, (C) 5. Read the statements one by one, and mark true or false next to the letter of each statement. The statement in choice (A) is false because both (A) and (B) have four shaded segments. The statement in choice (B) must be marked false because it is not entirely true. (B) is indeed less shaded than (C), but it is not more shaded than (A). To be true, a statement must be 100 percent true. The statement in choice (C) is true. (A) and (B) are equally shaded (4) and both are less shaded than (C) with its five shaded segments. Check out choice (D) just to be certain that you have not made an error. No problem here. The statement in choice (D) is clearly false.

2. The pie is divided into sixteen equal portions. Study the pie and find the best answer.

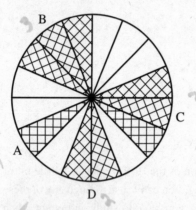

(A) A plus D equals B plus C.

(B) D minus A equals B minus C.

(C) C minus D equals A.

(D) B equals A plus C.

Begin by counting the pie wedges in each portion; write the number of wedges next to the letter—A (1), B (3), C (3), D (2). Now perform the very simple arithmetic for each statement.

    (A) $1 + 2 = 3 + 3$; $3 = 6$—false

    (B) $2 - 1 = 3 - 3$; $1 = 0$—false

    (C) $3 - 2 = 1$—true

    (D) $3 = 1 + 3$; $3 = 4$—false

NONGEOMETRIC COMPARISONS

1. Examine (A), (B), and (C) and find the best answer.

    (A) $(5 \times 4) - 10$

    (B) $(3 \times 6) + 4$

    (C) $(8 \times 3) - 6$

    (A) (B) is equal to (C) and greater than (A).

    (B) (C) is greater than (A) but less than (B).

    (C) (A) is greater than (C).

    (D) (A) is less than (C) but more than (B).

Obviously, you must begin by performing the indicated operations.

(A) $20 - 10 = 10$

(B) $18 + 4 = 22$

(C) $24 - 6 = 18$

Now you can substitute these numbers for the letters in the four statements and choose the correct one.

(A) 22 is equal to 18 and greater than 10—false

(B) 18 is greater than 10 but less than 22—true

(C) 10 is greater than 18—false

(D) 10 is less than 18 but more than 22—false

The correct answer is (B).

2. Examine (A), (B), and (C) and find the best answer.

(A) 4^3

(B) 3^4

(C) $(3 \times 4)(4)$

(A) $A > B > C$

(B) $A = B > C$

(C) $B > A > C$

(D) $A = C < B$

First, perform the operations.

(A) $4^3 = 64$

(B) $3^4 = 81$

(C) $(3 \times 4)(4) = 12 \times 4 = 48$

Substitute the numbers in the statements.

(A) 64 is greater than 81, which is greater than 48—false

(B) 64 equals 81, which is greater than 48—false

(C) 48 is smaller than 81, which is greater than 64—true

(D) 64 is equal to 48, which is smaller than 81—false

The correct answer is (C).

EXERCISES: COMPARISONS

Directions: Examine (A), (B), and (C) and find the best answer. The answer key and explanations follow this exercise.

1.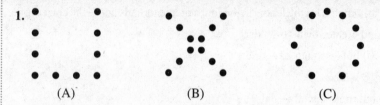
        (A)   (B)   (C)

    (A) (B) and (C) have the same number of dots.

    (B) (A) has fewer dots than (B) but more dots than (C).

    (C) (C) has more dots than (A).

    (D) (B) has more dots than (A) and (C), which have the same number of dots.

2. The distance from X to Y is one inch.

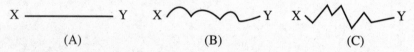
        (A)   (B)   (C)

    (A) Lines (A), (B), and (C) are of equal length.

    (B) Line (A) is longer than lines (B) and (C), which are of equal length.

    (C) Line (B) is shorter than line (A) but longer than line (C).

    (D) Line (A) is shorter than line (C).

3.
        (A)   (B)   (C)

    (A) (C) has more rings than (A).

    (B) (A) has the same number of rings as (B).

    (C) (B) and (C) have the same number of rings, which are more rings than (A).

    (D) (B) has fewer rings than either (A) or (C).

4.

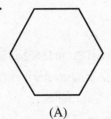 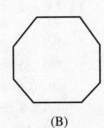 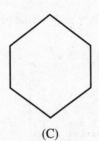

(A)   (B)   (C)

(A) (C) has more corners than (A).

(B) (B) has the same number of corners as (C) and more corners than (A).

(C) (A) has fewer corners than (B).

(D) (A), (B), and (C) all have the same number of corners.

5.

(A)   (B)   (C)

(A) (C) is more shaded than (B), which is more shaded than (A).

(B) (C) is more shaded than (A), which is not less shaded than (B).

(C) (B) and (C) are equally shaded.

(D) (A) and (B) are equally shaded.

6. Examine the rectangle and find the best answer.

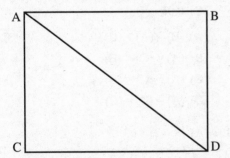

(A) AB is equal to CD, which is longer than AD.

(B) BD is shorter than AC.

(C) CD is longer than AD.

(D) AC is equal to BD.

7. Examine the graph and find the best answer.

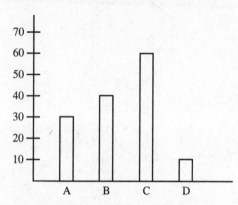

(A) C plus D minus A equals B.

(B) B plus D equals C.

(C) A plus B equals C.

(D) C minus D equals A plus B.

Directions: Examine (A), (B), and (C) and find the best answer.

8. (A) 30% of 30
   (B) 25% of 40
   (C) 20% of 50

   (A) (A), (B), and (C) are equal.

   (B) (A) and (C) are equal and are greater than (B).

   (C) (A) and (B) are equal and are less than (C).

   (D) (B) and (C) are equal and are greater than (A).

9. (A) $(4 + 8) \times 10$
   (B) $(8 + 10) \times 4$
   (C) $(4 + 10) \times 8$

   (A) (A) is greater than (B), which is smaller than (C).

   (B) (A) and (C) are equal and are greater than (B).

   (C) (C) is greater than (A), which is less than (B).

   (D) (A), (B), and (C) are equal.

10. (A) $(12 - 4) - 6$
    (B) $(12 - 6) - 4$
    (C) $12 - (6 - 4)$

    (A) (A) is greater than (B) but less than (C).

    (B) (C) is equal to (A) and greater than (B).

    (C) (A), (B), and (C) are equal.

    (D) (A) and (B) are equal but are less than (C).

11. (A) $\frac{2}{3}$ of 27
    (B) $\frac{2}{5}$ of 10
    (C) $\frac{3}{7}$ of 28

    (A) (A) is greater than (C) but less than (B).

    (B) (C) is smaller than (A) and (B).

    (C) (B) is smaller than (C), which is greater than (A).

    (D) (A) is greater than (C), which is greater than (B).

12. (A) $\frac{2}{5}\%$
    (B) $\frac{2}{5}$
    (C) 0.04

    (A) (B) > (A) > (C)

    (B) (A) < (C) < (B)

    (C) (A) = (C) < (B)

    (D) (A) = (B) = (C)

13. (A) $(8 \div 2) \times 12$
    (B) $(15 \div 3) \times 10$
    (C) $(22 \div 1) \times 4$

    (A) (A) is greater than (B), which is less than (C).

    (B) (C) is greater than (A), which is greater than (B).

    (C) (A) is equal to (B), which is less than (C).

    (D) (C) is greater than (A), which is less than (B).

14. (A) 160%

(B) $\sqrt{256}$

(C) 4^2

(A) (A) = (B) = (C)

(B) (B) = (C) < (A)

(C) (C) > (B) > (A)

(D) (A) < (C) = (B)

15. (A) $7(x + 2y)$

(B) $7x + 2y$

(C) $7(x + 2y) + 2x$

x and y are positive integers.

(A) (C) is greater than (B), which is smaller than (A).

(B) (B) is smaller than (C), which is smaller than (A).

(C) (A) is equal to (B), which is smaller than (C).

(D) (C) is greater than (A), which is smaller than (B).

ANSWER KEY AND EXPLANATIONS

1. C	4. C	7. A	10. D	13. D
2. D	5. A	8. D	11. D	14. D
3. B	6. D	9. A	12. B	15. A

1. **The correct answer is (C).** (A) has 10 dots; (B) has 12 dots; (C) has 11 dots. 11 is greater than 10, so (C) has more dots than (A). Test the other statements, and you will find them all false.

2. **The correct answer is (D).** A straight line is the shortest distance between two points, so line (A) is the shortest line. The statement in choice (D) declares that line (A) is shorter than either of the other two lines and therefore is the correct one.

3. **The correct answer is (B).** Each of the three figures has five rings, so any statement that speaks of more or fewer rings must be incorrect.

4. **The correct answer is (C).** Figures (A) and (C) are hexagons with 6 sides and 6 corners. Figure (B) is an octagon with 8 sides and 8 corners. The statement in choice (C) that figure (A) has fewer corners than figure (B) is correct.

5. **The correct answer is (A).** (C) is exactly half shaded; (B) is somewhat less than half shaded; (A) is very sparsely shaded. That is exactly the statement made in choice (A).

6. **The correct answer is (D).** In a rectangle, parallel sides are equal in length. Therefore, AB is equal to CD, and AC is equal to BD. AD is a hypotenuse. The hypotenuse is always the longest leg of a right triangle. AD cannot be shorter than any other line segment.

7. **The correct answer is (A).** Do the arithmetic. $60 + 10 - 30 = 40$. In other words, 40 equals 40, which is true. The other choices are all false. 40 plus 10 does not equal 60; 30 plus 40 does not equal 60; 60 minus 10 does not equal 30 plus 40.

8. **The correct answer is (D).** Do the arithmetic. (A): 30% of 30 = 9; (B): 25% of 40 = 10; (C): 20% of 50 = 10. Therefore, (B) and (C) are equal and are both greater than (A).

9. **The correct answer is (A).** Do the arithmetic. (A): $12 \times 10 = 120$; (B): $18 \times 4 = 72$; (C): $14 \times 8 = 112$. 120 is greater than 72, which is smaller than 112.

10. **The correct answer is (D).** Do the arithmetic. (A): $8 - 6 = 2$; (B): $6 - 4 = 2$; (C): $12 - 2 = 10$. (A) and (B), both equaling 2, are equal but are far less than the 10 of (C).

11. **The correct answer is (D).** Do the math. $\frac{2}{3}$ of 27 = 18; $\frac{2}{5}$ of 10 = 4; $\frac{3}{7}$ of 28 = 12. 18 is greater than 12, which is greater than 4. So, choice (D) is correct as it states: (A) is greater than (C), which is greater than (B).

12. **The correct answer is (B).** Convert all quantities to decimals. $\frac{2}{5} = 0.4$ and $\frac{2}{5}\% = 0.4\% = 0.004$. So, (A) < (C) < (B).

13. **The correct answer is (D).** Do the arithmetic. (A): $4 \times 12 = 48$; (B): $5 \times 10 = 50$; (C): $22 \times 4 = 88$. 88 is greater than 48, which is less than 50.

14. **The correct answer is (D).** Convert all quantities to decimals. 160% = 1.6 and both $\sqrt{256}$ and 42 equal 16. So, (A) < (C) = (B).

15. **The correct answer is (A).** You could substitute numerical values for x and y and arrive at the correct answer, but it is unnecessary to work with numbers. Simply perform the algebraic multiplications to make your comparisons. (A): $7(x + 2y) = 7x + 14y$; (B): $7x + 2y = 7x + 2y$; (C): $7(x + 2y) + 2x = 7x + 14y + 2x = 9x + 14y$. $9x + 14y$ is greater than $7x + 2y$, which is smaller than $7x + 14y$. That is what choice (A) states: (C) is greater than (B), which is smaller than (A).

SUMMING IT UP

- First, perform all of the operations for nongeometric comparison questions.

- Next, work through all of the answer choices one by one, and eliminate each statement that is false.

- Then, when you think you have found the correct answer, continue until you have tried each answer choice.

PART V

SIX PRACTICE TESTS

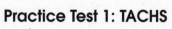

ANSWER SHEET PRACTICE TEST 1: TACHS

Reading

PART 1

1. Ⓐ Ⓑ Ⓒ Ⓓ   3. Ⓐ Ⓑ Ⓒ Ⓓ   5. Ⓐ Ⓑ Ⓒ Ⓓ   7. Ⓐ Ⓑ Ⓒ Ⓓ   9. Ⓐ Ⓑ Ⓒ Ⓓ
2. Ⓙ Ⓚ Ⓛ Ⓜ   4. Ⓙ Ⓚ Ⓛ Ⓜ   6. Ⓙ Ⓚ Ⓛ Ⓜ   8. Ⓙ Ⓚ Ⓛ Ⓜ   10. Ⓙ Ⓚ Ⓛ Ⓜ

PART 2

11. Ⓐ Ⓑ Ⓒ Ⓓ   13. Ⓐ Ⓑ Ⓒ Ⓓ   15. Ⓐ Ⓑ Ⓒ Ⓓ   17. Ⓐ Ⓑ Ⓒ Ⓓ   19. Ⓐ Ⓑ Ⓒ Ⓓ
12. Ⓙ Ⓚ Ⓛ Ⓜ   14. Ⓙ Ⓚ Ⓛ Ⓜ   16. Ⓙ Ⓚ Ⓛ Ⓜ   18. Ⓙ Ⓚ Ⓛ Ⓜ   20. Ⓙ Ⓚ Ⓛ Ⓜ

Language

PART 1

1. Ⓐ Ⓑ Ⓒ Ⓓ Ⓔ   6. Ⓙ Ⓚ Ⓛ Ⓜ Ⓝ   11. Ⓐ Ⓑ Ⓒ Ⓓ   16. Ⓙ Ⓚ Ⓛ Ⓜ
2. Ⓙ Ⓚ Ⓛ Ⓜ Ⓝ   7. Ⓐ Ⓑ Ⓒ Ⓓ Ⓔ   12. Ⓙ Ⓚ Ⓛ Ⓜ   17. Ⓐ Ⓑ Ⓒ Ⓓ
3. Ⓐ Ⓑ Ⓒ Ⓓ Ⓔ   8. Ⓙ Ⓚ Ⓛ Ⓜ Ⓝ   13. Ⓐ Ⓑ Ⓒ Ⓓ   18. Ⓙ Ⓚ Ⓛ Ⓜ
4. Ⓙ Ⓚ Ⓛ Ⓜ Ⓝ   9. Ⓐ Ⓑ Ⓒ Ⓓ Ⓔ   14. Ⓙ Ⓚ Ⓛ Ⓜ   19. Ⓐ Ⓑ Ⓒ Ⓓ
5. Ⓐ Ⓑ Ⓒ Ⓓ Ⓔ   10. Ⓙ Ⓚ Ⓛ Ⓜ Ⓝ   15. Ⓐ Ⓑ Ⓒ Ⓓ   20. Ⓙ Ⓚ Ⓛ Ⓜ

PART 2

21. Ⓐ Ⓑ Ⓒ Ⓓ   23. Ⓐ Ⓑ Ⓒ Ⓓ   25. Ⓐ Ⓑ Ⓒ Ⓓ   27. Ⓐ Ⓑ Ⓒ Ⓓ   29. Ⓐ Ⓑ Ⓒ Ⓓ
22. Ⓙ Ⓚ Ⓛ Ⓜ   24. Ⓙ Ⓚ Ⓛ Ⓜ   26. Ⓙ Ⓚ Ⓛ Ⓜ   28. Ⓙ Ⓚ Ⓛ Ⓜ   30. Ⓙ Ⓚ Ⓛ Ⓜ

Math

PART 1

1. Ⓐ Ⓑ Ⓒ Ⓓ   7. Ⓐ Ⓑ Ⓒ Ⓓ   13. Ⓐ Ⓑ Ⓒ Ⓓ   19. Ⓐ Ⓑ Ⓒ Ⓓ   25. Ⓐ Ⓑ Ⓒ Ⓓ
2. Ⓙ Ⓚ Ⓛ Ⓜ   8. Ⓙ Ⓚ Ⓛ Ⓜ   14. Ⓙ Ⓚ Ⓛ Ⓜ   20. Ⓙ Ⓚ Ⓛ Ⓜ   26. Ⓙ Ⓚ Ⓛ Ⓜ
3. Ⓐ Ⓑ Ⓒ Ⓓ   9. Ⓐ Ⓑ Ⓒ Ⓓ   15. Ⓐ Ⓑ Ⓒ Ⓓ   21. Ⓐ Ⓑ Ⓒ Ⓓ   27. Ⓐ Ⓑ Ⓒ Ⓓ
4. Ⓙ Ⓚ Ⓛ Ⓜ   10. Ⓙ Ⓚ Ⓛ Ⓜ   16. Ⓙ Ⓚ Ⓛ Ⓜ   22. Ⓙ Ⓚ Ⓛ Ⓜ   28. Ⓙ Ⓚ Ⓛ Ⓜ
5. Ⓐ Ⓑ Ⓒ Ⓓ   11. Ⓐ Ⓑ Ⓒ Ⓓ   17. Ⓐ Ⓑ Ⓒ Ⓓ   23. Ⓐ Ⓑ Ⓒ Ⓓ   29. Ⓐ Ⓑ Ⓒ Ⓓ
6. Ⓙ Ⓚ Ⓛ Ⓜ   12. Ⓙ Ⓚ Ⓛ Ⓜ   18. Ⓙ Ⓚ Ⓛ Ⓜ   24. Ⓙ Ⓚ Ⓛ Ⓜ   30. Ⓙ Ⓚ Ⓛ Ⓜ

PART 2

31. Ⓐ Ⓑ Ⓒ Ⓓ   33. Ⓐ Ⓑ Ⓒ Ⓓ   35. Ⓐ Ⓑ Ⓒ Ⓓ   37. Ⓐ Ⓑ Ⓒ Ⓓ   39. Ⓐ Ⓑ Ⓒ Ⓓ
32. Ⓙ Ⓚ Ⓛ Ⓜ   34. Ⓙ Ⓚ Ⓛ Ⓜ   36. Ⓙ Ⓚ Ⓛ Ⓜ   38. Ⓙ Ⓚ Ⓛ Ⓜ   40. Ⓙ Ⓚ Ⓛ Ⓜ

Ability

1. Ⓐ Ⓑ Ⓒ Ⓓ Ⓔ   4. Ⓙ Ⓚ Ⓛ Ⓜ Ⓝ   7. Ⓐ Ⓑ Ⓒ Ⓓ Ⓔ   9. Ⓐ Ⓑ Ⓒ Ⓓ Ⓔ
2. Ⓙ Ⓚ Ⓛ Ⓜ Ⓝ   5. Ⓐ Ⓑ Ⓒ Ⓓ Ⓔ   8. Ⓙ Ⓚ Ⓛ Ⓜ Ⓝ   10. Ⓙ Ⓚ Ⓛ Ⓜ Ⓝ
3. Ⓐ Ⓑ Ⓒ Ⓓ Ⓔ   6. Ⓙ Ⓚ Ⓛ Ⓜ Ⓝ

Practice Test 1: TACHS

READING

Part 1

5 Minutes

Directions: For each question, decide which one of the four possible answers has most nearly the same meaning as the underlined word above it. Then, on your answer sheet, find the row of answer spaces numbered the same as the question. Fill in the answer space that has the same letter as the answer you chose.

1. Lofty goals
   - (A) elevated
   - (B) unworthy
   - (C) apparent
   - (D) confusing

2. Pleasing demeanor
   - (J) smell
   - (K) sight
   - (L) mood
   - (M) understanding

3. A disheveled bedroom
   - (A) large
   - (B) messy
   - (C) complicated
   - (D) spacious

4. Move hastily
   - (J) slowly
   - (K) deliberately
   - (L) steadily
   - (M) quickly

5. To achieve recognition
   - (A) attain
   - (B) deserve
   - (C) seek
   - (D) squander

6. Placid waters
   - (J) stormy
   - (K) churning
   - (L) muddied
   - (M) peaceful

7. Many diverse cultures
   - (A) identical
   - (B) unknown
   - (C) varied
   - (D) ancient

8. Much rejoicing
   - (J) celebrating
   - (K) mourning
   - (L) relaxing
   - (M) studying

9. A large <u>segment</u>

   (A) hole

   (B) section

   (C) discussion

   (D) mystery

10. <u>Fascinating</u> new developments

   (J) boring

   (K) important

   (L) confusing

   (M) interesting

STOP If you finish before time is up, check over your work on this part only. Do not go on until the signal is given.

Part 2

15 Minutes

Directions: Read the passages below and then answer the questions. Four possible answers are given for each question. You are to choose the answer that you think is better than the others. Then, on your answer sheet, find the row of answer spaces numbered the same as the question. Fill in the best answer in the circles on your answer sheet.

Passage 1

My people are the people of Elu, the capital village of Ohafia in southeast Nigeria. Ours is a warrior tradition. We keep the tradition today primarily in name, but the warrior image is an important part of our identity, passed down through the generations.

We learn the tradition of the warrior through the process of many rituals, each taught to us by our elders, who ensure that our identity is maintained. I remember the first step of my manhood, when I reached the age of eight and was finally ready for the *nnu nnu mbu*, a ritual that proves that you are ready to enter the world of men. It is a sweltering morning, and my family has been preparing for the ceremony since dawn. My father is absorbed in the task of dressing me in a fine costume befitting the occasion, and he looks down upon me with pride as he completes his final touches and prepares me for show.

My father is beaming, and I feel his pride lift me as I move into the street to start the process of visiting others in the village who will honor me for my efforts. My chest swells and I hear my heart pounding in my ears, the blood rushing, as one by one I visit the huts of my kinfolk, receiving gifts of money and yams from each as they greet me. Some of the family member's from my mother's line are introduced to me during this ceremony for the first time. I feel the strength that comes with knowing that I am emerging into manhood.

11. How does the author's father feel about his son?

   (A) He is confused by his son's behavior.

   (B) He pays little attention to his son.

   (C) He is proud of his son's accomplishments.

   (D) He feels shamed by the actions of his son.

12. What happens when the author meets his mother's family?

   (J) His family members urge him to continue his target practice.

   (K) Some of his family members pretend that they do not know him.

   (L) He receives gifts of money and yams from the family members.

   (M) His family members come together to meet him in the village square.

Passage 2

Barrett had always dreamed of opening a photography studio. As soon as he finished photography school, he rented a small space in a strip mall just off the highway. For the first few years, he barely made ends meet. He took just enough photos to pay for rent and materials.

Barrett knew his business was not going to be successful if he continued to do business the way he had since he opened his studio. He researched a number of business strategies before he made his decision. Barrett advertised a month-long special in the newspaper. He decided to reduce his standard pricing by one third for the entire month. He knew this was a calculated risk, but it was one he felt he had to take.

13. The phrase "made ends meet" is another way of saying which of the following?

   (A) Opened the doors
   (B) Took nice pictures
   (C) Took care of customers
   (D) Balanced the budget

14. If Barrett was struggling financially, why did he reduce his prices?

   (J) He hoped to increase the number of customers.
   (K) He was giving up.
   (L) He was paying too many taxes.
   (M) His research was faulty.

Passage 3

History is full of "accidental inventions"—ingenious advances that were initially unintended but eventually served to benefit mankind in a variety of unique ways. Let's take a closer look at a few of these items, as well as their curious origins.

Many of us take for granted having a microwave to cook and reheat food quickly. However, individuals were without this useful appliance until 1945, when an engineer named Percy Spencer accidentally cooked a chocolate bar in his pants while tinkering with a magnetron for a radar-building project. This unexpected event led Spencer down an experimental path that ultimately resulted in the creation of the microwave oven.

Penicillin is an antibiotic used to treat a wide array of infections, and is widely considered one of the most essential medications in the world today. But did you know that its discovery was due to a careless mistake by a scientist? In 1928, Alexander Fleming, a Scottish scientist, noticed a unique mold strain on a Petri dish that was mistakenly left open on a lab table; a mold strain that inhibited the growth of bacteria surrounding it. Rigorous scientific testing of the curious new mold followed, leading to one of the most significant scientific and medical advances in history.

It's clear that scientific curiosity, when in the capable hands of an innovative thinker, can lead an individual down a path to greatness. But sometimes that path contains an unexpected detour, possibly due to a completely unforeseen mistake or accident, and the end result changes history forever.

15. Based on the information in the passage, what do the microwave oven and penicillin have in common?

   (A) Both the microwave and penicillin are essential inventions.
   (B) Both required the work of professional inventors to create them.
   (C) Both inventions are the direct result of an accident or mistake.
   (D) Both would have eventually been invented, even if the accidents mentioned in the passage didn't occur.

16. As used in the passage, "an unexpected detour," most likely refers to

    (J) a change in a driving route that leads to a new road.

    (K) an unintended event leading to a new innovation.

    (L) an unlikely inventor who becomes famous.

    (M) a world-changing invention that changes science.

Passage 4

In recent years, experts have not been able to make any substantial conclusions regarding the effect of e-mail and instant messaging on the social skills of computer users. Some experts in fields such as communications argue that e-mail and instant messaging have increased the social skills of computer users because people now communicate with each other more frequently than ever before. Others, however, maintain that computer users are able to hide behind their anonymity, thus allowing them to take on false personality traits and characteristics. Such experts further contend that the more communication takes place via e-mail and instant messaging, the less effective communication becomes in face-to-face settings. Experts on both sides of the debate do, however, agree that the frequency of communications has increased since the advent of electronic correspondence and that this alone should have some positive effect on the communication skills of computer users. After all, the adage says that practice makes perfect.

17. Which of the following would be the best title for the Passage above?

    (A) "The Problems with E-mail and Instant Messaging"

    (B) "The Electronic Communications Revolution"

    (C) "The Possible Effects of Electronic Communication on Communication Skills of Computer Users"

    (D) "The Debate over Instant Communications and Its Effects on E-mail"

18. The phrase "practice makes perfect" in the last sentence refers to which of the following?

    (J) The increased frequency of electronic communication

    (K) Public speaking engagements

    (L) Practice with computer software

    (M) Research conducted by experts in the field

Passage 5

The reality TV craze that began in the United States two decades ago apparently is here to stay, at least for several more years. Strangely, though, people who watch reality TV still have not caught on to the fact that there is little or no reality at all in reality television shows. Producers and directors often coerce reality show stars to say particular things or act in a particular manner. Filming stops frequently to re-shoot certain scenes or pieces of dialogue between cast members. Those who are chosen to be part of the reality show casts must sign contracts that require them to follow scores of rules. Furthermore, cast members are forbidden from revealing any secrets of the show. The public, though, is still being bombarded by staged, contrived shows that are being advertised as reality.

19. Which of the following is the main idea of the Passage above?

   (A) Reality shows are the most popular shows on TV.

   (B) Reality shows lure watchers through fancy advertising slogans and cute stars.

   (C) Reality TV actually consists of very little reality.

   (D) Reality show cast members usually become big stars and famous celebrities.

20. The author of the Passage above is most likely which of the following?

   (J) A reality show winner

   (K) A reality show producer

   (L) A critic of reality TV

   (M) An executive from a TV network

STOP   If you finish before time is up, check over your work on this part only. Do not go on until the signal is given.

WRITTEN EXPRESSION

Part 1

25 Minutes for Parts 1 and 2

Directions: This is a test of how well you can find mistakes in writing. For the questions with mistakes in spelling, capitalization, and punctuation, choose the answer with the same letter as the **line** containing the mistake. For the questions with mistakes in usage and expression, choose the answer with the same letter as the **line** containing the mistake, or choose the word, phrase, or sentence that is better than the others. When there is no mistake or no change needed, choose the last answer choice.

1. **(A)** dictionery
   (B) tragic
   (C) vintage
   (D) surprise
   (E) *(No mistakes)*

2. **(J)** vacation
   (K) discovery
   (L) collide
   (M) patience
   (N) *(No mistakes)*

3. **(A)** fortress
   (B) obtane
   (C) complete
   (D) interview
   (E) *(No mistakes)*

4. **(J)** invention
   (K) coffee
   (L) perswade
   (M) employer
   (N) *(No mistakes)*

5. **(A)** disscuss
   (B) manager
   (C) exam
   (D) advisory
   (E) *(No mistakes)*

6. **(J)** fortune
   (K) traffic
   (L) intrude
   (M) messinger
   (N) *(No mistakes)*

7. **(A)** referee
   (B) amature
   (C) against
   (D) believe
   (E) *(No mistakes)*

8. **(J)** cancellashun
   (K) invest
   (L) remark
   (M) mall
   (N) *(No mistakes)*

9. **(A)** wander
   (B) mygrate
   (C) functional
   (D) disappear
   (E) *(No mistakes)*

10. **(J)** mountain
    (K) progress
    (L) batter
    (M) profit
    (N) *(No mistakes)*

11. (A) Jamey is going to College
    (B) at Outback University, which
    (C) is located in Australia.
    (D) *(No mistakes)*

12. (J) The Mississippi river travels southward
    (K) toward the Gulf of Mexico
    (L) and passes many states along the way.
    (M) *(No mistakes)*

13. (A) Jovan couldn't wait to have lunch
    (B) at the new Chinese Restaurant
    (C) on the corner of Ridge Street and Dey Road.
    (D) *(No mistakes)*

14. (J) We're planning a nice dinner at the steak restaurant
    (K) to celebrate valentine's day; we're planning to watch
    (L) the movie *Shrek* after dinner.
    (M) *(No mistakes)*

15. (A) You just can't beat a cold drink
    (B) or a few scoops of Ben and Jerry's
    (C) on a scorching-hot Summer day.
    (D) *(No mistakes)*

16. (J) Mrs. Samson said that Archie,
    (K) her sister's third cousin, used to
    (L) live across the street from Taylor Swift.
    (M) *(No mistakes)*

17. (A) The astronauts aboard the Apollo rocket
    (B) said that the moon looked much different in Space
    (C) than it did from on the ground.
    (D) *(No mistakes)*

18. (J) He's so smart because he reads *Time* magazine
    (K) and the Newspaper in the morning
    (L) before he even gets to school.
    (M) *(No mistakes)*

19. (A) She accompanied her mother
    (B) on a visit to father O'Reilly to
    (C) thank him for visiting her brother in the hospital.
    (D) *(No mistakes)*

20. (J) The Dirt Road that wound through the woods
    (K) was just a few miles from Interstate 95,
    (L) which led to many major eastern cities.
    (M) *(No mistakes)*

Part 2

Directions: For questions 21 and 22, choose the best way of expressing the idea.

21. **(A)** Eldridge liked to tinker in his workshop and often came up with new product ideas.

    (B) Eldridge, who liked to tinker in his workshop; he often came up with new product ideas.

    (C) In his workshop, Eldridge liked to tinker, where he often came up with new product ideas.

    (D) Often coming up with new product ideas, Eldridge liked to tinker in his workshop where he was.

22. **(J)** The Garmin's house, their summer house in Maine, was built all month with a new bedroom by the carpenter.

    (K) In Maine, a summer house of the Garmin's, the carpenter spent all month building it—a new bedroom.

    (L) The carpenter spent all month building a new bedroom for the Garmins' summer house in Maine.

    (M) A summer house, which is the Garmin's, had a new bedroom built onto it by the carpenter, who spent all month building it.

Directions: For questions 23–30, choose the best answer based on the following paragraphs.

(1) Among the many scenic and storied lighthouses that still exist across the United States, there's one that stands above the rest—literally. (2) Cape Hatteras Lighthouse is America's tallest lighthouse, a 210-foot striped beacon to sailors and their sea vessels <u>since they were</u> first constructed in 1870. (3) It's located in a town called Buxton, on Hatteras Island—one of several islands that make up the Outer Banks along the coast of North Carolina. (4) <u>Obviously</u>, the current Cape Hatteras lighthouse is not the original; the original lighthouse was destroyed in 1862, during the Civil War. (5) Although the Cape Hatteras Lighthouse is the tallest in America, it currently ranks only 29th tallest in the world—it's dwarfed by the mammoth 436-foot Jeddah Lighthouse in Saudi Arabia.

23. What is the best way to write the underlined part of sentence 2?

    (A) when she was

    (B) when he were

    (C) since it was

    (D) *(No change)*

24. What is the best way to write the underlined part of sentence 4?

    (J) Therefore,

    (K) Interestingly,

    (L) In contrast,

    (M) *(No change)*

(1) Like many Impressionist painters working in France during the mid-to-late 19th century, Edgar Degas attempted to capture a fleeting moment in time on canvas. (2) Defined as an artistic movement in which painters tried to recreate the changing light and colors of a particular place and time, Impressionism featured heavy dabs of color painted with bold, swift strokes and subject matter rooted in nature. (3) Instead of painting the garden parties and floral landscapes embraced by his contemporaries, Degas preferred to paint a wide spectrum of human subjects. (4) Although best known for his depiction of dancers especially behind-the-scenes glimpses of ballerinas rehearsing or warming up backstage, he also painted everyday scenes of working class Parisian life at racetracks and cafes.

25. What is the best way to write the underlined part of sentence 2?

(A) bold swift

(B) bold; swift

(C) bold, Swift

(D) *(No change)*

26. What is the best way to write the underlined part of sentence 4?

(J) dancers. Especially

(K) dancers, especially

(L) dancers: especially

(M) *(No change)*

(1) When we think of the fastest members of the animal kingdom, mammals often come to mind. (2) Indeed, cheetahs can sprint at over 70 mph, and greyhounds have been clocked at 46 mph. (3) A more unlikely candidate, however, claims the title of the fastest creature on the Planet—the peregrine falcon. (4) After soaring high above its prey, the peregrine falcon plunges into a hunting dive with ever-increasing velocity and speeds topping 200 mph. (5) Known as the *stoop*, this dizzying maneuver not only makes the peregrine falcon a highly effective predator, but also allows this bird of prey to attain record speeds during its free-falling descent.

27. What is the best way to write the underlined part of sentence 2?

(A) Nonetheless,

(B) Conversely,

(C) Subsequently,

(D) *(No change)*

28. What is the best way to write the underlined part of sentence 3?

(J) Galaxy

(K) planet

(L) Hemisphere

(M) *(No change)*

(1) Described as the most famous diamond in the world, the Hope Diamond is housed in the <u>Smithsonian Natural History museum</u> in Washington, D.C. (2) The Hope Diamond was formed about 1.1 billion years ago and was first discovered in India during the seventeenth century. (3) Pear-shaped and uncommonly large, the diamond is the size of a walnut with a brilliant, deep-blue color attributed to traces of boron found within its crystal structure. (4) Since its founding, the diamond has frequently changed hands as it traveled from India to France and Britain before reaching its final destination in the United States. (5) Legends of a supposed curse on those who have worn or owned the Hope Diamond <u>abound</u>, but these stories of troubles and misfortune have never been proven.

29. What is the best way to write the underlined part of sentence 1?

(A) Smithsonian Natural History Museum

(B) Smithsonian natural history museum

(C) smithsonian natural history museum

(D) *(No change)*

30. What is the best way to write the underlined part of sentence 5?

(J) abounds

(K) abounded

(L) a bound

(M) *(No change)*

STOP If you finish before time is up, check over your work on this part only. Do not go on until the signal is given.

MATH

Part 1
30 Minutes

Directions: Four answers are given for each problem. Choose the best answer.

1. Which of the following is *not* a factor of 20?

   (A) 10

   (B) 5

   (C) 4

   (D) 3

2. The fraction $\frac{2}{3}$ is approximately which of the following?

   (J) $\frac{3}{2}$

   (K) 0.23

   (L) 0.67

   (M) 23.67

3. Which of the following is *not* a prime number?

   (A) 3

   (B) 9

   (C) 13

   (D) 19

4. Which of the following is a multiple of 3?

   (J) 29

   (K) 49

   (L) 69

   (M) 89

5. What is the product of 43 and 100?

   (A) 4,300

   (B) 143

   (C) 57

   (D) 0.43

6. The number 0.003 can also be represented by which of the following?

   (J) $\frac{3}{10}$

   (K) $\frac{3}{100}$

   (L) $\frac{3}{1000}$

   (M) $\frac{3}{10,000}$

7. Which of the following is the equivalent of 3^3?

   (A) 3×3

   (B) $3 \times 3 \div 3$

   (C) 27

   (D) 30

8. What is the sum of $\frac{1}{2} + \frac{2}{4} + \frac{3}{3}$?

   (J) 1

   (K) 2

   (L) $2\frac{1}{2}$

   (M) 3

9. What is the sum of $(3 \times 3) + (4 \times 4) + (5 \times 5)$?

   (A) 24

   (B) 50

   (C) 60

   (D) 345

10. Which of the following represents the reduced form for 1.6?

(J) $1\frac{6}{10}$

(K) $1\frac{3}{5}$

(L) $\frac{16}{10}$

(M) $\frac{32}{20}$

11. Jeff has 6 notebooks in his locker. Maggie has in her locker twice as many notebooks as Jeff. Darnell has in his locker twice as many notebooks as Maggie and Jeff combined. How many notebooks does Darnell have stuffed into his locker?

(A) 12

(B) 18

(C) 24

(D) 36

12. Baxter needed to replenish his supply of bottled water. The water dispenser in his kitchen holds 14 gallons of water. Baxter buys his water one half-gallon at a time at his local grocery store. How many half-gallon water purchases will Baxter need to make to fill his water dispenser?

(J) 7

(K) 14

(L) 21

(M) 28

13. McKenzie currently has $50 set aside to purchase a TV that costs $300. She earns $25 per week babysitting. How many weeks will it take her to earn enough money to buy the TV?

(A) 12

(B) 10

(C) 8

(D) 7

14. Sam's scooter gets 50 miles per gallon, and the scooter's gas tank holds 3 gallons of gasoline. If the gas tank in Sam's scooter is $\frac{2}{3}$ full, how many miles can Sam expect to travel before the tank is empty?

(J) 75

(K) 100

(L) 150

(M) 175

15. The rim on a basketball goal is 10 feet from the floor. If a player made 6 baskets, what is the sum of the distances that the ball would travel between the rim and the floor below?

(A) 60 feet

(B) 70 feet

(C) 160 feet

(D) Not given

16. If every car that travels along Highway 27 has four wheels and there are 72 cars driving on Highway 27, how many wheels are touching the road on Highway 27?

(J) 54

(K) 144

(L) 108

(M) 288

17. Ted can text 30 characters in 10 seconds. How many characters can Ted text in 2 minutes?

(A) 300

(B) 360

(C) 600

(D) 3,600

18. Aunt Ethel has 7 dozen antique ornaments for her Christmas tree. She anticipates needing a total of 200 ornaments to finish decorating her tree. How many ornaments should Aunt Ethel purchase at the antique fair to reach her goal of 200 antique ornaments for her tree?

(J) 84

(K) 96

(L) 116

(M) 124

19. Mandie and Mary Beth are planning to paint the concession stand at school. They have four walls to paint. Each wall is exactly the same size. The walls are each 12 feet long and 10 feet high. How many square feet of walls should they plan to paint if they are going to paint all four walls?

(A) 120 square feet

(B) 240 square feet

(C) 480 square feet

(D) 1,200 square feet

20. The penguins at the zoo eat 36,500 pounds of fish each year. How many pounds of fish do the penguins eat each day?

(J) 100

(K) 365

(L) 1,000

(M) Not given

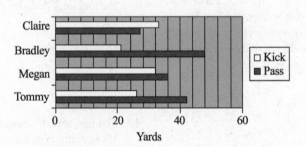

21. The city recently held a football skills competition at Barton Park. Based on the information in the chart above, which competitor passed the football the shortest distance?

(A) Claire

(B) Bradley

(C) Megan

(D) Tommy

22. Based on the information in the chart above, which competitor passed 4 more yards than he/she kicked the football?

(J) Claire

(K) Bradley

(L) Megan

(M) Tommy

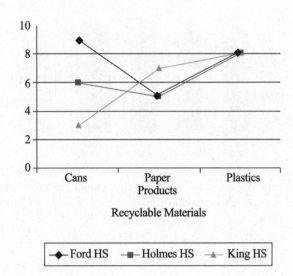

Recyclable Materials

◆ Ford HS ■ Holmes HS ▲ King HS

23. The City School District sponsored a week-long recycling campaign in which the three city high schools collected items to be recycled. The chart indicates the results of the campaign as measured in hundreds of pounds. Based on the information in the chart above, which of the high schools collected the most cans and paper products combined?

(A) Ford HS

(B) Holmes HS

(C) King HS

(D) Holmes HS and King HS

24. Based on the information in the chart above, what was the total weight of all plastics collected in the campaign?

(J) 800 pounds

(K) 1,600 pounds

(L) 2,400 pounds

(M) 6,900 pounds

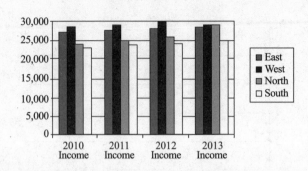

25. According to the bar graph above that illustrates per capita income by region in thousands of dollars, which region experienced the most income growth from 2010 to 2013?

(A) East

(B) West

(C) North

(D) South

26. According to the bar graph above, what was the approximate income of Southerners in 2013?

(J) $25,000

(K) $26,000

(L) $27,000

(M) $28,000

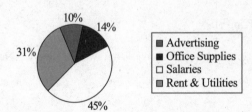

27. The pie chart above illustrates the proposed budget for a new company opening soon around the corner. Based on the information in the chart, what will be the most expensive part of running the new company?

(A) Advertising

(B) Office Supplies

(C) Salaries

(D) Rent & Utilities

28. Which two items in the proposed budget when added together equal the amount spent on salaries?

(J) Advertising and Office Supplies

(K) Rent & Utilities and Office Supplies

(L) Advertising and Salaries

(M) Advertising and Rent & Utilities

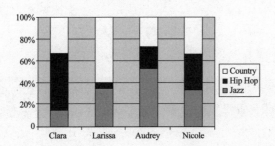

29. The chart above represents the music collections of 4 high school seniors. Based on the information in the chart, which of the girls has a music collection composed of approximately 60 percent country music?

    (A) Clara

    (B) Larissa

    (C) Audrey

    (D) Nicole

30. Based on the information in the chart, if all four collections are the same size, which girl seems to prefer jazz to both hip hop and country music?

    (J) Clara

    (K) Larissa

    (L) Audrey

    (M) Nicole

STOP   If you finish before time is up, check over your work on this part only. Do not go on until the signal is given.

Part 2

10 Minutes

Directions: For the following questions, <u>estimate</u> the answer in your head. No scratch work is allowed. Do NOT try to compute exact answers.

31. The closest estimate of 6544 – 3466 is
    _____.

    (A) 1000

    (B) 2000

    (C) 3000

    (D) 4000

32. The closest estimate of 82,122 ÷ 4055 is
    _____.

    (J) 20,000

    (K) 2,000

    (L) 200

    (M) 20

33. The average class size at Kennedy High School is 31 students. There are 30 classes in session at any one time. About how many Kennedy High students are in class at any given time?

    (A) 800

    (B) 900

    (C) 1000

    (D) Not given

34. The closest estimate of 3988 + 2177 is
    _____.

    (J) 5000

    (K) 5500

    (L) 6000

    (M) 6500

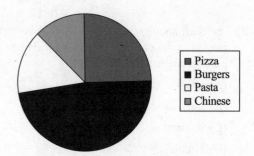

FAVORITE FOODS OF NEW YORK HIGH SCHOOL SENIORS

35. According to the chart above, about what percent of New York high school seniors prefers burgers?

    (A) 15%

    (B) 25%

    (C) 33%

    (D) 50%

36. According to the chart, if one hundred seniors were surveyed, about how many seniors prefer pizza?

    (J) 10

    (K) 15

    (L) 25

    (M) Not given

37. Most half-hour television shows are actually 23 minutes long once commercial time is deducted. If this is true, approximately how many seconds of commercials do viewers see in one half-hour show?

    (A) 300

    (B) 400

    (C) 500

    (D) 600

38. The closest estimate of 43 + 71 + 19 + 68 + 11 + 29 is _____.

(J) 200

(K) 210

(L) 240

(M) 300

39. The closest estimate of 63,977 ÷ 7,991 is _____.

(A) 8

(B) 80

(C) 256

(D) Not given

40. The closest estimate of 414 − 289 − 106 + 89 + 277 is _____.

(J) 600

(K) 500

(L) 400

(M) 300

practice test

ABILITY

5 Minutes

Directions: In questions 1–3, the first three figures are alike in certain ways. Choose the answer choice that corresponds to the first three figures.

1.

   (A) ☐   (B) ○   (C) ◺   (D) ▱   (E) ☐

2.

   (J) ⬠   (K) ⬭   (L) ▽   (M) ⋈   (N) ☐

3.

   (A) ⊠   (B)   (C) ⬡   (D) ◿   (E) ◔

Directions: In questions 4–7, the first figure is related to the second figure. Determine that relationship. The third figure is changed in the same way to make one of the answer choices. Choose the answer choice that relates to the third figure.

4.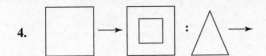

    (J)   (K)   (L)   (M)   (N)

5.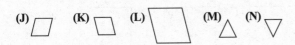

(A)   (B)   (C)   (D)   (E)

6.

Directions: In questions 8–10, look at the top row to see how a square piece of paper is folded and where holes are punched into it. Then look at the bottom row to decide which answer choice shows how the paper will look when it is completely unfolded.

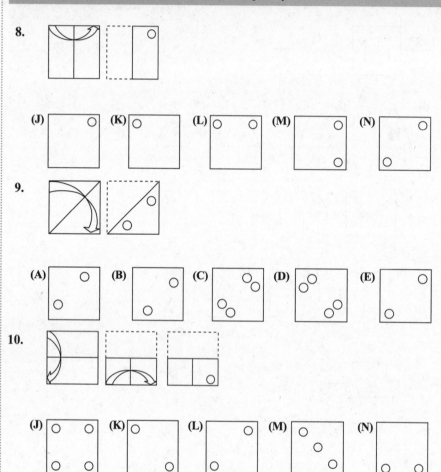

8.

(J) (K) (L) (M) (N)

9.

(A) (B) (C) (D) (E)

10.

(J) (K) (L) (M) (N)

STOP   If you finish before time is up, check over your work on this section only. Do not go back to any previous parts.

ANSWER KEYS AND EXPLANATIONS

Reading

Part 1

1. A	3. B	5. A	7. C	9. B
2. L	4. M	6. M	8. J	10. M

1. **The correct answer is (A)**, *elevated*. Other synonyms for *lofty* include "raised," "high," and "towering."

2. **The correct answer is (L)**, *mood*. Other synonyms for *demeanor* include "manner" and "deportment."

3. **The correct answer is (B)**, *messy*. *Disheveled* and *messy* are synonyms, both meaning "not tidy."

4. **The correct answer is (M)**, *quickly*. Other synonyms for *hastily* include "swiftly" and "hurriedly."

5. **The correct answer is (A)**, *attain*. Other synonyms for *achieve* include "accomplish," "gain," and "reach."

6. **The correct answer is (M)**, *peaceful*. Other synonyms for *placid* include "calm" and "serene."

7. **The correct answer is (C)**, *varied*. Other synonyms for *diverse* include "assorted" and "dissimilar."

8. **The correct answer is (J)**, *celebrating*. Other synonyms for *rejoicing* include "reveling" and "exulting."

9. **The correct answer is (B)**, *section*. Other synonyms for *segment* include "fragment" and "division."

10. **The correct answer is (M)**, *interesting*. Other synonyms for *fascinating* include "intriguing," "captivating," and "enticing."

Part 2

11. C	13. D	15. C	17. C	19. C
12. L	14. J	16. K	18. J	20. L

11. **The correct answer is (C)**. The passage shows that the author's father is proud of his son's accomplishments. In paragraph three, the fact that he is "beaming" indicates that he is happy and has a positive expression on his face. Answer choice (C) best reflects these qualities of the father, who is pleased with what his son has done. Answer choice (C) is correct.

12. **The correct answer is (L)**. Questions such as this one simply require you to identify certain details that were revealed in the story. To answer a "detail" question like this one, you might go back and refresh your memory by re-reading the part of the passage that describes what happened when the author met his mother's family. We are told in paragraph four that the author received gifts of money and yams from the family members as they greeted him. Answer choice (L) is therefore correct.

13. **The correct answer is (D)**. The phrase "making ends meet" is a common way of saying that a budget is balanced. In other words, when one makes ends meet, he or she makes their money last long enough to pay all expenses. The last sentence of the first paragraph gives the context clue about the phrase.

14. **The correct answer is (J).** He hoped to increase the number of customers. Barrett knew he needed more customers, and the first paragraph indicates that he had just enough customers to balance his budget; it is implied that he was not making much, if any, profit. In order to increase his profit, he needed more paying customers.

15. **The correct answer is (C).** The main idea of the passage is an exploration of accidental inventions—"ingenious advances that were initially unintended but eventually served to benefit mankind." The passage illustrates this topic by providing two examples—the microwave oven and penicillin, both described as inventions that are the direct result of an accident or mistake. Only penicillin is described as an essential invention, so choice (A) is incorrect. Choices B and D are incorrect because there is no indication that a "professional inventor" was required or that both the microwave and penicillin would have eventually been invented, even if the accidents mentioned in the passage hadn't occurred.

16. **The correct answer is (K).** The path, as described in the passage, refers to a line of scientific curiosity by an innovative thinker (like Spencer or Fleming) that is disrupted by an unintended event, but ultimately leads to a new innovation. For Percy Spencer, that led to the creation of the microwave oven. For Alexander Fleming, that led to the development of penicillin.

17. **The correct answer is (C).** "The Possible Effects of Electronic Communication on Communication Skills of Computer Users" is the best title because the Passage directly addresses the social skills of computer users and the ways that those skills are affected by communicating electronically, via e-mail and instant messaging.

18. **The correct answer is (J).** The phrase implies that the more something is practiced by someone, the better he or she becomes at whatever is practiced. The next-to-last sentence mentions increased communications, so it is implied that "practice makes perfect" refers to that increase in communications.

19. **The correct answer is (C).** Reality TV actually consists of very little reality. The author of the Passage contends that there is little reality in reality TV because the producers and directors still have a huge influence on the things that are filmed and televised, and this prevents reality TV from being real, which theoretically is the defining characteristic of reality.

20. **The correct answer is (L).** An author who criticizes and points out flaws or weaknesses is most likely a person who is a critic or opponent of that about which he or she writes.

Written Expression

Part 1

1. A	5. A	9. B	13. B	17. B
2. N	6. M	10. N	14. K	18. K
3. B	7. B	11. A	15. C	19. B
4. L	8. J	12. J	16. M	20. J

1. **The correct answer is (A).** The correct spelling is *dictionary*.

2. **The correct answer is (N).** *(No mistakes)*

3. **The correct answer is (B).** The correct spelling is *obtain*.

4. **The correct answer is (L).** The correct spelling is *persuade*.

5. **The correct answer is (A).** The correct spelling is *discuss*.

6. **The correct answer is (M).** The correct spelling is *messenger*.

7. **The correct answer is (B).** The correct spelling is *amateur.*

8. **The correct answer is (J).** The correct spelling is *cancellation.*

9. **The correct answer is (B).** The correct spelling is *migrate.*

10. **The correct answer is (N).** *(No mistakes)*

11. **The correct answer is (A).** The word "college" is only capitalized when included in a proper noun such as Boston College or Ithaca College.

12. **The correct answer is (J).** The word "river" is capitalized when included as part of a proper noun such as Mississippi River.

13. **The correct answer is (B).** Although the name of a country's cuisine is capitalized, the word "restaurant" is not capitalized unless it is used to begin a sentence or is part of a proper name.

14. **The correct answer is (K).** Holidays, because they are proper nouns, should be capitalized.

15. **The correct answer is (C).** Names of seasons are not proper nouns and do not need capitalization.

16. **The correct answer is (M).** *(No mistakes)*

17. **The correct answer is (B).** "Space" needs no capitalization because it is a common noun, but related terms such as "Haley's Comet" or "Jupiter" should be capitalized because they are proper nouns.

18. **The correct answer is (K).** The word "newspaper" is a common noun and would only be capitalized as part of a proper noun such as the "Baltimore Newspaper Publishing Company."

19. **The correct answer is (B).** Words like "father" or "sister" require capitalization when used as part of a person's name, as in the cases of "Father Dowling" or "Sister Wendy."

20. **The correct answer is (J).** Names of streets, roads, or avenues are to be capitalized, as in "Abbey Road" or "Penny Lane," but not when used as common nouns like "the dirt road" or "the winding country lane."

Part 2

| 21. A | 23. C | 25. D | 27. D | 29. A |
| 22. L | 24. M | 26. K | 28. K | 30. M |

21. **The correct answer is (A).** Choice (A) expresses the idea clearly with the correct punctuation, so it is correct. Choice (D) is incorrect because it contains the unnecessary phrase "where he was" at the end of the sentence.

22. **The correct answer is (L).** Choice (L) most efficiently and effectively expresses the ideas in this sentence, without the unnecessary wordiness, redundancy, and confusion that makes the other choices incorrect.

23. **The correct answer is (C).** As written, the underlined portion of the sentences incorrectly uses the plural pronoun they to replace the singular noun, *Cape Hatteras Lighthouse.* Choice C correctly uses the singular pronoun it to replace the singular noun.

24. **The correct answer is (K).** As written, the passage makes an incorrect assumption that the information about Cape Hatteras Lighthouse not being the original is obvious. This is more of an interesting bit of trivia than something obvious that everyone knows, so choice (K) would be a more effective way to begin this sentence, given the context of the passage.

25. **The correct answer is (D).** *(No change).* Both the words "bold" and "swift" are adjectives modifying the noun "strokes." Since two adjectives are used together to modify one noun, the two adjectives must be separated with a comma.

26. The correct answer is (K). Commas are needed to separate the phrase "especially behind-the-scenes glimpses of ballerinas rehearsing or warming up backstage" from the remainder of the sentence, so choice (K) is correct.

27. The correct answer is (D). *(No change).* The word "Indeed" signifies that a similar idea to what was presented in the first sentence will follow in the next sentence. Choices (A) and (B) both suggest information that opposes what has already been stated, and choice (C) would indicate a cause-and-effect relationship.

28. The correct answer is (K). The word "planet" is a common noun and would need capitalization only if used as part of a name, such as "Small Planet Institute."

29. The correct answer is (A). The word "museum" by itself is a common noun, but it requires capitalization when used as part of a proper noun naming a specific place. The other answer choices are incorrect since all four words in the name of the Smithsonian Natural History Museum must be capitalized.

30. The correct answer is (M). *(No change).* No change is necessary to the sentence, since the plural noun "Legends" takes a plural verb. Furthermore, the verb should be in present tense to match the rest of the sentence, ruling out choice (K). Choice (L) contains a different verb entirely based on the word "bound," or "compelled."

Math

Part 1

1. D	7. C	13. B	19. C	25. C
2. L	8. K	14. K	20. J	26. J
3. B	9. B	15. A	21. A	27. C
4. L	10. K	16. M	22. L	28. K
5. A	11. D	17. B	23. A	29. B
6. L	12. M	18. L	24. L	30. L

1. The correct answer is (D). 20 cannot be divided evenly by 3.

2. The correct answer is (L). $\frac{2}{3}$ is the same as 0.67, rounded to the nearest hundredth.

3. The correct answer is (B). 9 is divisible by three numbers—1, 3, and 9.

4. The correct answer is (L). 3 multiplied by 23 is 69.

5. The correct answer is (A). The term "product" means to multiply. $43 \times 100 = 4,300$.

6. The correct answer is (L). The third place to the right of the decimal is thousandths.

7. The correct answer is (C).
$3 \times 3 \times 3 = 3 \times 9 = 27$

8. The correct answer is (K).
$\frac{1}{2} + \frac{2}{4} + \frac{3}{3} = \frac{1}{2} + \frac{1}{2} + 1 = 1 + 1 = 2$

9. The correct answer is (B). $(3 \times 3) + (4 \times 4) + (5 \times 5) = 9 + 16 + 25 = 50$

10. The correct answer is (K). $1.6 = 1\frac{6}{10}$, which must be reduced to $1\frac{3}{5}$.

11. **The correct answer is (D).** Jeff has 6 notebooks. Maggie has 2 × 6 notebooks. Jeff and Maggie combined have 18 notebooks. Darnell has 2 × 18, or 36, notebooks.

12. **The correct answer is (M).** Baxter needs two half-gallons for each gallon, or 2 × 14 = 28.

13. **The correct answer is (B).** Since she already has $50, she must earn $250 to be able to purchase the $300 TV. Divide $250 by $25 (the amount earned per week) to see that it will take her 10 weeks to earn this money.

14. **The correct answer is (K).** A full tank would go 3 × 50, or 150 miles. $\frac{2}{3} \times 150 = 100$.

15. **The correct answer is (A).** 6 trips from rim to floor, or 6 × 10 = 60.

16. **The correct answer is (M).** 72 cars with 4 wheels each, or 72 × 4 = 288.

17. **The correct answer is (B).** Two minutes equals 2 × 60 = 120 seconds. In this amount of time, Ted can text 30 × 12 = 360 characters.

18. **The correct answer is (L).** Seven dozen is 7 × 12 = 84. 200 − 84 = 116.

19. **The correct answer is (C).** Each wall is 12 × 10, or 120 square feet. Four walls of 120 square feet is 4 × 120 = 480 square feet.

20. **The correct answer is (J).** 36,500 ÷ 365 days in a year is 100.

21. **The correct answer is (A).** Claire passed for only 27 yards.

22. **The correct answer is (L).** Megan passed for 36 yards and kicked 32 yards.

23. **The correct answer is (A).** Ford HS collected 900 pounds of cans and 500 pounds of paper products.

24. **The correct answer is (L).** Each school collected 800 pounds. 800 × 3 = 2400.

25. **The correct answer is (C).** The income in the North grew from about $24,000 to nearly $29,000.

26. **The correct answer is (J).** According the bar graph, the approximate income of Southerners (the white bar) in 2013 was $25,000.

27. **The correct answer is (C).** The money that will be spent on salaries is more than any other single expenditure.

28. **The correct answer is (K).** When added together, Rent & Utilities plus Office Supplies (31% + 14% = 45%) equals Salaries (45%).

29. **The correct answer is (B).** Larissa's collection consists of approximately 35% jazz, 5% hip hop, and 60% country.

30. **The correct answer is (L).** Audrey's collection consists of approximately 50% jazz, 20% hip hop, and 30% country.

Part 2

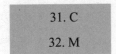 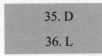

31. C	33. B	35. D	37. B	39. A
32. M	34. L	36. L	38. L	40. L

31. **The correct answer is (C).** 6544 − 3466 is approximately 6500 − 3500, or 3000.

32. **The correct answer is (M).** 82,122 ÷ 4055 is approximately 80,000 ÷ 4000, or 20.

33. **The correct answer is (B).** 31 × 30 is approximately 30 × 30, or 900.

34. **The correct answer is (L).** 3988 + 2177 is approximately 4000 + 2000, or 6000.

35. **The correct answer is (D).** About half, or 50 percent, chose burgers.

36. **The correct answer is (L).** About one fourth, or 25 percent, chose pizza. 100 × 25% = 25.

answers practice test 1

37. The correct answer is (B). Seven minutes is 7 × 60 seconds = 420 seconds, which is about 400.

38. The correct answer is (L). 43 + 71 + 19 + 68 + 11 + 29 can be approximated to 40 + 70 + 20 + 70 + 10 + 30, which is 240.

39. The correct answer is (A). 63,977 ÷ 7,991 is approximately 64,000 ÷ 8000, which is 8.

40. The correct answer is (L). 414 − 289 − 106 + 89 + 277 is approximately 400 − 300 − 100 + 100 + 300 = 400.

Ability

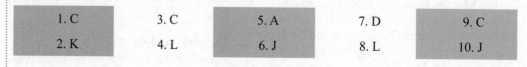

1. C	3. C	5. A	7. D	9. C
2. K	4. L	6. J	8. L	10. J

1. **The correct answer is (C).** The three given figures are all triangles.

2. **The correct answer is (K).** The three given figures are all ovals.

3. **The correct answer is (C).** Each of the three given figures has one line segment in its interior.

4. **The correct answer is (L).** For the first pair, the second figure has a smaller version of the first figure inside it. Thus, for the second figure of the second pair, we need a triangle drawn inside the given triangle and appearing in the same way. Answer choice (M) is incorrect because the triangle is upside down.

5. **The correct answer is (A).** For the first pair, the second figure results from pulling apart the two triangles where they are connected, then flipping over each triangle, and reconnecting them at a common point. Answer choices (B) and (C) are incorrect because one of the half-circles has not been flipped over.

6. **The correct answer is (J).** For the first pair, the second figure is simply a smaller version of the first figure. Answer choice (K) is incorrect because it appears different from the original first figure of the second pair.

7. **The correct answer is (D).** For the first pair, the second figure is one in which a smaller square is drawn inside the larger square, and the area between the two is shaded. Answer choice (D) follows that, with a smaller circle inside a larger circle and the area between the two shaded.

8. **The correct answer is (L).** After the figure is folded over the center vertical line, a hole is punched in the upper right-hand corner. When this figure is unfolded, a hole will appear in both the upper right and upper left portions of the original figure.

9. **The correct answer is (C).** This figure is folded over its diagonal, and then two holes are punched next to the diagonal. When unfolded, there will appear four holes next to the diagonal. Answer choice (D) is incorrect because the holes are too far away from the diagonal.

10. **The correct answer is (J).** This figure is folded first over a horizontal line and then folded again over a vertical line. After a hole is punched, when unfolded, there will be a hole in each corner.

ANSWER SHEET PRACTICE TEST 2: TACHS

Reading

PART 1

1. Ⓐ Ⓑ Ⓒ Ⓓ   3. Ⓐ Ⓑ Ⓒ Ⓓ   5. Ⓐ Ⓑ Ⓒ Ⓓ   7. Ⓐ Ⓑ Ⓒ Ⓓ   9. Ⓐ Ⓑ Ⓒ Ⓓ
2. Ⓙ Ⓚ Ⓛ Ⓜ   4. Ⓙ Ⓚ Ⓛ Ⓜ   6. Ⓙ Ⓚ Ⓛ Ⓜ   8. Ⓙ Ⓚ Ⓛ Ⓜ   10. Ⓙ Ⓚ Ⓛ Ⓜ

PART 2

11. Ⓐ Ⓑ Ⓒ Ⓓ   13. Ⓐ Ⓑ Ⓒ Ⓓ   15. Ⓐ Ⓑ Ⓒ Ⓓ   17. Ⓐ Ⓑ Ⓒ Ⓓ   19. Ⓐ Ⓑ Ⓒ Ⓓ
12. Ⓙ Ⓚ Ⓛ Ⓜ   14. Ⓙ Ⓚ Ⓛ Ⓜ   16. Ⓙ Ⓚ Ⓛ Ⓜ   18. Ⓙ Ⓚ Ⓛ Ⓜ   20. Ⓙ Ⓚ Ⓛ Ⓜ

Language

PART 1

1. Ⓐ Ⓑ Ⓒ Ⓓ Ⓔ   6. Ⓙ Ⓚ Ⓛ Ⓜ Ⓝ   11. Ⓐ Ⓑ Ⓒ Ⓓ   16. Ⓙ Ⓚ Ⓛ Ⓜ
2. Ⓙ Ⓚ Ⓛ Ⓜ Ⓝ   7. Ⓐ Ⓑ Ⓒ Ⓓ Ⓔ   12. Ⓙ Ⓚ Ⓛ Ⓜ   17. Ⓐ Ⓑ Ⓒ Ⓓ
3. Ⓐ Ⓑ Ⓒ Ⓓ Ⓔ   8. Ⓙ Ⓚ Ⓛ Ⓜ Ⓝ   13. Ⓐ Ⓑ Ⓒ Ⓓ   18. Ⓙ Ⓚ Ⓛ Ⓜ
4. Ⓙ Ⓚ Ⓛ Ⓜ Ⓝ   9. Ⓐ Ⓑ Ⓒ Ⓓ Ⓔ   14. Ⓙ Ⓚ Ⓛ Ⓜ   19. Ⓐ Ⓑ Ⓒ Ⓓ
5. Ⓐ Ⓑ Ⓒ Ⓓ Ⓔ   10. Ⓙ Ⓚ Ⓛ Ⓜ Ⓝ   15. Ⓐ Ⓑ Ⓒ Ⓓ   20. Ⓙ Ⓚ Ⓛ Ⓜ

PART 2

21. Ⓐ Ⓑ Ⓒ Ⓓ   23. Ⓐ Ⓑ Ⓒ Ⓓ   25. Ⓐ Ⓑ Ⓒ Ⓓ   27. Ⓐ Ⓑ Ⓒ Ⓓ   29. Ⓐ Ⓑ Ⓒ Ⓓ
22. Ⓙ Ⓚ Ⓛ Ⓜ   24. Ⓙ Ⓚ Ⓛ Ⓜ   26. Ⓙ Ⓚ Ⓛ Ⓜ   28. Ⓙ Ⓚ Ⓛ Ⓜ   30. Ⓙ Ⓚ Ⓛ Ⓜ

Math

PART 1

1. Ⓐ Ⓑ Ⓒ Ⓓ   7. Ⓐ Ⓑ Ⓒ Ⓓ   13. Ⓐ Ⓑ Ⓒ Ⓓ   19. Ⓐ Ⓑ Ⓒ Ⓓ   25. Ⓐ Ⓑ Ⓒ Ⓓ
2. Ⓙ Ⓚ Ⓛ Ⓜ   8. Ⓙ Ⓚ Ⓛ Ⓜ   14. Ⓙ Ⓚ Ⓛ Ⓜ   20. Ⓙ Ⓚ Ⓛ Ⓜ   26. Ⓙ Ⓚ Ⓛ Ⓜ
3. Ⓐ Ⓑ Ⓒ Ⓓ   9. Ⓐ Ⓑ Ⓒ Ⓓ   15. Ⓐ Ⓑ Ⓒ Ⓓ   21. Ⓐ Ⓑ Ⓒ Ⓓ   27. Ⓐ Ⓑ Ⓒ Ⓓ
4. Ⓙ Ⓚ Ⓛ Ⓜ   10. Ⓙ Ⓚ Ⓛ Ⓜ   16. Ⓙ Ⓚ Ⓛ Ⓜ   22. Ⓙ Ⓚ Ⓛ Ⓜ   28. Ⓙ Ⓚ Ⓛ Ⓜ
5. Ⓐ Ⓑ Ⓒ Ⓓ   11. Ⓐ Ⓑ Ⓒ Ⓓ   17. Ⓐ Ⓑ Ⓒ Ⓓ   23. Ⓐ Ⓑ Ⓒ Ⓓ   29. Ⓐ Ⓑ Ⓒ Ⓓ
6. Ⓙ Ⓚ Ⓛ Ⓜ   12. Ⓙ Ⓚ Ⓛ Ⓜ   18. Ⓙ Ⓚ Ⓛ Ⓜ   24. Ⓙ Ⓚ Ⓛ Ⓜ   30. Ⓙ Ⓚ Ⓛ Ⓜ

PART 2

31. Ⓐ Ⓑ Ⓒ Ⓓ   33. Ⓐ Ⓑ Ⓒ Ⓓ   35. Ⓐ Ⓑ Ⓒ Ⓓ   37. Ⓐ Ⓑ Ⓒ Ⓓ   39. Ⓐ Ⓑ Ⓒ Ⓓ
32. Ⓙ Ⓚ Ⓛ Ⓜ   34. Ⓙ Ⓚ Ⓛ Ⓜ   36. Ⓙ Ⓚ Ⓛ Ⓜ   38. Ⓙ Ⓚ Ⓛ Ⓜ   40. Ⓙ Ⓚ Ⓛ Ⓜ

Ability

1. Ⓐ Ⓑ Ⓒ Ⓓ Ⓔ   4. Ⓙ Ⓚ Ⓛ Ⓜ Ⓝ   7. Ⓐ Ⓑ Ⓒ Ⓓ Ⓔ   9. Ⓐ Ⓑ Ⓒ Ⓓ Ⓔ
2. Ⓙ Ⓚ Ⓛ Ⓜ Ⓝ   5. Ⓐ Ⓑ Ⓒ Ⓓ Ⓔ   8. Ⓙ Ⓚ Ⓛ Ⓜ Ⓝ   10. Ⓙ Ⓚ Ⓛ Ⓜ Ⓝ
3. Ⓐ Ⓑ Ⓒ Ⓓ Ⓔ   6. Ⓙ Ⓚ Ⓛ Ⓜ Ⓝ

answer sheet

Practice Test 2: TACHS

READING

Part 1

5 Minutes

Directions: For each question, decide which one of the four possible answers has most nearly the same meaning as the underlined word above it. Then, on your answer sheet, find the row of answer spaces numbered the same as the question. Fill in the answer space that has the same letter as the answer you chose.

1. Highly anticipated arrival
   - (A) expected
   - (B) late
   - (C) departed
   - (D) unclear

2. Decaying leaves
   - (J) growing
   - (K) falling
   - (L) rotting
   - (M) colorful

3. An alternate plan
   - (A) replacement
   - (B) ineffective
   - (C) ambitious
   - (D) inferior

4. To estimate the cost
   - (J) calculate approximately
   - (K) approve of
   - (L) discount
   - (M) pay for

5. A generic cereal brand
   - (A) individual
   - (B) common
   - (C) delicious
   - (D) expensive

6. Vibrant colors
   - (J) drab and dull
   - (K) bold and bright
   - (L) transparent
   - (M) black and white

7. A puzzling dilemma
   - (A) game
   - (B) answer
   - (C) appearance
   - (D) problem

8. Driving recklessly
   - (J) easily
   - (K) carelessly
   - (L) carefully
   - (M) for the first time

9. A <u>rambling</u> speaker
   (A) interesting
   (B) motivational
   (C) long-winded and wordy
   (D) loud

10. <u>Enormous</u> buildings
    (J) intricate
    (K) close together
    (L) huge
    (M) stone

STOP If you finish before time is up, check over your work on this part only. Do not go on until the signal is given.

Part 2

15 Minutes

Directions: Read the passages below and then answer the questions. Four answers are given for each question. You are to choose the answer that you think is better than the others. Then, on your answer sheet, find the row of answer spaces numbered the same as the question. Fill in the best answer in the ovals on your answer sheet.

Passage 1

Charlie finally decided that he had had enough of city life. He made up his mind that he was tired of riding the subway an hour to work every day, tired of living in a tiny apartment, and tired of not seeing the sunrise and sunset. Charlie gathered his family around the dinner table and informed them of his desire to escape the concrete jungle permanently. After a few hours, Charlie persuaded his wife and two kids to give the country life a try.

Two weeks after Charlie made his decision, the family moved into a ranch house in rural Texas. On the day the family moved in, Charlie's youngest, Laurie, got stung by a small scorpion. Only a few hours later, Charlie's wife began sneezing uncontrollably and developed red, watery eyes. Charlie's son found a rattlesnake in the shed shortly thereafter. Before the movers unloaded half the furniture from the truck, Charlie was on the phone with a Realtor back in New York City.

11. In sentence 1 of paragraph 2, what does the word "rural" mean?

(A) Western

(B) In the country

(C) Primitive

(D) Scenic

12. Why did Charlie call his Realtor before he was even unpacked in Texas?

(J) He was upset with the view from his porch.

(K) He wanted to double-check the price of his new house.

(L) The country life wasn't what he hoped for, and he was ready to move back to the city.

(M) He was disappointed in the movers.

Passage 2

In the nineteenth century, a wave of liberalism swept across Europe. Liberals—those who advocated liberalism—heavily favored liberty, equality, and natural rights for citizens of European nations. Specifically, liberals hoped to win for citizens such things as voting rights and equal protection under the law. Ironically, the vast majority of liberals sought these rights for men only and not for women.

Standing in the way of liberal reform were the wealthy nobles, aristocrats, and the monarchs seated precariously on the thrones of Europe. The nobility felt threatened by liberalism because nobles held nearly all political power in early nineteenth-century Europe. Because they held all the power, the common man was left with virtually no say in the government. The nobles knew that their political positions would be in jeopardy if the common citizens were allowed to choose government officials. Ultimately, liberalism proved too strong a force for the aristocracy to defeat.

13. What was the nobles' greatest fear about common citizens winning the right to vote?

(A) Citizens didn't know how to vote.

(B) Citizens might not exercise their right to vote.

(C) Nobles may not get the right to vote.

(D) Citizens probably would elect people who had not been the power-holding nobles prior to elections, thus leaving the nobles with little or no power.

14. Based on context clues in the second paragraph, the word "monarchs" probably means which of the following?

(J) Commoners

(K) Kings and queens

(L) Jesters

(M) Judges

Passage 3

Among the famous Seven Wonders of the Ancient World, do you know which one is truly the most ancient? It's the Great Pyramid of Giza, and curiously enough, it's also the only one of the Wonders that still exists, and remains largely unscathed by the ravages of time. Let's explore this architectural marvel, and discover what makes this structure a truly wonderful monument to human capability.

Based on extensive research by Egyptologists, it's believed that the Great Pyramid of Giza was built around 2560 BC, as a tomb for the Egyptian Pharaoh Khufu of the fourth dynasty. Pyramids commonly served as majestic resting places for dead royalty in Ancient Egypt, but the Great Pyramid of Giza is truly in a class all its own. Its initial height is a staggering 481 feet, and stood as the world's tallest man-made structure for nearly 4,000 years. The pyramid contains a series of chambers and levels for it's "royal residents," and is actually just one of several pyramids that make up the Giza pyramid complex in Cairo, which also includes the Great Sphinx, cemeteries, and an industrial complex. This grand structure is estimated to include over 2.3 million blocks of limestone and granite (some blocks weighing upwards of 50 tons), likely excavated from nearby quarries, and set with nearly half a million tons of mortar. Although there is a great amount of disagreement among experts regarding how the pyramid was constructed so long ago, one thing that is hardly in dispute is that it is truly a magnificent and awe-inspiring piece of human history.

15. Based on the information in the passage, the author refers to the Great Pyramid of Giza as "truly in a class all its own" because

   (A) there were no other pyramids located anywhere near it.

   (B) the pyramid is taller than the others created at the time.

   (C) you'll likely only learn about the pyramid in a classroom.

   (D) the original designers had a great deal of formal education.

16. As used in sentence two of the first paragraph, what does the word *unscathed* likely mean?

   (J) Gigantic

   (K) Modern

   (L) Not new

   (M) Unharmed

Passage 4

As Margie strolled through the mall, a muscular young man handed her a pamphlet advertising a brand new workout facility across town. Margie took the pamphlet; she had been pondering a new fitness routine. She read as she walked past store after store. On her way through the department store at the end of the mall, she stopped and browsed the fitness equipment in the store. Margie was convinced that she needed to do something to help herself feel better, have more energy, and generally lead a healthier life.

After much thought, Margie decided that an expensive exercise apparatus eventually would turn into an expensive clothes rack in her bedroom. Margie also decided that the new workout facility would be better than the exercise equipment. However, she wondered if a facility on the other side of town would actually deter her from working out regularly. Margie ultimately decided to spend a fraction of the money she would have spent otherwise, and she purchased small set of weights and some workout videos.

17. What was Margie's true feeling about purchasing the expensive exercise equipment?

   (A) She was afraid she wouldn't know how to use the equipment.

   (B) She wanted to hang clothes somewhere other than in her closet.

   (C) She feared that she wouldn't use the equipment enough to justify the price.

   (D) She didn't think the equipment would fit anywhere except in her bedroom.

18. Based on context clues, what does the word "deter" mean in the passage (paragraph 2)?

   (J) allow

   (K) include

   (L) encourage

   (M) discourage

Passage 5

The camp director stood in front of the staff late Friday evening to address her camp counselors. The counselors had been working for two weeks without a break and faced another two weeks of the same routine before camp was to be dismissed for the summer. The counselors directed or participated in activities with the campers for 12 or 14 hours every day. In addition, the counselors made themselves available to the campers for one-on-one attention, including giving advice and just listening. The counselors poured themselves into their jobs.

The director looked at the face of each counselor and smiled. She knew how much of themselves they invested in making the camp a success. She said, "When my elbows get rough, dry, and cracked from work and exposure, I rub lotion on them. It's amazing how that can relax and refresh. I want to give each of you some proverbial lotion to soothe your souls. You get tomorrow off!"

19. Which of the following most likely describes the counselors?

   (A) Unruly
   (B) Disinterested
   (C) Exhausted
   (D) Confused

20. Why did the director tell the counselors that she wanted to give them "some proverbial lotion"?

   (J) She wanted to give them real lotion, but she didn't have enough for everyone.
   (K) She wanted to help them be relaxed and refreshed by giving them a day off.
   (L) She wanted to give the counselors the hint that some of them had dry skin.
   (M) She wanted to encourage them to use suntan lotion when working with the campers.

STOP If you finish before time is up, check over your work on this part only. Do not go on until the signal is given.

WRITTEN EXPRESSION

Part 1

25 Minutes for Parts 1 and 2

Directions: This is a test of how well you can find mistakes in writing. For the questions with mistakes in spelling, capitalization, and punctuation, choose the answer with the same letter as the **line** containing the mistake. For the questions with mistakes in usage and expression, choose the answer with the same letter as the **line** containing the mistake, or choose the word, phrase, or sentence that is better than the others. When there is no mistake or no change needed, choose the last answer choice.

1. **(A)** ocean
   (B) calculater
   (C) trench
   (D) minute
   (E) *(No mistakes)*

2. **(J)** transport
   (K) attitude
   (L) sinse
   (M) evaluate
   (N) *(No mistakes)*

3. **(A)** receive
   (B) fault
   (C) liquid
   (D) lable
   (E) *(No mistakes)*

4. **(J)** notebook
   (K) famine
   (L) zebra
   (M) knolledge
   (N) *(No mistakes)*

5. **(A)** destination
   (B) declare
   (C) mischief
   (D) concquer
   (E) *(No mistakes)*

6. **(J)** liquid
   (K) scrumptious
   (L) agregate
   (M) conspicuous
   (N) *(No Mistakes)*

7. **(A)** finished
   (B) relyable
   (C) chrome
   (D) disappoint
   (E) *(No mistakes)*

8. **(J)** credible
   (K) starlight
   (L) venom
   (M) accelerate
   (N) *(No mistakes)*

9. **(A)** initiate
   (B) simply
   (C) govenor
   (D) decline
   (E) *(No mistakes)*

10. **(J)** monstrous
    (K) protection
    (L) fields
    (M) decieve
    (N) *(No mistakes)*

11. (A) To find my dog, rover, I
    (B) sailed across the ocean
    (C) to the Johnson's farm.
    (D) *(No mistakes)*

12. (J) The king's jet flew
    (K) over the Andes Mountains
    (L) and beyond the river.
    (M) *(No mistakes)*

13. (A) The New York Jets' kicker and
    (B) the Dallas cowboys' punter
    (C) are actually Atlanta Falcons' fans.
    (D) *(No mistakes)*

14. (J) President Jefferson once lived
    (K) in the famous Virginia Home
    (L) known as Monticello.
    (M) *(No mistakes)*

15. (A) For christmas last year,
    (B) mom and dad gave me
    (C) a coat just like Jamie's.
    (D) *(No mistakes)*

16. (J) The Basketball Coach sent
    (K) the injured basketball player
    (L) to see Dr. Moore.
    (M) *(No mistakes)*

17. (A) Dr. Jose Sandoz had never
    (B) expect to see his cousin
    (C) Jules at his office last Monday.
    (D) *(No Mistakes)*

18. (J) How many times did j.j.
    (K) take a bite of Buddy's ice cream
    (L) when Buddy was talking to Sally?
    (M) *(No mistakes)*

19. (A) The leading candy company,
    (B) Sweet Tooth, inc., just announced
    (C) a new candy bar called O Yum.
    (D) *(No mistakes)*

20. (J) I can't remember if California
    (K) is the biggest State
    (L) or if Texas is the biggest.
    (M) *(No mistakes)*

practice test

Part 2

Directions: For questions 21 and 22, choose the best way of expressing the idea.

21. **(A)** At Shara's office, with incredible food, there was great music, as well as there being an exciting midnight countdown—the New Year's Eve party was an amazing event.

    (B) There was incredible food. There was great music. There was an exciting countdown. At midnight, at Shara's office. There was a New Year's Eve party, an amazing event.

    (C) The New Year's Eve party at Shara's office was an amazing event, with incredible food, great music, and an exciting midnight countdown.

    (D) What an event, an amazing event. There was a party at Shara's office, a New Year's Eve party. There was lots of stuff that made it a great event. There was food, incredible food. Great music that was really great to listen to. And, there was an exciting countdown, at midnight it happened.

22. **(J)** To understand advanced calculus, Mr. Johnson has an uncanny knack for teaching his students.

    (K) Mr. Johnson has an uncanny knack for teaching his students to understand advanced calculus.

    (L) An uncanny knack for teaching his students, Mr. Johnson has to understand advanced calculus.

    (M) For teaching his students to understand advanced calculus, Mr. Johnson has an uncanny knack.

Directions: For questions 23–30, choose the best answer based on the following paragraphs.

(1) Although seventy-one percent of the Earth's surface is covered with water, freshwater makes up less than three percent of this total. (2) Access to safe drinking water has improved over the last decade; however, many people around the world still lack a reliable supply. (3) To ensure that clean water is available for current and future populations water conservation strategies and practices are essential. (4) These efforts must consider the sustainability of the water supply so that freshwater is not removed more quickly than it can be replaced by an ecosystem. (5) Water conservation policies must also focus on delivering safe drinking water efficiently and preserving freshwater habitats for local wildlife.

23. What is the best way to write the underlined part of sentence 1?

    (A) seventy one

    (B) seventyone

    (C) seventy, one

    (D) *(No change)*

24. What is the best way to write the underlined part of sentence 3?

    (J) populations, water

    (K) populations—water

    (L) populations. Water

    (M) *(No change)*

(1) Today's vloggers aren't just aimless and meandering individuals who have more free time on their hands than motivation and ambition. (2) As sources of media entertainment shift from corporate studios and major networks to creative individuals with cameras, vloggers represent burgeoning and evolving media brands. (3) Some of the most popular vlogs and <u>there</u> creators are now multi-million dollar empires, with legions of loyal fans and followers. (4) The entertainment landscape has truly <u>changed; according</u> to a recent study by the Interactive Advertising Bureau, more people watch original Internet video content than primetime network television. (5) This trend, spurned on by lightning-quick advances in technology, could hardly have been predicted just a few decades ago.

25. What is the best way to write the underlined part of sentence 3?

   (A) their

   (B) they are

   (C) they're

   (D) *(No change)*

26. What is the best way to write the underlined part of sentence 4?

   (J) changed according

   (K) changed, according

   (L) changed? According

   (M) *(No change)*

---

(1) Located 67 miles west of Key West, Florida, the Dry Tortugas are a remote collection of seven small islands, or keys, encompassing about 143 acres. (2) All of the keys' shorelines are affected by erosion; over the years, islands have disappeared and reappeared following strong storms. (3) Visitors arrive by seaplane or boat to visit Dry Tortugas National Park, which <u>included</u> all of the islands and the surrounding waters and is known for its clear blue waters, brilliant coral reefs, varied marine and bird life, and the former military fortress, Fort Jefferson. (4) Some of the keys are larger <u>then</u> others. (5) Loggerhead Key, Garden Key, and Bush Key make up over ninety percent of the Dry Tortugas, while other keys are merely sand bars rising out of the sea.

27. What is the best way to write the underlined part of sentence 3?

   (A) includes

   (B) had included

   (C) has been including

   (D) *(No change)*

28. What is the best way to write the underlined part of sentence 4?

   (J) as opposed to

   (K) regardless of

   (L) than

   (M) *(No change)*

(1) For many Commuters, being locked in gridlock traffic on crowded highways is a common frustration. (2) In the not-so-distant future, however, our daily commute to work, school, and other activities might involve flying instead of driving. (3) Developed after years of experimentation, the Skycar is the most promising flying car model to date. (4) Reaching speeds of 400 mph, the Skycar has a range of 900 miles and is fully automated using Global Positioning System (GPS) satellites. (5) Although their high costs now make them impractical, flying cars could cost about $60,000 each if they are eventually mass produced. (6) Flying cars taking to the open skies may finally move from the realm of science fiction to everyday reality.

29. What is the best way to write the underlined part of sentence 1?

(A) commuter

(B) commuters'

(C) commuters

(D) *(No change)*

30. What is the best way to write the underlined part of sentence 5?

(J) their

(K) there

(L) it's

(M) *(No change)*

STOP If you finish before time is up, check over your work on this part only. Do not go on until the signal is given.

MATH

Part 1

30 Minutes

Directions: Four answers are given for each problem. Choose the best answer.

1. Which of the following is a prime number?
   - (A) 27
   - (B) 28
   - (C) 29
   - (D) 30

2. The fraction $\frac{8}{4}$ can be reduced to which of the following?
   - (J) 84
   - (K) $\frac{1}{2}$
   - (L) $\frac{4}{8}$
   - (M) 2

3. Which of the following is the product of 16 and 4?
   - (A) 4
   - (B) 12
   - (C) 20
   - (D) 64

4. Which of the following is the equivalent of 6^7?
   - (J) 6×7
   - (K) $7 \times 6 \times 6 \times 6 \times 6 \times 6 \times 6$
   - (L) $6 \times 6 \times 6 \times 6 \times 6 \times 6 \times 6$
   - (M) $(6 + 6) \times 7$

5. The fraction $2\frac{6}{1000}$ can be expressed as a decimal by which of the following?
   - (A) 2.006
   - (B) 0.0026
   - (C) 26,000.000
   - (D) 26.1000

6. What is the difference between $\frac{7}{8}$ and $\frac{1}{2}$?
   - (J) $\frac{3}{8}$
   - (K) $\frac{6}{8}$
   - (L) $\frac{6}{2}$
   - (M) $\frac{3}{4}$

7. What is the sum of $(6 - 1) + (1 \times 5) + (10 \div 2) + (2.5 + 2.5)$?
   - (A) 25
   - (B) 20
   - (C) 15
   - (D) 125

8. Which of the following is *not* a multiple of 6?
   - (J) 72
   - (K) 112
   - (L) 402
   - (M) 246

9. Which of the following is the equivalent of $3 - (-6)$?

(A) -9

(B) -3

(C) 9

(D) 3

10. What is the least common multiple of 6, 12, and 72?

(J) 6

(K) 12

(L) 36

(M) 72

11. An accountant's fee for preparing a tax report for a customer is 40% more than his closest competitor. If the competitor charges $300, what is this accountant's fee?

(A) $360

(B) $400

(C) $420

(D) $500

12. Carl has collected 27 of the 32 available Captain Cosmos comic books, 19 of the 24 available Galactic General comic books, and 21 of the 23 available Larry the Laser comic books. If Carl wanted to acquire the missing comics from each series he collects, how many comic books would he need to buy?

(J) 7

(K) 67

(L) 79

(M) Not given

13. The school library recently relocated to a new building on campus. There are many new bookshelves in the new library. Each bookshelf holds 245 books. The library has 12 bookshelves that are 100 percent full and one bookshelf that is $\frac{4}{5}$ full. How many books are in the new library?

(A) $2,940$

(B) $3,136$

(C) $2,989$

(D) $294,000$

14. Paul's digital camera normally holds 200 images. If Paul sets his camera to take extra-high-quality pictures, his camera holds only 40 pictures. Paul has already saved 100 normal images on his camera, but he wants to take as many pictures as possible of the sunset over the bay. How many extra-high-quality pictures can Paul hold on his camera in addition to the 100 normal images he's already saved?

(J) 40

(K) 30

(L) 20

(M) 10

15. If Paige spends $3\frac{1}{4}$ hours per day practicing piano and she practices 4 days per week, how many hours does Paige practice piano each week?

(A) $12\frac{1}{4}$

(B) $12\frac{3}{4}$

(C) 13

(D) 14

16. Audrey and Ginnie volunteer each month to drive meals to elderly people. The first month they volunteered, they delivered a total of 60 meals. The next month they delivered $33\frac{1}{3}$ percent more than they did the first month. The third month they delivered twice as many meals as the first two months combined. How many meals did the two girls deliver in the third month?

(J) 80

(K) 90

(L) 160

(M) 280

17. If Taylor earns $7.50 per hour, how many 40-hour weeks will he need to work to earn enough to buy a new computer system that costs $1350?

(A) 3

(B) 4

(C) $4\frac{1}{2}$

(D) $12\frac{1}{2}$

18. Wallie wants to wallpaper her bedroom. Each roll of wallpaper covers 75 square feet of wall space. Her room has four walls that are 10 feet high and 15 feet wide. How many rolls of wallpaper will Wallie need to cover all four walls?

(J) 2

(K) 8

(L) 16

(M) 20

19. An amateur bowler practices daily and bowls four games per day. Today, his scores were 189, 243, 202, and 198. What was his average score?

(A) 200

(B) 208

(C) 189

(D) 220

20. Gee-Whiz electronics company exports 400,000 electronic devices each year. Gee-Whiz wants to merge with Go Electro, a new electronics company that exports 1,900 electronic devices each month. After the merger, how many electronic devices will the new company export per year?

(J) 35,233

(K) 401,900

(L) 422,800

(M) 6,333,333

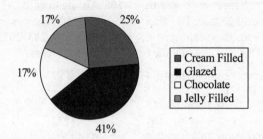

21. At Doodle's Donuts, the most popular item on the menu is Doodle's Dozen. The chart shows the typical distribution of donuts in each Doodle's Dozen that is sold. According to the chart, the single most widely consumed donut in Doodle's Dozen is which of the following?

    (A) Cream Filled

    (B) Glazed

    (C) Chocolate

    (D) Jelly Filled

22. Based on the information in the chart, Doodle's Dozen includes three of which type of donut?

    (J) Cream Filled

    (K) Glazed

    (L) Chocolate

    (M) Jelly Filled

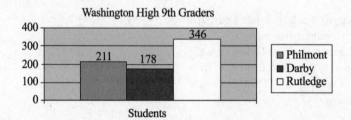

23. The chart above shows the feeder schools from which current ninth-graders at Washington High School came. If these are the only feeder schools that sent students to the ninth grade at Washington High School, which school sent the largest percentage of current Washington ninth-graders?

    (A) Philmont

    (B) Darby

    (C) Rutledge

    (D) Not given

24. Based on the information in the chart above, Washington High School currently has how many ninth-graders?

    (J) 211

    (K) 178

    (L) 346

    (M) 735

The Hudson Museum Portraits

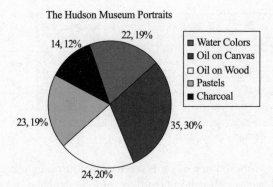

25. The pie chart above illustrates the number and types of portraits at the Hudson Museum. Based on the information in the chart, which of the following is true of the number of portraits in the museum?

    (A) There are fewer than 100 portraits.

    (B) There are 100 portraits.

    (C) There are more than 100 portraits.

    (D) Not given

26. The combination of which portrait types make up half of the entire collection?

    (J) Oils

    (K) Water Colors and Oil on Canvas

    (L) Charcoal and Pastels

    (M) Pastels and Water Colors

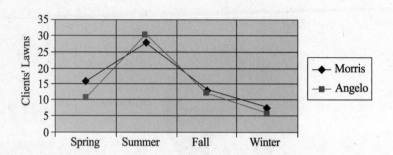

27. The chart above shows the amount of yards serviced by Morris and Angelo, each of whom runs a small lawn-care business. Based on the information in the chart, what is the busiest season for lawn care?

    (A) Spring

    (B) Summer

    (C) Fall

    (D) Winter

28. Based on the information in the chart, which of the following statements is true?

    (J) Morris experienced a bigger decline in business from the summer to the winter than did Angelo.

    (K) Angelo experienced a bigger decline in business from the summer to the winter than did Morris.

    (L) Angelo and Morris experienced the same decline in business from the summer to the winter.

    (M) Neither Morris nor Angelo experienced a decline in business from the summer to the winter.

Kensington Athletic Club Members

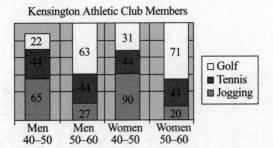

29. The chart above illustrates the members of the Kensington Athletic Club between the ages of 40 and 60 and the sports in which they currently participate. Based on the information in the chart, which sport becomes the most popular as both men and women grow older?

   (A) Golf

   (B) Tennis

   (C) Jogging

   (D) Not enough information available

30. Based on the information in the chart, which sport currently has the most total members participating in it?

   (J) Golf

   (K) Tennis

   (L) Jogging

   (M) Not enough information available

STOP   If you finish before time is up, check over your work on this part only. Do not go on until the signal is given.

Part 2

10 Minutes

Directions: For the following questions, <u>estimate</u> the answer in your head. No scratch work is allowed. Do NOT try to compute exact answers.

31. The closest estimate of 46,922 + 32,090 is
_____.

    (A) 70,000
    (B) 75,000
    (C) 80,000
    (D) 85,000

32. The closest estimate of 7988 ÷ 397 is
_____.

    (J) 20
    (K) 25
    (L) 200
    (M) 220

33. Rick decides to skate along the boardwalk at the local beach. He can skate at 6 miles per hour. If the boardwalk is 15 miles long, how long did it take him to complete the trip?

    (A) 90 minutes
    (B) 120 minutes
    (C) 150 minutes
    (D) 180 minutes

34. Coach Hollingsworth has a total of 653 wins in her career, and she has coached for 40 years. About how many wins has she averaged per year?

    (J) 13
    (K) 16
    (L) 19
    (M) 24

35. The closest estimate of 148 + 153.5 + 146 + 154.1 + 151 + 145.9 + 149 + 153 + 152.5 + 147.75 is _____.

    (A) 1375
    (B) 1400
    (C) 1500
    (D) 1575

36. A typical plain bagel has about 250 calories, and a typical glass of orange juice has about 160 calories. A jelly donut with chocolate icing and sprinkles has about 740 calories, and a large soda has about 255 calories. About how many bagel–juice combos would it take to equal the amount of calories in the jelly donut and a large soda?

    (J) $1\frac{1}{2}$
    (K) 2
    (L) $2\frac{1}{2}$
    (M) 3

37. The closest estimate of $385 - (2.9 \times 15.8)$ is _____.

    (A) 415
    (B) 360
    (C) 355
    (D) 337

38. George earns $10 per week. How many weeks will it take him to earn about $255?

    (J) 25
    (K) 52
    (L) 144
    (M) Not given

39. The closest estimate of 7.1×7.9 is _____.

(A) 49

(B) 56

(C) 63

(D) 70

40. The closest estimate of $221.8 \div 9.989$ is _____.

(J) 22

(K) 20

(L) 12

(M) 11

STOP If you finish before time is up, check over your work on this part only. Do not go on until the signal is given.

www.petersons.com

ABILITY

5 Minutes

Directions: In questions 1–2, the first three figures are alike in certain ways. Choose the answer choice that corresponds to the first three figures.

1.

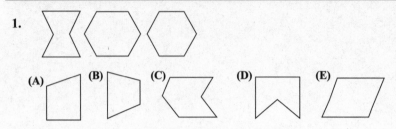

(A)   (B)   (C)   (D)   (E)

2.

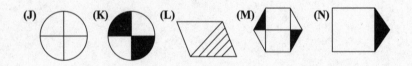

(J)   (K)   (L)   (M)   (N)

Directions: In questions 3–7, the first figure is related to the second figure. Determine that relationship. The third figure is changed in the same way to make one of the answer choices. Choose the answer choice that relates to the third figure.

3.

(A) (B) (C) (D) (E)
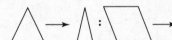

4.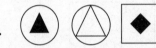

(J) (K) (L) (M) (N)
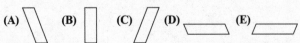

5.

(A) (B) (C) (D) (E)
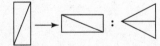

6.

(J) (K) (L) (M) (N)

7.

(A) (B) (C) (D) (E)

Directions: In questions 8–10, look at the top row to see how a square piece of paper is folded and where holes are punched in it. Then look at the bottom row to decide which answer choice shows how the paper will look when it is completely unfolded.

8.

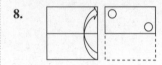

(J)   (K)   (L)   (M)   (N)

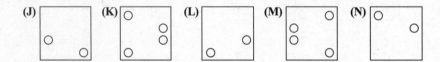

9.

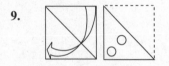

(A)   (B)   (C)   (D)   (E)

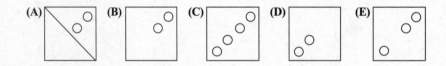

10.

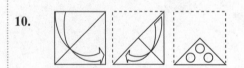

(J)   (K)   (L)   (M)   (N)

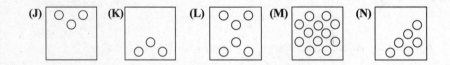

STOP   If you finish before time is up, check over your work on this section only. Do not go back to any previous parts.

ANSWER KEYS AND EXPLANATIONS

Reading

Part 1

1. A	3. A	5. B	7. D	9. C
2. L	4. J	6. K	8. K	10. L

1. **The correct answer is (A),** *expected*. Other synonyms for *anticipated* include "hoped for" and "awaited."

2. **The correct answer is (L),** *rotting*. Other synonyms for *decaying* include "decomposing" and "disintegrating."

3. **The correct answer is (A),** *replacement*. Other synonyms for *alternate* include "substitute" and "stand-in."

4. **The correct answer is (J),** *calculate approximately*. Other synonyms for *estimate* include "approximate" and "reckon."

5. **The correct answer is (B),** *common*. *Generic* and *common* are synonyms, both meaning "part of a broad group and not of a specific brand."

6. **The correct answer is (K),** *bold* and *bright*. Other synonyms for *vibrant* include "vivid" and "dazzling."

7. **The correct answer is (D),** *problem*. Other synonyms for *puzzling* include "predicament" and "quandary."

   Be careful to read the given word. Answer choice (A), game, might be a synonym for "puzzle," not puzzling.

8. **The correct answer is (K),** *carelessly*. Other synonyms for *recklessly* include "thoughtlessly" and "wildly."

9. **The correct answer is (C),** *long-winded* and *wordy*. Other synonyms for *rambling* include "verbose" and "garrulous."

10. **The correct answer is (L),** *huge*. Other synonyms for *enormous* include "gigantic," "immense," and "monstrous."

Part 2

11. B	13. D	15. B	17. C	19. C
12. L	14. K	16. M	18. M	20. K

11. **The correct answer is (B).** The word "rural" means "in the country." The last sentence of the first paragraph gives the context clue when it mentions "the country life."

12. **The correct answer is (L).** The country life wasn't what he hoped for, and he was ready to move back to the city. Charlie made a hurried and rash decision to move from the city to the country. Therefore, it was characteristic of Charlie to call his Realtor quickly and make another rushed decision, the decision that he didn't like life in the country.

13. **The correct answer is (D).** Citizens probably would elect people who had not been the power-holding nobles prior to elections, thus leaving the nobles with little or

no power. The nobles were people whose power didn't depend on the favor of those they controlled and exploited. The nobles knew that common citizens would most likely elect candidates with whom they had something in common.

14. **The correct answer is (K).** The reference to thrones in the first sentence of the second paragraph is the context clue that "monarchs" is synonymous with "kings and queens."

15. **The correct answer is (B).** The passage mentions that there were other pyramids in Egypt, and it then goes on to say that the Great Pyramid of Giza was different from the others because it was the tallest, setting it apart from all other structures at the time. Therefore, choice (B) is the best answer.

16. **The correct answer is (M).** The passage mentions that the Great Pyramid of Giza is the only one of the Seven Wonders that still exists, despite the ravages of time, which tends to harm or decay things. Choice (M), *unharmed*, is the correct answer.

17. **The correct answer is (C).** She feared that she wouldn't use the equipment enough to justify the price. Margie had a feeling that after a while, she would stop using the equipment for exercise. The line about the expensive clothes rack is a metaphor for exercise equipment that is not used for exercising.

18. **The correct answer is (M).** Based on context clues, the word "deter" means "discourage." The use of the word "however" at the beginning of the sentence indicates a shift in thought. Margie initially considered the new workout facility (as noted in the sentence before), but she wondered if the location on the other side of town would give her an excuse to not go—in other words, if it would deter or discourage her from working out regularly.

19. **The correct answer is (C).** The entire first paragraph describes the grueling and demanding schedule of the counselors. It is reasonable to expect people to be tired, or *exhausted,* after a schedule like the one described in the first paragraph.

20. **The correct answer is (K).** She wanted to help them be relaxed and refreshed by giving them a day off. The director was using "proverbial lotion" as a metaphor for something that would relax and refresh, i.e., a day off. A metaphor is symbolic and representative and, therefore, shouldn't be interpreted literally.

Written Expression

Part 1

1. B	5. D	9. C	13. B	17. B
2. L	6. L	10. M	14. K	18. J
3. D	7. B	11. A	15. A	19. B
4. M	8. N	12. M	16. J	20. K

1. **The correct answer is (B).** The correct spelling is *calculator*.

2. **The correct answer is (L).** The correct spelling is either *sense* or *since*.

3. **The correct answer is (D).** The correct spelling is *label*.

4. **The correct answer is (M).** The correct spelling is *knowledge*.

5. **The correct answer is (D).** The correct spelling is conquer.

6. **The correct answer is (L).** The correct spelling is *aggregate*.

7. **The correct answer is (B).** The correct spelling is *reliable*.

8. **The correct answer is (N).** *(No mistakes)*

9. **The correct answer is (C).** The correct spelling is *governor*.

10. **The correct answer is (M).** The correct spelling is *deceive*.

11. **The correct answer is (A).** The name "Rover" should be capitalized because a name is a proper noun.

12. **The correct answer is (M).** *(No mistakes)*

13. **The correct answer is (B).** The Dallas Cowboys is the name of a professional team and, as with names of other professional organizations, "Cowboys" should be capitalized because it is a proper noun.

14. **The correct answer is (K).** In this sentence, "home" simply means a house and is not part of a title. Therefore, "home" is a common noun and needs no capitalization.

15. **The correct answer is (A).** Holidays are proper nouns and should be capitalized.

16. **The correct answer is (J).** As used in this sentence, "basketball coach" is a common noun. If "coach" were included in a title like "Coach Van Gundy" or "Coach Parcells," then it would be capitalized.

17. **The correct answer is (B).** Because the action in the sentence occurred in the past, the correct form of the verb in choice (B) is the past tense *expected*.

18. **The correct answer is (J).** Even though these initials are abbreviated, they should be capitalized because they are a person's name, a proper noun.

19. **The correct answer is (B).** The abbreviation "Inc." is short for "Incorporated," which is part of the official name of a business organization and must be capitalized because it is a proper noun.

20. **The correct answer is (K).** The word "state" is a common noun; the names of states, Texas or New York, for example, are proper nouns and should be capitalized.

Part 2

21. C	23. D	25. A	27. A	29. C
22. K	24. J	26. M	28. L	30. M

21. The correct answer is (C). Choice (C) most efficiently and effectively expresses the ideas in this sentence without the unnecessary wordiness, redundancy, and confusion that makes the other choices incorrect.

22. The correct answer is (K). Although some of the alternate answer choices come close to expressing the main idea of the sentence, choices (J) and (L) lead us to the incorrect conclusion that Mr. Johnson needs to learn advanced calculus instead of teaching the subject to his students.

23. The correct answer is (D). *(No change).* No change is needed in the way the number "seventy-one" is written since the hyphenated form is correct.

24. The correct answer is (J). In this sentence, the subject "water conservation strategies and practices" and the verb "are" follow a long introductory phrase. The introductory phrase, or dependent clause, must be set off with a comma to link it to the main part of the sentence that follows.

25. The correct answer is (A). As written, the underlined portion of the sentence incorrectly uses the adverb *there*. The adjective *their* is required here to refer to the vlog creators.

26. The correct answer is (M). As written, the sentence correctly uses a semicolon to join these two independent clauses. The other choices introduce errors into the sentence.

27. The correct answer is (A). Since the passage is written in present tense, the verb "include" must be in agreement with the rest of the passage.

28. The correct answer is (L). The word "then" should be replaced with the word "than" in this sentence. Using "then" indicates a sequence of events, but "than" introduces a comparison of unequal items.

29. The correct answer is (C). The word "commuter" is not a proper noun, so it does not need capitalization. Choice (A) is incorrect since a plural form of the noun is needed, and choice (B) shows the plural possessive version of the word "commuter," which is not needed in this sentence.

30. The correct answer is (M). *(No change.)* No change is needed, because the phrase "they are" refers back to the subject of the sentence, "flying cars." Choices (J) and (K) are commonly confused with the correct answer because they sound very similar, and choice (L) is a singular pronoun form, so choices (J), (K), and (L) are incorrect.

Math

Part 1

1. C	7. B	13. B	19. B	25. C
2. M	8. K	14. L	20. L	26. J
3. D	9. C	15. C	21. B	27. B
4. L	10. M	16. M	22. J	28. K
5. A	11. C	17. C	23. C	29. A
6. J	12. M	18. K	24. M	30. L

1. **The correct answer is (C).** 29 is divisible only by 1 and 29.

2. **The correct answer is (M).** $\frac{8}{4}$ can be reduced to $\frac{2}{1}$, or 2.

3. **The correct answer is (D).** The term "product" is a clue to multiply.

4. **The correct answer is (L).** $6 \times 6 \times 6 \times 6 \times 6 \times 6 \times 6$; 6^7 means that 6 is multiplied by itself 7 times.

5. **The correct answer is (A).** The number 2.006 is the same as $2\frac{6}{1000}$.

6. **The correct answer is (J).** $\frac{7}{8} - \frac{1}{2}$ is the same as $\frac{7}{8} - \frac{4}{8}$, which equals $\frac{3}{8}$.

7. **The correct answer is (B).** $(6 - 1 = 5) + (1 \times 5 = 5) + (10 \div 2 = 5) + (2.5 + 2.5 = 5) = 5 + 5 + 5 + 5 = 20$

8. **The correct answer is (K).** Dividing 112 by 6 gives 18 remainder 4. Therefore, 112 is not a multiple of 6. The other choices all have a remainder of 0 when divided by 6.

9. **The correct answer is (C).** Subtracting a negative is the same as adding a positive. So, $3 - (-6) = 3 + 6 = 9$.

10. **The correct answer is (M).** 72 is the lowest number of which 6, 12, and 72 are all factors.

11. **The correct answer is (C).** 40% of $300 is $120. So, the accountant's fee is $420.

12. **The correct answer is (M).** $32 - 27 = 5$, $24 - 19 = 5$, and $23 - 21 = 2$. $5 + 5 + 2 = 12$ comic books that Carl needs to buy. 12 is not an answer choice.

13. **The correct answer is (B).** $12 \times 245 = 2940$ books on the 100 percent full book shelves. $\frac{4}{5}$ of 245 is the same as 80% of 245, or 0.8×245, which equals 196.

    $2940 + 196 = 3136$.

14. **The correct answer is (L).** 100 normal images is the same as $\frac{1}{2}$, or 50 percent, of the 200 high-quality images. If $\frac{1}{2}$ of the memory is already used, then only $\frac{1}{2}$ of the camera's memory is still available. $\frac{1}{2}$ of 40 high-quality images the camera normally would hold is 20.

15. **The correct answer is (C).** $4 \times 3\frac{1}{4} = 13$ hours each week.

16. **The correct answer is (M).** 60 meals in the first month plus $33\frac{1}{3}$ percent more meals in the second month $(60 + 20 = 80)$ equals 140 meals. In third month, they delivered 2 × 140, or 280 meals.

17. **The correct answer is (C).** $7.50 × 40 = $300. $1350 ÷ $300 = 4.5, or $4\frac{1}{2}$.

18. **The correct answer is (K).** There are 4 × (10 × 15 = 150) square feet of wall space, or 600 square feet. 600 ÷ 75 = 8 rolls.

19. **The correct answer is (B).** The average is $\frac{189 + 243 + 202 + 198}{4} = 208$.

20. **The correct answer is (L).** 1,900 devices × 12 = 22,800 devices per year. 400,000 + 22,800 = 422,800.

21. **The correct answer is (B).** Forty-one percent of the donuts consumed are glazed.

22. **The correct answer is (J).** Twenty-five percent of a dozen, or 12, equals 3. The chart shows that cream-filled donuts represent 25% of the Doodle's Dozen.

23. **The correct answer is (C).** Because Rutledge sent more students to Washington High than the other two schools, it represents the largest percentage.

24. **The correct answer is (M).** 211 + 178 + 346 = 735.

25. **The correct answer is (C).** There are more than 100 portraits. By adding the values, not the percentages, of each section it can be determined that there are 118 portraits.

26. **The correct answer is (J).** Oil on Wood and Oil on Canvas make up 59 of the 118 portraits, or 50 percent of the portraits.

27. **The correct answer is (B).** Morris had 28 lawns in the summer, and Angelo had 30 lawns in the summer.

28. **The correct answer is (K).** Angelo experienced a bigger decline in business from the summer to the winter than Morris did; Angelo's business went from 30 lawns in the summer to 6 lawns in the winter, whereas Morris' business went from 28 to 7 in that period.

29. **The correct answer is (A).** The number of members who play golf in the older-age category is much more than the number of members who play golf in the younger-age category.

30. **The correct answer is (L).** A total of 202 members currently participate in jogging, whereas 187 members participate in golf and 176 members participate in tennis.

Part 2

31. C	33. B	35. C	37. D	39. B
32. J	34. K	36. L	38. J	40. J

31. The correct answer is (C). $46,922 + 32,090$ is approximately $47,000 + 32,000$, which equals 79,000. 79,000 is approximately 80,000.

32. The correct answer is (J). $7988 \div 397$ is approximately $8000 \div 400 = 20$.

33. The correct answer is (B). Distance equals rate × time, so $15 = 6x$. Therefore, it takes him $\frac{15}{6} = 2.5$ hours, which equals $2.5(60) = 150$ minutes.

34. The correct answer is (K). $40 \times 16 = 640$, which is an approximation of 653.

35. The correct answer is (C). $148 + 153.5 + 146 + 154.1 + 151 + 145.9 + 149 + 153 + 152.5 + 147.75$ is approximately 150 added 10 times, or 1500.

36. The correct answer is (L). It would take $2\frac{1}{2}$ combos of about 400 calories to equal the approximately 1,000 calories of the donut-soda combo.

37. The correct answer is (D). $385 - (2.9 \times 15.8)$ is approximately equal to $385 - (3 \times 16) = 385 - 48 = 337$.

38. The correct answer is (J). $10 per week is about $500 per year, so it would take about 25 weeks to earn $255.

39. The correct answer is (B). 7.1×7.9 is approximately 7×8, which is 56.

40. The correct answer is (J). $221.8 \div 9.989$ is approximately $222 \div 10$. $222 \div 10$ is 22.2, or about 22.

Ability

1. C	3. B	5. C	7. A	9. C
2. K	4. M	6. J	8. K	10. M

1. **The correct answer is (C).** The first three figures each have six sides, as does choice (C).

2. **The correct answer is (K).** Each of the given figures has half its area shaded in black, as does choice (K).

3. **The correct answer is (B).** For the first pair, a segment parallel to one side is drawn in the interior, and then the figure is split into two parts.

4. **The correct answer is (M).** For the first pair, the second figure is one in which a smaller circle is drawn and the area between the two circles is shaded. Thus, the fourth figure would be a triangle inside the given triangle, and the area between them must be shaded. Choice (M) represents this description.

5. **The correct answer is (C).** For the first pair, the inside figure changes from black to white and the inside figure is enlarged so that its vertices touch the outside figure. Choice (C) shows the same changes, including the color change.

6. **The correct answer is (J).** For the first pair, the figure is simply rotated 90° clockwise. Choice (J) also shows a 90° clockwise rotation, without any other changes.

7. **The correct answer is (A).** For the first pair, the figure undergoes a dilation, which means it is kept similar, but changes in size. (In this case, it gets smaller.) Choice (A) represents the same change.

8. **The correct answer is (K).** After the figure is folded over a horizontal line, a hole is punched in the upper left and lower right corners. When unfolded, there will be four holes. The additional two holes will be, respectively, the same distance from the horizontal line as the original two holes.

9. **The correct answer is (C).** After the figure is folded over a diagonal, two holes are punched along the other diagonal (not drawn). When unfolded, there are four holes, all places on the other diagonal.

10. **The correct answer is (M).** This figure is folded over twice before three holes are punched. After unfolding, there are (3)(2)(2) = 12 holes positioned in the northern, eastern, southern, and western parts of the square, as shown by choice (M).

ANSWER SHEET PRACTICE TEST 3: COOP

Section 1. Sequences

1. Ⓐ Ⓑ Ⓒ Ⓓ   5. Ⓐ Ⓑ Ⓒ Ⓓ   9. Ⓐ Ⓑ Ⓒ Ⓓ   13. Ⓐ Ⓑ Ⓒ Ⓓ   17. Ⓐ Ⓑ Ⓒ Ⓓ
2. Ⓕ Ⓖ Ⓗ Ⓙ   6. Ⓕ Ⓖ Ⓗ Ⓙ   10. Ⓕ Ⓖ Ⓗ Ⓙ   14. Ⓕ Ⓖ Ⓗ Ⓙ   18. Ⓕ Ⓖ Ⓗ Ⓙ
3. Ⓐ Ⓑ Ⓒ Ⓓ   7. Ⓐ Ⓑ Ⓒ Ⓓ   11. Ⓐ Ⓑ Ⓒ Ⓓ   15. Ⓐ Ⓑ Ⓒ Ⓓ   19. Ⓐ Ⓑ Ⓒ Ⓓ
4. Ⓕ Ⓖ Ⓗ Ⓙ   8. Ⓕ Ⓖ Ⓗ Ⓙ   12. Ⓕ Ⓖ Ⓗ Ⓙ   16. Ⓕ Ⓖ Ⓗ Ⓙ   20. Ⓕ Ⓖ Ⓗ Ⓙ

Section 2. Analogies

1. Ⓐ Ⓑ Ⓒ Ⓓ   5. Ⓐ Ⓑ Ⓒ Ⓓ   9. Ⓐ Ⓑ Ⓒ Ⓓ   13. Ⓐ Ⓑ Ⓒ Ⓓ   17. Ⓐ Ⓑ Ⓒ Ⓓ
2. Ⓕ Ⓖ Ⓗ Ⓙ   6. Ⓕ Ⓖ Ⓗ Ⓙ   10. Ⓕ Ⓖ Ⓗ Ⓙ   14. Ⓕ Ⓖ Ⓗ Ⓙ   18. Ⓕ Ⓖ Ⓗ Ⓙ
3. Ⓐ Ⓑ Ⓒ Ⓓ   7. Ⓐ Ⓑ Ⓒ Ⓓ   11. Ⓐ Ⓑ Ⓒ Ⓓ   15. Ⓐ Ⓑ Ⓒ Ⓓ   19. Ⓐ Ⓑ Ⓒ Ⓓ
4. Ⓕ Ⓖ Ⓗ Ⓙ   8. Ⓕ Ⓖ Ⓗ Ⓙ   12. Ⓕ Ⓖ Ⓗ Ⓙ   16. Ⓕ Ⓖ Ⓗ Ⓙ   20. Ⓕ Ⓖ Ⓗ Ⓙ

Section 3. Quantitative Reasoning

1. Ⓐ Ⓑ Ⓒ Ⓓ   5. Ⓐ Ⓑ Ⓒ Ⓓ   9. Ⓐ Ⓑ Ⓒ Ⓓ   13. Ⓐ Ⓑ Ⓒ Ⓓ   17. Ⓐ Ⓑ Ⓒ Ⓓ
2. Ⓕ Ⓖ Ⓗ Ⓙ   6. Ⓕ Ⓖ Ⓗ Ⓙ   10. Ⓕ Ⓖ Ⓗ Ⓙ   14. Ⓕ Ⓖ Ⓗ Ⓙ   18. Ⓕ Ⓖ Ⓗ Ⓙ
3. Ⓐ Ⓑ Ⓒ Ⓓ   7. Ⓐ Ⓑ Ⓒ Ⓓ   11. Ⓐ Ⓑ Ⓒ Ⓓ   15. Ⓐ Ⓑ Ⓒ Ⓓ   19. Ⓐ Ⓑ Ⓒ Ⓓ
4. Ⓕ Ⓖ Ⓗ Ⓙ   8. Ⓕ Ⓖ Ⓗ Ⓙ   12. Ⓕ Ⓖ Ⓗ Ⓙ   16. Ⓕ Ⓖ Ⓗ Ⓙ   20. Ⓕ Ⓖ Ⓗ Ⓙ

Section 4. Verbal Reasoning—Words

1. Ⓐ Ⓑ Ⓒ Ⓓ   4. Ⓐ Ⓑ Ⓒ Ⓓ   7. Ⓐ Ⓑ Ⓒ Ⓓ   9. Ⓐ Ⓑ Ⓒ Ⓓ   11. Ⓐ Ⓑ Ⓒ Ⓓ
2. Ⓕ Ⓖ Ⓗ Ⓙ   5. Ⓕ Ⓖ Ⓗ Ⓙ   8. Ⓕ Ⓖ Ⓗ Ⓙ   10. Ⓕ Ⓖ Ⓗ Ⓙ   12. Ⓕ Ⓖ Ⓗ Ⓙ
3. Ⓐ Ⓑ Ⓒ Ⓓ   6. Ⓐ Ⓑ Ⓒ Ⓓ

Section 5. Verbal Reasoning—Context

1. Ⓐ Ⓑ Ⓒ Ⓓ   5. Ⓐ Ⓑ Ⓒ Ⓓ   9. Ⓐ Ⓑ Ⓒ Ⓓ   13. Ⓐ Ⓑ Ⓒ Ⓓ   17. Ⓐ Ⓑ Ⓒ Ⓓ
2. Ⓕ Ⓖ Ⓗ Ⓙ   6. Ⓕ Ⓖ Ⓗ Ⓙ   10. Ⓕ Ⓖ Ⓗ Ⓙ   14. Ⓕ Ⓖ Ⓗ Ⓙ   18. Ⓕ Ⓖ Ⓗ Ⓙ
3. Ⓐ Ⓑ Ⓒ Ⓓ   7. Ⓐ Ⓑ Ⓒ Ⓓ   11. Ⓐ Ⓑ Ⓒ Ⓓ   15. Ⓐ Ⓑ Ⓒ Ⓓ   19. Ⓐ Ⓑ Ⓒ Ⓓ
4. Ⓕ Ⓖ Ⓗ Ⓙ   8. Ⓕ Ⓖ Ⓗ Ⓙ   12. Ⓕ Ⓖ Ⓗ Ⓙ   16. Ⓕ Ⓖ Ⓗ Ⓙ   20. Ⓕ Ⓖ Ⓗ Ⓙ

answer sheet

Section 6. Mathematics

1. Ⓐ Ⓑ Ⓒ Ⓓ	9. Ⓐ Ⓑ Ⓒ Ⓓ	17. Ⓐ Ⓑ Ⓒ Ⓓ	25. Ⓐ Ⓑ Ⓒ Ⓓ	33. Ⓐ Ⓑ Ⓒ Ⓓ
2. Ⓕ Ⓖ Ⓗ Ⓙ	10. Ⓕ Ⓖ Ⓗ Ⓙ	18. Ⓕ Ⓖ Ⓗ Ⓙ	26. Ⓕ Ⓖ Ⓗ Ⓙ	34. Ⓕ Ⓖ Ⓗ Ⓙ
3. Ⓐ Ⓑ Ⓒ Ⓓ	11. Ⓐ Ⓑ Ⓒ Ⓓ	19. Ⓐ Ⓑ Ⓒ Ⓓ	27. Ⓐ Ⓑ Ⓒ Ⓓ	35. Ⓐ Ⓑ Ⓒ Ⓓ
4. Ⓕ Ⓖ Ⓗ Ⓙ	12. Ⓕ Ⓖ Ⓗ Ⓙ	20. Ⓕ Ⓖ Ⓗ Ⓙ	28. Ⓕ Ⓖ Ⓗ Ⓙ	36. Ⓕ Ⓖ Ⓗ Ⓙ
5. Ⓐ Ⓑ Ⓒ Ⓓ	13. Ⓐ Ⓑ Ⓒ Ⓓ	21. Ⓐ Ⓑ Ⓒ Ⓓ	29. Ⓐ Ⓑ Ⓒ Ⓓ	37. Ⓐ Ⓑ Ⓒ Ⓓ
6. Ⓕ Ⓖ Ⓗ Ⓙ	14. Ⓕ Ⓖ Ⓗ Ⓙ	22. Ⓕ Ⓖ Ⓗ Ⓙ	30. Ⓕ Ⓖ Ⓗ Ⓙ	38. Ⓕ Ⓖ Ⓗ Ⓙ
7. Ⓐ Ⓑ Ⓒ Ⓓ	15. Ⓐ Ⓑ Ⓒ Ⓓ	23. Ⓐ Ⓑ Ⓒ Ⓓ	31. Ⓐ Ⓑ Ⓒ Ⓓ	39. Ⓐ Ⓑ Ⓒ Ⓓ
8. Ⓕ Ⓖ Ⓗ Ⓙ	16. Ⓕ Ⓖ Ⓗ Ⓙ	24. Ⓕ Ⓖ Ⓗ Ⓙ	32. Ⓕ Ⓖ Ⓗ Ⓙ	40. Ⓕ Ⓖ Ⓗ Ⓙ

Section 7. Reading and Language Arts

1. Ⓐ Ⓑ Ⓒ Ⓓ	11. Ⓐ Ⓑ Ⓒ Ⓓ	21. Ⓐ Ⓑ Ⓒ Ⓓ	31. Ⓐ Ⓑ Ⓒ Ⓓ	41. Ⓐ Ⓑ Ⓒ Ⓓ
2. Ⓕ Ⓖ Ⓗ Ⓙ	12. Ⓕ Ⓖ Ⓗ Ⓙ	22. Ⓕ Ⓖ Ⓗ Ⓙ	32. Ⓕ Ⓖ Ⓗ Ⓙ	42. Ⓕ Ⓖ Ⓗ Ⓙ
3. Ⓐ Ⓑ Ⓒ Ⓓ	13. Ⓐ Ⓑ Ⓒ Ⓓ	23. Ⓐ Ⓑ Ⓒ Ⓓ	33. Ⓐ Ⓑ Ⓒ Ⓓ	43. Ⓐ Ⓑ Ⓒ Ⓓ
4. Ⓕ Ⓖ Ⓗ Ⓙ	14. Ⓕ Ⓖ Ⓗ Ⓙ	24. Ⓕ Ⓖ Ⓗ Ⓙ	34. Ⓕ Ⓖ Ⓗ Ⓙ	44. Ⓕ Ⓖ Ⓗ Ⓙ
5. Ⓐ Ⓑ Ⓒ Ⓓ	15. Ⓐ Ⓑ Ⓒ Ⓓ	25. Ⓐ Ⓑ Ⓒ Ⓓ	35. Ⓐ Ⓑ Ⓒ Ⓓ	45. Ⓐ Ⓑ Ⓒ Ⓓ
6. Ⓕ Ⓖ Ⓗ Ⓙ	16. Ⓕ Ⓖ Ⓗ Ⓙ	26. Ⓕ Ⓖ Ⓗ Ⓙ	36. Ⓕ Ⓖ Ⓗ Ⓙ	46. Ⓕ Ⓖ Ⓗ Ⓙ
7. Ⓐ Ⓑ Ⓒ Ⓓ	17. Ⓐ Ⓑ Ⓒ Ⓓ	27. Ⓐ Ⓑ Ⓒ Ⓓ	37. Ⓐ Ⓑ Ⓒ Ⓓ	47. Ⓐ Ⓑ Ⓒ Ⓓ
8. Ⓕ Ⓖ Ⓗ Ⓙ	18. Ⓕ Ⓖ Ⓗ Ⓙ	28. Ⓕ Ⓖ Ⓗ Ⓙ	38. Ⓕ Ⓖ Ⓗ Ⓙ	48. Ⓕ Ⓖ Ⓗ Ⓙ
9. Ⓐ Ⓑ Ⓒ Ⓓ	19. Ⓐ Ⓑ Ⓒ Ⓓ	29. Ⓐ Ⓑ Ⓒ Ⓓ	39. Ⓐ Ⓑ Ⓒ Ⓓ	49. Ⓐ Ⓑ Ⓒ Ⓓ
10. Ⓕ Ⓖ Ⓗ Ⓙ	20. Ⓕ Ⓖ Ⓗ Ⓙ	30. Ⓕ Ⓖ Ⓗ Ⓙ	40. Ⓕ Ⓖ Ⓗ Ⓙ	50. Ⓕ Ⓖ Ⓗ Ⓙ

Practice Test 3: COOP

SECTION 1. SEQUENCES

15 Minutes

Directions: For questions 1–20, choose the part that would continue the pattern or sequence. Mark the letter of your answer on the answer sheet.

1. △ △ ○ | ○ △ △ | △ ○ ○ | ○ ○ ____

    (A) △ (B) ● (C) ○ (D) ▽

2. + ✳ + ✳ | ✳ + ✳ + | + + ✳ + | ✳ ✳ ____

    (F) ✳ + (G) ✳ ✳ (H) + + (J) + ✳

3. (stick figures) ____

    (A) (B) (C) (D)

4. S S SS | S S SSS | S SS SSS | ____

    (F) S SSS SSS (G) SS SSS S (H) S SS SS (J) S SS SSS SS

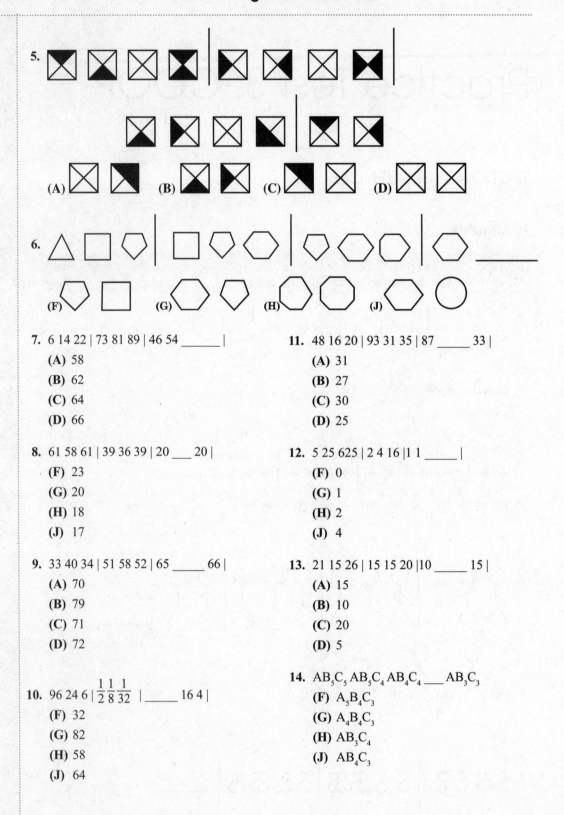

7. 6 14 22 | 73 81 89 | 46 54 _____ |
(A) 58
(B) 62
(C) 64
(D) 66

8. 61 58 61 | 39 36 39 | 20 ___ 20 |
(F) 23
(G) 20
(H) 18
(J) 17

9. 33 40 34 | 51 58 52 | 65 _____ 66 |
(A) 70
(B) 79
(C) 71
(D) 72

10. 96 24 6 | $\frac{1}{2}$ $\frac{1}{8}$ $\frac{1}{32}$ | _____ 16 4 |
(F) 32
(G) 82
(H) 58
(J) 64

11. 48 16 20 | 93 31 35 | 87 _____ 33 |
(A) 31
(B) 27
(C) 30
(D) 25

12. 5 25 625 | 2 4 16 | 1 1 _____ |
(F) 0
(G) 1
(H) 2
(J) 4

13. 21 15 26 | 15 15 20 | 10 _____ 15 |
(A) 15
(B) 10
(C) 20
(D) 5

14. AB_5C_5 AB_5C_4 AB_4C_4 _____ AB_3C_3
(F) $A_5B_4C_3$
(G) $A_4B_4C_3$
(H) AB_3C_4
(J) AB_4C_3

15. $F^1G^1H^1$ $F_2G^1H^1$ $F_2G_2H^1$ ___ $F^3G_2H_2$
    - **(A)** $F_2G_2H_2$
    - **(B)** $F^1G_2H^3$
    - **(C)** $F_2G_2H^3$
    - **(D)** $F^2G_2H_2$

16. W_1XY W_2X_1Y $W_3X_3Y_1$ $W_4X_5Y_2$ _____ $W_6X_9Y_4$
    - **(F)** $W_5X_6Y_3$
    - **(G)** $W_5X_7Y_3$
    - **(H)** $W_5X_6Y_4$
    - **(J)** $W_6X_7Y_3$

17. BCD FGH JKL MNP _____
    - **(A)** RST
    - **(B)** QUR
    - **(C)** QST
    - **(D)** QRS

18. CADA EAFA GAHA _____ KALA
    - **(F)** HAKA
    - **(G)** AIAJ
    - **(H)** MANA
    - **(J)** IAJA

19. PTL TLP LPT PTL _____
    - **(A)** LTP
    - **(B)** TLP
    - **(C)** LPT
    - **(D)** TPL

20. ABE FGJ KLO ____
    - **(F)** PRS
    - **(G)** PQT
    - **(H)** PQS
    - **(J)** QRU

STOP If you finish before time is up, check over your work on Section 1 only. Do not go on until the signal is given.

SECTION 2. ANALOGIES

7 Minutes

Directions: For questions 1–20, choose the picture that should go in the empty box so that the bottom two pictures are related in the same way that the top two are related.

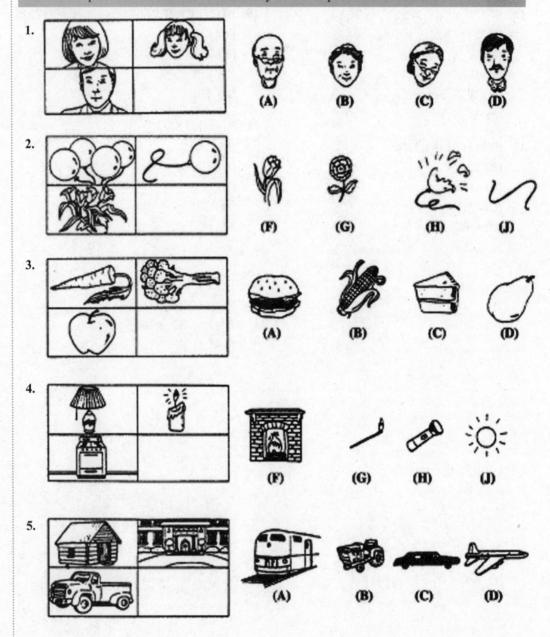

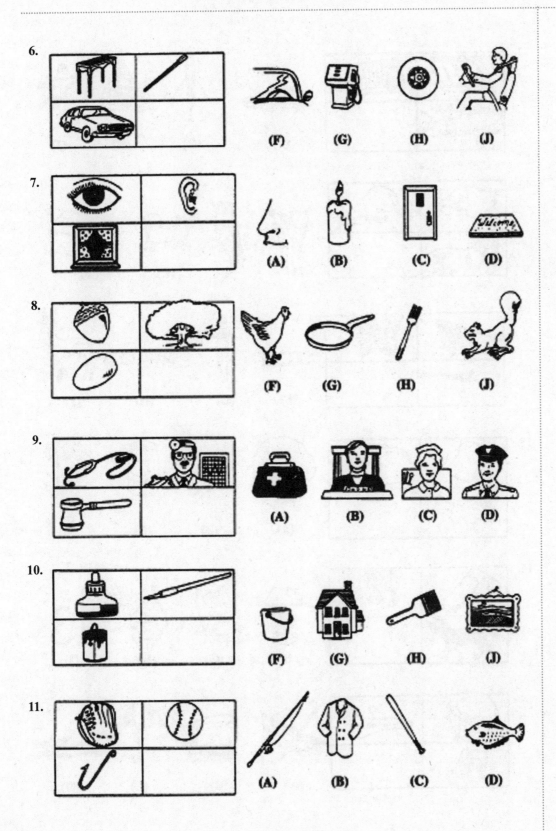

6.

(F)   (G)   (H)   (J)

7.

(A)   (B)   (C)   (D)

8.

(F)   (G)   (H)   (J)

9.

(A)   (B)   (C)   (D)

10.

(F)   (G)   (H)   (J)

11.

(A)   (B)   (C)   (D)

practice test

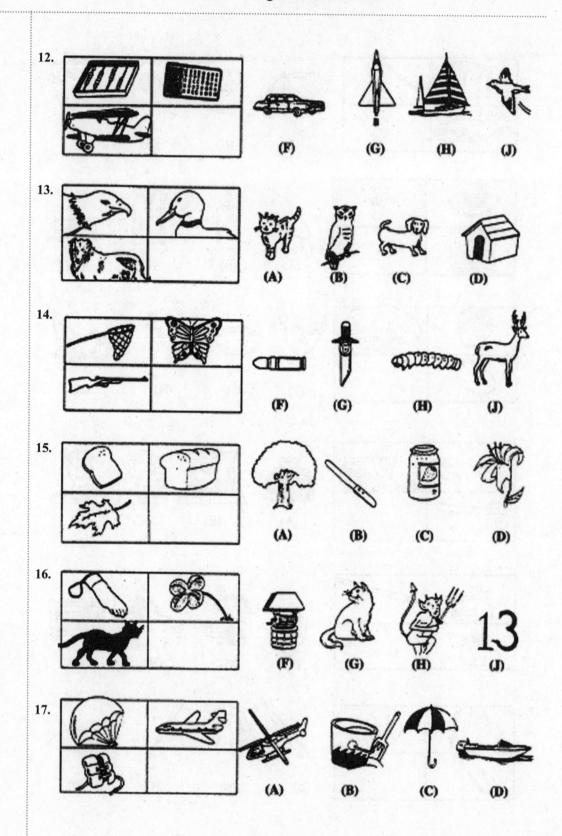

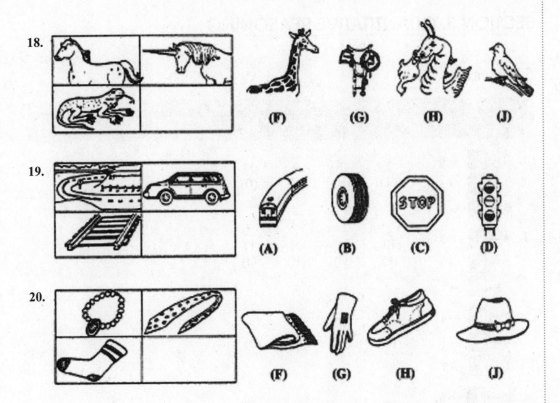

18.

(F) (G) (H) (J)

19.

(A) (B) (C) (D)

20.

(F) (G) (H) (J)

practice test

STOP If you finish before time is up, check over your work on Section 2 only. Do not go back to the previous section. Do not go on until the signal is given.

www.petersons.com

SECTION 3. QUANTITATIVE REASONING

5 Minutes

Directions: For questions 1–7, find the relationship of the numbers in one column to the numbers in the other column. Then find the missing number.

1. $2 \rightarrow \square \rightarrow 6$
   $1 \rightarrow \square \rightarrow 3$
   $3 \rightarrow \square \rightarrow ?$

3	7	9	12
(A)	(B)	(C)	(D)

2. $4 \rightarrow \square \rightarrow 8$
   $5 \rightarrow \square \rightarrow 9$
   $7 \rightarrow \square \rightarrow ?$

10	11	12	13
(F)	(G)	(H)	(J)

3. $7 \rightarrow \square \rightarrow 4$
   $4 \rightarrow \square \rightarrow 1$
   $1 \rightarrow \square \rightarrow ?$

−2	0	2	7
(A)	(B)	(C)	(D)

4. $36 \rightarrow \square \rightarrow 6$
   $54 \rightarrow \square \rightarrow 9$
   $84 \rightarrow \square \rightarrow ?$

12	14	39	54
(F)	(G)	(H)	(J)

5. $17 \rightarrow \square \rightarrow 24$
   $32 \rightarrow \square \rightarrow 39$
   $58 \rightarrow \square \rightarrow ?$

51	54	65	95
(A)	(B)	(C)	(D)

6. $\frac{2}{3} \rightarrow \square \rightarrow 2$
   $2 \rightarrow \square \rightarrow 6$
   $3 \rightarrow \square \rightarrow ?$

2	3	9	12
(F)	(G)	(H)	(J)

7. $\frac{1}{2} \rightarrow \square \rightarrow 1$
   $\frac{3}{2} \rightarrow \square \rightarrow 2$
   $3 \rightarrow \square \rightarrow ?$

$\frac{3}{2}$	$\frac{5}{2}$	$\frac{7}{2}$	$\frac{9}{2}$
(A)	(B)	(C)	(D)

Directions: For questions 8–14, find the fraction of the grid that is shaded.

8.

$$\frac{2}{5}$$ $$\frac{3}{4}$$ $$\frac{3}{10}$$ $$\frac{1}{5}$$
(F)   (G)   (H)   (J)

9.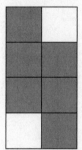

$$\frac{1}{2}$$ $$\frac{1}{3}$$ $$\frac{1}{6}$$ $$\frac{1}{8}$$
(A)   (B)   (C)   (D)

10.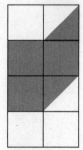

$$\frac{1}{2}$$ $$\frac{3}{4}$$ $$\frac{2}{3}$$ $$\frac{1}{4}$$
(F)   (G)   (H)   (J)

11.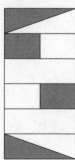

$$\frac{1}{2}$$ $$\frac{1}{3}$$ $$\frac{1}{4}$$ $$\frac{1}{6}$$
(A)   (B)   (C)   (D)

12.

$$\frac{2}{5}$$ $$\frac{1}{3}$$ $$\frac{3}{5}$$ $$\frac{1}{8}$$
(F)   (G)   (H)   (J)

13.

$\dfrac{5}{6}$ $\dfrac{4}{5}$ $\dfrac{3}{4}$ $\dfrac{5}{9}$
(A) (B) (C) (D)

14.

$\dfrac{1}{2}$ $\dfrac{1}{4}$ $\dfrac{1}{8}$ $\dfrac{1}{16}$
(F) (G) (H) (J)

Directions: For questions 15–20, look at the scale that shows sets of shapes of equal weight. Find an equivalent pair of sets that would also balance the scale.

15.

(A)

(B)

(C)

(D)

16.

(F)

(G)

(H)

(J)

17.

(A)

(B)

(C)

(D)

18.

(F)

(G)

(H)

(J)

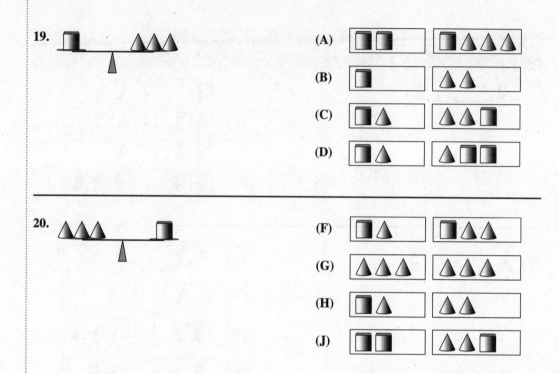

STOP If you finish before time is up, check over your work on Section 3 only. Do not go back to the previous sections. Do not go on until the signal is given.

Master the Catholic High School Entrance Exams 2018

SECTION 4. VERBAL REASONING—WORDS

15 Minutes

Directions: For questions 1–10, find the word that names a necessary part of the underlined word.

1. burning
   - (A) flame
   - (B) smoke
   - (C) ash
   - (D) heat

2. verbalize
   - (F) verb
   - (G) words
   - (H) hearing
   - (J) sound

3. legislation
   - (A) laws
   - (B) lawyers
   - (C) senate
   - (D) debate

4. bag
   - (F) carrier
   - (G) opening
   - (H) strap
   - (J) zipper

5. violin
   - (A) bow
   - (B) notes
   - (C) strings
   - (D) melody

6. chronometer
   - (F) watch
   - (G) standard
   - (H) time
   - (J) ticking

7. ocean
   - (A) wave
   - (B) sea
   - (C) water
   - (D) sand

8. hunger
   - (F) weakness
   - (G) lack
   - (H) starvation
   - (J) poverty

9. marriage
   - (A) Wedding
   - (B) Priest
   - (C) Love
   - (D) Relationship

10. science
    - (F) Technology
    - (G) Knowledge
    - (H) Physics
    - (J) Laboratory

Directions: In questions 11–20, the words in the top row are related in some way. The words in the bottom row are related in the same way. For each item, find the word that completes the bottom row of words.

11. vest   jacket   coat
    sandal   shoe

    (A) slipper
    (B) boot
    (C) ski
    (D) moccasin

12. eye   iris   pupil
    ear   lobe

    (F) hear
    (G) canal
    (H) body
    (J) audio

13. color   odor   sound
    feel   see

    (A) hear
    (B) soft
    (C) sound
    (D) tell

14 forsythia   tulip   crocus
    holly   poinsettia

    (F) lilac
    (G) mistletoe
    (H) wreath
    (J) tree

15. bird   dog   spider
    man   horse

    (A) crab
    (B) fly
    (C) eel
    (D) unicorn

16. baseball football basketball
    skiing   shotput

    (F) hockey
    (G) soccer
    (H) rugby
    (J) marathon

17. books   periodicals   library
    fish   water

    (A) pet store
    (B) school
    (C) aquarium
    (D) lobster

18. cumulus   stratus   cirrus
    molars   canines

    (F) mouth
    (G) incisors
    (H) bite
    (J) chew

19. tall   long   furry
    mailbox   letter

    (A) deliver
    (B) communicate
    (C) write
    (D) message

20. tigers panthers jaguars
    kangaroos   wallabees

    (F) Australia
    (G) koalas
    (H) animals
    (J) pouches

STOP If you finish before time is up, check over your work on Section 4 only. Do not go back to the previous sections. Do not go on until the signal is given.

SECTION 5. VERBAL REASONING—CONTEXT

15 Minutes

Directions: For questions 1–5, find the statement that is true according to the given information.

1. Jeffrey is a law student. On Monday evenings, he plays the violin in an orchestra. On Tuesdays and Thursdays, he goes square dancing. On Friday afternoon, Jeffrey fiddles for a children's folk dancing group.

   (A) Jeffrey plays the violin at least twice a week.

   (B) Jeffrey likes music better than the law.

   (C) Jeffrey dances three times a week.

   (D) Musicians are good dancers.

2. Debbie took the written Foreign Service Officer examination in December. Today, Debbie received an appointment date for her Oral Assessment. Debbie is very happy.

   (F) Debbie failed the written exam.

   (G) Debbie is now a Foreign Service officer.

   (H) Everyone who takes the Foreign Service Officer exam must take an oral exam as well.

   (J) Debbie is still under consideration for appointment as a Foreign Service officer.

3. Bill and Dan were exploring an abandoned house. The windows swung loose, the floorboards creaked, and dust and cobwebs filled the air. Suddenly, the two boys ran from the house.

   (A) The house was haunted.

   (B) Something frightened the boys.

   (C) There were bats flying about.

   (D) Someone told the boys to get out.

4. Daryl went to the Department of Motor Vehicles on Thursday afternoon to try and get a driver's license. The complete examination process includes both a written test and a road test. Daryl completed the examination process. He rode home in a new car later that day.

   (F) Daryl obtained his driver's license.

   (G) Daryl drove home from the Department of Motor Vehicles.

   (H) Daryl owns a new car.

   (J) Daryl took the written driver's test.

5. Mark was distracted by his dog while jumping on the trampoline; he slipped and broke his right arm. That same afternoon, the dog chased the cat up a tree. Another time Mark was walking his dog, the dog pulled Mark too fast; Mark fell and broke his right arm.

   (A) Mark's dog is dangerous and should be restrained at all times.

   (B) Mark should let his sister walk the dog.

   (C) Mark is left-handed.

   (D) Mark is accident-prone.

Directions: For questions 6–8, find the correct answer.

6. Here are some words translated from an artificial language.

   chekiruala means eating
   duangfrit means hidden
   duangruala means eaten

   Which word means *hiding*?
   (F) chekifrit
   (G) rualafrit
   (H) chekiduang
   (J) fritcheki

7. Here are some words translated from an artificial language.

   jokiohakaflis means creek
   luraohakaflis means river
   jokiohakasloo means pond

   Which word means *lake*?
   (A) slooohakalura
   (B) jokilurasloo
   (C) ohakasloolura
   (D) luraohakasloo

8. Here are some words translated from an artificial language.

   frushuwamba means dissolve
   uwambakuta means solution
   hamauwamba means resolve

   Which word means *resolution*?
   (F) kutafrush
   (G) hamauwambakuta
   (H) uwambakutahama
   (J) frushkutauwamba

Directions: For questions 9–20, find the statement that is true according to the given information.

9. Lexi's teacher tells her to write an essay of no more than 500 words on the French-Indian War. Lexi's essay is close to 1,000 words.
   (A) Lexi is on the honor roll.
   (B) Lexi really enjoys researching the French-Indian War.
   (C) Lexi exceeds the word limit on her assignment.
   (D) Lexi's teacher gives her a poor grade.

10. Bob used to live in Milwaukee, but he moved to Atlanta when he was 16. He lived in several other cities before settling in San Diego.
    (F) Bob likes city life.
    (G) Bob has moved more than three times.
    (H) Bob likes the West coast better than the Midwest or Northeast.
    (J) Bob enjoys living near the ocean.

11. Bud is taller than Chase but shorter than Rob. Pete is taller than Rob but shorter than Garrett.

(A) None of the boys are over six feet tall.

(B) Chase is five feet tall.

(C) Chase and Rob pick on Bud.

(D) Garrett is the tallest of the boys.

12. If Janice decides to go to the job interview at Gerringer's department store, she is excited about possibly working there. Janice started her new job last Monday.

(F) Janice is currently working at Gerringer's.

(G) Janice is excited about her new job.

(H) Janice was working last Monday.

(J) Janice is still looking for a new job.

13. Amber runs a 5K race and finishes in under an hour. Brittany runs the same race in a little over an hour.

(A) It is raining on race day.

(B) Amber places ahead of Brittany in the race.

(C) Brittany places ahead of several other racers.

(D) Amber's parents are in the crowd.

14. Shelly works at the blood drive but does not donate blood herself. Her shift ends at noon, and Shelly plans to eat lunch then.

(F) Shelly cannot donate blood.

(G) Shelly is afraid of needles.

(H) Shelly is too busy to donate blood.

(J) Shelly will not work at the blood drive after lunch.

15. Melanie is assigned three books to read over spring break. She reads two books over the break.

(A) Melanie is a slow reader.

(B) Melanie fails to complete her assignment of reading all three books.

(C) Melanie only likes science fiction books.

(D) Melanie reads two hours a day.

16. Andrew and Chelsea are on their school's Quiz Bowl team, and they attend every Quiz Bowl meet. There is a Quiz Bowl meet Thursday night.

(F) Andrew and Chelsea both take advanced placement classes.

(G) Andrew and Chelsea study together before Quiz Bowl meets.

(H) Andrew and Chelsea will be at a Quiz Bowl meet Thursday night.

(J) Andrew and Chelsea are co-captains of the Quiz Bowl team.

17. Art and Lee agree to meet at the Burger Palace at 6 p.m. Art brings his little sister Arianna.

(A) Art, Lee, and Arianna meet at the Burger Palace.

(B) Lee is upset with Art for bringing an uninvited guest.

(C) Lee orders for everyone.

(D) Arianna enjoys having dinner with Lee.

18. My cat always knows when I have been around other cats, and she snubs me when she smells other cats on me. When I returned from my friend Lisa's house, my cat smelled Lisa's cat on me.

(F) My cat does not like Lisa.

(G) My cat is very young.

(H) My cat dislikes strangers.

(J) My cat snubbed me.

19. Hilary scores higher on the math test than Gina, but lower than Amanda.

(A) Hilary studies more than the other girls.

(B) Gina scores lowest on the math test.

(C) Amanda and Hilary are the best math students in the class.

(D) Amanda scores lower than Hilary and Gina.

20. Shelly put together a scrapbook for her grandparents' fiftieth anniversary party. Her grandparents do not know about the surprise party, which will be held at their favorite Italian restaurant.

(F) Shelly's grandparents hate surprise parties.

(G) Shelly is an only grandchild.

(H) Shelly's grandparents love scrapbooks.

(J) Shelly's grandparents have been married for 50 years.

STOP   If you finish before time is up, check over your work on Section 5 only. Do not go back to the previous section. Do not go on until the signal is given.

SECTION 6. MATHEMATICS

35 Minutes

Directions: For questions 1–40, read each problem and find the answer.

1. Two hundred million, one hundred seventy-three thousand, and sixty-three =
   (A) 200,173,630
   (B) 2,173,063
   (C) 20,173,063
   (D) 200,173,063

2. Seventeen million sixty thousand thirty-four =
   (F) 1,760,034
   (G) 17,634
   (H) 17,060,034
   (J) 17,600,034

3. 0.5% is equal to
   (A) 0.5
   (B) 0.005
   (C) 0.05
   (D) $\frac{1}{2}$

4. A group of 6 people raised $690 for charity. One person raised 35% of the total. What was the amount raised by the other 5 people?
   (F) $241.50
   (G) $448.50
   (H) $449.50
   (J) $445.50

5. If a pie is divided into 20 parts, what percent is one part of the whole pie?
   (A) 20%
   (B) 5%
   (C) 2.0%
   (D) 0.5%

6. A centimeter is what part of a kilometer?
   (F) $\frac{1}{100}$
   (G) $\frac{1}{1,000}$
   (H) $\frac{1}{10,000}$
   (J) $\frac{1}{100,000}$

7. Find the area of a rectangle with a length of 176 feet and a width of 79 feet.
   (A) 13,904 sq. ft.
   (B) 13,854 sq. ft.
   (C) 13,304 sq. ft.
   (D) 13,804 sq. ft.

8. Mr. Lawson makes a weekly salary of $250 plus 7% commission on his sales. What will his income be for a week in which he made sales totaling $1250?
   (F) $337.50
   (G) $87.50
   (H) $267.50
   (J) $327.50

9. Complete the following statement:
   $3(\underline{\hspace{1cm}} \times 4) - 20 = 280$.
   (A) 5^3
   (B) 5
   (C) 5^2
   (D) 5×2

10. Find the area of a triangle whose dimensions are: $b = 14$ inches, $h = 20$ inches.
    (F) 208 sq. inches
    (G) 280 sq. inches
    (H) 140 sq. inches
    (J) 288 sq. inches

11. What is the sum of $(8 \times 10^2) + (6 \times 10) + 2$ and $(5 \times 10^3) + (2 \times 10^2) + (8 \times 10) + 9$?
    - **(A)** 6041
    - **(B)** 6151
    - **(C)** 50,041
    - **(D)** 51,151

12. The set of common factors for 30 and 24 is
    - **(F)** {1,2,3,6}
    - **(G)** {1,2,3,4,6}
    - **(H)** {1,2,4,6}
    - **(J)** {1,2,4,6,12}

13. If the scale on a blueprint is $\frac{1}{4}$ inch = 1 foot, give the blueprint dimensions of a room that is actually 29 feet long and 23 feet wide.
    - **(A)** $7\frac{1}{2}" \times 5\frac{1}{4}"$
    - **(B)** $6\frac{3}{4}" \times 6"$
    - **(C)** $7\frac{1}{4}" \times 5\frac{1}{2}"$
    - **(D)** $7\frac{1}{4}" \times 5\frac{3}{4}"$

14. A scalene triangle has
    - **(F)** two equal sides.
    - **(G)** two equal sides and one right angle.
    - **(H)** no equal sides.
    - **(J)** three equal sides.

15. On a recent trip, the Smiths drove at an average speed of 55 miles per hour. If the trip took $5\frac{1}{2}$ hours, how many miles did they drive?
    - **(A)** 320.75
    - **(B)** 312.50
    - **(C)** 320.5
    - **(D)** 302.5

16. $\frac{17}{30}$ is greater than
    - **(F)** $\frac{7}{8}$
    - **(G)** $\frac{9}{20}$
    - **(H)** $\frac{9}{11}$
    - **(J)** $\frac{22}{25}$

17. One millimeter equals what part of a meter?
    - **(A)** $\frac{1}{100}$
    - **(B)** $\frac{1}{1,000}$
    - **(C)** $\frac{1}{10,000}$
    - **(D)** $\frac{1}{100,000}$

18. A baseball team won 18 games, which was 40% of its season. How many games did the team lose?
    - **(F)** 25
    - **(G)** 45
    - **(H)** 32
    - **(J)** 27

19. If $-2 < q < -1$, which of the following is true?
    - **(A)** $q = \frac{1}{2}$
    - **(B)** $q > -1$
    - **(C)** $q > 0$
    - **(D)** $q > -2$

20. Which pair of values for x and $\square$ will make the following statement true?
    $2x \ \square \ 8$
    - **(F)** $(6, <)$
    - **(G)** $(4, >)$
    - **(H)** $(0, <)$
    - **(J)** $(-3, >)$

21. $(6 \times 2) + (7 \times 3) =$
    - **(A)** $(6 \times 7) + (2 \times 3)$
    - **(B)** $(7 - 6) + (3 - 2)$
    - **(C)** $(7 \times 3) + (6 \times 2)$
    - **(D)** $(7 \times 3) \times (6 \times 2)$

22. Which of the following will substitute for x and make the statement below true?
    $56 - (7 - x) = 53$
    - **(F)** 4
    - **(G)** 3
    - **(H)** 2
    - **(J)** 1

23. An angle that is greater than 90° and less than 180° is a(n)

    (A) acute angle.
    (B) right angle.
    (C) reflex angle.
    (D) obtuse angle.

24.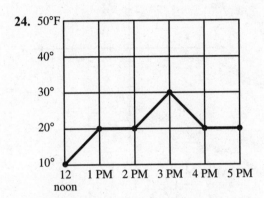

    What was the average temperature on the afternoon shown on the above graph?

    (F) 20°
    (G) 24°
    (H) 25°
    (J) 30°

25. Mr. Jones has agreed to borrow $3500 for one year at 10% interest. What is the total amount he will pay back to the bank?

    (A) $3675
    (B) $350
    (C) $3700
    (D) $3850

26. Which of the following statements is true?

    (F) $4 \times 5 < 4 \times 1 + 6$
    (G) $87 \div 3 < 30$
    (H) $25 = 2 \times 5$
    (J) $\frac{1}{4} < \frac{1}{5}$

27. If one angle of a triangle measures 115°, then the sum of the other two angles is

    (A) 245°
    (B) 75°
    (C) 195°
    (D) 65°

28. At 20 miles per hour, how long does it take to travel 1 mile?

    (F) 1 min.
    (G) 2 min.
    (H) 3 min.
    (J) 4 min.

29. Approximate the circumference of a circle whose radius is 21 feet. (Use $\pi = \frac{22}{7}$.)

    (A) 153 feet
    (B) 65.94 feet
    (C) 132 feet
    (D) 1769.4 feet

30. If $x > -4$, and $x < 2$, then $\{x\}$ includes

    (F) $-4, 0, 1, 2$
    (G) $-2, -1, 1, 2$
    (H) $1, 2, 3, 4$
    (J) $-3, -2, -1, 0, 1$

31.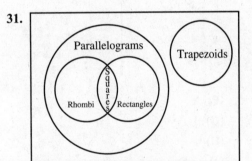

    From the diagram above, we know that

    (A) all trapezoids are parallelograms.
    (B) some rhombi are parallelograms.
    (C) some rectangles are rhombi.
    (D) all parallelograms are rectangles.

32. How many 2-inch tiles would have to be put around the outside edge of a 4-foot × 12-foot rectangle to completely frame the rectangle?

    (F) 32
    (G) 36
    (H) 192
    (J) 196

33. A certain highway intersection has had A accidents over a ten-year period, resulting in B deaths. What is the yearly average death rate for the intersection?

(A) $A + B - 10$

(B) $\dfrac{B}{10}$

(C) $10 - \dfrac{A}{B}$

(D) $\dfrac{AB}{12}$

34. Which point is named by the ordered pair $(-4,4)$?

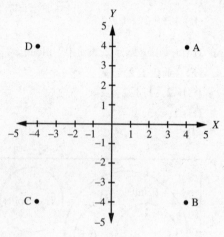

(F) A

(G) B

(H) C

(J) D

35. What are the coordinates of point P on the graph?

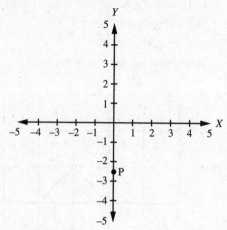

(A) $\left(-2\dfrac{1}{2}, 0\right)$

(B) $\left(0, -3\dfrac{1}{2}\right)$

(C) $\left(0, -2\dfrac{1}{2}\right)$

(D) $\left(-1, -2\dfrac{1}{2}\right)$

36. On a blueprint, 2 inches represent 24 feet. How long must a line be to represent 72 feet?

(F) 36 inches

(G) 12 inches

(H) 6 inches

(J) 4 inches

37. A store puts a pair of $14 jeans on sale at a 25% discount. What is the new selling price?

(A) $13.75

(B) $10.50

(C) $3.50

(D) $13.65

38.

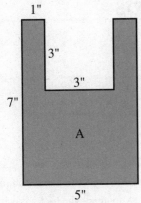

The area of figure A is

(F) 26 sq. in.

(G) 19 sq. in.

(H) 44 sq. in.

(J) 30 sq. in.

39. A boy *M* years old has a brother six years older and a sister four years younger. The combined age of the three is

(A) $M + 10$

(B) $3M + 2$

(C) $3M - 2$

(D) $2M - 6$

40. Event A occurs every 14 minutes and event B every 12 minutes. If they both occur at 1:00 p.m., when will be the next time that both occur together?

(F) 2:12 p.m.

(G) 1:48 p.m.

(H) 2:24 p.m.

(J) 3:48 p.m.

STOP If you finish before time is up, check over your work on Section 7 only. Do not go back to any previous sections.

practice test

SECTION 7. READING AND LANGUAGE ARTS

40 Minutes

Directions: For questions 1–40, read each passage and the questions following that passage. Find the answers.

QUESTIONS 1-4 REFER TO THE FOLLOWING PASSAGE.

Pearl was growing weary of working in the hot sun, having been there since early that morning, nailing shingle after shingle into the new church roof. Every time Pearl found herself wishing that she'd volunteered to help with the kitchen crew instead, she looked over at Reverend Cartwright working hard on his pile of shingles, and she found her inspiration in him. He had been the first to arrive on the roof that morning, and she was sure that he'd be the last to leave. Pearl had always admired Rev. Cartwright for his moving sermons and his ability to uplift any crowd of people. No matter how she was feeling, his Sunday messages always brought her back to looking on the positive side again. Seeing his hard work and dedication to the church rebuilding effort had made Pearl realize that she had only known a portion of Rev. Cartwright's caring up until now.

Each day and each night, Reverend Cartwright and his wife Mattie stood watch over the volunteer teams and lent their hands to the physical work whenever they could—whenever they weren't busy checking in supplies or organizing crews of people to start a new phase of the project. Every Wednesday night, the volunteers would pile into the makeshift sanctuary set up at old Cutter's barn just down the road and listen as Rev. Cartwright encouraged them to look for the silver lining in every cloud. He and Mattie refused to see the burning of their church as a setback. They chose instead, Rev. Cartwright preached, to see it as an opportunity: an opportunity to bring the congregation together in a united effort, which in fact was exactly what had happened.

1. Which word best describes the character of Reverend Cartwright in the story?
   (A) Playful
   (B) Angry
   (C) Dedicated
   (D) Frustrated

2. According to the passage, how was Pearl's church damaged?
   (F) By lightening
   (G) By a falling tree
   (H) By a flood
   (J) By a fire

3. In the opening of the passage, which of the following most likely explains why Pearl wishes she had volunteered for the kitchen crew instead of working on the roof?
   (A) She would meet more people on the kitchen crew.
   (B) The kitchen crew got to eat first.
   (C) Working on the kitchen crew was an easier job.
   (D) The kitchen crew held higher status.

4. Cutter's barn is used as a temporary
   (F) shelter for homeless people.
   (G) place of worship for the church members.
   (H) center for strategic planning.
   (J) kitchen for free meals.

QUESTIONS 5–7 REFER TO THE FOLLOWING PASSAGE.

The history of modern pollution problems shows that most have resulted from negligence and ignorance. We have an appalling tendency to interfere with nature before all of the possible consequences of our actions have been studied in depth. We produce and distribute radioactive substances, synthetic chemicals, and many other potent compounds before fully comprehending their effects on living organisms. Our education is dangerously incomplete.

It will be argued that the purpose of science is to move into unknown territory, to explore, and to discover. It can be said that similar risks have been taken before and that these risks are necessary to technological progress.

These arguments overlook an important element. In the past, risks taken in the name of scientific progress were restricted to a small place and a brief period of time. The effects of the processes we now strive to master are neither localized nor brief. Air pollution covers vast urban areas. Ocean pollutants have been discovered in nearly every part of the world. Synthetic chemicals spread over huge stretches of forest and farmland may remain in the soil for decades. Radioactive pollutants will be found in the biosphere for generations. The size and persistence of these problems have grown with the expanding power of modern science.

One might also argue that the hazards of modern pollutants are small compared to the dangers associated with other human activity. No estimate of the actual harm done by smog, fallout, or chemical residues can obscure the reality that the risks are being taken before being fully understood.

The importance of these issues lies in the failure of science to predict and control human intervention into natural processes. The true measure of the danger is represented by the hazards we will encounter if we enter the new age of technology without first evaluating our responsibility to the environment.

5. According to the author, the major cause of pollution problems is
   (A) designing synthetic chemicals to kill living organisms.
   (B) a lack of understanding of the history of technology.
   (C) scientists who are too willing to move into unknown territory.
   (D) changing our environment before understanding the effects of these changes.

6. The author believes that the risks taken by modern science are greater than those taken by earlier scientific efforts because
   (F) the effects may be felt by more people for a longer period of time.
   (G) science is progressing faster than ever before.

   (H) technology has produced more dangerous chemicals.
   (J) the materials used are more dangerous to scientists.

7. The author apparently believes that the problem of finding solutions to pollution depends on
   (A) the removal of present hazards to the environment.
   (B) the removal of all potential pollutants from their present uses.
   (C) overcoming technical difficulties.
   (D) the willingness of scientists to understand possible dangers before using new products in the environment.

QUESTIONS 8-12 REFER TO THE FOLLOWING PASSAGE.

Contrary to what we may have heard, not all of the fats that we eat are bad for our health. It is certainly wise to be cautious about how *much* fat we eat: many nutritionists recommend that we restrict our fat intake to about 30 percent of our total daily calories. Research now shows, however, that it is also important to be sure that we consume enough of the *good* fats in our diets, so that we can provide ourselves with optimal nutrition.

The fats that are particularly important for us belong to a group of fats that scientists call "essential fatty acids." These fats are termed "essential" because they are so vital to our health. Scientists have determined that there are two types of essential fatty acids that we humans must get from our diets: these are known as omega-3 and omega-6 fatty acids.

According to nutrition author Clara Felix, scientists now believe that we should consume at least one gram of omega-3 fatty acids for every 3 grams of omega-6 fatty acids that we eat. Although we tend to eat enough omega-6 fats, the American diet falls short when it comes to omega-3 fats. The best way to balance out our diets, Felix recommends, is to reduce the amount of omega-6 oils we are eating while at the same time increasing the amount of omega-3 fat.

We can do this by first limiting the amounts of salad dressing and margarine that we eat, as well as baked goods such as breads, muffins, cakes, and donuts. Next, to increase our omega-3 fats, we can add flaxseed oil and olive oil into our diets, as well as more walnuts and fish. The fish that provide the greatest sources of omega-3 fats, according to Felix, are herring, mackerel, salmon, sardines, trout, tuna, and whitefish.

8. Which of the following is true about Clara Felix?
   - **(F)** She has conducted experiments on dietary fat.
   - **(G)** She is a medical doctor.
   - **(H)** She has written works about nutrition.
   - **(J)** She has a degree in biology.

9. What is the author's opinion about omega-6 fatty acids?
   - **(A)** We should consume more of them.
   - **(B)** We get plenty of them in our diets already.
   - **(C)** We should not consume them in our diets.
   - **(D)** They are difficult to find in common foods.

10. This passage mainly focuses on how to
   - **(F)** lose weight by consuming less dietary fat.
   - **(G)** eliminate bad fats from our diet.
   - **(H)** improve nutrition by consuming more omega-3.
   - **(J)** analyze the importance of fat in the diet.

11. According to the passage, nutritionists recommend that we limit our consumption of fats to
   - **(A)** around 30 calories a day.
   - **(B)** a little more than 30 ounces a day.
   - **(C)** about 30 percent of total ounces of food consumed every day.
   - **(D)** about 30 percent of total calories consumed every day.

12. According to the passage, good sources of omega-3 fats include
   - **(F)** bread, salmon, and walnuts.
   - **(G)** olive oil, margarine, and sardines.
   - **(H)** salads, sardines, and white fish.
   - **(J)** olive oil, walnuts, and sardines.

QUESTIONS 13–17 REFER TO THE FOLLOWING PASSAGE.

Few people have seen the world from the vantage point of John Amatt. Some of those who have didn't live to tell about it.

Amatt was a leader and a climber on the 1982 Canadian expedition to Mount Everest, the tallest mountain in the world at 29,028 feet. This was the first Canadian expedition to Mount Everest. In the end, it was successful in placing two Canadian climbers on the summit of the great mountain. The journey to that goal, however, was extremely challenging.

The trip started with 16 Canadian climbers and 24 Sherpas, expert mountain guides who live in the Himalayas in Nepal. By the end of the trip, ten weeks later, only two Canadians and four Sherpas made it to the top of the mountain. One Canadian and three Sherpas had lost their lives in avalanche accidents during the early part of the trip. The accidents almost caused the climb to be called off, but the team chose to press on.

In his book, *Straight to the Top and Beyond*, Amatt describes how his experiences during the Everest expedition helped his team to learn from their setbacks. In Amatt's view, the experience of loss helped the team to strengthen their perspective on the reality of what they were up against. It also inspired them to approach their challenges with clarity and humbleness. He believes that the team learned from the accidents to take the risks that they faced more seriously. This lesson ultimately helped make the Everest expedition a success.

13. The main contrast in the article is between
- **(A)** the work of the Canadians and the work of the Sherpas.
- **(B)** those who have seen the world from Mount Everest and those who have not.
- **(C)** the success of the expedition and the losses it faced.
- **(D)** John Amatt and less successful climbers.

14. According to the passage, how many Sherpas reached the top of Mount Everest with the Canadian expedition?
- **(F)** 2
- **(G)** 4
- **(H)** 6
- **(J)** 24

15. The passage states that the expedition led by John Amatt was the
- **(A)** first expedition to scale Mount Everest.
- **(B)** only successful expedition to scale Mount Everest.
- **(C)** first Canadian expedition to scale Mount Everest.
- **(D)** last expedition that Amatt led up Mount Everest.

16. In his book, Amatt states that his team learned several lessons from their setbacks and challenges, including how to approach their efforts with
- **(F)** seriousness and indifference.
- **(G)** humbleness and pride.
- **(H)** skepticism and ambition.
- **(J)** humbleness and clarity.

17. In the following sentence in the last paragraph, "It also inspired them to approach their challenges with clarity and humbleness," the word "it" refers to the
- **(A)** experience of loss cited in the second sentence of the last paragraph.
- **(B)** experiences of Amatt's expedition cited in the first sentence of the last paragraph.
- **(C)** book written by Amatt cited in the first sentence of the last paragraph.
- **(D)** accidents cited in the fourth sentence of the last paragraph.

QUESTIONS 18–21 REFER TO THE FOLLOWING PASSAGE.

American inventor Dean Kamen began his career at an early age. His first invention, at age five, was a gadget that assisted him with making his bed in the mornings.

As an adult, Kamen said, "Education is . . . the most important thing you can do with your life." As a child, though, he didn't care much for school. He felt bored because his classes did not address the subjects he was interested in. So, he educated himself by reading all he could about the questions he wanted to answer.

In high school, Kamen converted his parents' basement into a workshop for his projects. By the time he graduated, he was making a living as an inventor. In fact, he made more money than his mother, a teacher, and his father, a comic book artist, put together.

Making money is not the primary force behind Kamen's work, however. When he discovers something the world needs, he does his best to create it. His inventions have included a high-tech prosthetic arm, a portable kidney dialysis machine, and a low-cost water-purifying system for people in developing countries.

Seeing a wheelchair user struggle to leap a curb inspired Kamen to invent a wheelchair that climbs stairs. The chair has six wheels, four large and two small. All four large wheels are powered. To ascend stairs, the large wheels roll up and over each other, while a gyroscope adjusts the balance of the chair to keep it upright.

Kamen believes scientists and engineers should be considered stars, like athletes and actors. To encourage young people's interest in science, he founded a robotics program for kids. Teams compete to develop the best robot for a given task, such as shooting hoops. The robot competitions are run like sporting events, complete with mascots and cheering crowds.

18. The wheelchair Kamen invented is extraordinary because it
   (F) holds the user in a standing position.
   (G) goes up and down stairs.
   (H) does not leap curbs.
   (J) has large wheels.

19. According to this article, Dean Kamen
   (A) was not concerned about his own education.
   (B) wants to increase student interest in athletics.
   (C) stopped attending school at an early age.
   (D) believes education is of the utmost importance.

20. Dean Kamen is inspired to be an inventor primarily because he wants
   (F) to earn a great deal of money.
   (G) to be treated like a movie star.
   (H) to solve problems he sees in the world.
   (J) young people to become interested in science.

21. All of the following are inventions by Kamen mentioned in the passage except a
   (A) prosthetic arm.
   (B) dialysis machine.
   (C) water purifier.
   (D) robotic athlete.

QUESTIONS 22–25 REFER TO THE FOLLOWING PASSAGE.

Have you ever experienced the ceremony known as potlatch? This centuries old traditional gift-giving feast is a common practice amongst various indigenous peoples who reside along the Pacific Northwest Coast of the United States and Canada. Among those who practice potlatch are the Nuxalk, Tlingit, Haida, Tsimshian, and Heiltsuk peoples, who honor long-standing customs and cultural tenets—like *potlatch*—through diligent adherence.

The origins of the word potlatch can be traced to the Chinook people, and means "a gift" or "to give away." Although there are subtle cultural variations in how this ceremony unfolds, it typically takes place in the less busy winter months, when people are not as preoccupied with hunting and gathering food. A potlatch is hosted by a numayn, a house within the community, to commemorate significant events such as weddings, adoptions, births, deaths, and transfers of power and leadership.

Potlatch ceremonies typically include elaborate displays of feasting and dancing that could last for several days, as well as intricate systems of gift giving. Gift giving behaviors are designed to communicate the relevant political, kinship, religious, or celebratory nature of the event taking place; and to establish or reinforce hierarchical relationships between individuals, houses, clans, villages, and nations. Items that are exchanged during a traditional potlatch include ornamental metals, animal skins, blankets, food, and canoes.

Unfortunately, history has often been harsh on the traditional customs of indigenous peoples when an occupying group grabs power and territory. In the latter part of the 19th century, the custom of potlatching was deemed "useless," "unproductive," and "uncivilized," and made illegal in Canada and the United States. Some saw the criminalization of indigenous traditions as a conscious push towards assimilation. The ban on potlatching persisted until 1951. Today, those eager to maintain traditions and reclaim a connection to their heritage have continued the noble and historical practice of potlatching.

22. The best title for this passage is
   (F) A Closer Look at a Traditional Custom
   (G) Relations between Canada and the United States
   (H) A Look Back at American Life in the 19th Century
   (J) A Snapshot of Traditional Life in Northeastern United States

23. Which of the following events would most likely not be cause to have a potlatching ceremony?
   (A) The accidental death of a village elder in a hunting accident
   (B) A wedding that joins two prominent families
   (C) The capture of a wild animal threatening people's safety
   (D) The celebration of a village elder becoming a new leader

24. Based on the information in the passage, all of the following items may have been given away during a potlatching ceremony *except*
   (F) a roasted pig.
   (G) a copper medallion.
   (H) a hand carved wooden canoe.
   (J) an ornate hunting spear.

25. According to the passage, one theory on why potlatching was made illegal in the 19th century was
   (A) fear of an unknown cultural practice.
   (B) an effort to assimilate an indigenous people.
   (C) an attempt to bring notoriety to an ancient culture.
   (D) a misguided attempt at initiating cultural unity.

QUESTIONS 26–29 REFER TO THE FOLLOWING PASSAGE.

As recently as the 1840s, most people believed that the Earth, and humans with it, was created a mere 6,000 to 7,000 years ago. For centuries, beautifully worked flints were regarded as the work of elves, a notion once far more plausible than the idea that man roamed the world's wildernesses in small bands long before the days of Greece and Rome. Even when these stones were accepted as man-made tools, they were attributed to the Romans or early Britons.

Today we think in wider terms. The earliest dated works of man have been found on the floor of Olduvai Gorge, a miniature Grand Canyon in East Africa, and include carefully made stone tools about 2,000,000 years old. Furthermore, fossil evidence suggests that members of the family of man used tools millions of years before that.

Opposition to these ideas began to fade during the late eighteenth and early nineteenth centuries. Excavators, mainly enthusiastic amateurs, pointed to material associated with the tools—fossil remains of men and extinct animals. Most geologists still thought in biblical terms, maintaining that such associations were accidental, that the Flood had mixed the bones of ancient animals and the tools and remains of recent man. But their last-ditch defenses crumbled with the finding of bones and tools together in unflooded and undisturbed deposits, including a number of important sites on the banks of the Somme River. British investigators came to check the French deposits, were convinced, and announced their conclusions in 1859, the year that saw publication of Darwin's *On the Origin of Species*. This date marks the beginning of modern research into human evolution.

26. All of the following types of archaeological information were mentioned except
    (F) carbon dating.
    (G) fossils.
    (H) flints.
    (J) extinct animals.

27. According to the article, man has lived on Earth for
    (A) about 7,000 years.
    (B) between 7,000 and 100,000 years.
    (C) about 2,000,000 years.
    (D) far more than 2,000,000 years.

28. The scientific turning point in theories about the age of man's existence was the
    (F) publication of *On the Origin of Species*.
    (G) discovery in France of the remains of extinct animals and men together.
    (H) new theological research of the Bible.
    (J) new theories about the Flood and its effects on mankind.

29. In the early nineteenth century,
    (A) small bands of Romans roamed the Earth.
    (B) geologists dated man's existence back 2,000,000 years.
    (C) the stones were accepted as ancient tools.
    (D) most people believed that man's existence was 6,000 to 7,000 years old.

QUESTIONS 30–34 REFER TO THE FOLLOWING PASSAGE.

Of all of the characters in the legend of King Arthur, perhaps the one who has received least credit for his achievements is the knight Perceval. Perceval is a relatively obscure knight compared to other famous characters such as Lancelot or Galahad. Nonetheless, he accomplished very lofty goals during his service to King Arthur.

The story of Perceval appears first in a work entitled *The Story of the Grail*, written by a French author named Chrétien de Troyes. According to author and translator Kirk McElhearn, who specializes in the Perceval literature, Chrétien de Troyes died some time in the 1180s, and the date of his birth remains unknown. His work, according to McElhearn, "marks the beginning of the Arthurian Legend, at least in what we know today."

Chrétien de Troyes' work tells the story of a young lad named Perceval, the son of a great warrior who was wounded in battle and later died of grief after his two oldest sons were killed in battle. Perceval at the time was very young, and his mother became determined that she would not lose her only remaining son. She lived with Perceval in the forest and tried to protect him from ever learning about knights, horses, armor, and battle.

As Perceval grows, he soon learns of knights who pass by on their way through the forest. He chooses to accompany the knights to learn of the world, much to his mother's sorrow. During his travels, Perceval gets a glimpse of the Holy Grail by chance in a castle. He does not understand the significance of the grail, and he neglects to ask about it. He realizes that he has missed his opportunity to learn about the grail, since he never asked about it, so he sets off on a quest to find the grail again.

Unfortunately, we never learn what happens to Perceval in Chrétien de Troyes' version of the story. Chrétien died before the story was finished, so the ending of his text remains a mystery. According to other versions of the legend, however, Perceval was extremely noble and pure of heart, and these qualities eventually caused him to be granted guardianship of the Holy Grail.

30. Which statement best reflects the main idea of the passage?

(F) Perceval is a less well-known character in the Arthurian legends who accomplished important goals for King Arthur.

(G) Perceval is an important character in the Arthurian legends who has received the least credit for his accomplishments.

(H) The legend of King Arthur's court emphasizes loyalty, courageousness, and honor.

(J) The story of Perceval concerns a knight who misses his opportunity to learn about the Holy Grail.

31. Kirk McElhearn is

(A) a translator who translated the works of Chrétien de Troyes.

(B) a translator who translated the Arthurian legends from English to French.

(C) an author and translator who specializes in the Perceval literature.

(D) an author who has published a book regarding Chrétien de Troyes.

32. In *The Story of the Grail*, why does Perceval's mother keep him from learning about knights, horses, armor, and battle?

   (F) She wants to honor the memory of Perceval's father, who was opposed to war.

   (G) She wants to protect Perceval, because he is her only remaining son.

   (H) She feels that Perceval is too young to begin learning about these things.

   (J) She would prefer for Perceval to be a poet or a scholar instead of a warrior.

33. The word *obscure* probably means

   (A) not very capable.

   (B) not very confident.

   (C) not well-known.

   (D) not very likable.

34. According to the passage, Chrétien de Troyes

   (F) completed the story of Perceval in the 1190s.

   (G) saw the Holy Grail himself.

   (H) died before completing the story of Perceval.

   (J) was unknown until his work was translated.

QUESTIONS 35–40 REFER TO THE FOLLOWING PASSAGE.

The dark and the sea are full of dangers to the fishermen of Norway. A whale might come and destroy the floating chain of corks that edges the nets, break it, and carry it off. Or a storm might come suddenly, unexpectedly, out of the night. The sea seems to turn somersaults. It opens and closes immense caverns with terrible clashes, chasing boats and fishermen who must flee from their nets and the expected catch. Then the fishermen might lift their nets as empty as they set them. At other times, the herring might come in such masses that the lines break from the weight when lifted, and the fishermen must return home empty-handed, without line, nets, or herring.

But often the nets are full of herring that shine and glisten like silver. Once in awhile, a couple of fishermen will venture in their boats along the net lines to see whether the herring are coming, and when the corks begin to bob and jerk as if something were hitting the nets to which they are attached, they then know that the herring are there. The nets are being filled, and all the fishermen sit in quiet excitement. They dare only to whisper to each other, afraid to disturb, and quite overcome by the over-helming generosity of the sea. Eyes shine happy anticipation; hands are folded in thanks. Then muscles strain with power. It is as though the strength of the body doubled. They can work day and night without a thought of weariness. They need neither food nor rest; the thought of success keeps their vigor up almost endlessly. They will take food and rest when it is all over.

35. The best title for this passage is
(A) "Hard Work in Norway."
(B) "The Perils and Rewards of Fishing."
(C) "Risky Business."
(D) "The Generosity of the Sea."

36. The difficulties faced by the Norwegian fishermen include
(F) the eating of the herring by whales.
(G) the difficulty of being very calm.
(H) interference by rough seas.
(J) the jerking of the corks.

37. At the first indication that herring are entering the nets, the fishermen
(A) try not to frighten the fish away.
(B) strain every muscle to haul in the catch.
(C) collect the nets quickly.
(D) row quickly along the edge of the nets.

38. When the article says that the sea opens and closes immense caverns, it is referring to
(F) caves along the shoreline.
(G) deep holes in the ocean floor.
(H) dangerous large boulders that get rolled around.
(J) hollow pockets beneath very high waves.

39. The fishermen are described as
(A) strong, angry, and excitable.
(B) skillful, religious, and impatient.
(C) patient, brave, and grateful.
(D) surly, hardworking, and cautious.

40. Of the following, the one that is *not* mentioned as posing a problem to the fishermen is
(F) destruction of the nets.
(G) theft of the nets by other fishermen.
(H) too large a catch.
(J) whales.

Directions: For questions 41–43, choose the topic sentence that best fits the paragraph.

41. _____

First, your ability to secure a position might depend on your English. Your prospective employer will notice how well you write the answers to the questions on your application blank. And when you are interviewed, he will notice how well you speak.

(A) As you move up the success ladder, what you write and what you say will determine in part your rate of climb.

(B) If you wish to enter business, there are three good reasons why you should study English.

(C) You will need to write reports accurately and interestingly.

(D) You will need to talk effectively with your fellow workers, with your superiors, and perhaps with the public.

42. _____

The first thing to do is gather several apples—a few good choices include Goldrush, Harrison, and Grimes Golden apples. Put your apples, and spices to taste, in a large pot and fill it with water until the apples are completely submerged. Bring it to a boil, stir for about an hour, strain it until you're left with the juice, refrigerate it, and serve your delicious beverage any time of day.

(F) If you're eager to make apple cider, here's an easy recipe for doing so.

(G) Did you know that most people don't drink enough fluids during the day?

(H) Apples are one of the most popular and versatile fruits in the United States.

(J) Do you know how to make a delicious homemade apple pie?

43. _____

There are important areas in our lives in which opinions play a major role. Every time we look into the future, we depend on opinions. Every time we attempt to judge facts, we depend on opinions. And every time we attempt to advance into the "not yet known area," we depend on opinions.

(A) Opinions should not be taken lightly.

(B) Newspaper editorials are based upon opinion rather than upon facts.

(C) In some ways, they actually go beyond facts.

(D) Scientific inquiry leaves no room for opinions.

Directions: For questions 44–46, choose the pair of sentences that best develops the topic sentence.

44. One of the most difficult problems in America today is that of homelessness.

(F) I think that homeless people tend to be dirty, lazy, and shiftless. They are an eyesore for honest, hardworking citizens.

(G) Homelessness was a problem during the Depression. The Salvation Army operated soup kitchens to feed the homeless.

(H) While the bulk of the homeless are single men, many are families with small children. Among the causes of homelessness are fires, poverty, and just plain hard luck.

(J) Some people are homeless by choice. Nomads like to wander from place to place without having to care for a stable residence.

45. Many city dwellers today are struggling to afford the rising cost of housing in urban areas.

(A) Most people should consider saving their money and buying property.

(B) It has always been quite expensive to live in a major city. There are a wide variety of clichés that are based on the notion of high rental costs in metropolitan areas.

(C) Many people are choosing to live in suburban or rural areas. The extra space and quiet that can be found outside of the city is very attractive to some people.

(D) Recent estimates indicate that the percentage of income that must be spent on renting an apartment has never been higher, and it's only going up. Many people have taken to sharing rooms or getting additional work to offset this growing expense.

46. One of the most important safety features on your car is the condition of the tires.

(F) The first tires were made of solid rubber and were very uncomfortable to ride on. Later tires had an inflatable inner tube that gave a softer ride.

(G) Studded tires give good traction on icy roads. Some states prohibit tire studs because they destroy the road surface.

(H) Today's steel-belted radial tires give long service. If you use radials, you should put them on all four wheels.

(J) Once the brakes are applied, it is the front tires that determine how quickly the car will stop and whether or not it will skid. Deep, matched treads on the two front tires will ensure a quick, smooth stop.

Directions: For question 47, choose the sentence that does not belong in the paragraph.

47. (1) Software developers and engineers are currently working on the next big innovation in mobile phone technology. (2) It might not be long before flexible, bendable phones are here. (3) This ingenious new technology would allow users to twist, roll up, and fold their phones without harming or affecting the device. (4) Last year, the percentage of people who used mobile phones on a daily basis was the highest ever recorded, according to a recent survey. (5) A major technological advance such as flexible phones might further stimulate interest in mobile phone technology and help sales of new phones.

(A) Sentence 2

(B) Sentence 3

(C) Sentence 4

(D) Sentence 5

Directions: For questions 48–50, read the paragraph and choose the sentence that best fills the blank.

48. A handy all-round wrench that is generally included in every toolbox is the adjustable open-end wrench. This wrench is not intended to take the place of the regular solid open-end wrench. _____
Its usefulness is achieved by its ability to fit.

(F) As the jaw opening increases, the length of the wrench increases.

(G) Adjustable wrenches are available in varying sizes, ranging from 4 to 24 inches in length.

(H) This flexibility is achieved although one jaw of the adjustable open-end wrench is fixed because the other jaw is moved along a slide by a thumbscrew adjustment.

(J) In addition, it is not built for use on extremely hard-to-turn items.

49. Geodes are geological structures that naturally occur in sedimentary and volcanic rocks. They are typically hollow and spherical in shape, and can vary greatly in size. _____ These crystals can come in a variety of colors, based on the chemicals and impurities involved in their formation. The colors inside of each geode, which remains a mystery until it is opened, and the dazzling crystalline world that waits within, is part of the reason why these objects are so prized and sought after.

(A) Geodes are quite valuable, and are collected by a variety of enthusiasts.

(B) Geodes commonly house an internal lining of quartz crystals.

(C) Geodes can typically be found in the Western United States.

(D) Any reputable science museum will contain a geode exhibit.

50. Along the shores of the Indian Ocean is found a pretty little shellfish that is noted for furnishing what may have been the first money ever used. _____ Millions of people around the ocean were using these cowries for money long before furs or cattle or other kinds of money were used anywhere, as far as is known. Cowries have been found in Assyria, many miles inland.

(F) Now, after thousands of years, there are still some tribes in Africa, India, and the South Seas that use cowries.

(G) In China, they were used with several other kinds of shells.

(H) Its shell, called a cowrie, is white or light yellow and is about one inch long.

(J) Tortoise shells had the highest value, so it might be said that the tortoise shells were the dollar bills while the cowries were the coins.

ANSWER KEYS AND EXPLANATIONS

Section 1. Sequences

1. A	5. A	9. D	13. A	17. D
2. J	6. H	10. J	14. J	18. J
3. B	7. B	11. B	15. A	19. B
4. G	8. J	12. G	16. G	20. G

1. **The correct answer is (A).** In the first three segments, the pattern is small figure, large figure, small figure. The fourth segment begins: small figure, large figure . . . The final figure should be small. Because none of the figures are filled in, there is no reason for the final figure to be filled in.

2. **The correct answer is (J).** The pattern in the second segment is exactly the opposite of that in the first. The first two figures in the fourth segment give every indication that the fourth segment will be the exact opposite of the third. Choice (J) carries this out.

3. **The correct answer is (B).** The position of the arms governs. In the first segment, down, up/down, up; in the second, down, down/up (a reversal), up; in the third, down, up, up/down; in the fourth, down, up . . . If a reversal is offered, it would be most reasonable. Choice (B) offers this completion.

4. **The correct answer is (G).** In each succeeding segment, the number of double S's (SS) increases by one. The fourth segment should have four double S's.

5. **The correct answer is (A).** The third figure is always blank. This information narrows your choice to (A) or (D). In addition, the fourth figure is always a combination of the first two. This confirms (A) as the correct answer.

6. **The correct answer is (H).** The basis of the sequence is the number of sides of the figures. In the first segment, the number of sides is 3, 4, 5; in the second, 4, 5, 6; in the third, 5, 6, 7; the fourth must be 6, 7, 8.

7. **The correct answer is (B).** This is a +8 series. Within each segment, each number is 8 more than the number before it. $54 + 8 = 62$.

8. **The correct answer is (J).** The pattern for each three-digit chunk is **x y x**, where **y** is 3 less than **x**. Applying this to the last three-digit chunk shows the blank should be filled in with 17.

9. **The correct answer is (D).** Within each segment, the pattern is +7, –6. So, $65 + 7 = 72$; $72 - 6 = 66$.

10. **The correct answer is (J).** The pattern is ÷4. In the first segment, $96 \div 4 = 24$, and $24 \div 4 = 6$; in the second segment, $\frac{1}{2} \div 4 = \frac{1}{8}$ and $\frac{1}{8} \div 4 = \frac{1}{32}$. Having established that the second number is the first divided by 4, multiply the second number of the fourth segment by 4 to find the first number.

11. **The correct answer is (B).** The pattern for each three-digit chunk is "divide by 3 to get the second number, and then add 4 to that to get the third number." So, the blank should be filled in with 29.

12. **The correct answer is (G).** Within each segment, the series consists of repeated squares. 5 squared is 25; 25 squared is 625. 2 squared is 4; 4 squared is 16. 1 squared is 1; 1 squared is 1.

13. **The correct answer is (A).** Each segment consists of a +5 series with 15 in the middle. $21 + 5 = 26$, 15 intervenes. $15 + 5 = 20$, with 15 intervening to confuse you. $10 + 5 = 15$. The 15 needed to fill the blank is the 15 that appears in each segment.

14. **The correct answer is (J).** The numbers and letters remain in the same relationship to one another throughout, that is, there is no number between A and B, and the numbers are always subscripts. The letters remain static. The pattern of the numbers appears to be 5 5, 5 4, 4 4, 4 3, 3 3. Isolating the numbers in this way, you can see the manner in which the numbers step down.

15. **The correct answer is (A).** The letters are static; each letter always has a number attached; odd numbers are superscripts, even numbers subscripts. The numbers are slowly increasing, with the changes occurring from left to right. The numbers in isolation read 111, 211, 221, 222, 322. Remember the superscript/subscript rule in choosing the answer.

16. **The correct answer is (G).** The letters are static, so only consider the sequence of subscripts: 1 _ _, then 21 _, then 331, then 452 … The first digit increases by 1 each time, the second digit increases by 2, and the third digit increases by 1. So, the term that goes into the blank is $W_5X_7Y_3$.

17. **The correct answer is (D).** The series consists of the consonants in alphabetical order.

18. **The correct answer is (J).** This series consists of the letters of the alphabet in alphabetical order, beginning with the letter *C*. The letter *A* appears after each letter in the series.

19. **The correct answer is (B).** This series consists of the three letters *P-T-L* in constant rotation. In each succeeding grouping of letters, the first letter of the group before moves to the end of the group, and the other two letters move to the left, so the letter that was second in the previous group becomes the first letter of the next. After *PTL*, the *P* must move to the rear, and the next group must begin with *T* followed by *LP*.

20. **The correct answer is (G).** The first grouping of three letters is obtained by starting at A, going to the next letter B, and then skipping two letters to get to E. The second grouping starts at the immediate next letter and repeats the pattern. Continuing in this manner, the term that goes into the blank is PQT.

Section 2. Analogies

1. B	5. C	9. B	13. C	17. D
2. F	6. H	10. H	14. J	18. H
3. D	7. C	11. D	15. A	19. A
4. F	8. F	12. G	16. J	20. H

1. **The correct answer is (B).** Mother is to daughter as father is to son. The analogy is one of parallel relationships.

2. **The correct answer is (F).** The analogy is that of the whole to one of its parts.

3. **The correct answer is (D).** Vegetable is to vegetable as fruit is to fruit. This is a part-to-part relationship. Carrot and broccoli are both part of the vegetable group. Apple and pear are both part of the fruit group.

4. **The correct answer is (F).** This is a relationship of new to old. A lamp is a modern version of the candle. A stove is a modern version of a fireplace.

5. **The correct answer is (C).** This is a relationship of degree. The mansion is a large, elegant version of the cabin. The stretch limousine is larger and more elegant than the pickup truck, though still a car.

6. **The correct answer is (H).** This is a functional relationship. The table leg holds up the table. The tire holds up the car. This could not be a simple part-to-whole relationship because too many car parts are offered as choices.

7. **The correct answer is (C).** This is a part-to-part relationship. Both eye and ear are parts of the head. Both window and door are parts of the house.

8. **The correct answer is (F).** This is a sequential relationship. From an acorn grows an oak tree; from an egg comes a chicken.

9. **The correct answer is (B).** This is a relationship between people and the tools they use. A stethoscope is used by a doctor; a gavel is used by a judge.

10. **The correct answer is (H).** The relationship is functional. Again, it is easiest read in reverse. A pen is used to apply ink; a brush is used to apply paint.

11. **The correct answer is (D).** This is another example of a functional relationship. This time, read forward. The baseball glove catches the ball. The hook catches the fish.

12. **The correct answer is (G).** This is a sequential relationship. The abacus preceded the calculator as a mathematical aid. The biplane preceded the jet.

13. **The correct answer is (C).** This relationship is part-to-part. The eagle and the duck are both part of the group of birds. Both the collie and the dachshund are part of the group of dogs.

14. **The correct answer is (J).** This relationship is between a hunting implement and the animal hunted with it. The butterfly net is used to hunt the butterfly. The rifle is used to hunt the deer.

15. **The correct answer is (A).** This is a part-to-whole relationship. A slice of bread is part of a loaf; a leaf is part of a tree.

16. **The correct answer is (J).** Call this one what you will—association or part-to-part relationship. The rabbit's foot and four leaf clover are considered good luck. The black cat and the number 13 are considered bad luck.

17. **The correct answer is (D).** A parachute is a safety device on planes; a life preserver is a safety device on boats.

18. **The correct answer is (H).** This is a relationship between real animals and mythical ones. A unicorn is a type of mythical horse; a dragon is a type of mythical reptile.

19. **The correct answer is (A).** Cars travel on roads, and trains travel on tracks.

20. **The correct answer is (H).** A necklace and a necktie are both worn around the neck. Socks and shoes are worn on your feet.

Section 3. Quantitative Reasoning

1. C	5. C	9. B	13. D	17. C
2. G	6. H	10. G	14. H	18. F
3. A	7. C	11. A	15. B	19. A
4. G	8. H	12. G	16. F	20. G

1. **The correct answer is (C).**

   $2 \times 3 = 6$

   $1 \times 3 = 3$

   $3 \times 3 = 9$

2. **The correct answer is (G).**

   $4 + 4 = 8$

   $5 + 4 = 9$

   $7 + 4 = 11$

3. **The correct answer is (A).**

   $7 - 3 = 4$

   $4 - 3 = 1$

   $1 - 3 = -2$

4. **The correct answer is (G).**

   $36 \div 6 = 6$

   $54 \div 6 = 9$

   $84 \div 6 = 14$

5. **The correct answer is (C).**

   $17 + 7 = 24$

   $32 + 7 = 39$

   $58 + 7 = 65$

6. **The correct answer is (H).**

   $\frac{2}{3} \times 3 = 2$

   $2 \times 3 = 6$

   $3 \times 3 = 9$

7. **The correct answer is (C).**

   $\frac{1}{2} + \frac{1}{2} = 1$

   $\frac{3}{2} + \frac{1}{2} = 2$

   $3 + \frac{1}{2} = \frac{7}{2}$

8. **The correct answer is (H).** The whole is divided into 10 equal pieces and 3 are shaded. So, the fraction is $\frac{3}{10}$.

9. **The correct answer is (B).** There are six squares. Two of them are shaded. We know that 2 over 6 is $\frac{2}{6}$, or $\frac{1}{3}$.

10. **The correct answer is (G).** There are eight squares. Six of them are shaded. We know that 6 over 8 is $\frac{6}{8}$, or $\frac{3}{4}$.

11. **The correct answer is (A).** There are eight squares. Three complete squares and two half-squares are shaded.

    If we add $3 + \frac{1}{2} + \frac{1}{2}$, the answer is 4. So, four squares are shaded. We know that 4 over 8 is $\frac{4}{8}$, or $\frac{1}{2}$.

12. **The correct answer is (G).** The whole is first divided into 6 equal rectangles. The triangles in the first and last rectangle each divide that rectangle in half, and the second and fourth rectangles are each divided in half using two smaller rectangles. So, if you think about the fact that there are 12 equal pieces (each of the 6 larger rectangles each divided in half), then 4 of 12 pieces are shaded. So, the fraction is $\frac{4}{12} = \frac{1}{3}$.

13. **The correct answer is (D).** There are nine squares. Five squares are shaded. We know that 5 over 9 is $\frac{5}{9}$.

14. **The correct answer is (H).** There are eight squares. One of them is shaded. We know that 1 over 8 is the same as $\frac{1}{8}$.

15. **The correct answer is (B).** The scale indicates that 1 cube = 1 cone. The only answer that maintains this relationship is choice (B), since it shows that 2 cubes = 1 cube + 1 cone.

16. **The correct answer is (F).** The scale indicates that 1 cube = 1 cone. The only answer that maintains this relationship is choice (F), since it has 1 cone + 1 cube = 2 cones.

17. **The correct answer is (C).** The scale indicates that 1 cube = 2 cones. The only answer that maintains this relationship is choice (C), since it shows that 2 cubes = 4 cones.

18. **The correct answer is (F).** The scale indicates that 1 cube = 2 cones. The only answer that maintains this relationship is choice (F), since it shows that 2 cubes + 1 cone = 1 cube + 3 cones.

19. **The correct answer is (A).** The scale indicates that 1 cube = 3 cones. The only answer that maintains this relationship is choice (A), since it shows that 2 cubes = 1 cube and 3 cones.

20. **The correct answer is (G).** The scale indicates that 1 cube = 3 cones. The only possible answer choice here is choice (G), since it shows that 3 cones = 3 cones.

Section 4. Verbal Reasoning—Words

1. D	5. C	9. D	13. A	17. C
2. G	6. H	10. B	14. G	18. G
3. A	7. C	11. B	15. A	19. D
4. G	8. B	12. H	16. J	20. G

1. **The correct answer is (D).** Flame and smoke often accompany burning, and ash often follows it. However, there can be no burning without heat; heat is the necessary component.

2. **The correct answer is (G).** To verbalize is to put into words; therefore, the essential ingredient of *verbalization* is *words*.

3. **The correct answer is (A).** Legislation is the enactment of laws. Laws may be enacted by any legislative body—city council, Congress, or a student organization. Debate is common but not required.

4. **The correct answer is (G).** Among the answer choices, the only necessary part of a bag is an opening, so that items can be placed inside for carrying. A bag can still be a bag if it doesn't currently have a carrier, a strap, or a zipper.

5. **The correct answer is (C).** The bow is an adjunct of a violin. Notes and melody are products. Strings are absolutely necessary to a violin.

6. **The correct answer is (H).** A chronometer is a device for measuring time. There must be time to measure. The chronometer may be a watch, a sundial, or even an hourglass.

7. **The correct answer is (C).** Among the answer choices, the only necessary part of an ocean is water. An ocean can still be an ocean if it does not have waves or sand. Seas are smaller than oceans.

8. **The correct answer is (B).** Hunger is the result of a lack of a food or nutrient. The other conditions can accompany hunger but are not essential.

9. **The correct answer is (D).** A marriage is a state of individuals being united in a relationship. A wedding, a priest, and love are not essential.

10. **The correct answer is (B).** Science refers to systematized knowledge. It does not require technology, physics, or a laboratory.

11. **The correct answer is (B).** The relationship is progressive: from light covering, to heavier or warmer covering, to heaviest or

most protective. So, choice (B) *boot* shows the right progression from sandal and shoe.

12. **The correct answer is (H).** The items above the line are all elements; those below the line are all compounds. Oxygen and helium are both elements. Atmosphere is a more general term than a simple compound.

13. **The correct answer is (A).** Color, odor, and sound are all properties of matter. Feeling, seeing, and hearing are all sensory means for being affected by the properties of matter.

14. **The correct answer is (G).** Above the line is a part of the human body (*eye*) followed by two of its parts, the *iris* and the *pupil*. Below the line is another part of the human body (*ear*), and two of its parts are the *lobe* and the *canal*, choice (G).

16. **The correct answer is (A).** Count the feet. Above the line: 2, 4, 8. Below the line: 2,

4, and the crab has 8. A fly has 6 legs; an eel, none at all; and a unicorn, 4.

16. **The correct answer is (J).** Above the line are team sports. Below the line are individual sports.

17. **The correct answer is (C).** Above the line are two items (*books* and *periodicals*) that are components of the third item (*library*). Below the line are two items (*fish* and *water*) that are components of an *aquarium*.

18. **The correct answer is (G).** Above the line are types of clouds. Below the line are types of teeth.

19. **The correct answer is (D).** Above the line are types of adjectives. Below the line are types of nouns.

20. **The correct answer is (G).** Above the line are specific types of jungle cats. Below the lines are specific types of marsupials.

Section 5. Verbal Reasoning—Context

1. A	5. D	9. C	13. B	17. A
2. J	6. F	10. G	14. J	18. J
3. B	7. D	11. D	15. B	19. B
4. J	8. G	12. H	16. H	20. J

1. **The correct answer is (A).** Jeffrey definitely plays the violin at least twice a week, on Monday and Friday. Although we know that Jeffrey enjoys both music and dancing, we have no way of knowing if he prefers either of these activities to the study of law. From this paragraph, you cannot tell how often Jeffrey dances.

2. **The correct answer is (J).** Chances are that Debbie did not fail the written exam because she is about to go for an Oral Assessment. Surely the person who failed the first step would not be called for the second. Likewise, we can assume that only people who pass the written exam take the oral exam. Otherwise, both exams could be scheduled in advance. However, we can't know for sure from the

information given. If Debbie were already a Foreign Service officer, she would not need to go for an Oral Assessment. You can assume from this paragraph that Debbie is happy because she passed the exam and is still under consideration for appointment as a Foreign Service officer.

3. **The correct answer is (B).** The only certainty is that something frightened the boys, and they got out in a hurry.

4. **The correct answer is (J).** The only statement that is definitely true among the answer choices is that Daryl took the written driver's test. The passage explicitly states that he "completed the examination process," which includes a written test. There is no indication that Daryl successfully

passed the complete examination process and obtained his license, so choice (F) is incorrect. In addition, there is no indication that he owns the new car he rode home in (choice H) or that he drove home from the Department of Motor Vehicles (choice G).

5. **The correct answer is (D).** Clearly Mark is accident-prone and breaks his right arm easily. His dog is not dangerous; we do not even know if Mark has a sister; he may be learning to use his left hand out of necessity, but we do not know if he is left- or right-handed.

6. **The correct answer is (F).** In this language, the suffix comes before the stem of the word.

   cheki means *ing*
   ruala means *eat*
   duang means *en*
   frit means *hide* or *hid*

7. **The correct answer is (D).** Because the three given English words do not contain common prefixes, suffixes, or stems, you must determine another basis on which to make your translation. All three words contain the central element *ohaka*. Chances are that this element refers to water and that it must appear in the middle of the word *lake* as well. The two words that refer to moving water end in *flis*. Since a pond and lake are both still, *lake* will probably end with *sloo*, as does pond. Creek and pond are basically small versions of river and lake. *Creek* and *pond* both begin with *joki*, which probably means small. So *lura* probably means large. Choice (D) allows you to form a word based on all these assumptions. "Large water still" means lake.

8. **The correct answer is (G).** Pull apart each word, then reassemble the pieces to suit.

   frush means *dis*
   uwamba means *solve* or *solute* as a
      combination form
   kuta means *tion*
   hama means *re*

   If you are alert, all you need do is isolate the prefix meaning *re* and put it in front of the given word for *solution*.

9. **The correct answer is (C).** While all the answers could be correct, only choice (C) must be true. It acknowledges the very definite fact that Lexi's essay is over its word limit.

10. **The correct answer is (G).** While all of the answers could be correct, only choice (G) is definitely true. Having moved to Atlanta, San Diego, and several other cities, Bob has moved more than three times.

11. **The correct answer is (D).** According to the statements, the boys, from shortest to tallest, are Chase, Bud, Rob, Pete, and Garrett. Therefore, Garrett is the tallest.

12. **The correct answer is (H).** The only definitely true statement is that Janice was working last Monday, the day she started her new job, so choice (H) is correct. We don't know if she got the job at Gerringer's department store, choice (F), or that she's excited about where she works, choice (G). We also cannot say for sure if she still has her new job or if she's looking for a new job again, so choice (J) is incorrect.

13. **The correct answer is (B).** Because Amber runs the race in less time than Brittany, she places ahead of Brittany in the race. While the other answer choices could be true, we can't be sure that they must be true.

14. **The correct answer is (J).** All of the answers could be true, but the only facts we know for certain are that Shelly's shift ends at noon and that she eats lunch when her shift ends. Thus, she will not be back after lunch to further assist with the blood drive.

15. **The correct answer is (B).** While any of the statements could be true, the only certain fact is that Melanie, by reading only two books, fell short of completing her assignment to read all three books over spring break.

16. **The correct answer is (H).** Any of the four statements could be true, but the only statement that must be true is that Andrew and Chelsea will be at the Thursday night meet. We know this because they are both members of the Quiz Bowl team, and they attend every meet.

17. The correct answer is (A). Since Art brings Arianna to the Burger Palace, we know that Art, Lee, and Arianna all meet at the Burger Palace. While the other choices could be true, there is not enough information to conclude that they are indeed true.

18. The correct answer is (J). The only fact we know for certain, based on the given statements, is that the narrator's cat snubbed her. The cat always snubs the narrator whenever she smells other cats on the narrator.

19. The correct answer is (B). In order of best math test scores to worst, the girls place as follows: Amanda, Hilary, and Gina. Thus, Gina scores lowest on the test.

20. The correct answer is (J). Shelly's grandparents must have been married for 50 years if their family is throwing them a fiftieth anniversary party. The other statements could be true, but we can't be sure that they must be true.

Section 6. Mathematics

1. D	9. C	17. B	25. D	33. B
2. H	10. H	18. J	26. G	34. J
3. B	11. B	19. D	27. D	35. C
4. G	12. F	20. H	28. H	36. H
5. B	13. D	21. C	29. C	37. B
6. J	14. H	22. F	30. J	38. F
7. A	15. D	23. D	31. C	39. B
8. F	16. G	24. F	32. J	40. H

1. The correct answer is (D). Remember, the hundreds place will not be mentioned if its value is zero.

2. The correct answer is (H). Notice that the 6 is in the ten-thousands place.

3. The correct answer is (B). 1% = 0.01; one-half of 1 percent is written 0.005.

4. The correct answer is (G). One person raised 35% of $690. $690 × 0.35 = $241.50. The remainder raised by the others was $690 − $241.50 = $448.50.

5. The correct answer is (B). The whole pie is 100%. Each part is $\frac{1}{20}$; 100 ÷ 20 = 5%.

6. The correct answer is (J). There are 100,000 centimeters in a kilometer. Each centimeter is $\frac{1}{100,000}$ of a kilometer.

7. The correct answer is (A).

Area = length × width

= 176 ft. × 79 ft.

= 13,904 sq. ft.

8. The correct answer is (F). Mr. Lawson's total income is equal to 7% of his sales plus $250. 7% of his sales is $1250 × 0.07 = $87.50 + $250 = $337.50.

9. The correct answer is (C).

$$3\left(5^2 \times 4\right) - 20 = 3\left(25 \times 4\right) - 20$$
$$= 3(100) - 20$$
$$= 300 - 20$$
$$= 280$$

10. **The correct answer is (H).** The area of a triangle is found by using the formula:

$$A = \frac{1}{2}bh$$

Since the base = 14 and the height = 20,

$$A = \frac{1}{2} \times 14 \times 20$$

$$A = 140 \text{ sq. in.}$$

11. **The correct answer is (B).**

$(8 \times 10^2) + (6 \times 10) + 2 = 862$ and $(5 \times 10^3) + (2 \times 10^2) + (8 \times 10) + 9 = 5289$. So, the sum is 6151.

12. **The correct answer is (F).** The set of factors for 24 is:

$\{1,2,3,4,6,8,12,24\}$

The set of factors for 30 is:

$\{1,2,3,5,6,10,15,30\}$

The set of common factors is: $\{1,2,3,6\}$

13. **The correct answer is (D).** For the length, 29 feet would be represented by 29 units of $\frac{1}{4}$ inch, resulting in $\frac{29}{4}$, or $7\frac{1}{4}$, inches. For the width, 23 feet would be represented by 23 units of $\frac{1}{4}$ inch, resulting in $\frac{23}{4}$, or $5\frac{3}{4}$, inches.

14. **The correct answer is (H).** A scalene triangle has no equal sides.

15. **The correct answer is (D).**

Distance = Rate × Time

$= 55 \text{ mph} \times 5\frac{1}{2} \text{ hours}$

$= 55 \text{ mph} \times 5.5 \text{ hours}$

$= 302.5 \text{ miles}$

16. **The correct answer is (G).** Note that $\frac{17}{30}$ is only slightly larger than $\frac{15}{30}$ or $\frac{1}{2}$. Choices (F), (H), and (J) are much closer in value to 1 than to $\frac{1}{2}$.

17. **The correct answer is (B).** One thousand millimeters equals 1 meter. So, 1 millimeter is $\frac{1}{1000}$ meter.

18. **The correct answer is (J).** If 18 games constituted 40% of the season, the season was $18 \div 0.40$, or 45 games long. If the team won 18 games, it lost $45 - 18$, or 27 games.

19. **The correct answer is (D).** The inequality should be conceptualized as "q is between -2 and -1." Because q must be closer to 0 than -2, it is *larger* than -2.

20. **The correct answer is (H).** If $x = 0$, then $2x < 8$ because $2(0) = 0$, which is less than 8. None of the other pairs results in a true statement.

21. **The correct answer is (C).** The order in which numbers are added does not affect the sum; changing the signs does.

22. **The correct answer is (F).** We want the amount in the parentheses to be equal to 3. The value of x that will make the amount in parentheses equal to 3 is 4.

23. **The correct answer is (D).** An angle that is greater than 90° and less than 180° is an obtuse angle.

24. **The correct answer is (F).** The temperature over the 6 hours graphed was $10° + 20° + 20° + 30° + 20° + 20° = 120° \div 6 = 20°$.

25. **The correct answer is (D).** He will pay back $3500 plus 10% interest. Ten percent of $3500 is $350. $3500 + $350 = $3850.

26. **The correct answer is (G).** $87 \div 3 = 29$, and 29 is less than 30. Choice (F) is incorrect because 4 times 5 is 20, which is not less than 10. Choice (H) is incorrect because 2^5 equals 32, which does not equal 2×5, or 10. Choice (J) is incorrect because $\frac{1}{4}$ is greater than (not less than) $\frac{1}{5}$.

27. **The correct answer is (D).** The sum of the angles of a triangle is 180°. Therefore, $180° - 115° = 65°$.

28. **The correct answer is (H).** Because Distance = Rate × Time, Time = Distance ÷ Rate. Therefore, time $= \frac{1}{20}$ of an hour $=$ 3 minutes. Or, because 60 mph is 1 mile per minute, 20 mph is 1 mile every 3 minutes.

29. The correct answer is (C).

Diameter = 2 × Radius

$$\pi = \frac{22}{7}$$

Circumference = π × Diameter

$$C = \pi \times 21 \times 2$$
$$C = \pi \times 42$$
$$= \frac{22}{7} \times 42$$
$$= 132 \text{ feet}$$

30. The correct answer is (J). The set {x} includes all those numbers larger than –4 and smaller than 2. Considering only whole numbers, this set includes –3, –2, –1, 0, and 1.

31. The correct answer is (C). Careful study of the Venn diagram shows overlap of the circles enclosing rectangles and rhombi, so some rectangles are rhombi as those same rhombi are rectangles. The other statements should read as follows: No trapezoids are parallelograms; all rhombi are parallelograms; and some parallelograms are rectangles, or all rectangles are parallelograms.

32. The correct answer is (J). Each tile is 2 inches wide, so there are 6 tiles per foot. 12 feet × 6 = 72 tiles across each length. Each width equals 4 feet × 6, or 24 tiles. Each corner needs 1 extra tile, so 4 addition tiles are needed.

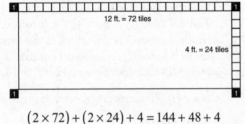

12 ft. = 72 tiles

4 ft. = 24 tiles

$$(2 \times 72) + (2 \times 24) + 4 = 144 + 48 + 4$$
$$= 196$$

Hence, 196 tiles are needed.

33. The correct answer is (B). The number of accidents is irrelevant to the question. *B* deaths occurred in 10 years, so each year, an average of one tenth of *B* deaths occurred.

34. The correct answer is (J). First read to the left along the negative *x*-axis, then read up on the *y*-axis.

35. The correct answer is (C). Because point P has not moved along the x-axis, the x-coordinate is 0. Moving down on the y-axis, point P is located at $-2\frac{1}{2}$.

36. The correct answer is (H). If 2 inches equal 24 feet, 1 inch equals 12 feet. A line representing 72 feet, therefore, must be 6 inches long (72 ÷ 12 = 6).

37. The correct answer is (B). Reduce the $14.00 price by 25%.

25% of $14.00 = $14 × 0.25 = $3.50

$14.00 – $3.50 = $10.50 (new price)

Therefore, (B) is the correct answer. Choice (A) indicates a reduction of only 25 cents. Choice (C) represents a reduction *to* 25% of the original price, or a 75% decrease in price.

38. The correct answer is (F). The area is most easily found by multiplying the length of the figure by its width, and then subtracting the area of the small 3" × 3" square.

(7" × 5") – (3" × 3") = area

35 sq. in. – 9 sq. in. = 26 sq. in.

Shapes such as this are often used for irregular pieces of carpeting or covering.

39. The correct answer is (B). The boy's age is *M* years. His older brother is *M* + 6 years old, and his younger sister is *M* – 4 years old. Adding the three ages together:

$$M + (M + 6) + (M - 4) = 3M + 2$$

40. The correct answer is (H). This problem requires two steps. First, find the smallest number divisible by both 14 and 12 (the least common multiple, or LCM). Second, add the number to 1:00 and rename it as time of day. The LCM of 14 and 12 is 84. Both events will occur simultaneously 84 minutes (1 hour 24 minutes) past 1:00, or 2:24 p.m.

Section 7. Reading and Language Arts

1. C	11. D	21. D	31. C	41. B
2. J	12. J	22. F	32. G	42. J
3. C	13. C	23. C	33. C	43. A
4. G	14. G	24. J	34. H	44. H
5. D	15. C	25. B	35. B	45. D
6. F	16. J	26. F	36. H	46. J
7. D	17. A	27. D	37. A	47. C
8. H	18. G	28. G	38. J	48. J
9. B	19. D	29. D	39. C	49. B
10. H	20. H	30. F	40. G	50. H

1. **The correct answer is (C).** Reverend Cartwright is described throughout the story as someone who is a hard worker and who is very devoted to his church. The passage tells us in paragraph one, for instance, that Reverend Cartwright has spent the entire day working hard on the roof and that he will continue to work until all of the volunteers have left. In the last paragraph, the passage tells us that Reverend Cartwright and his wife always help with the volunteer efforts themselves, doing the actual work when they are not coordinating projects. These descriptions of Reverend Cartwright show that he is very *dedicated* to the church, so choice (C) is correct.

   Choice (A) is incorrect, because nothing in the passage suggests that Reverend Cartwright is particularly *playful*. He is not described as joking or humorous, but as a hard worker who is very positive. Choices (B) and (D) are also incorrect because they express negative qualities, while Reverend Cartwright is described in the story in a very positive manner. He doesn't appear to be *angry* or *frustrated* about the damage to their church, for example; instead, he sees this as a positive opportunity.

2. **The correct answer is (J).** The answer to this question is buried a little bit in the passage, but it is still there. The last paragraph briefly mentions that Reverend Cartwright and his wife "refused to see the burning of their church as a setback." Thus, we know that the church was damaged by a fire, so choice (J) is correct.

3. **The correct answer is (C).** In the opening of the passage, Pearl is described as very tired and weary as she works on the roof. We can infer that she momentarily wishes she had been assigned to the kitchen crew because it is an easier job.

4. **The correct answer is (G).** The barn is described as a makeshift sanctuary. *Sanctuary*, in this case, means a holy place or a place of worship.

5. **The correct answer is (D).** Both the first and last paragraphs make the point that we have been too quick to put into use chemicals and other technological developments before fully understanding their long-range effects.

6. **The correct answer is (F).** The third paragraph discusses this aspect of the problem. Choice (F) is correct in that the author believes that the risks taken by modern science are greater than those taken by earlier scientific efforts because *the effects may be felt by more people for a longer period of time.*

7. **The correct answer is (D).** The author devotes his whole selection to the need for scientists to evaluate the impact of new products on the environment.

8. **The correct answer is (H).** In paragraph three, we are told that Felix is a "nutrition author," which means that she has written works on the subject of nutrition. Choice (H) is correct.

    Choices (F), (G), and (J) are incorrect, because each makes statements about Clara Felix that are not supported by the passage. The passage never tells us that Felix has conducted experiments on fats, that she is a medical doctor, or that she has a degree in biology. We cannot draw these conclusions without specific information from the passage, so each of these choices can be eliminated.

9. **The correct answer is (B).** The author tells us in paragraph two of the article that both omega-3 and omega-6 fats are essential for our health, so choice (C) is incorrect. We are then told, in the next paragraph, that "Americans tend to get plenty of omega-6 oils in their diets already." Therefore, choice (B) is correct.

10. **The correct answer is (H).** The second and third paragraphs of the passage, in particular, focus on the need for more omega-3 fats in the diet and which foods are good sources for omega-3 fats. Choice (J) is incorrect, because although the first two paragraphs mention the overall needs for fats in the diet, the passage deals specifically with reducing omega-6 and increasing omega-3, making this answer too general .

11. **The correct answer is (D).** The first paragraph states that we should restrict our intake of fats to 30 percent of the total number of calories we consume every day.

12. **The correct answer is (J).** Olive oil, walnuts, and sardines are three of the foods specifically mentioned in the last paragraph as good sources of omega-3 fats. Choice (H) is incorrect, because although salads in general are considered good for health, the passage does not say that they are good sources of omega-3 fats. Choices (F) and (G) are incorrect because the passage specifically states we should limit our consumption of salad dressing, margarine, bread, and other baked goods.

13. **The correct answer is (C).** The second paragraph tells us that though the expedition was successful in placing 6 climbers at the summit of Mount Everest, it had to overcome many challenges and setbacks. The next two paragraphs describe those challenges and their effect on the climbers.

14. **The correct answer is (G).** The third paragraph states that two Canadians and four Sherpas made it to the top of Mount Everest. Choice (H) is incorrect, as it refers to the total number of climbers who made it to the top, including both Canadians and Sherpas.

15. **The correct answer is (C).** The second paragraph states that this was the first Canadian expedition to Mount Everest, making choice (C) the correct answer. Choice (D) is incorrect, because the passage does not give us any information on whether this was the last expedition that Amatt led up Mount Everest.

16. **The correct answer is (J).** The last paragraph mentions that the expedition inspired Amatt's team to approach their challenges with clarity and humbleness, so choice (J) is the correct answer. Choice (F) is incorrect, because indifference would indicate that the team did not care about the accidents. Choice (G) is incorrect, because humbleness is the opposite of pride.

17. **The correct answer is (A).** The "it" refers back to the second sentence of the paragraph, which cites the experience of loss that Amatt and his team encountered. The noun "experience" is singular, so it agrees with the singular pronoun "it." Choice (B) is incorrect because the noun "experiences" in the first sentence is plural, and it would not use the singular pronoun "it."

18. **The correct answer is (G).** Check paragraph five to find this information. The article does not say the chair holds the

user in a standing position, so choice (F) is incorrect. All wheelchairs have at least one set of large wheels, so choice (J) is incorrect. Choice (H) is also incorrect, because if the chair climbs stairs, it could definitely leap a curb.

19. **The correct answer is (D).** The quote by Dean Kamen in paragraph two states his belief in the importance of education.

20. **The correct answer is (H).** Paragraph four, sentence two states, "When he [Kamen] discovers something the world needs, he does his best to create it."

21. **The correct answer is (D).** Paragraph four lists the items invented by Kamen. This list rules out each answer except choice (D), robotic athlete.

22. **The correct answer is (F).** The main purpose of this passage is to provide readers with a closer look at potlatching, a traditional custom practiced among the indigenous people of Pacific Northwest Canada and the United States. The title that best captures this notion is choice (F), A Closer Look at a Traditional Custom.

23. **The correct answer is (C).** The passage mentions that a potlatching ceremony would traditionally take place to commemorate "weddings, adoptions, births, deaths, and transfers of power and leadership." Therefore, among the answer choices, the capture of a wild animal threatening people's safety, choice (C), would most likely *not* be a reason to have a potlatching ceremony.

24. **The correct answer is (J).** According to the passage, among the types of items typically given as gifts during a potlatch ceremony are "ornamental metals, animal skins, blankets, food, and canoes." The only item among the answer choices that isn't mentioned is an ornate hunting spear, choice (J). There's no information provided regarding whether or not a weapon would be an appropriate gift.

25. **The correct answer is (B).** The fourth paragraph of the passage discusses the criminalization of potlatching in the late 19th century, along with the theory that "Some saw the criminalization of indigenous traditions as a conscious push towards assimilation." Therefore, choice (B) is correct.

26. **The correct answer is (F).** Carbon dating, the most recently developed method for determining the age of archeological finds and the most scientific, is not mentioned in this article.

27. **The correct answer is (D).** The second paragraph suggests that man used tools for a lot longer than only 2,000,000 years.

28. **The correct answer is (G).** This is stated toward the end of the last paragraph. The Somme River is in France, and it is there that the British investigators went to check the French deposits.

29. **The correct answer is (D).** The 1840s are in the early to mid-nineteenth century.

30. **The correct answer is (F).** The correct answer to a "main idea" question will always summarize the main idea that the author was trying to get across in writing the passage. In this case, the author starts the passage by telling us of the importance of Perceval's contributions to King Arthur's court. Then, he explains Perceval's story and states that in some versions of the story, Perceval was awarded the position of guardian of the Holy Grail. Choice (F) is therefore correct.

Choice (G) is incorrect, because the passage does not focus mainly on how little credit Perceval received but instead describes his accomplishments. Choice (H) is incorrect because it is too broad, and choice (J) is incorrect because it is too narrow to reflect the main idea.

31. **The correct answer is (C).** McElhearn is mentioned in paragraph two of the passage. Here we are told that McElhearn is an author and a translator and that he specializes in the Perceval literature. Choice (C) is therefore correct.

Choices (A), (B), and (D) bring up information that is not stated in the passage. The passage never mentions that McElhearn has translated the works of Chrétien de Troyes or the Arthurian legends. In addition, although McElhearn does seem knowledgeable about Chrétien de Troyes, we are never told that McElhearn has published a book regarding him.

32. **The correct answer is (G).** The answer to this question can be found in the third paragraph of the passage, which explains that Perceval's mother kept him sheltered because she wished to protect him. Perceval's mother did not want to lose her only remaining son, so she kept him from learning about the aspects of war. Choice (G) is therefore correct.

33. **The correct answer is (C).** To answer this vocabulary question, it is helpful to look for clues in the sentence and the paragraph around it that might help you to understand the meaning of the word *obscure*. The second sentence of paragraph one tells us that Perceval is *obscure* compared to other famous characters such as Lancelot or Galahad. Lancelot and Galahad are knights that many people know about. Perceval is being compared to them, and the sentence gives us the sense that Perceval doesn't quite measure up.

The sentence prior to this one also tells us that Perceval hasn't been given much credit for his accomplishments—in other words, people don't recognize him for what he achieved. This must mean that Perceval is not very famous, like Lancelot and Galahad are. The clues from the sentence and the paragraph suggest that the word *obscure* must mean the opposite of "famous," so choice (C) is correct.

34. **The correct answer is (H).** The last paragraph of the passage states that Chrétien de Troyes died before completing the story of Perceval, so choice (H) is the correct answer. We know from the second paragraph that he died in the 1180s, making choice (F) incorrect. Choice (J) is incorrect because the passage does not address how well known his work was before it was translated.

35. **The correct answer is (B).** The first paragraph speaks of the perils of fishing; the second speaks about its rewards.

36. **The correct answer is (H).** The middle of the first paragraph discusses the problems created by rough seas. None of the other choices is mentioned as a difficulty.

37. **The correct answer is (A).** In the middle of the second paragraph, we learn that when fishermen note that herring are entering the nets, they sit in quiet excitement so as not to frighten the fish away. They row along the net earlier in order to find out if the net is filling and haul in the nets later, when they are full.

38. **The correct answer is (J).** This phrase represents a powerful metaphor. Picture huge waves rising over empty space and crashing down upon fishermen and boats.

39. **The correct answer is (C).** All the other choices include at least one trait that is not ascribed to these fishermen.

40. **The correct answer is (G).** One might add honesty to the traits of the fishermen. Theft is not mentioned as a problem. If you had forgotten about the whales, reread the first sentence.

41. **The correct answer is (B).** Consider that this answer is practically a "gift." Because the second sentence begins with the word *first,* it is obvious that the sentence that is about to offer *three good reasons* will be the topic sentence. If choice (B) were not offered, choice (A) might well have served as a topic sentence, but choice (B) is clearly better. Choices (C) and (D) are quite obviously development sentences.

42. **The correct answer is (F).** The subordinate sentences in the paragraph are steps in a recipe. We are told that a "beverage" is being made, one that uses apples; therefore, choice (F) would be an appropriate topic sentence here. The paragraph isn't about getting enough fluids, choice (G), the popularity of apples, choice (H), or how to make an apple pie, choice (J).

43. **The correct answer is (A).** The first development sentence is practically a restatement of the topic sentence. If opinions play a major role in important areas in our lives, obviously they should not be taken lightly. Choice (B) is clearly a development

sentence; choice (C) could not possibly serve as a topic sentence because its subject is "they," which has no reference; choice (D) contradicts the paragraph; and choice (E) might be a development sentence or might even belong in the next paragraph.

44. **The correct answer is (H).** The first sentence tells us that homelessness presents a difficult problem. Develop the paragraph by describing the extent and causes of the problem. Choice (F) is a statement of opinion that does not really address the problem. Choice (G) digresses into a narrow aspect of homelessness—hunger; it might appear later in the paragraph or in another paragraph of the same article. Choice (J) is totally irrelevant.

45. **The correct answer is (D).** This is the only choice that directly addresses the notion that housing costs are rising in urban areas, which is a key component of the main topic sentence.

46. **The correct answer is (J).** Note that the topic sentence speaks of the *condition* of the tires. Only choice (J) follows that theme.

47. **The correct answer is (C).** The main point of this paragraph is the emergence of a new flexible mobile phone technology. Although choice (C) is an interesting statistic regarding mobile phones, it is the only choice that does not directly address this new technology.

48. **The correct answer is (J).** The second sentence tells of one use for which the open-end wrench is not intended. Choice (J) tells of additional unintended use. Choices (F) and (G) address the length of the wrench rather than the opening of its jaws. Choice (H) logically follows the last sentence of the paragraph.

49. **The correct answer is (B).** The sentence following the underline contains a key context clue for determining the correct sentence to fill the blank space. The phrase "these crystals" indicates that this subject is brought up earlier in the paragraph. Since there's no mention of the crystals in the existing sentences, the sentence that fits in this underline must introduce them; therefore, choice (B) is correct.

50. **The correct answer is (H).** In a paragraph about the use of cowries as money, an explanation of exactly what a cowrie is should be offered as early as possible.

SCORE SHEET

CTB/McGraw-Hill will score your actual exam and send your scaled scores and your percentile scores directly to the schools you indicated. Scaled scores are scores converted by a special formula to make comparable your performance on tests of unequal lengths and unequal importance. Percentile scores compare your performance on each test and the whole exam with the performance of other students who took the same exam at the same time. Your scores will not be reported either as raw scores—that is, number correct—nor as percents. Right now, however, you will find it very useful to convert your own scores on the practice exam into simple percentages. In this way you can compare your own performance on each test of the exam with your performance on each other test. You can then focus your study where it will do you the most good.

Subject	No. Correct ÷ No. of Questions	× 100 = _____ %
Sequences	_____ ÷ 20 =	_____ × 100 = _____ %
Analogies	_____ ÷ 20 =	_____ × 100 = _____ %
Quantitative Reasoning	_____ ÷ 20 =	_____ × 100 = _____ %
Verbal Reasoning—Words	_____ ÷ 12 =	_____ × 100 = _____ %
Verbal Reasoning—Context	_____ ÷ 20 =	_____ × 100 = _____ %
Mathematics	_____ ÷ 40 =	_____ × 100 = _____ %
Reading and Language Arts	_____ ÷ 50 =	_____ × 100 = _____ %
TOTAL EXAM	_____ ÷ 182 =	_____ × 100 = _____ %

ANSWER SHEET PRACTICE TEST 4: COOP

Section 1. Sequences

1. Ⓐ Ⓑ Ⓒ Ⓓ   5. Ⓐ Ⓑ Ⓒ Ⓓ   9. Ⓐ Ⓑ Ⓒ Ⓓ   13. Ⓐ Ⓑ Ⓒ Ⓓ   17. Ⓐ Ⓑ Ⓒ Ⓓ
2. Ⓕ Ⓖ Ⓗ Ⓙ   6. Ⓕ Ⓖ Ⓗ Ⓙ   10. Ⓕ Ⓖ Ⓗ Ⓙ   14. Ⓕ Ⓖ Ⓗ Ⓙ   18. Ⓕ Ⓖ Ⓗ Ⓙ
3. Ⓐ Ⓑ Ⓒ Ⓓ   7. Ⓐ Ⓑ Ⓒ Ⓓ   11. Ⓐ Ⓑ Ⓒ Ⓓ   15. Ⓐ Ⓑ Ⓒ Ⓓ   19. Ⓐ Ⓑ Ⓒ Ⓓ
4. Ⓕ Ⓖ Ⓗ Ⓙ   8. Ⓕ Ⓖ Ⓗ Ⓙ   12. Ⓕ Ⓖ Ⓗ Ⓙ   16. Ⓕ Ⓖ Ⓗ Ⓙ   20. Ⓕ Ⓖ Ⓗ Ⓙ

Section 2. Analogies

1. Ⓐ Ⓑ Ⓒ Ⓓ   5. Ⓐ Ⓑ Ⓒ Ⓓ   9. Ⓐ Ⓑ Ⓒ Ⓓ   13. Ⓐ Ⓑ Ⓒ Ⓓ   17. Ⓐ Ⓑ Ⓒ Ⓓ
2. Ⓕ Ⓖ Ⓗ Ⓙ   6. Ⓕ Ⓖ Ⓗ Ⓙ   10. Ⓕ Ⓖ Ⓗ Ⓙ   14. Ⓕ Ⓖ Ⓗ Ⓙ   18. Ⓕ Ⓖ Ⓗ Ⓙ
3. Ⓐ Ⓑ Ⓒ Ⓓ   7. Ⓐ Ⓑ Ⓒ Ⓓ   11. Ⓐ Ⓑ Ⓒ Ⓓ   15. Ⓐ Ⓑ Ⓒ Ⓓ   19. Ⓐ Ⓑ Ⓒ Ⓓ
4. Ⓕ Ⓖ Ⓗ Ⓙ   8. Ⓕ Ⓖ Ⓗ Ⓙ   12. Ⓕ Ⓖ Ⓗ Ⓙ   16. Ⓕ Ⓖ Ⓗ Ⓙ   20. Ⓕ Ⓖ Ⓗ Ⓙ

Section 3. Quantitative Reasoning

1. Ⓐ Ⓑ Ⓒ Ⓓ   5. Ⓐ Ⓑ Ⓒ Ⓓ   9. Ⓐ Ⓑ Ⓒ Ⓓ   13. Ⓐ Ⓑ Ⓒ Ⓓ   17. Ⓐ Ⓑ Ⓒ Ⓓ
2. Ⓕ Ⓖ Ⓗ Ⓙ   6. Ⓕ Ⓖ Ⓗ Ⓙ   10. Ⓕ Ⓖ Ⓗ Ⓙ   14. Ⓕ Ⓖ Ⓗ Ⓙ   18. Ⓕ Ⓖ Ⓗ Ⓙ
3. Ⓐ Ⓑ Ⓒ Ⓓ   7. Ⓐ Ⓑ Ⓒ Ⓓ   11. Ⓐ Ⓑ Ⓒ Ⓓ   15. Ⓐ Ⓑ Ⓒ Ⓓ   19. Ⓐ Ⓑ Ⓒ Ⓓ
4. Ⓕ Ⓖ Ⓗ Ⓙ   8. Ⓕ Ⓖ Ⓗ Ⓙ   12. Ⓕ Ⓖ Ⓗ Ⓙ   16. Ⓕ Ⓖ Ⓗ Ⓙ   20. Ⓕ Ⓖ Ⓗ Ⓙ

Section 4. Verbal Reasoning—Words

1. Ⓐ Ⓑ Ⓒ Ⓓ   4. Ⓐ Ⓑ Ⓒ Ⓓ   7. Ⓐ Ⓑ Ⓒ Ⓓ   9. Ⓐ Ⓑ Ⓒ Ⓓ   11. Ⓐ Ⓑ Ⓒ Ⓓ
2. Ⓕ Ⓖ Ⓗ Ⓙ   5. Ⓕ Ⓖ Ⓗ Ⓙ   8. Ⓕ Ⓖ Ⓗ Ⓙ   10. Ⓕ Ⓖ Ⓗ Ⓙ   12. Ⓕ Ⓖ Ⓗ Ⓙ
3. Ⓐ Ⓑ Ⓒ Ⓓ   6. Ⓐ Ⓑ Ⓒ Ⓓ

Section 5. Verbal Reasoning—Context

1. Ⓐ Ⓑ Ⓒ Ⓓ   5. Ⓐ Ⓑ Ⓒ Ⓓ   9. Ⓐ Ⓑ Ⓒ Ⓓ   13. Ⓐ Ⓑ Ⓒ Ⓓ   17. Ⓐ Ⓑ Ⓒ Ⓓ
2. Ⓕ Ⓖ Ⓗ Ⓙ   6. Ⓕ Ⓖ Ⓗ Ⓙ   10. Ⓕ Ⓖ Ⓗ Ⓙ   14. Ⓕ Ⓖ Ⓗ Ⓙ   18. Ⓕ Ⓖ Ⓗ Ⓙ
3. Ⓐ Ⓑ Ⓒ Ⓓ   7. Ⓐ Ⓑ Ⓒ Ⓓ   11. Ⓐ Ⓑ Ⓒ Ⓓ   15. Ⓐ Ⓑ Ⓒ Ⓓ   19. Ⓐ Ⓑ Ⓒ Ⓓ
4. Ⓕ Ⓖ Ⓗ Ⓙ   8. Ⓕ Ⓖ Ⓗ Ⓙ   12. Ⓕ Ⓖ Ⓗ Ⓙ   16. Ⓕ Ⓖ Ⓗ Ⓙ   20. Ⓕ Ⓖ Ⓗ Ⓙ

answer sheet

Section 6. Mathematics

1. Ⓐ Ⓑ Ⓒ Ⓓ	9. Ⓐ Ⓑ Ⓒ Ⓓ	17. Ⓐ Ⓑ Ⓒ Ⓓ	25. Ⓐ Ⓑ Ⓒ Ⓓ	33. Ⓐ Ⓑ Ⓒ Ⓓ
2. Ⓕ Ⓖ Ⓗ Ⓙ	10. Ⓕ Ⓖ Ⓗ Ⓙ	18. Ⓕ Ⓖ Ⓗ Ⓙ	26. Ⓕ Ⓖ Ⓗ Ⓙ	34. Ⓕ Ⓖ Ⓗ Ⓙ
3. Ⓐ Ⓑ Ⓒ Ⓓ	11. Ⓐ Ⓑ Ⓒ Ⓓ	19. Ⓐ Ⓑ Ⓒ Ⓓ	27. Ⓐ Ⓑ Ⓒ Ⓓ	35. Ⓐ Ⓑ Ⓒ Ⓓ
4. Ⓕ Ⓖ Ⓗ Ⓙ	12. Ⓕ Ⓖ Ⓗ Ⓙ	20. Ⓕ Ⓖ Ⓗ Ⓙ	28. Ⓕ Ⓖ Ⓗ Ⓙ	36. Ⓕ Ⓖ Ⓗ Ⓙ
5. Ⓐ Ⓑ Ⓒ Ⓓ	13. Ⓐ Ⓑ Ⓒ Ⓓ	21. Ⓐ Ⓑ Ⓒ Ⓓ	29. Ⓐ Ⓑ Ⓒ Ⓓ	37. Ⓐ Ⓑ Ⓒ Ⓓ
6. Ⓕ Ⓖ Ⓗ Ⓙ	14. Ⓕ Ⓖ Ⓗ Ⓙ	22. Ⓕ Ⓖ Ⓗ Ⓙ	30. Ⓕ Ⓖ Ⓗ Ⓙ	38. Ⓕ Ⓖ Ⓗ Ⓙ
7. Ⓐ Ⓑ Ⓒ Ⓓ	15. Ⓐ Ⓑ Ⓒ Ⓓ	23. Ⓐ Ⓑ Ⓒ Ⓓ	31. Ⓐ Ⓑ Ⓒ Ⓓ	39. Ⓐ Ⓑ Ⓒ Ⓓ
8. Ⓕ Ⓖ Ⓗ Ⓙ	16. Ⓕ Ⓖ Ⓗ Ⓙ	24. Ⓕ Ⓖ Ⓗ Ⓙ	32. Ⓕ Ⓖ Ⓗ Ⓙ	40. Ⓕ Ⓖ Ⓗ Ⓙ

Section 7. Reading and Language Arts

1. Ⓐ Ⓑ Ⓒ Ⓓ	11. Ⓐ Ⓑ Ⓒ Ⓓ	21. Ⓐ Ⓑ Ⓒ Ⓓ	31. Ⓐ Ⓑ Ⓒ Ⓓ	41. Ⓐ Ⓑ Ⓒ Ⓓ
2. Ⓕ Ⓖ Ⓗ Ⓙ	12. Ⓕ Ⓖ Ⓗ Ⓙ	22. Ⓕ Ⓖ Ⓗ Ⓙ	32. Ⓕ Ⓖ Ⓗ Ⓙ	42. Ⓕ Ⓖ Ⓗ Ⓙ
3. Ⓐ Ⓑ Ⓒ Ⓓ	13. Ⓐ Ⓑ Ⓒ Ⓓ	23. Ⓐ Ⓑ Ⓒ Ⓓ	33. Ⓐ Ⓑ Ⓒ Ⓓ	43. Ⓐ Ⓑ Ⓒ Ⓓ
4. Ⓕ Ⓖ Ⓗ Ⓙ	14. Ⓕ Ⓖ Ⓗ Ⓙ	24. Ⓕ Ⓖ Ⓗ Ⓙ	34. Ⓕ Ⓖ Ⓗ Ⓙ	44. Ⓕ Ⓖ Ⓗ Ⓙ
5. Ⓐ Ⓑ Ⓒ Ⓓ	15. Ⓐ Ⓑ Ⓒ Ⓓ	25. Ⓐ Ⓑ Ⓒ Ⓓ	35. Ⓐ Ⓑ Ⓒ Ⓓ	45. Ⓐ Ⓑ Ⓒ Ⓓ
6. Ⓕ Ⓖ Ⓗ Ⓙ	16. Ⓕ Ⓖ Ⓗ Ⓙ	26. Ⓕ Ⓖ Ⓗ Ⓙ	36. Ⓕ Ⓖ Ⓗ Ⓙ	46. Ⓕ Ⓖ Ⓗ Ⓙ
7. Ⓐ Ⓑ Ⓒ Ⓓ	17. Ⓐ Ⓑ Ⓒ Ⓓ	27. Ⓐ Ⓑ Ⓒ Ⓓ	37. Ⓐ Ⓑ Ⓒ Ⓓ	47. Ⓐ Ⓑ Ⓒ Ⓓ
8. Ⓕ Ⓖ Ⓗ Ⓙ	18. Ⓕ Ⓖ Ⓗ Ⓙ	28. Ⓕ Ⓖ Ⓗ Ⓙ	38. Ⓕ Ⓖ Ⓗ Ⓙ	48. Ⓕ Ⓖ Ⓗ Ⓙ
9. Ⓐ Ⓑ Ⓒ Ⓓ	19. Ⓐ Ⓑ Ⓒ Ⓓ	29. Ⓐ Ⓑ Ⓒ Ⓓ	39. Ⓐ Ⓑ Ⓒ Ⓓ	49. Ⓐ Ⓑ Ⓒ Ⓓ
10. Ⓕ Ⓖ Ⓗ Ⓙ	20. Ⓕ Ⓖ Ⓗ Ⓙ	30. Ⓕ Ⓖ Ⓗ Ⓙ	40. Ⓕ Ⓖ Ⓗ Ⓙ	50. Ⓕ Ⓖ Ⓗ Ⓙ

Practice Test 4: COOP

SECTION 1. SEQUENCES

15 Minutes

Directions: For questions 1–20, choose the part that would continue the pattern or sequence. Mark the letter of your answer on the answer sheet.

1.

(A) (B) (C) (D)

2.

(F) (G) (H) (J)

3.

(A) (B) (C) (D)

4.

(F) (G) (H) (J)

5.

(A) (B) (C) (D)

6.

(F)   (G)   (H)   (J)

7. 44 39 35 | 87 82 78 | 61 56 _____
   (A) 53
   (B) 52
   (C) 50
   (D) 48

8. 3 6 3 | 12 24 12 | 9 _____ 9
   (F) 18
   (G) 3
   (H) 6
   (J) 27

9. 4 6 18 | 4 7 21 | _____ 2 6
   (A) 14
   (B) 12
   (C) 4
   (D) 2

10. 75 25 8.$\overline{3}$ | 90 30 10 | _____ 7 2.3
    (F) 23
    (G) 21
    (H) 30
    (J) 15

11. 23 41 41 | 7 25 25 | 41 _____ 59
    (A) 23
    (B) 25
    (C) 59
    (D) 41

12. 5 9 13 | 9 17 25 | 17 29 _____
    (F) 16
    (G) 10
    (H) 12
    (J) 32

13. 100 80 90 | 60 40 50 | 80 _____ 70
    (A) 60
    (B) 90
    (C) 50
    (D) 100

14. $R_1S_2T^3$ | $R^3S_1T_2$ | $R_2S^3T_1$ | _____ $R^3S_1T_2$
    (F) $R^1S_2T_3$
    (G) $R^3S_2T_1$
    (H) $R_3S_1T^2$
    (J) $R_1S_2T^3$

15. $W^2X^4Z_6$ | $W^4X^6Z_{10}$ | $W^7X^2Z_9$ | _____
    (A) $W^9X^7Z^{16}$
    (B) $W^9X^5Z_{14}$
    (C) $W_6X_1Z^7$
    (D) $W^2X^5Z_{10}$

16. $L^5M^5N_4$ | $L^5M_4N_4$ | $L_4M_4N_4$ | _____ $L_4M^3N^3$
    (F) $L_4M_4N^3$
    (G) $L^5M_4N^3$
    (H) $L^5M^5N^5$
    (J) $L_4M^5N_3$

17. ABC FED GHI LKJ _____
- **(A)** ONM
- **(B)** NOP
- **(C)** MNO
- **(D)** MON

18. ABDB ACEB ADFB _____ AFHB
- **(F)** ADGB
- **(G)** AEGB
- **(H)** AFGB
- **(J)** ACGB

19. ABC EFG IJK _____
- **(A)** PQR
- **(B)** UVW
- **(C)** STU
- **(D)** OMN

20. ZYWX VUST RQOP _____ JIGH
- **(F)** MNKL
- **(G)** LKMN
- **(H)** NMKL
- **(J)** NMLK

STOP If you finish before time is up, check over your work on Section 1 only. Do not go on until the signal is given.

practice test

SECTION 2. ANALOGIES

7 Minutes

Directions: For questions 1–20, choose the picture that should go in the empty box so that the bottom two pictures are related in the same way that the top two are related.

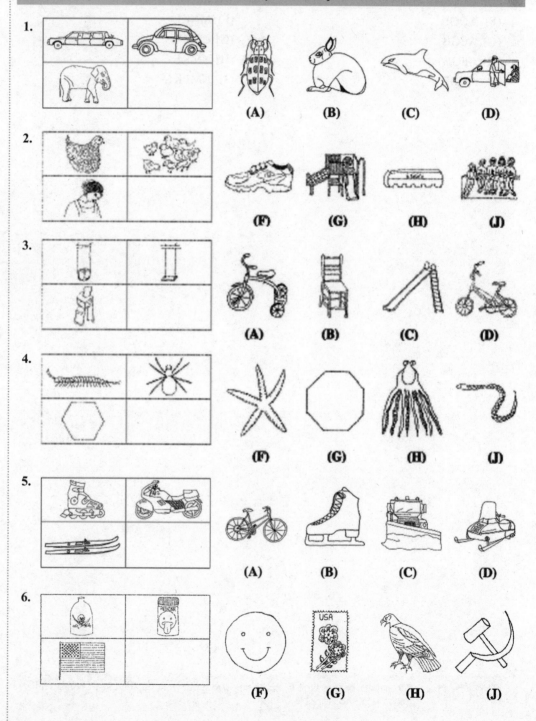

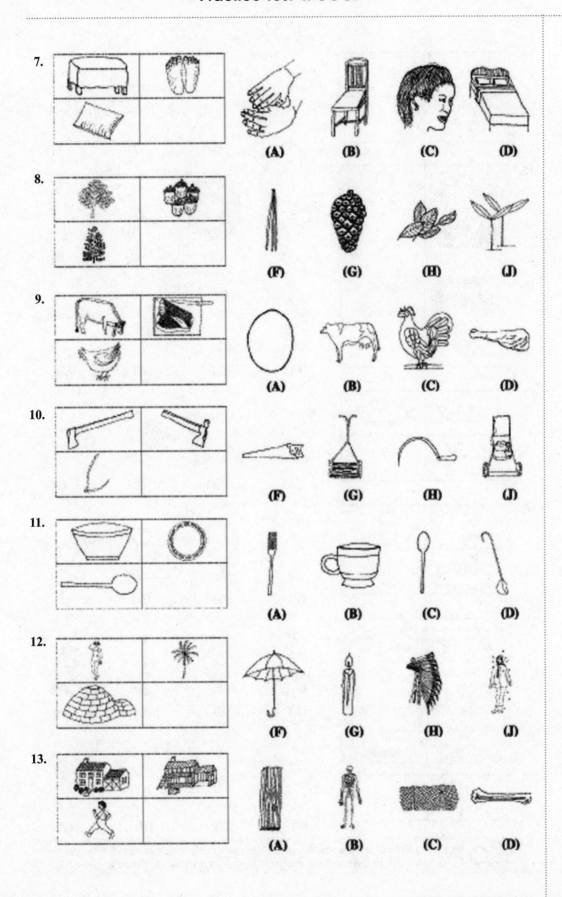

practice test

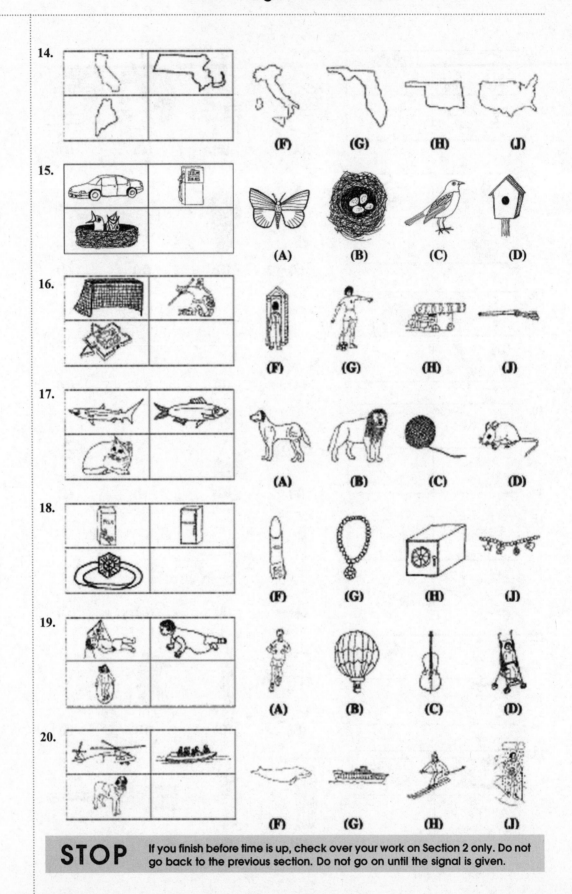

14.

(F)   (G)   (H)   (J)

15.

(A)   (B)   (C)   (D)

16.

(F)   (G)   (H)   (J)

17.

(A)   (B)   (C)   (D)

18.

(F)   (G)   (H)   (J)

19.

(A)   (B)   (C)   (D)

20.

(F)   (G)   (H)   (J)

STOP   If you finish before time is up, check over your work on Section 2 only. Do not go back to the previous section. Do not go on until the signal is given.

SECTION 3. QUANTITATIVE REASONING

5 Minutes

Directions: For questions 1–6, find the relationship of the numbers in one column to the numbers in the other column. Then find the missing number.

1.
$$2 \rightarrow \boxed{} \rightarrow 6$$
$$3 \rightarrow \boxed{} \rightarrow 7$$
$$5 \rightarrow \boxed{} \rightarrow ?$$

9	11	13	15
(A)	(B)	(C)	(D)

2.
$$43 \rightarrow \boxed{} \rightarrow 38$$
$$34 \rightarrow \boxed{} \rightarrow 29$$
$$28 \rightarrow \boxed{} \rightarrow ?$$

29	27	23	22
(F)	(G)	(H)	(J)

3.
$$30 \rightarrow \boxed{} \rightarrow 27$$
$$20 \rightarrow \boxed{} \rightarrow 17$$
$$10 \rightarrow \boxed{} \rightarrow ?$$

3	7	10	13
(A)	(B)	(C)	(D)

4.
$$8 \rightarrow \boxed{} \rightarrow 6$$
$$5 \rightarrow \boxed{} \rightarrow 3$$
$$3 \rightarrow \boxed{} \rightarrow ?$$

1	2	3	4
(F)	(G)	(H)	(J)

5.
$$2 \rightarrow \boxed{} \rightarrow 4$$
$$5 \rightarrow \boxed{} \rightarrow 10$$
$$9 \rightarrow \boxed{} \rightarrow ?$$

16	17	18	19
(A)	(B)	(C)	(D)

6.
$$42 \rightarrow \boxed{} \rightarrow 6$$
$$84 \rightarrow \boxed{} \rightarrow 29$$
$$105 \rightarrow \boxed{} \rightarrow ?$$

15	18	33	69
(F)	(G)	(H)	(J)

Directions: For questions 7–13, find the fraction of the grid that is shaded.

7.

    $\frac{1}{2}$ $\frac{1}{3}$ $\frac{1}{4}$ $\frac{1}{5}$
    (A)   (B)   (C)   (D)

8.

    $\frac{2}{3}$ $\frac{5}{12}$ $\frac{2}{5}$ $\frac{1}{3}$
    (F)   (G)   (H)   (J)

9.

    $\frac{1}{2}$ $\frac{1}{3}$ $\frac{1}{4}$ $\frac{1}{5}$
    (A)   (B)   (C)   (D)

10.

    $\frac{5}{9}$ $\frac{1}{2}$ $\frac{5}{6}$ $\frac{4}{9}$
    (F)   (G)   (H)   (J)

11.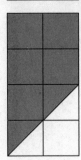

    $\frac{4}{5}$ $\frac{3}{4}$ $\frac{2}{3}$ $\frac{1}{2}$
    (A)   (B)   (C)   (D)

12.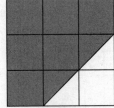

$\dfrac{7}{9}$ $\dfrac{5}{6}$ $\dfrac{1}{3}$ $\dfrac{2}{9}$

(F) (G) (H) (J)

13.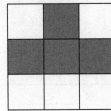

$\dfrac{1}{2}$ $\dfrac{1}{3}$ $\dfrac{1}{4}$ $\dfrac{4}{9}$

(A) (B) (C) (D)

practice test

Directions: For questions 14–20, look at the scale showing sets of shapes of equal weight. Find an equivalent pair of sets that would also balance the scale.

14.

(F)

(G)

(H)

(J)

15.

(A)

(B)

(C)

(D)

16.

(F)

(G)

(H)

(J)

17.

(A)

(B)

(C)

(D)

18.

(F)

(G)

(H)

(J)

19.

(A)

(B)

(C)

(D)

20.

(F)

(G)

(H)

(J)

STOP If you finish before time is up, check over your work on Section 3 only. Do not go back to the previous sections. Do not go on until the signal is given.

practice test

SECTION 4. VERBAL REASONING—WORDS

15 Minutes

Directions: For questions 1–10, find the word that names a necessary part of the underlined word.

1. cartoon
   - **(A)** humor
   - **(B)** animation
   - **(C)** drawing
   - **(D)** message

2. heroine
   - **(F)** hero
   - **(G)** woman
   - **(H)** crisis
   - **(J)** victim

3. music
   - **(A)** sound
   - **(B)** voice
   - **(C)** instruments
   - **(D)** hearing

4. lantern
   - **(F)** light
   - **(G)** glass
   - **(H)** handle
   - **(J)** fuel

5. data
   - **(A)** numbers
   - **(B)** information
   - **(C)** charts
   - **(D)** words

6. biography
   - **(F)** facts
   - **(G)** book
   - **(H)** life
   - **(J)** fame

7. table
   - **(A)** surface
   - **(B)** legs
   - **(C)** chair
   - **(D)** meal

8. student
   - **(F)** assignment
   - **(G)** grade
   - **(H)** books
   - **(J)** teacher

9. inch
   - **(A)** yard
   - **(B)** ruler
   - **(C)** measure
   - **(D)** height

10. patriotism
    - **(F)** nation
    - **(G)** flag
    - **(H)** anthem
    - **(J)** leader

Directions: In questions 11–20, the words in the top row are related in some way. The words in the bottom row are related in the same way. For each item, find the word that completes the bottom row of words.

11. red   yellow   blue
    orange   green

    (A) turquoise
    (B) aqua
    (C) violet
    (D) gray

12. wind   water   sun
    coal   gas

    (F) uranium
    (G) fission
    (H) wood
    (J) oil

13. Monday   Thursday   week
    branches   leaves

    (A) nature
    (B) tree
    (C) parks
    (D) organic

14. saturated   wet   damp
    doctorate   master's

    (F) nurse
    (G) baccalaureate
    (H) mistress
    (J) hospital

15. apple   tomato   watermelon
    plum   mango

    (A) pear
    (B) cherry
    (C) strawberry
    (D) papaya

16. toe   foot   ankle
    finger   hand

    (F) leg
    (G) nail
    (H) arm
    (J) wrist

17. infancy   adolescence   adulthood
    kindergarten   high   school

    (A) college
    (B) student
    (C) learning
    (D) education

18. sight   smell   hearing
    index   thumb

    (F) hand
    (G) pinky
    (H) touch
    (J) pinch

19. skates   sticks   pads
    racket   balls

    (A) net
    (B) sports
    (C) tennis
    (D) serve

20. speak   eat   laugh
    walk   run

    (F) see
    (G) hear
    (H) lick
    (J) dance

STOP If you finish before time is up, check over your work on Section 4 only. Do not go back to the previous sections. Do not go on until the signal is given.

SECTION 5. VERBAL REASONING—CONTEXT

15 Minutes

Directions: For questions 1–5, find the statement that is true according to the given information.

1. Bob walked into the convenience store and requested a package of cigarettes. The clerk asked Bob some questions. Bob left the store without cigarettes.

    (A) Bob is too young to purchase cigarettes in this state.

    (B) The store does not carry the brand that Bob prefers.

    (C) Bob did not have enough money with him.

    (D) The clerk did not sell cigarettes to Bob.

2. Tara purchased an airplane ticket for a vacation trip to Bermuda. The airplane crashed at takeoff. Tara's name was not among the list of injured passengers.

    (F) Tara missed the flight and was not on the airplane.

    (G) Tara survived the crash.

    (H) Tara was not injured.

    (J) Tara never got to Bermuda.

3. A lavishly staged new play based on a very successful movie recently opened at a Broadway theater. A popular, but temperamental, aging actress was cast in the leading role. After three weeks, the play closed.

    (A) The star walked out on the show.

    (B) The movie was not suited to be performed as a stage play.

    (C) The play was not a box office success.

    (D) The play had only been scheduled for a three-week run.

4. Before Bernie left Tucson for a two-week vacation trip, he brought his dog, Michelle, to the home of his son Jack. Jack was unexpectedly called out of town on a business trip, so he took Michelle to a kennel. Jack's business kept him away from Tucson for three days.

    (F) Michelle spent some time at a kennel.

    (G) The kennel is in Tucson.

    (H) Jack took Michelle out of the kennel after three days.

    (J) Michelle eagerly awaited Bernie's return.

5. Glendale Junior High School served lunch in the cafeteria each weekday at noon. Every student had the option of choosing an entrée, side dish, and drink. Sara entered the cafeteria at noon on Thursday. She ate lunch and left for class at 1 p.m. that day.

    (A) Sara had a cafeteria lunch on Thursday.

    (B) Glendale Junior High School serves lunch every day of the week.

    (C) Every Glendale Junior High School student had an entrée during lunch.

    (D) Lunch was available at noon every Wednesday at Glendale Junior High School.

Directions: For questions 6–8, find the correct answer.

6. Here are some words translated from an artificial language.

adabamikula means north pole
bomanitinkipu means south wind
adabagotono means north star

Which word means *east wind*?

- (F) adabatinkipu
- (G) manitutinkipu
- (H) mikulamanitu
- (J) manitugotono

7. Here are some words translated from an artificial language.

pataracolufax means biography
pataragantropo means biology
lognosocolufax means cartography

Which word means *geophysics*?

- (A) damaniposiflo
- (B) lognosodamani
- (C) damanigantropo
- (D) pataraposiflo

8. Here are some words translated from an artificial language.

elemehotuto means red fruit
zigarunaftama means green vegetable
zigarubiganinaftama means green leafy vegetable

Which word means *red flower*?

- (F) hotutotoribuz
- (G) biganieleme
- (H) zigaruhotuto
- (J) toribuzhotuto

Directions: For questions 9–20, find the statement that is true according to the given information.

9. Angela's student advisor tells her that taking advanced biology will help her get into her first choice college. Angela really wants to go to her first choice college, and she always follows her advisor's recommendations.

- (A) Angela signs up for the advanced biology course.
- (B) Duke University is Angela's first choice college.
- (C) Angela wants to go into pre-med studies at college.
- (D) Angela's advisor tells all college-bound students to take advanced biology.

10. All predators eat meat. Harvey is a panther that lives in the Cincinnati Zoo. His favorite breakfast is a big raw steak.

- (F) Harvey the panther was born at the zoo.
- (G) The Cincinnati Zoo houses a wide variety of animals.
- (H) Harvey the panther is not a vegetarian.
- (J) Harvey the panther is a dangerous predator.

11. Sharon, Kelly, Peter, and Alex all run for senior class president. They are the only candidates for the position. Sharon and Alex both get the least number of votes, while Peter only gets five fewer votes than Kelly.

    (A) Sharon and Alex are not very popular.

    (B) Peter thinks the role of class president will look good on his scholarship application.

    (C) Peter has a strong campaign team.

    (D) Kelly is the new senior class president.

12. If Heather does not leave school by 3 p.m., she will miss her dance class at the community center. Heather leaves school at 2:50 p.m. after the last bell.

    (F) Heather leaves school in time to make it to her dance class.

    (G) Heather hates hurrying around on Wednesday afternoons for dance practice.

    (H) Heather wants to win a dance scholarship.

    (J) Heather cannot perform in dance competitions if she misses more than three classes.

13. The Agriculture Club cannot host its annual Farm Day if there is bad weather. On the morning of Farm Day, the sky is dark and thunderstorms are moving through the area.

    (A) The Agriculture Club moves Farm Day activities to the gymnasium.

    (B) The Agricultural Club does not host Farm Day.

    (C) Farm Day is always in the spring.

    (D) Farm Day has been rained out for the past two years.

14. Renee leaves Charleston at 3 p.m. It takes her 4 hours to get to Charlotte.

    (F) Renee is a careful driver and obeys the speed limit.

    (G) Renee's car gets very good gas mileage.

    (H) Renee arrives in Charlotte at about 7 p.m.

    (J) Renee stops to eat at 5 p.m.

15. Cindy has an important business meeting at her office on Thursday afternoon. It takes her precisely 45 minutes to get to her office from her home. Cindy leaves her home 2 hours later than she originally planned on Thursday. Cindy leaves her office at 7 p.m. to go home that same day.

    (A) Cindy was looking forward to her business meeting on Thursday afternoon.

    (B) Cindy spent time commuting on Thursday.

    (C) Cindy was late for her business meeting on Thursday afternoon.

    (D) Cindy is successful and well-respected at her job.

16. Abby's parents warn that if she does not get at least a "C" on her history exam, she cannot go out with her friends on Saturday. Abby gets a "B+" on the history test.

    (F) Abby's parents take her out for a celebratory dinner.

    (G) Abby scores high enough to be allowed to go out with her friends on Saturday.

    (H) Abby's history teacher tells her she applied herself well.

    (J) Abby plans to go to the mall with her friends on Saturday.

17. Jack and his friend Tim meet at their friend Rick's house. Rick's parents do not want the boys playing soccer in the house, and the boys uphold this rule.

    (A) Jack, Tim, and Rick play video games inside the house.

    (B) Jack, Tim, and Rick decide to go to Jack's house.

    (C) Jack, Tim, and Rick think Rick's parents are too strict.

    (D) If Jack, Tim, and Rick play soccer at Rick's house, they play outside.

18. Rob places better than Nancy and Georgia in the spelling contest. Rob also does better than Joe and Diego, but Martha places better than Rob.

(F) Martha places best out of the students mentioned.

(G) Joe and Diego both miss words ending in consonants.

(H) Nancy and Georgia both miss difficult words.

(J) Diego wishes he had placed higher than Rob in the contest.

19. The yearbook staff can only take pictures when the school's camera is not in use by the student newspaper staff. The newspaper staff members never take pictures on the paper's publishing day, which is every Thursday.

(A) The newspaper staff only uses black and white film.

(B) The newspaper editor does not like the yearbook editor.

(C) The school's publication budget is smaller than the sports budget.

(D) The yearbook staff can use the school's camera on Thursdays.

20. Amber starts a community service group to visit residents at a local nursing home. She can visit nursing home residents on nights when she is not working. Amber works at the Ice Cream Palace every weeknight, but never on weekends.

(F) Amber can visit with the nursing home residents on weekends.

(G) Amber's favorite ice cream flavor is peanut butter fudge.

(H) Amber brings ice cream to the nursing home staff members.

(J) Amber's great aunt is a resident at the nursing home.

STOP If you finish before time is up, check over your work on Section 5 only. Do not go back to the previous section. Do not go on until the signal is given.

SECTION 6. MATHEMATICS

35 Minutes

Directions: For questions 1–40, read each problem and find the answer.

1. If $x = 2\frac{2}{5}$, the reciprocal of x equals

   (A) $\frac{12}{5}$

   (B) $\frac{5}{4}$

   (C) $\frac{5}{12}$

   (D) $\frac{5}{2}$

2. The product of $\frac{7}{16}$ and a number x is 1. The number is

   (F) $1\frac{7}{16}$

   (G) $\frac{16}{7}$

   (H) $\frac{31}{14}$

   (J) 1

3. $\dfrac{\frac{1}{x} + 1}{1 + \frac{1}{x}}$ is equivalent to

   (A) 1

   (B) $\frac{1}{x}$

   (C) $\frac{1}{x} + 2$

   (D) $1 + x$

4. $\dfrac{\frac{5}{12} - \frac{7}{24}}{\frac{1}{2} - \frac{3}{8}} =$

   (F) $\frac{1}{2}$

   (G) $\frac{3}{8}$

   (H) 1

   (J) 8

5. In the formula $L = \frac{3}{4}bxh$, if $b = 2$, $x = 7$, and $h = \frac{1}{2}$, L equals

   (A) $\frac{21}{2}$

   (B) $\frac{21}{4}$

   (C) $\frac{21}{8}$

   (D) $\frac{7x}{4}$

6. Two angles of a triangle are 45° and 75°. What is the measure of the third angle?

   (F) 60°

   (G) 35°

   (H) 180°

   (J) 45°

7.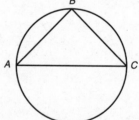

   Isosceles $\triangle ABC$ is inscribed in a circle that has a diameter of 10 centimeters. The area of the triangle is

   (A) 78.5 sq. cm.

   (B) 12.5 sq. cm.

   (C) 25 sq. cm.

   (D) 50 sq. cm.

8. The volume of a small warehouse measuring 75 feet long, 50 feet wide, and 30 feet high is

(F) 1,112,500 cubic feet.

(G) 112,500 square feet.

(H) 112,500 feet.

(J) 112,500 cubic feet.

9. A department store marks up its clothing 80% over cost. If it sells blue jeans for $14, how much did the store pay for them?

(A) $7.78

(B) $17.50

(C) $11.20

(D) $1.12

10. The monthly finance charge on a charge account is $1\frac{1}{2}$% on the unpaid amount up to $500 and 1% on the unpaid amount over $500. What is the finance charge on an unpaid amount of $750?

(F) $22.50

(G) $1.00

(H) $10.00

(J) $100.00

11.

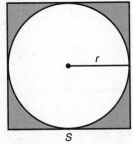

The square above has a side 4" long. The area of the shaded portion is approximately

(A) $\frac{22}{7}$ sq. in.

(B) 16 sq. in.

(C) $3\frac{3}{7}$ sq. in.

(D) $4\frac{3}{7}$ sq. in.

12. The ratio of teachers to students in a certain school is 1:14. If there are fourteen teachers in the school, how many students are there?

(F) 14

(G) 196

(H) 206

(J) 176

13. Evaluate $\frac{10^4}{100^5}$.

(A) $\frac{1}{10}$

(B) $\frac{1}{1,000}$

(C) $\frac{1}{100,000}$

(D) $\frac{1}{1,000,000}$

14. If x is an odd whole number, which of the following also represents an odd number?

(F) $2x + 1$

(G) $x - 2$

(H) $4x - 3$

(J) All of the above

15. Sum of 4 hours 17 minutes, 3 hours 58 minutes, 45 minutes, and 7 hours 12 minutes is

(A) 15 hr. 32 min.

(B) 17 hr. 32 min.

(C) 16 hr. 12 min.

(D) 14 hr. 50 min.

16. If 8 lb. 12 oz. of fruit were to be divided among eight people, how much would each receive?

(F) 1 lb. 1.5 oz.

(G) 10.5 oz.

(H) 2.0 lb.

(J) 13.5 oz.

17. In how much less time does a runner who finishes a marathon in 2 hours 12 minutes 38 seconds complete the race than a runner who finishes in 3 hours 2 minutes 24 seconds?

(A) 48 min. 56 sec.

(B) 49 min. 46 sec.

(C) 1 hr. 51 min. 22 sec.

(D) 1 hr. 26 min. 12 sec.

18. The drawing of a wheel in a book is done at $\frac{1}{16}$ scale. If the drawing is 1.8 inches in diameter, what is the wheel's diameter?

(F) 32 inches

(G) 28.8 inches

(H) 24 inches

(J) 0.1125 inch

19. If a man runs M miles in T hours, his speed is

(A) M/T

(B) $M + T$

(C) $M - T$

(D) MT

20. How many square yards are there in x rooms in a house, each having y square feet?

(F) $9xy$

(G) $\frac{xy}{9}$

(H) $144xy$

(J) $\frac{xy}{144}$

21. The ratio of the six inches to six feet is

(A) 1:6

(B) 12:1

(C) 1:12

(D) 24:1

22. Event A occurs every 4 years, event B every 11 years, and event C every 33 years. If they last occurred together in 1950, what is the next year they will occur simultaneously?

(F) 3402

(G) 1983

(H) 2082

(J) 6804

23.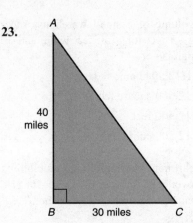

Two drivers begin at point C simultaneously. One drives from C to B to A. The other drives directly to A at 50 mph. How fast must the first person drive to get to A first?

(A) Less than 50 mph

(B) Less than 60 mph

(C) Less than 70 mph

(D) More than 70 mph

24.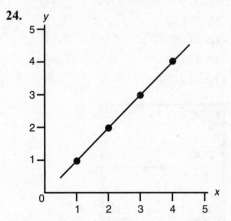

The graph above shows

(F) x increasing faster than y.

(G) y increasing faster than x.

(H) x increasing as fast as y.

(J) no relationship between x and y.

25. In the number 6,000,600,000, there are

(A) 6 billions and 6 hundred thousands.

(B) 6 millions and 6 thousands.

(C) 6 billions and 6 millions.

(D) 6 millions and 60 thousands.

26. One of the scales used in drawing topographic maps is 1:24,000. On a scale of this sort, 1 inch on the map would equal how much distance on the ground?

    (F) 1 inch

    (G) 2,000 feet

    (H) 24,000 feet

    (J) 1 mile

27. If A number of people each make L things, the total number of things made is

    (A) A/L

    (B) $A + L$

    (C) $A - L$

    (D) AL

28.
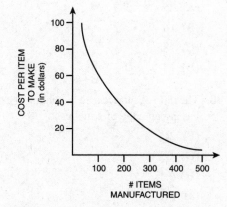

    Based upon the graph above, what is the cost per item if 300 items are manufactured?

    (F) $40

    (G) $28

    (H) $20

    (J) < $20

29.
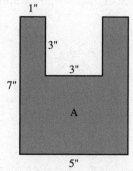

    Note: In the figure above, assume that any angle which appears to be a right angle is a right angle.

    The perimeter of figure A is

    (A) 19 in.

    (B) 30 in.

    (C) 23 in.

    (D) 24 in.

30. Of 27 people in a certain group, 15 are men and 12 are women. In simplest form, what is the ratio of men to women?

    (F) 15:12

    (G) 12:15

    (H) 5:4

    (J) 27:12

31.
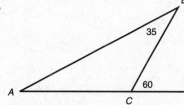

    The measure of angle A is

    (A) 15°

    (B) 20°

    (C) 25°

    (D) 35°

32. The difference between 1,001,000 and 999,999 is

    (F) 101,001

    (G) 1999

    (H) 10,001

    (J) 1001

33. The surface area of a brick with the dimensions 6" × 3" × 2" is

    (A) 36 sq. in.

    (B) 72 sq. in.

    (C) 128 sq. in.

    (D) 72 cu. in.

34. Simplify: $-3 - [-2 + (5 - 6) - 3]$

    (F) +3

    (G) −1

    (H) +1

    (J) −3

35. Simplify: $0.6 + 1\frac{1}{2} + \frac{3}{4}$

    (A) 2.31

    (B) 2.52

    (C) 2.85

    (D) $2\frac{13}{20}$

36. Simplify: $-6 - [2 - (3a - b) + b] + a$

    (F) $4 - 3a + 2b$

    (G) $-6 + 3a + b$

    (H) $-8 + 4a - 2b$

    (J) $-8 + 3a - b$

37. Simplify: $-2\,[-4\,(2 - 1) + (3 + 2)]$

    (A) 18

    (B) 2

    (C) −18

    (D) −2

38.

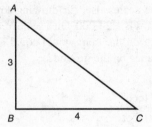

The length of AC in the right triangle above is

    (F) 4.5

    (G) 3.5

    (H) 5

    (J) 4

39. 5:6 as 15:?

    (A) 25

    (B) 16

    (C) 18

    (D) 12

40. The ratio of surface area to volume of a cube having an edge of 2 inches is

    (F) 2:3

    (G) 1:3

    (H) 6:1

    (J) 3:1

STOP   If you finish before time is up, check over your work on Section 7 only. Do not go back to any previous sections.

SECTION 7. READING AND LANGUAGE ARTS

40 Minutes

Directions: For questions 1–40, read each passage and the questions following that passage. Find the answers.

QUESTIONS 1–4 REFER TO THE FOLLOWING PASSAGE.

Using new tools and techniques, scientists, almost unnoticed, are remaking the world of plants. They have already remodeled 65 sorts of flowers, fruits, vegetables, and trees, giving us, among other things, tobacco that resists disease, cantaloupes that are immune to the blight, and lettuce with crisper leaves. The chief new tool they are using is colchicine, a poisonous drug that has astounding effects upon growth and upon heredity. It creates new varieties with astonishing frequency, whereas such mutations occur rarely in nature. Colchicine has thrown new light on the fascinating jobs of the plant hunters. The Department of Agriculture sends agents all over the world to find plants native to other lands that can be grown here and that are superior to those already here. Scientists have crossed these foreign plants with those at home, thereby adding to our farm crops many desirable characteristics. The colchicine technique has enormously facilitated their work because hybrids so often can be made fertile and because it takes so few generations of plants now to build a new variety with the qualities desired.

1. The title that best expresses the ideas of the paragraph is
   (A) "Plant Growth and Heredity."
   (B) "New Plants for Old."
   (C) "Remodeling Plant Life."
   (D) "A More Abundant World."

2. Mutation in plant life results in
   (F) diseased plants.
   (G) hybrids.
   (H) new varieties.
   (J) fertility.

3. Colchicine speeds the improvement of plant species because it
   (A) makes possible the use of foreign plants.
   (B) makes use of natural mutations.
   (C) creates new varieties very quickly.
   (D) can be used with 65 different vegetables, fruits, and flowers.

4. According to the passage, colchicine is a
   (F) poisonous drug.
   (G) blight.
   (H) kind of plant hunter.
   (J) hybrid plant.

QUESTIONS 5–8 REFER TO THE FOLLOWING PASSAGE.

The peopling of the Northwest Territory by companies from the eastern states, such as the Ohio Company under the leadership of Reverend Manasseh Cutler of Ipswich, Massachusetts, furnishes us with many interesting historical tales.

The first towns to be established were Marietta, Zanesville, Chillocothe, and Cincinnati. After the Ohio Company came the Connecticut Company, which secured all the territory bordering Lake Erie save a small portion known as fire lands and another portion known as Congress lands. The land taken up by the Connecticut people was called the Western Reserve and was settled almost entirely by New England people. The remainder of the state of Ohio was settled by Virginians and Pennsylvanians. Because the British controlled Lakes Ontario and Erie, the Massachusetts and Connecticut people made their journey into the Western Reserve through the southern part of the state. General Moses Cleaveland, the agent for the Connecticut Land Company, led a body of surveyors to the tract, proceeding by way of Lake Ontario. He quieted the Indian claims to the eastern portion of the reserve by giving them five hundred pounds, two heads of cattle, and one hundred gallons of whiskey. Landing at the mouth of the Conneaut River, General Moses Cleaveland and his party of fifty, including two women, celebrated Independence Day, 1796, with a feast of pork and beans with bread. A little later, a village was established at the mouth of the Cuyahoga River and was given the name of Cleaveland in honor of the agent of the company. It is related that the name was afterward shortened to Cleveland by one of the early editors because he could not get so many letters into the heading of his newspaper.

5. Reverend Manasseh Cutler
   (A) led the Ohio Company.
   (B) owned the Western Reserve.
   (C) led the Connecticut Land Company.
   (D) settled the Congress lands.

6. The title that best expresses the main idea of this selection is
   (F) "Control of the Great Lake Region."
   (G) "The Accomplishments of Reverend Manasseh Cutler."
   (H) "The Naming of Cleveland, Ohio."
   (J) "The Settling of the Northwest Territory."

7. In the last sentence of the selection, the word *related* is used to mean
   (A) associated with.
   (B) rumored.
   (C) reported.
   (D) thought.

8. The selection suggests that General Cleaveland at first found the Indians to be
   (F) extremely noisy people.
   (G) hostile to his party of strangers.
   (H) starving.
   (J) eager to work with him.

QUESTIONS 9–12 REFER TO THE FOLLOWING PASSAGE.

From Gettysburg to the Battle of the Bulge, carrier pigeons have winged their way through skies fair and foul to deliver the vital messages of battle. Today, in spite of electronics and atomic weapons, these feathered heroes are still an important communication link in any army.

No one could be surer of this than the men at Fort Monmouth, New Jersey, the sole Army pigeon breeding and training center in this country. On the roosts at Fort Monmouth perch many genuine battle heroes, among them veteran G. I. Joe.

In 1943, 1,000 British troops moved speedily ahead of the Allied advance in Italy to take the small town of Colvi Vecchia. Since communications could not be established in time to relay the victory to headquarters, the troops were due for a previously planned Allied bombing raid. Then one of the men released carrier pigeon G. I. Joe. With a warning message on his back, he flew 20 miles in 20 minutes, arriving just as the bombers were warming up their engines. For saving the day for the British, the Lord Mayor of London later awarded G. I. Joe the Dickin Medal, England's highest award to an animal.

Even when regular message channels are set up, equipment can break or be overloaded or radio silence must be observed. Then the carrier pigeon comes into his own. Ninety-nine times out of a hundred, he completes his mission. In Korea, Homer the homing pigeon was flying from the front to a rear command post when he developed wing trouble. Undaunted, Homer made a forced landing, hopped the last two miles, and delivered his message. For initiative and loyalty, Homer was promoted to Pfc.—Pigeon First Class!

9. The writer of this selection evidently believes that carrier pigeons
    (A) have no usefulness in modern warfare.
    (B) should be forced to fly only in emergencies.
    (C) are remarkably reliable as message carriers.
    (D) should receive regular promotions.

10. G. I. Joe was rewarded for
    (F) preventing unnecessary loss of life.
    (G) guiding a bomber's flight.
    (H) returning in spite of an injured wing.
    (J) bringing the news of an allied victory.

11. G. I. Joe's reward was a
    (A) promotion.
    (B) reception given by the Lord Mayor.
    (C) chance to retire to Fort Monmouth.
    (D) medal.

12. Choose the sentence that is written correctly.
    (F) For initiative and loyalty, Homer was promoted to Pfc.— Pigeon First Class.
    (G) Homer for initiative and loyalty, was promoted to Pfc.—Pigeon First Class.
    (H) For initiative and loyalty Homer promoted to Pfc.—Pigeon First Class!
    (J) Initiative and loyalty was the reason why Homer was promoting to Pfc.—Pigeon First Class.

QUESTIONS 13–17 REFER TO THE FOLLOWING PASSAGE.

"There are many things from which I might have derived good, by which I have not profited, I dare say, Christmas among the rest. But I am sure I have always thought of Christmastime, when it has come round— apart from the veneration due to its sacred origin, if anything belonging to it *can* be apart from that—as a good time; a kind, forgiving, charitable, pleasant time; the only time I know of, in the long calendar of the year, when men and women seem by one consent to open their shut-up hearts freely and to think of people below them as if they really were fellow travelers to the grave, and not another race of creatures bound on other journeys. And therefore, Uncle, though it has never put a scrap of gold or silver in my pocket, I believe that it *has* done me good, and *will* do me good; and I say, God bless it!" The clerk in the tank involuntarily applauded.

"Let me hear another sound from *you*," said Scrooge, "and you'll keep your Christmas by losing your situation! You're quite a powerful speaker, sir," he added, turning to his nephew. "I wonder you don't go into Parliament."

—From *A Christmas Carol*
by Charles Dickens

13. The word *veneration* probably means

(A) worship.

(B) disapproval.

(C) agreement.

(D) love.

14. The first speaker

(F) is a very religious person.

(G) enjoys and celebrates Christmas.

(H) is defending Christmas.

(J) has been fired by Scrooge.

15. The first speaker believes that Christmas

(A) is a pleasant nuisance.

(B) brings out the best in people.

(C) has been separated from its religious origin.

(D) could be a profitable time of year.

16. The phrase by *one consent* is synonymous with

(F) affirmatively.

(G) contractually.

(H) partially.

(J) unanimously.

17. Scrooge probably is angry with

(A) the speaker and the clerk.

(B) only the speaker.

(C) only the clerk.

(D) people who celebrate Christmas.

practice test

QUESTIONS 18–22 REFER TO THE FOLLOWING PASSAGE.

When an art form—any art form—becomes widespread, it usually becomes the subject of scholarly study. Scholars examine the art form to understand its roots and its history. The art form of hip-hop music is no exception.

Author John Richardson discusses how hip-hop has continued as a music form, even though it has been mass-produced. The style first emerged to reflect the views of a specific minority group. It was a type of "underground" music, as Richardson states. It followed a similar path as did punk rock and other underground music styles.

First, it was supported by major corporations who realized they could make a great profit from it. Then, hip-hop became mainstream. Next, it became standardized and mass-produced. Through this process, hip-hop lost some of its subtle qualities. It also lost some of its originality.

Normally, in a path such as this, underground forms of music would lose their uniqueness as well, states Richardson. Eventually, the music form would lose its identity entirely. It would fall out of favor as a popular style and would disappear. This never happened to hip-hop, however. It has continued to maintain its emphasis on the underground, focusing on "the street" and on "keeping it real."

18. When does an art form usually become the subject of scholarly study?

   (F) When it begins to generate profits

   (G) When it becomes widespread

   (H) When it is one century old

   (J) When it disappears from public view

19. According to the passage, which of the following happened to hip-hop?

   (A) It lost its popularity and disappeared.

   (B) It became standardized and mass-produced.

   (C) It developed a sound similar to punk rock.

   (D) It maintained an emphasis on big business.

20. According to John Richardson, why has hip-hop music not lost its identity entirely?

   (F) It has become standardized and highly uniform.

   (G) It has shifted its focus away from "the street."

   (H) It has continued to maintain its emphasis on the underground.

   (J) It has been supported by major corporations.

21. According to the passage, hip-hop first developed to express the views and experiences of

   (A) the mainstream public.

   (B) a major corporation.

   (C) an underground music business.

   (D) a minority group.

22. What happened after hip-hop became a mainstream form of music?

   (F) Hip-hop lost some of its subtle qualities.

   (G) Hip-hop gained more originality.

   (H) Hip-hop stopped being mass-produced.

   (J) Hip-hop fell out of favor as a popular style.

QUESTIONS 23–26 REFER TO THE FOLLOWING PASSAGE.

Nine-banded armadillos, the only type of armadillo that lives in the United States, are fascinating and unusual mammals. Originally located in South America, armadillos have gradually extended their geographical range northward, and they can now be found across the southeastern U.S. and as far north as Kansas. The armadillo is particularly popular in Texas, where it is the official state small mammal.

Instead of being covered with skin, the armadillo's body is covered with hard, bony plates, reminiscent of armor. These plates gave the armadillo its name, which means "little armored one" in Spanish. Nine-banded armadillos have nine separate segments of bony plate around their midsections. This allows them to bend.

About the size of large house cats, armadillos have poor eyesight but a superb sense of smell. Their strong legs and extra-large front claws make them excellent diggers, a trait they use to build underground burrow homes. Their digging skills, plus their long, sticky tongues, enable armadillos to search for and trap insects, one of their favorite foods.

Because of their heavy outer covering, it would be easy to assume that armadillos cannot function in water. However, this is far from the truth. An armadillo can hold its breath for four to six minutes. If it needs to cross a small body of water, it simply holds its breath and walks across the bottom. For longer aquatic encounters, the armadillo gulps in air to inflate its intestines. This makes its body quite buoyant, enabling the armadillo to become a capable swimmer.

Shy creatures, armadillos prefer to escape rather than face confrontation. When frightened, they have the rather strange ability to jump, straight up, three to four feet in the air. This propensity makes armadillos a roadway hazard, both to drivers and themselves. An armadillo senses a moving vehicle and leaps just high enough to be struck by the vehicle's bumper.

23. According to the article, a nine-banded armadillo would be least likely to be found in
(A) Texas.
(B) Florida.
(C) Michigan.
(D) Oklahoma.

24. Nine-banded armadillos can bend in the middle because their armor
(F) is flexible.
(G) has nine sections.
(H) has hinges.
(J) is bony and thick.

25. When an armadillo faces danger, it will most likely not
(A) stand and fight.
(B) jump high in the air.
(C) dig a hole to hide in.
(D) run away quickly.

26. Although it seems unlikely, the armadillo is a good swimmer because its
(F) oversized front claws make it excellent at paddling.
(G) poor eyesight and keen sense of smell are assets in the water.
(H) bony plates are lightweight and act like a boat in the water.
(J) ability to fill its intestines with air enables it to float easily.

QUESTIONS 27–30 REFER TO THE FOLLOWING PASSAGE.

You know, of course, that in China the Emperor is a Chinaman, and all the people around him are Chinamen, too. It happened a good many years ago, but that's just why it's worthwhile to hear the story, before it is forgotten. The Emperor's palace was the most splendid in the world; entirely and altogether made of porcelain, so costly, but so brittle, so difficult to handle that one had to be terribly careful. In the garden were to be seen the strangest flowers, and to the most splendid of them silver bells were tied, which tinkled so that nobody should pass by without noticing the flowers. Oh, the Emperor's garden had been laid out very smartly, and it extended so far that the gardener himself didn't know where the end was. If you went on and on, you came into the loveliest forest with high trees and deep lakes. The forest went right down to the sea, which was blue and deep; tall ships could sail right in under the branches of the trees; and in the trees lived a nightingale which sang so sweetly that even the poor fisherman, who had many other things to do, stopped still and listened when he had gone out at night to take up his nets and then heard the nightingale.

—From *The Nightingale*
by Hans Christian Andersen

27. The author wants to tell this story
    (A) before it is forgotten.
    (B) because he is enchanted by China.
    (C) because he is a writer and storyteller.
    (D) in order to describe the garden.

28. The Emperor's palace was made of
    (F) silver bells.
    (G) high trees.
    (H) porcelain.
    (J) large stones and boulders.

29. Silver bells were tied to flowers in the garden to
    (A) further enhance their beauty.
    (B) draw attention to their beauty.
    (C) accompany the singing of the nightingale.
    (D) discourage flower picking.

30. The Emperor's garden
    (F) was too large to care for.
    (G) led into a lovely forest.
    (H) housed a rare nightingale.
    (J) was a source of pleasure for all in the kingdom.

QUESTIONS 31–35 REFER TO THE FOLLOWING PASSAGE.

Our planet is made up of three separate layers, known as the crust, mantle, and core. The core of the Earth is also made up of two layers, an outer core and an inner core.

Just as the Earth rotates on its axis, the parts of the Earth also move over time. This movement occurs in a horizontal direction and is very slow. Most parts of the Earth are believed to move at a rate of only 10 centimeters per year—about the same rate as the growth of a human fingernail, according to writer David Schneider.

Recently, scientists investigating the inner core of the Earth have discovered that this part of the Earth moves much faster than the surrounding parts. Exactly how fast the inner core moves, however, is still a subject of debate.

Up until recently, most of our knowledge about the content of the Earth's inner core has come through using scientific logic. Scientists deduced that the Earth's core was composed mainly of iron. In addition to using logic, scientists have gathered some direct evidence regarding the Earth's core. This evidence comes from seismic studies, which investigate waves traveling through the Earth from earthquakes and explosives. Seismic studies show that the Earth contains not just iron, but a lighter element as well. Scientists aren't sure which lighter element is contained in the core, but they have narrowed down the possibilities. They believe it could be one of these five: oxygen, sulfur, silicon, hydrogen, or carbon.

Recently, new experiments show that silicon may be the key element. These studies, conducted at the University of Chicago, encouraged scientists to pinpoint silicon as the most likely light element for three reasons. First, like iron, silicon is very abundant in our solar system. Second, it combines easily with iron to create an iron alloy. Third, silicon lowers the density of iron when the two elements are placed together under high pressure conditions.

31. The inner core of the Earth is most likely made up mainly of
    (A) iron and silicon.
    (B) iron and oxygen.
    (C) silicon and sulfur.
    (D) oxygen and hydrogen.

32. Which statement best describes the inner core of the Earth?
    (F) It moves at a rate of about 10 centimeters per year.
    (G) It is divided into two layers: crust and mantle.
    (H) It moves at a rate of about 10 kilometers per year.
    (J) It moves faster than the other parts of the Earth.

33. The Earth is made up of three separate layers called the
    (A) outer core, the inner core, and the iron core.

    (B) surface, spindle, and core.
    (C) crust, mantle, and core.
    (D) crust, the outer core, and the inner core.

34. Scientist have been learning about the Earth's core by analyzing waves traveling through the Earth caused by
    (F) explosives and earthquakes.
    (G) explosives and volcanoes.
    (H) earthquakes and asteroids.
    (J) explosives and meteors.

35. According to the passage, what effect does silicon have upon iron when the two are placed together under high pressure?
    (A) Silicon increases the specific gravity of iron.
    (B) Silicon makes iron more explosive.
    (C) Silicon decreases the temperature of iron.
    (D) Silicon decreases the density of iron.

QUESTIONS 36–40 REFER TO THE FOLLOWING PASSAGE.

In caffeine-fueled cultures across the globe, it has never been easier to enjoy a great cup of coffee, regardless of where you may find yourself in the world. Coffee has become one of the most profitable—and revered—businesses in the world, with ever-increasing numbers of coffee houses opening up, some of which proclaim to make and serve the best cup of coffee around. While individual coffee tastes and preferences are as varied as the number of bean varieties that exist, it would be hard to find a coffee more interesting—or expensive—than kopi luwak.

Kopi luwak is also referred to as civet coffee, and for good reason. These prized beans are harvested from the digested remains of coffee cherries that have been eaten by Asian palm civets, small squirrel-like creatures that inhabit Southeast Asia. The vast majority of kopi luwak is produced in the islands of Java, Bali, Sumatra, Sulawesi, and the Philippines. Many coffee experts proclaim that civets naturally select only the best, most fleshy coffee cherries to consume—and ultimately eliminate—and that during the digestion process, a process of fermentation occurs within the civets that diminishes the coffee bean's natural acidity, reduces bitterness, and ultimately leads to a smoother and more satisfying beverage.

After the fruity pulp of the coffee cherries are consumed by the civets, the remains are excreted and collected for cleaning and roasting. Because of the unique conditions in which the beans are obtained, their limited supply, and its prized taste, kopi luwak is widely recognized as one of the most expensive and rare coffees in the world. Prices have been known to go as high as several hundred dollars or more for a pound of beans. As a result, farmers and harvesters, keen on profiting from the prized droppings, have taken to extreme methods to increase supply, including trapping and caging these creatures in overcrowded civet farms, which have raised concerns regarding the welfare and safety of these animals. Unsavory merchants have also taken to selling inferior beans under the kopi luwak name in an effort to turn a profit.

While kopi luwak certainly has its critics—not everyone believes this process yields a superior cup of coffee—there are certainly enough people who either greatly enjoy the beans or who are at least curious enough to try it to keep harvesting kopi luwak a profitable enterprise. One could argue that when it comes to kopi luwak, the old adage "there's no accounting for taste" is on full display.

36. The title that best expresses the main idea of this passage is:
    (F) Kopi Luwak: A Prized Cup of Coffee
    (G) Exploring the Life of the Civet
    (H) Discover How Coffee is Made
    (J) What's Your Favorite Beverage?

37. What bodily process helps kopi luwak achieve its distinct flavor?
    (A) respiration
    (B) digestion
    (C) perspiration
    (D) circulation

38. Based on how it's used in the final sentence of the passage, the word adage most nearly means
    (F) a warning.
    (G) a saying.
    (H) a joke.
    (J) a secret code.

39. According to the passage, kopi luwak can most likely be found in all of the following places except
    (A) Java.
    (B) Sumatra.
    (C) Bali.
    (D) Nicaragua.

40. Which of the following happens to coffee beans during the fermentation process within civets?

(F) The color is changed.

(G) The thickness is diminished.

(H) The bitterness is reduced.

(J) The sweetness is increased.

Directions: For questions 41–43, choose the topic sentence that best fits the paragraph.

41. _____

Today, more people spend time on their mobile phones than reading books or newspapers. People can pay bills and keep in touch with friends and family online. Now, we can purchase virtually anything we need from the comfort of our home computers.

(A) Technology is changing the way we live.

(B) Everyone has a mobile phone these days.

(C) Advances in technology are more trouble than they're worth.

(D) People love shopping online.

42. _____

Mass and weight are not the same. Mass is the amount of matter any object contains. Weight is the pull of gravity on that mass.

(F) Matter is anything that has mass and occupies space.

(G) The phenomenon of weightlessness in outer space is created by the weak pull of gravity.

(H) Matter is composed of basic substances known as *elements*.

(J) Atomic weight is the weight of one atom of an element expressed in atomic mass units.

43. _____

In some cases, it consists only of ordinances, with little or no attempt at enforcement. In other cases, good control is obtained through wise ordinances and an efficient inspecting force and laboratory. While inspection alone can do much toward controlling the quality and production of milk, there must also be frequent laboratory tests of the milk.

(A) The bacterial count of milk indicates the condition of the dairy and the methods of milk handling.

(B) When the milk-producing animals are free from disease, the milk that they provide registers a low bacterial count.

(C) Inefficient sterilization of equipment and utensils represented a source of milk contamination in dairies at the turn of the century.

(D) Most cities carrying on public health work exercise varying degrees of inspection and control over their milk supplies.

Directions: For questions 44–46, choose the pair of sentences that best develops the topic sentence.

44. A passage leads from the outer ear to a membrane called the eardrum.

(F) Earaches are caused by infection within the ear. Untreated chronic earaches may lead to eventual deafness.

(G) Sound waves striking the eardrum make it vibrate. On the other side of the eardrum lies a space called the middle ear.

(H) This tube ends near the throat opening of the nose, close to the tonsils. Doctors often remove both tonsils and adenoids in the same operation.

(J) The sounds we hear are created by the vibration of air waves. The frequency of the vibrations determines the pitch of the sound.

45. Urban open-air markets originally came into existence spontaneously when groups of pushcart peddlers congregated in spots where business was good.

(A) There was confusion and disorder in these open-air markets because the peddlers paid no licensing fees. The strongest and toughest peddlers secured the best locations.

(B) One problem created by open-air markets is that of garbage in the streets. Another is obstruction of traffic.

(C) In some Asian countries, fixed stores represent a very small percent of all commerce. Nearly all buying and selling is done by merchants in the streets.

(D) Good business induced them to return to these spots daily, and unofficial open-air markets thus arose. These peddlers paid no fees, and cities received no revenue from them.

46. Crowdfunding is an effective way for new entrepreneurs and businesses to achieve success.

(F) Obtaining money for new projects from corporate partnerships is another way to make a new business work. Entrepreneurs can also sell their inventions or ideas for a profit.

(G) In today's challenging economic environment, starting a new business is risky. It may make more sense to try and find employment in an existing and established business.

(H) New ventures can obtain essential startup funding from small contributions made by multiple people in their networks, or crowds. Funds raised this way can finance projects and pay for necessary business expenses, such as staffing and office space.

(J) Who knows what the future holds for funding new business endeavors? Technology is rapidly changing, and with it we may see new and exciting opportunities for entrepreneurs and businesses.

Directions: For question 47, choose the sentence that does not belong in the paragraph.

47. (1) Making iced tea is a relatively simple process that anyone can do at home. (2) All you need are two tea bags, four cups of water, and a large heatproof container, such as a pitcher. (3) Heat the water until boiling, pour it into your container, and set the teabags in it to steep for at least five minutes. (4) Iced tea is delicious when mixed with other drinks, such as lemonade. (5) After it has steeped, serve over ice, add in fruit or sugar to taste, and enjoy your delicious beverage.

(A) Sentence 2

(B) Sentence 3

(C) Sentence 4

(D) Sentence 5

Directions: For questions 48–50, read the paragraph and choose the sentence that best fills the blank.

48. Pufferfish, also known as blowfish, balloonfish, or puffers, are members of the *Tetraodontidae* family. They are typically found in warm, tropical, aquatic environments, such as South America. _____ When threatened, they use their natural defense mechanisms to protect themselves from danger.

(F) Viewing tropical fish in their native habitats is a popular tourist attraction in resorts around the world.

(G) The meat of pufferfish is considered by many cultures to be a delicacy, and can be found on menus in Japan, Korea, and China.

(H) Some individuals and marine hobbyists attempt to add pufferfish to their exotic personal aquariums.

(J) Most pufferfish are highly poisonous, and can fill their bodies with water or air to inflate themselves to help fend off predators.

49. Kindling temperature is the lowest temperature at which a substance catches fire and continues to burn. Different fuels have different kindling temperatures. _____ Coal, because of its high kindling temperature, requires much heat before it will begin to burn. Matches are tipped with phosphorus or some other low kindling material to permit the small amount of heat produced by friction to ignite the match.

(A) Safety matches are so called because they can be ignited only by striking on a strip on the package in which they are sold.

(B) Paper catches fire easily because it has a low kindling temperature.

(C) The United States consumes so much energy that it is rapidly consuming its store of fossil fuels.

(D) Thin dry twigs are used as kindling wood for open fires.

50. Arsonists are persons who set fires deliberately. They don't look like criminals, but they cost the nation millions of dollars in property loss and sometimes loss of life. _____ Sometimes a shopkeeper sees no way out of losing his business and sets fire to it to collect the insurance. Some arsonists just like the excitement of seeing the fire burn and watching the firefighters at work.

(F) Arsonists set fires for many different reasons.

(G) Forest fires usually stem from carelessness or from natural causes rather than from the acts of arsonists.

(H) Another type of arsonist wants revenge and sets fire to the home or shop of someone he feels has treated him unfairly.

(J) Arsonists have even been known to help fight the fire.

STOP If you finish before time is up, check over your work on Section 6 only. Do not go back to the previous sections. Do not go on until the signal is given.

ANSWER KEYS AND EXPLANATIONS

Section 1. Sequences

1. B	5. C	9. C	13. A	17. C
2. H	6. G	10. G	14. J	18. G
3. A	7. B	11. C	15. B	19. D
4. J	8. F	12. H	16. F	20. H

1. **The correct answer is (B).** The little circle is moving around the box in a counter-clockwise direction. In the first frame, the circle is on the outside of the box. After one complete circuit, the little circle straddles the perimeter of the box as it continues its counter-clockwise travel in the second frame. After the straddling circuit, the little circle moves into the box. The correct answer represents continuation of the circle in its counterclockwise travel inside the box.

2. **The correct answer is (H).** Look at the first three frames and note that in each frame, the first and last elements are identical. Eliminate choice (F). Look again at the first three frames and note that in each of the central elements, only one segment is darkened. Eliminate choice (G). Now notice that within each frame, the single darkened elements are positioned opposite each other.

3. **The correct answer is (A).** In each of the first three frames, the two dark-headed arrows are of the same length and point in the same direction on the right. This pattern is carried out only in choice (A). Check to be certain of your choice by looking at the other two arrows. One is long, one short; both heads are clear; they point in opposite directions. This is consistent with the behavior of the left-hand arrows in the first three frames. All other choices break the pattern in more than one way.

4. **The correct answer is (J).** In the first three frames, the first figure stands on both legs. Eliminate choice (G). Looking again at the first figure, in each of the first three frames, the arms are in a different position. Choice

(J) offers the fourth position for this figure's arms. Confirm this by looking at the other two figures. The arm and leg positions are exactly reversed in the first and third frames. The arm and leg positions of the second and third figures in choice (J) are the reverse of those in the second frame.

5. **The correct answer is (C).** Of the four figures in each frame, the first two are always alike while the other two vary. There are only three different figures. The easiest way to derive a pattern is to assign a number to each figure. Thus, in the first frame, we have 1-1-2-3; in the second, 2-2-3-1; and in the third, 3-3-1-2. The progression shows that in each succeeding frame, the figure in the third position in the preceding frame is doubled. Thus, the fourth frame should consist of 1-1-2-3, as found in choice (C).

6. **The correct answer is (G).** Name the patterns. First frame: plain, vee, left up, right down. Second frame: plain, vee, left down, right up. Third frame: plain, vee, right up, left down. Fourth frame must follow the up-down, left-right reversal pattern established: plain, vee, right down, left up.

7. **The correct answer is (B).** In the first frame, $44 - 5 = 39$ and $39 - 4 = 35$. Try this pattern in the second frame, and you will see that the -5, -4 rule holds. In the third frame, $61 - 5 = 56$, so the answer is $56 - 4 = 52$.

8. **The correct answer is (F).** In each frame, the first and last numbers are the same, so you need only figure the relationship of the middle number to each of these. In both the first and second frames, the central number is $2 \times$ the first, so choose $2 \times 9 = 18$ for your answer.

9. **The correct answer is (C).** In each three-digit frame, the third number is 3 times the second. The first number remains 4 from frame to frame. So, the blank should be filled in with 4.

10. **The correct answer is (G).** The rule appears most clearly in the second frame: divide by 3, divide by 3. Applied to the first frame, it works. To choose the answer, you must choose the number that yields 7 when divided by 3. Multiply 7×3 to find 21.

11. **The correct answer is (C).** In each frame, the second number is repeated, so you really might just guess that the middle number in the last frame will be the same as the last. To double check, you might note that the second number in each frame is 18 more than the first.

12. **The correct answer is (H).** In the first frame, the numbers increase by 4; in the second, they increase by 8, and in the third frame they increase by 12. So, the blank should be filled in with 41.

13. **The correct answer is (A).** In each frame, the first and second numbers set the limits, and the last number is halfway between. So, in the last frame, 70 is halfway between 80 and the correct answer 60.

14. **The correct answer is (J).** Look carefully and you will see that in every case, *1* and *2* are subscripts and *3* is a superscript. The letters remain in the same order, and the numbers simply move one letter to the right and then back to the first letter.

15. **The correct answer is (B).** The pattern is that within each frame, the superscripts on *W* and *X* sum to the subscript on *Z*. Since $9 + 5 = 14$, and these numbers are correctly positioned as subscripts and superscripts, the correct answer is choice (B).

16. **The correct answer is (F).** Again the letters remain the same and in the same order, but here the numbers both change and change their positions. Looking carefully, you will note that the odd numbers are superscripts while the even numbers are subscripts. Furthermore, the numbers themselves are decreasing in value one at a time. Concentrate on numbers alone: 5-5-4; 5-4-4; 4-4-4; fill in 4-4-3; then 4-3-3.

17. **The correct answer is (C).** This series is basically the alphabet, but every other set presents the letters in reverse order. As we reach the next set, we are back to alphabetical order again. If you quickly write the alphabet across the page in your test booklet, you will find alphabetic series questions much easier to figure out.

18. **The correct answer is (G).** Each set begins with *A* and ends with *B*. Then we find an alphabetic sequence beginning with *B* at the second position in each set and an alphabetic sequence beginning with *D* in the third position in each set.

19. **The correct answer is (D).** Each frame starts with a vowel and is followed by the two consecutive consonants that come after it in the alphabet. So, OMN should fill in the blank.

20. **The correct answer is (H).** This is a difficult question. You can see immediately that we are dealing with the alphabet in reverse and that no letters have been skipped. But what is the rule that governs? Assign a number to each letter in the first group, basing the number on natural sequence. Thus, figure W-X-Y-Z would be 1-2-3-4; here they appear Z-Y-W-X or 4-3-1-2. Follow through with the remaining groupings and you will find that all adhere to the same 4-3-1-2 rule. Now it is easy to choose the answer.

Section 2. Analogies

1. B	5. D	9. D	13. B	17. D
2. J	6. H	10. H	14. G	18. H
3. B	7. C	11. A	15. C	19. A
4. F	8. G	12. J	16. F	20. J

1. **The correct answer is (B).** Large four-footed mammal is to small four-footed mammal as large four-wheeled vehicle is to small four-wheeled vehicle. Large is to small is not an adequate formulation of the relationship because the elephant is also larger than the bug. You must refine your relationship until you find only one answer.

2. **The correct answer is (J).** The mother has lots of children as the hen has lots of chickens.

3. **The correct answer is (B).** The analogy here is sequential. Progress is from high chair to chair as it is from baby swing to swing. If asked to locate another analogous relationship, you would choose that of the tricycle to the bicycle.

4. **The correct answer is (F).** The relationship here is that of more to fewer. The centipede has more legs than the spider. The hexagon has more sides than the starfish has arms. The octagon and the octopus both sport eight sides or arms (more than the hexagon, not fewer), and the snake has none at all.

5. **The correct answer is (D).** In-line skates are wheeled vehicles worn on the feet and propelled by the person wearing them; a motorcycle is a wheeled vehicle ridden by a person and propelled by a motor. Analogously, skis are runnered, worn on the feet, and propelled by the person wearing them; a snowmobile is a runnered vehicle ridden by a person and propelled by a motor.

6. **The correct answer is (H).** The skull and crossbones and the "Mister Yuk" face on containers are both symbols for poisons. They say, "Danger. Don't eat or drink me." The American flag and the American eagle are both symbols for the United States. The hammer and sickle is the symbol for Russia. When faced with two possible choices to fit an analogy, you must refine the relationship. Here you must go beyond *symbol* to *symbol for the same thing*.

7. **The correct answer is (C).** A head goes on a pillow as feet go on a hassock. The relationship is one of purpose. The pillow goes on the bed, but that represents a reversal of the analogy.

8. **The correct answer is (G).** Pine cones are the seed carriers of the pine tree as acorns are the seed of the oak. Pine needles are part of the pine tree but not the seed-carrying part.

9. **The correct answer is (D).** Steak is an edible part of the steer; a drumstick is an edible part of the chicken. The egg is an edible product of the chicken, but it is not part of the meat of the chicken that is eaten.

10. **The correct answer is (H).** The analogy is of large to small of objects with similar functions. Thus, an axe is a long-handled wood-chopping tool, while the hatchet serves the same function but has a short handle. Similarly, the scythe is a long-handled grass-cutting tool, while the sickle serves the same function but has a short handle.

11. **The correct answer is (A).** Sometimes it is easier to explain an analogy by reading down instead of across. Thus, one eats from a soup bowl with a soup spoon and from a plate with a fork. Actually, this analogy is easy enough to solve visually, without words at all.

12. **The correct answer is (J).** This analogy is based on association. The swimsuited woman is associated with the palm tree; think "hot." The igloo is associated with the parka-clad person; think "cold."

13. **The correct answer is (B).** To solve this analogy, think "outside is to inside." The human body bears the same relationship to its skeleton as the full, finished house bears to its framework.

14. **The correct answer is (G).** California is a coastal state of the far west; Massachusetts is its counterpart on the east coast. Maine is the northernmost state on the east coast, while Florida is southernmost. You could articulate this analogy as: "west is to east as north is to south." Actually, this analogy need not be so carefully refined. It would be adequate to say: "coastal state is to coastal state as coastal state is to coastal state." No other choice makes sense in the analogy.

15. **The correct answer is (C).** The car consumes gasoline; the source of that fuel is the gas pump. The baby birds consume worms, moths, and insects; the source of their fuel is the mother bird. Do not confuse the source of the fuel with the fuel itself.

16. **The correct answer is (F).** The hockey goal is guarded by the goalie; the fort is guarded by the sentry. The goalie and the sentry are both guardians of the gates; they have analogous functions.

17. **The correct answer is (D).** The analogy is that of the eater to the eaten. The shark eats the little fish; the cat eats the mouse.

18. **The correct answer is (H).** Milk, when not being drunk, is preserved in the refrigerator. A diamond ring, when not being worn, is preserved in a safe.

19. **The correct answer is (A).** The analogy is based on activities at different stages of development. The infant plays lying down and gets around by crawling. The child plays by jumping rope, for example, and gets around running. The child in the stroller is getting around passively. It does not fit into the analogy.

20. **The correct answer is (J).** The analogy is that of the rescuer to the rescued. The helicopter comes to the rescue of the people adrift in the lifeboat. The St. Bernard comes to the rescue of the hiker stranded in bad weather.

Section 3. Quantitative Reasoning

1. A	5. C	9. C	13. D	17. B
2. H	6. F	10. F	14. F	18. H
3. B	7. A	11. B	15. D	19. A
4. F	8. J	12. F	16. H	20. F

1. **The correct answer is (A).**

   $2 + 4 = 6$

   $3 + 4 = 7$

   $5 + 4 = 9$

2. **The correct answer is (H).**

   $43 - 5 = 38$

   $34 - 5 = 29$

   $28 - 5 = 23$

3. **The correct answer is (B).**

   $30 - 3 = 27$

   $20 - 3 = 17$

   $10 - 3 = 7$

4. **The correct answer is (F).**

   $8 - 2 = 6$

   $5 - 2 = 3$

   $3 - 2 = 1$

5. **The correct answer is (C).**

   $2 \times 2 = 4$

   $5 \times 2 = 10$

   $9 \times 2 = 18$

6. **The correct answer is (F).**

   $42 \div 7 = 6$

   $84 \div 7 = 12$

   $105 \div 7 = 15$

7. **The correct answer is (A).** There are six squares in the grid. The line is drawn exactly from one corner to the other corner, which means that exactly half the total grid is shaded. Half the grid is $\frac{1}{2}$.

8. **The correct answer is (J).** The whole rectangle is divided into 12 equal smaller rectangles. Two of the smaller rectangles are further divided into two equal triangles. So, two such triangles are equal in area to one smaller rectangle. Therefore, the shaded part represents $\frac{4}{12} = \frac{1}{3}$ of the whole.

9. **The correct answer is (C).** There are eight squares. One complete square and two half-squares are shaded. $1 + \frac{1}{2} + \frac{1}{2}$ is 2. Two squares are shaded. 2 over 8 is $\frac{2}{8}$, or $\frac{1}{4}$.

10. **The correct answer is (F).** The whole rectangle is divided into 9 equal smaller rectangles. Five of these are shaded. So, the shaded part represents $\frac{5}{9}$ of the whole.

11. **The correct answer is (B).** There are eight squares in the grid. Five complete squares and two half-squares are shaded. $5 + \frac{1}{2} + \frac{1}{2}$ is 6. 6 over 8 is $\frac{6}{8}$, or $\frac{3}{4}$.

12. **The correct answer is (F).** There are nine squares. Six complete and two half-squares are shaded. $6 + \frac{1}{2} + \frac{1}{2} = 7$. 7 over 9 is $\frac{7}{9}$.

13. **The correct answer is (D).** There are nine squares. Four squares are shaded. 4 over 9 is $\frac{4}{9}$.

14. **The correct answer is (F).** The scale indicates that 1 cube = 1 cone. The only answer that maintains this relationship is choice (F), since it has 2 cubes = 2 cones.

15. **The correct answer is (D).** The scale indicates that 1 cube = 1 cone. The only answer that maintains this relationship is choice (D), since it has 1 cube + 2 cones = 2 cubes + 1 cone.

16. **The correct answer is (H).** The scale indicates that 1 cube = 1 cone. The only answer that maintains this relationship is choice (H), since it has 2 cubes + 1 cone = 3 cones.

17. **The correct answer is (B).** The scale indicates that 1 cube = 2 cones. The only answer that maintains this relationship is choice (B), since it has 2 cones = 2 cones.

18. **The correct answer is (H).** The scale indicates that 1 cube = 2 cones. The only answer that maintains this relationship is choice (H), since it has 1 cube + 1 cone = 3 cones.

19. **The correct answer is (A).** The scale indicates that 1 cube = 3 cones. The only answer that maintains this relationship is choice (A), since it has 2 cubes + 3 cones = 3 cubes.

20. **The correct answer is (F).** The scale indicates that 1 cube = 4 cones. The only answer that maintains this relationship is choice (F), since it has 1 cube + 4 cones = 2 cubes.

Section 4. Verbal Reasoning—Words

1. C	5. B	9. C	13. B	17. A
2. G	6. H	10. A	14. G	18. G
3. A	7. A	11. C	15. B	19. A
4. F	8. D	12. J	16. J	20. J

1. **The correct answer is (C).** A cartoon always involves some sort of drawing. A cartoon usually involves animation, but animation may be lacking in a political cartoon. Humor and a message are common ingredients, but a cartoon may be simply decorative.

2. **The correct answer is (G).** The heroine must be a woman.

3. **The correct answer is (A).** Among the answer choices, the only necessary part of music is sound. Music can still exist if it doesn't have a voice, instruments, or someone to hear it.

4. **The correct answer is (F).** The necessary part of a lantern is light. The source of the light might be a bulb, and the light can shine through mica or plastic as well as through glass.

5. **The correct answer is (B).** Information is absolutely necessary to the existence of data. Numbers, words, and charts all constitute information.

6. **The correct answer is (H).** A biography is the story of a life.

7. **The correct answer is (A).** An essential component of a table is a surface on which to place things. Legs are not essential, as a solid piece of wood or other item might be used as a table. Likewise, a table does not require a chair or a meal.

8. **The correct answer is (D).** The concept of student requires a teacher. It does not require assignments, grades, or books.

9. **The correct answer is (C).** An inch is a unit of measurement. While a ruler can help measure, it is not an essential part. Likewise, an inch does not require a yard or height.

10. **The correct answer is (A).** Among the answer choices, a nation or country is the only necessary part of patriotism. It does not require a flag, anthem, or ruler.

11. **The correct answer is (C).** Above the line are the primary colors of the spectrum, in order. Below the line are the mixed colors, also in order of appearance.

12. **The correct answer is (J).** Above the line are natural energy sources. Below the line are fossil fuels. Wood, uranium, and fission are all sources of power, but only oil is a fossil fuel.

13. **The correct answer is (B).** Above the line are two parts (*Monday* and *Thursday*) followed by the whole they make up (*week*). Below the line is two parts (*branches* and *leaves*) of a whole—a *tree*, choice (B).

14. **The correct answer is (G).** Above the line are degrees of wetness, from left to right most wet to least wet. Below the lines are academic degrees, from left to right the most highly educated doctorate to the master's and the baccalaureate degree.

15. **The correct answer is (B).** Above the line are seed fruits; below the line, the common factor is that all are stone fruits.

16. **The correct answer is (J).** The structures are connected in order.

17. **The correct answer is (A).** Above the line are the ordered stages of the human life-cycle, from infancy to adulthood. Above the line are ordered stages of education, from kindergarten to college.

18. **The correct answer is (G).** Above the line are types of connected items (*human senses*). Below the line are types of connected items (*human fingers*).

19. **The correct answer is (A).** Above the line are types of equipment used in the sport of hockey. Below the line are types of equipment used in the sport of tennis.

20. **The correct answer is (J).** Above the line are things you can do with your mouth. Below the line are things you can do with your feet.

Section 5. Verbal Reasoning—Context

1. D	5. D	9. A	13. B	17. D
2. H	6. G	10. H	14. H	18. F
3. C	7. A	11. D	15. B	19. D
4. F	8. J	12. F	16. G	20. F

1. **The correct answer is (D).** Because Bob went into the store alone and walked out empty-handed, we can safely conclude that the clerk did not sell cigarettes to Bob. No other assumption is supported by the facts as presented.

2. **The correct answer is (H).** If Tara's name was not on the injured list, Tara was not injured. She might have survived unscathed or have been killed. She might have missed the flight. As for choice (J), she might have changed her plans and taken a cruise to Bermuda instead. The possibility of an airline error in compiling the list of injured is not offered. Strictly on the basis of the situation described, you may correctly assume that Tara was not injured.

3. **The correct answer is (C).** Producers plan lavish stage productions to become long-running shows and always have contingency plans to replace actors as needed. There are many reasons why a show might not draw large audiences, but you can be certain that the reason for the premature closing was that the play was not a box office success.

4. **The correct answer is (F).** Michelle definitely spent some time at the kennel. We have no way of knowing where the kennel is nor at what point during Bernie's vacation Jack was called out of town. Bernie might have returned while Jack was out of town and might have taken Michelle home himself. And maybe Michelle was perfectly happy at the kennel or with Jack.

5. The correct answer is (D). The only statement that is definitely true among the answer choices is that lunch was available at noon every Wednesday at Glendale Junior High School. The passage explicitly states that "Glendale Junior High School served lunch in the cafeteria each weekday at noon," which would include every Wednesday, choice (D). There is no evidence that Sara ate a cafeteria lunch on Thursday (she could have brought lunch from home). Glendale Junior High School only serves lunch on weekdays, not on weekends. There's also no evidence that every student had an entrée during lunch.

6. The correct answer is (G).

adaba means *north*
mikula means *pole*
bomani means *south*
tinkipu means *wind*
gotono means *star*

Therefore, *manitu* must mean *east* and *manitutinkipu* must mean *east wind*.

7. The correct answer is (A). If you study this question carefully, you do not need to actually translate at all. The word that you are trying to identify, *geophysics*, has no elements in common with any of the three words for which you are given translations. You can therefore eliminate any choice that contains any element that appears in any of the three initial words.

8. The correct answer is (J). In this language, the modifiers follow the noun.

eleme means *fruit*
naftama means *vegetable*
hotuto means *red*
zigaru means *green*
bigani means *leafy*

Therefore, *toribuz* must mean *flower*. Remember that in this language, the modifier follows the noun. Choice (A) reverses this order. *Toribuzhotuto* means *red flower*.

9. The correct answer is (A). Angela always follows her advisor's recommendations, and her advisor suggests taking the advanced biology course. So, it must be true that Angela takes advanced biology. That is the only answer choice that is definitely true.

10. The correct answer is (H). The only statement that is definitely true among the answer choices is that Harvey the panther is not a vegetarian, as we are told "his favorite breakfast is a big raw steak." We are not told where Harvey was born (choice F), what other animals live at the zoo (choice G), or whether or not Harvey is a dangerous predator (choice J).

11. The correct answer is (D). Based on the statements, Kelly has to be the new class president. She received five more votes than Peter, the runner up.

12. The correct answer is (F). Since Heather leaves school before 3 p.m., she leaves in enough time to make her dance class. We don't have enough information to conclude that the other statements are true.

13. The correct answer is (B). The statements tell us that Farm Day cannot be held during bad weather, and the thunderstorms and dark skies indicate bad weather.

14. The correct answer is (H). Renee leaves Charleston at 3 p.m., and it takes her 4 hours to get to Charlotte. That puts her in Charlotte at about 7 p.m. The statements don't give us any information about the other answer choices, including driving ability or her means of travel.

15. The correct answer is (B). The only statement that is definitely true among the answer choices is that Cindy spent time commuting from her home to her office on Thursday, choice (B). We are not told whether she was looking forward to her business meeting, whether or not she was late for her meeting (it is possible that she left with plenty of time to get to her meeting, even if she did leave later than planned), or whether or not she's successful and well-respected at her job, making choices A, C, and D incorrect.

16. The correct answer is (G). Any of the four statements could be true, but the only thing we know for sure is that Abby scores high enough to be allowed to go out with her friends on Saturday. We know that if she earned at least a "C" on the history test, she would score high enough to be allowed to go. She ended up scoring a B+, which is better than a "C."

17. **The correct answer is (D).** We know that the boys obey Rick's parents. So, if they choose to play soccer at Rick's house, they must play outside. While the other choices could be true, there is not enough information to determine that they must be true.

18. **The correct answer is (F).** Because Rob places better than everyone in the spelling

contest except Martha, she is the highest placer in the group. We aren't given enough information to know if the other answer choices are true, including the difficulty of the words Nancy and Georgia missed.

19. **The correct answer is (D).** The newspaper staff does not use the school camera on Thursdays. Therefore, the yearbook staff is free to use the camera on Thursdays. Answer choice (D) must be true.

20. **The correct answer is (F).** Since Amber does not work on weekends, she can visit the nursing home on these nights. The other answer choices may or may not be true; we can't tell for sure that they're definitely true.

Section 6. Mathematics

1. C	9. A	17. B	25. A	33. B
2. G	10. H	18. G	26. G	34. F
3. A	11. C	19. A	27. D	35. C
4. J	12. G	20. G	28. H	36. H
5. B	13. D	21. C	29. B	37. D
6. F	14. J	22. H	30. H	38. H
7. C	15. C	23. D	31. C	39. C
8. J	16. F	24. H	32. J	40. J

1. **The correct answer is (C).** Convert x to an improper fraction and then flip it over to get the reciprocal:

$x = 2\frac{2}{5} = \frac{12}{5}$, so the reciprocal is $\frac{5}{12}$.

2. **The correct answer is (G).** The product of any number and its reciprocal is 1. Therefore, $\frac{7}{16} \times \frac{16}{7} = 1$, and making choice (G) the correct answer. Even if you didn't know this rule, you could have examined the answers and eliminated choice (F) because that product was greater than 1 and choice (J) because its product was less than 1.

3. **The correct answer is (A).** This problem looks much harder than it really is. The numerator of this complex fraction is the same as the denominator. When numerator and denominator are equivalent, the fraction is equal to 1.

4. **The correct answer is (H).** First, simplify the numerator:

$$\frac{5}{12} - \frac{7}{24} = \frac{10}{24} - \frac{7}{24}$$

$$= \frac{3}{24}$$

$$= \frac{1}{8}$$

Next, simplify the denominator:

$$\frac{1}{2} - \frac{3}{8} = \frac{4}{8} - \frac{3}{8} = \frac{1}{8}.$$

So, $\dfrac{\dfrac{5}{12} - \dfrac{7}{24}}{\dfrac{1}{2} - \dfrac{3}{8}} = \dfrac{\dfrac{1}{8}}{\dfrac{1}{8}} = 1$.

5. **The correct answer is (B).** This is a problem in which you must substitute the values given into the formula. After you do that, it is a simple problem.

$$L = \frac{3}{4} \times 2 \times 7 \times \frac{1}{2}$$

$$\frac{3 \times 2 \times 7 \times 1}{4 \times 2} = \frac{42}{8} = \frac{21}{4}$$

Therefore, choice (B) is the correct answer. The other answers would have resulted if you had forgotten to multiply one of the numbers in the numerator. Choice (D) might have been chosen by someone who didn't know what to do but thought the most difficult-looking answer would be the best.

6. **The correct answer is (F).** The sum of the angles of a triangle is always 180°. The correct answer, therefore, is choice (F) because 45° + 75° + 60° = 180°.

7. **The correct answer is (C).** Note that the base of the triangle is the same as the diameter of the circle. Because ΔABC is isosceles, its altitude is the same length as the radius of the circle. Use the formula for the area of a triangle, and substitute the correct values:

$$A = \frac{1}{2}bh$$

$$= \frac{1}{2} \times 10 \times 5$$

$$= 25 \text{ cm}^2$$

Choice (A) is the area of the circle.

8. **The correct answer is (J).** These measurements describe a large rectangular room 30 feet high. Use the formula $V = l \times w \times h$ to find the volume:

$V = 75$ feet × 50 feet × 30 feet

$V = 112{,}500$ cubic feet

Choices (G) and (H) use the wrong units. Volume is always measured in *cubic* units.

9. **The correct answer is (A).** A store markup of 100% would exactly double the price. An 80% markup almost doubles the price. The $14 jeans are priced at almost double their cost to the store. By estimation, the best answer is choice (A). To figure precisely, remember that an 80% markup is the equivalent of multiplying the cost by 180%, or 1.80.

cost × 1.80 = 14.00

cost = 14.00 ÷ 1.80

cost = $7.78

10. **The correct answer is (H).** The finance charge will be the sum of $1\frac{1}{2}\%$ of $500, plus 1% of $250. You can write this as follows:

(0.015 × 500) + (0.01 × 250) = 7.50 + 2.50 = $10.00

You can estimate the answer if you remember that percent means "hundredths of." One hundredth of $500 is $5.00; one hundredth of $250 is $2.50. The only answer near this sum is choice (H), $10.00. Choices (G) and (J) would have resulted if you had misplaced a decimal point.

11. **The correct answer is (C).** The area of the shaded portion is equal to the area of the square, less the area of the circle. The length of the side of the square is equal to the diameter of the circle. Therefore, using $\frac{22}{7}$ for pi:

$$(4" \times 4") - (\pi 2^2) = 16 \text{ sq. in.} - \frac{88}{7} \text{ sq. in.}$$
$$= 3\frac{3}{7} \text{ sq. in.}$$

The correct answer is (C). If you selected choice (D), $4\frac{3}{7}$, check your skills in subtracting fractions from whole numbers.

12. **The correct answer is (G).** For each teacher, there are 14 students. Because there are 14 teachers, there must be 14×14, or 196, students.

13. **The correct answer is (D).**

$$\frac{10^4}{100^5} = \frac{10^4}{(10^2)^5}$$
$$= \frac{10^4}{10^{10}}$$
$$= \frac{1}{10^6}$$
$$= \frac{1}{1,000,000}$$

14. **The correct answer is (J).** In the whole number system, every other number is odd and every other number is even. If x is odd, $x + 1$ is even, $x + 2$ is odd, $x + 3$ is even, and so forth. Also, if x is odd, $x - 1$ is even, $x - 2$ is odd, and $x - 3$ is even. If an even or odd number is doubled, the outcome is even. Therefore, if x is odd, $2x + 1$ is odd, $x - 2$ is odd, and $4x - 3$ is odd.

15. **The correct answer is (C).** Arrange the periods of time in columns and add as you would add whole numbers.

```
  4 hr.    17 min.
  3 hr.    58 min.
           45 min.
+ 7 hr.    12 min.
 14 hr.   132 min.
```

We know there are 60 minutes in each hour. Therefore, 132 minutes equal 2 hours 12 minutes. The correct answer for this addition is 16 hours 12 minutes, or choice (C). When working with units that measure time, volume, and length, it is usually best to represent the answer using as many larger units as possible. That's why 16 hours 12 minutes is preferable to 14 hours 132 minutes as an answer.

16. **The correct answer is (F).** You do not have to calculate this answer. If eight people share equally of 8 pounds and some ounces of fruit, each person would receive 1 pound and a few ounces. Only choice (F) is possible.

17. **The correct answer is (B).** This is a subtraction problem. You must find the difference between the lengths of time required to finish the race. As with other problems involving units of measurement, you must work carefully.

```
  3 hr.  2 min. 24 sec.
- 2 hr. 12 min. 38 sec.
```

Because 38 seconds is larger than 24 seconds and 12 minutes is larger than 2 minutes, borrow from the minutes column and the hour column and rewrite the problem as follows:

```
  2 hr. 61 min. 84 sec.
- 2 hr. 12 min. 38 sec.
  0 hr. 49 min. 46 sec.
```

18. **The correct answer is (G).** If the drawing is at $\frac{1}{16}$ scale, it means that the drawing is $\frac{1}{16}$ the size of the actual wheel. Therefore, multiply the size of the drawing by 16. $1.8 \times 16 = 28.8$ inches

19. **The correct answer is (A).** This problem asks you to find speed or rate. Speed or rate is found by dividing the distance traveled by the time required. The choice in which distance is divided by time is (A).

20. **The correct answer is (G).** There are 9 square feet in 1 square yard. So, y square feet equals $\frac{y}{9}$ square yards. Since there are x rooms with the same area, multiply this by x to get $x\left(\frac{y}{9}\right) = \frac{xy}{9}$ square yards.

21. **The correct answer is (C).**

    Step 1. To find the correct ratio, write it as:

    $$\frac{6 \text{ inches}}{6 \text{ feet}}$$

    Step 2. Rewrite each quantity in inches.

    $$\frac{6 \text{ inches}}{72 \text{ inches}}$$

    Step 3. Simplify the ratio.

    $$\frac{6}{72} = \frac{1}{12} = 1:12$$

22. **The correct answer is (H).** Here, three events occur periodically, so we must find the LCM of 4, 11, and 33 and add that number to 1950. That year will be the next common occurrence. The LCM of 4, 11, and 33 is 132. $1950 + 132 = 2082$.

23. **The correct answer is (D).** This is a two-step problem. First, find the length of the hypotenuse, so you know how far the other person is driving.

    $$(AC)^2 = (AB)^2 + (BC)^2$$
    $$= (40)^2 + (30)^2$$
    $$= 1600 + 900$$
    $$(AC) = \sqrt{2500} = 50 \text{ miles}$$

    This tells you that the person driving directly from C to A is driving 50 miles at 50 mph. He or she will get there in 1 hour. The other driver going from C to B to A is driving 70 miles. To get there first, he or she must drive faster, or more than 70 miles per hour (mph), choice (D).

24. **The correct answer is (H).** This graph contains a line that has points with coordinates (1,1), (2,2), (3,3) and (4,4). From one point to another, the value of the x-coordinate changes just as much as the value of the y-coordinate. This line is at a 45° angle from the x-axis and will be created whenever the x- and y-coordinates are equal.

25. **The correct answer is (A).** The first 6 is in the billions place; the second, in the hundred-thousands place. If you had trouble with this problem, review the sections on how to read numbers and determine place values in your math textbook.

26. **The correct answer is (G).** A scale of 1:24,000 means that 1 inch on the map equals 24,000 inches on the ground. 24,000 inches equals 2,000 feet ($24,000 \div 12 = 2,000$).

27. **The correct answer is (D).** This is a *literal problem* requiring you to "think without numbers." Creating mental pictures might help you solve this type of problem. If each person in a group makes L number of things, the group's output will be the product of the number of people in the group and the number of things each makes. Choice (D) represents the product and is the correct answer.

28. The correct answer is (H). Find 300 on the horizontal axis. Draw a vertical line upward until you touch the line. Move horizontally from this point on the line to the vertical axis. Note that you touch the vertical axis at a point roughly equivalent to $20. We suggest you use a ruler to sketch your line.

29. The correct answer is (B). To find the perimeter, we add up the dimensions of all of the sides. Note that there are some parts that have not been assigned measurements, so we should infer that they are the same as those corresponding parts whose measurements have been designated because we are told to assume that there are right angles in the figure. Beginning at the bottom and moving clockwise, the dimensions are:

5" + 7" + 1" + 3" + 3" + 3" + 1" + 7"

These equal 30 inches. If you selected choices (A), (C), or (D), you failed to add up all of the segments.

30. The correct answer is (H). The ratio of men to women is 15:12, but this ratio must be expressed in simplest form. Because 15 and 12 have 3 as a common factor, the ratio expressed correctly is 5:4. The ratio of women to men would be 12:15 or 4:5.

31. The correct answer is (C). A straight line represents a "straight angle" of 180°. An angle of 60° is given, so m∠C must be 120° to complete the line. Knowing that all the angles in a triangle added together equal 180°,

$$m\angle A + m\angle B + m\angle C = 180°$$
$$m\angle A + 35° + 120° = 180°$$
$$m\angle A = 180° - 155°$$
$$m\angle A = 25°$$

32. The correct answer is (J). This is a simple subtraction problem designed to test how carefully you can subtract. It is possible to calculate the correct answer without pencil and paper. 999,999 is only 1 less than a million, and 1,001,000 is 1000 greater than a million. The difference, then, is 1000 + 1, or 1001. Or, you may figure the problem in the following way:

```
  1001000
−  999999
     1001
```

33. The correct answer is (B). The surface of a rectangular solid such as a brick is found by calculating the area of each face of the brick and finding the sum of the areas of the faces. The brick has 6 faces:

Two faces 6" × 3"; total 36 sq. in.

Two faces 6" × 2"; total 24 sq. in.

Two faces 3" × 2"; total 12 sq. in.

Total 72 sq. in.

Surface area of a solid figure, is expressed in square measure. Only volume is expressed in cubic measure.

34. The correct answer is (F).

Step 1. $-3 - [-2 + (5 - 6) - 3]$

Step 2. $-3 - [-2 + (-1) - 3]$

Step 3. $-3 - [-2 - 1 - 3]$

Step 4. $-3 - [-6]$

Step 5. $-3 + 6 = +3$

35. The correct answer is (C). By far the easiest way to solve this problem is to rename the fractions as decimals: 0.6 + 1.5 + 0.75 = 2.85. If you were to rename as fractions, the correct answer would be $2\frac{17}{20}$.

36. The correct answer is (H). When simplifying, begin with the innermost grouping symbols first, and work your way outward.

Step 1. $-6 - [2 - (3a - b) + b] + a$

Step 2. $-6 - [2 - 3a + b + b] + a$

Step 3. $-6 - [2 - 3a + 2b] + a$

Step 4. $-6 - 2 + 3a - 2b + a$

Step 5. $-8 + 4a - 2b$

37. The correct answer is (D). Begin with the innermost parentheses and work your way outward. Note that a negative sign in front of a grouping symbol reverses the signs of all numbers within.

Step 1. $-2\,[\,-4\,(2-1)+(3+2)]$

Step 2. $-2\,[\,-4\,(1)+(5)]$

Step 3. $-2\,[\,-4+5]$

Step 4. $-2\,[+1]=-2$

38. The correct answer is (H). The Pythagorean theorem is used to find the length of the sides of right triangles. The square of the length of the longest side (the hypotenuse) is equal to the sum of the squares of the other two sides. Once we know the square of the length of the longest side, it is easy to find the length.

$$(AC)^2 = (AB)^2 + (BC)^2$$
$$(AC)^2 = 3^2 + 4^2$$
$$(AC)^2 = 25$$
$$AC = \sqrt{25} = 5$$

39. The correct answer is (C). This proportion asks you to find the missing element. A proportion is a statement of equality between two ratios, so we know that 5 bears the same relationship to 15 as 6 does to the unknown number. Since 3×5 equals 15, we know 3×6 equals the unknown number. The number, thus, is 18. The completed proportion should read: 5:6 as 15:18. Proportions may also be written with a set of two colons replacing the word "as." In this case, the proportion would read: 5:6::15:18.

40. The correct answer is (J). Calculate the surface area of the cube. It has six faces, each 2" × 2". Its surface area, then, is 6×4 sq. in., or 24 sq. in. Its volume is found by multiplying its length × width × height, or $2" \times 2" \times 2" = 8$ cu. in. The ratio of surface area to volume is 24:8, or 3:1.

Section 7. Reading and Language Arts

1. C	11. D	21. D	31. A	41. A
2. H	12. F	22. F	32. J	42. F
3. C	13. A	23. C	33. C	43. D
4. F	14. H	24. G	34. G	44. G
5. A	15. B	25. A	35. D	45. D
6. J	16. J	26. J	36. F	46. H
7. C	17. A	27. A	37. B	47. C
8. G	18. G	28. H	38. H	48. J
9. C	19. B	29. B	39. D	49. B
10. F	20. H	30. G	40. H	50. F

1. The correct answer is (C). Choosing the title for this paragraph takes more than one reading of the paragraph. This is not an easy question. After a couple of readings, however, you should be able to conclude that the all-inclusive subject of the paragraph is the remodeling of plants. An equally correct title, not offered here, might be "Uses and Effects of Colchicine."

2. **The correct answer is (H).** Buried in the middle of the paragraph is the sentence: "It creates new varieties with astonishing frequency, whereas such mutations occur but rarely in nature."

3. **The correct answer is (C).** This question becomes easy to answer after you have dealt with the previous question. Colchicine speeds the improvement of plant species because it creates new varieties very quickly.

4. **The correct answer is (F).** The third sentence states that colchicine is a poisonous drug.

5. **The correct answer is (A).** The answer to this question of fact is in the first sentence, where it states that the Ohio Company was *under the leadership of Reverend Manasseh Cutler.*

6. **The correct answer is (J).** Do not be misled by the first sentence, which introduces Reverend Manasseh Cutler, nor by the last portion of the selection, which discusses the naming of Cleveland. The entire selection has to do with the settling of the Northwest Territory.

7. **The correct answer is (C).** In this context, the word *related* means reported or simply told.

8. **The correct answer is (G).** Read carefully. General Cleaveland *quieted the Indian claims*; he did not quiet the Indians. If the Indians were making claims, they were not eager to work with him. The selection suggests that General Cleaveland bought off the Indians with money, cattle, and whiskey.

9. **The correct answer is (C).** Clearly the writer of the selection is an admirer of carrier pigeons, praising their usefulness and reliability.

10. **The correct answer is (F).** G. I. Joe brought the news of an allied victory, but he was rewarded for the results of his bringing the news, for preventing unnecessary loss of life. If the British had not received news that their troops were already in the town of Colvi Vecchia, they would have sent out the raid and bombed their own soldiers. When two answers to a question seem right, you must choose the one that more specifically answers what is asked.

11. **The correct answer is (D).** At the end of paragraph 3, it states that the Lord Mayor of London gave G. I. Joe the Dickin *Medal*, England's highest award to an animal.

12. **The correct answer is (F).** This sentence is written correctly. The other answer choices contain errors of usage and grammar.

13. **The correct answer is (A).** The context in which it is used should help you to choose this answer. ". . . veneration due to its sacred origin . . ." implies something religious and related to worship.

14. **The correct answer is (H).** The speaker probably does celebrate and enjoy Christmas, but the primary reason for this speech is to defend the holiday to Uncle Scrooge by listing its advantages to mankind.

15. **The correct answer is (B).** This is the whole point of the first paragraph. The passage states that the expedition led by John Amatt was the only successful expedition to scale Mount Everest.

16. **The correct answer is (J).** Again, use of the word in context should lead you to its meaning. The paragraph speaks of goodwill among all men and women. This *one consent* therefore is *unanimous* good feeling.

17. **The correct answer is (A).** Read the last paragraph carefully. Scrooge is first reacting to the clerk who has just applauded the speech in defense of Christmas. Scrooge threatens the clerk with firing. He then turns and makes a sarcastic remark to his nephew. It can be assumed that he is angry with both characters.

18. **The correct answer is (G).** Choices (F), (H), and (J) are incorrect, because they contain ideas that are not mentioned in the passage. The first sentence explains that an art form will become the subject of scholarly study when it becomes

widespread, not when it generates profits, becomes a century old, or disappears from public view. Choice (G) is therefore correct.

19. **The correct answer is choice (B).** According to the third paragraph, after hip-hop became mainstream, the music then became standardized and mass-produced. Choice (A) is incorrect because the author makes it clear that although some music loses popularity and disappears after becoming mass-produced, this did not happen to hip-hop.

20. **The correct answer is (H).** This question is a "cause and effect" question. It asks you to identify the *reason why* hip-hop music has not lost its identity, according to John Richardson. The answer to this question can be found in the last paragraph of the passage. Here, we are told that in Richardson's view, part of the reason why hip-hop did not lose its identity entirely is because it kept its emphasis on the underground, so choice (H) is correct.

21. **The correct answer is (D).** The second paragraph states that hip-hop originally reflected the view of a specific minority group, so choice (D) is the correct answer. Choice (C) is incorrect, because although hip-hop is a form of underground music, the passage indicates that it first emerged to express the views of a minority group, not a business.

22. **The correct answer is (F).** In the third paragraph of the passage, we are told that when hip-hop became mainstream, it lost some of its subtle qualities. Choice (F) states accurately that hip-hop lost some of its subtle qualities in the process of becoming mainstream, so choice (F) is correct.

Choices (G), (H), and (J) are incorrect, because they contradict the information in the passage. According to the third paragraph, when hip-hop became mainstream, it *lost* some of its originality. Also, once hip-hop became mainstream, it next became "standardized and mass-produced." Finally, the last paragraph tells us that hip-hop never fell out of favor as a popular style.

23. **The correct answer is (C).** The first paragraph of the article states that armadillos are found in the southeastern United States and as far north as Kansas. Michigan is on the northern border of the United States.

24. **The correct answer is (G).** This information is found in the third and fourth sentences of paragraph two: *Nine-banded armadillos have nine separate segments of bony plate around their midsections. This allows them to bend.*

25. **The correct answer is (A).** Check the first sentence of paragraph five to note that armadillos are not likely to stand their ground when threatened.

26. **The correct answer is (J).** In paragraph four, sentences five and six explain how an armadillo inflates its intestines when it has a need to swim: *For longer aquatic encounters, the armadillo gulps in air to inflate its intestines. This makes its body quite buoyant, enabling the armadillo to become a capable swimmer.*

27. **The correct answer is (A).** Any one of the reasons might be accurate, but the author specifically tells you his reason in the second sentence, which states that "... it's worthwhile to hear the story, before it is forgotten."

28. **The correct answer is (H).** The answer can be found in the third sentence: "The Emperor's palace was the most splendid in the world; entirely and altogether made of porcelain.."

29. **The correct answer is (B).** The answer is in the fourth sentence, where it states that the silver bells were tied to the flowers so that no one would be able to pass without noticing the flowers' beauty.

30. **The correct answer is (G).** The selection says that the garden extended so far that the gardener did not know where it ended, but it does not say that he was unable to care for it because of its size. In the sixth sentence, we learn that the garden led into a lovely forest. The nightingale lived in the forest, not in the garden.

answers practice test 4

31. The correct answer is (A). The passage tells us in paragraph four that the Earth's inner core is made up mainly of iron and a lighter element, so choices (C) and (D) can be eliminated. Paragraph five states that silicon may be the key element in addition to iron, so choice (A) is correct.

32. The correct answer is (J). The passage tells us that most parts of the Earth move at a rate of about 10 centimeters per year. Paragraph three states that the inner core moves faster than the other parts of the Earth, but the exact speed of the inner core is not mentioned. Choice (J) is therefore correct.

33. The correct answer is (C). The first paragraph of the passage states that the Earth has three separate layers and that these are the crust, mantle, and core, so choice (C) is the correct answer.

34. The correct answer is (G). The fourth paragraph states the scientists have learned about the Earth's core through seismic studies, which investigate waves traveling through the Earth caused by earthquakes and explosives.

35. The correct answer is (D). The last paragraph states the silicon lowers the density of iron when the two elements are placed together under high pressure conditions, making choice (D) the correct answer.

36. The correct answer is (F). This passage is about kopi luwak coffee, the process it undergoes to be created, and why it's such a prized and expensive beverage. The title that best expresses the main idea of this passage is "Kopi Luwak: A Prized Cup of Coffee," choice (F).

37. The correct answer is (B). The passage explicitly mentions that "these prized beans are harvested from the digested remains of coffee cherries that have been eaten by Asian palm civets," so choice (B) is correct.

38. The correct answer is (G). The word *adage*, which appears in the final sentence of the passage, appears right before the following quoted material: "'there's no accounting for taste' is on full display." Scanning the answer choices, this is most closely a

saying, so choice (G) is correct. This isn't a warning, joke, or secret code, so choices (F), (H), and (J) are incorrect.

39. The correct answer is (D). The passage mentions that "the vast majority of kopi luwak is produced in the islands of Java, Bali, Sumatra, Sulawesi, and the Philippines." The only choice not mentioned in the passage is Nicaragua, choice (D).

40. The correct answer is (H). The passage discusses some of the properties of the fermentation process, and how the coffee beans are changed. This includes a reduction in the bitterness of the coffee beans, choice (H). The other choices are not mentioned in the passage.

41. The correct answer is (A). The subordinate sentences in the paragraph support the notion that technology is changing the way we live, choice (A). Choices (B) and (D) would better serve as supporting details than topic sentences. Choice (C) runs counter to the argument in the paragraph.

42. The correct answer is (F). Because the first development sentence tells of two dimensions that are not the same, and the remainder of the paragraph proceeds to define these two dimensions, it is reasonable to expect the topic sentence to lead into discussion of at least one of these dimensions.

43. The correct answer is (D). What consists only of ordinances with little or no attempt at enforcement? Only "the varying degrees of inspection and control" answers this question, so it must be the topic sentence.

44. The correct answer is (G). The topic sentence introduces the structure of the ear and specifically mentions the eardrum. Choice (G) tells of the function of the eardrum and then continues describing the structure of the ear. Choice (H) speaks of "this tube," but the reference is unclear. All other choices lead off on various tangents, all of them ear-related but none of them logically developing the topic sentence.

45. The correct answer is (D). The topic sentence promises a history of the development of open-air markets in urban locations. Choice (D) picks right up on the theme. Choices (A) and (B) focus in on the negative aspects of the open-air markets. Choice (C) digresses to the nature of open-air markets in other cultures.

46. **The correct answer is (H).** This is the only choice that directly addresses the concept of crowdfunding and how it could be an effective way for new entrepreneurs and businesses to achieve success.

47. **The correct answer is (C).** The main point of this paragraph is to inform readers how to make iced tea. Although choice (C) is an interesting idea about how iced tea can be used once it's made, it is the only choice that does not directly discuss how iced tea is made.

48. **The correct answer is (J).** The sentence following the underline discusses how pufferfish employ their natural defense mechanisms to protect themselves from danger. A logical preceding sentence would detail what these defense mechanisms are, which choice (J) does.

49. **The correct answer is (B).** The second sentence, telling us that different fuels have different kindling temperatures, sets the stage. What follows should be a discussion of a number of fuels with respect to their kindling temperatures, and the sentence in choice (B) does just that: *Paper catches fire easily because it has a low kindling temperature.*

50. **The correct answer is (F).** The next two sentences tell some reasons for which an arsonist might set a fire. Choice (H) also gives a reason, but "another" must come later in the paragraph. Choice (F) is correct as it states: *Arsonists set fires for many different reasons.*

SCORE SHEET

CTB/McGraw-Hill will score your actual exam and send your scaled scores and your percentile scores directly to the schools you indicated. Scaled scores are scores converted by a special formula to make comparable your performance on tests of unequal lengths and unequal importance. Percentile scores compare your performance on each test and the whole exam with the performance of other students who took the same exam at the same time. Your scores will not be reported either as raw scores—that is, number correct—nor as percents. Right now, however, you will find it very useful to convert your own scores on the practice exam into simple percentages. In this way, you can compare your own performance on each test of the exam with your performance on each other test. You can then focus your study where it will do you the most good.

Subject	No. Correct ÷ No. of Questions	× 100 = ____ %
Sequences	____ ÷ 20 =	____ × 100 = ____ %
Analogies	____ ÷ 20 =	____ × 100 = ____ %
Quantitative Reasoning	____ ÷ 20 =	____ × 100 = ____ %
Verbal Reasoning—Words	____ ÷ 12 =	____ × 100 = ____ %
Verbal Reasoning—Context	____ ÷ 20 =	____ × 100 = ____ %
Mathematics	____ ÷ 40 =	____ × 100 = ____ %
Reading and Language Arts	____ ÷ 50 =	____ × 100 = ____ %
TOTAL EXAM	____ ÷ 182 =	____ × 100 = ____ %

Now compare the percentage scores you just earned on the Practice Test 4: COOP with the scores you achieved on the Practice Test 3: COOP. If you have paid attention to the study chapters in this book and if you have concentrated especially on your areas of previous weakness, you should see a marked improvement in your performance. If you still see trouble spots, review the applicable study chapters again and, perhaps, consult a textbook or a teacher for further help and suggestions.

Subject	Practice Test 3	Practice Test 4
Sequences	%	%
Analogies	%	%
Quantitative Reasoning	%	%
Verbal Reasoning--Words	%	%
Verbal Reasoning--Context	%	%
Mathematics	%	%
Reading and Language Arts	%	%
TOTAL EXAM	%	%

Practice Test 5: HSPT®

VERBAL SKILLS

16 Minutes

Directions: Mark one answer—the answer you think is best—for each problem.

1. Which word does *not* belong with the others?
   - **(A)** oven
   - **(B)** toaster
   - **(C)** cook
   - **(D)** microwave

2. Which word does *not* belong with the others?
   - **(A)** run
   - **(B)** walk
   - **(C)** jog
   - **(D)** sneaker

3. Red is to pink as black is to
   - **(A)** beige.
   - **(B)** white.
   - **(C)** dark.
   - **(D)** gray.

4. Ann reads faster than Sue. Karen reads faster than Ann. Karen reads more slowly than Sue. If the first two statements are true, the third is
   - **(A)** true.
   - **(B)** false.
   - **(C)** uncertain.

5. *Create* most nearly means
   - **(A)** destroy.
   - **(B)** despise.
   - **(C)** discover.
   - **(D)** invent.

6. Youth is to young as age is to
   - **(A)** people.
   - **(B)** parents.
   - **(C)** grandmother.
   - **(D)** old.

7. Which word does *not* belong with the others?
   - **(A)** quality
   - **(B)** honesty
   - **(C)** sincerity
   - **(D)** integrity

8. Sand is to beach as black dirt is to
   - **(A)** earth.
   - **(B)** plants.
   - **(C)** water.
   - **(D)** farm.

9. Which word does *not* belong with the others?
   - **(A)** day
   - **(B)** time
   - **(C)** month
   - **(D)** hour

10. A *salamander* is a(n)
    - **(A)** amphibian.
    - **(B)** hammock.
    - **(C)** spice.
    - **(D)** fish.

11. *Arrogant* most nearly means
    (A) poised.
    (B) superior.
    (C) fragrant.
    (D) haughty.

12. North is to south as left is to
    (A) west.
    (B) down.
    (C) right.
    (D) sideways.

13. One is to two as three is to
    (A) two.
    (B) five.
    (C) thirty.
    (D) six.

14. Which word does *not* belong with the others?
    (A) figure
    (B) number
    (C) add
    (D) letter

15. Paul is taller than Peter. Peter is shorter than John. Paul is taller than John. If the first two statements are true, the third is
    (A) true.
    (B) false.
    (C) uncertain.

16. A *mellow* peach is
    (A) ripe.
    (B) rotten.
    (C) yellow.
    (D) green.

17. *Gossamer* most nearly means
    (A) beautiful.
    (B) flimsy.
    (C) eerie.
    (D) supernatural.

18. *Coddle* most nearly means
    (A) handle.
    (B) embrace.
    (C) pamper.
    (D) love.

19. Books are to libraries as rides are to
    (A) carnivals.
    (B) fun.
    (C) roller coaster.
    (D) bookstore.

20. Choir is to director as team is to
    (A) sport.
    (B) coach.
    (C) player.
    (D) athlete.

21. *Diversify* most nearly means
    (A) vary.
    (B) oppose.
    (C) change.
    (D) strengthen.

22. Harry is more intelligent than George. Sam is more intelligent than Ralph. Harry is more intelligent than Ralph. If the first two statements are true, the third is
    (A) true.
    (B) false.
    (C) uncertain.

23. A *superficial* wound is
    (A) serious.
    (B) deep.
    (C) facial.
    (D) shallow.

24. Jackie can throw a javelin farther than Elsa. Liandra can throw a javelin farther than Shelley but not as far as Jackie. Shelley won the javelin-throwing contest. If the first two sentences are true, the third is
    (A) true.
    (B) false.
    (C) uncertain.

25. A *bellicose* general is:
  (A) peaceful
  (B) combative
  (C) understanding
  (D) weak

26. A *sadistic* remark is
  (A) sad.
  (B) silly.
  (C) hurtful.
  (D) sudden.

27. Which word does *not* belong with the others?
  (A) college
  (B) university
  (C) school
  (D) dormitory

28. *Truncate* most nearly means
  (A) pack.
  (B) cut.
  (C) sound.
  (D) transport.

29. A *facetious* game show host is:
  (A) serious.
  (B) intelligent.
  (C) humorous.
  (D) boring.

30. An *indigent* person is
  (A) delicate.
  (B) intelligent.
  (C) indignant.
  (D) needy.

31. Table is to leg as automobile is to
  (A) wheel.
  (B) axle.
  (C) door.
  (D) fuel.

32. Which word does *not* belong with the others?
  (A) dungeon
  (B) residence
  (C) dwelling
  (D) domicile

33. Bishop's house is the largest on his street. Terrence and Arianna both live on Oakville Lane, but Arianna's house is much larger than Terrence's house. Arianna and Bishop live on the same street. Arianna's house is the largest on Oakville Lane. If the first two sentences are true, the fourth is
  (A) true.
  (B) false.
  (C) uncertain.

34. Which word does *not* belong with the others?
  (A) prison
  (B) jail
  (C) reformatory
  (D) punishment

35. Refuse means the *opposite* of
  (A) reheat.
  (B) accept.
  (C) reveal.
  (D) tidy.

36. Ink is to pen as paint is to
  (A) canvas.
  (B) bucket.
  (C) wall.
  (D) brush.

37. Acquire means the *opposite* of
  (A) solo.
  (B) buy.
  (C) release.
  (D) collect.

38. River A is wider than River B. River B is narrower than River C. River A is wider than River C. If the first two statements are true, the third is
(A) true.
(B) false.
(C) uncertain.

39. Scant means the *opposite* of
(A) sparse.
(B) scoundrel.
(C) abundant.
(D) straight.

40. Pinnacle means the *opposite* of
(A) bridge.
(B) base.
(C) wall.
(D) rummy.

41. Team is to captain as office is to
(A) secretary.
(B) accountant.
(C) staff.
(D) manager.

42. Which word does *not* belong with the others?
(A) window
(B) drape
(C) shade
(D) curtain

43. Corpulent means the *opposite* of
(A) bulky.
(B) singular.
(C) company.
(D) slender.

44. Naive means the *opposite* of
(A) rural.
(B) dull.
(C) sophisticated.
(D) funny.

45. Which word does *not* belong with the others?
(A) fez
(B) turban
(C) glove
(D) derby

46. Which word does *not* belong with the others?
(A) gallery
(B) audience
(C) congregation
(D) podium

47. *Pledge* most nearly means
(A) promise.
(B) beg.
(C) join.
(D) obey.

48. Depression is the *opposite* of
(A) incline.
(B) valley.
(C) hill.
(D) oppression.

49. Grapes cost more than apples but less than pineapples. Oranges cost more than apples but less than lemons. Apples cost the least of the fruits. If the first two statements are true, the third is
(A) true.
(B) false.
(C) uncertain.

50. Which word does *not* belong with the others?
(A) oak
(B) elm
(C) maple
(D) fir

51. Diminish is the *opposite* of
    (A) trim.
    (B) augment.
    (C) decorate.
    (D) decrease.

52. Jay's batting average is better than Michael's. Michael's batting average is higher than Tom's. Jay's batting average is lower than Tom's. If the first two statements are true, the third is
    (A) true.
    (B) false.
    (C) uncertain.

53. Abandon is the *opposite* of
    (A) abdicate.
    (B) keep.
    (C) maintain.
    (D) encourage.

54. Which word does *not* belong with the others?
    (A) flexible
    (B) feasible
    (C) supple
    (D) malleable

55. A is northeast of B. C is southwest of D but northwest of A. C is north of B. If the first two statements are true, the third is
    (A) true.
    (B) false.
    (C) uncertain.

56. Which word does *not* belong with the others?
    (A) leather
    (B) cotton
    (C) wool
    (D) fur

57. Which word does *not* belong with the others?
    (A) zipper
    (B) button
    (C) snap
    (D) seam

58. *Dwindle* most nearly means
    (A) shrink.
    (B) ooze.
    (C) leak.
    (D) spoil.

59. Which word does *not* belong with the others?
    (A) oxygen
    (B) water
    (C) helium
    (D) gold

60. Jon ran faster than Carl. Ron ran faster than George but not as fast as Jon. Carl was the fastest runner. If the first two statements are true, the third is
    (A) true.
    (B) false.
    (C) uncertain.

STOP End of Verbal Skills section. If you have any time left, go over your work in this section only. Do not work in any other section of the test.

QUANTITATIVE SKILLS

30 Minutes

Directions: Mark one answer—the answer you think is best—for each problem.

61. What number is 3 more than 20% of 40?

(A) 11

(B) 8

(C) 5

(D) 9

62. Look at this series: 32, 39, 46, 53, ...
What number should come next?

(A) 68

(B) 61

(C) 59

(D) 60

63. Look at this series: 48, 39, 30, 21, ...
What number should come next?

(A) 17

(B) 20

(C) 29

(D) 12

64. Examine (A), (B), and (C) and find the best
answer.

(A)   (B)   (C)

(A) (A) plus (C) is less than (B).

(B) (C) is equal to (A).

(C) (A) is greater than (C).

(D) (C) is less than (B) and greater
than (A).

65. Examine (A), (B), and (C) and find the best
answer.

(A) 0.625

(B) $\frac{4}{7}$

(C) 0.297 × 2.1

(A) (B) is less than (A) but greater than
(C).

(B) (A) and (C) are equal and greater than
(B).

(C) (C) is greater than (A) and (B).

(D) (B) is less than (A) and (C).

66. What number is the cube of 5 divided by 5?

(A) 15

(B) 25

(C) 75

(D) 125

67. What number is $\frac{1}{2}$ of the average of 7, 18,
5, 39, 11?

(A) 40

(B) 5

(C) 8

(D) 20

68. Examine (A), (B), and (C) and find the best
answer.

(A)   (B)   (C)

(A) (A) is more shaded than (B).

(B) (B) and (C) are equally shaded.

(C) (C) is less shaded than either (A) or
(B).

(D) (A) and (C) are both less shaded than
(B).

69. Look at this series: 1, 4, 11, _____, 21, 24, 31, ... What number should fill the blank in the middle of the series?

  (A) 3
  (B) 14
  (C) 20
  (D) 22

70. Examine (A), (B), and (C) and find the best answer.

  (A) 10% of 80
  (B) 80% of 10
  (C) 10% of 80%

  (A) (B) is greater than (A) or (C).
  (B) (A), (B), and (C) are equal.
  (C) (A) is equal to (B) and smaller than (C).
  (D) (A) is greater than (C).

71. Look at this series: 1, 2, 4, 5, 10, 11, ...
  What number should come next?

  (A) 22
  (B) 12
  (C) 15
  (D) 21

72. Look at this series: 56, 51, 47, 48, 43, 39, 40, ... What three numbers come next?

  (A) 36, 37, 32
  (B) 36, 31, 32
  (C) 35, 31, 32
  (D) 34, 30, 31

73. What number subtracted from 30 leaves 7 more than $\dfrac{3}{5}$ of 25?

  (A) 8
  (B) 15
  (C) 22
  (D) 23

74. What number is 7 more than $\dfrac{1}{4}$ of 64?

  (A) 4
  (B) 9
  (C) 18
  (D) 23

75. Examine (A), (B), and (C) and find the best answer.

  (A) $(8 \times 3) - 10$
  (B) $(5 \times 2) + 4$
  (C) $(4 \times 4) - 2$

  (A) (C) is greater than (A) and (B).
  (B) (A) is greater than (B) and equal to (C).
  (C) (A), (B), and (C) are equal.
  (D) (B) is greater than (A) and less than (C).

76. Look at this series: 821, 812, 804, 797, ... What number should come next?

  (A) 791
  (B) 788
  (C) 787
  (D) 790

77. Examine (A), (B), and (C) and find the best answer.

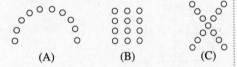

  (A)   (B)   (C)

  (A) (A) has more circles than (B).
  (B) (B) and (C) have the same number of circles.
  (C) (B) and (C) each have more circles than (A).
  (D) (A) and (C) each have fewer circles than (B).

78. Examine (A), (B), and (C) and find the best answer.

  (A)   (B)   (C)

  (A) (C) is more shaded than (B).
  (B) (A) and (C) are equally shaded, and both are more shaded than (B).
  (C) (B) is more shaded than (A) and less shaded than (C).
  (D) (A), (B), and (C) are equally shaded.

79. Look at this series: 95, 99, _____, 107, 111. What number should fill the blank in the middle of the series?

(A) 104

(B) 98

(C) 106

(D) 103

80. What number divided by 4 is $\frac{1}{5}$ of 100?

(A) 400

(B) 20

(C) 80

(D) 200

81. Look at this series: 1, V, 6, X, ... What number should come next?

(A) XV

(B) 11

(C) 10

(D) IX

82. Examine (A), (B), and (C) and find the best answer.

(A) $\frac{1}{3}$ of 15

(B) $\frac{1}{4}$ of 16

(C) $\frac{1}{5}$ of 20

(A) (A) and (B) are each greater than (C).

(B) (A), (B), and (C) are equal.

(C) (C) is greater than (A).

(D) (B) and (C) are equal.

83. $\frac{1}{2}$ of what number is 7 times 3?

(A) 21

(B) 42

(C) 20

(D) 5

84. Examine (A), (B), and (C) and find the best answer.

(A)   (B)   (C)

(A) (A), (B), and (C) are equally shaded.

(B) (B) is less shaded than (C) and more shaded than (A).

(C) (A) is more shaded than (B) or (C).

(D) (C) is more shaded than (A).

85. What number added to 6 is 3 times the product of 5 and 2?

(A) 16

(B) 4

(C) 30

(D) 24

86. Look at this series: 50, 48, 52, 50, 54, 52, ... What number should come next?

(A) 50

(B) 56

(C) 54

(D) 58

87. Examine (A), (B), and (C) and find the best answer.

(A) 125%

(B) 1.25

(C) $\frac{25}{2}$

(A) (A) is greater than (C), and (C) is greater than (b).

(B) (A) and (B) are equal, and both are less than (C).

(C) (A) and (C) are equal, and both are greater than (B).

(D) (A), (B), and (C) are all equal.

$\frac{3}{2} \cdot \frac{2}{3}x = 27 \cdot \frac{3}{2} = \frac{81}{2} = 40.5$

88. $\frac{3}{4}$ of what number is 6 times 4?

(A) 18
(B) 24
(C) 32
(D) 8

$\frac{3}{3} \cdot \frac{3}{4}x = 24 \cdot 4$

$= 8 \cdot 4 = 3.2$

89. Look at this series: 12, 14, 28, _____, 60, ... What number should fill the blank in this series?

(A) 19
(B) 16
(C) 40
(D) 30

90. Look at this series: 4, 5, 8, 11, 12, 15, 18, 19, ... What number should come next?

(A) 20
(B) 22
(C) 23
(D) 21

91. Examine the triangle and find the best answer.

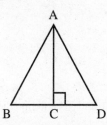

(A) AD is greater than CD.
(B) BA and AD are each less than BC.
(C) AB is equal to BC.
(D) AB is equal to AC plus BC.

92. What number multiplied by 3 is 5 less than 29?

(A) 6
(B) 24
(C) 8
(D) 21

93. Look at this series: 23, 29, 32, 38, 41, _____, 50, ... What number should fill the blank in this series?

(A) 42
(B) 47
(C) 44
(D) 51

94. Examine (A), (B), and (C) and find the best answer.

(A) $(10 \div 5) \times 10$ 20
(B) $(5 \div 1) \times 4$ 20
(C) $(20 \div 5) \times 5$ 20

(A) (A) is equal to (B), which is equal to (C).
(B) (A) is equal to (B) and less than (C).
(C) (B) is equal to (C) and less than (A).
(D) (C) is greater than (A) and (B).

95. Look at this series: 100, 101, 91, 92, 82, ... What two numbers should come next?

(A) 72, 74
(B) 72, 73
(C) 83, 73
(D) 84, 74

96. Examine the cube and find the best answer.

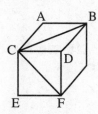

(A) CF is greater than CB.
(B) EF is less than AB.
(C) CB is equal to CE.
(D) CF is greater than AB.

97. What number divided by 2 leaves 4 more than 6?

(A) 5
(B) 10
(C) 20
(D) 4

98. Examine (A), (B), and (C). Find the best answer if $1 < x < y$ and x and y are whole numbers.

(A) $xy =$

(B) $y^2 =$

(C) $x^2 =$

(A) (A) is less than (B) and (B) is less than (C).

(B) (C) is less than (A) and (A) is less than (B).

(C) (B) is less than (A) and (A) is less than (C).

(D) (C) is less than (B) and (B) is less than (A).

99. Look at this series: 14, 28, 32, 64, 68, ... What number should come next?

(A) 136

(B) 138

(C) 72

(D) 76

100. What number subtracted from 7 leaves $\frac{1}{4}$ of 20?

(A) 13

(B) 5

(C) 12

(D) 2

101. Look at this series: A24, C28, E18, G22, ... What comes next?

(A) H26

(B) J14

(C) I12

(D) F20

102. Examine the graph and find the best answer.

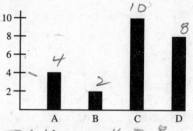

(A) B plus C minus A equals D.

(B) C minus A minus B equals D.

(C) C plus D equals A plus B.

(D) D minus B equals A plus C.

103. What number is 2 less than $\frac{3}{5}$ of 10?

(A) 4

(B) 8

(C) 6

(D) 2

104. Look at this series: 4, 16, 5, 25, 6, ... What number should come next?

(A) 36

(B) 30

(C) 6

(D) 20

105. Examine (A), (B), and (C) and find the best answer.

(A) 5^2

(B) 4^3

(C) 2^4

(A) $A > B > C$

(B) $B > A > C$

(C) $A = B = C$

(D) $B > A = C$

106. Look at this series: 10, $7\frac{1}{2}$, 5, $2\frac{1}{2}$, ...

What number should come next?

(A) 1

(B) $1\frac{1}{2}$

(C) $\frac{1}{2}$

(D) 0

107. What number is 8 times $\frac{1}{2}$ of 20?

(A) 10

(B) 80

(C) 24

(D) 28

108. Look at this series: 26, 30, 28, 27, 31, 29, 28, ... What three numbers should come next?

(A) 32, 38, 24

(B) 30, 28, 27

(C) 32, 30, 29

(D) 24, 26, 27

109. $\frac{1}{3}$ of what number added to 6 is 2 times 9?

(A) 12

(B) 36

(C) 18

(D) 3

110. Examine the parallelogram and find the best answer.

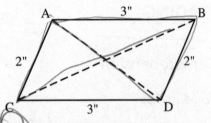

(A) The perimeter of the parallelogram is 10 inches.

(B) The area of the parallelogram is 5 square inches.

(C) The area of triangle ABD is greater than the area of triangle ACD.

(D) The perimeter of triangle BAC is equal to the perimeter of the parallelogram.

111. What number is 10 more than $\frac{4}{9}$ of 27?

(A) 37

(B) 12

(C) 2

(D) 22

112. What number is 11 more than 5 squared?

(A) 36

(B) 21

(C) 14

(D) 1

STOP End of Quantitative Skills section. If you have any time left, go over your work in this section only. Do not work in any other section of the test.

READING

Comprehension

25 Minutes

Directions: Read each passage carefully. Then mark one answer—the answer you think is best—for each item.

QUESTIONS 113–122 REFER TO THE FOLLOWING PASSAGE.

Our planet Earth is divided into seven separate layers. The outer layer is called the crust and appears to be approximately twenty miles thick. Next in line are the four layers of the mantle. These layers <u>vary</u> in thickness from 250 to 1,000 miles. The <u>remaining</u> two layers are divided into the outer core and inner core. The thickness of the outer core has been determined to be slightly more than 1,200 miles, while that of the inner core is <u>slightly</u> less than 800 miles. Scientists calculate the location and depth of these layers by measuring and studying the speed and direction of earthquake waves. They have also determined that both temperature and pressure are much greater at the core than at the crust.

113. The thickest portion of the Earth is the
- **(A)** crust.
- **(B)** outer core.
- **(C)** mantle.
- **(D)** inner core.

114. How many separate layers does the Earth have?
- **(A)** Two
- **(B)** Twenty
- **(C)** Seven
- **(D)** Four

115. Which of the following is correct?
- **(A)** No two sets of earthquake waves ever travel in the same direction.
- **(B)** Earthquakes usually travel in the same direction.
- **(C)** Earthquake waves travel at different speeds.
- **(D)** Earthquake waves travel at the same speed but in different directions.

116. You would expect to find the kind of information in this passage in
- **(A)** an encyclopedia.
- **(B)** a science book.
- **(C)** neither of these.
- **(D)** both of these.

117. In going from the surface to the center of the Earth, in which order would you pass through the layers?
- **(A)** crust, outer core, mantle, inner core
- **(B)** outer core, inner core, crust, mantle
- **(C)** outer core, crust, inner core, mantle
- **(D)** crust, mantle, outer core, inner core

118. The word <u>vary</u>, as underlined and used in this passage, most nearly means
- **(A)** stabilize.
- **(B)** increase.
- **(C)** range.
- **(D)** arbitrate.

119. Which of the following is correct?

- **(A)** Scientists know the exact thickness of the crust.
- **(B)** Scientists believe they know the thickness of the crust.
- **(C)** The thickness of the crust cannot be determined.
- **(D)** Scientists cannot agree on the thickness of the crust.

120. In comparing the core with the crust, you would find that at the core,

- **(A)** temperature and pressure are less.
- **(B)** pressure is greater, temperature is less.
- **(C)** temperature is greater, pressure is less.
- **(D)** temperature and pressure are greater.

121. The word <u>slightly</u>, as underlined and used in this passage, most nearly means

- **(A)** scarcely.
- **(B)** considerably.
- **(C)** a little.
- **(D)** at least.

122. The word <u>remaining</u>, as underlined and used in this passage, most nearly means

- **(A)** previous.
- **(B)** outer.
- **(C)** last.
- **(D)** prior.

QUESTIONS 123–132 REFER TO THE FOLLOWING PASSAGE.

The man is in <u>utter</u> darkness. Only the <u>wavering</u> beam of light from his flashlight pierces the blackness. The air, damp and cold, smells of dank, unseen, decaying material.

The man stumbles over stones, splashes into a hidden puddle. He bangs into a cold rocky wall. The flashlight cocks upward, and suddenly, the air is filled with the flutter of thousands of wings and the piping of tiny animal wails. He ducks, startled, then grins. He's found what he's looking for—bats!

For this man is a spelunker, another name for someone who explores caves for the fun of it. Spelunkers actually enjoy crawling on their stomachs in narrow, rocky tunnels far below the surface of the earth.

Spelunkers have discovered new caves. Some have formed clubs, sharing safety knowledge, developing new techniques, and teaching novices.

Spelunkers believe that Earth's inner spaces are as exciting as the universe's outer spaces.

123. The first two paragraphs of this passage describe a cave's

- **(A)** rocks.
- **(B)** depth.
- **(C)** atmosphere.
- **(D)** streams.

124. The word <u>wavering</u>, as underlined and used in this passage, most nearly means

- **(A)** swaying.
- **(B)** steady.
- **(C)** strong.
- **(D)** shining.

125. The author of this passage is most likely a
    (A) spelunker.
    (B) cave scientist.
    (C) medical doctor.
    (D) magazine writer.

126. The cave the man was exploring was probably
    (A) large and dry.
    (B) deep underground.
    (C) near the surface.
    (D) dangerous.

127. According to this passage, what started the bats to suddenly fly about?
    (A) The spelunker
    (B) The damp and cold air
    (C) The flashlight
    (D) The sudden noise

128. The man ducked when the bats flew because he was
    (A) angry.
    (B) afraid.
    (C) surprised.
    (D) hurt.

129. The word utter, as underlined and used in this passage, most nearly means
    (A) bovine.
    (B) unspeakable.
    (C) oppressive.
    (D) great.

130. According to this passage, spelunkers ignore
    (A) safety rules.
    (B) light.
    (C) discomfort.
    (D) other spelunkers.

131. A good title for this passage would be
    (A) "Batty about Bats."
    (B) "Spelunkers—Underground Explorers."
    (C) "Inner Space."
    (D) "The Life of a Spelunker."

132. According to this passage, which word would most nearly describe spelunkers?
    (A) Experimental
    (B) Cautious
    (C) Antisocial
    (D) Adventurous

QUESTIONS 133–142 REFER TO THE FOLLOWING PASSAGE.

Even adventurous eaters may have very little experience encountering the kohlrabi, also known as the turnip cabbage or German turnip. Often misidentified as a root vegetable because of its bulbous, root-like appearance, kohlrabi is both a resilient crop and a protean menu ingredient—it can be eaten raw or cooked, and is an excellent addition to a wide array of recipes. Many of its fans insist that it deserves a wider audience and more attention than it currently receives.

This versatile—but largely unknown—vegetable is a member of the *Brassica oleracea* species, which also includes broccoli, kale, cauliflower, and Brussels sprouts. This may not come as a surprise to those who have eaten kohlrabi, as the taste is similar to these other vegetables. Kohlrabi grows above ground, and comes in both green and purple colors. Among the many currently available varietals are the White Danube, Purple Danube, White Vienna, and Purple Vienna, perhaps a reflection of the vegetable's popularity in Germany.

Need a few more reasons to give kholrabi a try? This hearty vegetable is a great addition to salads, stews, and slaws, and also packs a nutrient-rich punch—it's an excellent source of vitamin C, vitamin B, potassium, and fiber and helps promote good muscle and nerve function, vision and digestive health, bone strength, and more. The next time you're doing some meal planning, think beyond the usual ingredients and consider adding kohlrabi.

133. The author's opinion on kohlrabi as a food is most likely
    (A) pessimistic.
    (B) cautious.
    (C) enthusiastic.
    (D) curious.

134. A good title for this passage would be:
    (A) "Consider Kohlrabi"
    (B) "Exploring German Foods"
    (C) "Mix Up Your Menu"
    (D) "A Brand New Vegetable"

135. The word protean, as underlined and used in this passage, most nearly means
    (A) delicious.
    (B) versatile.
    (C) expensive.
    (D) nutritious.

136. According to the passage, kohlrabi is a good source of
    (A) calories.
    (B) energy.
    (C) spice.
    (D) potassium.

137. What is the most logical explanation for the author's statement regarding kohlrabi's popularity in Germany?
    (A) The Danube and Vienna are of German origin.
    (B) The author of the passage is from Germany.
    (C) Germany often leads the world in new food trends.
    (D) It's well known that Germans love eating vegetables.

138. The word varietal, as underlined and used in this passage, most nearly means the
    (A) flavor of kohlrabi.
    (B) price of kohlrabi.
    (C) use of kohlrabi.
    (D) type of kohlrabi.

139. According to the passage, what is the main reason why kohlrabi is often mistaken as a root vegetable?
    (A) Its taste
    (B) Its color
    (C) Its appearance
    (D) Its name

140. Kohlrabi is *not* in the same vegetable species as
    (A) turnips.
    (B) broccoli.
    (C) kale.
    (D) cauliflower.

141. All of the following are mentioned in the passage as benefits of kohlrabi *except*
    (A) muscle and nerve function.
    (B) heart health.
    (C) vision and digestive health.
    (D) bone strength.

142. What is most likely the author's purpose in writing this passage?
    (A) To compare kohlrabi with other vegetables
    (B) To get people interested in trying kohlrabi
    (C) To convince individuals to cook more
    (D) To promote a healthy vegetarian lifestyle

QUESTIONS 143-152 REFER TO THE FOLLOWING PASSAGE.

The superstition of witchcraft, which most people laugh at today, is still a matter of mystery and speculation.

Hundreds of thousands of people in Europe who were accused of being witches were executed during the Middle Ages and even as late as the early eighteenth century. Their deaths probably resulted from hysterical fears. Yet the judges undoubtedly were sincere in their desire to eliminate what they thought was a real danger. Some modern psychologists have theorized that so-called witches actually were dangerous. In essence, they say that a person who believes in the powers of witchcraft can be affected emotionally or physically—may even die—because of a "witch's spell."

When Europeans immigrated to America, they brought their beliefs with them. There were a number of witchcraft trials in Massachusetts during the 1600s; however, after the execution of twenty Salem "witches" in 1692, prosecution for witchcraft didn't survive long in the New World.

Most people in the civilized world no longer believe in witchcraft. Nonetheless, the subject is fascinating for many people. As an example, the TV show *Bewitched* was a very popular program for more than five years.

143. This passage was probably printed in a(n)
(A) history book.
(B) magazine.
(C) psychology book.
(D) encyclopedia.

144. According to this passage, the mystery of witchcraft is
(A) a major problem for psychologists.
(B) of very little interest today.
(C) still unsolved.
(D) a major problem for sincere judges.

145. One of today's reminders of ancient witchcraft beliefs is
(A) Halloween.
(B) April Fools' Day.
(C) the use of brooms.
(D) the death penalty for certain crimes.

146. Which group can we be sure has had members who believed in witchcraft?
(A) Judges
(B) TV producers
(C) Psychologists
(D) Newspaper reporters

147. This passage calls witchcraft a "superstition." Which of these would also be a superstition?
(A) "Many hands make light work."
(B) "Breaking a mirror brings bad luck."
(C) "Eating sweets causes pimples."
(D) "Great oaks from little acorns grow."

148. According to some psychologists, persons who *do* believe in witchcraft
(A) can be harmed by it.
(B) tend to laugh at it today.
(C) are crazy.
(D) tend to be dangerous.

149. The phrase <u>In essence</u>, as underlined and used in this passage, most nearly means

(A) probably.

(B) basically.

(C) briefly.

(D) finally.

150. The word <u>fascinating</u>, as underlined and used in this passage, most nearly means

(A) frightening.

(B) enjoyable.

(C) frustrating.

(D) interesting.

151. This passage suggests that what you believe

(A) can hurt you.

(B) should be based on facts.

(C) does not affect you.

(D) changes as you grow older.

152. A good title for this passage might be

(A) "Witchcraft—Fact or Fiction?"

(B) "The End of Witchcraft."

(C) "Witchcraft in the New World."

(D) "The Powers of Witchcraft."

Vocabulary

Directions: Choose the word that means the same or about the same as the underlined word.

153. a new <u>perspective</u>
- (A) receptacle
- (B) sight
- (C) picture
- (D) view

154. <u>impair</u> his vision
- (A) test
- (B) weaken
- (C) improve
- (D) destroy

155. strong business <u>acumen</u>
- (A) intelligence
- (B) speed
- (C) flexibility
- (D) confusion

156. <u>subjugate</u> the enemy
- (A) confront
- (B) bargain with
- (C) trick
- (D) overpower

157. to <u>reproach</u>
- (A) approach
- (B) praise
- (C) blame
- (D) steal

158. to be <u>elated</u>
- (A) happy
- (B) akin
- (C) moved
- (D) upset

159. his <u>brusque</u> manner
- (A) foreign
- (B) subtle
- (C) soft
- (D) abrupt

160. <u>depress</u> the key
- (A) put away
- (B) insert
- (C) turn
- (D) push down

161. <u>quench</u> your thirst
- (A) end
- (B) increase
- (C) continue
- (D) decrease

162. a famous <u>exploit</u>
- (A) crime
- (B) deed
- (C) reputation
- (D) game

163. A <u>precipitous</u> incline
- (A) gradual
- (B) steep
- (C) unavoidable
- (D) delicate

164. an interesting <u>chronicle</u>
- (A) fairy tale
- (B) record
- (C) time
- (D) item

165. that <u>amiable</u> soul
    (A) casual
    (B) honest
    (C) fine
    (D) likable

166. her <u>astute</u> mind
    (A) shrewd
    (B) careful
    (C) stupid
    (D) astounding

167. to <u>sever</u> contact
    (A) cut
    (B) maintain
    (C) seek
    (D) establish

168. the <u>eminent</u> man
    (A) wicked
    (B) destitute
    (C) ancient
    (D) outstanding

169. to <u>terminate</u> a contract
    (A) end
    (B) enter
    (C) make
    (D) determine

170. to <u>hinder</u> someone
    (A) assist
    (B) follow
    (C) impede
    (D) slight

171. a spirit of <u>contention</u>
    (A) debate
    (B) content
    (C) inquiry
    (D) calm

172. to <u>concede</u> defeat
    (A) suspect
    (B) admit
    (C) realize
    (D) refuse

173. to <u>forego</u> his rights
    (A) usurp
    (B) insure
    (C) insist on
    (D) give up

174. your <u>canny</u> guess
    (A) uncertain
    (B) mistaken
    (C) clever
    (D) insincere

STOP   End of Reading section. If you have any time left, go over your work in this section only. Do not work in any other section of the test.

practice test

MATHEMATICS

Concepts

45 Minutes

Directions: Mark one answer—the answer you think is best—for each problem. You may use scratch paper when working on these problems.

175. Which of the following is *not* a quadrilateral?
- (A) Square
- (B) Trapezoid
- (C) Triangle
- (D) Rectangle

176. $\{4, 7, 9\} \cup \{4, 9, 12, 15\} =$
- (A) $\{4, 9\}$
- (B) $\{4, 7, 9\}$
- (C) $\{4, 7, 9, 12, 15\}$
- (D) $\{ \}$

177. To the nearest tenth, 63.594 is written
- (A) 63.6
- (B) 64
- (C) 63.59
- (D) 64.5

178. Simplify: $3(-2)^3 =$
- (A) -216
- (B) -18
- (C) 1
- (D) -24

179. As a fraction, 0.24 is
- (A) $\dfrac{24}{1000}$
- (B) $\dfrac{6}{25}$
- (C) $\dfrac{1}{4}$
- (D) $\dfrac{100}{24}$

180. The measure of angle A is

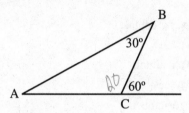

- (A) $15°$
- (B) $20°$
- (C) $30°$
- (D) $35°$

181. To multiply a number by 100, move the decimal point
- (A) one place to the right.
- (B) two places to the left.
- (C) three places to the right.
- (D) two places to the right.

182. Which of the following is a pair of reciprocals?
- (A) $(3, -3)$
- (B) $\left(3\dfrac{1}{3}, \dfrac{3}{10}\right)$
- (C) $(2^3, 3^2)$
- (D) $(0, 1)$

183. The circumference of this circle is

(A) 32π

(B) 16

(C) 8π

(D) 4

184. The ratio of 3 yards to 18 inches is

(A) 3 to 18

(B) 1 to 6

(C) 3 to 2

(D) 6 to 1

185. How many integers are between $\frac{33}{7}$ and 8.001?

(A) 3

(B) 6

(C) 5

(D) 4

186. Which of the following is true?

(A) $a \div (b + c) = \frac{a}{b} + \frac{a}{c}$

(B) $a(x + b) = ax + b$

(C) $a(x + b) = a(x) + a(b)$

(D) $a \div b = b\left(\frac{1}{a}\right)$

187. The square root of 198 is between

(A) 19 and 20

(B) 98 and 100

(C) 90 and 100

(D) 14 and 15

188. In a base-five system of numeration, what are the next three counting numbers after $43_{(5)}$?

(A) $44_{(5)}, 45_{(5)}, 50_{(5)}$

(B) $44_{(5)}, 45_{(5)}, 46_{(5)}$

(C) $44_{(5)}, 50_{(5)}, 52_{(5)}$

(D) $44_{(5)}, 100_{(5)}, 101_{(5)}$

189. Which of these is a correctly written scientific notation?

(A) $0.038 = 3.8 \times 10^{-2}$

(B) $380 = 3.8 \times 10^{3}$

(C) $0.38 = 3.8 \times 10^{-2}$

(D) $3800 = 3.8 \times 10^{2}$

190. Which fraction shows the greatest value?

(A) $\frac{5}{9}$

(B) $\frac{2}{3}$

(C) $\frac{6}{7}$

(D) $\frac{7}{8}$

191. Which of the following is true?

(A) $8 \leq 6$

(B) $6 \geq 6$

(C) $0.080 > 0.08$

(D) $15 < 8$

192. $\triangle ABC$ is similar to $\triangle DBE$. The length of AB is

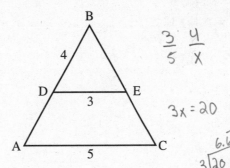

(A) $8\frac{1}{3}$

(B) $6\frac{1}{3}$

(C) $6\frac{2}{3}$

(D) $8\frac{2}{3}$

193. It is possible to have a right triangle that is also

(A) equilateral.

(B) equiangular.

(C) obtuse.

(D) isosceles.

194. Which one of the following is *not* equal to $62\frac{1}{2}\%$?

(A) $\frac{10}{16}$

(B) $\frac{5}{8}$

(C) 0.625

(D) 62.5

195. The prime factorization of 12 is

(A) $2 \cdot 2 \cdot 3$

(B) $4 + 8$

(C) $6 \cdot 2$

(D) $4 \cdot 3$

196. The least common multiple of 2 and 6 is

(A) 6

(B) 12

(C) 3

(D) 2

197. If Bill can mow a lawn in x hours, what part of the lawn can he mow in 2 hours?

(A) $\frac{2}{x}$

(B) $\frac{x}{2}$

(C) $\frac{1}{2}$

(D) $\frac{1}{x}$

198. Which of the following illustrates the commutative property of multiplication?

(A) $3 \cdot (0.2 + 9.8) = 3 \cdot (0.2) + 3 \cdot (9.8)$

(B) $\frac{3}{8}\left(5+\frac{1}{2}\right) = \left(5+\frac{1}{2}\right)\frac{3}{8}$

(C) $\frac{1}{6}(4 \cdot 8) = \left(\frac{1}{6} \cdot 4\right)8$

(D) $\frac{4}{3} \cdot 1 = \frac{4}{3}$

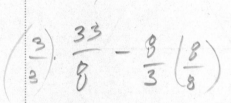

Problem-Solving

199. A movie theater sold 130 student tickets at $1.25 each and 340 adult tickets at $1.90 each. How much was collected?

(A) $798.50

(B) $708.50

(C) $808.50

(D) $818.50

200. Solve: $12 - 2\frac{3}{16} =$

(A) $10\frac{3}{16}$

(B) $9\frac{13}{16}$

(C) $10\frac{13}{16}$

(D) $9\frac{3}{16}$

201. Mr. Allen paid $542.40 for his telephone bills last year. How much did he pay, on average, per month?

(A) $46.20

(B) $54.20

(C) $55.20

(D) $45.20

202. Bob has $10 less than four times the amount Tim has. If Bob has $88, how much does Tim have?

(A) $48

(B) $22

(C) $16

(D) $24.50

203. Simplify: $(-2) \cdot (-4) \cdot (3) \cdot (-1)$

(A) -24

(B) -4

(C) 12

(D) 24

204. The formula $F = \frac{9}{5}C + 32$ converts temperature from Centigrade to Fahrenheit. What is the Fahrenheit temperature for 85° Centigrade?

(A) $153°$

(B) $185°$

(C) $175°$

(D) $130°$

205. If the 5% sales tax on a snowmobile was $42, what was the price of the snowmobile not including the tax?

(A) $840

(B) $210

(C) $820

(D) $640

206. Solve: $4\frac{1}{8} - 2\frac{2}{3} =$

(A) $2\frac{13}{24}$

(B) $2\frac{11}{24}$

(C) $1\frac{13}{24}$

(D) $1\frac{11}{24}$

207. If $-5 + 4x = 21$, $x =$

(A) 6.5

(B) 4

(C) 8.5

(D) 5.75

208. Solve: $3\frac{1}{3} \times 3\frac{3}{4} \times \frac{2}{5} =$

(A) $9\frac{1}{4}$

(B) 6

(C) 5

(D) $6\frac{2}{5}$

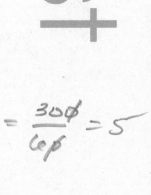

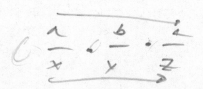

209. Mr. Symon paid $58.50 interest on a loan that had a 6% simple interest rate. How much did he borrow?

(A) $975

(B) $351

(C) $898

(D) $410

210. If a flagpole has a shadow 56 feet long when a 6-foot man's shadow is 14 feet long, what is the height of the flagpole?

(A) 24 feet

(B) 28 feet

(C) 20 feet

(D) 32 feet

$$\frac{6}{14} = \frac{x}{56}$$

211. If the perimeter of a rectangular region is 50 units, and the length of one side is 7 units, what is the area of the rectangular region?

(A) 291 square units

(B) 301 square units

(C) 126 square units

(D) 226 square units

212. If $5(1 - 2x) + 25 = 0$, then x = _____.

(A) 20

(B) 15

(C) 3

(D) –3

213. If 18 is added to an integer, and the result is $\frac{5}{4}$ of the integer, what is the integer?

(A) 72

(B) 36

(C) 24

(D) –18

214. If $A = 6$ and $B = 3$, then $7A - 3B =$

(A) 7

(B) 5

(C) 36

(D) 33

215. Four years ago, Jim's father was 5 times as old as Jim. How old is Jim's father now if Jim is 12?

(A) 56

(B) 44

(C) 40

(D) 36

216. Solve: $2\frac{1}{2} + 7\frac{2}{3} + \frac{3}{4} =$

(A) $9\frac{1}{4}$

(B) $11\frac{1}{2}$

(C) $10\frac{11}{12}$

(D) $10\frac{1}{4}$

217. If $N\%$ of 60 is 24, $N =$

(A) 40

(B) 25

(C) 125

(D) 150

218. If $10x - 3 = 2x + 4$, then x equals

(A) $\frac{9}{8}$

(B) $\frac{7}{8}$

(C) $\frac{8}{7}$

(D) $\frac{6}{7}$

219. The ratio of $\frac{3}{4}$ to $\frac{5}{2}$ is

(A) 10 to 3

(B) 15 to 8

(C) 3 to 10

(D) 8 to 15

$$\frac{3}{4} : 2 \qquad \frac{3}{4} : \frac{10}{4}$$

220. What is the cost of carpeting a square room that is 27 feet by 27 feet if the carpet costs $11 per square yard?

(A) $594

(B) $729

(C) $891

(D) $8019

221. Solve: $6.41\overline{)3.6537}$

(A) 67

(B) 57

(C) 0.57

(D) 0.67

222.

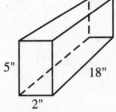

What is the volume of this rectangular solid?

(A) 90 cu. in.

(B) 160 cu. in.

(C) 140 cu. in.

(D) 180 cu. in.

223. If $A = 3$, $B = 2$, and $C = 6$, then $\dfrac{3ABC}{2A} =$

(A) 18

(B) 24

(C) $4\dfrac{1}{2}$

(D) $4\dfrac{1}{6}$

224. Simplify: $4\dfrac{2}{5} \times 2\dfrac{3}{11}$

(A) $1\dfrac{117}{125}$

(B) $6\dfrac{1}{2}$

(C) $8\dfrac{6}{55}$

(D) 10

225. If $\dfrac{5}{6}x = 30$, then $x =$

(A) 42

(B) 25

(C) 20

(D) 36

226. Solve: 65.14×0.093

(A) 6.05802

(B) 60.5802

(C) 605.602

(D) 6.05602

227. 26.80, 26.86, 26.92, 26.98, _____

What number should come next in this sequence?

(A) 27.04

(B) 27.02

(C) 26.02

(D) 26.04

228. Solve: $72,528 \times 109$

(A) 1,377,032

(B) 7,805,452

(C) 1,378,032

(D) 7,905,552

229. The product of 11 and 12 is 3 more than N. What is N?

(A) 135

(B) 129

(C) 132

(D) 126

230. How many boards $1\dfrac{1}{3}$ feet long can be cut from a board $9\dfrac{1}{2}$ feet long?

(A) 9

(B) 6

(C) 7

(D) 8

231. Solve for x: $3x + 3 < 9 + x$

(A) $x = 6$

(B) $x > 3$

(C) $x < 3$

(D) $x > 6$

232. Solve: $0.602 + 4.2 + 5.03 =$

(A) 11.47

(B) 9.802

(C) 9.832

(D) 10.441

233. Solve for x: $2.5x + 12.5 = 30$

(A) 7

(B) 9

(C) 17

(D) 70

234. Solve: $28\overline{)54,900}$

(A) 1960 R20

(B) 1858 R20

(C) 1642 R12

(D) 1868 R16

235. Solve: If $\sqrt{x + 36} = 10$, then $x =$

(A) 8

(B) 64

(C) −16

(D) −4

236. Add in base 5:

$$143_{(5)}$$
$$+\quad 33_{(5)}$$

(A) $131_{(5)}$

(B) $221_{(5)}$

(C) $231_{(5)}$

(D) $211_{(5)}$

237. Solve for x: $\left(\dfrac{2}{3} + \dfrac{1}{5}\right) - \left(\dfrac{1}{4} + \dfrac{1}{2}\right) = x$

(A) $\dfrac{13}{30}$

(B) $\dfrac{7}{60}$

(C) $\dfrac{51}{60}$

(D) $\dfrac{37}{60}$

238. If the tax rate is $3.62 per $100, how much tax must be paid on a home assessed at $25,000?

(A) $90.50

(B) $80.50

(C) $805

(D) $905

STOP End of Mathematics section. If you have any time left, go over your work in this section only. Do not work in any other section of the test.

LANGUAGE

25 Minutes

Directions: In questions 239–278, look for errors in capitalization, punctuation, or usage. Mark the answer choice that contains the error. If you find no mistake, mark (D) on your answer sheet.

239. (A) Jeff asked, "What color is the Easter bunny?"
     (B) Steve won the annual polka contest.
     (C) The letter was mailed on Memorial day.
     (D) *No mistakes*

240. (A) Joris read the *daily cryer* newspaper each morning.
     (B) Mr. Judson prepared the annual quarterly report for his presentation.
     (C) Gemma ordered the cod entrée from the restaurant's expansive menu options.
     (D) *No mistakes*

241. (A) We will be vacationing in sunny Italy.
     (B) Dave will arrive at Kennedy international airport.
     (C) We decided to have Charlie read the report.
     (D) *No mistakes*

242. (A) Dallas is one of the most populous cities in Texas.
     (B) Michigan Avenue is a main tourist attraction in Chicago.
     (C) New York is the larger city in the United States.
     (D) *No mistakes*

243. (A) Kim's birthday is in June.
     (B) Jared was the second person in line.
     (C) August falls between july and September.
     (D) *No mistakes*

244. (A) The greedy lion ate an entire sirloin steak in just a few seconds.
     (B) Sari yearned to travel to America and see the grand canyon.
     (C) Have you ever cooked a turkey for Thanksgiving?
     (D) *No mistakes*

245. (A) Where in the world did you leave your gloves?
     (B) The dog licked its chops after the meal.
     (C) "Oh, that's terrible!" Sally cried.
     (D) *No mistakes*

246. (A) Detroit is the center of the automobile industry.
     (B) Governor Jones was an officer in the Navy.
     (C) Their making a terrible mistake.
     (D) *No mistakes*

247. (A) How is your cold?
     (B) The rabbit got sick and died.
     (C) Who's book is this?
     (D) *No mistakes*

248. (A) That is a pretty dress, isn't it, Sheila?
     (B) How old is your pet, Alfie?
     (C) Why are you so tired?
     (D) *No mistakes*

249. (A) Katie's final exam grade was the highest in her geometry class.
     (B) Anderson's favorite movie of all time is *Star Wars*.
     (C) Sherman thinks the Bronx zoo is his favorite place to visit.
     (D) *No mistakes*

250. (A) Don told us where he'd bought his coat.
(B) What's your name, little girl?
(C) Yellowstone is run by the National Park Service.
(D) *No mistakes*

251. (A) How are you, Jim?
(B) I'm fine, thank you.
(C) Did you notice that John left early?
(D) *No mistakes*

252. (A) The town of Springsburgh held its annual pie eating contest on Tuesday afternoon.
(B) The science museum held an impressive collection of meteorites.
(C) Are you going to vote in the next Presidential Election?
(D) *No mistakes*

253. (A) Will, you're parents are very nice.
(B) Ted's family is buying a boat.
(C) My father is a textbook publisher.
(D) *No mistakes*

254. (A) It was the most beautiful sight I've ever saw.
(B) Ed's aunt and uncle lived in the South for many years.
(C) Mattie is the older of the two.
(D) *No mistakes*

255. (A) What is the matter with Sam's leg?
(B) The first show is at 2:30, isn't it?
(C) How much is your plane ticket?
(D) *No mistakes*

256. (A) The award was given jointly to Deirdre and I.
(B) John asked if he might go home early.
(C) Cats and dogs sometimes play well together.
(D) *No mistakes*

257. (A) Have you seen Marie's new coat?
(B) Sue said, "I'm taking dancing lessons this year."
(C) People lay down when they are tired.
(D) *No mistakes*

258. (A) Anne said, "we really should go now."
(B) You can always say Sam eats well—and often!
(C) I told them my study hall was second period.
(D) *No mistakes*

259. (A) The boy threw his shoe in anger.
(B) I laid in bed all night without sleeping.
(C) Keep this as a secret between you and me.
(D) *No mistakes*

260. (A) Yesterday, Valerie came to visit me.
(B) The package arrived hear around 5 p.m.
(C) Arnold and I went to dinner at the Panda Palace, which has great egg rolls.
(D) *No mistakes*

261. (A) She and I consider ourselves to be best friends.
(B) Do you know which of the spellings of too means also?
(C) There is a narrow path beside the railroad track.
(D) *No mistakes*

262. (A) We would have called you if we'd known.
(B) May I open my eyes now?
(C) My brother-in-law lives in Butte, Montana.
(D) *No mistakes*

263. (A) Actually, ice hockey is exciting to watch.
(B) Janet plays guitar almost as well as Tom.
(C) Does Dave like to talk to Debby Ann?
(D) *No mistakes*

264. **(A)** Ken will graduate from Stanford this June.
     (B) Jack is learning Kay to draw.
     (C) Before we knew it, the class was over.
     (D) *No mistakes*

265. **(A)** When will you know what the assignment is?
     (B) You should of seen the crowd at Paul's yesterday.
     (C) Joe will be stationed at Fort Benning, Georgia.
     (D) *No mistakes*

266. **(A)** Dad's going fishing in Canada next week.
     (B) Barb didn't know whether to laugh or to cry.
     (C) Mom put to much baking powder in the cake.
     (D) *No mistakes*

267. **(A)** We have already sold too many tickets.
     (B) If I knew the answer, I would be rich now.
     (C) The artist works less hours than the carpenter.
     (D) *No mistakes*

268. **(A)** The tiny kitten sat licking it's wounds.
     (B) If you wish, we will have chicken for dinner.
     (C) It is so cloudy that we cannot see the Milky Way tonight.
     (D) *No mistakes*

269. **(A)** Everyone must sign their name on the register.
     (B) I am all ready, but the taxi is not here yet.
     (C) I do not believe that I have only two choices.
     (D) *No mistakes*

270. **(A)** If you don't know the answer, don't raise your hand.
     (B) The baby is playing in her crib.
     (C) Jeff is the taller of my three sons.
     (D) *No mistakes*

271. **(A)** Neither Lisa nor Liz has made the Honor Roll.
     (B) I have much more free time than you.
     (C) Everyone wants to have his own way.
     (D) *No mistakes*

272. **(A)** When he said that, everyone applauded.
     (B) He was much more interesting than I thought he'd be.
     (C) Helen asked Molly and I to come to her party.
     (D) *No mistakes*

273. **(A)** The sun set at 5:15 this afternoon.
     (B) Mary set the table for dinner yesterday.
     (C) Please set those books over there, Jim.
     (D) *No mistakes*

274. **(A)** The horse ran swiftly and won the race.
     (B) I feel badly that I cannot attend your wedding.
     (C) Most birds and some people fly south for the winter.
     (D) *No mistakes*

275. **(A)** This kind of movie may frighten small children.
     (B) I'm glad to hear that you're planning to go to college.
     (C) Myself has bought a new dress for the party.
     (D) *No mistakes*

276. (A) How many eggs did you use in this cake?

(B) I can't hardly wait for the school year to be over.

(C) Neither Shawn nor Sylvia has to work for her spending money.

(D) *No mistakes*

277. (A) The childrens' boots got mixed up in the coatroom.

(B) Sheila is trying out for the marching band today.

(C) My sisters and I all went to camp last summer.

(D) *No mistakes*

278. (A) I'll let you know if my parents can pick us up.

(B) Our whole class sent get-well cards to Hilda.

(C) Harry said he hadn't done nothing wrong.

(D) *No mistakes*

Directions: For questions 279–288, look for mistakes in spelling only.

279. (A) Clarence Darrow was a distinguished trial lawyer.

(B) Apparantly Suzy couldn't find her umbrella.

(C) Alice will be married next Wednesday.

(D) *No mistakes*

280. (A) Are you sure you can complete the assignment on time?

(B) The entire crew worked very efficently.

(C) Mary went to the library yesterday.

(D) *No mistakes*

281. (A) It occured to me that I should write home.

(B) "What a dreadful comparison," Ida remarked.

(C) Bob's temperature was back to normal yesterday.

(D) *No mistakes*

282. (A) Mary Lou is eligible for the committee.

(B) Discussion and argument are not the same thing.

(C) The chemist analized the solution in his laboratory.

(D) *No mistakes*

283. (A) My brother's going out for athletics next year.

(B) "This is a small token of my esteem," he told his teacher.

(C) Mary dropped her handkerchief in the corridor.

(D) *No mistakes*

284. (A) Tyler noticed a mispelled word in the book he just purchased.

(B) The steering committee couldn't wait to vote on the new referendum.

(C) The inn was unable to accommodate the large group of tourists.

(D) *No mistakes*

285. (A) The schedule is posted on the bulletin board in the hall.

(B) Don discribed the play with sweeping gestures.

(C) Occasionally our class runs over into the next period.

(D) *No mistakes*

286. (A) Pete perfers to sit by the door.

(B) Joy has a very agreeable personality.

(C) We struggle with ourselves to overcome our faults.

(D) *No mistakes*

287. (A) Did you hear the announcement about the picnic?

(B) While the initial cost is high, the maintenance is low.

(C) Jan's coat is similar to mine.

(D) *No mistakes*

288. **(A)** Al said it was not neccessary to read all of the plays.

(B) It's disappointing to have missed the picture.

(C) The original order was difficult to decipher.

(D) *No mistakes*

Directions: For questions 289–298, look for errors in composition. Follow the directions for each question.

289. Choose the best word or words to join the thoughts together.

I left my books at school; _____ I won't be able to do my homework.

(A) therefore,

(B) nevertheless,

(C) however,

(D) None of these

290. Choose the best word or words to join the thoughts together.

That area is experiencing great economic hardship; _____ its unemployment rate is very high.

(A) for example,

(B) in contrast,

(C) suprisingly,

(D) None of these

291. Choose the group of words that best completes this sentence.

After a hard day at work, _____

(A) sleep was something Mary did very well.

(B) Mary slept very well.

(C) Mary slept well afterwards.

(D) sleeping was what Mary did

292. Which of these expresses the idea most clearly?

(A) Tom, every morning at breakfast, the paper he liked to read.

(B) At breakfast every morning it was the paper that Tom liked to read.

(C) At breakfast, reading the paper was what Tom liked to do every morning.

(D) Tom liked to read the paper every morning at breakfast.

293. Which of these expresses the idea most clearly?

(A) In order to hear her favorite musician perform, 50 miles it was that she drove.

(B) She drove 50 miles in order to hear her favorite musician perform.

(C) She drove, in order to hear her favorite musician perform, 50 miles.

(D) Her favorite musician performed, and she drove 50 miles in order to hear him perform.

294. Which of these best fits under the topic "History of the Automobile"?

(A) Cars require a great deal of attention and care in order to prevent problems from developing.

(B) The legal driving age varies from one state to another.

(C) The invention of the automobile cannot be credited to any one person.

(D) None of these

295. Which of these expresses the idea most clearly?

(A) His brother, and Stuart, were eager to experience—never on an airplane voyaging in the skies.

(B) Stuart and his brother had never been on an airplane, and they were eager to experience their first voyage in the skies.

(C) Voyage in the skies? Eager Stuart and his brother haven't. They've never been on an airplane.

(D) Never on an airplane, never voyaging—in the skies—Stuart or his brother have never had this eager experience.

296. Which sentence does *not* belong in the paragraph?

(1) Everyone in the class was looking forward to the Halloween party. (2) Five students had difficulty with their math homework from the previous day. (3) Each student had prepared a snack to bring. (4) The costumes included four ghosts, five space creatures, and two pumpkins.

(A) Sentence 1

(B) Sentence 2

(C) Sentence 3

(D) Sentence 4

297. Which topic is best for a one-paragraph theme?

(A) How to Open Your Own Business

(B) Child Psychology

(C) The Geography of Asia and Africa

(D) None of these

298. Where should the sentence, "The government has set up laws restricting or forbidding the hunting of certain animals," be placed in the paragraph below?

(1) Many animal species are now becoming or have recently become extinct. (2) Both government and private efforts are being made to protect those species currently in danger. (3) It has also attempted to educate the public about the problem.

(A) Between sentences 1 and 2

(B) Between sentences 2 and 3

(C) After sentence 3

(D) The sentence does not fit in this paragraph.

STOP   End of Language section. If you have any time left, go over your work in this section only. Do not work in any other section of the test.

ANSWER KEYS AND EXPLANATIONS

Verbal Skills

1. C	13. D	25. B	37. C	49. A
2. D	14. C	26. C	38. C	50. D
3. D	15. C	27. D	39. C	51. B
4. B	16. A	28. B	40. B	52. B
5. D	17. B	29. C	41. D	53. B
6. D	18. C	30. D	42. A	54. B
7. A	19. A	31. A	43. D	55. A
8. D	20. B	32. A	44. C	56. B
9. B	21. A	33. B	45. C	57. D
10. A	22. C	34. D	46. D	58. A
11. D	23. D	35. B	47. A	59. B
12. C	24. C	36. D	48. C	60. B

1. **The correct answer is (C).** Choices (A), (B), and (D) are all types of appliances that are used for cooking. Cook, choice (C), does not share this common characteristic with the other words.

2. **The correct answer is (D).** The common feature among three of the answer choices is that they're all verbs—*run*, *walk*, and *jog*. Choice (D), sneaker, is a noun, not a verb.

3. **The correct answer is (D).** Cause-effect relationship. The effect of lightening red is pink; the effect of lightening black is gray.

4. **The correct answer is (B).** Because the first two statements are true and Karen reads faster than Ann, she must also read faster than Sue.

5. **The correct answer is (D).** *Create* means to bring into existence or to invent.

6. **The correct answer is (D).** Noun-adjective relationship.

7. **The correct answer is (A).** *Quality* is a general classification. The other choices are examples of good qualities.

8. **The correct answer is (D).** Part-whole relationship. Sand is part of the beach; black dirt is part of a farm.

9. **The correct answer is (B).** *Time* is a general classification. The other choices are measures of time.

10. **The correct answer is (A).** A *salamander* is an amphibian resembling a lizard.

11. **The correct answer is (D).** *Arrogant* means proud or haughty.

12. **The correct answer is (C).** The first part of the analogy establishes opposite directions. The opposite direction of left is right, choice (C).

13. **The correct answer is (D).** Part-whole relationship. 1 is half of 2; 3 is half of 6.

14. The correct answer is (C). *Add* is a function. The others are general classifications of symbols.

15. The correct answer is (C). From the first two statements, it is only certain that Peter is the shortest of the three boys. The relationship between Paul and John cannot be determined.

16. The correct answer is (A). A *mellow* fruit is one that is tender and sweet, or *ripe*.

17. The correct answer is (B). Other synonyms for *gossamer* are insubstantial, delicate, or tenuous.

18. The correct answer is (C). *Coddle* means to treat with extreme care, or *pamper*.

19. The correct answer is (A). The first part of the analogy establishes a type of item (books) and a place where they're usually found (libraries). Rides are a type of item that are usually found in carnivals, choice (A).

20. The correct answer is (B). Object-purpose relationship. The purpose of a director is to lead a choir; the purpose of a coach is to lead a team.

21. The correct answer is (A). *Diversify* means to make or become more varied.

22. The correct answer is (C). The first two statements indicate no relationship between Harry and Ralph; therefore, the third statement is uncertain.

23. The correct answer is (D). A *superficial* wound is a surface wound, or *shallow*.

24. The correct answer is (C). Although Shelley cannot throw a Javelin farther than Liandra, we are not told who took part in the javelin-throwing contest, so we cannot be certain who won.

25. The correct answer is (B). Someone who is *bellicose* is eager to fight, or combative, choice (B).

26. The correct answer is (C). A *sadistic* remark is intended to inflict pain, or *hurtful*.

27. The correct answer is (D). A *dormitory* is only one part of a school, university, or college.

28. The correct answer is (B). *Truncate* means to shorten or to cut off.

29. The correct answer is (C). Someone who is *facetious* is clever and humorous, choice (C).

30. The correct answer is (D). An *indigent* person is impoverished, or *needy*.

31. The correct answer is (A). Part-whole relationship. A leg is a part of a table on which the table rests; a wheel is a part of a car on which the car rests.

32. The correct answer is (A). A *dungeon* is a place where people may be forced to stay. The other choices are places in which people choose to live.

33. The correct answer is (B). We are told early on that "Bishop's house is the largest on his street." We are also told that "Arianna and Bishop live on the same street." Therefore, even though Arianna's house is much larger than Terrence's house, it is false that Arianna's house is the largest on Oakville Lane, since Bishop's house is the largest on his street, and he lives on the same street as Arianna.

34. The correct answer is (D). *Punishment* is a general classification. The other choices describe specific types or places of punishment.

35. The correct answer is (B). *Refuse* means to decline; the opposite is *to accept*.

36. The correct answer is (D). Object-user relationship. Ink is used in a pen when applied; paint is used on a brush when applied.

37. The correct answer is (C). *Acquire* means to gain possession of; the opposite is *to release*.

38. The correct answer is (C). Though the first two statements are considered true, they do not provide any information as to the direct relationship between rivers A and C.

39. **The correct answer is (C).** *Scant* means meager; the opposite is *abundant*.

40. **The correct answer is (B).** *Pinnacle* means peak; the opposite is *base*.

41. **The correct answer is (D).** Part-whole relationship. The captain is the part of a team that guides the team; the manager is the part of an office that guides the office.

42. **The correct answer is (A).** A *window* may be covered by the other three choices.

43. **The correct answer is (D).** *Corpulent* means obese; the opposite is *slender*.

44. **The correct answer is (C).** *Naive* means lacking experience or knowledge; the opposite is *sophisticated*.

45. **The correct answer is (C).** A *glove* is a hand covering; all the other choices are head coverings.

46. **The correct answer is (D).** A *podium* is positioned at the front of an auditorium or theater. The other choices represent those who face the podium.

47. **The correct answer is (A).** To *pledge* is to promise.

48. **The correct answer is (C).** A *depression* is a low spot or a *hollow;* the opposite is a *hill*.

49. **The correct answer is (A).** Because the first two statements are true and all the fruits cost more than apples, apples must cost the least.

50. **The correct answer is (D).** A *fir tree* is an evergreen; all of the other trees are deciduous, losing their leaves.

51. **The correct answer is (B).** *Diminish* means to decrease; the opposite is *to augment*.

52. **The correct answer is (B).** Because the first two statements are true, Jay's batting average must be higher than Tom's.

53. **The correct answer is (B).** *Abandon* means to give up; the opposite is *to keep*.

54. **The correct answer is (B).** *Feasible* is an attribute of abstract things or ideas. The other choices are generally attributes applied to concrete objects.

55. **The correct answer is (A).** Because the first two statements are true and C is north of A, it must also be north of B.

56. **The correct answer is (B).** *Cotton* is a vegetable product; leather, wool, and fur are animal products.

57. **The correct answer is (D).** A *seam* is a type of closing. The other choices are things for opening and closing.

58. **The correct answer is (A).** *Dwindle* means to grow smaller.

59. **The correct answer is (B).** Oxygen, helium, and gold are elements; water is a compound of hydrogen and oxygen.

60. **The correct answer is (B).** Because the first two statements are true and the third statement is in direct opposition to the first, it cannot be true.

Quantitative Skills

61. A	72. C	83. B	93. B	103. A
62. D	73. A	84. A	94. A	104. A
63. D	74. B	85. D	95. C	105. B
64. C	75. C	86. B	96. D	106. D
65. D	76. A	87. B	97. C	107. B
66. B	77. C	88. C	98. B	108. C
67. C	78. D	89. D	99. A	109. B
68. D	79. D	90. B	100. D	110. A
69. B	80. C	91. A	101. C	111. D
70. D	81. B	92. C	102. A	112. A
71. A	82. D			

61. **The correct answer is (A).** Start by finding 20% of 40: $0.20 \times 40 = 8$. Then add 3:

$$8 + 3 = 11.$$

62. **The correct answer is (D).** The pattern in this series is made by adding 7 to each number.

63. **The correct answer is (D).** The pattern in this series is made by subtracting 9 from each number.

64. **The correct answer is (C).** Determine the amount of money for (A), (B), and (C). Then test the alternatives given to see which is correct.

65. **The correct answer is (D).** (A) is 0.625; (B) is 0.571; (C) is 0.6237. Clearly (B) is less than both (A) and (C), which are not equal to each other.

66. **The correct answer is (B).** The cube of 5 is 125. 125 divided by 5 = 25.

67. **The correct answer is (C).** The sum of $7 + 18 + 5 + 39 + 11 = 80$.

$80 \div 5 = 16$. $\frac{1}{2}$ of 16 = 8.

68. **The correct answer is (D).** Determine how much of each box is shaded. Then test each alternative to see which is correct.

69. **The correct answer is (B).** The pattern in this series is +3, +7, +3, +7, and so on.

70. **The correct answer is (D).** Determine the amounts for (A), (B), and (C). Here, (A) = 8, (B) = 8, and (C) = 0.08. When you test each alternative to see which is correct, you see that choice (D) is the correct answer: (A) is greater than (C).

71. **The correct answer is (A).** The pattern in this series is +1, ×2, +1, ×2, and so on.

72. **The correct answer is (C).** The pattern in this series is −5, −4, +1, −5, −4, +1, … So, the next three numbers in the series are 35, 31, 32.

73. **The correct answer is (A).** Start this problem from the end and work forward:

$$\frac{3}{5} \times \frac{25}{1} = 15$$
$$15 + 7 = 22$$

The number you're looking for is found by setting up an equation.

$$30 - x = 22$$
$$x = 30 - 22$$
$$x = 8$$

74. **The correct answer is (B).** $\frac{1}{4}$ of 64 is 16, and 7 less than 16 is 9.

75. The correct answer is (C). First determine the amounts of (A), (B), and (C). In this case, (A), (B), and (C) all equal 14. When you test each alternative, you see that choice (C) is the correct answer: (A), (B), and (C) are equal.

76. The correct answer is (A). The pattern in this series is –9, –8, –7, –6, and so on.

77. The correct answer is (C). Count the circles in (A), (B), and (C). Test each alternative to find the one that is true. You will see that (B) has 12 circles and (C) has 13 circles—both of which are more than (A), which has only 10 circles.

78. The correct answer is (D). Determine how much of each figure is shaded. Then test each alternative to find the one that is true. In this case, (A), (B), and (C) each have 3 parts shaded, so they're equally shaded.

79. The correct answer is (D). The pattern in this series is made by adding 4 to each number. $99 + 4 = 103$.

80. The correct answer is (C). Determine $\frac{1}{5}$ of 100: $\frac{1}{5} \times \frac{100}{1} = 20$. Multiply this result by 4 to find the answer:

$20 \times 4 = 80$.

81. The correct answer is (B). The pattern in this series is +4, +1, +4, +1, and so on. Also, whenever 1 is added, the result is expressed as an Arabic numeral; whenever 4 is added, the result is expressed as a Roman numeral.

82. The correct answer is (D). Determine the amounts for (A), (B), and (C). Here, (A) = 5, (B) = 4, and (C) = 4. When you test each alternative to find the one that is true, you see that choice (D) is the correct answer: (B) and (C) are equal.

83. The correct answer is (B). First find 7 times 3: $7 \times 3 = 21$. Double this result to find the answer: $2 \times 21 = 42$.

84. The correct answer is (A). Each box is shaded by $\frac{1}{2}$. Therefore, only (A) can be true.

85. The correct answer is (D). Figure this problem from the end and work forward:

$$5 \times 2 = 10$$
$$3 \times 10 = 30$$
$$6 + x = 30$$
$$x = 30 - 6 = 24$$

86. The correct answer is (B). The pattern in this series is –2, +4, –2, +4, and so on.

87. The correct answer is (B). 125% = 1.25, so (A) and (B) are equal. But $\frac{25}{2} = 12.5$, which is greater than (A) and (B). So, (A) and (B) are both less than (C).

88. The correct answer is (C). You can figure out this problem with algebra:

$$\frac{3}{4} \times x = 6 \times 4$$
$$\frac{3}{4} \times x = 24$$
$$x = \frac{24}{1} \times \frac{4}{3}$$
$$x = 32$$

89. The correct answer is (D). The pattern in this series is +2, ×2, +2, ×2, and so on.

90. The correct answer is (B). The pattern in this series is +1, +3, +3, +1, +3, +3, +1, and so on.

91. The correct answer is (A). The line drawn from point A to the base of triangle ABD divides this triangle into two right triangles, one of which is ∆ACD. AD is the hypotenuse of this right triangle whose length must be greater than the length CD, a leg of ∆ACD.

92. The correct answer is (C). Begin by subtracting 5 from 29. This number divided by 3 will provide the answer:

$$29 - 5 = 24$$
$$24 \div 3 = 8$$

93. The correct answer is (B). The pattern in this series is +6, +3, +6, +3, and so on.

94. The correct answer is (A). Determine the amounts for (A), (B), and (C). Then choose the best alternative. Be sure to do the operations in the parentheses first when figuring.

95. The correct answer is (C). The pattern in this series is $+1, -10, +1, -10$, and so on.

96. The correct answer is (D). Because the figure is a cube, all edges and sides are equal. When a diagonal line is drawn across one side, like CF, it forms a hypotenuse of a right triangle whose length is longer than the length of either of its sides (CE and EF). Because the sides of the cube are all equal, CF must also be longer than AB.

97. The correct answer is (C). This can be done with algebra. If x is the number you are looking for:

$$x \div 2 = 6 + 4$$
$$2(x \div 2) = (6 + 4)2$$
$$x = 20$$

98. The correct answer is (B). Since $x < y$, multiplying both sides by x gives $x^2 < xy$. So, (C) is less than (A). Likewise, since $x < y$, multiplying both sides by y gives $xy < y^2$. So, (A) is less than (B).

99. The correct answer is (A). The pattern in this series is $\times 2, +4, \times 2, +4$, and so on.

100. The correct answer is (D). To begin, find $\frac{1}{4}$ of 20. This is the same as saying $20 \div 4$, which equals 5. If x is the number you are looking for:

$$7 - x = 5$$
$$x = 2$$

101. The correct answer is (C). The pattern for the letters in this series is made by using every other letter starting with A. The pattern for the numbers is $+4, -10, +4, -10$, and so on.

102. The correct answer is (A). Determine the values for each bar in the graph by using the number scale to the left. Then choose the correct alternative. Choice (A) is correct because $2 + 10 - 4 = 8$ or $12 - 4 = 8$.

103. The correct answer is (A). This can be set up as an algebraic equation. If x is the number you are looking for:

$$x = \frac{3}{5}(10) - 2$$
$$x = 6 - 2$$
$$x = 4$$

104. The correct answer is (A). The pattern in this series is made by taking numbers in sequential order (4, 5, 6, and so on) and following each number with its square.

105. The correct answer is (B). Determine the amounts for (A), (B), and (C). Then, decide which alternative is true.

(A) $5^2 = 25$

(B) $4^3 = 64$

(C) $2^4 = 16$

So, (B) is greater than (A), which is greater than (C).

106. The correct answer is (D). The pattern in this series is made by subtracting $2\frac{1}{2}$ from each number.

107. The correct answer is (B). Begin by figuring $\frac{1}{2}$ of 20. This number multiplied by 8 will provide the answer:

$$\frac{1}{2} \times 20 = 10$$
$$8 \times 10 = 80$$

108. The correct answer is (C). The pattern in this series is $+4, -2, -1, +4, -2, -1$, and so on.

109. The correct answer is (B). This can be set up as an algebraic equation. If x is the number you are looking for:

$$6 + \frac{1}{3}x = 2 \times 9$$
$$6 + \frac{1}{3}x = 18$$
$$\frac{1}{3}x = 12$$
$$x = 36$$

110. The correct answer is (A). Test each of the alternatives to find the true one. To find the perimeter, add the length of all four sides together: $2 + 3 + 2 + 3 = 10$.

111. The correct answer is (D). This can be set up as an algebraic equation. If x is the number you are looking for:

$$x = \frac{4}{9}(27) + 10$$
$$x = 12 + 10$$
$$x = 22$$

112. The correct answer is (A). 5 squared is 25, and 11 more than 25 is 36.

answers practice test 5

Reading
COMPREHENSION

113. B	121. C	129. D	137. A	145. A
114. C	122. C	130. C	138. D	146. A
115. C	123. C	131. B	139. C	147. B
116. D	124. A	132. D	140. A	148. A
117. D	125. D	133. C	141. B	149. B
118. C	126. B	134. A	142. B	150. D
119. B	127. C	135. B	143. B	151. A
120. D	128. C	136. D	144. C	152. A

113. The correct answer is (B). Sentence 6 states that the thickness of the outer core is "slightly more than 1,200 miles, while that of the inner core is slightly less than 800 miles. The crust, choice (A), is about 20 miles thick, as noted in sentence 2.

114. The correct answer is (C). The answer is in sentence 1: "Our planet Earth is divided into *seven* separate layers."

115. The correct answer is (C). This is an inferential question. Based on sentence 7, we know that both the speed and direction of earthquake waves vary. We do not know from this information if choice (A) is true, so we must assume that (C) is the best answer.

116. The correct answer is (D). Because of the nature of the information, it would be found in both an encyclopedia and a science book.

117. The correct answer is (D). This answer is determined by the entire passage, which describes the layers in order. The answer can be verified by eliminating choices (A), (B), and (C).

118. The correct answer is (C). *Vary* most closely means *range*.

119. The correct answer is (B). This is an inferential question. Though not specifically stated, the answer can be assumed based on sentence 2 and the phrase "appears to be."

120. The correct answer is (D). The last sentence of the paragraph states that "both temperature and pressure are much greater at the core than at the crust."

121. The correct answer is (C). In this passage, *slightly* most nearly means *a little*.

122. The correct answer is (C). *Remaining* most closely means *last*.

123. The correct answer is (C). This answer may be verified by eliminating choices (A), (B), and (D). Though rocks are mentioned, they are only a part of the entire description.

124. The correct answer is (A). In this case, *wavering* most nearly means *swaying*.

125. The correct answer is (D). This answer may be verified by eliminating choices (A), (B), and (C). A clue to the answer is the way the passage is written—without technical terms and in the third person.

126. The correct answer is (B). The cave the man was exploring was probably deep underground. This is an inferential question. The answer may be verified by eliminating the other choices.

127. The correct answer is (C). This is the most specific, direct answer, though the other choices may have been indirectly related. The answer is found in paragraph 2, where it states that it was the flashlight that started the bats to suddenly fly about.

128. The correct answer is (C). In paragraph 2, sentence 4 states: "He ducks, startled, then grins." So he is surprised.

129. The correct answer is (D). *Utter* most nearly means *great.*

130. The correct answer is (C). Spelunkers ignore *discomfort.* This is an inferential question. The answer may be verified by eliminating the other choices. See paragraphs 3 and 4.

131. The correct answer is (B). A good title for this passage would be "Spelunkers—Underground Explorers." Though the author mentions bats, the passage covers the more general topic of spelunkers.

132. The correct answer is (D). According to this passage, adventurous is the word that would most nearly describe spelunkers. The answer may be verified by eliminating the other choices.

133. The correct answer is (C). This passage provides positive information about kohlrabi, and based on the optimistic tone, readers can determine that the author's opinion on kohlrabi as a food is most likely *enthusiastic,* choice (C).

134. The correct answer is (A). This passage is a persuasive piece that highlights the many merits of this type of vegetable in an effort to get readers to try it. Therefore, "Consider Kohlrabi," choice (A), would be the best title for this passage.

135. The correct answer is (B). As used in the passage, the word *protean* is used to describe the type of menu ingredient that "can be eaten raw or cooked and is an excellent addition to a wide array of recipes." This description attempts to portray kohlrabi as a versatile ingredient, making choice (B) the correct answer.

136. The correct answer is (D). According to the passage, kohlrabi is a good source of vitamin C, vitamin B, fiber, and *potassium,* choice (D). There is no mention of kohlrabi being a source of calories, energy, or spice, so choices (A), (B), and (C) are incorrect.

137. The correct answer is (A). The author mentions "the vegetable's popularity in Germany" in the same sentence as the types of kohlrabi (White Danube, Purple Danube, White Vienna, and Purple Vienna). The most likely scenario is that these names are of German origin, making choice (A) the correct answer.

138. The correct answer is (D). Within the passage, the word varietal is used to introduce the White Danube, Purple Danube, White Vienna, and Purple Vienna—each a *type* of kohlrabi. Therefore, choice (D) is correct.

139. The correct answer is (C). According to the passage, the main reason why kohlrabi is often mistaken as a root vegetable is its bulbous, root-like *appearance* (choice C). The kohlrabi's taste, color, and name have nothing to do with its being mistaken for a root vegetable, so choices (A), (B), and (D) are incorrect.

140. The correct answer is (A). Kohlrabi is a member of the *Brassica oleracea* species, which also includes broccoli, kale, cauliflower, and Brussels sprouts. There is no mention of it being in the same species as turnips, so choice (A) is correct.

141. The correct answer is (B). In the passage, the only item among the answer choices that's *not* mentioned as a benefit of kohlrabi is heart health, making choice (B) the correct answer.

142. The correct answer is (B). This passage is an enthusiastic piece of writing that is in full support of giving kohlrabi a try. It discusses a wide array of kohlrabi's benefits and positive characteristics, and it suggests trying kohlrabi "the next time you're doing some meal planning." Therefore, choice (B) is correct.

143. The correct answer is (B). The passage was probably printed in a magazine. This answer may be verified by eliminating the other three choices. The passage covers several aspects of the topic—more than would be contained in just one type of book.

144. The correct answer is (C). See paragraph 1. According to this passage, the mystery of witchcraft is *still unsolved*.

145. The correct answer is (A). One of today's reminders of ancient witchcraft beliefs is *Halloween*. This is a question based on your general knowledge.

146. The correct answer is (A). Judges, according to the passage, are the group that has had members who believed in witchcraft. In paragraph 2, it states: ... *the judges undoubtedly were sincere in their desire to eliminate what they thought was a real danger.*

147. The correct answer is (B). Another superstition is *"Breaking a mirror brings bad luck."* This answer is actually testing your vocabulary.

148. The correct answer is (A). As stated in paragraph 3, according to some psychologists, persons who do believe in witchcraft *can be harmed by it.*

149. The correct answer is (B). As it is used in the passage, *in essence* most closely means *basically.*

150. The correct answer is (D). *Interesting* is the best answer; it could be substituted for *fascinating.*

151. The correct answer is (A). This is an inferential question. The answer is implied in paragraph 3. This passage suggests that what you believe *can hurt you.*

152. The correct answer is (A). A good title for this passage might be *"Witchcraft—Fact or Fiction?"* This answer may be verified by eliminating the other choices.

Vocabulary

153. D	158. A	163. B	167. A	171. A
154. B	159. D	164. B	168. D	172. B
155. A	160. D	165. D	169. A	173. D
156. D	161. A	166. A	170. C	174. C
157. C	162. B			

153. The correct answer is (D). *Perspective* means "aspect," "attitude," or "view."

154. The correct answer is (B). To *impair* is to "spoil," "damage," or "weaken."

155. The correct answer is (A). *Acumen* refers to a "keen intelligence."

156. The correct answer is (D). To *subjugate* means to "dominate," or "overpower."

157. The correct answer is (C). To *reproach* is to "condemn," "chide," or "blame."

158. The correct answer is (A). To be *elated* is to be "jubilant," "exhilarated," or "happy."

159. The correct answer is (D). *Brusque* means to be "curt," "blunt," or "abrupt."

160. The correct answer is (D). To *depress* something is to "squash," "flatten," or "push down."

161. The correct answer is (A). To *quench* is to "allay," "stifle," or "end."

162. The correct answer is (B). An *exploit* is an "escapade," "deed," or "venture."

163. The correct answer is (B). A *precipitous* incline is "steep."

164. The correct answer is (B). A *chronicle* is an "account," a "history," or a "record" of something.

165. The correct answer is (D). To be an *amiable* person means to be "likeable."

166. The correct answer is (A). The meaning of the word *astute* is to be "keen," "shrewd," or "clever."

167. The correct answer is (A). To *sever* something means to "divide," "split," or "cut" the object.

168. The correct answer is (D). *Eminent* means to be "distinguished," "important," or "outstanding."

169. The correct answer is (A). To *terminate* is to "end," "cancel," or "stop" something.

170. The correct answer is (C). To *hinder* means to "obstruct," "interfere," or "impede" something.

171. The correct answer is (A). To be in *contention* means to be in "strife," "discord," or "debate."

172. The correct answer is (B). To *concede* means to "admit," "allow," or "acknowledge."

173. The correct answer is (D). To *forego* means to "concede," "give up," or "relinquish."

174. The correct answer is (C). For something to be *canny* means to be "clever."

Mathematics

CONCEPTS

175. C	180. C	185. D	190. D	195. A
176. C	181. D	186. C	191. B	196. A
177. A	182. B	187. D	192. C	197. A
178. D	183. C	188. D	193. D	198. B
179. B	184. D	189. A	194. D	

175. The correct answer is (C). A quadrilateral is defined as a figure with four sides. A triangle has only three sides.

176. The correct answer is (C). The union of two sets is the set containing all of the elements that are in *at least one* of the sets. So, $\{4,7,9\} \cup \{4,9,12,15\} = \{4, 7, 9, 12, 15\}$.

177. The correct answer is (A). This problem requires you to "round off" the given number to the place one digit to the right of the decimal point.

178. The correct answer is (D). Always start with the operations in the parentheses first:

$(-2)^3 = (-2) \times (-2) \times (-2)$

$(-2)^3 = -8$

Then continue with the operations outside the parentheses:

$3 \times (-8) = -24$

Remember, a negative number times a positive number equals a negative number; a negative times a negative equals a positive number.

179. The correct answer is (B). The digits 2 and 4 end in the hundredths place. This means $0.24 = \frac{24}{100}$. When simplified to simplest form, $\frac{24}{100} = \frac{6}{25}$.

180. The correct answer is (C). A straight line represents a "straight angle" of 180°. An angle of 60° is given, so m∠C must be 120° to complete the line. All the angles in a triangle added together equal 180°, therefore:

$m\angle A + m\angle B + m\angle C = 180°$

$m\angle A + 30° + 120° = 180°$

$m\angle A = 180° - 150°$

$m\angle A = 30°$

181. The correct answer is (D). When multiplying by 10, 100, 1000, etc., move the decimal point one place to the right for each zero in the multiplier. In this example, 100 has two zeros, so the decimal point would be moved two places to the right.

182. The correct answer is (B). The reciprocal of a fraction is the fraction "reversed." To find the answer, you would have to rename $3\frac{1}{3}$ as an improper fraction: $3\frac{1}{3} = \frac{10}{3}$; $\frac{10}{3}$ is the reciprocal of $\frac{3}{10}$.

183. The correct answer is (C). The formula for finding the circumference of a circle is π times the diameter. The diameter is 2 times the radius. In this case, $2 \times 4 = 8$ is the diameter. Therefore:

$C = d\pi$

$C = 8\pi$

184. The correct answer is (D). The components of this problem must be stated in the same units. Therefore, 3 yards = 108 inches. The ratio of 108 to 18 is simplified to 6 to 1.

185. The correct answer is (D). State $\frac{33}{7}$ as a decimal number. $\frac{33}{7} = 4.714$.

An integer is a whole number.

186. The correct answer is (C). The distributive property makes choice (C) true.

187. The correct answer is (D). $14^2 = 196$; $15^2 = 225$. So, the square root of 198 would fall between 14 and 15.

188. The correct answer is (D). The base-five system uses only five symbols: 1, 2, 3, 4, and 0. Because of this, the other three alternatives are eliminated.

189. The correct answer is (A). When working with scientific notation, the exponent represents the number of places to move the decimal point in the multiplier. If the exponent of 10 is positive, the decimal point moves to the right. If it is negative, the decimal point moves to the left.

190. The correct answer is (D). This problem may be done without computation. The larger the denominator, the smaller the parts of the whole have been divided. The larger the numerator, the more parts are being considered. An alternative to this method is to find a common denominator and compare numerators. The largest numerator in this case shows the greatest value.

191. The correct answer is (B). The symbol ≥ means "greater than or equal to," and 6 is equal to 6.

192. The correct answer is (C). Figures are "similar" when their corresponding angles are equal and their corresponding sides are in proportion.

$$\frac{4}{AB} = \frac{3}{5}$$

$$3AB = 20$$

$$AB = \frac{20}{3} = 6\frac{2}{3}$$

193. The correct answer is (D). By definition, an isosceles triangle is any triangle with two sides equal. Therefore, it is the only possible answer.

194. The correct answer is (D). For choice (D) to be equal, it would need the percent symbol after it.

195. The correct answer is (A). Prime factorization is factoring a number to the point where all factors are prime.

196. The correct answer is (A). The least common multiple is the least number divisible by both given numbers.

197. The correct answer is (A). This is done by ratios. The relationship between part of the lawn and the whole lawn is the same as the relationship between the time it takes to mow part of the lawn and the time it takes to mow the whole lawn.

198. The correct answer is (B). The commutative property of multiplication tells us that we can switch the order in which numbers are multiplied and still get the same result. This is illustrated by $\frac{3}{8}\left(5+\frac{1}{2}\right) = \left(5+\frac{1}{2}\right)\frac{3}{8}$ since only the order in which $\left(5+\frac{1}{2}\right)$ and $\frac{3}{8}$ are being multiplied has changed.

PROBLEM-SOLVING

199. C	207. A	215. B	223. A	231. C
200. B	208. C	216. C	224. D	232. C
201. D	209. A	217. A	225. D	233. A
202. D	210. A	218. B	226. A	234. A
203. A	211. C	219. C	227. A	235. B
204. B	212. C	220. A	228. D	236. C
205. A	213. A	221. C	229. B	237. B
206. D	214. D	222. D	230. C	238. D

199. The correct answer is (C). This involves multiplication and addition.

Student

    tickets 130 × $1.25 = $162.50

Adult

    tickets 340 × $1.90 =+ $646.00

               Total = $808.50

200. The correct answer is (B). When subtracting fractional numbers, you must first rename the numbers with a common denominator.

$$12 - 2\frac{3}{16} = \frac{192}{16} - \frac{35}{16}$$

$$= \frac{157}{16}$$

$$= 9\frac{13}{16}$$

201. The correct answer is (D). There are 12 months in 1 year. If $542.40 is the total amount paid in a year, the average amount paid per month is $542.40 ÷ 12 = $45.20.

202. The correct answer is (D). First, add $10 to Bob's $88:

$88 + $10 = $98

Then, divide by 4:

$98 ÷ 4 = $24.50

203. The correct answer is (A). Multiply the numbers as you would whole numbers. Then, since there are an odd number of negative signs, affix a negative sign to the product. Doing so yields $(-2) \cdot (-4) \cdot (3) \cdot (-1) = -24$.

204. The correct answer is (B). Replace the C in the formula with 85 and solve:

$$F = \frac{9}{5}(85) + 32 = 153 + 32$$
$$= 185$$

205. The correct answer is (A). This can be set up as an algebraic equation. If n equals the price of the snowmobile, 5% of n equals $42, or

$0.05n = \$42$

$n = \$42 \div 0.05$

$n = \$840$

206. The correct answer is (D). Rename the fractions of the equation with a common denominator.

$$4\frac{1}{8} - 2\frac{2}{3} = \frac{33}{8} - \frac{8}{3}$$
$$= \frac{99}{24} - \frac{64}{24}$$
$$= \frac{35}{24}$$
$$= 1\frac{11}{24}$$

207. The correct answer is (A). Solve for x:

$-5 + 4x = 21$

$4x = 21 + 5$

$4x = 26$

$x = \frac{26}{4}$

$x = 6.5$

208. The correct answer is (C). Before multiplying, rename the mixed numbers as improper fractions:

$$3\frac{1}{3} \times 3\frac{3}{4} \times \frac{2}{5} = \frac{10}{3} \times \frac{15}{4} \times \frac{2}{5}$$
$$= \frac{300}{60} = 5$$

209. The correct answer is (A). This can be set up as an algebraic equation. If n is the amount Mr. Symon borrowed:

$6\%(n) = 58.50$

$n = \frac{58.50}{6\%}$

$= \frac{58.50}{0.06}$

$= 975$

210. The correct answer is (A). This problem is done by ratios:

$$\frac{n}{6} = \frac{56}{14}$$
$$336 = 14n$$
$$\frac{336}{14} = n$$
$$24 = n$$

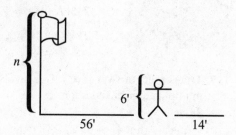

211. The correct answer is (C). By definition, the opposite sides of a rectangle are equal to each other. Because of this, if one side is 7 units, the opposite side is also 7 units. Consequently, 14 units account for two sides (7 + 7). The other two sides are each equal to $(50 - 14) \div 2$, or 18 units. Area is length times width—in this case: $7 \times 18 = 126$ square units.

212. The correct answer is (C). Solve for x:

$$5(1 - 2x) + 25 = 0$$
$$5 - 10x + 25 = 0$$
$$30 - 10x = 0$$
$$30 = 10x$$
$$3 = x$$

213. The correct answer is (A). Solve this as an algebraic equation with n as the unknown integer:

$$n + 18 = \frac{5}{4}n$$
$$18 = \frac{5}{4}n - n$$
$$18 = \frac{1}{4}n$$
$$72 = n$$

214. The correct answer is (D). Replace the letters with the given numbers and solve:

$$7A - 3B =$$
$$7(6) - 3(3) =$$
$$42 - 9 = 33$$

215. The correct answer is (B). Because Jim is now 12, four years ago he was 8. His father was then 5 times older, or 40. Now, 4 years later, Jim's father is 44.

216. The correct answer is (C). Convert the mixed numbers into improper fractions, then find the common denominator and add:

$$2\frac{1}{2} + 7\frac{2}{3} + \frac{3}{4} = \frac{5}{2} + \frac{23}{3} + \frac{3}{4}$$
$$= \frac{30}{12} + \frac{92}{12} + \frac{9}{12}$$
$$= \frac{131}{12}$$
$$= 10\frac{11}{12}$$

217. The correct answer is (A).

$$N\% \times 60 = 24$$
$$N\% = \frac{24}{60}$$
$$N\% = \frac{2}{5}$$
$$N\% = 0.4$$
$$N = 40$$

218. The correct answer is (B). Solve for x:

$$10x - 3 = 2x + 4$$
$$10x - 2x = 4 + 3$$
$$8x = 7$$
$$x = \frac{7}{8}$$

219. The correct answer is (C). To determine ratios, multiply the first numerator by the second denominator and the first denominator by the second numerator. Then reduce:

$$\frac{3}{4} \text{ to } \frac{5}{2}$$

6 to 20

3 to 10

220. The correct answer is (A). The area to be carpeted is $(27 \times 27) = 729$ square feet. Since there are 9 square feet in one yard, this is equivalent to 81 square yards, and since it costs $11 per square yard, the total cost is $(81 \times 11) = \$891$.

221. The correct answer is (C).

$$
\begin{array}{r}
0.57 \\
6.41\overline{)3.6537} \\
3205 \\
\hline
4487 \\
4487 \\
\hline
0
\end{array}
$$

222. The correct answer is (D).

$$V = lwh$$
$$V = 18 \times 2 \times 5$$
$$V = 180 \text{ cu. in.}$$

223. The correct answer is (A). Replace the letters in the problem with the given numbers.

$$\frac{3ABC}{2A} = \frac{3 \times 3 \times 2 \times 6}{2 \times 3}$$
$$= \frac{108}{6}$$
$$= 18$$

224. The correct answer is (D). Convert the mixed numbers to improper fractions and then multiply:

$$4\frac{2}{5} \times 2\frac{3}{11} = \frac{22}{5} \times \frac{25}{11}$$
$$= \frac{550}{55}$$
$$= 10$$

225. The correct answer is (D).

$$\frac{5}{6}x = 30$$
$$x = \frac{30}{1} \cdot \frac{6}{5}$$
$$x = \frac{180}{5}$$
$$x = 36$$

226. The correct answer is (A). When solving this problem, remember that the number of decimal places to the right of the decimal point in the answer should equal the total number of places to the right of the decimal points in the two factors being multiplied.

$$\begin{array}{r} 65.14 \\ \times 0.093 \\ \hline 19542 \\ 586260 \\ \hline 6.05802 \end{array}$$

227. The correct answer is (A). The pattern in this sequence is made by adding 0.06 to each number.

228. The correct answer is (D).

$$\begin{array}{r} 72528 \\ \times\ 109 \\ \hline 652\ 752 \\ 000\ 00 \\ 7\ 252\ 8 \\ \hline 7,905,552 \end{array}$$

229. The correct answer is (B). Set this problem up as an algebraic equation.

$$11 \times 12 = N + 3$$
$$132 = N + 3$$
$$132 - 3 = N$$
$$129 = N$$

230. The correct answer is (C). Convert the mixed numbers into improper fractions. Then, divide the total length of the board by the length into which it will be cut.

$$9\frac{1}{2} \div 1\frac{1}{3} = \frac{19}{2} \div \frac{4}{3}$$
$$= \frac{19}{2} \times \frac{3}{4}$$
$$= \frac{57}{8}$$
$$= 7\frac{1}{8}$$

Though $\frac{1}{8}$ of a board is left, only 7 full-size boards can be made.

231. The correct answer is (C).

$$3x + 3 < 9 + x$$
$$3x - x < 9 - 3$$
$$2x < 6$$
$$x < \frac{6}{2}$$
$$x < 3$$

232. The correct answer is (C). When adding decimal numbers, line up the decimal points.

$$\begin{array}{r} 0.602 \\ 4.200 \\ +\ 5.030 \\ \hline 9.832 \end{array}$$

233. The correct answer is (A).

$$2.5x + 12.5 = 30$$
$$2.5x = 30 - 12.5$$
$$2.5x = 17.5$$
$$x = \frac{17.5}{2.5}$$
$$x = 7$$

234. The correct answer is (A).

$$\begin{array}{r} 1960 \\ 28\overline{)54900} \\ 28 \\ \hline 269 \\ 252 \\ \hline 170 \\ 168 \\ \hline 20 \end{array}$$

235. The correct answer is (B).

$$\sqrt{x + 36} = 10$$
$$x + 36 = 10^2$$
$$x + 36 = 100$$
$$x = 100 - 36$$
$$x = 64$$

236. The correct answer is (C).

$$\begin{array}{r} 143_{(5)} \\ + 33_{(5)} \\ \hline 231_{(5)} \end{array}$$

237. The correct answer is (B). Rename the fractions with a common denominator. Do the operations in parentheses first.

$$\left(\frac{2}{3} + \frac{1}{5}\right) - \left(\frac{1}{4} + \frac{1}{2}\right) = x$$
$$\left(\frac{10}{15} + \frac{3}{15}\right) - \left(\frac{1}{4} + \frac{2}{4}\right) = x$$
$$\frac{13}{15} - \frac{3}{4} = x$$
$$\frac{52}{60} - \frac{45}{60} = \frac{7}{60}$$

238. The correct answer is (D). First determine how many times 25,000 can be divided by 100: $25,000 \div 100 = 250$.

For *every* $100 in 25,000, $3.62 must be paid in taxes: $250 \times 3.62 = \$905.00$.

Language

239. C	251. D	263. D	275. C	287. D
240. A	252. C	264. B	276. B	288. A
241. B	253. A	265. B	277. A	289. A
242. C	254. A	266. C	278. C	290. A
243. C	255. D	267. C	279. B	291. B
244. B	256. A	268. A	280. B	292. D
245. D	257. C	269. A	281. A	293. B
246. C	258. A	270. C	282. C	294. C
247. C	259. B	271. D	283. D	295. B
248. D	260. B	272. C	284. A	296. B
249. C	261. D	273. D	285. B	297. D
250. D	262. D	274. B	286. A	298. B

answers practice test 5

239. The correct answer is (C). *Day* should be capitalized.

240. The correct answer is (A). The names of newspapers are both capitalized and italicized: *Daily Cryer*.

241. The correct answer is (B). *International* and *Airport* should both be capitalized.

242. The correct answer is (C). The use of the word *larger* is incorrect since New York is being compared with more than one city in the United States. The correct word is *largest*.

243. The correct answer is (C). The first letter of the word *July* should be capitalized.

244. The correct answer is (B). The proper names of places are capitalized: Grand Canyon.

245. The correct answer is (D). No mistakes.

246. The correct answer is (C). The word *Their* is incorrect in this context. The word should be *They're* (they are).

247. The correct answer is (C). The word *Who's* (who is) is incorrect in this context. The word should be *Whose*.

248. The correct answer is (D). No mistakes.

249. The correct answer is (C). "Zoo" is part of the name so it should be capitalized: Bronx Zoo.

250. The correct answer is (D). No mistakes.

251. The correct answer is (D). No mistakes.

252. The correct answer is (C). There's no reason to capitalize a non-specific event such as a presidential election.

253. The correct answer is (A). The word *you're* (you are) is incorrect in this context. The word should be *your*.

254. The correct answer is (A). The tense is incorrect. The last part of the sentence should read *I'd ever seen*.

255. The correct answer is (D). No mistakes.

256. The correct answer is (A). The object of the preposition *to* is Deirdre and *me*.

257. The correct answer is (C). The word *lay* is incorrect in this context. The word should be *lie*.

258. The correct answer is (A). The word *we* should be capitalized.

259. The correct answer is (B). The past tense of the verb *to lie* is *lay*.

260. The correct answer is (B). This sentence contains a misspelled word. The word *hear*, which means the act of hearing, should be replaced with the word *here*, which means a place.

261. The correct answer is (D). No mistakes.

262. The correct answer is (D). No mistakes.

263. The correct answer is (D). No mistakes.

264. The correct answer is (B). The word *learning* is incorrect in this context. The word should be *teaching*.

265. The correct answer is (B). The word *of* is incorrect in this context. The word should be *have*.

266. The correct answer is (C). The preposition *to* is incorrect in this context. The word should be *too*, meaning excessive.

267. The correct answer is (C). The number of hours can be counted—therefore, *fewer*.

268. The correct answer is (A). The possessive of *it* is *its*. *It's* is the contraction for *it is*.

269. The correct answer is (A). *Everyone* is singular. The pronoun must be singular as well. Either *his* or *her* would be correct.

270. The correct answer is (C). There are three, so the comparative term must be *tallest*.

271. The correct answer is (D). No mistakes.

272. The correct answer is (C). The subjective *I* is incorrect in this context. The correct word is *me,* the object of the verb *asked.*

273. The correct answer is (D). No mistakes.

274. The correct answer is (B). I feel *bad.* I would feel *badly* if something were wrong with my hands.

275. The correct answer is (C). The subject/verb of the sentence is *I have.*

276. The correct answer is (B). I *can hardly* wait. The double negative is incorrect.

277. The correct answer is (A). The apostrophe in *childrens'* should be placed before the *s* since *children* is a plural word.

278. The correct answer is (C). The word *nothing* is incorrect in this context. The correct word is *anything.* The double negative is unacceptable.

279. The correct answer is (B). The correct spelling is *apparently.*

280. The correct answer is (B). The correct spelling is *efficiently.*

281. The correct answer is (A). The correct spelling is *occurred.* (See Spelling—Rule 9.)

282. The correct answer is (C). The correct spelling is *analyzed.*

283. The correct answer is (D). No mistakes.

284. The correct answer is (A). The correct spelling of the word is *misspelled.*

285. The correct answer is (B). The correct spelling is *described.*

286. The correct answer is (A). The correct spelling is *prefers.*

287. The correct answer is (D). No mistakes.

288. The correct answer is (A). The correct spelling is *necessary.*

289. The correct answer is (A). *Therefore* indicates the cause-and-effect relationship of the two clauses.

290. The correct answer is (A). The second clause provides an example.

291. The correct answer is (B). The subject (*Mary*) must follow the introductory phrase.

292. The correct answer is (D). This sentence expresses the idea most clearly.

293. The correct answer is (B). The second clause offers the reason why she drove 50 miles.

294. The correct answer is (C). The invention of the automobile definitely belongs in a discussion of the history of the automobile.

295. The correct answer is (B). This choice most clearly and succinctly presents the ideas provided here.

296. The correct answer is (B). Sentences 1, 3, and 4 all concern preparation for the Halloween party.

297. The correct answer is (D). All of these topics are too broad for a one-paragraph theme.

298. The correct answer is (B). The given sentence should fall before sentence 3, because it refers to a singular noun and sentence 2 contains a plural noun. By placing the sentence between 2 and 3, the paragraph makes sense.

SCORE SHEET

Although your actual exam scores will not be reported as percentages, it might be helpful to convert your test scores to percentages so that you can see at a glance where your strengths and weaknesses lie. The numbers in parentheses represent the questions that test each skill.

Subject	No. Correct ÷ No. of Questions	× 100 = _____ %
Verbal Analogies (3, 6, 8, 12, 13, 19, 20, 31, 36, 41)	_____ ÷ 10 = _____	× 100 = _____ %
Synonyms (5, 10, 11, 16, 17, 18, 21, 23, 25, 26, 28, 29, 30, 47, 58)	_____ ÷ 15 = _____	× 100 = _____ %
Logic (4, 15, 22, 24, 33, 38, 49, 52, 55, 60)	_____ ÷ 10 = _____	× 100 = _____ %
Verbal Classification (1, 2, 7, 9, 14, 27, 32, 34, 42, 45, 46, 50, 54, 56, 57, 59)	_____ ÷ 16 = _____	× 100 = _____ %
Antonyms (35, 37, 39, 40, 43, 44, 48, 51, 53)	_____ ÷ 9 = _____	× 100 = _____ %
TOTAL VERBAL SKILLS	_____ ÷ 60 = _____	× 100 = _____ %
Number Series (62, 63, 69, 71, 72, 76, 79, 81, 86, 89, 90, 93, 95, 99, 101, 104, 106, 108)	_____ ÷ 18 = _____	× 100 = _____ %
Geometric Comparisons (68, 77, 78, 84, 91, 96, 102, 110)	_____ ÷ 8 = _____	× 100 = _____ %
Nongeometric Comparisons (64, 65, 70, 75, 82, 87, 94, 98, 105)	_____ ÷ 9 = _____	× 100 = _____ %
Number Manipulation (61, 66, 67, 73, 74, 80, 83, 85, 88, 92, 97, 100, 103, 107, 109, 111, 112)	_____ ÷ 17 = _____	× 100 = _____ %
TOTAL QUANTITATIVE SKILLS	_____ ÷ 52 = _____	× 100 = _____ %
Reading—Comprehension (113–152)	_____ ÷ 40 = _____	× 100 = _____ %
Reading—Vocabulary (153–174)	_____ ÷ 22 = _____	× 100 = _____ %
TOTAL READING	_____ ÷ 62 = _____	× 100 = _____ %
Mathematics—Concepts (175–198)	_____ ÷ 24 = _____	× 100 = _____ %
Mathematics—Problem-Solving (199–238)	_____ ÷ 40 = _____	× 100 = _____ %
TOTAL MATHEMATICS	_____ ÷ 64 = _____	× 100 = _____ %
Punctuation and Capitalization (239–241, 243, 248–251, 255, 258, 260, 277)	_____ ÷ 12 = _____	× 100 = _____ %
Usage (242, 244–247, 252–254, 256, 257, 259, 261–276, 278)	_____ ÷ 28 = _____	× 100 = _____ %
Spelling (279–288)	_____ ÷ 10 = _____	× 100 = _____ %
Composition (289–298)	_____ ÷ 10 = _____	× 100 = _____ %
TOTAL LANGUAGE	_____ ÷ 60 = _____	× 100 = _____ %
TOTAL EXAM	_____ ÷ 298 = _____	× 100 = _____ %

ANSWER SHEET PRACTICE TEST 6: HSPT®

Verbal Skills

1. Ⓐ Ⓑ Ⓒ Ⓓ   13. Ⓐ Ⓑ Ⓒ Ⓓ   25. Ⓐ Ⓑ Ⓒ Ⓓ   37. Ⓐ Ⓑ Ⓒ Ⓓ   49. Ⓐ Ⓑ Ⓒ Ⓓ
2. Ⓐ Ⓑ Ⓒ Ⓓ   14. Ⓐ Ⓑ Ⓒ Ⓓ   26. Ⓐ Ⓑ Ⓒ Ⓓ   38. Ⓐ Ⓑ Ⓒ Ⓓ   50. Ⓐ Ⓑ Ⓒ Ⓓ
3. Ⓐ Ⓑ Ⓒ   15. Ⓐ Ⓑ Ⓒ   27. Ⓐ Ⓑ Ⓒ   39. Ⓐ Ⓑ Ⓒ Ⓓ   51. Ⓐ Ⓑ Ⓒ
4. Ⓐ Ⓑ Ⓒ Ⓓ   16. Ⓐ Ⓑ Ⓒ Ⓓ   28. Ⓐ Ⓑ Ⓒ Ⓓ   40. Ⓐ Ⓑ Ⓒ Ⓓ   52. Ⓐ Ⓑ Ⓒ Ⓓ
5. Ⓐ Ⓑ Ⓒ Ⓓ   17. Ⓐ Ⓑ Ⓒ Ⓓ   29. Ⓐ Ⓑ Ⓒ Ⓓ   41. Ⓐ Ⓑ Ⓒ Ⓓ   53. Ⓐ Ⓑ Ⓒ Ⓓ
6. Ⓐ Ⓑ Ⓒ Ⓓ   18. Ⓐ Ⓑ Ⓒ Ⓓ   30. Ⓐ Ⓑ Ⓒ   42. Ⓐ Ⓑ Ⓒ Ⓓ   54. Ⓐ Ⓑ Ⓒ Ⓓ
7. Ⓐ Ⓑ Ⓒ Ⓓ   19. Ⓐ Ⓑ Ⓒ Ⓓ   31. Ⓐ Ⓑ Ⓒ Ⓓ   43. Ⓐ Ⓑ Ⓒ Ⓓ   55. Ⓐ Ⓑ Ⓒ Ⓓ
8. Ⓐ Ⓑ Ⓒ Ⓓ   20. Ⓐ Ⓑ Ⓒ   32. Ⓐ Ⓑ Ⓒ Ⓓ   44. Ⓐ Ⓑ Ⓒ   56. Ⓐ Ⓑ Ⓒ Ⓓ
9. Ⓐ Ⓑ Ⓒ Ⓓ   21. Ⓐ Ⓑ Ⓒ Ⓓ   33. Ⓐ Ⓑ Ⓒ Ⓓ   45. Ⓐ Ⓑ Ⓒ Ⓓ   57. Ⓐ Ⓑ Ⓒ Ⓓ
10. Ⓐ Ⓑ Ⓒ   22. Ⓐ Ⓑ Ⓒ Ⓓ   34. Ⓐ Ⓑ Ⓒ Ⓓ   46. Ⓐ Ⓑ Ⓒ Ⓓ   58. Ⓐ Ⓑ Ⓒ
11. Ⓐ Ⓑ Ⓒ Ⓓ   23. Ⓐ Ⓑ Ⓒ Ⓓ   35. Ⓐ Ⓑ Ⓒ Ⓓ   47. Ⓐ Ⓑ Ⓒ Ⓓ   59. Ⓐ Ⓑ Ⓒ Ⓓ
12. Ⓐ Ⓑ Ⓒ Ⓓ   24. Ⓐ Ⓑ Ⓒ Ⓓ   36. Ⓐ Ⓑ Ⓒ   48. Ⓐ Ⓑ Ⓒ Ⓓ   60. Ⓐ Ⓑ Ⓒ Ⓓ

Quantitative Skills

61. Ⓐ Ⓑ Ⓒ Ⓓ   72. Ⓐ Ⓑ Ⓒ Ⓓ   83. Ⓐ Ⓑ Ⓒ Ⓓ   94. Ⓐ Ⓑ Ⓒ Ⓓ   105. Ⓐ Ⓑ Ⓒ Ⓓ
62. Ⓐ Ⓑ Ⓒ Ⓓ   73. Ⓐ Ⓑ Ⓒ Ⓓ   84. Ⓐ Ⓑ Ⓒ Ⓓ   95. Ⓐ Ⓑ Ⓒ Ⓓ   106. Ⓐ Ⓑ Ⓒ Ⓓ
63. Ⓐ Ⓑ Ⓒ Ⓓ   74. Ⓐ Ⓑ Ⓒ Ⓓ   85. Ⓐ Ⓑ Ⓒ Ⓓ   96. Ⓐ Ⓑ Ⓒ Ⓓ   107. Ⓐ Ⓑ Ⓒ Ⓓ
64. Ⓐ Ⓑ Ⓒ Ⓓ   75. Ⓐ Ⓑ Ⓒ Ⓓ   86. Ⓐ Ⓑ Ⓒ Ⓓ   97. Ⓐ Ⓑ Ⓒ Ⓓ   108. Ⓐ Ⓑ Ⓒ Ⓓ
65. Ⓐ Ⓑ Ⓒ Ⓓ   76. Ⓐ Ⓑ Ⓒ Ⓓ   87. Ⓐ Ⓑ Ⓒ Ⓓ   98. Ⓐ Ⓑ Ⓒ Ⓓ   109. Ⓐ Ⓑ Ⓒ Ⓓ
66. Ⓐ Ⓑ Ⓒ Ⓓ   77. Ⓐ Ⓑ Ⓒ Ⓓ   88. Ⓐ Ⓑ Ⓒ Ⓓ   99. Ⓐ Ⓑ Ⓒ Ⓓ   110. Ⓐ Ⓑ Ⓒ Ⓓ
67. Ⓐ Ⓑ Ⓒ Ⓓ   78. Ⓐ Ⓑ Ⓒ Ⓓ   89. Ⓐ Ⓑ Ⓒ Ⓓ   100. Ⓐ Ⓑ Ⓒ Ⓓ   111. Ⓐ Ⓑ Ⓒ Ⓓ
68. Ⓐ Ⓑ Ⓒ Ⓓ   79. Ⓐ Ⓑ Ⓒ Ⓓ   90. Ⓐ Ⓑ Ⓒ Ⓓ   101. Ⓐ Ⓑ Ⓒ Ⓓ   112. Ⓐ Ⓑ Ⓒ Ⓓ
69. Ⓐ Ⓑ Ⓒ Ⓓ   80. Ⓐ Ⓑ Ⓒ Ⓓ   91. Ⓐ Ⓑ Ⓒ Ⓓ   102. Ⓐ Ⓑ Ⓒ Ⓓ
70. Ⓐ Ⓑ Ⓒ Ⓓ   81. Ⓐ Ⓑ Ⓒ Ⓓ   92. Ⓐ Ⓑ Ⓒ Ⓓ   103. Ⓐ Ⓑ Ⓒ Ⓓ
71. Ⓐ Ⓑ Ⓒ Ⓓ   82. Ⓐ Ⓑ Ⓒ Ⓓ   93. Ⓐ Ⓑ Ⓒ Ⓓ   104. Ⓐ Ⓑ Ⓒ Ⓓ

Reading

COMPREHENSION

113. Ⓐ Ⓑ Ⓒ Ⓓ   121. Ⓐ Ⓑ Ⓒ Ⓓ   129. Ⓐ Ⓑ Ⓒ Ⓓ   137. Ⓐ Ⓑ Ⓒ Ⓓ   145. Ⓐ Ⓑ Ⓒ Ⓓ
114. Ⓐ Ⓑ Ⓒ Ⓓ   122. Ⓐ Ⓑ Ⓒ Ⓓ   130. Ⓐ Ⓑ Ⓒ Ⓓ   138. Ⓐ Ⓑ Ⓒ Ⓓ   146. Ⓐ Ⓑ Ⓒ Ⓓ
115. Ⓐ Ⓑ Ⓒ Ⓓ   123. Ⓐ Ⓑ Ⓒ Ⓓ   131. Ⓐ Ⓑ Ⓒ Ⓓ   139. Ⓐ Ⓑ Ⓒ Ⓓ   147. Ⓐ Ⓑ Ⓒ Ⓓ
116. Ⓐ Ⓑ Ⓒ Ⓓ   124. Ⓐ Ⓑ Ⓒ Ⓓ   132. Ⓐ Ⓑ Ⓒ Ⓓ   140. Ⓐ Ⓑ Ⓒ Ⓓ   148. Ⓐ Ⓑ Ⓒ Ⓓ
117. Ⓐ Ⓑ Ⓒ Ⓓ   125. Ⓐ Ⓑ Ⓒ Ⓓ   133. Ⓐ Ⓑ Ⓒ Ⓓ   141. Ⓐ Ⓑ Ⓒ Ⓓ   149. Ⓐ Ⓑ Ⓒ Ⓓ
118. Ⓐ Ⓑ Ⓒ Ⓓ   126. Ⓐ Ⓑ Ⓒ Ⓓ   134. Ⓐ Ⓑ Ⓒ Ⓓ   142. Ⓐ Ⓑ Ⓒ Ⓓ   150. Ⓐ Ⓑ Ⓒ Ⓓ
119. Ⓐ Ⓑ Ⓒ Ⓓ   127. Ⓐ Ⓑ Ⓒ Ⓓ   135. Ⓐ Ⓑ Ⓒ Ⓓ   143. Ⓐ Ⓑ Ⓒ Ⓓ   151. Ⓐ Ⓑ Ⓒ Ⓓ
120. Ⓐ Ⓑ Ⓒ Ⓓ   128. Ⓐ Ⓑ Ⓒ Ⓓ   136. Ⓐ Ⓑ Ⓒ Ⓓ   144. Ⓐ Ⓑ Ⓒ Ⓓ   152. Ⓐ Ⓑ Ⓒ Ⓓ

answer sheet

VOCABULARY

153. Ⓐ Ⓑ Ⓒ Ⓓ   158. Ⓐ Ⓑ Ⓒ Ⓓ   163. Ⓐ Ⓑ Ⓒ Ⓓ   168. Ⓐ Ⓑ Ⓒ Ⓓ   173. Ⓐ Ⓑ Ⓒ Ⓓ
154. Ⓐ Ⓑ Ⓒ Ⓓ   159. Ⓐ Ⓑ Ⓒ Ⓓ   164. Ⓐ Ⓑ Ⓒ Ⓓ   169. Ⓐ Ⓑ Ⓒ Ⓓ   174. Ⓐ Ⓑ Ⓒ Ⓓ
155. Ⓐ Ⓑ Ⓒ Ⓓ   160. Ⓐ Ⓑ Ⓒ Ⓓ   165. Ⓐ Ⓑ Ⓒ Ⓓ   170. Ⓐ Ⓑ Ⓒ Ⓓ
156. Ⓐ Ⓑ Ⓒ Ⓓ   161. Ⓐ Ⓑ Ⓒ Ⓓ   166. Ⓐ Ⓑ Ⓒ Ⓓ   171. Ⓐ Ⓑ Ⓒ Ⓓ
157. Ⓐ Ⓑ Ⓒ Ⓓ   162. Ⓐ Ⓑ Ⓒ Ⓓ   167. Ⓐ Ⓑ Ⓒ Ⓓ   172. Ⓐ Ⓑ Ⓒ Ⓓ

Mathematics

CONCEPTS

175. Ⓐ Ⓑ Ⓒ Ⓓ   180. Ⓐ Ⓑ Ⓒ Ⓓ   185. Ⓐ Ⓑ Ⓒ Ⓓ   190. Ⓐ Ⓑ Ⓒ Ⓓ   195. Ⓐ Ⓑ Ⓒ Ⓓ
176. Ⓐ Ⓑ Ⓒ Ⓓ   181. Ⓐ Ⓑ Ⓒ Ⓓ   186. Ⓐ Ⓑ Ⓒ Ⓓ   191. Ⓐ Ⓑ Ⓒ Ⓓ   196. Ⓐ Ⓑ Ⓒ Ⓓ
177. Ⓐ Ⓑ Ⓒ Ⓓ   182. Ⓐ Ⓑ Ⓒ Ⓓ   187. Ⓐ Ⓑ Ⓒ Ⓓ   192. Ⓐ Ⓑ Ⓒ Ⓓ   197. Ⓐ Ⓑ Ⓒ Ⓓ
178. Ⓐ Ⓑ Ⓒ Ⓓ   183. Ⓐ Ⓑ Ⓒ Ⓓ   188. Ⓐ Ⓑ Ⓒ Ⓓ   193. Ⓐ Ⓑ Ⓒ Ⓓ   198. Ⓐ Ⓑ Ⓒ Ⓓ
179. Ⓐ Ⓑ Ⓒ Ⓓ   184. Ⓐ Ⓑ Ⓒ Ⓓ   189. Ⓐ Ⓑ Ⓒ Ⓓ   194. Ⓐ Ⓑ Ⓒ Ⓓ

PROBLEM-SOLVING

199. Ⓐ Ⓑ Ⓒ Ⓓ   207. Ⓐ Ⓑ Ⓒ Ⓓ   215. Ⓐ Ⓑ Ⓒ Ⓓ   223. Ⓐ Ⓑ Ⓒ Ⓓ   231. Ⓐ Ⓑ Ⓒ Ⓓ
200. Ⓐ Ⓑ Ⓒ Ⓓ   208. Ⓐ Ⓑ Ⓒ Ⓓ   216. Ⓐ Ⓑ Ⓒ Ⓓ   224. Ⓐ Ⓑ Ⓒ Ⓓ   232. Ⓐ Ⓑ Ⓒ Ⓓ
201. Ⓐ Ⓑ Ⓒ Ⓓ   209. Ⓐ Ⓑ Ⓒ Ⓓ   217. Ⓐ Ⓑ Ⓒ Ⓓ   225. Ⓐ Ⓑ Ⓒ Ⓓ   233. Ⓐ Ⓑ Ⓒ Ⓓ
202. Ⓐ Ⓑ Ⓒ Ⓓ   210. Ⓐ Ⓑ Ⓒ Ⓓ   218. Ⓐ Ⓑ Ⓒ Ⓓ   226. Ⓐ Ⓑ Ⓒ Ⓓ   234. Ⓐ Ⓑ Ⓒ Ⓓ
203. Ⓐ Ⓑ Ⓒ Ⓓ   211. Ⓐ Ⓑ Ⓒ Ⓓ   219. Ⓐ Ⓑ Ⓒ Ⓓ   227. Ⓐ Ⓑ Ⓒ Ⓓ   235. Ⓐ Ⓑ Ⓒ Ⓓ
204. Ⓐ Ⓑ Ⓒ Ⓓ   212. Ⓐ Ⓑ Ⓒ Ⓓ   220. Ⓐ Ⓑ Ⓒ Ⓓ   228. Ⓐ Ⓑ Ⓒ Ⓓ   236. Ⓐ Ⓑ Ⓒ Ⓓ
205. Ⓐ Ⓑ Ⓒ Ⓓ   213. Ⓐ Ⓑ Ⓒ Ⓓ   221. Ⓐ Ⓑ Ⓒ Ⓓ   229. Ⓐ Ⓑ Ⓒ Ⓓ   237. Ⓐ Ⓑ Ⓒ Ⓓ
206. Ⓐ Ⓑ Ⓒ Ⓓ   214. Ⓐ Ⓑ Ⓒ Ⓓ   222. Ⓐ Ⓑ Ⓒ Ⓓ   230. Ⓐ Ⓑ Ⓒ Ⓓ   238. Ⓐ Ⓑ Ⓒ Ⓓ

Language

239. Ⓐ Ⓑ Ⓒ Ⓓ   251. Ⓐ Ⓑ Ⓒ Ⓓ   263. Ⓐ Ⓑ Ⓒ Ⓓ   275. Ⓐ Ⓑ Ⓒ Ⓓ   287. Ⓐ Ⓑ Ⓒ Ⓓ
240. Ⓐ Ⓑ Ⓒ Ⓓ   252. Ⓐ Ⓑ Ⓒ Ⓓ   264. Ⓐ Ⓑ Ⓒ Ⓓ   276. Ⓐ Ⓑ Ⓒ Ⓓ   288. Ⓐ Ⓑ Ⓒ Ⓓ
241. Ⓐ Ⓑ Ⓒ Ⓓ   253. Ⓐ Ⓑ Ⓒ Ⓓ   265. Ⓐ Ⓑ Ⓒ Ⓓ   277. Ⓐ Ⓑ Ⓒ Ⓓ   289. Ⓐ Ⓑ Ⓒ Ⓓ
242. Ⓐ Ⓑ Ⓒ Ⓓ   254. Ⓐ Ⓑ Ⓒ Ⓓ   266. Ⓐ Ⓑ Ⓒ Ⓓ   278. Ⓐ Ⓑ Ⓒ Ⓓ   290. Ⓐ Ⓑ Ⓒ Ⓓ
243. Ⓐ Ⓑ Ⓒ Ⓓ   255. Ⓐ Ⓑ Ⓒ Ⓓ   267. Ⓐ Ⓑ Ⓒ Ⓓ   279. Ⓐ Ⓑ Ⓒ Ⓓ   291. Ⓐ Ⓑ Ⓒ Ⓓ
244. Ⓐ Ⓑ Ⓒ Ⓓ   256. Ⓐ Ⓑ Ⓒ Ⓓ   268. Ⓐ Ⓑ Ⓒ Ⓓ   280. Ⓐ Ⓑ Ⓒ Ⓓ   292. Ⓐ Ⓑ Ⓒ Ⓓ
245. Ⓐ Ⓑ Ⓒ Ⓓ   257. Ⓐ Ⓑ Ⓒ Ⓓ   269. Ⓐ Ⓑ Ⓒ Ⓓ   281. Ⓐ Ⓑ Ⓒ Ⓓ   293. Ⓐ Ⓑ Ⓒ Ⓓ
246. Ⓐ Ⓑ Ⓒ Ⓓ   258. Ⓐ Ⓑ Ⓒ Ⓓ   270. Ⓐ Ⓑ Ⓒ Ⓓ   282. Ⓐ Ⓑ Ⓒ Ⓓ   294. Ⓐ Ⓑ Ⓒ Ⓓ
247. Ⓐ Ⓑ Ⓒ Ⓓ   259. Ⓐ Ⓑ Ⓒ Ⓓ   271. Ⓐ Ⓑ Ⓒ Ⓓ   283. Ⓐ Ⓑ Ⓒ Ⓓ   295. Ⓐ Ⓑ Ⓒ Ⓓ
248. Ⓐ Ⓑ Ⓒ Ⓓ   260. Ⓐ Ⓑ Ⓒ Ⓓ   272. Ⓐ Ⓑ Ⓒ Ⓓ   284. Ⓐ Ⓑ Ⓒ Ⓓ   296. Ⓐ Ⓑ Ⓒ Ⓓ
249. Ⓐ Ⓑ Ⓒ Ⓓ   261. Ⓐ Ⓑ Ⓒ Ⓓ   273. Ⓐ Ⓑ Ⓒ Ⓓ   285. Ⓐ Ⓑ Ⓒ Ⓓ   297. Ⓐ Ⓑ Ⓒ Ⓓ
250. Ⓐ Ⓑ Ⓒ Ⓓ   262. Ⓐ Ⓑ Ⓒ Ⓓ   274. Ⓐ Ⓑ Ⓒ Ⓓ   286. Ⓐ Ⓑ Ⓒ Ⓓ   298. Ⓐ Ⓑ Ⓒ Ⓓ

Practice Test 6: HSPT®

VERBAL SKILLS

16 Minutes

Directions: Mark one answer—the answer you think is best—for each problem.

1. Which word does *not* belong with the others?
   - (A) one
   - (B) three
   - (C) fourth
   - (D) nine

2. Arouse is to pacify as agitate is to
   - (A) smooth.
   - (B) ruffle.
   - (C) understand.
   - (D) ignore.

3. Henri is a much better juggler than Jerome. Francine is a better juggler than Jerome. Francine is a better juggler than Henri. If the first two statements are true, the third is
   - (A) true.
   - (B) false.
   - (C) uncertain.

4. Query means the *opposite* of
   - (A) argument.
   - (B) answer.
   - (C) square.
   - (D) loner.

5. *Impair* most nearly means
   - (A) direct.
   - (B) improve.
   - (C) stimulate.
   - (D) weaken.

6. Which word does *not* belong with the others?
   - (A) rotate
   - (B) revolve
   - (C) spin
   - (D) planet

7. If the wind is *variable,* it is
   - (A) shifting.
   - (B) mild.
   - (C) chilling.
   - (D) steady.

8. Egg is to beat as potato is to
   - (A) yam.
   - (B) bake.
   - (C) eye.
   - (D) mash.

9. If you *obstruct* the entrance to a building, you
   - (A) block it.
   - (B) enter it.
   - (C) leave it.
   - (D) cross it.

practice test 6

10. The red balloon is higher in the sky than the green balloon. The yellow balloon is higher in the sky than the red balloon. The green balloon is higher in the sky than the yellow balloon. If the first two statements are true, the third is

    (A) true.
    (B) false.
    (C) uncertain.

11. Which word does *not* belong with the others?

    (A) blended
    (B) stirred
    (C) mixing
    (D) whisked

12. Cause means the *opposite* of

    (A) affect.
    (B) result.
    (C) question.
    (D) accident.

13. Weight is to gain as lemonade is to

    (A) blast.
    (B) drink.
    (C) tart.
    (D) cold.

14. Which word does *not* belong with the others?

    (A) tent
    (B) igloo
    (C) cabin
    (D) cave

15. Pepper is the shaggiest dog in the obedience school class. Pretzel is a dachshund. Pepper and Pretzel are in the same obedience school class. If the first two statements are true, the third is

    (A) true.
    (B) false.
    (C) uncertain.

16. Camera is to lens as lightbulb is to

    (A) filament.
    (B) lamp.
    (C) bright.
    (D) watts.

17. *Revenue* most nearly means

    (A) taxes.
    (B) income.
    (C) expenses.
    (D) produce.

18. Which word does *not* belong with the others?

    (A) trapeze
    (B) wedge
    (C) lever
    (D) pulley

19. Which word does *not* belong with the others?

    (A) joy
    (B) sadness
    (C) tears
    (D) glee

20. Linda jumps rope faster than Mary but slower than Inez. Lori jumps faster than Inez but slower than Cleo. Mary is the slowest jumper in the group. If the first two statements are true, the third is

    (A) true.
    (B) false.
    (C) uncertain.

21. If a machine has *manual* controls, the machine is

    (A) self-acting.
    (B) simple.
    (C) hand-operated.
    (D) handmade.

22. *Marshy* most nearly means

    (A) swampy.
    (B) sandy.
    (C) wooded.
    (D) rocky.

23. Seal is to fish as bird is to
    (A) wing.
    (B) minnow.
    (C) worm.
    (D) snail.

24. Profit means the *opposite* of
    (A) ratio.
    (B) gross.
    (C) net.
    (D) loss.

25. Rest means the *opposite* of
    (A) sleep.
    (B) activity.
    (C) wake.
    (D) speak.

26. Which word does *not* belong with the others?
    (A) wind
    (B) gale
    (C) hurricane
    (D) zephyr

27. All people eaters are purple. No cyclops eat people. No cyclops are purple. If the first two statements are true, the third is
    (A) true.
    (B) false.
    (C) uncertain.

28. A *churlish* old cat is
    (A) small.
    (B) tired.
    (C) surly.
    (D) energetic.

29. The judge who rules evidence to be *immaterial* means it is
    (A) unclear.
    (B) unimportant.
    (C) unpredictable.
    (D) not debatable.

30. Green books are heavier than red books but not as heavy as orange books. Orange books are lighter than blue books but not as light as yellow books. Yellow books are heavier than green books. If the first two statements are true, the third is
    (A) true.
    (B) false.
    (C) uncertain.

31. Shoe is to leather as highway is to
    (A) passage.
    (B) road.
    (C) trail.
    (D) asphalt.

32. Mend means the *opposite* of
    (A) give back.
    (B) change.
    (C) destroy.
    (D) clean.

33. Abstract means the *opposite* of
    (A) art.
    (B) absurd.
    (C) sculpture.
    (D) concrete.

34. A computer that does not *function* does not
    (A) operate.
    (B) finish.
    (C) stop.
    (D) overheat.

35. Which word does *not* belong with the others?
    (A) vitamin
    (B) protein
    (C) meat
    (D) calcium

36. All Ts are either green-eyed Ys or blue-tailed Gs. All blue-tailed Gs have brown eyes and red noses. Some Ts have red noses. If the first two statements are true, the third is
    (A) true.
    (B) false.
    (C) uncertain.

37. A *cacophony* of sirens is
    (A) loud.
    (B) pleasant.
    (C) melodic.
    (D) helpful.

38. Which word does *not* belong with the others?
    (A) stag
    (B) monkey
    (C) bull
    (D) ram

39. Taste is to tongue as touch is to
    (A) finger.
    (B) eye.
    (C) feeling.
    (D) borrow.

40. Discord means the *opposite* of
    (A) reward.
    (B) record.
    (C) harmony.
    (D) music.

41. Which word does *not* belong with the others?
    (A) aroma
    (B) odor
    (C) scent
    (D) fumes

42. Which word does *not* belong with the others?
    (A) ride
    (B) creep
    (C) hop
    (D) run

43. *Fatal* most nearly means
    (A) accidental.
    (B) deadly.
    (C) dangerous.
    (D) beautiful.

44. Terry has won more races than Bill. Bill has won more races than Luis. Terry has won fewer races than Luis. If the first two statements are true, the third is
    (A) true.
    (B) false.
    (C) uncertain.

45. Which word does *not* belong with the others?
    (A) glass
    (B) gauze
    (C) brick
    (D) lattice

46. If the packages were kept in a *secure* place, the place was
    (A) distant.
    (B) safe.
    (C) convenient.
    (D) secret.

47. Garish means the *opposite* of
    (A) dull.
    (B) damp.
    (C) sweet.
    (D) closed.

48. Horse is to foal as mother is to
    (A) mare.
    (B) son.
    (C) stallion.
    (D) father.

49. Which word does *not* belong with the others?
    (A) gelatin
    (B) tofu
    (C) gum
    (D) sourball

50. *Counterfeit* most nearly means
   (A) mysterious.
   (B) false.
   (C) unreadable.
   (D) priceless.

51. The thruway has more lanes than the parkway. The parkway has fewer lanes than the highway. The thruway has more lanes than the highway. If the first two statements are true, the third is
   (A) true.
   (B) false.
   (C) uncertain.

52. Dog is to flea as horse is to
   (A) rider.
   (B) mane.
   (C) fly.
   (D) shoe.

53. The foghorn that sounded *intermittently* sounded
   (A) constantly.
   (B) annually.
   (C) using intermediaries.
   (D) at intervals.

54. Which word does *not* belong with the others?
   (A) Greek
   (B) Acrylic
   (C) Latin
   (D) Arabic

55. Diverse means the *opposite* of
   (A) definite.
   (B) understandable.
   (C) similar.
   (D) boring.

56. Finder is to reward as repenter is to
   (A) religion.
   (B) sin.
   (C) absolution.
   (D) contrition.

57. Which word does *not* belong with the others?
   (A) bend
   (B) explode
   (C) shatter
   (D) burst

58. The grocery store is south of the drugstore, which is between the gas station and the dry cleaner. The bookstore is north of the gas station. The grocery store is north of the dry cleaner. If the first two statements are true, the third is
   (A) true.
   (B) false.
   (C) uncertain.

59. *Deception* most nearly means
   (A) secrets.
   (B) fraud.
   (C) mistrust.
   (D) hatred.

60. Which word does *not* belong with the others?
   (A) cotton
   (B) linen
   (C) silk
   (D) nylon

STOP End of Verbal Skills section. If you have any time left, go over your work in this section only. Do not work in any other section of the test.

QUANTITATIVE SKILLS

30 Minutes

Directions: Mark one answer—the answer you think is best—for each problem.

61. Look at this series: 23, 22, 20, 19, 16, 15, 11, ... What number should come next?

- **(A)** 9
- **(B)** 10
- **(C)** 7
- **(D)** 6

62. Examine (A), (B), (C), and (D) and find the best answer.

(A)

(B)

(C)

(D)

- **(A)** (A) is longer than (C) but shorter than (D).
- **(B)** (C) is shorter than (A) minus (D).
- **(C)** (B) and (D) together are longer than (A).
- **(D)** (C) plus (D) is longer than (A) plus (B).

63. Examine (A), (B), and (C) and find the best answer.

(A) $(5 + 8)^2$

(B) $5^2 + 8^2$

(C) $2(5) + 2(8)$

- **(A)** (A) equals (B) and (C) is less than (A)
- **(B)** (A) equals (B) and (B) equals (C)
- **(C)** (B) is less than (C) and (C) is less than (A)
- **(D)** (C) is less than (B) and (B) is less than (A)

64. What number is 5 less than 60% of 40?

- **(A)** 24
- **(B)** 19
- **(C)** 29
- **(D)** 20

65. Look at this series: 50, 52, 48, 50, 46, 48, 44, ... What number should come next?

- **(A)** 46
- **(B)** 40
- **(C)** 50
- **(D)** 48

66. What number is 3 more than the cube of 4 divided by 4?

- **(A)** 61
- **(B)** 39
- **(C)** 67
- **(D)** 19

67. What number is 2 times the average of 6 + 12 + 4 + 41 + 7?

- **(A)** 140
- **(B)** 14
- **(C)** 28
- **(D)** 30

68. Look at this series: 42, 40, 38, 35, 32, 28, 24, ... What two numbers should come next?

- **(A)** 20, 18
- **(B)** 18, 14
- **(C)** 19, 14
- **(D)** 20, 16

69. Look at this series: 34, 41, 43, 50, 52, ... What is the next number in the series?

(A) 54
(B) 59
(C) 61
(D) 68

70. Examine the triangle and find the best answer.

(A) AB is equal to AC.
(B) m∠B is greater than m∠C.
(C) AB minus AC is equal to BC.
(D) m∠A + m∠B = m∠C.

71. $\frac{2}{3}$ of what number is 6 times 4?

(A) 16
(B) 36
(C) 48
(D) 32

72. What number divided by $\frac{1}{4}$ is 3 less than 79?

(A) 304
(B) 328
(C) 20.5
(D) 19

73. Examine (A), (B), and (C) and find the best answer.

(A) (B) (C)

(A) (B) is less shaded than (A).
(B) (B) and (C) are equally shaded.
(C) (A) and (B) are both less shaded than (C).
(D) (A) and (C) are both more shaded than (B).

74. Look at this series: 2, 11, 21, 32, 44, 57, ... What three numbers should come next?

(A) 71, 86, 102
(B) 68, 72, 94
(C) 70, 85, 101
(D) 72, 85, 105

75. Examine (A), (B), and (C) and find the best answer.

(A) 0.875

(B) 0.33 × 2.6

(C) $\frac{7}{8}$

(A) (A), (B), and (C) are all equal.
(B) (B) is greater than (C).
(C) (B) is less than (A).
(D) (A) is greater than (C).

76. The number that is 6 less than 69 is the product of 7 and what other number?

(A) 9
(B) 12
(C) 8
(D) 6

77. Examine (A), (B), and (C) and find the best answer.

(A) $\frac{1}{5}$ of 20

(B) $\frac{1}{4}$ of 24

(C) $\frac{1}{8}$ of 32

(A) (B) is equal to (C).
(B) (A) is less than (B) and equal to (C).
(C) (A) plus (C) equals (B).
(D) (B) minus (A) equals (C).

78. Examine the pictograph and find the best answer.

Number of New Houses Built in XYZ Town, Years A to D

(A)

(B) (three houses)

(C) (five houses)

(D) (four houses)   Each (house) represents 100 houses.

(A) One-half as many houses were built in year (A) as in year (B).

(B) More houses were built in years (A) and (B) combined than in year (C).

(C) Fewer houses were built in years (A) and (D) combined than in year (C).

(D) An equal number of houses were built in years (A) and (B) combined as in year (D).

79. Look at this series: 8, 16, 9, 18, 11, _____, 15, 30, ... What number should fill the blank in this series?

(A) 12

(B) 22

(C) 19

(D) 7

80. Look at this series: 6, 7, 8, 10, 12, 15, 18, ... What number should come next?

(A) 20

(B) 21

(C) 22

(D) 23

81. The product of 25% of a positive number and 40% of the same number is 14.4. What is the number?

(A) 1.2

(B) 12

(C) 14.4

(D) 144

82. By how much does the average of 12, 87, 72, and 41 exceed 25?

(A) 28

(B) 78

(C) 53

(D) 25

83. Look at this series: 24, 25, 23, 24, 21, 22, 18, ... What number should come next?

(A) 17

(B) 23

(C) 21

(D) 19

84. Examine (A), (B), (C), and (D) and find the best answer.

    (A)   (B)   (C)   (D)

(A) (A) has fewer paddles than (B) but more than (D).

(B) (A) and (D) together are equal to (B) and (C) together.

(C) (B) has fewer paddles than (A) and (C) together.

(D) (B) has more paddles than (C) and (D) together.

85. What number subtracted from 82 leaves 3 more than $\frac{4}{5}$ of 80?

(A) 64

(B) 5

(C) 15

(D) 67

86. Look at this series: 5, 15, 24, 32, _____, 45, 50, ... What number should fill the blank in this series?

(A) 39

(B) 40

(C) 37

(D) 55

87. Examine (A), (B), and (C) and find the best answer.

   (A) 6^2

   (B) 2^6

   (C) $(2 \times 6) (6 \times 2)$

   (A) (A) + (B) = (C).

   (B) (C) − (B) = (A).

   (C) (A) = (B) and both are smaller than (C).

   (D) (C) is greater than either (A) or (B).

88. Examine (A), (B), and (C) and find the best answer.

   (A) $(9 \times 5) + 6$

   (B) $(7 \times 8) - 5$

   (C) $(15 \times 3) + (2 \times 3)$

   (A) (A) is equal to (B), which is equal to (C).

   (B) (C) is greater than (B) but equal to (A).

   (C) (A) is greater than (B), which is less than (C).

   (D) (C) is greater than (A).

89. What number added to 30 is 3 times the product of 8 and 4?

   (A) 63

   (B) 93

   (C) 39

   (D) 66

90. What number divided by 6 is $\frac{1}{8}$ of 96?

   (A) 48

   (B) 72

   (C) 12

   (D) 84

91. Look at this series: 0.125, 0.250, 0.375, 0.500, ... What number should come next?

   (A) 0.620

   (B) 0.625

   (C) 0.728

   (D) 0.875

92. Examine (A), (B), and (C) and find the best answer.

   (A)   (B)   (C)

   (A) (C) is more shaded than (A).

   (B) (A) and (B) are equally shaded and are more shaded than (C).

   (C) (A) is less shaded than (B) and more shaded than (C).

   (D) (A) and (C) are equally shaded.

93. What number is 15 more than $\frac{5}{9}$ of 99?

   (A) 45

   (B) 60

   (C) 70

   (D) 81

94. What number divided by $\frac{3}{4}$ yields a quotient that is equal to the divisor?

   (A) $\frac{5}{8}$

   (B) $\frac{7}{16}$

   (C) $\frac{9}{16}$

   (D) $\frac{3}{4}$

95. Examine (A), (B), and (C) and find the best answer.

   (A) 0.8

   (B) 80%

   (C) $\frac{8}{10}$ %

   (A) (B) is greater than (A) or (C).

   (B) (A) is greater than (B) plus (C).

   (C) (A), (B), and (C) are equal.

   (D) (C) is smaller than both (A) and (B).

96. Examine the figure and find the best answer.

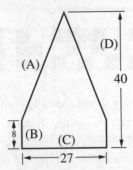

(A) Line segment (A) is shorter than line segment (D), which is longer than line segment (C).

(B) Line segment (B) is shorter than line segment (A), which is longer than line segment (D).

(C) Line segment (C) is longer than line segment (D), which is longer than line segment (B).

(D) Line segment (B) plus line segment (C) together equal the length of line segment (D).

97. Look at this series: 81, 9, 64, 8, _____ , 7, 36, ... What number should fill the blank in this series?

(A) 9

(B) 56

(C) 63

(D) 49

98. Look at this series: B25, E21, H17, K13, ... What comes next?

(A) M9

(B) N9

(C) N10

(D) O8

99. Look at this series: 1, 3, 3, 9, 9, 27, 27, ... What three numbers should come next?

(A) 81, 81, 729

(B) 27, 36, 36

(C) 27, 81, 81

(D) 81, 81, 243

100. If $\frac{3}{8}$ of a number is 9, then $83\frac{1}{3}\%$ of the number is

(A) 20

(B) 27

(C) 14

(D) 54

101. Examine the figure and choose the best answer.

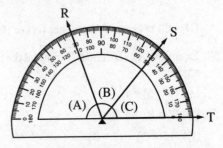

(A) Angle (B) plus angle (C) equals a right angle.

(B) Angle (A) is greater than angle (C), which is smaller than angle (B).

(C) Angle (B) minus angle (C) equals angle (A).

(D) Angle (A) is equal to angle (C).

102. Examine (A), (B), and (C) and choose the best answer.

(A) $\frac{1}{5}$ of 200

(B) 2^2 times 10

(C) $\frac{1}{2}$ of 8^2

(A) (A) is equal to (B) and greater than (C).

(B) (A), (B), and (C) are all equal.

(C) (B) is greater than (A), which is equal to (C).

(D) (A) is greater than (C), which is greater than (B).

103. Look at this series: –19, –14, –12, –7, –5 . . . .

What number should come next?

(A) 0
(B) 5
(C) –1
(D) 1

104. What number when subtracted from 75 is twice the sum of 9 and 3?

(A) 24
(B) 51
(C) 61
(D) 99

105. Look at this series: 0.2, 0.1, 0.05, 0.025, ... What number should come next?

(A) 0.00625
(B) 0.0025
(C) 0.0125
(D) 0.055

106. What number is 12 less than $\frac{5}{8}$ of 96?

(A) 56
(B) 65
(C) 60
(D) 48

107. Examine (A), (B), and (C) and find the best answer.

(A)   (B)   (C)

(A) (A) is equal to (C).
(B) (B) is greater than (A) and less than (C).
(C) (A) is not greater than (C), which is not greater than (B).
(D) (A) plus (B) is not greater than (C).

108. Look at this series: VI, IX, 12, 15, XVIII, ... What should come next?

(A) XXI
(B) 21
(C) XXII
(D) 22

109. Look at this series: $\frac{16}{2}, \frac{8}{2}, \frac{8}{4}, \frac{8}{8}, \frac{8}{16}$, ... What number should come next?

(A) $\frac{16}{16}$
(B) $\frac{8}{32}$
(C) $\frac{16}{32}$
(D) $\frac{4}{8}$

110. Examine (A), (B), and (C) and find the best answer.

(A) 100% of 95
(B) 100% of 195%
(C) 95% of 100

(A) (B) is greater than (A).
(B) (C) is greater than (A) plus (B).
(C) (A) and (C) are equal and are greater than (B).
(D) (A) and (C) are equal and are smaller than (B).

111. What number decreased by 40% of itself is 90?

(A) 150
(B) 36
(C) 60
(D) 145

112. Look at this series: 26, 18, 18, 12, 12, 8, 8, ... What two numbers should come next?

(A) 7, 7
(B) 8, 6
(C) 6, 4
(D) 6, 6

STOP End of Quantitative Skills section. If you have any time left, go over your work in this section only. Do not work in any other section of the test.

READING

Comprehension

25 *Minutes*

> **Directions:** Read each passage carefully. Then mark one answer—the answer you think is best—for each item.

Questions 113–122 refer to the following passage.

Early in the nineteenth century, American youth was playing a game, somewhat like the English game of rounders, that contained all the elements of modern baseball. It was neither scientifically planned nor skillfully played, but it furnished considerable excitement for players and spectators alike. The playing field was a sixty-foot square with goals, or bases, at each of its four corners. A pitcher stationed himself at the center of the square, and a catcher and an indefinite number of fielders supported the pitcher and completed the team. None of these players, usually between 8 and 20 on a side, covered the bases. The batter was out on balls caught on the fly or the first bounce, and a base runner was out if he was hit by a thrown ball while off base. The bat was nothing more than a stout paddle with a two-inch-thick handle. The ball was apt to be an impromptu affair composed of a bullet, cork, or metal slug tightly wound with wool yarn and string. With its simple equipment and only a few rules, this game steadily increased in popularity during the first half of the century.

113. The title that best expresses the main idea of this selection is
    (A) "Baseball Rules."
    (B) "An English Game."
    (C) "Baseball's Predecessor."
    (D) "American Pastimes."

114. The rules of this game required
    (A) 8 fielders.
    (B) a pitcher, a catcher, and one fielder for each base.
    (C) 20 fielders.
    (D) no specific number of players.

115. The shape of the playing field was
    (A) oblong.
    (B) irregular.
    (C) square.
    (D) subject to no rules.

116. The game was
    (A) scientifically planned.
    (B) exciting for the players but boring to watch.
    (C) boring for the players but exciting to watch.
    (D) similar to an English game called "rounders."

117. The word impromptu, as underlined and used in this passage, most nearly means
    (A) proven.
    (B) unrehearsed.
    (C) improvised.
    (D) argued about.

118. This passage places the playing of this un-named game roughly between the years of
    (A) 1900 to 1950.
    (B) 1800 to 1850.
    (C) 1700 to 1750.
    (D) 1760 to 1790.

119. This selection suggests that
    (A) the game of baseball has grown more complicated over the years.
    (B) the game described was very dangerous.
    (C) baseball originated in the United States.
    (D) the game described required skilled players.

120. According to the author, the popularity of this game was based largely upon
    (A) the excitement of watching skillful players.
    (B) the low cost of equipment.
    (C) the fact that none of the players covered the bases.
    (D) its being a new, strictly American game.

121. The word stout, as underlined and used in this passage, most nearly means
    (A) courageous.
    (B) fat.
    (C) that the bat was made from a stave of a beer barrel.
    (D) sturdy.

122. The writer of this selection
    (A) disdains this game because of its unprofessional aspects.
    (B) is nostalgic for days when games were simpler.
    (C) has prepared a factual report.
    (D) admires the ingenuity of American youth.

Questions 123–132 refer to the following passage.

The most common way in which nuclear power is generated is through a process known as *nuclear fission*. The term "fission" means "to split." Nuclear fission occurs when an atom absorbs an extra *neutron*, or an atomic particle that has no electrical charge. If an atom is hit by a neutron traveling at high speed, the atom will split into two or more parts. Two types of atoms that split very easily are those found in the radioactive elements uranium and plutonium. When uranium or plutonium atoms are split, they release a great deal of energy. They also release more neutrons, which causes the splitting process to continue. This continued splitting process is known as a "nuclear chain reaction." It is the process that enables nuclear fission to create power.

Most nuclear reactors today use uranium as the main element in the fission process. Uranium is found naturally in the earth and is extracted through mining. When natural uranium is first mined, it contains two components known as Uranium-235 and Uranium-238. The first component, Uranium-235, splits easily in a nuclear reaction and can therefore be used for the fission process. The second component, Uranium-238, cannot be used as well in the normal fission process. However, most natural uranium is made up of 99.3 percent U-238 and only 0.07 percent U-235. Before the uranium is used in nuclear reactions, then, it first goes through a process known as *enrichment*. The enriched uranium contains much more of the usable U-235 than natural uranium—about 4 or 5 percent.

123. When natural uranium is first mined, how much usable uranium does it usually contain?
    (A) 0.07 percent
    (B) 4 percent
    (C) 96 percent
    (D) 99. 3 percent

124. In a nuclear chain reaction, what causes the nuclear splitting process to continue?
    (A) The neutrons that are released when uranium or plutonium atoms are split
    (B) The energy that is released when uranium or plutonium atoms are split
    (C) The radioactive waste that is produced when uranium or plutonium atoms are split
    (D) The fuel rods that are used to house the fission process, during which uranium atoms are split

125. The word extracted, as underlined and used in this passage, most nearly means
    (A) examined.
    (B) defined.
    (C) removed.
    (D) exacted.

126. The word enriched, as underlined and used in this passage, most nearly means
    (A) weakened.
    (B) strengthened.
    (C) wealthier.
    (D) lightened.

127. A neutron is a particle that has
    (A) a negative electrical charge.
    (B) a positive electrical charge.
    (C) no electrical charge.
    (D) alternating electrical charge.

128. What do the elements uranium and plutonium have in common?
    (A) They both contain atoms that split very easily.
    (B) They do not possess any neutrons.
    (C) They both are enriched by one another.
    (D) They both have a positive electrical charge.

129. A nuclear chain reaction is the process that creates
    (A) enriched uranium.
    (B) nuclear reactors.
    (C) electrical charge.
    (D) nuclear power.

130. How many uranium components are found in uranium in its natural state?
    (A) None
    (B) One
    (C) Two
    (D) Four

131. The author's purpose in writing this selection was most probably to
    (A) warn people of the dangers of nuclear power.
    (B) explain how nuclear power is created.
    (C) promote the benefits of nuclear power.
    (D) explore alternatives to fossil fuels.

132. The title that best expresses the main idea of this passage is
    (A) "The Discovery of Nuclear Fission."
    (B) "The Uses of Nuclear Fission."
    (C) "The Process of Nuclear Fission."
    (D) "The Varieties of Nuclear Fission."

Questions 133–142 refer to the following passage.

Have you ever wondered about the origins of the humble and unassuming fortune cookie? Many people have been introduced to these curious little treats at the cessation of a meal at a Chinese restaurant—after eating, your waiter or waitress had brought you a small plate with fortune cookies for your table on it. You'd then carefully select a cookie, crack it open, and read your fortune on the small slip of paper inside while eating the cookie. These intriguing slips of paper may contain a wise saying, a prophecy, or even a good luck phrase and numbers. Whether or not that slip of paper truly holds your fortune is best left to fate to decide. For many, their first experience with fortune cookies have left an indelible mark on their memories. But where do these cookies come from?

Believe it or not, the origins of the fortune cookie are as mysterious as the messages found inside of them. Traditional fortune cookies were made by hand, and claims as to who invented the fortune cookie are varied and far reaching, and span countries across the globe—folks in the United States, Japan, and China all make claims as to having invented the fortune cookie. Variations of the fortune cookie go back at least as far as 19th century Japan, although they didn't resemble the modern cookies many people recognize today. Some even claim that the roots of the fortune cookie go back as far as the late 17th century in Romania, where "note pies" were commonly served as part of elegant royal feasts. Others declare that Japanese mooncakes from the Ming revolution, which contained hidden messages, are the direct ancestors of modern fortune cookies. Regarding the origins of the fortune cookie, only one thing seems certain—the dispute as to who invented them may never be definitively settled.

Today's fortune cookies, typically made with vanilla, butter, flour, sugar, and sesame oil, are often manufactured by huge machines—a big change from traditional cookies. Approximately 3 billion fortune cookies are made worldwide every year, and they are always a welcome site at meals, gatherings, and special events. We may not always be able to predict the future, but hopefully we'll always have fortune cookies around to help us get a glimpse of what's in store for us.

133. A good title for this passage would be
  (A) Fortune Cookies: A Mysterious Treat with Mysterious Origins
  (B) What is Your Favorite Treat after a Good Meal?
  (C) An Exploration of Hidden Messages and Secret Codes
  (D) A History of the World's Most Popular and Beloved Cookie

134. The word cessation, as underlined and used in this passage, most nearly means
  (A) ending.
  (B) beginning.
  (C) climax.
  (D) middle.

135. The best word to sum up the author's beliefs regarding the origins of the fortune cookie is
    (A) obvious.
    (B) unclear.
    (C) traceable.
    (D) humorous.

136. Why does the author refer to modern, machine-made fortune cookies as "a big change from traditional cookies"?
    (A) Because no one knows who invented traditional fortune cookies.
    (B) Because traditional cookies were larger and had different ingredients.
    (C) Because traditional fortune cookies were made by hand.
    (D) Because traditional fortune cookies tasted better.

137. The word indelible, as underlined and used in this passage, most nearly means
    (A) uneatable.
    (B) brief.
    (C) unimaginable.
    (D) unforgettable.

138. Based on the information in the passage, can we conclude that fortune cookies are the author's favorite cookie?
    (A) Yes, the author says that this is his or her favorite type of cookie.
    (B) Yes, that's the only reason why the author would write this passage.
    (C) No, there's not enough information in the passage to determine this.
    (D) No, the author most likely prefers another type of cookie.

139. According to the information in the passage, all of the following ingredients make up the modern fortune cookie except
    (A) vanilla.
    (B) cinnamon.
    (C) butter.
    (D) flour.

140. According to the information in the passage, all of the following are possible things you'd find in a fortune cookie fortune except a
    (A) funny riddle.
    (B) wise saying.
    (C) prophecy.
    (D) good luck phrase.

141. What is most likely the author's purpose in writing this passage?
    (A) To practice writing an investigative essay
    (B) To confess an obsession with a type of cookie
    (C) To inform readers about the origin of the fortune cookie
    (D) To persuade readers to eat more fortune cookies

142. According to the information in the passage, which of the following places are potentially where fortune cookies were invented?
    (A) Thailand
    (B) Brazil
    (C) Bali
    (D) Japan

Questions 143–152 refer to the following passage.

"Sophistication by the reel" is the motto of Peretz Johannes, who selects juvenile films for Saturday viewing at the Museum of the City of New York. Sampling the intellectual climate of the young fans in this city for the past two years has convinced him that many people underestimate the taste level of young New Yorkers. Consequently, a year ago he began to show films ordinarily restricted to art movie distribution. The series proved enormously successful, and in September, when the program commenced for this season, youngsters from the five boroughs filled the theater.

As a student of history, Mr. Johannes has not confined himself to productions given awards in recent years, but has spent many hours among dusty reels <u>ferreting out</u> such prewar favorites as the silhouette films Lotte Reiniger made in Germany. One program included two films based on children's stories, "The Little Red Lighthouse" and "Mike Mulligan and His Steam Shovel." The movies are shown at 11 a.m. and 3 p.m., with a short program of stories and a demonstration of toys presented during the intermission.

143. Mr. Johannes is a

(A) filmmaker.

(B) film critic.

(C) film selector.

(D) student of film.

144. Admission to the program described is

(A) limited to children in the neighborhood of the museum.

(B) for Manhattan only.

(C) available for all the city.

(D) for teenagers only.

145. By his motto, "sophistication by the reel," Mr. Johannes means to imply that he

(A) can convince students to remain in school through the lessons taught by his films.

(B) introduces complex ideas and new perceptions by means of the movies.

(C) considers all moviegoers to be immature.

(D) feels that education on film is more effective than education in the classroom.

146. The words <u>ferreting out</u>, as underlined and used in the passage, most nearly mean

(A) searching out.

(B) dusting off.

(C) editing.

(D) protesting against.

147. The films are shown

(A) year-round.

(B) twice every day.

(C) at the Museum of Modern Art.

(D) on Saturday.

148. Mr. Johannes

(A) followed an established policy in planning his programs.

(B) has failed so far to secure a good audience.

(C) limits his programs to the newest award-winning pictures.

(D) evidently is a good judge of children's tastes.

149. Mr. Johannes found that children's taste in motion pictures
- **(A)** was more varied than had been thought.
- **(B)** ruled out pictures made before their own day.
- **(C)** was limited to cartoons.
- **(D)** was even poorer than adults had suspected.

150. Mr. Johannes would probably *not* choose to show a(n)
- **(A)** film about a ballet dancer.
- **(B)** X-rated film.
- **(C)** film about the plight of migrant farmers.
- **(D)** silent movie.

151. In the first sentence of the second paragraph, the reels are described as "dusty." The writer chose this word because
- **(A)** the cans in which the films were kept were very dirty.
- **(B)** the movies had not been shown in a long time.
- **(C)** many of the prewar films were about the plight of the farmers in the dust bowl of the Southwest.
- **(D)** the word *dusty* is a synonym for *stuffy*.

152. The silhouette films were probably popular with children because they
- **(A)** were made in Germany.
- **(B)** were not very colorful.
- **(C)** allowed for free run of the imagination to fill details.
- **(D)** had lively background music.

Vocabulary

Directions: Choose the word that means the same or about the same as the underlined word.

153. tedious work
- **(A)** technical
- **(B)** interesting
- **(C)** tiresome
- **(D)** confidential

154. to rescind an order
- **(A)** revise
- **(B)** cancel
- **(C)** misinterpret
- **(D)** confirm

155. a histrionic reaction
- **(A)** confusing
- **(B)** impressive
- **(C)** dramatic
- **(D)** productive

156. the problem of indigence
- **(A)** poverty
- **(B)** corruption
- **(C)** intolerance
- **(D)** laziness

157. a vindictive person
- **(A)** prejudiced
- **(B)** unpopular
- **(C)** petty
- **(D)** revengeful

158. unsatisfactory remuneration
- **(A)** payment
- **(B)** summary
- **(C)** explanation
- **(D)** estimate

159. a deficient program
- **(A)** excellent
- **(B)** inadequate
- **(C)** demanding
- **(D)** interrupted

160. a detrimental influence
- **(A)** favorable
- **(B)** lasting
- **(C)** harmful
- **(D)** restraining

161. accurate information
    (A) correct
    (B) good
    (C) ample
    (D) useful

162. to amplify one's remarks
    (A) soften
    (B) simplify
    (C) enlarge upon
    (D) repeat

163. to be legally competent
    (A) expert
    (B) ineligible
    (C) accused
    (D) able

164. a shrewd comment
    (A) clever
    (B) boring
    (C) tired
    (D) meaningless

165. a relevant magazine article
    (A) applicable
    (B) controversial
    (C) miscellaneous
    (D) recent

166. an office manual
    (A) laborer
    (B) handbook
    (C) typewriter
    (D) handle

167. a computational device
    (A) calculator
    (B) adder
    (C) mathematician
    (D) machine

168. a conventional test
    (A) agreeable
    (B) public
    (C) large-scale
    (D) ordinary

169. the subject of controversy
    (A) annoyance
    (B) debate
    (C) envy
    (D) review

170. a diplomatic person
    (A) well-dressed
    (B) tactful
    (C) domineering
    (D) tricky

171. an irate student
    (A) irresponsible
    (B) untidy
    (C) insubordinate
    (D) angry

172. durable paint
    (A) cheap
    (B) long-lasting
    (C) easily applied
    (D) quick-drying

173. an intense skirmish
    (A) conversation
    (B) conflict
    (C) meal
    (D) package

174. the inception of the program
    (A) beginning
    (B) discussion
    (C) rejection
    (D) purpose

STOP End of Reading section. If you have any time left, go over your work in this section only. Do not work in any other section of the test.

MATHEMATICS

Concepts

45 Minutes

Directions: Mark one answer—the answer you think is best—for each problem. You may use scratch paper when working on these problems.

175. Three hundred twenty-six million nine hundred thousand six hundred nineteen =
    - **(A)** 3,269,619
    - **(B)** 32,690,619
    - **(C)** 326,960,019
    - **(D)** 326,900,619

176. A number is changed if
    - **(A)** 0 is added to it.
    - **(B)** 1 is subtracted from it.
    - **(C)** it is divided by 1.
    - **(D)** it is multiplied by 1.

177. In the number 4,000,400,000, there are
    - **(A)** 4 billions and 4 hundred thousands.
    - **(B)** 4 millions and 4 thousands.
    - **(C)** 4 billions and 4 millions.
    - **(D)** 4 millions and 40 thousands.

178. Which is the longest time?
    - **(A)** 1,440 minutes
    - **(B)** 25 hours
    - **(C)** $\frac{1}{2}$ day
    - **(D)** 3,600 seconds

179. $5^3 \times 3^4 =$
    - **(A)** $5 \times 3 \times 3 \times 4$
    - **(B)** $5 \times 5 \times 5 \times 3 \times 3 \times 3$
    - **(C)** $5 \times 5 \times 5 \times 3 \times 3 \times 3 \times 3$
    - **(D)** $5 \times 5 \times 5 \times 5 \times 3 \times 3 \times 3$

180. $\dfrac{3 \times 8}{6 \times 5} =$
    - **(A)** $\frac{2}{3}$
    - **(B)** $\frac{1}{6}$
    - **(C)** $\frac{3}{4}$
    - **(D)** $\frac{4}{5}$

181. Which of the following has the same value as $1\frac{3}{4}\%$?
    - **(A)** 1.75
    - **(B)** 0.0175
    - **(C)** $\frac{7}{4}$
    - **(D)** $\frac{7}{40}$

182. What is the total number of degrees found in angles A and C in the triangle below?

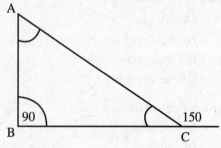

    - **(A)** 100°
    - **(B)** 180°
    - **(C)** 90°
    - **(D)** 60°

183. If $x > 9$, then

(A) $x^2 > 80$

(B) $x^2 - 2 = 47$

(C) $x^2 < 65$

(D) $x^2 - 2 < 90$

184. Any number that is divisible by both 3 and 4 is also divisible by

(A) 8

(B) 9

(C) 12

(D) 16

185. Which symbol belongs in the circle?

0.023 ○ 0.0086

(A) >

(B) <

(C) =

(D) ≅

186. The greatest common factor of 50 and 10 is

(A) 1

(B) 5

(C) 10

(D) 25

187. What number belongs in the box?

$+ 5 + \square = -3$

(A) +3

(B) −3

(C) +8

(D) −8

188. Which of these numbers might be a value of x in the following inequality?

$3x + 2 > 12$

(A) 1

(B) 2

(C) 3

(D) 4

189. The area of the circle is

(A) 3π cm.

(B) 6π sq. cm.

(C) 9π sq. cm.

(D) 36π sq. cm.

190. If $x - 3 < 12$, x is

(A) less than 15

(B) greater than 16

(C) equal to 15

(D) less than 18

191. The ratio of 3 quarts to 3 gallons is

(A) 3:1

(B) 1:4

(C) 6:3

(D) 4:1

192. Which pair of values for x and $\square$ will make the following statement true?

$2x \square 8$

(A) (6, <)

(B) (4, >)

(C) (0, <)

(D) (−3, >)

193. How many fifths are there in $4\frac{1}{4}$?

(A) $21\frac{1}{4}$

(B) 20

(C) $\frac{4}{85}$

(D) $\frac{17}{20}$

194. Set M = {1,2,3,4}; Set N = {2,5,6}. The intersection ∩ of the two sets is

(A) {2}

(B) {1,2,3,4,5}

(C) {3}

(D) {26}

195. If Mary is x years old now and her sister is 3 years younger, then 5 years from now her sister will be what age?

    (A) $x + 5$ years

    (B) $x + 3$ years

    (C) $x + 2$ years

    (D) 8 years

196. Write 493 in expanded form, using exponents.

    (A) $(4 \times 10^2) + (9 \times 10) + 3$

    (B) $(4 \times 10^3) + (9 \times 10^2) + (3 \times 10)$

    (C) $(4 \times 10^1) + (9 \times 10) + 3$

    (D) None of the above

197. Which of the following statements is true?

    (A) $7 \times 11 > 78$

    (B) $6 + 4 < 10.5$

    (C) $8 - 3 = 7 + 4$

    (D) $16 \div 2 > 9$

198.

$$\overline{AB} \cup \overline{BC}$$

    (A) $\overline{BD}$

    (B) $\overline{BC}$

    (C) $\overline{AD}$

    (D) $\overline{AC}$

Problem-Solving

199. The ratio of teachers to students in a certain school is 1:12. If there are 16 teachers in the school, how many students are there?

    (A) 16

    (B) 192

    (C) 202

    (D) 176

200. The legend on a trail map indicates that 1.2 inches represents 50 feet. How many feet is represented by 6 inches?

    (A) 200

    (B) 250

    (C) 360

    (D) 400

201. A department store marks up its clothing 75% over cost. If it sells khaki pants for $17, how much did the store pay for them?

    (A) $9.71

    (B) $17.50

    (C) $11.20

    (D) $1.12

202. The same store puts the same $17 pants on sale at a 20% discount. What is the new selling price?

    (A) $16.80

    (B) $13.60

    (C) $3.40

    (D) $16.75

203.

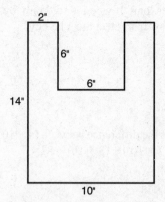

Note: In the figure above, assume that any angle which appears to be a right angle is a right angle.

The perimeter of the figure above is

(A) 38 in.

(B) 60 in.

(C) 46 sq. in.

(D) 38 sq. in.

204. The area of the figure above is

(A) 104 sq. in.

(B) 120 sq. in.

(C) 276 sq. in.

(D) 240 sq. in.

205. The charge for a particular long-distance call was $1.56 for the first 3 minutes and $0.22 for each additional minute. What was the total charge for a 16-minute call?

(A) $5.80

(B) $5.08

(C) $2.86

(D) $4.42

206. The winner of a race received $\frac{1}{3}$ of the total purse. The third-place finisher received $\frac{1}{3}$ of the winner's share. If the winner's share was $2700, what was the total purse?

(A) $2700

(B) $8100

(C) $900

(D) $1800

207. As a train departs from station A, it has 12 empty seats, 14 seated passengers, and 4 standing passengers. At the next stop, 8 passengers get off, 13 passengers get on, and everyone takes a seat. How many empty seats are there?

(A) 1

(B) 2

(C) 3

(D) 4

208. In order to increase revenues, a municipality considers raising its sales tax from 5% to 8%. How much more will it cost to buy a $250 television set if the 8% sales tax is approved?

(A) $7.50

(B) $10.00

(C) $12.50

(D) $15.50

209. Solve: $\dfrac{1\frac{3}{4} - \frac{1}{8}}{\frac{1}{8}} =$

(A) 12

(B) 13

(C) 14

(D) 1

210. Solve: $2.01 \div 1.02 =$

(A) 1.97

(B) 0.507

(C) 3.03

(D) 2.0001

211. Simplify: $-2[3 - 2(1 - 5) - 6]$

(A) −10

(B) −28

(C) 22

(D) 34

212. 140% of 70 is

(A) 150

(B) 9.8

(C) 9800

(D) 98

213.   5 gallons 2 quarts 1 pint
      −1 gallon 3 quarts
      _____

   (A) 4 gal. 9 qt. 1 pt.
   (B) 2 gal. 2 qt. 1 pt.
   (C) 3 gal. 3 qt. 1 pt.
   (D) 2 gal. 6 qt. 2 pt.

214. Solve: $6 \div \frac{1}{3} + \frac{2}{3} \times 9 =$

   (A) $\frac{2}{3}$
   (B) 24
   (C) 168
   (D) 54

215. If $x = -3$, $y = 5$, and $z = -2$, the value of $x(y - z)^2$ is

   (A) 147
   (B) 27
   (C) −27
   (D) −147

216. 7 is to 21 as $\frac{2}{3}$ is to

   (A) 2
   (B) 1
   (C) $\frac{4}{3}$
   (D) 3

217. The average of −10, 6, 0, −3, and 22 is

   (A) 2
   (B) −3
   (C) −6
   (D) 3

218. The number of phones in Adelaide, Australia, is 48,000. If this represents 12.8 phones per 100 persons, the population of Adelaide to the nearest thousand is

   (A) 128,000
   (B) 375,000
   (C) 378,000
   (D) 556,000

219. A carpenter needs four boards, each 2 feet 9 inches long. If wood is sold only by the foot, how many feet must he buy?

   (A) 9
   (B) 10
   (C) 11
   (D) 12

220. What is the difference between $(4 \times 10^3) + 6$ and $(2 \times 10^3) + (3 \times 10) + 8$?

   (A) 168
   (B) 55,968
   (C) 3765
   (D) 1968

221. A square has an area of 49 sq. in. The number of inches in its perimeter is

   (A) 7
   (B) 28
   (C) 14
   (D) 98

222. $r = 35 - (3 + 6)(-n)$
    $n = 2$
    $r =$

   (A) 53
   (B) 17
   (C) −53
   (D) −17

223. $(3 + 4)^3 =$

   (A) 21
   (B) 91
   (C) 343
   (D) 490

224. Aluminum bronze consists of copper and aluminum, usually in the ratio of 10:1 by weight. If an object made of this alloy weighs 77 pounds, how many pounds of aluminum does it contain?

   (A) 7.7
   (B) 7.0
   (C) 70.0
   (D) 10

225. Mr. Wilson makes a weekly salary of $175 plus 8% commission on his sales. What will his income be for a week in which he makes sales totaling $1025?

 (A) $257.00

 (B) $260.50

 (C) $247.00

 (D) $267.00

226. Solve for x: $x^2 + 5 = 41$

 (A) ±6

 (B) ±7

 (C) ± 8

 (D) ± 9

227. If 5 pints of water are needed to water each square foot of lawn, the minimum number of gallons of water needed for a lawn 8' by 12' is

 (A) 60

 (B) 56

 (C) 80

 (D) 30

228. Solve for x : $\frac{x}{2} + 36 = 37.25$

 (A) 18.5

 (B) 3.5

 (C) 2.5

 (D) 12.5

229.

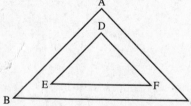

In the figure above, the sides of △ABC are respectively parallel to the sides of △DEF. If the complement of ∠A is 40°, then the complement of ∠D is

 (A) 20°

 (B) 50°

 (C) 60°

 (D) 40°

230. Find the area of a rectangle with a length of 168 feet and a width of 82 feet.

 (A) 13,776 sq. ft.

 (B) 13,856 sq. ft.

 (C) 13,306 sq. ft.

 (D) 13,706 sq. ft.

231. Solve: $63 \div \frac{1}{9} =$

 (A) 56

 (B) 67

 (C) 7

 (D) 567

232. A house was valued at $83,000 and insured for 80% of that amount. Find the yearly premium if it is figured at $0.45 per $100 of value.

 (A) $298.80

 (B) $252.63

 (C) $664.00

 (D) $83.80

233. Solve: $72.61 \div 0.05 =$

 (A) 1.45220

 (B) 145.220

 (C) 1452.20

 (D) 14.522

234. Find the area of a triangle whose dimensions are $b = 12'$, $h = 14'$.

 (A) 168 sq. ft.

 (B) 84 sq. ft.

 (C) 42 sq. ft.

 (D) 24 sq. ft.

235. Increased by 150%, the number 72 becomes

 (A) 188

 (B) 108

 (C) 180

 (D) 170

236. If $17x - 3y = 1$ and $2y - 17x = 5$, then $y = $ _____.

(A) 6

(B) 1

(C) −1

(D) −6

237. If $ab + 4 = 52$, and $a = 6$, $b = $

(A) 42

(B) 8

(C) 21

(D) 4

238. A group left on a trip at 8:50 a.m. and reached its destination at 3:30 p.m. How long, in hours and minutes, did the trip take?

(A) 3 hours 10 minutes

(B) 4 hours 40 minutes

(C) 5 hours 10 minutes

(D) 6 hours 40 minutes

STOP End of Mathematics section. If you have any time left, go over your work in this section only. Do not work in any other section of the test.

LANGUAGE

25 *Minutes*

Directions: In questions 239–278, look for errors in capitalization, punctuation, or usage. Mark the answer choice that contains the error. If you find no error, mark (D) on your answer sheet.

239. **(A)** We had swum across the lake before the sun rose.

   (B) Clearly visible on the desk were those letters he claimed to have mailed yesterday.

   (C) John Kennedy effected many executive reforms during the tragically few years that he served as president of the United States.

   (D) *No mistakes*

240. **(A)** John and I are meeting friends on Sunday afternoon to shop for prom wear.

   (B) We are going to Milner Farms on Saturday.

   (C) He hadn't seen none of the movies the others talked about.

   (D) *No mistakes*

241. **(A)** Rather than go with John, he decided to stay at home.

   (B) Each of the nurses were scrupulously careful about personal cleanliness.

   (C) His education had filled him with anger against those who he believed had hurt or humiliated him.

   (D) *No mistakes*

242. **(A)** July is a spectacular month for an exotic beach vacation.

   (B) Harold visited his Grandmother in Paramus, New Jersey

   (C) Randy needs to go to the Morningvale Mall on Tuesday.

   (D) *No mistakes*

243. **(A)** Neither tears nor protests effected the least change in their parents' decision.

   (B) Being able to trust one's sources is indispensable for the investigative reporter.

   (C) When you go to the library tomorrow, please take this book to the librarian who sits in the reference room.

   (D) *No mistakes*

244. **(A)** It's not good to have too much cholesterol in your diet.

   (B) Jack waited for his favorite newspaper, *The Haverford Courier*, to be delivered.

   (C) Frieda ate Muriel's signature dish, Eggplant Lasagna, on Sunday night.

   (D) *No mistakes*

245. **(A)** If you prepare systematically and diligently for the examination, one can be confident of passing it.

   (B) Mary was so uninterested in the baseball game that she yawned unashamedly.

   (C) If he had had the forethought to arrange an appointment, his reception might have been more friendly.

   (D) *No mistakes*

246. **(A)** Carlie, Gracie, and Sammie are members of the swim team.

    (B) Sheila and Margie are the school's best pitchers.

    (C) My favorite zoo exhibit is the snake house.

    (D) *No mistakes*

247. **(A)** In the Bennington household, Claudia's Graduation Day was a big event.

    (B) The Niborg Aquarium, which is in Sweden, has an amazing stingray exhibit.

    (C) Lars's favorite book is *The Catcher in the Rye*.

    (D) *No mistakes*

248. **(A)** Was it really she whom you saw last night?

    (B) The distraught traveler asked Tom and I to give her directions to the nearest bus stop.

    (C) Making friends is more rewarding than being antisocial.

    (D) *No mistakes*

249. **(A)** In his tales of adventure and romance, he predicted many scientific achievements of the twentieth century.

    (B) Today's *Times* has headlines about another woman who has just swum the English Channel.

    (C) Some Third World Countries have suggested that they be given the right to regularly censor what foreign journalists tell about their countries.

    (D) *No mistakes*

250. **(A)** Even if history does not repeat itself, knowledge of history can give current problems a familiar look.

    (B) He proved to his own satisfaction that he was as clever as, if not more clever than, she.

    (C) The citizens of Washington, like Los Angeles, prefer to commute by automobile.

    (D) *No mistakes*

251. **(A)** I have found one of those books that teaches how to build a model airplane.

    (B) There are less derelicts in the downtown area since the crumbling building was razed.

    (C) The ceremonies were opened by a colorful drum and bugle corps.

    (D) *No mistakes*

252. **(A)** Do not make a choice that changed the meaning of the original sentence.

    (B) I would appreciate your treating me as if I were your sister.

    (C) The contract should not have been awarded to the secretary's nephew.

    (D) *No mistakes*

253. **(A)** "To eat sparingly is advisable," said the doctor.

    (B) "Which is the way to the science building?" asked the new student.

    (C) She inquired, "Are you going to hand in your report before lunch?"

    (D) *No mistakes*

254. **(A)** There is a fantastic miniature golf course in Ocean City, Maryland.

    (B) At the time, the titanic was the largest passenger liner ever built.

    (C) Emily has to have her wisdom teeth removed by a dentist.

    (D) *No mistakes*

255. **(A)** You must explain that in the United States, there is no government interference with the arts.

    (B) The failure to pay back loans is a major cause of the failure of banks.

    (C) The former Soviet Union was unsuccessful in curbing youth's "addiction" to hard rock and heavy metal.

    (D) *No mistakes*

256. (A) The convicted spy was hanged at sunrise.

(B) The lady looked well in her new boots.

(C) Neither the manager nor the employees want to work overtime.

(D) *No mistakes*

257. (A) The town consists of three distinct sections, of which the western one is by far the larger.

(B) His speech is so precise as to seem affected.

(C) The door opens, and in walk John and Mary.

(D) *No mistakes*

258. (A) His testimony today is different from that of yesterday.

(B) If you had studied the problem carefully, you would have found the solution more quickly.

(C) The flowers smelled so sweet that the whole house was perfumed.

(D) *No mistakes*

259. (A) Band practice is every other Tuesday.

(B) Charlotte and Kelly are planning a Memorial Day tribute with the local Firefighters.

(C) The deadline for signing up for soccer is next Friday.

(D) *No mistakes*

260. (A) My parents love to go on vacations with my sister and me.

(B) Last year, we went to Honolulu, Hawaii.

(C) We went to a luau and watched fire eaters.

(D) *No mistakes*

261. (A) That business is good appears to be true.

(B) The school secretary was pleased that the courses she had taken were relevant to her work.

(C) Strict accuracy is a necessary requisite in record keeping.

(D) *No mistakes*

262. (A) The expression "Thanking you in advance" is unacceptable in modern practice.

(B) I like Burns's poem "To a Mountain Daisy."

(C) Venetian blinds—called that even though they probably did not originate in Venice, are no longer used in most homes.

(D) *No mistakes*

263. (A) You see, you did mail the letter to yourself!

(B) Your introduction to your new classmates has been a pleasant experience, has it not.

(C) During the broadcast, you are expected to stand, to salute, and to sing the fourth stanza of "America."

(D) *No mistakes*

264. (A) Participation in active sports produces both release from tension as well as physical well-being.

(B) One or the other of those clerks is responsible for these errors.

(C) None of the rocks that form the solid crust of our planet is more than two billion years old.

(D) *No mistakes*

265. (A) We all prefer those other kinds of candy.

(B) The law prescribes when, where, and to whom the tax should be paid.

(C) Everything would have turned out right if she had only waited.

(D) *No mistakes*

266. (A) Yesterday they laid their uniforms aside with the usual end-of-the-season regret.

(B) John told William that he was sure he had seen it.

(C) He determined to be guided by the opinion of whoever spoke first.

(D) *No mistakes*

267. (A) Because a man understands a woman does not mean they are necessarily compatible.

    (B) After much talk and haranguing, the workers received an increase in wages.

    (C) If I am chosen, I will try and attend every meeting that is called.

    (D) *No mistakes*

268. (A) While driving through the mountain pass, the breathtaking scenes awed the travelers.

    (B) I do not understand why mother should object to my playing the piano at the party.

    (C) My experience in South Africa taught me that the climate there is quite different from ours.

    (D) *No mistakes*

269. (A) To learn to speak a foreign language fluently requires much practice.

    (B) Buzzing around the picnic basket, a bumblebee flew into Sam's open mouth.

    (C) It would be interesting to compare the interior of one of the pyramids in Mexico with that of one of the pyramids in Egypt.

    (D) *No mistakes*

270. (A) "Complaints from the public," reports a government official, "are no longer considered to be a mere nuisance."

    (B) Statistics tell us, "that heart disease kills more people than any other illness."

    (C) According to a report released by the Department of Agriculture, the labor required to produce a bushel of wheat in 1830 was 3 hours.

    (D) *No mistakes*

271. (A) His written work has been done in so careless a manner that I refuse to read it.

    (B) I never feel badly if after trying hard I fail to win a prize; the effort gives me satisfaction.

    (C) Neither the United States nor, for that matter, any other country has seriously regretted having joined the United Nations.

    (D) *No mistakes*

272. (A) My landlord does not approve of my sending that letter to the local rent control agency.

    (B) My artist friend and myself were the only guests in the gallery to truly appreciate the abstract paintings on display.

    (C) The messenger will have gone to the airport before the package can be sent to the shipping room.

    (D) *No mistakes*

273. (A) Between you and me, I must say that I find this whole situation to be ridiculous.

    (B) The dimensions of the envelope determine the quantity of material that can be enclosed.

    (C) The reason why the train was so late today was because the previous train had been derailed.

    (D) *No mistakes*

274. (A) Due to the impending snowstorm, we will go directly home instead of stopping for ice cream.

    (B) The eraser was lost after it had lain alongside the typewriter for weeks.

    (C) Please distribute these newly arrived booklets among all the teachers in the building.

    (D) *No mistakes*

275. (A) The lecture was interrupted by the whirring, often much too loud, of the street-repair machinery right outside the window.

(B) Mandated school courses include mathematics, literature, history, and science; optional subjects include drama, marching band, and weaving.

(C) The pupil's account of his lateness is incredible, I will not give him a classroom pass.

(D) *No mistakes*

276. (A) Winter came before the archaeologists could do anything more than mark out the burial site.

(B) Since her concentration was disrupted by the loud noise, she decided to wash her hair.

(C) Let's you and me settle the matter between ourselves.

(D) *No mistakes*

277. (A) I recommend that you participate in all the discussions and heed the council of your elders.

(B) Upon graduation from the training course, my friend will be assigned to a permanent position.

(C) He finally realized that the extra practice had had a visible effect on his accuracy at the foul line.

(D) *No mistakes*

278. (A) That unfortunate family faces the problem of adjusting itself to a new way of life.

(B) The teacher promptly notified the principal of the fire for which he was highly praised.

(C) All questions regarding procedure should be referred to a disinterested expert.

(D) *No mistakes*

Directions: For questions 279–288, look for mistakes in spelling only.

279. (A) A novocaine shot promises only transient pain in place of agony from prolonged drilling.

(B) I will join the theater party next week if I am able to locate a responseble babysitter.

(C) That painting is so valuable that it is described as priceless.

(D) *No mistakes*

280. (A) Zach thinks downhill skiing is an absolutely exhilarating event.

(B) Nala understood that being successful on the gymnastic team would require great disipline.

(C) Gloria knew she wanted a red convertible immediately after getting her license.

(D) *No mistakes*

281. (A) Zach thinks downhill skiing is an absolutely exhilarating event.

(B) Nala understood that being successful on the gymnastic team would require great disipline.

(C) Gloria knew she wanted a red convertible immediately after getting her license.

(D) *No mistakes*

282. (A) The eager young politician stood at the street corner handing out political pamphlets.

(B) If you do not watch your eating habits in a foreign country, you may return with an intestinal paresite.

(C) My childhood heroes were mainly cartoon characters.

(D) *No mistakes*

283. **(A)** Begin to descend into the cave by way of the staircase just beyond the huge copper beech tree.

(B) Admissible evidence is evidence that has been collected in entirely legal ways.

(C) Since our army is so outnumbered, we might as well conceed defeat and limit our casualties.

(D) *No mistakes*

284. **(A)** The scavengers desecrated many native graves.

(B) Be sure you enter your figures in a straight column.

(C) Even an exorbitant charge does not guarantee that the doctor will perform a thorough examination.

(D) *No mistakes*

285. **(A)** The prologue to the play greatly enhanced its meaning.

(B) All students in attendance today will join together for an assembly program and physical education class.

(C) The error on the scoreboard was immediately noticable to all.

(D) *No mistakes*

286. **(A)** The union and management agreed that the reccomendation of the arbitrator would be binding.

(B) Parallel lines never meet.

(C) Drinking and driving often combine to conclude with a tragic accident.

(D) *No mistakes*

287. **(A)** The hospital issued a daily bulletin regarding the movie star's medical condition.

(B) Please do not interrup my telephone conversation.

(C) The newest soft contact lenses allow for extended wear.

(D) *No mistakes*

288. **(A)** The manufacturer's reply was terse but cordial.

(B) Every student who was questioned gave a similar explanation.

(C) The writer has created a clever psuedonym for himself.

(D) *No mistakes*

Directions: For questions 289–298, look for errors in composition. Follow the directions for each question.

289. Choose the best word or words to join the thoughts together.

The soldiers will not come home _____ the war is over.

(A) while

(B) since

(C) before

(D) None of these

290. Choose the best word or words to join the thoughts together.

We enjoyed the movie _____ the long wait in line.

(A) during

(B) despite

(C) because of

(D) None of these

291. Choose the group of words that best completes this sentence.

Darren, a responsible security guard, could not leave his post _____ his shift replacement arrived each night.

(A) however

(B) because

(C) until

(D) but

292. Which of these expresses the idea most clearly?

(A) You can swim in tropical waters and see glass-bottomed boats, colorful fish, and coral reefs.

(B) You can see glass-bottomed fish swimming among coral reefs and colorful boats in tropical waters.

(C) In tropical waters you can see glass-bottomed boats, colorful fish, and coral reefs swimming.

(D) From glass-bottomed boats you can see colorful fish swimming in tropical waters among coral reefs.

293. Which of these expresses the idea most clearly?

(A) Backgammon is a complex game, and you must change strategies often to learn it well.

(B) Though backgammon is easy to learn, it is a complex game which requires frequent shifts of strategy when played well.

(C) To learn to play backgammon you must shift complex strategies easily.

(D) You must easily learn to shift strategies to play the complex game of backgammon well.

294. Choose the pair of sentences that best develops this topic sentence.

Computers came along at just the right moment.

(A) Cities were growing larger and spreading farther. People found they couldn't gather facts fast enough to make needed decisions.

(B) The computer is a mass of complex parts and flashing lights. However, it is still just a machine made by humans to serve humans.

(C) The most unusual use for computers lately has been in the supermarket. At the wave of a wand, the computer can read what a person has bought.

(D) The computer aids business by storing information. It is able to provide this information almost as soon as a problem comes up.

295. Which of the following sentences offers *least* support to the topic "The Need to Protect the Bald Eagle"?

(A) In flight, the bald eagle is beautiful.

(B) Today, it enjoys the full protection of the law and seems to be slowly increasing.

(C) It is so plentiful that it is seen as a dangerous rival to the fishing industry.

(D) The game laws of Alaska are under local jurisdiction.

296. Which of these best fits under the topic "The Squid—A Master of Disguise"?

(A) Because the squid is shy, it is often misunderstood.

(B) Little sacs of pigment enable the squid to change its color.

(C) In reality, they are adaptable, intelligent, and often beautiful.

(D) They propel themselves backward by squirting water out of a nozzle located near their heads.

297. Which sentence does *not* belong in the paragraph?

(1) Intense religious zeal was the main reason for the Crusades, but it was not the only reason. (2) The Crusades weakened feudalism. (3) Businessmen saw good opportunities to set up new markets in the East. (4) Some knights hoped to win military glory, and many just sought adventure.

(A) Sentence 1

(B) Sentence 2

(C) Sentence 3

(D) Sentence 4

298. Where should the sentence "Man is learning" be placed in the paragraph below?

(1) His past experiences have taught him well. (2) He imports ladybugs to destroy aphids. (3) He irrigates, fertilizes, and rotates his crops.

(A) Before sentence 1

(B) Between sentences 1 and 2

(C) Between sentences 2 and 3

(D) The sentence does not fit in this paragraph.

STOP   End of Language section. If you have any time left, go over your work in this section only. Do not work in any other section of the test.

ANSWER KEYS AND EXPLANATIONS

Verbal Skills

1. C	13. B	25. B	37. A	49. D
2. A	14. D	26. A	38. B	50. B
3. C	15. C	27. C	39. A	51. C
4. B	16. A	28. C	40. C	52. C
5. D	17. B	29. B	41. D	53. D
6. D	18. A	30. C	42. A	54. B
7. A	19. C	31. D	43. B	55. C
8. D	20. A	32. C	44. B	56. C
9. A	21. C	33. D	45. C	57. A
10. B	22. A	34. A	46. B	58. C
11. C	23. C	35. C	47. A	59. B
12. B	24. D	36. A	48. B	60. D

1. **The correct answer is (C).** *Fourth* is an ordinal number. The other three are cardinal numbers.

2. **The correct answer is (A).** *Arouse* and *pacify* are antonyms, as are *agitate* and *smooth*. *Ruffle* is a synonym for *agitate*.

3. **The correct answer is (C).** If the first two statements are true, then the only thing we can be certain of is that both Francine and Henri are better jugglers than Jerome. It is uncertain if Francine is a better juggler than Henri, or vice versa, so choice (C) is correct.

4. **The correct answer is (B).** A query is a question, which is the opposite of *answer*.

5. **The correct answer is (D).** To *impair* is to damage or to *weaken*.

6. **The correct answer is (C).** *Death* is the fact of dying. The other choices are crimes, one of which just happens to cause death.

7. **The correct answer is (A).** That which is *variable* is changeable, fluctuating, or *shifting*.

8. **The correct answer is (D).** The relationship is that of object to action. When one *beats* an *egg,* one performs a violent act upon the substance of the egg in preparation for eating. When one *mashes* a *potato,* one performs an analogous act upon the potato. Baking a potato prepares it for eating, but the act of baking is not analogous to the act of beating. If *mash* were not offered as a choice, *bake* might have served as the answer. You must always choose the best answer available.

9. **The correct answer is (A).** To *obstruct* is to "clog" or to *block*.

10. **The correct answer is (B).** The green balloon is lower in the sky than the red balloon. Since the yellow balloon is higher in the sky than the red balloon, the green balloon cannot be higher than the yellow balloon, so the third statement must be false.

11. **The correct answer is (C).** The common feature among three of the answer choices is that they're all in the past tense. Choice (C), *mixing*, is in the present tense.

12. **The correct answer is (B).** The *result* is the end product of a *cause*. A synonym for *result* is "effect." Do not confuse "effect" with *affect,* which means "influence."

13. **The correct answer is (B).** The first part of the analogy establishes a noun (*weight*) and a verb that is typically used with it (*gain*). *Lemonade* is a beverage that one typically *drinks*, choice (B).

14. **The correct answer is (D).** A cave is a naturally occurring shelter that might be used as a dwelling place. All the other choices are man-made.

15. **The correct answer is (C).** Pretzel, the dachshund, is clearly less shaggy than Pepper and so could be in the same dog obedience class, but there is no information to suggest that Pretzel even goes to obedience school.

16. **The correct answer is (A).** The first part of the analogy establishes an item (*camera*) and a part that it comprises (*lens*). *Lightbulb* is an item and a *filament*, choice (A), is part of it.

17. **The correct answer is (B).** *Revenue* means *income.* Taxes produce revenue, but they are not in themselves revenue.

18. **The correct answer is (A).** A *trapeze* is a short horizontal bar that gymnasts and aerialists swing from and upon which they perform. All the other choices are tools that make work easier.

19. **The correct answer is (C).** *Tears* may well come as a sign of emotion. All the other choices are emotions themselves.

20. **The correct answer is (A).** From fastest to slowest jumper, we have: Cleo—Lori—Inez—Linda—Mary.

21. **The correct answer is (C).** *Manual,* as opposed to automatic or mechanical, means *hand-operated.*

22. **The correct answer is (A).** *Marshy* means "boggy" or *swampy.*

23. **The correct answer is (C).** The relationship is that of actor to object or, if you like, eater to eaten. A *seal* eats *fish;* a *bird* eats *worms.*

24. **The correct answer is (D).** *Loss* is the opposite of *profit.*

25. **The correct answer is (B).** *Activity* is motion. *Rest* is freedom from activity.

26. **The correct answer is (A).** *Wind* is the general term for air in motion. All the other choices are descriptions of winds based upon wind speed.

27. **The correct answer is (C).** All people eaters are purple, but it does not necessarily follow that all things purple eat people. We cannot tell whether or not there are some cyclops that are purple even though they do not eat people.

28. **The correct answer is (C).** *Churlish* most nearly means *surly,* choice (C).

29. **The correct answer is (B).** The word *immaterial* means *unimportant.*

30. **The correct answer is (C).** From the heaviest to the lightest books, the order is blue, orange, green, and red. Although we are told that orange books are not as light as yellow books, we cannot tell whether yellow books are heavier or lighter than the green books.

31. **The correct answer is (D).** A *shoe* is made of *leather;* a *highway* is made of *asphalt.*

32. **The correct answer is (C).** To *mend* is to *repair,* which is the opposite of *destroy.*

33. **The correct answer is (D).** *Concrete* means "specific" or "particular." *Abstract* means "general" or "theoretical."

34. **The correct answer is (A).** To *function* is to *operate* or to "work."

35. **The correct answer is (C).** *Meat* is food. All the other choices are nutrients found in food.

36. **The correct answer is (A).** Because all Ts are either green-eyed Ys or blue-tailed Gs, it is reasonable to assume that some are blue-tailed Gs. Because all blue-tailed Gs have red noses, we can safely assume that some Ts, at least those that are blue-tailed Gs, have red noses.

37. **The correct answer is (A).** A *cacophony* of sirens is harsh and loud, choice (A).

38. **The correct answer is (B).** *Monkey* is the general term describing a whole class of primates, regardless of gender. All the other choices are specifically male animals.

39. **The correct answer is (A).** You *taste* with your *tongue;* you *touch* with your *finger.* The sense of touch has to do with feeling, but the organ of touch to be found among the choices is *finger,* which is analogous to *tongue* in its relation to *taste.*

40. **The correct answer is (C).** *Discord* means "deep disagreement." Music may be either harmonious or discordant.

41. **The correct answer is (D).** *Fumes* are gas, smoke, or vapor emanations. The other choices describe the smell of fumes.

42. **The correct answer is (A).** *Riding* is a passive act; an animal or machine does the transporting. All the other choices are active ways in which to move from one place to another.

43. **The correct answer is (B).** *Fatal* means "causing death" or *deadly.*

44. **The correct answer is (B).** Terry has won the most races of all.

45. **The correct answer is (C).** A *brick* is opaque. All the other choices are translucent.

46. **The correct answer is (B).** *Secure* means *safe,* as in "not exposed to danger."

47. **The correct answer is (A).** *Garish* means "gaudy" and "glaring," the opposite of *dull.*

48. **The correct answer is (B).** This is a sequential relationship. The sequence is from parent to child. *Horse* is the parent; *foal* the child. *Mother* is the parent; *son* the child. The gender of the parent and child is irrelevant to this analogy.

49. **The correct answer is (D).** A *sourball* is a very hard food. All the other choices are soft foods.

50. **The correct answer is (B).** That which is *counterfeit* is an "imitation made with intent to defraud" and, hence, *false.*

51. **The correct answer is (C).** All you know is that the thruway and the highway have more lanes then the parkway.

52. **The correct answer is (C).** In this actor-and-object relationship, the actor serves as an irritant to the object. Thus, a *flea* irritates a *dog;* a *fly* irritates a *horse.* A rider might at times irritate a horse but not with such consistency as a fly.

53. **The correct answer is (D).** The word *intermittently* means "recurring from time to time."

54. **The correct answer is (B).** *Acrylic* refers to a resin product—fiber, paint, or adhesive. The other choices refer to languages that are printed in different alphabets. If you had trouble with this, you were probably thinking of *Cyrillic,* the alphabet in which the Russian language is written.

55. **The correct answer is (C).** *Diverse* means "different."

56. **The correct answer is (C).** The *finder* seeks and receives a *reward;* the *repenter* seeks and receives *absolution* (from sin). *Contrition* is the feeling the repenter must have in order to repent. *Religion* may be associated with *repentance* but without the same essential actor-to-object relationship.

57. **The correct answer is (A).** When an object *bends,* it changes shape or orientation but remains intact. All the other choices refer to breaking apart.

58. **The correct answer is (C).** We are told only relative positions with regard to north and south but have no information as to proximity or what is adjacent to what. We cannot tell from this information exactly where the grocery store is in relation to the dry cleaner.

59. **The correct answer is (B).** *Deception* means *fraud* or "subterfuge."

60. **The correct answer is (D).** *Nylon* is a synthetic fiber. All the other choices are natural fibers.

Quantitative Skills

61. B	72. D	83. D	93. C	103. A
62. C	73. C	84. B	94. C	104. B
63. D	74. A	85. C	95. D	105. C
64. B	75. C	86. A	96. A	106. D
65. A	76. A	87. D	97. D	107. C
66. D	77. B	88. A	98. B	108. A
67. C	78. A	89. D	99. D	109. B
68. C	79. B	90. B	100. A	110. C
69. B	80. C	91. B	101. B	111. A
70. D	81. B	92. D	102. A	112. D
71. B	82. A			

61. **The correct answer is (B).** If you write the direction and amount of change between the numbers of the series, you see that the pattern of the series is −1, −2, −1, −3, −1, −4, ... The next step is −1. 11 − 1 = 10.

62. **The correct answer is (C).** The relationships are clearly visible. Just read and examine carefully.

63. **The correct answer is (D).** Evaluate each separately:

(A) = $(5 + 8)^2 = 13^2 = 169$

(B) = $5^2 + 8^2 = 25 + 64 = 89$

(C) = $2(5) + 2(8) = 10 + 16 = 26$

So, (C) is less than (B), and (B) is less than (A).

64. **The correct answer is (B).** 60% of 40 = 24 − 5 = 19.

65. **The correct answer is (A).** The pattern is +2, −4, +2, −4, and so on. 44 + 2 = 46.

66. **The correct answer is (D).** The cube of 4 divided by 4 is the square of 4 = 16.

16 + 3 = 19.

67. **The correct answer is (C).** 6 + 12 + 4 + 41 + 7 = 70 ÷ 5 = 14 × 2 = 28.

68. **The correct answer is (C).** The series so far is: −2, −2, −3, −3, −4, −4; next should come −5, −5. 24 − 5 = 19 − 5 = 14.

69. **The correct answer is (B).** The pattern is to add 7, then add 2, add 7, then add 2, . . . So, the next number is 52 + 7 = 59.

70. **The correct answer is (D).** Angle C is a right angle (90°). The three angles of a triangle must add up to 180°. Therefore, the sum of the other two angles is equal to 90°.

71. **The correct answer is (B).**

$$6 \times 4 = 24$$

$$\frac{2}{3}x = 24$$

$$x = 24\frac{3}{2}$$

$$x = 36$$

72. **The correct answer is (D).** Let x denote the number. Then, translate the number sentence into the equation $\frac{x}{\frac{1}{4}} = 79 - 3$.

Solve as follows:

$$\frac{x}{\frac{1}{4}} = 79 - 3$$

$$4x = 76$$

$$x = 19$$

73. **The correct answer is (C).** Count up the shaded areas, taking note of the fact that some areas are larger than others. Then choose your answer by inspection and careful reading.

74. **The correct answer is (A).** The series reads: +9, +10, +11, +12, +13. Continue: 57 + 14 = 71 + 15 = 86 + 16 = 102.

75. **The correct answer is (C).** Doing the math, (B) = 0.858. The decimal form of (C) = 0.875, which makes it equal to (A). Now you can see that there is only one true statement.

76. **The correct answer is (A).**

69 − 6 = 63 ÷ 7 = 9.

77. **The correct answer is (B).** (A) is 4; (B) is 6; (C) is 4. Now just be careful.

78. **The correct answer is (A).** (A) is 150; (B) is 300; (C) is 500; and (D) is 350.

79. **The correct answer is (B).** Sometimes you must shift gears. Most series are based upon addition and subtraction but not all. You cannot make sense of this series if you stick to the + 8 with which you probably started out. The relationship between 9 and 18 and between 15 and 30 should make you think of multiplication. The series reads: ×2, −7, ×2, −7, ×2, −7, ... 11 × 2 = 22. To confirm: 22 − 7 = 15.

80. **The correct answer is (C).** You should see that the pattern is developing: +1, +1, +2, +2, +3, +3, +4, ... 18 + 4 = 22.

81. **The correct answer is (B).** Let x represent the number. 25% of x is $0.25x$, and 40% of x is $0.40x$. The product is $(0.25x)(0.40x) = 14.4$. Simplifying the equation yields the equivalent equation $0.1x^2 = 14.4$. Divide by 0.1 to get $x^2 = 144$. Taking the square root gives $x = 12$.

82. **The correct answer is (A).** 12 + 87 + 72 + 41 = 212 ÷ 4 = 53 − 25 = 28.

83. **The correct answer is (D).** The series +1, −2, +1, −3, +1, −4 now continues with +1. 18 + 1 = 19.

84. **The correct answer is (B).** Read, count, and reason carefully.

85. **The correct answer is (C).** $\frac{4}{5}$ of 80 = 64 + 3 = 67. 82 − 67 = 15.

86. **The correct answer is (A).** The series as we see it reads +10, +9, +8, _____ , +6, +5. Fill in with 32 + 7 = 39.

87. **The correct answer is (D).** (A) is 36; (B) is 64; and (C) is 144. Plug in the numbers and find the answer.

88. **The correct answer is (A).** Work out the arithmetic and learn that (A), (B), and (C) all are equal to 51. Now there is only one true statement.

89. **The correct answer is (D).** 8 × 4 = 32 × 3 = 96 − 30 = 66.

90. **The correct answer is (B).** $\frac{1}{8}$ of 96 = 12 × 6 = 72.

91. **The correct answer is (B).** The series may be interpreted as a repetition of +0.125 or as increasing decimals of $\frac{1}{8}$, $\frac{2}{8}$, $\frac{3}{8}$ and so on.

92. **The correct answer is (D).** Count, then read carefully.

93. **The correct answer is (C).** $\frac{5}{9}$ of 99 = 55 + 15 = 70.

94. **The correct answer is (C).** The easiest way to find the solution is to try out each of the answers.

$\frac{9}{16} \div \frac{3}{4} = \frac{9}{16} \times \frac{4}{3} = \frac{3}{4}$; $\frac{5}{8} \div \frac{3}{4} = \frac{5}{6}$; $\frac{7}{16} \div \frac{3}{4} = \frac{7}{12}$; $\frac{3}{4} \div \frac{3}{4} = 1$.

95. **The correct answer is (D).** 0.8 and 80% are equal, but $\frac{8}{10}$% is only 0.008. Now it's easy.

96. **The correct answer is (A).** The order of the lengths of the line segments, shortest to longest, is (B), (C), (A), (D).

97. **The correct answer is (D).** You should see quite readily that the series is based on squares followed by their positive number square roots in descending order. The missing number is the square of 7.

98. The correct answer is (B). The letters progress by +3. The numbers progress by −4. Three letters after K is N. $13 − 4 = 9$.

99. The correct answer is (D). After you look beyond the first two numbers, you can see that the progression is ×3, repeat the number, ×3, repeat the number, ×3, repeat the number. We pick up the series at $27 × 3 = 81$. Then repeat the number 81. Then, $81 × 3 = 243$.

100. The correct answer is (A). If $\frac{3}{8}x = 9$, then

$3x = 72$ and $x = \frac{72}{3}$. So, $x = 24$.

$83\frac{1}{3}$%, or $\frac{5}{6}$, of 24 = 20.

101. The correct answer is (B). The size of the angle is easily read on the arc of the protractor. (A) = 70°; (B) = 60°; and (C) = 50°. A right angle is 90°. Now, plug the angle sizes into the statements to find the answer.

102. The correct answer is (A). (A) is 40; (B) is 40; and (C) is 32. Use numbers in place of the letters and solve.

103. The correct answer is (A). Don't be thrown by the negative numbers. The series is: +5, +2, +5, +2. Next comes +5. $−5 + 5 = 0$.

104. The correct answer is (B). Let x represent the number. We translate the number sentence into the following equation:

$75 − x = 2(9 + 3)$. Solve for x, as follows:

$$75 − x = 2(12)$$
$$75 − x = 24$$
$$75 − 24 = x$$
$$51 = x$$

105. The correct answer is (C). This is a simple ÷ 2 series; the decimals make it a bit confusing. $0.025 ÷ 2 = 0.0125$

106. The correct answer is (D).

$\frac{5}{8}$ of 96 = 60 − 12 = 48.

107. The correct answer is (C). (A) is 21¢; (B) is 28¢; and (C) is 25¢. Replace letters with money amounts and answer the question.

108. The correct answer is (A). The progress of the series is +3. $18 + 3 = 21$. However, in the small segment that we see, the series alternates two Roman numerals and two Arabic numbers. Having no reason to suppose that this alternation will change later in the series, we must assume that the next entry will be a Roman numeral. Hence, XXI is the correct form for the next number in the series.

109. The correct answer is (B). This is a ÷2 series, which you might find somewhat hard to visualize in the fraction form. Rename the improper fractions as whole numbers to make this clear:

$\frac{16}{2} = 8$; $\frac{8}{2} = 4$; $\frac{8}{4} = 2$; $\frac{8}{8} = 1$; $\frac{8}{16} = \frac{1}{2}$.

The correct answer, $\frac{8}{32}$, is $\frac{8}{16} ÷ 2$.

$$\frac{8}{16} ÷ 2 = \frac{8}{16} × \frac{1}{2} = \frac{8}{32}$$

110. The correct answer is (C). (A) is 95; (B) is 1.95; (C) is 95. Work with the numbers instead of the letters to find the answer.

111. The correct answer is (A). This is another instance in which it is easiest to try out the answers. 40% of 150 = 60. $150 − 60 = 90$. Because the first choice works, there is no reason to continue. Choices (B) and (C), being less than 90, could not possibly be correct. If you wanted to be doubly sure (and if you had spare time), you could try 40% of 145 = 58. $145 − 58 = 87$, which is not 90.

112. The correct answer is (D). The pattern being established is: −8, repeat the number, −6, repeat the number, −4, repeat the number. Logically, the next step is −2, repeat the number. $8 − 2 = 6$; then repeat the 6.

Reading

COMPREHENSION

113. C	121. D	129. D	137. D	145. B
114. D	122. C	130. C	138. C	146. A
115. C	123. A	131. B	139. B	147. D
116. D	124. A	132. C	140. A	148. D
117. C	125. C	133. A	141. C	149. A
118. B	126. B	134. A	142. D	150. B
119. A	127. C	135. B	143. C	151. B
120. B	128. A	136. C	144. C	152. C

113. The correct answer is (C). The selection is about a game that appears to be an early version of modern baseball.

114. The correct answer is (D). There were "usually between 8 and 20 players." The number of players was not fixed by rule. In fact, according to the last sentence, there were very few rules.

115. The correct answer is (C). One of the few rules defined the playing field as a 60-foot square.

116. The correct answer is (D). The first sentence tells us that the game was similar to the English game of rounders. The game probably derived its name from the fact that players ran around the bases. The second sentence assures us that the game was exciting for both players and spectators.

117. The correct answer is (C). The ball is described as a bullet, cork, or metal slug wound with yarn and string, obviously improvised to be put into service by that moment's group of players.

118. The correct answer is (B). The nineteenth century consists of the years in the 1800s. The game is placed in the early nineteenth century, from 1800 on. Its popularity increased throughout the first half of the century, so it clearly was played at least until 1850—and probably beyond.

119. The correct answer is (A). Compare your knowledge of the game of baseball as it is played today with the description of the game in the selection. You can readily see how much more complicated the game is today.

120. The correct answer is (B). The simple, improvised equipment made this a low-cost pastime. The players were not exceptionally skillful, and the game was only an American adaptation of an English game.

121. The correct answer is (D). The paddle with the thick handle was sturdy.

122. The correct answer is (C). The writer of the passage expresses no feeling whatsoever. This is nothing more than a clear, factual report.

123. The correct answer is (A). The answer to this detail question can be found by re-reading paragraph two of the passage, which discusses the percentage of usable uranium found in natural uranium when it is first mined. The passage tells us that most natural uranium contains only 0.07 percent of the usable type of uranium, which is known as U-235. Therefore, choice (A) is correct.

124. The correct answer is (A). This question is a "cause and effect" question. In this case, you're asked to identify what causes the nuclear splitting process to continue in a chain reaction. The answer to this question can be found in the first paragraph of the passage. Here, we are told that the release of neutrons that occurs during fission causes the nuclear splitting process to continue. Choice (A) pinpoints the cause as "the neutrons that are released" when uranium and plutonium atoms are split, so choice (A) is correct.

125. **The correct answer is (C).** To *extract* means to remove, making choice (C) the correct answer. The passage states that uranium is extracted through mining, and raw materials are removed from the earth during the mining process, so choice (C) makes sense. *Exacted* is a similar word, but to *exact* means to obtain something such as payment usually by threatening a person or group, so choice (D) is incorrect.

126. **The correct answer is (B).** The passage states that the process of enrichment makes the uranium contain a higher percentage of U-235. Enriched uranium is therefore a more powerful type of uranium, so the word *strengthened* is the correct answer. Choice (B) is incorrect, because *enriched* does not mean "more wealthy" in this context.

127. **The correct answer is (C).** The first paragraph states that a neutron is an atomic particle with no electrical charge, so choice (C) is correct.

128. **The correct answer is (A).** The first paragraph states that two types of atoms that split very easily are found in uranium and plutonium, making choice (A) the correct answer.

129. **The correct answer is (D).** The first paragraph states that a nuclear chain reaction is the process that creates power, making choice (D) the correct answer. Choice (B) is incorrect, because a nuclear reactor is a device in which nuclear power is created. Nuclear chain reactions do not create reactors, but instead take place *within* nuclear reactors.

130. **The correct answer is (C).** The second paragraph states that natural uranium contains two components, Uranium-235 and Uranium-238, making choice (C) the correct answer.

131. **The correct answer is (B).** In the passage, the author explains the process of nuclear fission and the use of uranium in this process, making choice (B) the correct answer. Choices (A) and (C) are incorrect, because the author does not reveal any personal opinions regarding either the dangers or benefits of nuclear power. Choice (D) is incorrect because the author does not discuss nuclear power as an alternative to fossil fuels or present other alternatives.

132. **The correct answer is (C).** The passage focuses almost entirely on the process of nuclear fission and how it creates nuclear power, so choice (C) is the correct answer. The passage does not explore or expand upon the ways in which nuclear power may be employed, so choice (B) is incorrect.

133. **The correct answer is (A).** The purpose of the passage is to inform readers about the history of the fortune cookie, and the mystery that surrounds its origins. Therefore, the most appropriate title for this passage would be: "Fortune Cookies: A Mysterious Treat with Mysterious Origins," which is choice (A).

134. **The correct answer is (A).** The word *cessation* is used to describe the point at which fortune cookies come during the meal, and the author mentions that the cookies are served "after eating." Therefore, it most nearly means "ending," which is choice (A).

135. **The correct answer is (B).** The author states that "regarding the origins of the fortune cookie, only one thing seems certain—the dispute as to who invented them may never be definitively settled." Therefore, *unclear* is the best word to sum up the author's beliefs regarding the origins of the fortune cookie.

136. **The correct answer is (C).** The author refers to modern, machine-made fortune cookies as "a big change from traditional cookies" because traditional cookies were made by hand, as mentioned in the second paragraph.

137. **The correct answer is (D).** The word *indelible* is used in the passage to describe the lasting and unforgettable memory that one's first experience with fortune cookies likely created. Therefore, choice (D) is the correct answer.

138. **The correct answer is (C).** It may or may not be true that the fortune cookie is the author's favorite cookie, but there's not enough information in the passage to determine this. Therefore, choice (C) is the correct answer.

139. **The correct answer is (B).** The only ingredient among the answer choices that is not explicitly mentioned in the passage is cinnamon, which is choice (B).

140. **The correct answer is (A).** The only choice among the answer choices that is not explicitly stated in the passage as something you could potentially find in a fortune cookie is a funny riddle, which is choice (A).

141. **The correct answer is (C).** This is an informative piece of writing regarding the fortune cookie and its origins, and the author's most likely purpose in writing this passage is to inform readers about the origin of the fortune cookie, making choice (C) the correct answer.

142. **The correct answer is (D).** The passage explicitly states that Japan is one of the places where individuals claim that the fortune cookie was invented. Therefore, choice (D) is the correct answer.

143. **The correct answer is (C).** Mr. Johannes selects films for showing. He is a student of history.

144. **The correct answer is (C).** The last sentence of the first paragraph tells us that youngsters from all five boroughs of the City of New York attend the program.

145. **The correct answer is (B).** Mr. Johannes makes no far-reaching claims for long-term effects of his films. All he claims is that children are open to a broader range of concepts and visual presentations than those of their daily experience.

146. **The correct answer is (A).** To *ferret out* is to "dig" or to "search out." A ferret is a weasel-like animal that hunts out small rodents by flushing them out of their burrows.

147. **The correct answer is (D).** Read carefully. The film series begins in September. The films are shown at the Museum of the City of New York at 11 a.m. and 3 p.m. on Saturdays only.

148. **The correct answer is (D).** Because Mr. Johannes chooses a wide variety of films and regularly fills his theater, he is obviously a good judge of children's tastes.

149. **The correct answer is (A).** Mr. Johannes found that children's taste in motion pictures was more varied than had been thought. You can find the answer is in the first paragraph.

150. **The correct answer is (B).** The audience consists of children.

151. **The correct answer is (B).** The word *dusty* is a metaphor for "long-unused" or "almost forgotten." The cans may well have been dust-laden from long disuse, but the reels were well preserved if he was able to show them. At any rate, choice (B) is certainly true while choice (A) only possibly might be true. Without (B) as a choice, (A) might have been correct. You must always choose the best answer.

152. **The correct answer is (C).** Silhouettes are one-color dark outline shapes against a light background. As such, the shapes present motion, form, and limited features, mainly profiles. Details can be filled by an active imagination. Choice (B), if anything, would argue against popularity.

answers practice test 6

Vocabulary

153. C	158. A	163. D	167. D	171. D
154. B	159. B	164. A	168. D	172. B
155. C	160. C	165. A	169. B	173. B
156. A	161. A	166. B	170. B	174. A
157. D	162. C			

153. The correct answer is (C). *Tedious* means "monotonous," "boring," or *"tiresome."*

154. The correct answer is (B). To *rescind* is "to take back," "to revoke," or *to cancel.*

155. The correct answer is (C). *Histrionic* refers to something or someone "dramatic."

156. The correct answer is (A). *Indigence* is "destitution," or *poverty.* The word that means "laziness" is "indolence."

157. The correct answer is (D). *Vindictive* means "eager to get even," or *revengeful.*

158. The correct answer is (A). *Remuneration* is "compensation," "reward," or *payment.*

159. The correct answer is (B). *Deficient* means "lacking," "incomplete," or *inadequate.*

160. The correct answer is (C). *Detrimental* means "causing damage," or *harmful.*

161. The correct answer is (A). *Accurate* means "precise," or *correct.*

162. The correct answer is (C). To *amplify* is "to make larger or stronger" or "to develop more fully," or *enlarge upon* as with details and examples.

163. The correct answer is (D). To be *competent* is to be "sufficient," "permissible," "authorized," or *able.*

164. The correct answer is (A). *Shrewd* refers to something or someone that is "clever."

165. The correct answer is (A). *Relevant* means "related to the matter at hand," or *applicable.*

166. The correct answer is (B). A *manual* is a "book of instructions," or a *handbook.*

167. The correct answer is (D). A *device* is a machine devised for a specific purpose. Be careful to define only the underscored word. A *calculator* is a "computational device."

168. The correct answer is (D). *Conventional* means "customary," "usual," or *ordinary.*

169. The correct answer is (B). *Controversy* is "difference of opinion," "argument," or *debate.*

170. The correct answer is (B). *Diplomatic* means *tactful* when dealing with people.

171. The correct answer is (D). *Irate* means *angry.*

172. The correct answer is (B). *Durable* means *long-lasting,* even under conditions of hard use.

173. The correct answer is (B). A *skirmish* refers to a "conflict."

174. The correct answer is (A). The *inception* is the *beginning.*

Mathematics

CONCEPTS

175. D	180. D	185. A	190. A	195. C
176. B	181. B	186. C	191. B	196. A
177. A	182. C	187. D	192. C	197. B
178. B	183. A	188. D	193. A	198. D
179. C	184. C	189. C	194. A	

175. The correct answer is (D). The millions begin with the seventh digit to the left of the decimal place. Because you need 326 million, you can immediately eliminate choices (A) and (B). Read on: 900 thousand. You need look no further for the correct answer.

176. The correct answer is (B). A number is changed if 1 is subtracted from it. You should know this answer instantly. If you do not, try out each option.

177. The correct answer is (A). The first 4 is in the billions place; the second, in the hundred-thousands place. If you had trouble with this problem, review the sections on how to read numbers and determine place values in your math textbook.

178. The correct answer is (B). You should recognize immediately that $\frac{1}{2}$ day is shorter than 25 hours and that 3,600 seconds is far shorter than 1,440 minutes. Narrowing down to the first two choices, you probably know that there are 1,440 minutes in a day. If you do not know this, multiply 24 by 60 to see for yourself.

179. The correct answer is (C). You should know what the exponents mean. Count the 5s and 3s carefully.

180. The correct answer is (D). Multiply and simplify.

$$\frac{3 \times 8}{6 \times 5} = \frac{24}{30} = \frac{4}{5}$$

181. The correct answer is (B).

$$1\frac{3}{4}\% = 1.75\% = 0.0175$$

182. The correct answer is (C). Because the sum of the angles of a triangle must always equal 180°, and because m∠B = 90°, angles A and C together must equal 90°. Do not allow yourself to be diverted by extra information. m∠C of the triangle is equal to 30°, so m∠A = 60°, but this knowledge is irrelevant to the question being asked. Do not waste time on unnecessary calculations.

183. The correct answer is (A). $9^2 = 81$. Because x is greater than 9, x^2 would have to be greater than 81. Obviously, then, x^2 is greater than 80.

184. The correct answer is (C). Many numbers are divisible by either 3 or 4 but not by both. All numbers that are divisible by both 3 and 4 are also divisible by their multiple, 12.

185. The correct answer is (A). Compare the digit in the hundredths place. 0.023 is greater than 0.0086.

186. The correct answer is (C). The *greatest* common factor of 50 and 10 is 10 itself. 1 and 5 are also common factors, but they are smaller.

187. The correct answer is (D). For the sum to be smaller than the given number of an addition problem, the missing number must be negative.

answers practice test 6

188. **The correct answer is (D).** Begin as if you were solving an equation; subtract 2 from both sides. Now $3x > 10$. Quick inspection will show you that only 3×4 is greater than 10.

189. **The correct answer is (C).** The formula for determining the area of a circle is πr^2. $r = 3$; $r^2 = 3^2 = 9$.

190. **The correct answer is (A).** Because $x - 3 < 12$, x can be any number less than 15.

191. **The correct answer is (B).** Three gallons contain 12 quarts. The ratio is 3:12, or, in simplest form, 1:4.

192. **The correct answer is (C).** If $x = 0$, then $2x < 8$ because $2(0) < 8$. None of the other pairs results in a true statement.

193. **The correct answer is (A).**

$$4\frac{1}{4} \div \frac{1}{5} = \frac{17}{4} \div \frac{1}{5}$$
$$= \frac{17}{4} \times 5$$
$$= \frac{85}{4}$$
$$= 21\frac{1}{4}$$

194. **The correct answer is (A).** The intersection ($\cap$) of two sets has as its elements only those numbers that are in both original sets. In this case, only "2" is found in both sets.

195. **The correct answer is (C).** Mary's age now = x. Her sister's age now $x - 3$. In 5 years, her sister's age will be $x - 3 + 5 = x + 2$.

196. **The correct answer is (A).** Choice (B) is 4930; choice (C) is 133.

197. **The correct answer is (B).** $10 < 10.5$.

198. **The correct answer is (D).** The union of the two adjacent line segments creates one continuous line segment.

Problem-Solving

199. B	207. C	215. D	223. C	231. D
200. B	208. A	216. A	224. B	232. A
201. A	209. B	217. D	225. A	233. C
202. B	210. A	218. B	226. A	234. B
203. B	211. A	219. C	227. A	235. C
204. A	212. D	220. D	228. C	236. D
205. D	213. C	221. B	229. D	237. B
206. B	214. B	222. A	230. A	238. D

199. **The correct answer is (B).** For each teacher, there are 12 students. Because there are 16 teachers, there must be 12×16, or 192, students.

200. The correct answer is (B).

Set up a proportion:

$$\frac{1.2 \text{ inches}}{50 \text{ feet}} = \frac{6 \text{ inches}}{x \text{ feet}}$$

Solve for x, as follows:

$$1.2x = (6)(50)$$
$$1.2x = 300$$

$$x = \frac{300}{1.2} = 250$$

201. The correct answer is (A). A store markup of 100% would exactly double the price. A 75% markup almost doubles the price. The $17 pants are priced at almost double their cost to the store. By estimation, the best answer is (A). To figure precisely, remember that a 75% markup is the equivalent of multiplying the cost by 175%, or 1.75.

$$\text{cost} \times 1.75 = 17.00$$
$$\text{cost} = 17.00 \div 1.75$$
$$\text{cost} = \$9.71$$

202. The correct answer is (B). Reduce the $17.00 price by 20%.

20% of 17.00 = $17 × 0.20 = $3.40

$17.00 − 3.40 = $13.60 (new price)

Therefore, (B) is the correct answer. Choice (A) indicates a reduction of only 20 cents. Choice (C) represents a reduction *to* 20% of the original price, or an 80% decrease in price.

203. The correct answer is (B). To find the perimeter, we add up the dimensions of all of the sides. Note that there are some parts that have not been assigned measurements, so we should infer that they are the same as those corresponding parts whose measurements have been designated because we are told to assume that there are right angles in the figure. Beginning at the bottom and moving clockwise, the dimensions are:

10" + 14" + 2" + 6" + 6" + 6" + 2" + 14"

These equal 60 inches. The correct answer is (B). If you selected choices (A), (C), or (D), you failed to add up all of the segments.

204. The correct answer is (A). The area is most easily found by multiplying the length of the figure by its width, and then subtracting the area of the small 6" × 6" square.

(14" × 10") − (6" × 6") = area

140 sq. in. − 36 sq. in. = 104 sq. in.

Shapes such as this are often used for irregular pieces of carpeting or covering.

205. The correct answer is (D). A 16-minute call would cost $1.56 for the first 3 minutes, plus 22¢ for each of the 13 additional minutes. The total cost is found by $1.56 + 13(0.22) = $1.56 + $2.86 = $4.42.

206. The correct answer is (B). You have to read only the first and third sentences of the problem. The information in the second sentence is not relevant to the problem. The winner received $\frac{1}{3}$ of the total, or $2700. Thus, the total purse was $2700 × 3 = $8100.

207. The correct answer is (C). Number of seats = 12 + 14 = 26

Number of passengers at station A = 14 + 4 = 18

Number of passengers at next stop = 18 − 8 + 13 = 23

Number of empty seats = 26 − 23 = 3

208. The correct answer is (A). Raising the sales tax from 5% to 8% is a raise of 3%. 3% of $250 = 0.03 × $250 = $7.50.

209. The correct answer is (B). Simplify the numerator of the fraction, and then divide.

$$\frac{1\frac{3}{4} - \frac{1}{8}}{\frac{1}{8}} = \frac{1\frac{6}{8} - \frac{1}{8}}{\frac{1}{8}}$$

$$= \frac{1\frac{5}{8}}{\frac{1}{8}} = 1\frac{5}{8} \cdot \frac{8}{1}$$

$$= \frac{13}{8} \cdot \frac{8}{1} = 13$$

210. The correct answer is (A).

$$1.02\overline{)2.01000}$$

$$\begin{array}{r} 1.970 \\ \hline 1\ 02 \\ \hline 99\ 0 \\ 91\ 8 \\ \hline 7\ 20 \\ 7\ 14 \\ \hline 60 \end{array}$$

211. The correct answer is (A). Use the order of operations:

$$-2\big[3-2(1-5)-6\big]=-2\big[3-2(-4)-6\big]$$
$$=-2\big[3+8-6\big]$$
$$=-2\big[11-6\big]$$
$$=-2[5]$$
$$=-10$$

212. The correct answer is (D). This is a good problem to do in your head. Note that 10% of 70 is 7. 140%, then, is 14×7, or 98.

213. The correct answer is (C). Borrow a gallon and add it to 2 quarts. Rewrite the problem. Remember that you borrowed.

$$\begin{array}{l} \ \ \ 4 \text{ gallons } 6 \text{ quarts } 1 \text{ pint} \\ -\ 1 \text{ gallon} \ \ \ 3 \text{ quarts } 0 \text{ pints} \\ \hline \ \ \ 3 \text{ gallons } 3 \text{ quarts } 1 \text{ pint} \end{array}$$

214. The correct answer is (B). Bracket the multiplication and division first, and solve the problem.

$$\left(6 \div \frac{1}{3}\right) + \left(\frac{2}{3} \times 9\right)$$
$$= 18 + 6$$
$$= 24$$

215. The correct answer is (D). Substitute in the values of $x, y,$ and z and simplify using the order of operations:

$$x\left(y-z\right)^2 = -3(5-(-2))^2$$
$$= -3(7)^2$$
$$= -3(49)$$
$$= -147$$

216. The correct answer is (A). 7 is one-third of 21, and $\frac{2}{3}$ is one-third of 2.

217. The correct answer is (D). To find the average, find the sum of the addends and divide that sum by the number of addends.

$$-10 + 6 + 0 + -3 + 22 = 15$$
$$15 \div 5 = 3$$

218. The correct answer is (B). By knowing how many phones are in Adelaide (48,000) and how many serve each group of 100 in the population (12.8), we can find how many groups of 100 are in the population. 48,000 phones ÷ 12.8 phones per 100 of population = 3,750 groups of 100 in the population. $3,750 \times 100 = 375,000$ people.

219. The correct answer is (C). Four boards, each 2'9" long, total 11 feet. The carpenter must buy 11 feet of wood.

220. The correct answer is (D).

$$(4 \times 10^3) + 6 = 4006$$
$$(2 \times 10^3) + (3 \times 10) + 8 = 2038$$

The difference is 1968.

221. The correct answer is (B).

$$\text{Area of a square} = s^2$$
$$49 = 7^2$$
$$\text{one side} = 7 \text{ inches}$$
$$P = 4s$$
$$P = 4 \times 7" = 28 \text{ inches}$$

222. The correct answer is (A).

$$r = 35 - (9)(-n)$$
$$r = 35 - (9)(-2)$$
$$r = 35 - (-18)$$
$$r = 35 + 18 = 53$$

To subtract signed numbers, change the sign of the subtrahend and proceed as in algebraic addition.

223. The correct answer is (C). First perform the operation within the parentheses. To cube a number, multiply it by itself, two times.

$$(3 + 4)^3 = (7)^3 = 7 \times 7 \times 7 = 343$$

224. The correct answer is (B). Copper and aluminum in the ratio of 10:1 means 10 parts copper to 1 part aluminum.

Let x = weight of aluminum, then $10x$ = weight of copper

$$10x + x = 77$$
$$11x = 77$$
$$x = 7$$

225. The correct answer is (A). His total income is equal to 8% of his sales plus $175. 8% of his sales is $1025 × 0.08 = $82: $82 + $175 = $257.

226. The correct answer is (A).

$$x^2 + 5 = 41$$
$$x^2 = 41 - 5$$
$$x^2 = 36$$
$$x = \pm 6$$

227. The correct answer is (A). The lawn is 8' × 12' = 96 sq. ft.

96 × 5 = 480 pints of water needed

8 pts. in 1 gal.; 480 ÷ 8 = 60 gallons needed

228. The correct answer is (C).

$$\frac{x}{2} + 36 = 37.25$$
$$\frac{x}{2} = 37.25 - 36$$
$$\frac{x}{2} = 1.25$$
$$x = 2.50$$

229. The correct answer is (D). If the sides are parallel, the angles are congruent.

230. The correct answer is (A).

Area = length × width

Area = 168 ft. × 82 ft.

Area = 13,776 sq. ft.

231. The correct answer is (D).

$$63 \div \frac{1}{9} = 63 \times \frac{9}{1} = 567$$

This is a good answer to estimate. By dividing a number by $\frac{1}{9}$, you are, in effect, multiplying it by 9. Only one of the suggested answers is close.

232. The correct answer is (A). The amount the house was insured for is 80% of $83,000, or $66,400. The insurance is calculated at 45¢ per hundred, or $4.50 per thousand of value. Because there are 66.4 thousands of value, 66.4 × $4.50 per thousand equals the yearly premium of $298.80.

233. The correct answer is (C). Move the decimal point of the divisor two places to the right; do the same for the dividend. Then divide.

234. The correct answer is (B). The formula for the area of a triangle is

$A = \frac{1}{2}bh$. Plug in the numbers:

$$A = \frac{1}{2} \cdot 12 \cdot 14$$
$$A = 84 \text{ sq. ft.}$$

235. The correct answer is (C). This is a tricky question. It doesn't ask for 150% of 72, but rather to increase 72 by 150%. Because 150% of 72 = 108, we add 72 and 108 for the correct answer. Careful reading is an important factor in test success.

236. The correct answer is (D). Add the equations to eliminate x: $-y = 6$, so that $y = -6$.

237. The correct answer is (B). If $a = 6$, $ab + 4 = 52$ becomes $6b + 4 = 52$.

If $6b + 4 = 52$

$$6b = 52 - 4$$
$$6b = 48$$
$$b = 8$$

238. The correct answer is (D). First convert to a 24-hour clock.

3:30 p.m. = 15:30

$$\begin{array}{r} 15:30 \\ -\ 8:50 \\ \hline 6:40 \end{array} = 6 \text{ hours 40 minutes}$$

To subtract a greater number of minutes from a lesser number of minutes, "borrow" 60 minutes from the hour to enlarge the lesser number.

Language

239. C	251. B	263. B	275. C	287. B
240. C	252. A	264. A	276. D	288. C
241. B	253. D	265. D	277. A	289. C
242. B	254. B	266. B	278. B	290. B
243. D	255. D	267. C	279. B	291. C
244. C	256. B	268. A	280. B	292. D
245. A	257. A	269. D	281. D	293. B
246. D	258. D	270. B	282. B	294. A
247. A	259. B	271. B	283. C	295. C
248. B	260. D	272. B	284. D	296. B
249. C	261. C	273. C	285. C	297. B
250. C	262. C	274. A	286. A	298. A

239. **The correct answer is (C).** *President of the United States* must be capitalized.

240. **The correct answer is (C).** The use of double negatives, *hadn't* and *none,* makes this sentence incorrect. It should read *hadn't seen any.*

241. **The correct answer is (B).** Each of the nurses, one at a time, *was* careful. In choice (C), *who,* rather than *whom,* is correctly the subject of the clause "who had hurt or humiliated him."

242. **The correct answer is (B).** The word *grandmother* is not a proper noun, so it shouldn't be capitalized.

243. **The correct answer is (D).** No mistakes.

244. **The correct answer is (C).** *Eggplant lasagna* is not a proper noun, and shouldn't be capitalized unless it's at the beginning of a sentence.

245. **The correct answer is (A).** Maintain the same voice throughout the sentence. "If *you* prepare, *you* can be confident." The statement, "If *one* prepares, *one* can be confident" would also be correct.

246. **The correct answer is (D).** No mistakes.

247. **The correct answer is (A).** *Graduation day* is not an official holiday, and shouldn't be capitalized unless it's at the beginning of a sentence.

248. **The correct answer is (B).** Tom and *me* are the objects of the verb *asked.*

249. **The correct answer is (C).** There is no reason for the word *countries* to begin with a capital letter.

250. **The correct answer is (C).** You cannot compare people with a city. "The citizens of Washington, like *those* of Los Angeles . . . ."

251. **The correct answer is (B).** *Less* is a measure of bulk amount. *Fewer* gives the count of individuals.

252. **The correct answer is (A).** The choice that you have not yet made cannot have already changed the meaning of the sentence "Do not make a choice that *changes* . . . ."

253. **The correct answer is (D).** No mistakes.

254. **The correct answer is (B).** The name of a ship, such as *The Titanic,* is a proper noun and should be capitalized.

255. **The correct answer is (D).** No mistakes.

256. **The correct answer is (B).** It is unlikely that the new boots made the lady look healthy; they made her look *good,* that is, attractive.

257. **The correct answer is (A).** Three sections are being compared, so the superlative, *largest,* must be used. Choice (C) might sound awkward, but both verbs are in the present tense, and the sentence is correct.

258. **The correct answer is (D).** No mistakes.

259. **The correct answer is (B).** The word *firefighters* is not a proper noun, so it should not be capitalized.

260. **The correct answer is (D).** No mistakes.

261. **The correct answer is (C).** A *requisite* is a *necessity.* "Necessary requisite" is redundant.

262. **The correct answer is (C).** Dashes used to set apart amplifying but extraneous information must be used in pairs. The comma after *Venice* should be replaced by a dash.

263. **The correct answer is (B).** This direct question should end with a question mark. In choice (C), a period *always* goes inside the quotation marks, regardless of meaning.

264. **The correct answer is (A).** "Both" requires two objects connected by "and." Sports produce both release from tension *and* physical well-being.

265. **The correct answer is (D).** No mistakes.

266. **The correct answer is (B).** This sentence is ambiguous. To whom does the second *he* refer? Is John sure that he personally had seen it, or is John sure that William had seen it? In choice (A), *laid* is correctly used as the past tense of lay. In choice (C), *whoever* is the subject of the clause.

267. **The correct answer is (C).** Proper idiomatic form demands *try to attend.*

268. **The correct answer is (A).** The breathtaking scenes did not drive, but that is what the sentence implies. The *travelers* must be cast as the subject of the sentence. "While driving . . ., the travelers were awed by . . . ."

269. **The correct answer is (D).** No mistakes.

270. **The correct answer is (B).** There is no direct quote here, so quotation marks are inappropriate, as is the comma following "us."

271. **The correct answer is (B).** Feeling *badly* refers to one's sense of touch. When referring to health or emotions, one feels *bad.*

272. **The correct answer is (B).** The correct subject of the sentence is "my artist friend and *I.*" The reflexive *myself* is used only when something is reflecting back on me as, for instance, "I was beside myself with grief."

273. **The correct answer is (C).** The *reason why* is not *because;* The *reason why is* that . . . . Or the *reason that* is *because* . . . . In choice (A), *you and me* are correctly the objects of the preposition *between.*

274. **The correct answer is (A).** It is poor form to begin a sentence with "due to." The correct introduction to such an explanatory statement is "because of." In choice (B), the past participle of the verb *to lie* is *lain.*

275. **The correct answer is (C).** This error is called a "comma splice." The cure might be to create two sentences, with a period at the end of the first, or to join the two independent clauses with either a semicolon or a conjunction such as "so."

276. **The correct answer is (D).** No mistakes.

277. **The correct answer is (A).** The wrong word has been used. A "council" is a group; *counsel,* the required word, means "advice."

278. **The correct answer is (B).** Was the teacher highly praised for the fire? Was the principal highly praised for the fire? If the sentence means to say that the teacher was highly praised for promptly notifying the principal, then that is what the sentence should say.

279. **The correct answer is (B).** The correct spelling is *responsible*.

280. **The correct answer is (B).** The correct spelling is *discipline*.

281. **The correct answer is (D).** No mistakes.

282. **The correct answer is (B).** The correct spelling is *parasite*.

283. **The correct answer is (C).** The correct spelling is *concede*.

284. **The correct answer is (D).** No mistakes.

285. **The correct answer is (C).** The correct spelling is *noticeable*. (See Spelling—Rule 4.)

286. **The correct answer is (A).** The correct spelling is *recommendation*.

287. **The correct answer is (B).** The correct spelling is *interrupt*.

288. **The correct answer is (C).** The correct spelling is *pseudonym*.

289. **The correct answer is (C).** The point is that the soldiers are busy fighting a war but will return when the war is over. They will not return before the war is over because they are busy fighting it.

290. **The correct answer is (B).** Choice (A) represents an impossibility, and choice (C) is ridiculous. If the movie is very good, one might consider it to have been worth the wait.

291. **The correct answer is (C).** *Until* is the correct choice to complete this sentence: *Darren, a responsible security guard, could not leave his post until his shift replacement arrived each night.*

292. **The correct answer is (D).** "Glass-bottomed fish" and "coral reefs swimming" make no sense at all. Choice (A) is technically correct, but the whole purpose of glass-bottomed boats is to peer down to observe the fish swimming among the coral reefs.

293. **The correct answer is (B).** Choice (D) is totally garbled. Choices (A) and (C) suggest that changing strategies is part of the learning process. The statement made by choice (B) is more reasonable.

294. **The correct answer is (A).** The growth of cities and the information explosion define the moment at which computers were needed.

295. **The correct answer is (C).** The threat that the bald eagle poses to the fishing industry counters the need to protect the bird.

296. **The correct answer is (B).** Changing one's color is a means for disguise.

297. **The correct answer is (B).** This sentence is an effect, not a reason.

298. **The correct answer is (A).** This sentence serves as a topic sentence and provides a subject. All the other sentences begin with pronouns referring to "man" and offer examples to bolster the topic sentence.

SCORE SHEET

Although your actual exam scores will not be reported as percentages, it may be helpful to convert your test scores to percentages so that you can see at a glance where your strengths and weaknesses lie. The numbers in parentheses represent the questions that test each skill area.

Subject	No. Correct ÷ No. of Questions	× 100 = _____ %
Verbal Analogies (2, 8, 13, 16, 23, 31, 39, 48, 52, 56)	_____ ÷ 10 = _____	× 100 = _____ %
Synonyms (5, 7, 9, 17, 21, 22, 28, 29, 34, 37, 43, 46, 50, 53, 59)	_____ ÷ 15 = _____	× 100 = _____ %
Logic (3, 10, 15, 20, 27, 30, 36, 44, 51, 58)	_____ ÷ 10 = _____	× 100 = _____ %
Verbal Classification (1, 6, 11, 14, 18, 19, 26, 35, 38, 41, 42, 45, 49, 54, 57, 60)	_____ ÷ 16 = _____	× 100 = _____ %
Antonyms (4, 12, 24, 25, 32, 33, 40, 47, 55)	_____ ÷ 9 = _____	× 100 = _____ %
TOTAL VERBAL SKILLS	_____ ÷ 60 = _____	× 100 = _____ %
Number Series (61, 65, 68, 69, 74, 79, 80, 83, 86, 91, 97, 98, 99, 103, 105, 108, 109, 112)	_____ ÷ 18 = _____	× 100 = _____ %
Geometric Comparisons (62, 70, 73, 78, 84, 92, 96, 101)	_____ ÷ 8 = _____	× 100 = _____ %
Nongeometric Comparisons (63, 75, 77, 87, 88, 95, 102, 107, 110)	_____ ÷ 9 = _____	× 100 = _____ %
Number Manipulation (64, 66, 67, 71, 72, 76, 81, 82, 85, 89, 90, 93, 94, 100, 104, 106, 111)	_____ ÷ 17 = _____	× 100 = _____ %
TOTAL QUANTITATIVE SKILLS	_____ ÷ 52 = _____	× 100 = _____ %
Reading—Comprehension (113–152)	_____ ÷ 40 = _____	× 100 = _____ %
Reading—Vocabulary (153–174)	_____ ÷ 22 = _____	× 100 = _____ %
TOTAL READING	_____ ÷ 62 = _____	× 100 = _____ %
Mathematics—Concepts (175–198)	_____ ÷ 22 = _____	× 100 = _____ %
Mathematics—Problem-Solving (199–238)	_____ ÷ 40 = _____	× 100 = _____ %
TOTAL MATHEMATICS	_____ ÷ 64 = _____	× 100 = _____ %
Punctuation and Capitalization (239, 242, 244, 247, 249, 253–255, 259, 262, 263, 270, 275)	_____ ÷ 13 = _____	× 100 = _____ %
Usage (240, 241, 243, 245, 246, 248, 250–252, 256–258, 260, 261, 264–269, 271–274, 276–278)	_____ ÷ 27 = _____	× 100 = _____ %
Spelling (279–288)	_____ ÷ 10 = _____	× 100 = _____ %
Composition (289–298)	_____ ÷ 10 = _____	× 100 = _____ %
TOTAL LANGUAGE	_____ ÷ 60 = _____	× 100 = _____ %
TOTAL EXAM	_____ ÷ 298 = _____	× 100 = _____ %

APPENDIXES

Word List

A

abbreviate (verb) to make briefer, to shorten. *Because time was running out, the speaker had to abbreviate his remarks.* **abbreviation** (noun).

abrasive (adjective) irritating, grinding, rough. *The manager's rude, abrasive way of criticizing the workers was bad for morale.* **abrasion** (noun).

abridge (verb) to shorten, to reduce. *The Bill of Rights is designed to prevent Congress from abridging the rights of Americans.* **abridgment** (noun).

absolve (verb) to free from guilt, to exonerate. *The criminal jury absolved Mr. Callahan of the murder of his neighbor.* **absolution** (noun).

abstain (verb) to refrain, to hold back. *After his heart attack, William was warned by his doctor to abstain from smoking, drinking, and overeating.* **abstinence** (noun), **abstemious** (adjective).

accentuate (verb) to emphasize, to stress. *The overcast skies and chill winds only accentuate our gloomy mood.* **accentuation** (noun).

acrimonious (adjective) biting, harsh, caustic. *The election campaign became acrimonious, as the candidates traded insults and accusations.* **acrimony** (noun).

adaptable (adjective) able to be changed to be suitable for a new purpose. *Some scientists say that the mammals outlived the dinosaurs because they were more adaptable to a changing climate.* **adapt** (verb), **adaptation** (noun).

adulation (noun) extreme admiration. *The young actress received great adulation from critics and fans following her performance in the Broadway play.* **adulate** (verb), **adulatory** (adjective).

adversary (noun) an enemy or opponent. *When Germany became an American ally, the United States lost a major adversary.* **adversarial** (adjective).

adversity (noun) misfortune. *It's easy to be patient and generous when things are going well; a person's true character is revealed under adversity.* **adverse** (adjective).

aesthetic (adjective) relating to art or beauty. *Mapplethorpe's photos may be attacked on moral grounds, but no one questions their aesthetic value—they are beautiful.* **aestheticism** (noun).

affected (adjective) false, artificial. *At one time, Japanese women were taught to speak in an affected high-pitched voice, which was thought girlishly attractive.* **affect** (verb), **affectation** (noun).

aggressive (adjective) forceful, energetic, and attacking. *Some believe that a football player needs a more aggressive style of play than a soccer player.* **aggression** (noun).

alacrity (noun) promptness, speed. *Thrilled with the job offer, he accepted with alacrity—"Before they can change their minds!" he thought.* **alacritous** (adjective).

allege (verb) to state without proof. *Some have alleged that Foster was murdered, but all the evidence points to suicide.* **allegation** (noun).

alleviate (verb) to make lighter or more bearable. *Although no cure for AIDS has been found, doctors are able to alleviate the suffering of those with the disease.* **alleviation** (noun).

ambiguous (adjective) having two or more possible meanings. *The phrase, "Let's table that discussion" is ambiguous; some think it means, "Let's discuss it now," while others think it means, "Let's save it for later."* **ambiguity** (noun).

ambivalent (adjective) having two or more contradictory feelings or attitudes; uncertain. *She was ambivalent toward her impending marriage; at times she was eager to go ahead, while at other times she wanted to call it off.* **ambivalence** (noun).

amiable (adjective) likable, agreeable, friendly. *He was an amiable lab partner, always smiling, on time, and ready to work.* **amiability** (noun).

amicable (adjective) friendly, peaceable. *Although they agreed to divorce, their settlement was amicable and they remained friends afterward.*

amplify (verb) to enlarge, expand, or increase. *Uncertain as to whether they understood, the students asked the teacher to amplify his explanation.* **amplification** (noun).

anachronistic (adjective) out of the proper time. *The reference, in Shakespeare's Julius Caesar to "the clock striking twelve" is anachronistic, since there were no striking timepieces in ancient Rome.* **anachronism** (noun).

anarchy (noun) absence of law or order. *For several months after the Nazi government was destroyed, there was no effective government in parts of Germany, and anarchy ruled.* **anarchic** (adjective).

anomaly (noun) something different or irregular. *Tiny Pluto, orbiting next to the giants Jupiter, Saturn, and Neptune, had long appeared to be an anomaly.* **anomalous** (adjective).

antagonism (noun) hostility, conflict, opposition. *As more and more reporters investigated the Watergate scandal, antagonism between Nixon and the press increased.* **antagonistic** (adjective), **antagonize** (verb).

antiseptic (adjective) fighting infection; extremely clean. *A wound should be washed with an antiseptic solution. The all-white offices were bare and almost antiseptic in their starkness.*

apathy (noun) lack of interest, concern, or emotion. *Tom's apathy toward his job could be seen in his lateness, his sloppy work, and his overall poor attitude.* **apathetic** (adjective).

arable (adjective) able to be cultivated for growing crops. *Rocky New England has relatively little arable farmland.*

arbiter (noun) someone able to settle disputes; a judge or referee. *The public is the ultimate arbiter of commercial value; it decides what sells and what doesn't.*

arbitrary (adjective) based on random or merely personal preference. *Both computers cost the same and had the same features, so in the end I made an arbitrary decision about which one to buy.*

arcane (adjective) little-known, mysterious, obscure. *Eliot's* Waste Land *is filled with arcane lore, including quotations in Latin, Greek, French, German, and Sanskrit.* **arcana** (noun, plural).

ardor (noun) a strong feeling of passion, energy, or zeal. *The young revolutionary proclaimed his convictions with an ardor that excited the crowd.* **ardent** (adjective).

arid (adjective) very dry; boring and meaningless. *The arid climate of Arizona makes farming difficult. Some find the law a fascinating topic, but for me it is an arid discipline.* **aridity** (noun).

ascetic (adjective) practicing strict self-discipline for moral or spiritual reasons. *The so-called Desert Fathers were hermits who lived an ascetic life of fasting, study, and prayer.* **asceticism** (verb).

assiduous (adjective) working with care, attention, and diligence. *Although Karen is not a naturally gifted math student, by assiduous study she managed to earn an A in trigonometry.* **assiduity** (noun).

astute (adjective) observant, intelligent, and shrewd. *The reporter's years of experience in Washington and his personal acquaintance with many political insiders made him an astute commentator on politics.*

atypical (adjective) not typical; unusual. *In* Hyde Park on Hudson, *Bill Murray, best known as a comic actor, gave an atypical dramatic performance.*

audacious (adjective) bold, daring, adventurous. *Her plan to cross the Atlantic single-handed in a 12-foot sailboat was audacious, if not reckless.* **audacity** (noun).

audible (adjective) able to be heard. *Although she whispered, her voice was picked up by the microphone, and her words were audible throughout the theater.* **audibility** (noun).

auspicious (adjective) promising good fortune; propitious. *The news that a team of British climbers had reached the summit of Everest seemed an auspicious sign for the reign of newly crowned Queen Elizabeth II.*

authoritarian (adjective) favoring or demanding blind obedience to leaders. *Despite Americans' belief in democracy,* the American government has supported authoritarian regimes in other countries. **authoritarianism** (noun)

B

belated (adjective) delayed past the proper time. *She called her mother on January 5th to offer her a belated "Happy New Year."*

belie (verb) to present a false or contradictory appearance. *Lena Horne's youthful appearance belied her long, distinguished career in show business.*

benevolent (adjective) wishing or doing good. *In old age, Carnegie used his wealth for benevolent purposes, donating large sums to found libraries and schools.* **benevolence** (noun).

berate (verb) to scold or criticize harshly. *The judge angrily berated the two lawyers for their unprofessional behavior.*

bereft (adjective) lacking or deprived of something. *Bereft of parental love, orphans sometimes grow up to be insecure.*

bombastic (adjective) inflated or pompous in style. *Old-fashioned bombastic political speeches don't work on television, which demands a more intimate style of communication.* **bombast** (noun).

bourgeois (adjective) middle class or reflecting middle-class values. *The Dadaists of the 1920s produced art deliberately designed to offend bourgeois art collectors, with their taste for respectable, refined, uncontroversial pictures.* **bourgeois** (noun).

buttress (noun) something that supports or strengthens; a projecting structure of masrony or wood. *The endorsement of the American Medical Association is a powerful buttress for the claims made about this new medicine. The buttress on the south wall of the Medieval castle was beginning to crumble.* **buttress** (verb).

C

camaraderie (noun) a spirit of friendship. *Spending long days and nights together on the road, the members of a traveling theater group develop a strong sense of camaraderie.*

candor (noun) openness, honesty, frankness. *In his memoir about the Vietnam War,* former defense secretary McNamara described his mistakes with remarkable candor. **candid** (adjective).

capricious (adjective) unpredictable, whimsical. *The pop star changes her image so many times that each new transformation now appears capricious rather than purposeful.* **caprice** (noun).

carnivorous (adjective) meat-eating. *The long, dagger-like teeth of the Tyrannosaurus make it obvious that this was a carnivorous dinosaur.* **carnivore** (noun).

carping (adjective) unfairly or excessively critical; querulous. *New York is famous for its demanding critics, but none is harder to please than the carping John Simon, said to have single-handedly destroyed many acting careers.* **carp** (verb).

catalytic (adjective) bringing about, causing, or producing some result. *The conditions for revolution existed in America by 1765; the disputes about taxation that arose later were the catalytic events that sparked the rebellion.* **catalyze** (verb).

caustic (adjective) burning, corrosive. *No one was safe when the satirist H. L. Mencken unleashed his caustic wit.*

censure (noun) blame, condemnation. *The news that the senator had harassed several women brought censure from many feminists.* **censure** (verb).

chaos (noun) disorder, confusion, chance. *The first few moments after the explosion were pure chaos: no one was sure what had happened, and the area was filled with people running and yelling.* **chaotic** (adjective).

circuitous (adjective) winding or indirect. *We drove to the cottage by a circuitous route so we could see as much of the surrounding countryside as possible.*

circumlocution (noun) speaking in a roundabout way; wordiness. *Legal documents often contain circumlocutions that make them difficult to understand.*

circumscribe (verb) to define by a limit or boundary. *Originally, the role of the executive branch of government was clearly circumscribed, but that role has greatly expanded over time.* **circumscription** (noun).

circumvent (verb) to get around. *When James was caught speeding, he tried to circumvent the law by offering the police officer a bribe.*

clandestine (adjective) secret, surreptitious. *As a member of the underground, Balas took part in clandestine meetings to discuss ways of sabotaging the Nazi forces.*

cloying (adjective) overly sweet or sentimental. *The deathbed scenes in the novels of Dickens are famously cloying: as Oscar Wilde said, "One would need a heart of stone to read the death of Little Nell without dissolving into tears . . . of laughter."*

cogent (adjective) forceful and convincing. *The committee members were won over to the project by the cogent arguments of the chairman.* **cogency** (noun).

cognizant (adjective) aware, mindful. *Cognizant of the fact that it was getting late, the master of ceremonies cut short the last speech.* **cognizance** (noun).

cohesive (adjective) sticking together, unified. *An effective military unit must be a cohesive team, all its members working together for a common goal.* **cohere** (verb), **cohesion** (noun).

collaborate (verb) to work together. *To create a truly successful movie, the director, writers, actors, and many others must collaborate closely.* **collaboration** (noun), **collaborative** (adjective).

colloquial (adjective) informal in language; conversational. *Some expressions from Shakespeare, such as the use of thou and thee, sound formal today but were colloquial English in Shakespeare's time.*

competent (adjective) having the skill and knowledge needed for a particular task; capable. *Any competent lawyer can draw up a will.* **competence** (noun).

complacent (adjective) smug, self-satisfied. *Until recently, American auto makers were complacent, believing that they would continue to be successful with little effort.* **complacency** (noun).

composure (noun) calm, self-assurance. *The company's president managed to keep his composure during his speech even when the teleprompter broke down, leaving him without a script.* **composed** (adjective).

conciliatory (adjective) seeking agreement, compromise, or reconciliation. *As a conciliatory gesture, the union leaders agreed to postpone a strike and to continue negotiations with management.* **conciliate** (verb), **conciliation** (noun).

concise (adjective) expressed briefly and simply; succinct. *Less than a page long, the Bill of Rights is a concise statement of the freedoms enjoyed by all Americans.* **concision** (noun).

condescending (adjective) having an attitude of superiority toward another; patronizing. *"What a cute little car!" she remarked in a condescending style. "I suppose it's the nicest one someone like you could afford!"* **condescension** (noun).

condolence (noun) pity for someone else's sorrow or loss; sympathy. *After the sudden death of Princess Diana, thousands of messages of condolence were sent to her family.* **condole** (verb).

confidant (noun) someone entrusted with another's secrets. *No one knew about Jane's engagement except Sarah, her confidant.* **confide** (verb), **confidential** (adjective).

conformity (noun) agreement with or adherence to custom or rule. *In my high school, conformity was the rule: everyone dressed the same, talked the same, and listened to the same music.* **conform** (verb), **conformist** (noun, adjective).

consensus (noun) general agreement among a group. *Among Quakers, voting traditionally is not used; instead, discussion continues until the entire group forms a consensus.*

consolation (noun) relief or comfort in sorrow or suffering. *Although we miss our dog very much, it is a consolation to know that she died quickly, without suffering.* **console** (verb).

consternation (noun) shock, amazement, dismay. *When a voice in the back of the church shouted out, "I know why they should not be married!" the entire gathering was thrown into consternation.*

consummate (verb) to complete, finish, or perfect. *The deal was consummated with a handshake and the payment of the agreed-upon fee.* **consummate** (adjective), **consummation** (noun).

contaminate (verb) to make impure. *Chemicals dumped in a nearby forest had seeped into the soil and contaminated the local water supply.* **contamination** (noun).

contemporary (adjective) modern, current; from the same time. *I prefer old-fashioned furniture rather than contemporary styles.*

The composer Vivaldi was roughly contemporary with Bach. **contemporary** (noun).

contrite (adjective) sorry for past misdeeds. *The public is often willing to forgive celebrities who are involved in some scandal, as long as they appear contrite.* **contrition** (noun).

conundrum (noun) a riddle, puzzle, or problem. *The question of why an all-powerful, all-loving God allows evil to exist is a conundrum many philosophers have pondered.*

convergence (noun) the act of coming together in unity or similarity. *A remarkable example of evolutionary convergence can be seen in the shark and the dolphin, two sea creatures that developed from different origins to become very similar in form.* **converge** (verb).

convoluted (adjective) twisting, complicated, intricate. *Tax law has become so convoluted that it's easy for people to accidentally violate it.* **convolute** (verb), **convolution** (noun).

corroborating (adjective) supporting with evidence; confirming. *A passerby who had witnessed the crime gave corroborating testimony about the presence of the accused person.* **corroborate** (verb), **corroboration** (noun).

corrosive (adjective) eating away, gnawing, or destroying. *Years of poverty and hard work had a corrosive effect on her beauty.* **corrode** (verb), **corrosion** (noun).

credulity (noun) willingness to believe, even with little evidence. *Con artists fool people by taking advantage of their credulity.* **credulous** (adjective).

criterion (noun) a standard of measurement or judgment. *In choosing a design for the new taxicabs, reliability will be our main criterion.* **criteria** (plural).

critique (noun) a critical evaluation. *The editor gave a detailed critique of the manuscript, explaining its strengths and its weaknesses.* **critique** (verb).

culpable (adjective) deserving blame, guilty. *Although he committed the crime, because he was mentally ill he should not be considered culpable for his actions.* **culpability** (noun).

cumulative (adjective) made up of successive additions. *Smallpox was eliminated only through the cumulative efforts of several generations of doctors and scientists.*

accumulation (noun), **accumulate** (verb).

curtail (verb) to shorten. *The opening round of the golf tournament was curtailed by the severe thunderstorm.*

D

debased (adjective) lowered in quality, character, or esteem. *The quality of TV journalism has been debased by the many new tabloid-style talk shows.* **debase** (verb).

debunk (verb) to expose as false or worthless. *Magician James Randi loves to debunk psychics, mediums, clairvoyants, and others who claim supernatural powers.*

decorous (adjective) having good taste; proper, appropriate. *Prior to her visit to Buckingham Palace, the young woman was instructed to demonstrate the most decorous behavior.* **decorum** (noun).

decry (verb) to criticize or condemn. *The workers continued to decry the lack of safety in their factory.*

deduction (noun) a logical conclusion, especially a specific conclusion based on general principles. *Based on what is known about the effects of greenhouse gases on atmospheric temperature, scientists have made several deductions about the likelihood of global warming.* **deduce** (verb).

delegate (verb) to give authority or responsibility. *The president delegated the vice president to represent the administration at the peace talks.* **delegate** (noun).

deleterious (adjective) harmful. *About thirty years ago, scientists proved that working with asbestos could be deleterious to one's health, producing cancer and other diseases.*

delineate (verb) to outline or describe. *Naturalists had long suspected the fact of evolution, but Darwin was the first to delineate a process—natural selection— through which evolution could occur.* **delineation** (noun)

demagogue (noun) a leader who plays dishonestly on the prejudices and emotions of his followers. *Senator Joseph McCarthy was a demagogue who used the paranoia of the anti-Communist 1950s as a way of seizing fame and power in Washington.* **demagoguery** (noun).

demure (adjective) modest or shy. *The demure heroines of Victorian fiction have given way to today's stronger, more opinionated, and more independent female characters.*

denigrate (verb) to criticize or belittle. *The firm's new president tried to explain his plans for improving the company without appearing to denigrate the work of his predecessor.* **denigration** (noun).

depose (verb) to remove from office, especially from a throne. *Iran was once ruled by a monarch called the Shah, who was deposed in 1979.*

derelict (adjective) neglecting one's duty. *The train crash was blamed on a switchman who was derelict, having fallen asleep while on duty.* **dereliction** (noun).

derivative (adjective) taken from a particular source. *When a person first writes poetry, her poems are apt to be derivative of whatever poetry she most enjoys reading.* **derivation** (noun), **derive** (verb).

desolate (adjective) empty, lifeless, and deserted; hopeless, gloomy. *Robinson Crusoe was shipwrecked and had to learn to survive alone on a desolate island. The murder of her husband left Mary Lincoln desolate.* **desolation** (noun).

destitute (adjective) very poor. *Years of rule by a dictator who stole the wealth of the country had left the people of the Philippines destitute.* **destitution** (noun).

deter (verb) to discourage from acting. *The best way to deter crime is to ensure that criminals will receive swift and certain punishment.* **deterrence** (noun), **deterrent** (adjective).

detractor (noun) someone who belittles or disparages. *Neil Diamond has many detractors who consider his music boring, inane, and sentimental.* **detract** (verb).

deviate (verb) to depart from a standard or norm. *Having agreed upon a spending budget for the company, we mustn't deviate from it; if we do, we may run out of money soon.* **deviation** (noun).

devious (adjective) tricky, deceptive. *The CEO's devious financial tactics were designed to enrich his firm while confusing or misleading government regulators.*

didactic (adjective) intended to teach, instructive. *The children's TV show Sesame Street is designed to be both entertaining and didactic.*

diffident (adjective) hesitant, reserved, shy. *Someone with a diffident personality should pursue a career that involves little public contact.* **diffidence** (noun).

diffuse (verb) to spread out, to scatter. *The red dye quickly became diffused through the water, turning it a very pale pink.* **diffusion** (noun).

digress (verb) to wander from the main path or the main topic. *My high school biology teacher loved to digress from science into personal anecdotes about his college adventures.* **digression** (noun), **digressive** (adjective).

dilatory (adjective) delaying, procrastinating. *The lawyer used various dilatory tactics, hoping that his opponent would get tired of waiting for a trial and drop the case.*

diligent (adjective) working hard and steadily. *Through diligent efforts, the townspeople were able to clear away the debris from the flood in a matter of days.* **diligence** (noun).

diminutive (adjective) unusually small, tiny. *Children are fond of Shetland ponies because their diminutive size makes them easy to ride.* **diminution** (noun).

discern (verb) to detect, notice, or observe. *I could discern the shape of a whale off the starboard bow, but it was too far away to determine its size or species.* **discernment** (noun).

disclose (verb) to make known; to reveal. *Election laws require candidates to disclose the names of those who contribute large sums of money to their campaigns.* **disclosure** (noun).

discomfit (verb) to frustrate, thwart, or embarrass. *Discomfited by the interviewer's unexpected question, Peter could only stammer in reply.* **discomfiture** (noun).

disconcert (verb) to confuse or embarrass. *When the hallway bells began to ring halfway through her lecture, the speaker was disconcerted and didn't know what to do.*

discredit (verb) to cause disbelief in the accuracy of some statement or the reliability of a person. *Although many people still believe in UFOs, among scientists the reports of "alien encounters" have been thoroughly discredited.*

discreet (adjective) showing good judgment in speech and behavior. *Be discreet when* *discussing confidential business matters— don't talk among strangers on the elevator, for example.* **discretion** (noun).

discrepancy (noun) a difference or variance between two or more things. *The discrepancies between the two witnesses' stories show that one of them must be lying.* **discrepant** (adjective).

disdain (noun) contempt, scorn. *The professor could not hide his disdain for those students who were perpetually late to his class.* **disdain** (verb), **disdainful** (adjective).

disingenuous (adjective) pretending to be candid, simple, and frank. *When Texas billionaire H. Ross Perot ran for president, many considered his "jest plain folks" style disingenuous.*

disparage (verb) to speak disrespectfully about, to belittle. *Many political ads today both praise their own candidate and disparage his or her opponent.* **disparagement** (noun), **disparaging** (adjective).

disparity (noun) difference in quality or kind. *There is often a disparity between the kind of high-quality television people say they want and the low-brow programs they actually watch.* **disparate** (adjective).

disregard (verb) to ignore, to neglect. *If you don't write a will, when you die, your survivors may disregard your wishes about how your property should be handled.* **disregard** (noun).

disruptive (adjective) causing disorder, interrupting. *When the senator spoke at our college, angry demonstrators picketed, heckled, and engaged in other disruptive activities.* **disrupt** (verb), **disruption** (noun).

dissemble (verb) to pretend, to simulate. *When the police questioned her about the crime, she dissembled innocence.*

dissipate (verb) to spread out or scatter. *The windows and doors were opened, allowing the smoke that had filled the room to dissipate.* **dissipation** (noun).

dissonance (noun) lack of music harmony; lack of agreement between ideas. *Most modern music is characterized by dissonance, which many listeners find hard to enjoy. There is a noticeable dissonance between two common beliefs of most conservatives: their faith in unfettered free markets and their preference for traditional social values.* **dissonant** (adjective).

diverge (verb) to move in different directions. *Frost's poem* The Road Less Traveled *tells of the choice he made when "Two roads diverged in a yellow wood."* **divergence** (noun), **divergent** (adjective).

diversion (noun) a distraction or pastime. *During the two hours he spent in the doctor's waiting room, the game on his cell phone was a welcome diversion.* **divert** (verb).

divination (noun) the art of predicting the future. *In ancient Greece, people wanting to know their fate would visit the priests at Delphi, supposedly skilled at divination.* **divine** (verb).

divisive (adjective) causing disagreement or disunity. *Throughout history, race has been the most divisive issue in American society.*

divulge (verb) to reveal. *The people who count the votes for the Oscar awards are under strict orders not to divulge the names of the winners.*

dogmatic (adjective) holding firmly to a particular set of beliefs with little or no basis. *Believers in Marxist doctrine tend to be dogmatic, ignoring evidence that contradicts their beliefs.* **dogmatism** (noun).

dominant (adjective) greatest in importance or power. *Turner's* Frontier Thesis *suggests that the existence of the frontier had a dominant influence on American culture.* **dominate** (verb), **domination** (noun).

dubious (adjective) doubtful, uncertain. *Despite the chairman's attempts to convince the committee members that his plan would succeed, most of them remained dubious.* **dubiety** (noun).

durable (adjective) long lasting. *Denim is a popular material for work clothes because it is strong and durable.*

duress (noun) compulsion or restraint. *Fearing that the police might beat him, he confessed to the crime, not willingly but under duress.*

E

eclectic (adjective) drawn from many sources; varied, heterogeneous. *The Mellon family art collection is an eclectic one, including works ranging from ancient Greek* *sculptures to modern paintings.* **eclecticism** (noun).

efficacious (adjective) able to produce a desired effect. *Though thousands of people today are taking herbal supplements to treat depression, researchers have not yet proved them efficacious.* **efficacy** (noun).

effrontery (noun) shameless boldness. *The sports world was shocked when a professional basketball player had the effrontery to choke his head coach during a practice session.*

effusive (adjective) pouring forth one's emotions very freely. *Having won the Oscar for Best Actress, Sally Field gave an effusive acceptance speech in which she marveled, "You like me! You really like me!"* **effusion** (noun).

egotism (noun) excessive concern with oneself; conceit. *Robert's egotism was so great that all he could talk about was the importance—and the brilliance—of his own opinions.* **egotistic** (adjective).

egregious (adjective) obvious, conspicuous, flagrant. *It's hard to imagine how the editor could allow such an egregious error to appear.*

elated (adjective) excited and happy; exultant. *When the Washington Redskins' last, desperate pass was intercepted, the elated fans of the Philadelphia Eagles began to celebrate.* **elate** (verb), **elation** (noun).

elliptical (adjective) very terse or concise in writing or speech; difficult to understand. *Rather than speak plainly, she hinted at her meaning through a series of nods, gestures, and elliptical half sentences.*

elusive (adjective) hard to capture, grasp, or understand. *Though everyone thinks they know what "justice" is, when you try to define the concept precisely, it proves to be quite elusive.*

embezzle (verb) to steal money or property that has been entrusted to your care. *The church treasurer was found to have embezzled thousands of dollars by writing phony checks on the church bank account.* **embezzlement** (noun).

emend (verb) to correct. *Before the letter is mailed, please emend the two spelling errors.* **emendation** (noun).

emigrate (verb) to leave one place or country to settle elsewhere. *Millions of Irish emigrated to the New World in the wake of the great Irish famines of the 1840s.* **emigrant** (noun), **emigration** (noun).

eminent (adjective) noteworthy, famous. *Vaclav Havel was an eminent author before he was elected president of the Czech Republic.* **eminence** (noun).

emissary (noun) someone who represents another. *In an effort to avoid a military showdown, former President Jimmy Carter was sent as an emissary to Korea to negotiate a settlement.*

emollient (noun) something that softens or soothes. *She used a hand cream as an emollient on her dry, work-roughened hands.* **emollient** (adjective).

empathy (noun) imaginative sharing of the feelings, thoughts, or experiences of another. *It's easy for a parent to have empathy for the sorrow of another parent whose child has died.* **empathetic** (adjective).

empirical (adjective) based on experience or personal observation. *Although many people believe in ESP, scientists have found no empirical evidence of its existence.* **empiricism** (noun).

emulate (verb) to imitate or copy. *The British band Oasis admitted their desire to emulate their idols, the Beatles.* **emulation** (noun).

encroach (verb) to go beyond acceptable limits; to trespass. *By quietly seizing more and more authority, Robert Moses continually encroached on the powers of other government leaders.* **encroachment** (noun).

enervate (verb) to reduce the energy or strength of someone or something. *The extended exposure to the sun along with dehydration enervated the shipwrecked crew, leaving them almost too weak to spot the passing vessel.*

engender (verb) to produce, to cause. *Countless disagreements over the proper use of national forests have engendered feelings of hostility between ranchers and environmentalists.*

enhance (verb) to improve in value or quality. *New kitchen appliances will enhance your house and increase the amount of money you'll make when you sell it.* **enhancement** (noun).

enmity (noun) hatred, hostility, ill will. *Long-standing enmity, like that between the*

word list

Protestants and Catholics in Northern Ireland, is difficult to overcome.

enthrall (verb) to enchant or charm. *The Swedish singer Jenny Lind enthralled American audiences in the nineteenth century with her beauty and talent.*

ephemeral (adjective) quickly disappearing; transient. *Stardom in pop music is ephemeral; many of the top acts of ten years ago are forgotten today.*

equanimity (noun) calmness of mind, especially under stress. *FDR had the gift of facing the great crises of his presidency—the Depression and the Second World War—with equanimity and even humor.*

eradicate (verb) to destroy completely. *American society has failed to eradicate racism, although some of its worst effects have been reduced.*

espouse (verb) to take up as a cause; to adopt. *No politician in America today will openly espouse racism, although some behave and speak in racially prejudiced ways.*

euphoric (adjective) a feeling of extreme happiness and well-being; elation. *One often feels euphoric during the earliest days of a new love affair.* **euphoria** (noun).

evanescent (adjective) vanishing like a vapor; fragile and transient. *As she walked by, the evanescent fragrance of her perfume reached me for just an instant.*

exacerbate (verb) to make worse or more severe. *The roads in our town already have too much traffic; building a new shopping mall will exacerbate the problem.*

exasperate (verb) to irritate or annoy. *Because she was trying to study, Sharon was exasperated by the yelling of her neighbors' children.*

exculpate (verb) to free from blame or guilt. *When someone else confessed to the crime, the previous suspect was exculpated.* **exculpation** (noun), **exculpatory** (adjective).

exemplary (adjective) worthy to serve as a model. *The Baldrige Award is given to a company with exemplary standards of excellence in products and service.* **exemplar** (noun), **exemplify** (verb).

exonerate (verb) to free from blame. *Although the truck driver was suspected at first of being involved in the bombing, later evidence exonerated him.* **exoneration** (noun), **exonerative** (adjective).

expansive (adjective) broad and large; speaking openly and freely. *The LBJ Ranch is located on an expansive tract of land in Texas. Over dinner, she became expansive in describing her dreams for the future.*

expedite (verb) to carry out promptly. *As the flood waters rose, the governor ordered state agencies to expedite their rescue efforts.*

expertise (noun) skill, mastery. *The software company was eager to hire new graduates with programming expertise.*

expiate (verb) to atone for. *The president's apology to the survivors of the notorious Tuskegee experiments was his attempt to expiate the nation's guilt over their mistreatment.* **expiation** (noun).

expropriate (verb) to seize ownership of. *When the Communists came to power in China, they expropriated most businesses and turned them over to government-appointed managers.* **expropriation** (noun).

extant (adjective) currently in existence. *Of the seven ancient Wonders of the World, only the pyramids of Egypt are still extant.*

extenuate (verb) to make less serious. *Jeanine's guilt is extenuated by the fact that she was only twelve when she committed the theft.* **extenuating** (adjective), **extenuation** (noun).

extol (verb) to greatly praise. *At the party convention, speaker after speaker rose to extol their candidate for the presidency.*

extricate (verb) to free from a difficult or complicated situation. *Much of the humor in the TV show I Love Lucy comes in watching Lucy try to extricate herself from the problems she creates by fibbing or trickery.* **extricable** (adjective).

extrinsic (adjective) not an innate part or aspect of something; external. *The high price of old baseball cards is due to extrinsic factors, such as the nostalgia felt by baseball fans for the stars of their youth, rather than the inherent beauty or value of the cards themselves.*

exuberant (adjective) wildly joyous and enthusiastic. *As the final seconds of the game ticked away, the fans of the winning team began an exuberant celebration.* **exuberance** (noun).

F

facile (adjective) easy; shallow or superficial. *The one-minute political commercial favors a candidate with facile opinions rather than serious, thoughtful solutions.* **facilitate** (verb), **facility** (noun).

fallacy (noun) an error in fact or logic. *It's a fallacy to think that "natural" means "healthful"; after all, the deadly poison arsenic is completely natural.* **fallacious** (adjective).

felicitous (adjective) pleasing, fortunate, apt. *The sudden blossoming of the dogwood trees on the morning of Matt's wedding seemed a felicitous sign of good luck.* **felicity** (noun).

feral (adjective) wild. *The garbage dump was inhabited by a pack of feral dogs that had escaped from their owners and become completely wild.*

fervent (adjective) full of intense feeling; ardent, zealous. *In the days just after his religious conversion, his piety was at its most fervent.* **fervid** (adjective), **fervor** (noun).

flagrant (adjective) obviously wrong; offensive. *Nixon was forced to resign the presidency after a series of flagrant crimes against the U.S. Constitution.* **flagrancy** (noun).

flamboyant (adjective) very colorful, showy, or elaborate. *At Mardi Gras, partygoers compete to show off the most wild and flamboyant outfits.*

florid (adjective) flowery, fancy; reddish. *The grand ballroom was decorated in a florid style. Years of heavy drinking had given him a florid complexion.*

foppish (adjective) describing a man who is foolishly vain about his dress or appearance. *The foppish character of the 1890s wore bright-colored spats and a top hat; in the 1980s, he wore fancy suspenders and a shirt with a contrasting collar.* **fop** (noun).

formidable (adjective) awesome, impressive, or frightening. *According to his plaque in the Baseball Hall of Fame, pitcher Tom Seaver turned the New York Mets "from lovable losers into formidable foes."*

fortuitous (adjective) lucky, fortunate. *Although the mayor claimed credit for the falling crime rate, it was really caused by several fortuitous trends.*

fractious (adjective) troublesome, unruly. *Members of the British Parliament are often fractious, shouting insults and sarcastic questions during debates.*

fragility (noun) the quality of being easy to break; delicacy, weakness. *Because of their fragility, few stained-glass windows from the early Middle Ages have survived.* **fragile** (adjective).

fraternize (verb) to associate with on friendly terms. *Although baseball players aren't supposed to fraternize with their opponents, players from opposing teams often chat before games.* **fraternization** (noun).

frenetic (adjective) chaotic, frantic. *The floor of the stock exchange, filled with traders shouting and gesturing, is a scene of frenetic activity.*

frivolity (noun) lack of seriousness; levity. *The frivolity of the Mardi Gras carnival is in contrast to the seriousness of the religious season of Lent that follows.* **frivolous** (adjective).

frugal (adjective) spending little. *With our last few dollars, we bought a frugal dinner: a loaf of bread and a piece of cheese.* **frugality** (noun).

fugitive (noun) someone trying to escape. *When two prisoners broke out of the local jail, police were warned to keep an eye out for the fugitives.* **fugitive** (adjective).

G

gargantuan (adjective) huge, colossal. *The building of the Great Wall of China was one of the most gargantuan projects ever undertaken.*

genial (adjective) friendly, gracious. *A good host welcomes all visitors in a warm and genial fashion.*

grandiose (adjective) overly large, pretentious, or showy. *Among Hitler's grandiose plans for Berlin was a gigantic building with a dome several times larger than any ever built.* **grandiosity** (noun).

gratuitous (adjective) given freely or without cause. *Since her opinion was not requested, her harsh criticism of his singing seemed a gratuitous insult.*

gregarious (adjective) enjoying the company of others; sociable. *Naturally gregarious, Emily is a popular member of several clubs and a sought-after lunch companion.*

guileless (adjective) without cunning; innocent. *Deborah's guileless personality and complete honesty make it hard for her to survive in the harsh world of politics.*

gullible (adjective) easily fooled. *When the sweepstakes entry form arrived bearing the message, "You may be a winner!" my gullible neighbor tried to claim a prize.* **gullibility** (noun).

H

hackneyed (adjective) without originality, trite. *When someone invented the phrase, "No pain, no gain," it was clever, but now it is so commonly heard that it seems hackneyed.*

haughty (adjective) overly proud. *The fashion model strode down the runway, her hips thrust forward and a haughty expression, like a sneer, on her face.* **haughtiness** (noun).

hedonist (noun) someone who lives mainly to pursue pleasure. *Having inherited great wealth, he chose to live the life of a hedonist, traveling the world in luxury.* **hedonism** (noun), **hedonistic** (adjective).

heinous (adjective) very evil, hateful. *The massacre by Pol Pot of more than a million Cambodians is one of the twentieth century's most heinous crimes.*

hierarchy (noun) a ranking of people, things, or ideas from highest to lowest. *A cabinet secretary ranks just below the president and vice president in the hierarchy of the executive branch.* **hierarchical** (adjective).

hypocrisy (noun) a false pretense of virtue. *When the sexual misconduct of the television preacher was exposed, his followers were shocked at his hypocrisy.* **hypocritical** (adjective).

I

iconoclast (noun) someone who attacks traditional beliefs or institutions. *Comedian Stephen Colbert enjoys his reputation as an iconoclast, though people in power often resent his satirical jabs.* **iconoclasm** (noun), **iconoclastic** (adjective).

idiosyncratic (adjective) peculiar to an individual; eccentric. *Cyndi Lauper sings pop music in an idiosyncratic style, mingling high-pitched whoops and squeals with throaty gurgles.* **idiosyncrasy** (noun).

idolatry (noun) the worship of a person, thing, or institution as a god. *In Communist China, Chairman Mao was the subject of idolatry; his picture was displayed everywhere, and millions of Chinese memorized his sayings.* **idolatrous** (adjective).

impartial (adjective) fair, equal, unbiased. *If a judge is not impartial, then all of her rulings are questionable.* **impartiality** (noun).

impeccable (adjective) flawless. *The crooks printed impeccable copies of the Super Bowl tickets, making it impossible to distinguish them from the real ones.*

impetuous (adjective) acting hastily or impulsively. *Stuart's resignation was an impetuous act; he did it without thinking, and he soon regretted it.* **impetuosity** (noun).

impinge (verb) to encroach upon, touch, or affect. *You have a right to do whatever you want, so long as your actions don't impinge on the rights of others.*

implicit (adjective) understood without being openly expressed; implied. *Although most clubs had no rules excluding minorities, many had an implicit understanding that no member of a minority group would be allowed to join.*

impute (verb) to credit or give responsibility to; to attribute. *Although Helena's comments embarrassed me, I don't impute any ill will to her; I think she didn't realize what she was saying.* **imputation** (noun).

inarticulate (adjective) unable to speak or express oneself clearly and understandably. *A skilled athlete may be an inarticulate public speaker, as demonstrated by many post-game interviews.*

incisive (adjective) clear and direct expression. *Franklin settled the debate with a few incisive remarks that summed up the issue perfectly.*

incompatible (adjective) unable to exist together; conflicting. *Many people hold seemingly incompatible beliefs: for example, supporting the death penalty while believing in the sacredness of human life.* **incompatibility** (noun).

inconsequential (adjective) of little importance. *When the flat screen TV was delivered, it was a different shade of gray* than I expected, but the difference was inconsequential.

incontrovertible (adjective) impossible to question. *The fact that Alexandra's fingerprints were the only ones on the murder weapon made her guilt seem incontrovertible.*

incorrigible (adjective) impossible to manage or reform. *Lou is an incorrigible trickster, constantly playing practical jokes no matter how much his friends complain.*

incremental (adjective) increasing gradually by small amounts. *Although the initial cost of the Medicare program was small, the incremental expenses have grown to be very large.* **increment** (noun).

incriminate (verb) to give evidence of guilt. *The fifth amendment to the Constitution says that no one is required to reveal information that would incriminate him or her in a crime.* **incriminating** (adjective).

incumbent (noun) someone who occupies an office or position. *It is often difficult for a challenger to win a seat in Congress from the incumbent.* **incumbency** (noun), **incumbent** (adjective).

indeterminate (adjective) not definitely known. *The college plans to enroll an indeterminate number of students; the size of the class will depend on the number of applicants and how many accept offers of admission.* **determine** (verb).

indifferent (adjective) unconcerned, apathetic. *The mayor's small proposed budget for education suggests that he is indifferent to the needs of our schools.* **indifference** (noun).

indistinct (adjective) unclear, uncertain. *We could see boats on the water, but in the thick morning fog their shapes were indistinct.*

indomitable (adjective) unable to be conquered or controlled. *The world admired the indomitable spirit of Nelson Mandela; he remained courageous despite years of imprisonment.*

induce (verb) to cause. *The doctor prescribed a medicine that was supposed to induce a lowering of the blood pressure.* **induction** (noun).

ineffable (adjective) difficult to describe or express. *He gazed in silence at the sunrise over the Taj Mahal, his eyes reflecting an ineffable sense of wonder.*

inevitable (adjective) unable to be avoided. *Once the Japanese attacked Pearl Harbor, American involvement in World War II was inevitable.* **inevitability** (noun).

inexorable (adjective) unable to be deterred; relentless. *It's difficult to imagine how the mythic character of Oedipus could have avoided his evil destiny; his fate appears inexorable.*

ingenious (adjective) showing cleverness and originality. *The Post-it note is an ingenious solution to a common problem—how to mark papers without spoiling them.* **ingenuity** (noun).

inherent (adjective) naturally part of something. *Compromise is inherent in democracy, since everyone cannot get his or her way.* **inhere** (verb), **inherence** (noun).

innate (adjective) inborn, native. *Not everyone who takes piano lessons becomes a fine musician, which shows that music requires innate talent as well as training.*

innocuous (adjective) harmless, inoffensive. *I was surprised that Melissa took offense at such an innocuous joke.*

inoculate (verb) to prevent a disease by infusing with a disease-causing organism. *Pasteur found he could prevent rabies by inoculating patients with the virus that causes the disease.* **inoculation** (noun).

insipid (adjective) flavorless, uninteresting. *Some TV shows are so insipid that you can watch them while reading without missing a thing.* **insipidity** (noun).

insolence (noun) an attitude or behavior that is bold and disrespectful. *Some feel that news reporters who shout questions at the president are behaving with insolence.* **insolent** (adjective).

insular (adjective) narrow or isolated in attitude or viewpoint. *Americans are famous for their insular attitudes; they seem to think that nothing important has ever happened outside of their country.* **insularity** (noun).

insurgency (noun) uprising, rebellion. *The angry townspeople had begun an insurgency bordering on downright revolution; they were collecting arms, holding secret meetings, and refusing to pay certain taxes.* **insurgent** (adjective).

integrity (noun) honesty, uprightness; soundness, completeness. *"Honest Abe" Lincoln is considered a model of political* *integrity. Inspectors examined the building's support beams and foundation and found no reason to doubt its structural integrity.*

interlocutor (noun) someone taking part in a dialogue or conversation. *Annoyed by the constant questions from someone in the crowd, the speaker challenged his interlocutor to offer a better plan.* **interlocutory** (adjective).

interlude (noun) an interrupting period or performance. *The two most dramatic scenes in* King Lear *are separated, strangely, by a comic interlude starring the king's jester.*

interminable (adjective) endless or seemingly endless. *Addressing the United Nations, Castro announced, "We will be brief"—then delivered an interminable 4-hour speech.*

intransigent (adjective) unwilling to compromise. *Despite the mediator's attempts to suggest a fair solution, the two parties were intransigent, forcing a showdown.* **intransigence** (noun).

intrepid (adjective) fearless and resolute. *Only an intrepid adventurer is willing to undertake the long and dangerous trip by sled to the South Pole.* **intrepidity** (noun).

intrusive (adjective) forcing a way in without being welcome. *The legal requirement of a search warrant is supposed to protect Americans from intrusive searches by the police.* **intrude** (verb), **intrusion** (noun).

intuitive (adjective) known directly, without apparent thought or effort. *An experienced chess player sometimes has an intuitive sense of the best move to make, even if she can't explain it.* **intuit** (verb), **intuition** (noun).

inundate (verb) to flood; to overwhelm. *As soon as the playoff tickets went on sale, eager fans inundated the box office with orders.*

invariable (adjective) unchanging, constant. *When writing a book, it was her invariable habit to rise at 6 a.m. and work at her desk from 7 to 12.* **invariability** (noun).

inversion (noun) a turning backwards, inside-out, or upside-down; a reversal. *Latin poetry often features inversion of word order; for example, the first line of Virgil's* Aeneid: *"Arms and the man I sing."* **invert** (verb), **inverted** (adjective).

inveterate (adjective) persistent, habitual. *It's very difficult for an inveterate gambler to give up the pastime.* **inveteracy** (noun).

invigorate (verb) to give energy to, to stimulate. *As her car climbed the mountain road, Lucinda felt invigorated by the clear air and the cool breezes.*

invincible (adjective) impossible to conquer or overcome. *For three years at the height of his career, boxer Mike Tyson seemed invincible.*

inviolable (adjective) impossible to attack or trespass upon. *In the president's remote hideaway at Camp David, guarded by the Secret Service, his privacy is, for once, inviolable.*

irrational (adjective) unreasonable. *Richard knew that his fear of insects was irrational, but he was unable to overcome it.* **irrationality** (noun).

irresolute (adjective) uncertain how to act, indecisive. *The line in the ice cream shop grew as the irresolute child wavered between her two favorite ice cream flavors before finally choosing one.* **irresolution** (noun).

J

jeopardize (verb) to put in danger. *Terrorist attacks jeopardize the fragile peace in the Middle East.* **jeopardy** (noun).

juxtapose (verb) to put side by side. *Juxtaposing the two editorials revealed the enormous differences in the writers' opinions.* **juxtaposition** (noun).

L

languid (adjective) without energy; slow, sluggish, listless. *The hot, humid weather of late August can make anyone feel languid.* **languish** (verb), **languor** (noun).

latent (adjective) not currently obvious or active; hidden. *Although he had committed only a single act of violence, the examining psychiatrist said it's likely he always had a latent tendency toward violence.* **latency** (noun).

laudatory (adjective) giving praise. *The ads for the movie are filled with laudatory comments from critics.*

lenient (adjective) mild, soothing, or forgiving. *The judge was known for his lenient disposition; he rarely imposed long jail sentences on criminals.* **leniency** (noun).

lethargic (adjective) lacking energy; sluggish. *Visitors to the zoo are surprised that the lions appear so lethargic, but, in the wild, lions sleep up to 18 hours a day.* **lethargy** (noun).

liability (noun) an obligation or debt; a weakness or drawback. *The insurance company had a liability of millions of dollars after the town was destroyed by a tornado. Slowness afoot is a serious liability in an aspiring basketball player.* **liable** (adjective).

lithe (adjective) flexible and graceful. *The ballet dancer was almost as lithe as a cat.*

longevity (noun) length of life; durability. *The reduction in early deaths from infectious diseases is responsible for most of the increase in human longevity over the past two centuries.*

lucid (adjective) clear and understandable. *Hawking's A Short History of the Universe is a lucid explanation of modern scientific theories about the origin of the universe.* **lucidity** (noun).

lurid (adjective) shocking, gruesome. *While the serial killer was on the loose, the newspapers were filled with lurid stories about his crimes.*

M

malediction (noun) curse. *In the fairy tale "Sleeping Beauty," the princess is trapped in a death-like sleep because of the malediction uttered by an angry witch.*

malevolence (noun) hatred, ill will. *Critics say that Iago, the villain in Shakespeare's* Othello, *seems to exhibit malevolence with no real cause.* **malevolent** (adjective).

malinger (verb) to pretend incapacity or illness to avoid a duty or work. *During the labor dispute, hundreds of employees malingered, forcing the company to slow production and costing it millions in profits.*

malleable (adjective) able to be changed, shaped, or formed by outside pressures. *Gold is a very useful metal because it is so malleable. A child's personality is malleable and deeply influenced by the things his or her parents say and do.* **malleability** (noun).

mandate (noun) order, command. *The new policy of using only organic produce in the restaurant went into effect as soon as the manager issued his mandate about it.* **mandate** (verb), **mandatory** (adjective).

maturation (noun) the process of becoming fully grown or developed. *Free markets in the former Communist nations are likely to operate smoothly only after a long period of maturation.* **mature** (adjective and verb), **maturity** (noun).

mediate (verb) to act to reconcile differences between two parties. *During the baseball strike, both the players and the club owners were willing to have the president mediate the dispute.* **mediation** (noun).

mediocrity (noun) the state of being middling or poor in quality. *The New York Mets finished in ninth place in 1968 but won the world's championship in 1969, going from horrible to great in a single year and skipping mediocrity.* **mediocre** (adjective).

mercurial (adjective) changing quickly and unpredictably. *The mercurial personality of Robin Williams, with his many voices and styles, made him perfect for the role of the ever-changing genie in* Aladdin.

meticulous (adjective) very careful with details. *Repairing watches calls for a craftsperson who is patient and meticulous.*

mimicry (noun) imitation, aping. *The continued popularity of Elvis Presley has given rise to a class of entertainers who make a living through mimicry of "The King."* **mimic** (noun and verb).

misconception (noun) a mistaken idea. *Columbus sailed west with the misconception that he would reach the shores of Asia.* **misconceive** (verb).

mitigate (verb) to make less severe; to relieve. *Wallace certainly committed the assault, but the verbal abuse he'd received helps to explain his behavior and somewhat mitigates his guilt.* **mitigation** (noun).

modicum (noun) a small amount. *The plan for your new business is well designed; with a modicum of luck, you should be successful.*

mollify (verb) to soothe or calm; to appease. *Samantha tried to mollify the angry customer by promising him a full refund.*

morose (adjective) gloomy, sullen. *After Chuck's girlfriend dumped him, he lay* around the house for a couple of days, feeling morose.

mundane (adjective) everyday, ordinary, commonplace. *Moviegoers in the 1930s liked the glamorous films of Fred Astaire because they provided an escape from the mundane problems of life during the Great Depression.*

munificent (adjective) very generous; lavish. *Ted Turner's billion-dollar donation to the United Nations was one of the most munificent acts of charity in history.* **munificence** (noun).

mutable (adjective) likely to change. *A politician's reputation can be highly mutable, as seen in the case of Harry Truman—mocked during his lifetime, revered afterward.*

N

narcissistic (adjective) showing excessive love for oneself; egoistic. *Andre's room, decorated with photos of himself and the sports trophies he has won, suggests a narcissistic personality.* **narcissism** (noun).

nocturnal (adjective) of the night; active at night. *Travelers on the Underground Railroad escaped from slavery to the North by a series of nocturnal flights. The eyes of nocturnal animals must be sensitive in dim light.*

nonchalant (adjective) appearing to be unconcerned. *Unlike the other players on the football team who pumped their fists when their names were announced, John ran on the field with a nonchalant wave.* **nonchalance** (noun).

nondescript (adjective) without distinctive qualities; drab. *The bank robber's clothes were nondescript; none of the witnesses could remember their color or style.*

notorious (adjective) famous, especially for evil actions or qualities. *Warner Brothers produced a series of movies about notorious gangsters such as John Dillinger and Al Capone.* **notoriety** (noun).

novice (noun) beginner. *Lifting your head before you finish your swing is a typical mistake committed by the novice at golf.*

nuance (noun) a subtle difference or quality. *At first glance, Monet's paintings of water lilies all look much alike, but the more you study them, the more you appreciate the nuances of color and shading that distinguish them.*

nurture (verb) to nourish or help to grow. *The money given by the National Endowment for the Arts helps nurture local arts organizations throughout the country.* **nurture** (noun).

O

obdurate (adjective) unwilling to change; stubborn, inflexible. *Despite the many pleas he received, the governor was obdurate in his refusal to grant clemency to the convicted murderer.*

objective (adjective) dealing with observable facts rather than opinions or interpretations. *When a legal case involves a shocking crime, it may be hard for a judge to remain objective in his rulings.*

oblivious (adjective) unaware, unconscious. *Karen practiced her oboe with complete concentration, oblivious to the noise and activity around her.* **oblivion** (noun), **obliviousness** (noun).

obscure (adjective) little known; hard to understand. *Mendel was an obscure monk until decades after his death when his scientific work was finally discovered. Most people find the writings of James Joyce obscure; hence the popularity of books that explain his books.* **obscure** (verb), **obscurity** (noun).

obsessive (adjective) haunted or preoccupied by an idea or feeling. *His concern with cleanliness became so obsessive that he washed his hands twenty times every day.* **obsess** (verb), **obsession** (noun).

obsolete (adjective) no longer current; old-fashioned. *W. H. Auden said that his ideal landscape would include water wheels, wooden grain mills, and other forms of obsolete machinery.* **obsolescence** (noun).

obstinate (adjective) stubborn, unyielding. *Despite years of effort, the problem of drug abuse remains obstinate.* **obstinacy** (noun).

obtrusive (adjective) overly prominent. *Philip should sing more softly; his bass is so obtrusive that the other singers can barely be heard.* **obtrude** (verb), **obtrusion** (noun).

ominous (adjective) foretelling evil. *Ominous black clouds gathered on the horizon, for* *a violent storm was fast approaching.* **omen** (noun).

onerous (adjective) heavy, burdensome. *The hero Hercules was ordered to clean the Augean Stables, one of several onerous tasks known as "the labors of Hercules."* **onus** (noun).

opportunistic (adjective) eagerly seizing chances as they arise. *When Princess Diana died suddenly, opportunistic publishers quickly released books about her life and death.* **opportunism** (noun).

opulent (adjective) rich, lavish. *The mansion of newspaper tycoon Hearst is famous for its opulent decor.* **opulence** (noun).

ornate (adjective) highly decorated, elaborate. *Baroque architecture is often highly ornate, featuring surfaces covered with carving, sinuous curves, and painted scenes.*

ostentatious (adjective) overly showy, pretentious. *To show off his wealth, the millionaire threw an ostentatious party featuring a full orchestra, a famous singer, and tens of thousands of dollars' worth of food.*

ostracize (verb) to exclude from a group. *In Biblical times, those who suffered from the disease of leprosy were ostracized and forced to live alone.* **ostracism** (noun).

P

pallid (adjective) pale; dull. *Working all day in the coal mine had given him a pallid complexion. The new musical offers only pallid entertainment: the music is lifeless, the acting dull, the story absurd.*

parched (adjective) very dry; thirsty. *After two months without rain, the crops were shriveled and parched by the sun.* **parch** (verb).

pariah (noun) outcast. *Accused of robbery, he became a pariah; his neighbors stopped talking to him, and people he'd considered friends no longer called.*

partisan (adjective) reflecting strong allegiance to a particular party or cause. *The vote on the president's budget was strictly partisan: every member of the president's party voted yes, and all others voted no.* **partisan** (noun).

pathology (noun) disease or the study of disease; extreme abnormality. *Some people believe that high rates of crime are symptoms of an underlying social pathology.* **pathological** (adjective).

pellucid (adjective) very clear; transparent; easy to understand. *The water in the mountain stream was cold and pellucid. Thanks to the professor's pellucid explanation, I finally understand relativity theory.*

penitent (adjective) feeling sorry for past crimes or sins. *Having grown penitent, he wrote a long letter of apology, asking forgiveness.*

penurious (adjective) extremely frugal; stingy. *Haunted by memories of poverty, he lived in penurious fashion, driving a 12-year-old car and wearing only the cheapest clothes.* **penury** (noun).

perceptive (adjective) quick to notice, observant. *With his perceptive intelligence, Holmes was the first to notice the importance of this clue.* **perceptible** (adjective), **perception** (noun).

perfidious (adjective) disloyal, treacherous. *Although he was one of the most talented generals of the American Revolution, Benedict Arnold is remembered today as a perfidious betrayer of his country.* **perfidy** (noun).

perfunctory (adjective) unenthusiastic, routine, or mechanical. *When the play opened, the actors sparkled, but by the thousandth night their performance had become perfunctory.*

permeate (verb) to spread through or penetrate. *Little by little, the smell of gas from the broken pipe permeated the house.*

persevere (adjective) to continue despite difficulties. *Although several of her teammates dropped out of the marathon, Gail persevered.* **perseverance** (noun).

perspicacity (noun) keenness of observation or understanding. *Journalist Murray Kempton was famous for the perspicacity of his comments on social and political issues.* **perspicacious** (adjective).

peruse (verb) to examine or study. *Caroline perused the contract carefully before she signed it.* **perusal** (noun).

pervasive (adjective) spreading throughout. *As news of the disaster reached the town, a pervasive sense of gloom could be felt.* **pervade** (verb).

phlegmatic (adjective) sluggish and unemotional in temperament. *It was surprising* to see Tom, *who is normally so phlegmatic, acting excited.*

placate (verb) to soothe or appease. *The waiter tried to placate the angry customer with the offer of a free dessert.* **placatory** (adjective).

plastic (adjective) able to be molded or reshaped. *Because it is highly plastic, clay is an easy material for beginning sculptors to use.*

plausible (adjective) apparently believable. *According to the judge, the defense attorney's argument was both powerful and plausible.* **plausibility** (noun).

polarize (verb) to separate into opposing groups or forces. *For years, the abortion debate has polarized the American people, with many people voicing extreme views and few trying to find a middle ground.* **polarization** (noun).

portend (verb) to indicate a future event; to forebode. *According to folklore, a red sky at dawn portends a day of stormy weather.*

potentate (noun) a powerful ruler. *The Tsar of Russia was one of the last hereditary potentates of Europe.*

pragmatism (noun) a belief in approaching problems through practical rather than theoretical means. *Roosevelt's approach to the Great Depression was based on pragmatism: "Try something," he said. "If it doesn't work, try something else."* **pragmatic** (adjective).

preamble (noun) an introductory statement. *The preamble to the Constitution begins with the famous words, "We the people of the United States of America..."*

precocious (adjective) mature at an unusually early age. *Picasso was so precocious as an artist that, at nine, he is said to have painted far better pictures than his teacher.* **precocity** (noun).

predatory (adjective) living by killing and eating other animals; exploiting others for personal gain. *The tiger is the largest predatory animal native to Asia. Microsoft has been accused of predatory business practices that prevent other software companies from competing with it.* **predation** (noun), **predator** (noun).

predilection (noun) a liking or preference. *To relax from his presidential duties, Kennedy had a predilection for spy novels featuring James Bond.*

predominant (adjective) greatest in numbers or influence. *Although hundreds of religions are practiced in India, the predominant faith is Hinduism.* **predominance** (noun), **predominate** (verb).

prepossessing (adjective) attractive. *Smart, lovely, and talented, she has all the prepossessing qualities that mark a potential movie star.*

presumptuous (adjective) going beyond the limits of courtesy or appropriateness. *The senator winced when the presumptuous young staffer addressed him as "Chuck."* **presume** (verb), **presumption** (noun).

pretentious (adjective) claiming excessive value or importance. *For a shoe salesman to call himself a "Personal Foot Apparel Consultant" seems awfully pretentious.* **pretension** (noun).

procrastinate (verb) to put off, to delay. *If you habitually procrastinate, try this technique: never touch a piece of paper without either filing it, responding to it, or throwing it out.* **procrastination** (noun).

profane (adjective) impure, unholy. *It is inappropriate and rude to use profane language in a church.* **profane** (verb), **profanity** (noun).

proficient (adjective) skillful, adept. *A proficient artist, Louise quickly and accurately sketched the scene.* **proficiency** (noun).

proliferate (verb) to increase or multiply. *Over the past twenty-five years, high-tech companies have proliferated in northern California, Massachusetts, and Seattle.* **proliferation** (noun).

prolific (adjective) producing many offspring or creations. *With more than 300 books to his credit, Isaac Asimov was one of the most prolific writers of all time.*

prominence (noun) the quality of standing out; fame. *Barack Obama rose to political prominence after his keynote address to the 2004 Democratic National Convention.* **prominent** (adjective).

promulgate (verb) to make public, to declare. *Lincoln signed the proclamation that freed the slaves in 1862, but he waited several months to promulgate it.*

propagate (verb) to cause to grow; to foster. *John Smithson's will left his fortune for the founding of an institution to propagate knowledge, without saying whether that meant a university, a library, or a museum.* **propagation** (noun).

propriety (noun) appropriateness. *The principal questioned the propriety of the discussion the teacher had with her students about another instructor's gambling addiction.*

prosaic (adjective) everyday, ordinary, dull. *"Paul's Case" tells the story of a boy who longs to escape from the prosaic life of a clerk into a world of wealth, glamour, and beauty.*

protagonist (noun) the main character in a story or play; the main supporter of an idea. *Leopold Bloom is the protagonist of James Joyce's great novel* Ulysses.

provocative (adjective) likely to stimulate emotions, ideas, or controversy. *The demonstrators began chanting obscenities, a provocative act that they hoped would cause the police to lose control.* **provoke** (verb), **provocation** (noun).

proximity (noun) closeness, nearness. *Neighborhood residents were angry over the proximity of the sewage plant to the local school.* **proximate** (adjective).

prudent (adjective) wise, cautious, and practical. *A prudent investor will avoid putting all of her money into any single investment.* **prudence** (noun), **prudential** (adjective).

pugnacious (adjective) combative, bellicose, truculent; ready to fight. *Ty Cobb, the pugnacious outfielder for the Detroit Tigers, got into more than his fair share of brawls, both on and off the field.* **pugnacity** (noun).

punctilious (adjective) very concerned about proper forms of behavior and manners. *A punctilious dresser like James would rather skip the party altogether than wear the wrong color tie.* **punctilio** (noun).

pundit (noun) someone who offers opinions in an authoritative style. *The Sunday morning talk shows are filled with pundits, each with his or her own theory about the week's political news.*

punitive (adjective) inflicting punishment. *The jury awarded the plaintiff one million dollars in punitive damages, hoping to teach the defendant a lesson.*

purify (verb) to make pure, clean, or perfect. *The new plant is supposed to purify the drinking water provided to everyone in the nearby towns.* **purification** (noun).

Q

quell (verb) to quiet, to suppress. *It took a huge number of police officers to quell the rioting.*

querulous (adjective) complaining, whining. *The nursing home attendant needed a lot of patience to care for the three querulous, unpleasant residents on his floor.*

R

rancorous (adjective) expressing bitter hostility. *Many Americans are disgusted by recent political campaigns, which seem more rancorous than ever before.* **rancor** (noun).

rationale (noun) an underlying reason or explanation. *Looking at the sad faces of his employees, it was hard for the company president to explain the rationale for closing the business.*

raze (verb) to completely destroy; demolish. *The old Coliseum building will soon be razed to make room for a new hotel.*

reciprocate (verb) to give and take mutually. *If you'll watch my children tonight, I'll reciprocate by taking care of yours tomorrow.* **reciprocity** (noun).

reclusive (adjective) withdrawn from society. *During the last years of her life, actress Greta Garbo led a reclusive existence, rarely appearing in public.* **recluse** (noun).

reconcile (verb) to make consistent or harmonious. *FDR's greatness as a leader can be seen in his ability to reconcile the demands and values of the varied groups that supported him.* **reconciliation** (noun).

recrimination (noun) a retaliatory accusation. *After the governor called his opponent unethical, his opponent angrily replied with recriminations that the governor was a hypocrite.* **recriminate** (verb), **recriminatory** (adjective).

recuperate (verb) to regain health after an illness. *Although Marie left the hospital two days after her operation, it took her a few weeks to fully recuperate.* **recuperation** (noun), **recuperative** (adjective).

redoubtable (adjective) inspiring respect, awe, or fear. *Johnson's knowledge, experience, and personal clout made him a redoubtable political opponent.*

refurbish (verb) to fix up; renovate. *It took three days' work by a team of carpenters, painters, and decorators to completely refurbish the apartment.*

refute (verb) to prove false. *The company invited reporters to visit their plant in an effort to refute the charges of unsafe working conditions.* **refutation** (noun).

relevance (noun) connection to the matter at hand; pertinence. *Testimony in a criminal trial may be admitted only if it has clear relevance to the question of guilt or innocence.* **relevant** (adjective).

remedial (adjective) serving to remedy, cure, or correct some condition. *Affirmative action can be justified as a remedial step to help minority members overcome the effects of past discrimination.* **remediation** (noun), **remedy** (verb).

remorse (noun) a painful sense of guilt over wrongdoing. *In Poe's story* The Tell-Tale Heart, *a murderer is driven insane by remorse over his crime.* **remorseful** (adjective).

remuneration (noun) pay. *In a civil lawsuit, the attorney often receives part of the financial settlement as his or her remuneration.* **remunerate** (verb), **remunerative** (adjective).

renovate (verb) to renew by repairing or rebuilding. *The television program* This Old House *shows how skilled craftspeople renovate houses.* **renovation** (noun).

renunciation (noun) the act of rejecting or refusing something. *King Edward VII's renunciation of the British throne was caused by his desire to marry an American divorcee, something he couldn't do as king.* **renounce** (verb).

replete (adjective) filled abundantly. *Graham's book is replete with wonderful stories about the famous people she has known.*

reprehensible (adjective) deserving criticism or censure. *Although Pete Rose's misdeeds were reprehensible, not all fans agree that he deserves to be excluded from the Baseball Hall of Fame.* **reprehend** (verb), **reprehension** (noun).

repudiate (verb) to reject, to renounce. *After it became known that Duke had been a leader of the Ku Klux Klan, most Republican leaders repudiated him.* **repudiation** (noun).

reputable (adjective) having a good reputation; respected. *Find a reputable auto mechanic by asking your friends for recommendations based on their own experiences.* **reputation** (noun), **repute** (noun).

resilient (adjective) able to recover from difficulty. *A professional athlete must be resilient, able to lose a game one day and come back the next with confidence and enthusiasm.* **resilience** (noun).

resplendent (adjective) glowing, shining. *In late December, midtown New York is resplendent with holiday lights and decorations.* **resplendence** (noun).

responsive (adjective) reacting quickly and appropriately. *The new director of the Internal Revenue Service has promised to make the agency more responsive to public complaints.* **respond** (verb), **response** (noun).

restitution (noun) return of something to its original owner; repayment. *Some Native American leaders are demanding that the U.S. government make restitution for the lands taken from them.*

revere (verb) to admire deeply, to honor. *Millions of people around the world revered Mother Teresa for her saintly generosity.* **reverence** (noun), **reverent** (adjective).

rhapsodize (verb) to praise in a wildly emotional way. *That critic is such a huge fan of Toni Morrison that she will surely rhapsodize over the writer's next novel.* **rhapsodic** (adjective).

S

sagacious (adjective) discerning, wise. *Only a leader as sagacious as Nelson Mandela could have united South Africa so successfully and peacefully.* **sagacity** (noun).

salvage (verb) to save from wreck or ruin. *After the hurricane destroyed her home, she was able to salvage only a few of her belongings.* **salvage** (noun), **salvageable** (adjective).

sanctimonious (adjective) showing false or excessive piety. *The sanctimonious prayers of the TV preacher were interspersed with requests that the viewers send him money.* **sanctimony** (noun).

scapegoat (noun) someone who bears the blame for others' acts; someone hated for no apparent reason. *Although Buckner's error was only one reason the Red Sox lost, many fans made him the scapegoat, booing him mercilessly.*

scrupulous (adjective) acting with extreme care; painstaking. *Disney theme parks are famous for their scrupulous attention to small details.* **scruple** (noun).

scrutinize (verb) to study closely. *The lawyer scrutinized the contract, searching for any sentence that could pose a risk for her client.* **scrutiny** (noun).

secrete (verb) to emit; to hide. *Glands in the mouth secrete saliva, a liquid that helps in digestion. The jewel thieves secreted the necklace in a tin box buried underground.*

sedentary (adjective) requiring much sitting. *When Officer Samson was given a desk job, she had trouble getting used to sedentary work after years on the street.*

sequential (adjective) arranged in an order or series. *The courses for the chemistry major are sequential; you must take them in order, since each course builds on the previous ones.* **sequence** (noun).

serendipity (noun) the act of lucky, accidental discoveries. *Great inventions sometimes come about through deliberate research and hard work, sometimes through pure serendipity.* **serendipitous** (adjective).

servile (adjective) like a slave or servant; submissive. *The tycoon demanded that his underlings behave in a servile manner, agreeing quickly with everything he said.* **servility** (noun).

simulated (adjective) imitating something else; artificial. *High-quality simulated gems must be examined under a magnifying glass to be distinguished from real ones.* **simulate** (verb), **simulation** (noun).

solace (verb) to comfort or console. *There was little the rabbi could say to solace the husband after his wife's death.* **solace** (noun).

spontaneous (adjective) happening without plan. *When the news of Kennedy's assassination broke, people everywhere gathered in a spontaneous effort to share their shock and grief.* **spontaneity** (noun).

spurious (adjective) false, fake. *The so-called Piltdown Man, supposed to be the fossil of a primitive human, turned out to be spurious, although who created the hoax is still uncertain.*

squander (verb) to use up carelessly, to waste. *Those who had made donations to the charity were outraged to learn that its director had squandered millions on fancy dinners and first-class travel.*

stagnate (verb) to become stale through lack of movement or change. *Having had no contact with the outside world for generations, Japan's culture gradually stagnated.* **stagnant** (adjective), **stagnation** (noun).

staid (adjective) sedate, serious, and grave. *This college is definitely not a "party school"; the students all work hard, and the campus has a reputation for being staid.*

stimulus (noun) something that excites a response or provokes an action. *The arrival of merchants and missionaries from the West provided a stimulus for change in Japanese society.* **stimulate** (verb).

stoic (adjective) showing little feeling, even in response to pain or sorrow. *A soldier must respond to the death of his comrades in stoic fashion, since the fighting will not stop for his grief.* **stoicism** (noun).

strenuous (adjective) requiring energy and strength. *Hiking in the foothills of the Rockies is fairly easy, but climbing the higher peaks can be strenuous.*

submissive (adjective) accepting the will of others; humble, compliant. *At the end of Ibsen's play* A Doll's House, *Nora leaves her husband and abandons the role of submissive housewife.*

substantiate (verb) verified or supported by evidence. *The charge that Nixon had helped to cover up crimes was substantiated by his comments about it on a series of audio tapes.* **substantiated** (adjective), **substantiation** (noun).

sully (verb) to soil, stain, or defile. *Nixon's misdeeds as president did much to sully the reputation of the American government.*

superficial (adjective) on the surface only; without depth or substance. *Her wound was superficial and required only a light bandage. His superficial attractiveness hides the fact that his personality is lifeless and his mind is dull.* **superficiality** (noun).

superfluous (adjective) more than is needed, excessive. *Once you've won the debate,* *don't keep talking; superfluous arguments will only bore and annoy the audience.*

suppress (verb) to put down or restrain. *As soon as the unrest began, thousands of helmeted police were sent into the streets to suppress the riots.* **suppression** (noun).

surfeit (noun) an excess. *Most American families have a surfeit of food and drink on Thanksgiving Day.* **surfeit** (verb).

surreptitious (adjective) done in secret. *Because Iraq avoided weapons inspections, many believed it had a surreptitious weapons development program.*

surrogate (noun) a substitute. *When the congressman died in office, his wife was named to serve the rest of his term as a surrogate.* **surrogate** (adjective).

sustain (verb) to keep up, to continue; to support. *Because of fatigue, he was unable to sustain the effort needed to finish the marathon.*

T

tactile (adjective) relating to the sense of touch. *The thick brush strokes and gobs of color give the paintings of van Gogh a strongly tactile quality.* **tactility** (noun).

talisman (noun) an object supposed to have magical effects or qualities. *Superstitious people sometimes carry a rabbit's foot, a lucky coin, or some other talisman.*

tangential (adjective) touching lightly; only slightly connected or related. *Having enrolled in a class on African-American history, the students found the teacher's stories about his travels in South America of only tangential interest.* **tangent** (noun).

tedium (noun) boredom. *For most people, watching the Weather Channel for 24 hours would be sheer tedium.* **tedious** (adjective).

temerity (noun) boldness, rashness, excessive daring. *Only someone who didn't understand the danger would have the temerity to try to climb Everest without a guide.* **temerarious** (adjective).

temperance (noun) moderation or restraint in feelings and behavior. *Most professional athletes practice temperance in their personal habits; too much eating or drinking, they know, can harm their performance.* **temperate** (adjective).

tenacious (adjective) clinging, sticky, or persistent. *Tenacious in pursuit of her goal, she applied for the grant unsuccessfully four times before it was finally approved.* **tenacity** (noun).

tentative (adjective) subject to change; uncertain. *A firm schedule has not been established, but the Super Bowl in 2019 has been given the tentative date of February 3.*

terminate (verb) to end, to close. *The Olympic Games terminate with a grand ceremony attended by athletes from every participating country.* **terminal** (noun), **termination** (noun).

terrestrial (adjective) of the Earth. *The movie* Close Encounters of the Third Kind *tells the story of the first contact between beings from outer space and terrestrial humans.*

therapeutic (adjective) curing or helping to cure. *Hot-water spas were popular in the nineteenth century among the sickly, who believed that soaking in the water had therapeutic effects.* **therapy** (noun).

timorous (adjective) fearful, timid. *The cowardly lion approached the throne of the wizard with a timorous look on his face.*

toady (noun) someone who flatters a superior in hopes of gaining favor; a sycophant. *"I can't stand a toady!" declared the movie mogul. "Give me someone who'll tell me the truth—even if it costs him his job!"* **toady** (verb).

tolerant (adjective) accepting, enduring. *San Franciscans have a tolerant attitude about lifestyles: "Live and let live" seems to be their motto.* **tolerate** (verb), **toleration** (noun).

toxin (noun) poison. *DDT is a powerful toxin once used to kill insects but now banned in the United States because of the risk it poses to human life.* **toxic** (adjective).

tranquillity (noun) freedom from disturbance or turmoil; calm. *She moved from New York City to rural Vermont seeking the tranquillity of country life.* **tranquil** (adjective).

transgress (verb) to go past limits; to violate. *No one could fathom why the honor student transgressed by shoplifting hundreds of dollars of merchandise from his favorite clothing store.* **transgression** (noun).

transient (adjective) passing quickly. *Long-term visitors to this hotel pay a* *different rate than transient guests who stay for just a day or two.* **transience** (noun).

transitory (adjective) quickly passing. *Public moods tend to be transitory; people may be anxious and angry one month but relatively content and optimistic the next.* **transition** (noun).

translucent (adjective) letting some light pass through. *Panels of translucent glass let daylight into the room while maintaining privacy.*

transmute (verb) to change in form or substance. *In the Middle Ages, the alchemists tried to discover ways to transmute metals such as iron into gold.* **transmutation** (noun).

treacherous (adjective) untrustworthy or disloyal; dangerous or unreliable. *Nazi Germany proved to be a treacherous ally, first signing a peace pact with the Soviet Union, then invading. Be careful crossing the rope bridge; parts are badly frayed and treacherous.* **treachery** (noun).

tremulous (adjective) trembling or shaking; timid or fearful. *Never having spoken in public before, he began his speech in a tremulous, hesitant voice.*

trite (adjective) boring because of over-familiarity; hackneyed. *Her letters were filled with trite expressions, like "All's well that ends well" and "So far so good."*

truculent (adjective) aggressive, hostile, belligerent. *Hitler's truculent behavior in demanding more territory for Germany made it clear that war was inevitable.* **truculence** (noun).

truncate (verb) to cut off. *The poor copying job truncated the playwright's manuscript: the last page ended in the middle of a scene, halfway through the first act.*

turbulent (adjective) agitated or disturbed. *The night before the championship match, Serena Williams was unable to sleep, her mind turbulent with fears and hopes.* **turbulence** (noun).

U

unheralded (adjective) little known, unexpected. *In a year of big-budget, much-hyped, mega-movies, this unheralded foreign film has surprised everyone with its popularity.*

unpalatable (adjective) distasteful, unpleasant. *Although I agree with the candidate on many issues, I can't vote for her because I find her position on capital punishment unpalatable.*

unparalleled (adjective) with no equal; unique. *Tiger Woods's victory in the Masters golf tournament by a full twelve strokes was an unparalleled accomplishment.*

unstinting (adjective) giving freely and generously. *Eleanor Roosevelt was much admired for her unstinting efforts on behalf of the poor.*

untenable (adjective) impossible to defend. *The theory that this painting is a genuine van Gogh became untenable when the artist who actually painted it came forth.*

untimely (adjective) out of the natural or proper time. *The untimely death of a youthful Princess Diana seemed far more tragic than Mother Teresa's death of old age.*

unyielding (adjective) firm, resolute, obdurate. *Despite criticism, Mario Cuomo was unyielding in his opposition to capital punishment; he vetoed several death penalty bills as governor.*

usurper (noun) someone who takes a place or possession without the right to do so. *Kennedy's most devoted followers tended to regard later presidents as usurpers, holding the office they felt he or his brothers should have held.* **usurp** (verb), **usurpation** (noun).

utilitarian (adjective) purely of practical benefit. *The design of the Model T car was simple and utilitarian, lacking the luxuries found in later models.*

utopia (noun) an imaginary, perfect society. *Those who founded the Oneida community dreamed that it could be a kind of utopia— a prosperous state with complete freedom and harmony.* **utopian** (adjective).

V

validate (verb) to officially approve or confirm. *The election of the president is validated when the members of the Electoral College meet to confirm the choice of the voters.* **valid** (adjective), **validity** (noun).

variegated (adjective) spotted with different colors. *The brilliant, variegated* appearance of butterflies makes them popular among collectors. **variegation** (noun).

venerate (verb) to admire or honor. *In Communist China, Chairman Mao Zedong was venerated as an almost god-like figure.* **venerable** (adjective), **veneration** (noun).

verdant (adjective) green with plant life. *Southern England is famous for its verdant countryside filled with gardens and small farms.* **verdancy** (noun).

vestige (noun) a trace or remainder. *Today's tiny Sherwood Forest is the last vestige of a woodland that once covered most of England.* **vestigial** (adjective).

vex (verb) to irritate, annoy, or trouble. *It vexes me that she never helps with any chores around the house.* **vexation** (noun).

vicarious (adjective) experienced through someone else's actions by way of the imagination. *Great literature broadens our minds by giving us vicarious participation in the lives of other people.*

vindicate (verb) to confirm, justify, or defend. *Lincoln's Gettysburg Address was intended to vindicate the objectives of the Union in the Civil War.*

virtuoso (noun) someone very skilled, especially in an art. *Vladimir Horowitz was one of the great piano virtuosos of the twentieth century.* **virtuosity** (noun).

vivacious (adjective) lively, sprightly. *The role of Maria in* The Sound of Music *is usually played by a charming, vivacious young actress.* **vivacity** (noun).

volatile (adjective) quickly changing; fleeting, transitory; prone to violence. *Public opinion is notoriously volatile; a politician who is very popular one month may be voted out of office the next.* **volatility** (noun).

W

whimsical (adjective) based on a capricious, carefree, or sudden impulse or idea; fanciful, playful. *Dave Barry's* Book of Bad Songs *is filled with the kind of goofy jokes that are typical of his whimsical sense of humor.* **whim** (noun).

Z

zealous (adjective) filled with eagerness, fervor, or passion. *A crowd of the candidate's most zealous supporters greeted her at the airport with banners, signs, and a marching band.* **zeal** (noun), **zealot** (noun), **zealotry** (noun).

word list

List of Synonyms and Antonyms

A

abbreviate
Synonyms—shorten, make concise
Antonyms—lengthen, elongate (to make longer)

abrasive
Synonyms—harsh, rough, irritating
Antonyms—smooth, soft, soothing

abstain
Synonyms—refrain, give up, hold back
Antonyms—give in, indulge (to allow oneself to partake or participate)

acclaim
Synonyms—praise, approve, applaud
Antonyms—blame, condemn, censure (to criticize)

accumulate
Synonyms—acquire, gain, hoard
Antonyms—diminish, give away, squander (to waste)

accuse
Synonyms—challenge, blame, incriminate (to attribute responsibility)
Antonyms—forgive, exonerate (to free from guilt)

adaptable
Synonyms—flexible, changeable
Antonyms—inflexible, rigid

adept
Synonyms—skillful, proficient, competent
Antonyms—inexperienced, incompetent, unskillful

adhere
Synonyms—attach, stick, follow, uphold
Antonyms—detach, disengage, reject

adversary
Synonyms—enemy, opponent, foe, nemesis (an arch enemy)
Antonyms—friend, collaborator, ally (one who collaborates)

adverse
Synonyms—bad, negative
Antonyms—good, positive

aggressive
Synonyms—combative, belligerent (hostile)
Antonyms—peaceful, conciliatory (easily makes amends)

agitate
Synonyms—irritate, anger, upset, stir
Antonyms—soothe, calm, pacify (to calm)

agreeable
Synonyms—pleasant, likeable, delightful
Antonyms—mean, unkind, unpleasant

ambiguous
Synonyms—unclear, vague
Antonyms—clear, straightforward

ambitious
Synonyms—determined, driven, motivated
Antonyms—lazy, unmotivated, unenthusiastic

ambivalent
Synonyms—indecisive, wishy-washy, unsure
Antonyms—decided, determined, sure

amplify
Synonyms—expand, heighten, enlarge
Antonyms—decrease, minimize, diminish

animated
Synonyms—energetic, lively, spirited
Antonyms—lazy, sluggish, depressed

animosity
Synonyms—hostility, resentment, hatred
Antonyms—kindness, friendliness, warmth, compassion (caring)

anomalous
Synonyms—odd, inconsistent, irregular, unusual
Antonyms—commonplace, ordinary, normal, regular

anonymous
Synonyms—nameless, unknown, unidentified
Antonyms—identified, known, recognized

antagonize
Synonyms—irritate, bother, annoy
Antonyms—help, aid, soothe

apathy
Synonyms—indifference, unconcern, disregard (lack of interest)
Antonyms—interest, concern

arbitrary
Synonyms—random, chance, inconsistent
Antonyms—steady, unchanging, reliable, predictable

arid
Synonyms—dry, barren, parched (lacking water)
Antonyms—humid, soaked, well-watered

attentive
Synonyms—interested, observant, aware
Antonyms—unaware, unconcerned, neglectful

astute
Synonyms—quick-witted, intelligent, smart
Antonyms—inept, foolish, slow-witted

atypical
Synonyms—not normal, uncommon, unnatural
Antonyms—normal, regular, common, typical

audacious
Synonyms—outrageous, bold, daring
Antonyms—meek, mild, quiet

audible
Synonyms—perceptible, discernible, distinct (able to be heard)
Antonyms—silent, indistinct (quiet or not able to be heard)

authentic
Synonyms—original, trustworthy, credible
Antonyms—corrupt, untrustworthy, fake

autonomous
Synonyms—independent, self-governing
Antonyms—dependent, helpless, subjugated (controlled by others)

B

baffle
Synonyms—confuse, stump, puzzle
Antonyms—clarify, elucidate (to make clear)

banal
Synonyms—usual, common, ordinary
Antonyms—unusual, different, special

barren
Synonyms—lifeless, empty, unfruitful (not able to support life)
Antonyms—productive, fruitful (able to support life)

belated
Synonyms—late, overdue
Antonyms—prompt, punctual (on time)

benevolent
Synonyms—kind, good-hearted
Antonyms—cruel, evil, malevolent (willing to cause harm)

benign
Synonyms—mild, peaceable, harmless
Antonyms—deadly, dangerous, harmful

berate
Synonyms—scold, criticize, reprimand (to scold or blame)
Antonyms—praise, encourage, uplift

bleak
Synonyms—grim, hopeless, desolate (deserted and empty)
Antonyms—hopeful, cheerful, encouraging

boisterous
Synonyms—noisy, loud, rambunctious (uncontrolled)
Antonyms—quiet, orderly, subdued (calm and under control)

bombastic
Synonyms—boastful, ostentatious (showy), pompous (full of oneself)
Antonyms—restrained, quiet, humble, reserved (private)

buttress
Synonyms—bolster, reinforce, support
Antonyms—weaken

C

cajole
Synonyms—coax, persuade, wheedle (to convince by asking nicely)
Antonyms—order, force, compel

camaraderie
Synonyms—friendship, companionship, togetherness
Antonyms—animosity, isolation

candid
Synonyms—truthful, straightforward, unrehearsed
Antonyms—dishonest, staged, set up

candor
Synonyms—honesty, directness, veracity (truthfulness)
Antonyms—insincerity, deceit, lying

capricious
Synonyms—willful, arbitrary, impulsive (acting without thought)
Antonyms—predictable, steady, sensible

captivate
Synonyms—dazzle, enchant, fascinate
Antonyms—bore, offend, repulse

caustic
Synonyms—burning, hurtful, sarcastic
(cutting or mocking)
Antonyms—soothing, mild, innocuous
(harmless)

chaos
Synonyms—disorder, confusion,
pandemonium (an uproar or hubbub)
Antonyms—harmony, order, tranquility
(peace)

circumvent
Synonyms—go around, avoid, elude (to get
away from)
Antonyms—take on, confront, face

clandestine
Synonyms—secret, undercover, covert,
surreptitious (hidden)
Antonyms—public, open, aboveboard, overt
(open)

cloying
Synonyms—sticky, sentimental, clingy
Antonyms—independent, detached, cool

coerce
Synonyms—force, bully, pressure
Antonyms—coax, cajole, encourage

cogent
Synonyms—powerful, logical, persuasive
Antonyms—unconvincing, ineffective,
illogical

cognizant
Synonyms—aware, informed, sentient
(conscious)
Antonyms—ignorant, oblivious (not
attentive)

coherent
Synonyms—understandable, clear
Antonyms—confused, meaningless

cohesive
Synonyms—close-knit, unified,
interconnected
Antonyms—scattered, disorganized,
fragmented

collaborate
Synonyms—work together, cooperate, join
forces
Antonyms—separate, part ways, conflict

commend
Synonyms—praise, applaud, honor
Antonyms—criticize, put down, disapprove

compatible
Synonyms—harmonious, well-suited,
congenial (friendly)
Antonyms—mismatched, clashing,
incompatible

compel
Synonyms—force, require, pressure
Antonyms—discourage, prevent, dissuade (to
advise against)

competent
Synonyms—skilled, qualified, proficient
(good at)
Antonyms—inept, useless, bungling (prone
to making mistakes)

complacent
Synonyms—self-satisfied, comfortable, smug
(self-satisfied)
Antonyms—restless, dissatisfied, discontent

comply
Synonyms—obey, conform, follow
Antonyms—rebel, resist, defy

comprehensive
Synonyms—thorough, inclusive, complete
Antonyms—limited, partial, restricted

concise
Synonyms—short, to the point, succinct
(brief)
Antonyms—rambling, long-winded, wordy

condescending
Synonyms—rude, snobbish
Antonyms—down-to-earth, friendly, kind

confident
Synonyms—sure, convinced, positive
Antonyms—insecure, shy, fearful

conform
Synonyms—comply, submit, follow
Antonyms—defy, disobey, flout (to go against
or disregard)

conformity
Synonyms—compliance, submission
Antonyms—defiance, disobedience

congested
Synonyms—packed, jammed, blocked
Antonyms—empty, free, wide-open

congruent
Synonyms—alike, matching, harmonious
(goes well together)
Antonyms—incompatible, mismatched,
dissimilar

consensus
Synonyms—agreement, compromise,
harmony
Antonyms—difference, disparity,
confrontation

consequential
Synonyms—important, major, meaningful
Antonyms—trivial, insignificant

conservative
Synonyms—traditional, old-fashioned, conventional
Antonyms—progressive, adventurous, avant-garde (extremely modern)

constant
Synonyms—steady, persistent, incessant (unceasing)
Antonyms—irregular, occasional

constrain
Synonyms—hold back, restrict, inhibit (to slow down or prevent)
Antonyms—expand, develop, increase

consummate
Synonyms—ideal, perfect, superlative (the best)
Antonyms—inferior, awful, abysmal (very bad)

contaminate
Synonyms—pollute, spoil, taint (to spoil or damage)
Antonyms—purify, cleanse

contemporary
Synonyms—modern, up to date, new
Antonyms—old-fashioned, antique

contradict
Synonyms—disagree, oppose, challenge
Antonyms—support, concur (to agree)

conventional
Synonyms—usual, established, typical
Antonyms—uncommon, odd, original

converge
Synonyms—meet, come together, join
Antonyms—diverge, separate

convey
Synonyms—tell, express, communicate
Antonyms—hold back, contain

convoluted
Synonyms—complex, difficult
Antonyms—simple, uncomplicated, straightforward

corroborate
Synonyms—confirm, support, substantiate (to back up with evidence)
Antonyms—contradict, deny, challenge, refute

corrupt
Synonyms—dishonest, shady, crooked
Antonyms—truthful, honest, moral, upstanding

covert
Synonyms—secret, hidden, underground
Antonyms—open, public, exposed

criticize
Synonyms—disparage (to cut down), denigrate (to put down)
Antonyms—praise, commend

culpable
Synonyms—responsible, guilty, at fault
Antonyms—innocent, blameless

curtail
Synonyms—cut back, limit, shorten, restrict
Antonyms—increase, expand, lengthen

D

debased
Synonyms—corrupted, depraved (wicked)
Antonyms—upright, noble, dignified

decisive
Synonyms—determined, conclusive, sure
Antonyms—undetermined, indecisive, irresolute (unsure)

decorous
Synonyms—polite, proper, suitable
Antonyms—indecent, wrong, unsuitable

decry
Synonyms—devalue, disparage (to criticize), demean (to put down)
Antonyms—respect, approve, praise

deficient
Synonyms—lacking, insufficient, not enough
Antonyms—ample, adequate, enough

deficit
Synonyms—deficiency, loss, shortage
Antonyms—excess, surplus, sufficient amount

definite
Synonyms—certain, explicit, indubitable (not questionable)
Antonyms—uncertain, questionable, refutable

defy
Synonyms— disregard, flout (to go against)
Antonyms—obey, respect, follow

delete
Synonyms—remove, take away, expunge (to get rid of)
Antonyms—add, build up, create

deleterious
Synonyms—damaging, hurtful, injurious (harmful)
Antonyms—helpful, good for the health, beneficial, harmless

denigrate
Synonyms— malign, impugn, slander (to put down)
Antonyms— encourage, boost, celebrate

deplete
Synonyms—diminish, reduce, use up
Antonyms—fill, increase, enhance

deplore
Synonyms—despise, hate, undervalue
Antonyms—appreciate, accept, value

deprecate
Synonyms—ridicule, disparage (to criticize), denigrate (to put down)
Antonyms—commend, approve, bolster, support

deprive
Synonyms—take away, rob, remove
Antonyms—give, confer, bestow (to give)

desire
Synonyms—want, longing, craving
Antonyms—disinterest, apathy (lack of interest), repulsion (extreme dislike)

desolate
Synonyms—barren, lifeless, devoid (empty)
Antonyms—inhabited, lively, fruitful (productive)

destitute
Synonyms—poor, indigent (without money)
Antonyms—wealthy, secure, prosperous

destroy
Synonyms—eliminate, obliterate (to wipe out), raze (to completely destroy)
Antonyms—build, fix, improve

detach
Synonyms—remove, segregate, separate
Antonyms—join, put together, assemble

deter
Synonyms—stop, halt, hinder
Antonyms—aid, inspire, incite (to promote)

detractor
Synonyms—critic, enemy
Antonyms—supporter, benefactor, friend

detrimental
Synonyms—bad, harmful, unfavorable
Antonyms—positive, helpful, useful

devastate
Synonyms—destroy, wreck, annihilate (to demolish)
Antonyms—save, protect, expand, augment (to add to)

devious
Synonyms—dishonest, evil, duplicitous (scheming)
Antonyms—honest, forthright, righteous

diffuse
Synonyms—spread out, expanded, propagated (spread out)
Antonyms—condensed, confined, succinct (brief)

digress
Synonyms—stray, ramble, deviate (to go off in another direction)
Antonyms—focus, be direct, stay on course

diligent
Synonyms—hard-working, earnest, persistent
Antonyms—thoughtless, careless, lazy

diminish
Synonyms—decrease, dwindle, reduce
Antonyms—prolong, increase, enhance, extend

diminutive
Synonyms—petite, small, short
Antonyms—big, enormous, huge

dire
Synonyms—critical, very important, desperate, grave (serious)
Antonyms—trivial, unimportant, silly

disagree
Synonyms—conflict, go against, dissent (to differ in opinion)
Antonyms—agree, concur (to have the same opinion), acquiesce (to accept without protesting)

discern
Synonyms—recognize, distinguish, perceive
Antonyms—confuse, misunderstand, discombobulate (to confuse)

disclose
Synonyms—tell, expose, reveal, make known
Antonyms—suppress, hide, disavow (to deny)

discomfort
Synonyms—unpleasantness, irritation, pain, anguish (great pain)
Antonyms—comfort, peacefulness, ease

disconcerting
Synonyms—disturbing, unbalancing, upsetting
Antonyms—quieting, calming, comforting

discord
Synonyms—disharmony, conflict
Antonyms—harmony, peacefulness

discrepancy
Synonyms—variation, difference, incongruity (difference)
Antonyms—consistency, sameness, reliability

dismal
Synonyms—bleak, sad, horrible
Antonyms—bright, hopeful, encouraging

dismay
Synonyms—disappointment, discouragement, trepidation (anxiety or fear)
Antonyms—encouragement, security, confidence

dismiss
Synonyms—send away, discard, push aside
Antonyms—permit, allow, keep, maintain

disparage
Synonyms— mock, criticize, belittle (to put down)
Antonyms—lift up, support, encourage, sanction (to support)

disparate
Synonyms—at variance, contrasting, different
Antonyms—similar, invariable, like

disparity
Synonyms—imbalance, gap, inequity
Antonyms—equity, likeness, sameness

dispute
Synonyms—bicker, argue, contend
Antonyms—harmonize, agree, go along with

disruptive
Synonyms—disorderly, disturbing
Antonyms—unifying, peaceful, calming

disseminate
Synonyms—publicize, scatter, radiate, disperse
Antonyms—condense, conceal, hide

dissipate
Synonyms—deplete, use up, squander (to waste)
Antonyms—save, preserve, conserve (to save)

distinct
Synonyms—separate, clearly defined, explicit (obvious)
Antonyms—vague, unsure, ambiguous (poorly defined)

distorted
Synonyms—warped, bent out of shape, perverted
Antonyms—straight, pure, invariable

diverge
Synonyms—separate, deviate (to go off course)
Antonyms—converge, join

diverse
Synonyms—dissimilar, different, varied
Antonyms—conforming, uniform, similar

divide
Synonyms—split up, disjoin, partition (to cut up)
Antonyms—join, add, combine

divulge
Synonyms—bring to light, confess, tell
Antonyms—protect, suppress, hide, conceal

dominant
Synonyms—superior, controlling, main
Antonyms—subordinate, inferior, auxiliary (additional)

dominate
Synonyms—rule over, influence, overshadow
Antonyms—follow, submit, acquiesce (to go along with)

dubious
Synonyms—suspicious, doubtful, disputable
Antonyms—reliable, true, unambiguous

duplicitous
Synonyms—two-faced, shady, dishonest
Antonyms—trustworthy, reliable, truthful, honest

durable
Synonyms—rugged, tough, tenacious (persistent)
Antonyms—flimsy, fragile, weak

duress
Synonyms—hardship, suffering, threat
Antonyms—ease, support, peacefulness

E

endure
Synonyms—bear, withstand, suffer, tolerate, cope with
Antonyms—give up, surrender, cave in

effusive
Synonyms—expressive, gushing, unrestrained
Antonyms—reserved, restrained, aloof

egotism
Synonyms—narcissism, self-absorption (focusing only on one's self and one's own desires)
Antonyms—selflessness, compassion, thoughtfulness

elaborate
Synonyms—ornate, refined, complicated
Antonyms—plain, simple, uncomplicated

elated
Synonyms—thrilled, joyful, euphoric (extremely happy)
Antonyms—deflated, melancholy, disappointed

elusive
Synonyms—mysterious, puzzling, baffling (difficult to understand)
Antonyms—clear, understandable, concise (brief and clear)

eminent
Synonyms—prestigious, well-known, illustrious (well-known in a positive manner)
Antonyms—unimportant, ordinary, unknown

emulate
Synonyms—copy, mimic, act like
Antonyms—act independently

encompass
Synonyms—include, circumscribe, encircle
Antonyms—exclude, leave out, remove

enervate
Synonyms—weaken, incapacitate, drain
Antonyms—animate, empower, strengthen

engage
Synonyms—deal with, undertake, employ
Antonyms—avoid, repulse, ignore, fire

engender
Synonyms—incite, provoke, rouse (to move to action)
Antonyms—calm, discourage, hinder (to block or stop), dissuade (to advise against)

enhance
Synonyms—heighten, improve, increase
Antonyms—devalue, weaken, reduce, lessen, undermine (to weaken)

enrich
Synonyms—improve, enhance, aggrandize (to make bigger)
Antonyms—decrease, impoverish (to make poorer)

enthrall
Synonyms—charm, captivate, mesmerize (to capture the attention of)
Antonyms—bore, disgust, repel

eradicate
Synonyms—eliminate, destroy, get rid of
Antonyms—maintain, protect

erratic
Synonyms—irregular, unpredictable, volatile (explosive)
Antonyms—steadfast, predictable, regular

espouse
Synonyms—advocate, defend, support
Antonyms—disallow, reject, forsake (to abandon)

essential
Synonyms—necessary, requisite (required), indispensable (very much needed)
Antonyms—trivial, unnecessary, extra

euphoric
Synonyms—excited, thrilled, very happy
Antonyms—depressed, grieving, sorrowful

exacerbate
Synonyms—embitter, intensify, irritate
Antonyms— calm down, alleviate (to lesson), placate (to please)

exasperate
Synonyms—provoke, rile up, infuriate (to make angry)
Antonyms—mollify (to soothe), tranquilize (to calm down)

exclude
Synonyms—keep out, omit, ostracize (to ban someone from a group)
Antonyms—include, welcome, allow in

exculpate
Synonyms—forgive, excuse, acquit (to free from guilt)
Antonyms—punish, accuse, incriminate (to make appear responsible for a crime)

exempt
Synonyms—not required to, immune
Antonyms—responsible, required to

exonerate
Synonyms—hold blameless, vindicate (to free from guilt), exculpate (to free from guilt)
Antonyms—condemn, convict, hold accountable

expand
Synonyms—enlarge, increase, swell
Antonyms—decrease, minimize, reduce

expansive
Synonyms—all-inclusive, broad, widespread
Antonyms—exclusive, narrow, limited

expedite
Synonyms—quicken, hurry, hasten
Antonyms—delay, slow down, retard

expert
Synonyms—skilled, knowledgeable, experienced
Antonyms— amateur, inept (unskilled), novice (new at something)

extenuate
Synonyms—diminish, lessen
Antonyms—increase, worsen, exacerbate (to make worse)

extol
Synonyms—praise, exalt, acclaim (to rave about)
Antonyms—disapprove, condemn, disparage (to complain about)

extraneous
Synonyms—extra, not needed, unnecessary, irrelevant
Antonyms—vital, relevant

extricate
Synonyms—liberate, free
Antonyms—restrain, involve, constrain (to limit)

extrinsic
Synonyms—foreign, alien, external (outside)
Antonyms—native, natural, inherent (originating from within)

exuberant
Synonyms—cheerful, buoyant (high-spirited), ebullient (full of positive energy)
Antonyms—unenthusiastic, dull, lethargic (slow)

F

fabricate
Synonyms—manufacture, make up, formulate
Antonyms—disassemble, break apart

fallacy
Synonyms—falsehood, lie, deception
Antonyms—truth, fact, reality

fanatic
Synonyms—lunatic, zealot, radical (extremist)
Antonyms—conservative, disinterested party, unbeliever, infidel (non-believer)

fecund
Synonyms—propagating, fertile, fruitful (able to reproduce)
Antonyms—infertile, sterile, barren (unable to have children)

felicitous
Synonyms—appropriate, suitable, apropos (appropriate)
Antonyms—inopportune, poorly-timed, irrelevant

feral
Synonyms—wild, savage, untamed
Antonyms—tamed, mild-mannered, civilized

fervent
Synonyms—sincere, impassioned
Antonyms—unenthusiastic, unfeeling, dispassionate (unmoved)

flagrant
Synonyms—shameless, undisguised, brazen (brash)
Antonyms—obscure, contained, camouflaged (hidden)

flamboyant
Synonyms—glamorous, over-the-top, pretentious (showy)
Antonyms—refined, dull, common

forbid
Synonyms—prohibit, disallow, ban
Antonyms—facilitate, advance, admit (to allow)

formal
Synonyms—official, established, conventional
Antonyms—casual, informal, unofficial

forthright
Synonyms—sincere, honest, candid (open and direct)
Antonyms—dishonest, sneaky, lying

fortitude
Synonyms—courage, endurance, tenacity (persistence)
Antonyms—cowardice, laziness

foster
Synonyms—champion, support, nurture
Antonyms—neglect, halt, starve, deprive (to withhold support)

fragile
Synonyms—breakable, weak, frail
Antonyms—strong, durable, sturdy, rugged

frenetic
Synonyms—obsessive, overwrought (very upset), maniacal (frenzied, like a madman)
Antonyms—normal, balanced, calm

frivolity
Synonyms—whimsicality, silliness, childishness, playfulness
Antonyms—seriousness, sternness

frugal
Synonyms—economical, penny-pinching, thrifty
Antonyms—wasteful, spendthrift, lavish

furtive
Synonyms—secretive, clandestine (hidden), stealthy (done in a sneaky way)
Antonyms—candid, straightforward, overt (done in an obvious way)

futile
Synonyms—pointless, purposeless, trifling (having no value)
Antonyms—useful, worthwhile, efficacious (effective)

G

gargantuan
Synonyms—huge, gigantic, enormous
Antonyms—tiny, infinitesimal (infinitely small), minute (really small or insignificant)

generate
Synonyms—make, create, produce
Antonyms—end, terminate, destroy

genial
Synonyms—cordial, amiable, kindly (likeable)
Antonyms—disagreeable, unfriendly, surly (gruff)

grandiose
Synonyms—exaggerating, pompous (full of oneself), ostentatious (acting like a "show-off")
Antonyms—humble, lowly, unimposing (humble)

gratuitous
Synonyms—excessive, uncalled for, unnecessary
Antonyms—warranted, necessary, vital

greedy
Synonyms—gluttonous, insatiable (strong desire for selfish gain)
Antonyms—generous, giving, satisfied, metered (controlled)

gregarious
Synonyms—sociable, outgoing, good-natured
Antonyms—shy, introverted (turning inward to oneself), antisocial (unfriendly or aloof)

guileless
Synonyms—truthful, honest, straightforward
Antonyms—cunning, deceitful, tricky

gullible
Synonyms—simple, credulous (easily fooled)
Antonyms—sophisticated, skeptical, incredulous (unbelieving)

H

hackneyed
Synonyms—stale, common, trite (something overdone or constantly repeated)
Antonyms—original, fresh, authentic

haughty
Synonyms—snotty, narcissistic (focused on the self), arrogant (feeling superior to others)
Antonyms—humble, polite, self-effacing (humble)

heinous
Synonyms—wicked, repugnant (very bad), atrocious (awful)
Antonyms—honorable, wonderful, pleasing

heretic
Synonyms—pagan, unbeliever, iconoclast (one who goes against a belief system)
Antonyms—believer, loyalist, adherent (one who follows a belief system)

hesitate
Synonyms—pause, defer (to put off), balk (to refuse to move forward)
Antonyms—charge into, perform, hasten (to speed up)

honorable
Synonyms—well-regarded, law-abiding, esteemed (well-respected)
Antonyms—unethical, unjust, corrupt, dishonorable, base (lowly)

hypocrisy
Synonyms—phoniness, fraudulence (fakeness), duplicity (lying)
Antonyms—honesty, sincerity, genuineness

hypothetical
Synonyms—supposed, presumed, guessed
Antonyms—factual, actual, real

I

imitate
Synonyms—copy, mimic (copy), impersonate (to act like someone), emulate (to strive to be like)
Antonyms—differ from, diverge from (to differ from)

immature
Synonyms—childish, infantile (like an infant)
Antonyms—experienced, mature, adult, seasoned (experienced)

impede
Synonyms—block, hinder, stymie (thwart)
Antonyms—facilitate, accelerate, bolster (to support), expedite (to speed up)

impersonate
Synonyms—mimic, copy, imitate (to act like)
Antonyms—differ from

impetuous
Synonyms—hasty, rash (acting with little thought)
Antonyms—cautious, thoughtful, planned

impulsive
Synonyms—unpredictable, erratic (irregular), hasty (acting quickly, without thought)
Antonyms—deliberate, planned, designed (well-thought-out)

inarticulate
Synonyms—stammering, incomprehensible, tongue-tied (not well-spoken)
Antonyms—intelligible, clear, understandable, eloquent (well-spoken)

incisive
Synonyms—clever, acute, sharp (quick-witted)
Antonyms—dull, half-witted, incompetent (not capable)

incompatible
Synonyms—opposite, clashing (conflicting), disparate (different)
Antonyms—suitable, harmonious, simpatico (compatible)

incongruent
Synonyms—unlike, conflicting, inconsistent
Antonyms—alike, equal, analogous (similar)

incontrovertible
Synonyms—irrefutable, unquestionable, sure
Antonyms—questionable, inconclusive, unconvincing

incorporate
Synonyms—include, join, merge, mix
Antonyms—exclude, divide, separate

incriminate
Synonyms— accuse, involve, blame
Antonyms—free, exonerate (to remove from guilt)

indecision
Synonyms—ambivalence, hesitancy, tentativeness
Antonyms—certainty, assurance, decisiveness

independent
Synonyms—self-determining, free, self-sufficient, liberated
Antonyms—dependent

indeterminate
Synonyms—inexact, inconclusive, imprecise (not accurate)
Antonyms—conclusive, definite, irrefutable (certain)

indict
Synonyms—accuse, condemn, blame
Antonyms—hold blameless, exonerate (to excuse), acquit (to find not guilty)

indifference
Synonyms—disinterest, apathy (lack of interest)
Antonyms—concern, involvement, interest

indistinct
Synonyms—poorly defined, murky (unclear), ambiguous (not clearly marked or understood)
Antonyms—obvious, well-defined, discernible (distinct)

induce
Synonyms—motivate, cause, instigate (to set in motion)
Antonyms—hinder, block, impede (to slow or stop), dissuade (to advise against)

inept
Synonyms—unskillful, clumsy, incompetent (not capable), bungling (prone to making mistakes)
Antonyms—skillful, masterful, competent (capable), dexterous (demonstrating skill)

inevitable
Synonyms—unavoidable, impending (happening soon), destined (bound by destiny to happen)
Antonyms—avoidable, unlikely, uncertain

infamous
Synonyms—disreputable (having a bad reputation), notorious (well-known in a negative way)
Antonyms—righteous, noble, goodly

informal
Synonyms—casual, unofficial, unfussy
Antonyms—fussy, formal, stiff (acting in a strict manner)

ingenious
Synonyms—gifted, intelligent, resourceful (clever)
Antonyms—foolish, dumb, dull-witted

inherent
Synonyms—built-in, natural, innate (found naturally within)
Antonyms—acquired, unnatural, learned

inhibit
Synonyms—constrain, suppress, restrain, prevent
Antonyms—assist, encourage, support

inhibited
Synonyms—shy, subdued, reserved (quiet or timid in manner)
Antonyms—outrageous, loud, boisterous (noisy)

initiate
Synonyms—start, begin, inaugurate (to implement)
Antonyms—end, finish, cease (to stop)

initiative
Synonyms—drive, motivation, gumption
Antonyms—idleness, laziness

innocuous
Synonyms—inoffensive, mild, harmless
Antonyms—offensive, shocking, wild

insipid
Synonyms—dull, tedious, boring
Antonyms—exciting, interesting, fun

insolence
Synonyms— crudeness, disrespect, impertinence (lack of respect)
Antonyms—respect, obedience, humility

instigate
Synonyms—start, initiate (to begin), foment (to stimulate to action)
Antonyms—suppress, not allow, dissuade (to advise against)

integrate
Synonyms—put together, merge, harmonize
Antonyms—separate, leave out, cast aside

intimidating
Synonyms—coercive, threatening, compelling
Antonyms—easy-going, non-threatening

intrepid
Synonyms—fearless, courageous, undaunted (unafraid)
Antonyms—cautious, fearful, afraid

inundate
Synonyms—overload, flood, overwhelm
Antonyms—relieve, lessen

invariable
Synonyms—unchanging, consistent, constant, steady
Antonyms—variable, changing, inconsistent, wavering

invigorate
Synonyms—energize, stimulate, enliven
Antonyms—drain, discourage, deflate

invincible
Synonyms—strong, unbeatable, indomitable (unable to be conquered)
Antonyms—weak, downtrodden, conquerable

irate
Synonyms—angry, furious, enraged
Antonyms—calm, peaceful, pacified (soothed)

irrational
Synonyms—illogical, nonsensical
Antonyms—rational, logical, sensible

irregular
Synonyms—variable, unsteady, inconsistent, unusual, variegated (full of variety)
Antonyms—regular, steady, predictable, consistent, normal, uniform

irresolute
Synonyms—uncertain, undecided, indecisive
Antonyms—resolute, certain, decisive

irritate
Synonyms—annoy, upset, aggravate
Antonyms—please, soothe, placate (to make happy)

J

jeopardize
Synonyms—endanger, threaten
Antonyms—protect, support, empower

jovial
Synonyms—happy, upbeat, good-natured
Antonyms—cranky, grumpy, glum (sullen)

judicious
Synonyms—thoughtful, cautious, prudent (wise)
Antonyms—reckless, ill-considered, imprudent (unwise)

K

keen
Synonyms—sharp, quick, astute (smart)
Antonyms—dull, slow, unintelligent

L

laborious
Synonyms—difficult, hard, demanding
Antonyms—easy, relaxed, undemanding

lackluster
Synonyms—dull, boring, uninteresting
Antonyms—brilliant, captivating, interesting

lament
Synonyms—mourn, regret, grieve
Antonyms—celebrate

languid
Synonyms—slow, sluggish, weak
Antonyms—energetic, vital, strong

languish
Synonyms—droop, decline, suffer
Antonyms—thrive, grow, flourish (to grow)

latent
Synonyms—unexpressed, inactive, hidden, undeveloped
Antonyms—expressed, active, actualized, developed

lavish
Synonyms—extravagant, posh, opulent (abundant)
Antonyms—poor, bare, understated, low-key

lax
Synonyms—relaxed, loose, permissive, lenient (not strict)
Antonyms—strict, tight, rigid

lazy
Synonyms—unmotivated, unenergetic, indolent (avoiding work)
Antonyms—driven, energetic, hardworking, industrious

legitimate
Synonyms—actual, real, verified (shown to be true)
Antonyms—illegitimate, false, fake, unreal

lenient
Synonyms—allowing, permissive, forgiving, lax (not strict)
Antonyms—strict, rigid, restrictive, punishing

lethargic
Synonyms—slow, lazy, sluggish, inactive
Antonyms—quick, energetic, vital, active

liability
Synonyms—obligation, debt, weakness, disadvantage
Antonyms—asset, strength, advantage

linger
Synonyms—stay, loiter, delay
Antonyms—leave, flee, rush, expedite (to hurry)

livid
Synonyms—angry, irate, furious
Antonyms—calm, pleased, contented

lofty
Synonyms—high, ambitious, pretentious (showy)
Antonyms—low, lowly, meager (very poor or not enough)

loquacious
Synonyms—talkative, chatty, wordy, garrulous (talkative)
Antonyms—silent, unresponsive, concise (brief), taciturn (unexpressive), terse (short)

lucid
Synonyms—clear, understandable, rational
Antonyms—unclear, muddled, confusing

M

malevolence
Synonyms—hatred, ill will, malice (intent to harm)
Antonyms—goodness, kindness, benevolence (good will)

malingering
Synonyms—lazy, shirking (avoiding duties)
Antonyms—hardworking, industrious

malignant
Synonyms—harmful, dangerous
Antonyms—beneficial, harmless, benign (not harmful)

malleable
Synonyms—changeable, bendable, pliable (easy to bend)
Antonyms—unchangeable, inflexible, rigid

mature
Synonyms—full-grown, developed, ripe
Antonyms—immature, undeveloped, underdeveloped

mediocre
Synonyms—unimpressive, ordinary, average, so-so
Antonyms—impressive, extraordinary, excellent, stellar (outstanding)

mercurial
Synonyms—ever-changing, unpredictable, fickle (not loyal), capricious (quick to change)
Antonyms—steady, constant, predictable

meticulous
Synonyms—neat, careful, detailed, precise (accurate)
Antonyms—messy, sloppy, imprecise (lacking accuracy)

misconception
Synonyms—misunderstanding, misperception, false belief
Antonyms—fact, truth

mitigate
Synonyms—reduce, lessen, relieve
Antonyms—worsen, exacerbate (to make more severe)

moderate
Synonyms—mild, medium, average
Antonyms—extreme, excessive, intense

modicum
Synonyms—bit, tidbit, morsel (a tiny amount)
Antonyms—load, large amount

mollify
Synonyms—soothe, calm, pacify (to calm)
Antonyms—enrage, aggravate, irritate, anger

moribund
Synonyms—dying, ending, declining, terminal (at the end)
Antonyms—vital, thriving, alive, living

morose
Synonyms—negative, dark, sullen (gloomy)
Antonyms—positive, happy, cheerful

mundane
Synonyms—ordinary, commonplace, everyday
Antonyms—extraordinary, unique, original

munificent
Synonyms—generous, lavish, liberal (giving freely)
Antonyms—stingy, miserly, withholding

mutable
Synonyms—changeable, flexible, malleable (able to be changed)
Antonyms—inflexible, rigid, steadfast

N

naive
Synonyms—innocent, trusting, newcomer
Antonyms—experienced, sophisticated

narcissistic
Synonyms—self-absorbed, conceited, selfish
Antonyms—generous, altruistic (helping others)

nebulous
Synonyms—vague, unclear
Antonyms—precise, specific, well-defined

neglect
Synonyms—forget, abandon, overlook
Antonyms—nurture, care for, foster

nemesis
Synonyms—arch enemy, opponent, adversary
Antonyms—best friend, collaborator, ally (friend)

nocturnal
Synonyms—nighttime, vampirish
Antonyms—daytime, diurnal (during the day)

nonchalant
Synonyms—casual, relaxed, laid-back
Antonyms—formal, stiff, uptight

notorious
Synonyms—disreputable (having a bad reputation), infamous (well-known for a bad reason)
Antonyms—unknown, unfamiliar, unheard of

novel
Synonyms—new, unique, imaginative
Antonyms—ordinary, everyday, unoriginal

novice
Synonyms—beginner, trainee, neophyte (new learner)
Antonyms—expert, authority, professional

nurture
Synonyms—care for, foster, protect
Antonyms—neglect, abandon, ignore, harm

O

objective
Synonyms—fair, unbiased, open-minded
Antonyms—prejudiced, partial, subjective (biased)

obliterate
Synonyms—demolish, eliminate, eradicate (wipe out)
Antonyms—assemble, build, create

oblivious
Synonyms—unresponsive, unaware, forgetting
Antonyms—mindful, conscious, alert

obscure
Synonyms—unknown, minor, unseen
Antonyms—famous, prominent, recognized

obsolete
Synonyms—outdated, irrelevant, archaic (old)
Antonyms—contemporary, current, trendy, modern

obstinate
Synonyms—stubborn, headstrong, obdurate (stubborn), tenacious (determined)
Antonyms—obedient, yielding (giving in), accommodating (eager to please others)

obtrusive
Synonyms—obvious, prominent, blatant (highly noticeable)
Antonyms—ordinary, unremarkable, inconspicuous (unnoticeable)

occlude
Synonyms—block, obstruct, impede (to hold back)
Antonyms—assist, facilitate, ease

omnipotent
Synonyms—supreme, invincible (unstoppable)
Antonyms—powerless, weak, helpless

onerous
Synonyms—burdensome, tedious (repetitive and boring), arduous (difficult and demanding)
Antonyms—easy, effortless, trouble-free

opinionated
Synonyms—inflexible, unbending, dogmatic (having rigid opinions)
Antonyms—mellow, easygoing, laid-back

opponent
Synonyms—rival, foe, challenger
Antonyms—friend, colleague, teammate, ally (friend)

opportune
Synonyms—well-timed, advantageous (helpful)
Antonyms—inconvenient, unfortunate

optimistic
Synonyms—hopeful, positive, sanguine (confident)
Antonyms—pessimistic, gloomy

opulent
Synonyms—lavish, luxurious, sumptuous (expensive)
Antonyms—inadequate, meager (very poor or not enough), impoverished (poor)

ordinary
Synonyms—common, usual, regular, normal
Antonyms—extraordinary, exceptional, unique

ornate
Synonyms—lavish, bejeweled, adorned (decorated)
Antonyms—plain, simple, basic

orthodox
Synonyms—conventional, mainstream, usual
Antonyms—innovative, pioneering, ground-breaking

ostentatious
Synonyms—flashy, flamboyant, pretentious (showy)
Antonyms—modest, down-to-earth, humble

ostracize
Synonyms—banish, ignore, cast out
Antonyms—welcome, include, embrace

overt
Synonyms—open, unconcealed, blatant (obvious)
Antonyms—hidden, covert (concealed), clandestine (secret)

P

parched
Synonyms—dry, dehydrated, waterless
Antonyms—wet, saturated, drenched

pariah
Synonyms—outcast, untouchable, exile
Antonyms—insider, hero, idol

passion
Synonyms—enthusiasm, zeal, delight
Antonyms—indifference, apathy (lack of interest)

passive
Synonyms—sluggish, lifeless, inert (inactive)
Antonyms—active, lively, energetic

pathetic
Synonyms—pitiful, wretched, lame
Antonyms—admirable, excellent, worthy

penitent
Synonyms—sorry, apologetic, contrite (sorry)
Antonyms—unrepentant, shameless, unremorseful

perceptive
Synonyms—insightful, observant
Antonyms—insensitive, oblivious (unaware)

perish
Synonyms—die, pass away, expire
Antonyms—live, survive, endure

perplexing
Synonyms—puzzling, bewildering, mystifying
Antonyms—simple, effortless, trouble-free, clear, understandable

persevere
Synonyms—persist, continue, keep on
Antonyms—quit, surrender, give up

perturb
Synonyms—annoy, disturb, bother
Antonyms—please, delight, gratify (make happy)

pervasive
Synonyms—omnipresent, all-encompassing (found everywhere)
Antonyms—contained, limited

pessimistic
Synonyms—gloomy, negative
Antonyms—optimistic, hopeful

pious
Synonyms—religious, reverent
Antonyms—disrespectful, heretical (going against established beliefs)

placate
Synonyms—soothe, pacify, appease (to calm down)
Antonyms—enrage, anger, infuriate (to anger)

placid
Synonyms—calm, peaceful, easygoing
Antonyms—anxious, stressed, agitated (upset)

plausible
Synonyms—believable, possible, likely
Antonyms—improbable, far-fetched, questionable

popular
Synonyms—appealing, well-liked, admired
Antonyms—disliked, ill-favored, unpopular

potent
Synonyms—powerful, strong, effective
Antonyms—weak, unsuccessful, incapable

practical
Synonyms—useful, sensible, no-nonsense
Antonyms—unrealistic, unreasonable, impractical

precede
Synonyms—lead, go before
Antonyms—follow, trail

predatory
Synonyms—aggressive, rapacious (out to kill)
Antonyms—harmless, passive (inactive)

predominant
Synonyms—major, principal, most common
Antonyms—secondary, insignificant

pretentious
Synonyms—showy, conceited, self-important
Antonyms—practical, down-to-earth, humble

privilege
Synonyms—advantage, benefit
Antonyms—disadvantage, drawback, shortcoming

procrastinate
Synonyms—postpone, delay
Antonyms—advance, proceed, progress, hurry

proficient
Synonyms—skilled, talented, capable
Antonyms—incompetent, clumsy, inept (unskilled)

proliferate
Synonyms—increase, flourish, spread, thrive (to do well)
Antonyms—reduce, diminish, dwindle

propagate
Synonyms—spread, transmit, publicize
Antonyms—suppress, hold back

propensity
Synonyms—tendency, inclination, penchant (tendency)
Antonyms—reluctance, aversion (dislike)

proponent
Synonyms—supporter, advocate, fan
Antonyms—opponent, foe, antagonist (enemy)

propriety
Synonyms—respectability, politeness
Antonyms—rudeness, discourtesy

prosaic
Synonyms—dull, ordinary, commonplace
Antonyms—inspiring, stirring, exciting

prosperous
Synonyms—wealthy, affluent, abundant
Antonyms—unsuccessful, disadvantaged

proximity
Synonyms—closeness, convenience, nearness
Antonyms—distance, remoteness

prudent
Synonyms—wise, cautious, practical
Antonyms—foolish, risky, reckless

punitive
Synonyms—penalizing, disciplinary, retaliatory (punishing)
Antonyms—rewarding, incentivizing, inducing (encouraging), enticing (tempting)

purify
Synonyms—cleanse, distill, filter, sanitize
Antonyms—soil, pollute, muddy

Q

quell
Synonyms—crush, defeat, conquer, suppress
Antonyms—incite, provoke, inflame, encourage

querulous
Synonyms—difficult, irritable, argumentative, cantankerous (argumentative)
Antonyms—amiable, friendly, good-natured, genial (likeable)

quarrelsome
Synonyms—querulous, cranky, grouchy, bad-tempered
Antonyms—affable, likable, good-humored, kind

quiescent
Synonyms—quiet, sluggish, passive
(inactive), dormant (inactive)
Antonyms—active, lively, energetic, vigorous

R

random
Synonyms—accidental, haphazard, chance,
casual
Antonyms—predictable, intentional,
planned, on purpose

rational
Synonyms—sane, normal, coherent (makes
sense)
Antonyms—unreasonable, absurd, illogical

rebut
Synonyms—deny, disprove, invalidate
Antonyms—accept, believe, recognize,
support

recede
Synonyms—ebb, diminish, draw back
Antonyms—advance, press forward, progress

reclusive
Synonyms—isolated, solitary, withdrawn
Antonyms—outgoing, friendly, sociable

reconcile
Synonyms—reunite, resolve, bring together
Antonyms—separate, split, break up

recuperate
Synonyms—recover, get well, improve
Antonyms—decline, weaken, deteriorate (to
get worse)

refined
Synonyms—polished, developed, cultivated
Antonyms—coarse, crude, rough

remedy
Synonyms—cure, restore, fix
Antonyms—worsen, aggravate, exacerbate
(make worse)

remorse
Synonyms—guilt, sorrow, regret, shame
Antonyms—indifference, hard-heartedness,
pride

remote
Synonyms—distant, isolated, far
Antonyms—close, nearby

renovate
Synonyms—renew, refresh, repair
Antonyms—demolish, destroy

renounce
Synonyms—reject, abandon, deny
Antonyms—accept, embrace

replete
Synonyms—full, stuffed, plentiful
Antonyms—hungry, empty, bare

reprehensible
Synonyms—criminal, wicked, disgraceful
Antonyms—honorable, noble, praiseworthy

repress
Synonyms—restrain, control, suppress, stifle
(to hold back)
Antonyms—express, release, free (to let go)

reputable
Synonyms—trustworthy, dependable,
respectable, legitimate
Antonyms—questionable, shady, dishonest

resilient
Synonyms—flexible, elastic, rebounding
Antonyms—rigid, unyielding, stiff

resplendent
Synonyms—dazzling, magnificent, glorious,
stunning
Antonyms—unimpressive, ordinary,
forgettable

restrain
Synonyms—control, confine, hold back
Antonyms—free, release, liberate

retain
Synonyms—keep, save, preserve
Antonyms—discard, throw away, let go

revere
Synonyms—admire, respect, esteem (to
regard highly)
Antonyms—disapprove, dislike, object to

robust
Synonyms—healthy, strong, vigorous
Antonyms—weak, feeble, frail

routine
Synonyms—usual, ordinary, normal
Antonyms—exceptional, uncommon

rupture
Synonyms—break, burst, rip open
Antonyms—heal, mend, repair

S

sagacious
Synonyms—wise, shrewd, learned,
perceptive
Antonyms—foolish, thoughtless, irrational

saturate
Synonyms—soak, flood, inundate (to
overwhelm)
Antonyms—dehydrate, desiccate (to dry)

scrutinize
Synonyms—examine, inspect, analyze
Antonyms—ignore, disregard, overlook

secrete
Synonyms—conceal, hide, stash
Antonyms—reveal, disclose, divulge (to reveal)

sedentary
Synonyms—inactive, immobile, lethargic (slow)
Antonyms—active, lively, energetic

sequential
Synonyms—in order, chronological (sorted by time)
Antonyms—disordered, chaotic, random

serene
Synonyms—calm, peaceful, tranquil
Antonyms—busy, lively, hectic

skeptical
Synonyms—doubtful, unconvinced, disbelieving
Antonyms—persuaded, converted, won over

solace
Synonyms—comfort, support, relief
Antonyms—irritation, annoyance, hurt

soporific
Synonyms—dull, sleep-inducing, monotonous (boring)
Antonyms—stimulating, exciting, lively, energizing

sparse
Synonyms—limited, scarce, inadequate, scant (a small amount)
Antonyms—abundant, plentiful, profuse (in good supply)

spontaneous
Synonyms—unplanned, spur-of-the-moment, impromptu (unplanned)
Antonyms—structured, deliberate, premeditated (planned)

squander
Synonyms—waste, spend, misuse
Antonyms—save, keep, conserve (to save)

stagnant
Synonyms—still, inactive, inert (not active)
Antonyms—moving, mobile, dynamic

sterile
Synonyms—antiseptic, disinfected, sanitary
Antonyms—contaminated, dirty, soiled

stimulate
Synonyms—encourage, motivate, inspire
Antonyms—discourage, dampen, stifle (to hold back)

strenuous
Synonyms—taxing, straining, demanding, arduous (difficult)
Antonyms—easy, effortless, painless

strict
Synonyms—firm, exacting, rigorous
Antonyms—lenient, relaxed, easygoing

submissive
Synonyms—obedient, passive (inactive), compliant (willing to obey)
Antonyms—assertive, pushy, aggressive

substantial
Synonyms—considerable, extensive, sizeable, significant
Antonyms—minor, insignificant, limited

substantiate
Synonyms—verify, prove, corroborate (to prove)
Antonyms—disprove, refute, invalidate

subtle
Synonyms—slight, understated, delicate
Antonyms—obvious, noticeable, apparent

sullen
Synonyms—brooding, grim, gloomy
Antonyms—cheerful, smiling, joyful

summon
Synonyms—call, beckon, gather
Antonyms—dismiss, release

superficial
Synonyms—shallow, surface
Antonyms—deep, profound, meaningful

superfluous
Synonyms—extra, surplus (more than is needed)
Antonyms—indispensable, necessary, vital, essential

supply
Synonyms—provide, give, contribute
Antonyms—remove, take away, deprive (to withhold from)

support
Synonyms—maintain, encourage, sustain (to keep going)
Antonyms—abandon, ignore, forsake (to abandon)

suppress
Synonyms—prevent, repress (to hold down), stifle (to hold back), constrain (to limit)
Antonyms—spread, express, distribute

surge
Synonyms—rush, flow, pour, gush
Antonyms—stagnate, stand still, pool (to gather in one place)

surplus
Synonyms—extra, spare, leftover
Antonyms—basic, essential

surreptitious
Synonyms—secret, sneaky, stealthy (sneaky), covert (hidden)
Antonyms—open, honest, direct

surrogate
Synonyms—substitute, replacement, stand-in
Antonyms—real, permanent, genuine

sustain
Synonyms—support, maintain, keep going
Antonyms—quit, stop, give up, abandon

T

tame
Synonyms—domestic, friendly, docile (obedient)
Antonyms—wild, untamed, feral (not domesticated)

tardy
Synonyms—late, slow, delayed
Antonyms—prompt, punctual, timely

tedious
Synonyms—boring, dull, dreary, monotonous (boring)
Antonyms—interesting, motivating, fascinating

temperate
Synonyms—moderate, pleasant, mild
Antonyms—extreme, severe, intense

temperamental
Synonyms—unpredictable, moody, volatile (explosive)
Antonyms—reliable, dependable, even-tempered

tenacious
Synonyms—stubborn, persistent, determined
Antonyms—unsure, hesitant, irresolute (undecided)

tentative
Synonyms—cautious, hesitant, uncertain
Antonyms—sure, definite, secure

tenuous
Synonyms—weak, flimsy, fragile
Antonyms—strong, sound, robust (strong)

tense
Synonyms—worried, anxious, stressed, uptight
Antonyms—relaxed, calm, tranquil, peaceful

terminate
Synonyms—end, finish, conclude, cease
Antonyms—begin, commence, originate

terse
Synonyms—abrupt, brief, concise (to the point), brusque (abrupt)
Antonyms—rambling, long-winded, wordy

therapeutic
Synonyms—healing, beneficial, helpful
Antonyms—harmful, destructive, unsafe, detrimental (harmful)

tolerant
Synonyms—broadminded, understanding, forbearing (patient)
Antonyms—intolerant, unforgiving, rigid, impatient

toxic
Synonyms—poisonous, deadly, lethal (deadly)
Antonyms—harmless, safe

tranquil
Synonyms—peaceful, calm, relaxing, serene (peaceful)
Antonyms—noisy, chaotic, frenzied

transgression
Synonyms—wrongdoing, disobedience, offense
Antonyms—good deed, kindness, favor

transient
Synonyms—temporary, brief, fleeting, short-lived
Antonyms—permanent, lasting, eternal, enduring

translucent
Synonyms—clear, transparent, see-through
Antonyms—opaque, dense, thick

treacherous
Synonyms—unsafe, dangerous, hazardous, perilous (dangerous)
Antonyms—harmless, safe, risk-free

trepidation
Synonyms—fear, anxiety, apprehension (fear)
Antonyms—composure, level-headedness, equanimity (calmness)

trivial
Synonyms—minor, insignificant, petty, negligible (not important)
Antonyms—crucial, essential, important, necessary, vital

truncate
Synonyms—shorten, abbreviate, trim
Antonyms—lengthen, extend, elongate (to make longer)

turbulent
Synonyms—chaotic, confused, tumultuous (in turmoil)
Antonyms—orderly, calm

U

unheralded
Synonyms—unannounced, unpredicted, unexpected
Antonyms—forecasted, foretold, expected

uniform
Synonyms—unchanging, unvarying, standardized, homogeneous (the same)
Antonyms—different, dissimilar, unlike, diverse (different)

unpalatable
Synonyms—unpleasant, distasteful, disagreeable
Antonyms—enjoyable, pleasing, satisfying

unparalleled
Synonyms—matchless, unequaled, incomparable, supreme
Antonyms—common, ordinary, everyday, regular

unstinting
Synonyms—generous, giving
Antonyms—stingy, tightfisted

untenable
Synonyms—indefensible, unreasonable
Antonyms—justifiable, understandable

utilitarian
Synonyms—useful, practical, functional
Antonyms—ineffective, nonfunctional

utopian
Synonyms—perfect, ideal
Antonyms—problematic, flawed

V

vague
Synonyms—unclear, hazy, indistinct (not clear)
Antonyms—definite, distinct, evident (clear)

valid
Synonyms—legitimate, reasonable, sensible
Antonyms—invalid, illegitimate, unsound, fallacious (not true)

validate
Synonyms—confirm, approve, certify, authorize
Antonyms—invalidate, cancel, disapprove, deny

valid
Synonyms—authentic, legal, legitimate, official
Antonyms—invalid, worthless, void (not valid)

verdant
Synonyms—green, lush, luxuriant
Antonyms—bare, stripped, withered

versatile
Synonyms—adaptable, resourceful, multitalented
Antonyms—limited, narrow, restricted

vex
Synonyms—annoy, pester, irritate, exasperate (frustrate)
Antonyms—please, satisfy, calm

virtuoso
Synonyms—expert, master, ace, whiz
Antonyms—amateur, beginner, dabbler, hobbyist

viscous
Synonyms—thick, sticky, gluey
Antonyms—thin, runny

vitality
Synonyms—energy, liveliness, durability
Antonyms—weariness, sluggishness, lethargy (lack of energy)

vital
Synonyms—essential, fundamental, crucial
Antonyms—unimportant, insignificant, trivial

vivacious
Synonyms—lively, cheerful, spirited
Antonyms— slow, languid (lacking energy), lethargic (slow)

vivid
Synonyms—bright, vibrant, colorful
Antonyms—dull, dreary, faded, lackluster (dull)

volatile
Synonyms—explosive, unpredictable, unstable
Antonyms— calm, placid (calm), inert (inactive)

voluntary
Synonyms—unpaid, honorary, pro bono (done without pay)
Antonyms—paid, compensated, remunerated (paid)

vulnerable
Synonyms—unprotected, in danger, at risk
Antonyms—secure, protected

List of Synonyms and Antonyms

W

wane
Synonyms—diminish, decline, fade
Antonyms—increase, develop, wax (to fade or decline)

waver
Synonyms—hesitate, fluctuate, vacillate (to be indecisive)
Antonyms—decide, resolve, choose

whimsical
Synonyms—fanciful, quirky, eccentric (unusual)
Antonyms—normal, regular, ordinary

wordy
Synonyms—rambling, long-winded, verbose (full of words)
Antonyms—concise (brief), taciturn (quiet), reticent (quiet)

Y

youthful
Synonyms—young, vigorous, vital
Antonyms—aged, decrepit (old), infirm (ill)

Z

zealous
Synonyms—eager, passionate, fervent (full of passion)
Antonyms— bored, lethargic (slow), listless (lacking energy)

zeal
Synonyms—enthusiasm, passion, eagerness
Antonyms—disinterest, indifference, apathy (lack of interest)